AF443278

GLOBAL DATA MANAGEMENT

Emerging Communication

Studies in New Technologies and Practices in Communication

Emerging Communication is publishing state-of-the-art papers that examine a broad range of issues in communication technology, theories, research, practices and applications.

It presents the latest development in the field of traditional and computer-mediated communication with emphasis on novel technologies and theoretical work in this multidisciplinary area of pure and applied research.

Since Emerging Communication seeks to be a general forum for advanced communication scholarship, it is especially interested in research whose significance crosses disciplinary and sub-field boundaries.

Volume 8

Previously published in this series:

ISSN 1566-7677

Global Data Management

Edited by

Roberto Baldoni
*Dipartimento di Informatica e Sistemistica "Antonio Ruberti",
Università degli Studi Roma "La Sapienza", Rome, Italy*

Giovanni Cortese
Interplay Software, Trento, Italy

Fabrizio Davide
Telecom Italia, Rome, Italy

and

Angelo Melpignano
Telecom Italia, Rome, Italy

IOS
Press

Amsterdam • Berlin • Oxford • Tokyo • Washington, DC

ISBN 1-58603-629-7
Library of Congress Control Number: 2006928210

Publisher
IOS Press
Nieuwe Hemweg 6B
1013 BG Amsterdam
Netherlands
fax: +31 20 687 0019
e-mail: order@iospress.nl

Distributor in the UK and Ireland
Gazelle Books Services Ltd.
White Cross Mills
Hightown
Lancaster LA1 4XS
United Kingdom
fax: +44 1524 63232
e-mail: sales@gazellebooks.co.uk

Distributor in the USA and Canada
IOS Press, Inc.
4502 Rachael Manor Drive
Fairfax, VA 22032
USA
fax: +1 703 323 3668
e-mail: iosbooks@iospress.com

v

Foreword

Managing Diversity in Knowledge

In the vision of pervasive communications and computing, information and communication technologies seamlessly and invisibly pervade into everyday objects and environments, delivering services adapted to the person and the context of their use. The communication and computing landscape will be sensing the physical world via a huge variety of sensors, and controlling it via a plethora of actuators. Applications and services will therefore have to be greatly based on the notions of context and knowledge.

In such foreseeable technology rich environments, the role of content providers and content consumers is being reshaped due to their immense and unprecedented number, and the way they generate, preserve, discover, use and abandon information. Pervasive communications call for new architectures based on device autonomy, fragmented connectivity, spatial awareness and data harnessing inside each network node. The realisation of this vision will then depend on the ability to access decentralized data, with demanding performance, scalability, security requirements than cannot be matched by centralized approaches. One of the key research challenges is then how to design a distributed data management infrastructure, allowing the handling of very high levels of complexity in the management of distributed highly heterogeneous data and knowledge sources (as they can be found in the Web), the integration of continuously changing data flows, and in general the management of multimedia data (e.g. personal, cultural heritage, education).

Global Data Management is playing a crucial role in the development of our networked distributed society. Its importance has been recognised in the IST programme since several years, in particular in its long-term research part, Future and Emerging Technologies (FET). Many of the papers included in this book refer to IST and FET projects currently running or recently completed. This subject is also one of the focal points identified for long-term FET research in the 7th Framework Programme for Community Research. The basic principles identified in the areas *"Pervasive Computing and Communications"* and *"Managing Diversity in Knowledge"* (see http://cordis.europa.eu/ist/fet/), as summarised in this foreword, are very much in line with the goals of this book.

An unforeseen growth of the volume and diversity of the data, content and knowledge is being generated all over the globe. Several factors lead to this growing complexity, among them: *Size* (the sheer increase in the numbers of knowledge producers and users, and in their production/use capabilities), *Pervasiveness* (in space and time of knowledge, knowledge producers and users), *Dynamicity* (new and old knowledge items will appear and disappear virtually at any moment), *Unpredictability* (the future dynamics of knowledge are unknown not only at design time but also at run time). The situation is made worse by the fact that the complexity of knowledge grows exponentially with the number of interconnected components.

The traditional approach of knowledge management and engineering is top-down and centralised, and depends on fixing at design time what can be expressed and how.

The key idea is to design a "general enough" reference representation model. Examples of this *top-down* approach are the work on (relational) databases, the work on distributed databases, and, lately, the work on information integration (both with databases and ontologies).

There are many reasons why this approach has been and is still largely successful. From a technological point of view it is conceptually simple, and it is also the most natural way to extend the technology developed for relational databases and single information systems. From an organisational point of view, this approach satisfies the companies' desire to centralise and, consequently, to be in control, of their data. Finally, from a cultural point of view, this approach is very much in line with the way knowledge is thought of in the western culture and philosophy, and in particular with the basic principle (rooted in ancient Greek philosophy) that it must be possible to say whether a knowledge statement is (universally) true or false. This property is reassuring and also efficient from an organisational point of view in that it makes it "easy" to decide what is "right" and what is "wrong".

However, as applications become increasingly open, complex and distributed, the knowledge they contain can no longer be managed in this way, as the requirements are only partially known at design time. The standard solution so far has been to handle the problems which arise during the life time of a knowledge system as part of the maintenance process. This however comes at a high price because of the increased cost of maintenance (exponentially more complex than the knowledge parts integrated inside it), the decreased life time of systems, and the increased load on the users who must take charge of the complexity which cannot be managed by the system. In several cases this approach has failed simply because people did not come to an agreement on the specifics of the unique global representation.

In pervasive distributed systems, the top-down approach must be combined with a new, bottom-up approach in which the different knowledge parts are designed and kept 'locally' and independently, and new knowledge is obtained by adaptation and combination of such items.

The key idea is to make a paradigm shift and to consider *diversity as a feature* which must be maintained and exploited and not as a defect that must be absorbed in some general schema. People, organisations, communities, populations, cultures build diverse representations of the world for a reason, and this reason lies in the local *context*, representing a notion of contextual, local knowledge which satisfies, in an optimal way, the (diverse) needs of the knowledge producer and knowledge user.

The bottom-up approach provides a flexible, incremental solution where diverse knowledge parts can be built and used independently, with some degree of complexity arising in their integration.

A second paradigm shift moves from the view where knowledge is mainly assembled by combining basic building blocks to a view where new knowledge is obtained by the design- or run-time *adaptation* of existing, independently designed, knowledge parts. Knowledge will no longer be produced *ab initio*, but more and more as adaptations of other, existing knowledge parts, often performed in run-time as a result of a process of evolution. This process will not always be controlled or planned externally but induced by changes perceived in the environment in which systems are embedded.

The challenge is to develop theories, methods, algorithms and tools for harnessing, controlling and using the emergent properties of large, distributed and heterogeneous collections of knowledge, as well as knowledge parts that are created through combination of others. The ability to manage diversity in knowledge will allow the creation of adaptive and, when necessary, self-adaptive knowledge systems.

The complexity in knowledge is a consequence of the complexity resulting from globalisation and the vitalisation of space and time produced by the current computing and networking technology, and of the effects that this has on the organisation and social structure of knowledge producers and users. This includes the following focus issues:

- *Local vs. global knowledge.* The key issue will be to find the right balance and interplay between operations for deriving local knowledge and operations which construct global knowledge.
- *Autonomy vs. coordination,* namely how the peer knowledge producers and users find the right balance between their desired level of autonomy of and the need to achieve coordination with the others.
- *Change and adaptation*, developing organisation models which facilitate the combination and coordination of knowledge and which can effectively adapt to unpredictable dynamics.
- *Quality*, namely how to maintain good enough quality e.g. through self-certifying algorithms, able to demonstrate correct answers (or answers with measurable incorrectness) in the presence of inconsistent, incomplete, or conflicting knowledge components.
- *Trust, reputation, and security* of knowledge and knowledge communities, for instance as a function of the measured quality; how to guard against deliberate introduction of falsified data.

Europe is very well positioned given the investment already done in many of these areas. This book represents a further step in the right direction.

Fabrizio Sestini[1]
Future Emerging Technologies Program
European Commission
Brussel, Belgium

---

[1] This text presents solely the opinions of the author, which do not prejudice in any way those of the European Commission.

Preface

Not many years ago, some researcher created the vision of the 'data utility' as a key enabler towards ubiquitous and pervasive computing. As for the water and power grid, there should be a utility infrastructure, designed for worldwide availability, providing continuous access to persistent information. Such utility service should provide appropriate guarantees in terms of security, data availability and survivability, and performance independent of location from which it is accessed. Decentralization and replication would be the approach to make it resistant against security attacks.

Several projects have explored (and still are exploring) the feasibility of the vision, each having a different emphasis on individual features such as data durability, uniform geographic access, privacy and support for uncensorship, mobility support, or other.

Applications which benefit from such global data service would be many, ranging from distributed, Internet-wide, file services, to mobile data provisioning, content distribution, data backup, digital libraries, information retrieval. Similarly, information systems for national security, world-wide safety infrastructures and other systems which rely on sensors (physical or logical e.g. firewalls, packet filters), all require a decentralized, inter-organisational data collection and processing infrastructure, able to process in real time a huge amount of data, and filter, correlate and securely distribute information to many users.

It is interesting to observe, that most of the researchers working towards this vision are also bringing forward, as an integral part of the vision, the so called 'self-*' or autonomic design approach. They share a common awareness that such a global scale service can be realized only by leveraging high numbers of nodes, through technologies that do not rely on human administration but are able by themselves to take care of their configuration, performance, and of data availability and survivability.

As another common driver, many of them are aiming at a 'no big brother' business model, and often assume cooperative sharing of resources among users of the service, or collaborative federation of service providers, as a key design choice.

Today, progressive ubiquitous deployment of broadband (both in fixed and mobile setting), together with successful deployment of several peer-to-peer applications, which raised public awareness of the potential of this paradigm for building global scale services, are bringing us significantly closer to that vision.

Most of the prominent goals of pervasive computing seem to depend on the ability to access decentralized data, with demanding performance, scalability, security requirements than cannot be matched by centralized approaches.

The key research challenge is then how to design a distributed data management infrastructure, in such a way that can be flexible and scalable enough to support a wide variety of tasks.

This volume aims at presenting an organic view on the research and technologies that are bringing us towards the realization of the vision.

We see two main, complementary problems to be tackled for building an infrastructure of this kind.

First, we need to design a data management 'fabric', providing storage, data replication, query and data distribution services, fit for such decentralized, large-scale setting. Differently from a distributed database, the data management fabric we seek must be able to operate in untrusted environments, must be opportunistic in using all the available storage, processing and communication resources, and must be able to configure itself, and recover from failures with minimum user intervention.

However, in the large scale, dynamic environment we envision we cannot expect all nodes use data which is consistent with an agreed and immutable schema. The problem of information integration and interoperability, heavily studied in traditional data management research, needs novel approaches, possibly rooted in complex system research, which are consistent with the 'million of peers' view we take.

The book is accordingly organized as follows.

Section 1. Data Management in Dynamic Networks of Agents

The opening section covers architectures and techniques, which deliver data management services in large, dynamic networks of agents.

Peer-to-peer *data storage and query techniques,* which are strategic to building highly decentralised repositories of data, as well as *data distribution* architectures which facilitate distribution of information from many sources to many destination nodes, are the main subjects we cover.

In Chapter 1.1, Milani, Querzoni, Tucci Piergiovanni provide a survey of methods for distributed data storage, with a focus on replication strategies which are peculiar to peer-to-peer architectures.

In Chapter 1.2, Aekaterinidis, Ntarmos, Pitoura, Triantafillou discuss methods for implementing complex queries in structured peer-to-peer networks, as embodied into the authors' RangeGuards architecture, and also introduce the notion of altruism and selfishness of peers, which is exploited in the PLANES architecture to improve the performance of the network of peers.

A special case of complex queries, aggregation services are a most important technology when querying many decentralised data sources is the task at hand, like in monitoring applications. In Chapter 1.3, by Cortese, Morabito, Davide, Virgillito, Beraldi, Quema, existing architectures for data aggregation in highly distributed systems are surveyed, taking into considerations both research originated in peer-to-peer and sensor network communities. The chapter includes the discussion of GREG, the author's architecture providing data indexing and aggregation services.

Chapter 1.4, by Corsaro, Querzoni, Scipioni, Tucci Piergiovanni, Virgillito, is specifically focused on data dissemination, specifically in selective data dissemination based on the publish-subscribe paradigm. This chapter also represents a bridge between research and industry viewpoints, by bringing into this book a standard-oriented perspective. The chapter features a survey of approaches to the design of publish-subscribe communication infrastructures, together with a presentation of the OMG standards in this area.

In Chapter 1.5, Akbarinia, Martins, Pacitti, Valduriez, present a complete architecture for peer-to-peer data management, termed Atlas Peer-to-Peer Architecture (APPA), which the authors at INRIA and LINA designed and implemented. This chapter presents together in a single view all the main components of a peer-to-peer data management system, so it may be also an alternative option for the reader to start with. APPA also aims at semantic interoperability in a peer-to-peer world which is focus of Section 2.

Wireless and mobile settings pose some distinct challenges to the designer. While sheer scalability with respect to the size of the network may be a less important requirement, the dynamics of the network, the unreliability of communication and resource scarceness are important concerns here.

In Chapter 1.6, Miranda, Rodrigues, Leggio, Raatikainen describe an algorithm for efficiently replicating and retrieving data items in a mobile ad-hoc network environment (MANET), which could be used for implementing a distributed name service, a service discovery protocol, or a directory service. The approach aims at addressing the peculiar issues of the MANET environment, by using gossip-based protocols for disseminating data, and achieving the desired replication of data items.

Chapter 1.7, by Carreras, De Pellegrini, Kiraly, Chlamtac, after an introductory part on Wireless Sensor Networks, describes a data management architecture for the so called 'Nomadic Sensor Networks' which are built out of mobile, personal user devices and tiny sensors scattered in the environment. Nomadic Sensor Networks spread information using a combination of multi-hopping and ad-hoc interactions between mobile nodes, and exploit physical mobility of users and devices to transport information.

The last chapter in this section has a distinct flavor and brings us closer to complex systems research.

Chapter 1.8, by Gupta, provides a mind-stimulating perspective on design methodologies for peer-to-peer data overlays and storage data structures. While current overlays have been designed using an informal approach, a few recent studies aim at specification of overlay protocols using formal, declarative approaches such as logic languages and algebras. Also, the author discusses how nature-inspired approaches can be translated into distributed protocols with a sound and systematic approach.

Section 2. Semantic Interoperability in the Large

The subject of Section 2 is semantic interoperability in widely distributed information systems with large numbers of agents.

It is a fact that several research communities (e.g. peer-to-peer data management, information agents, Semantic Web or Web data mining) are striving to address semantic interoperability using a self-organising, emergent approach. In many applications of global data management, it is unrealistic to expect that interaction between peers or agent can happen on the basis of data structured according to immutable, ex-ante agreed schemas. The vision of emergent schema management is to resolve these heterogeneities automatically in a self-organizing, emergent way by taking advantage of mediation capabilities in the network. The emerging schema information can be used in various ways, i.e. to drive the construction of an overlay network, and to route queries through the network.

Calvanese, De Giacomo, Lembo, Lenzerini, Rosati introduce us (Chapter 2.1) to the specific issues of data integration in the context of P2P systems. After providing both an informal and theoretical characterization of such issues, they propose a new semantics for P2P systems based on epistemic logic, and explore the benefits that such choice delivers in building query answering techniques which are not restricted in their generality.

In Chapter 2.2, by Cudré-Mauroux, Aberer, the problem of decentralized creation and maintenance of schema mappings, which can be created by independent parties, and are used by each peer to reformulate queries locally, is approached; a probabilistic technique for detecting erroneous schema mappings is proposed, which is part of a broader scope research aiming at having correct schema mappings emerge from local interactions among the peers.

Felix Heine, in Chapter 2.3, is similarly concerned with the problem of Emergent Schema Management. To address information integration problems in decentralized environments, he researches the usage of rich data representation models supporting taxonomical reasoning, such as RDF Schema, and proposes novel techniques for storage and query of data structured along rich data models in DHT-based peer-to-peer data management systems. Support of taxonomical reasoning, when searching semi-structured data, is an important requirement for several applications, ranging from information directories in GRID and network management, to decentralized information retrieval.

Chapter 2.4, by Altherr, Baehni, Bezençon, Eugster, Guerraoui, and Monod, is related to a slightly different aspect: type interoperability. The problem of how to make interoperability easier in a widely distributed programming environment, is tackled; specifically, the chapter addresses the ability for types representing the same software module, but possibly defined by different programmers, in different languages and running on different distributed platforms, to be treated as one single type.

Section 3. Applications

As mentioned earlier in this introduction, there are many potential global data management applications, beyond the generic, database and publish-subscribe type of applications, which have been documented in Section 1.

We selected two specific application areas to be documented, namely distributed information retrieval and content distribution. By this selection, we also intend to underline the broad scope of the global data utility, which must be able to work both with structured data, as well as with semi-structured data and unstructured content.

In Chapter 3.1, Zezula, Dohnal, Novak introduce the base concept and algorithms for similarity searching, a general information retrieval technique which is applicable to both textual and multimedia search, and discuss its possible implementations using structured peer-to-peer overlay networks. The intent of this work is to enable next-generation search engines, whose design instead is the specific focus of next chapter.

Chapter 3.2, by Bender, Michel, Triantafillou, Weikum, Zimmer, describes Minerva, an architecture for a fully decentralized, peer-to-peer search engine which is being developed as part of the IST project Delis.

In Chapter 3.3, Pierre, van Steen, Szymaniak, Sivasubramanian describe several architectures for large-scale content distribution. Alongside with traditional Content Distribution Networks (CDN), the architecture of peer-to-peer, collaborative CDNs, and of fully peer-to-peer content distribution systems (e.g. BitTorrent), are presented; the relative merits and drawbacks are analyzed and compared.

Last, Chapter 3.4 by Schiely, Felber presents Crossflux, a peer-to-peer architecture for media streaming. Crossflux demonstrates how the data distribution infrastructure can dynamically adapt to changes in network topology, in this case to maintain optimal end-to-end latency and overall bandwidth utilisation.

Contents

Section 1

Data Management in Dynamic Networks of Agents

Global Data Management
R. Baldoni et al. (Eds.)
IOS Press, 2006

3

Data Object Storage in Large Scale Distributed Systems[1]

Alessia Milani, Leonardo Querzoni and Sara Tucci Piergiovanni
Dipartimento di Informatica e Sistemistica "A. Ruberti",
Università di Roma "La Sapienza", Rome, Italy

Abstract. During the last decade, we assisted to an astounding revolution in the computer world. The widespread usage of internet-enabled applications, together with the advent of community-based interactions, completely changed our concept of collaborative work. One of the most important steps in this direction is the development of new technologies for data object storage, able to guarantee high degrees of reliability, while permitting the access in a nomadic environment through heterogeneous devices. In this chapter, we will study the problem of implementing a global data object storage system, exploring the current state of the art for correlated technologies, and surveying the most interesting proposals.

Keywords. Peer-to-peer systems, data storage, efficient data location and routing, availability, load balancing, data consistency management

1. Introduction

The enormous steps ahead home PCs underwent in the last decade, with respect to computing power, storage space and network bandwidth, completely transformed the way we were used to think about collaborative work. In a modern networked environment, the resources available to the sum of all home PCs used by clients, often greatly overwhelm the possibility of any available server. From this idea, the peer-to-peer interaction model arose, quickly imposing a revolution in the way people think about distributed applications. Peer-to-peer communication techniques try to leverage the *wasted* resources available on home PCs to benefit the whole collectivity.

Meanwhile, users access applications via Internet through a large variety of different devices (e.g. PDAs, cellular phones). This makes fundamental the need of a *persistent* data storage system, both distributed and Internet-based, to share data and preserve information even when devices are lost or damaged. The need of a distributed global data storage system arises from the scale of the system, i.e. the potential number of connected client devices implies such a storage system must eventually consist of thousands or millions of Internet-connected nodes.

---

[1]   This work was partially supported by the RESIST project, funded by the European Community.

In the last five years, many research efforts have been spent on this topic. The goal is to build a distributed system such that:

- Users can store their data objects efficiently and safely.
- Any authorized user can efficiently retrieve data objects.
- Data objects remain available besides nodes or network failures.
- Data object coherence is maintained beside concurrent accesses.

All the implementation issues related to these points should remain completely hidden from user perspective. Ideally, these systems should offer to the final user an interface for data access very close to the one used to access local data objects.

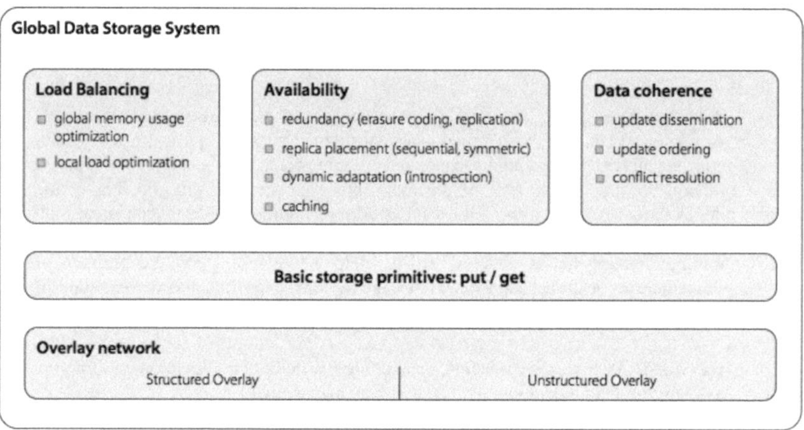

Figure 1. Conceptual architecture for a global data storage system.

To this end, a global data storage system consists of several services with defined and specific goals. **Figure 1** describes a conceptual architecture for a global data storage system. The architecture consists of three layers. The first layer arranges participants in a connected network, called overlay network, built on top of TCP/IP, and provides nodes with mechanisms to join and leave this network. The difference between structured and unstructured refers to the types of neighborhood relations among participants: stringent and precise relations in structured overlays and more random in unstructured ones. The second layer provides each node with the basic primitives to store and retrieve objects, i.e. the put and get functions. The third layer provides more sophisticate services. The load balance management is in charge of (i) maximizing the memory usage of nodes in order to exploit the total capacity of the system, and (ii) equally distributing the load of get requests among all participants, accommodating objects depending on their popularity. The availability management consists of several techniques aimed at augmenting the likelihood that a user gets the requested object besides nodes and network failures. Replication and erasure coding are basic techniques providing object redundancy. Replica placement concerns the identification of the most appropriate network nodes where storing replicas (or blocks for erasure coding) to cope with multiple simultaneous failures and with the goal of augmenting the replica survival probability. Availability does not only concern with the actual presence of a given object in the system along the time, but even with the possibility of obtaining the object in a reasonable time. In order to address this point several techniques (e.g. caching) try to augment the so-called system responsiveness. Data coherence management involves issues arising when the system provides, besides read operations (read operations map easily to several get function invocations), even write/update operations. In this case, consistency among different replicas of the same object must hold. Different strategies for update dissemination, ordering and conflicts resolution may be pursued.

Various systems [8, 9, 10, 11, 12] currently support many of the services described in the general architecture. For instance, Oceanstore [9] uses Tapestry [4] as basic infrastructure for get/put functions. Availability and load balancing are supported by means of several mechanisms like introspection to place/create/remove object replicas, or erasure coding to provide redundancy (see later for details). Oceanstore provides also support for data updating based on: epidemic update dissemination, a total update ordering decided from a small group of servers and conflict resolutions techniques.

Other systems like CFS [8] and PAST [10] do not support data updating but provides sophisticate mechanism aimed at optimizing the memory usage. PAST relies on Pastry [2] as basic infrastructure while CFS uses Chord [1]. Both systems provide mechanisms to maximize the usage of the total memory available and to optimize the load locally at each node by evenly sharing it. Different techniques are used like virtual servers, replica diversion, block fragmentation, and various cache policies.

Goal of this chapter is to give the reader a better knowledge on the many different issues related to the implementation of each global data object storage system layer, along with an overview of the existing solutions. The approach is completely orthogonal with respect to existing systems: for each layer presented in the conceptual architecture all techniques available in existing systems will be presented, discussed and, where appropriate, compared.

The chapter is organized as follows: Section 2 presents the first two basic layers of the conceptual architecture under the name of data object access facilities. Section 3 introduces mechanisms of higher level, able to provide data object availability and load balancing. Section 4 presents the issues related to data coherence under the name of data object updating. Data object updating is currently a new feature supported only by a few global data object storage systems, but due to its importance, many systems are currently being extended to support it.

2. Data Object Access Facilities

Storing and accessing data object in a global setting is an old idea pursued for a long time. Nowadays the environment in which well-known solutions should be deployed is becoming more and more challenging for the following reasons:
- Entities are unreliable, dispersed on a wide geographical area, and connected through unreliable WANs (often Internet).
- Resources are extremely heterogeneous, both for their capacity and availability.
- A centralized management of resources is not available.

From this point of view, research recently focused on the development of network abstractions able to hide to developers at least part of all the complexities arising from the environment. These abstractions take usually the form of an application level *overlay network* built on top of standard TCP/IP communication primitives.

In the following, we will analyze how overlay networks are realized, from a general point of view, to later explore in detail some implementations.

2.1. *The Overlay Network Approach to Data Object Storage*

An *overlay network* is, as the name implies, a communication network built on top of another communication network. An overlay network takes charge of various aspects like: basic connectivity among participants, message routing, management of participants joining or leaving the network, faults management. From its definition and objectives, an obvious question immediately arises: which is the meaning in building a network over an existing one?

The justification to these structures comes from the peculiar characteristics of the underlying infrastructure: the Internet. Due to its implicit unreliability, the TCP-IP network constituting Internet is unable to directly address the needs of a wide range of various modern applications that require fast, reliable and complex communication primitives. Due to the practical difficulties that an extension of the TCP/IP protocols would imply, the researcher efforts moved toward a layered approach where the existing network is left in its current state, and on top of it new algorithms and protocols are deployed in order to maintain "virtual" networks and provide through them the required communication primitives.

Overlay networks for object storage and retrieval in a completely distributed fashion provide two fundamental primitives:
- A *put* function: to store an object somewhere in the overlay
- A *get* function: to locate and retrieve an object previously stored.

These fundamental primitives are at the basis of a global storage infrastructure.
Three aspects characterize an overlay network:
- How the overlay is built and maintained. This implies all the algorithms used to manage new nodes joining the network, old nodes leaving it and node faults.
- Which strategy is exploited to store objects in the network, i.e. on which node an object is physically stored once a *put* operation is invoked.
- Which strategy is used to locate and retrieve objects through the *get* primitive.

Basing on how these aspects are treated, we can distinguish between two groups of overlay network systems: *structured systems* and *unstructured systems*.

Structured systems build and maintain some distributed data object structure. This structure is then used both to organize nodes in the overlay and to place stored objects. All these overlay networks organize nodes in a precise structure. Node joining the system must follow a defined join algorithm to become part of the overlay. This algorithm is able to organize connections between nodes in order to build, in a distributed fashion, complex regular structures. Various types of graphs are employed: besides rings [1,2] and their derivatives, we can encounter *d*-dimensional thoroidal spaces [3], general meshes [4], butterflies [5], De Bruijn graphs [6], etc. Note that, the usage of a specific structure for node connections is not necessarily a pre-requisite for the implementation of specific algorithms for *put* and *get* primitives. Nevertheless, algorithms can leverage structures to increase overall performance.

Object placement is usually executed just using the structure previously deployed. The implementation of the *put* primitive consists of an algorithm which selects in which point (node) of this structure the object will be placed. Given this placement strategy the *get* primitive can be implemented exploiting some high performance traversal technique appropriate for the chosen structure.

Structured overlay networks, in their various forms, are by far the most used infrastructures for global data object storage systems. Systems exploiting such overlays are, for example, CFS [8], PAST [10], Glacier [11], Oceanstore [9], P-Grid [12] and Ivy [13].

Unstructured systems approach the problem from a completely different perspective: their goal is to maximize independence and self-organization among nodes; for this reason systems based on this approach usually employs random algorithms for overlay network's construction and maintenance. Actually, the unstructured approach did not attained a wide success in the area of global data object storage (with the noteworthy exception of the Pangaea [14] system).

2.2.　　Current Solutions

In this section we will show the insights of four overlay networks, namely Chord, Tapestry, Pastry and P-Grid. The systems here introduced allow us to highlight in a clear manner basic characteristics proper of any structured overlay network, since they are simple but represent a wider range of more complex and sophisticate systems.

2.2.1.　　Chord

Chord [1] is the implementation of a *distributed hash table* (DHT). It is able to create and maintain a distributed abstract space, called *key space*, where objects can be easily stored and retrieved, exactly as in a standard centralized hash table.

The *key space* can be imagined as a sequence of ordered locations, each identified by a key, that constitute a ring-shaped sequence (i.e. the location with the smallest key follows the one with the larger key); keys are represented by integer numbers chosen in a predefined interval $[0,2^h]$ with $h \in N$. h is a predefined constant used to control the size of the keyspace, i.e. the maximum number of locations it contains. The *key space* is continuous, i.e. does not contain holes: a location exists for each possible key; this is achieved in Chord decoupling the *key space* from the set of nodes that effectively maintains this space. Each node constituting the Chord network is represented in the *key space* by a key that is usually calculated applying a consistent hash function [7], namely $h(x)$, to the node's IP address; this key is defined as the node's *id*.

Keys are assigned to nodes in a straightforward way: each location, identified by its key k, is stored on the first node whose identifier *id*, is equal to or follows k in the key space. This node is called the *successor node* of key k, and is denoted by *successor(k)*.

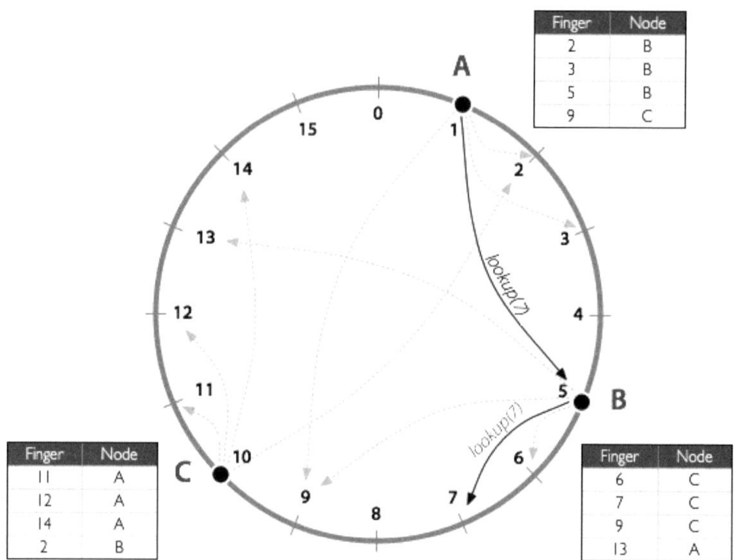

Figure 2. Chord network.

In Figure 2 a key space (h=4) populated by three nodes (id=1,5,10) is represented. If we consider the location identified by key 7, it is physically stored in the node with id 10, i.e. its successor.

Each node n maintains a table with h entries, called the *finger table*. The i-th entry in the table at node n contains the identity (i.e. the IP address) of the first node n' whose id follows n's id by at least 2^{i-1} on the key space, i.e. n'=*successor(id+2^{i-1})*, where $1 \leq i \leq h$ (and all arithmetic is modulo 2^h). We call node n' the i-th *finger* of node n. Figure 2 reports the finger tables of the three nodes that constitute the network. Dotted grey lines departing from each node represent keys pointed by the respective fingers.

The *put* primitive in Chord is called *insert(key, value)* and take two parameters: a valid key and the object that we want to store on the location corresponding to that key. The key is used to globally identify the object and is thus usually obtained applying the hash function to a globally known and unique property of the object (e.g. its name). The implementation of *insert* is based on another function: *lookup(key)*. The sole purpose of *lookup* is to return the node that stores *key*. When a node n executes *lookup(k)*, and k does not appear in its finger table, i.e. n does not know *successor(k)*, it forwards the message to another node in the network, closer than itself to the desired key. To accomplish this task, n searches its finger table for the closest finger preceding k, and forwards the message to that node: intuitively, each step toward the destination halves the distance to it; this means that, with high probability, the number of nodes that must be visited by a message to reach its destination in a M-node network is $O(\log M)$. Let us explain this through an example based on the small Chord network depicted in Figure 2. Suppose *lookup(7)* is executed on the node with id 1, i.e. node A. This node does not have a finger pointing directly to key 7, thus it looks in its finger table and forwards the *lookup(7)* query to the node associated with the 3rd finger pointing toward key 5, i.e. node B. As soon as node B receives this query it looks in its finger table and finds a finger pointing directly toward key 7. The node associated with this key is the one with *id*=10, i.e. C, actually the successor of key 7. The message will be thus forwarded to node C, its final destination.

The implementation of the *insert* function is straightforward through this powerful *lookup* function. The *lookup* function is also used to realize the *get* primitive, whose implementation is also rather obvious. Chord also includes smart algorithms used to dynamically handle nodes joining or leaving the overlay network. The reader can refer to [1] for the details. The Chord overlay network is used as a distributed storage service by CFS [8] and Glacier [11].

2.2.2. Tapestry

Also Tapestry [4] is the implementation of a DHT, but it uses a completely different overlay structure. In fact it is mostly based on the routing mechanism introduced by Plaxton et al. in [15].

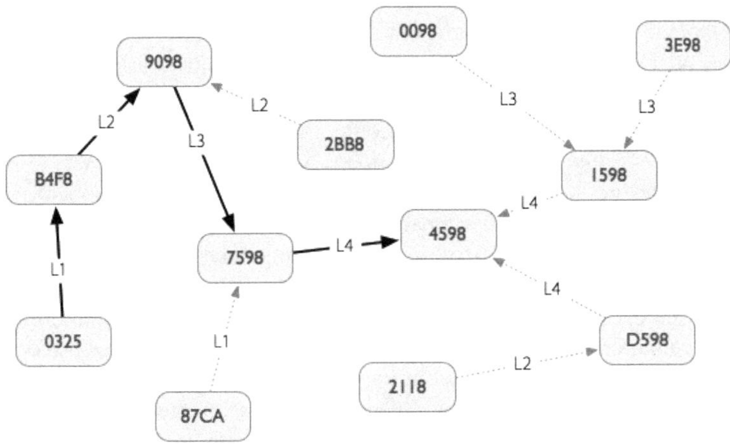

Figure 3. Tapestry mesh.

The work in [15] proposed a mesh-like structure. Each node in the system is assigned an *id* (it is always possible to apply a hash function on the node's IP address). The *id*s are then used to construct a mesh among nodes, as shown in **Figure 3** (where *id*s are expressed with hexadecimal values). In this figure, each link is labeled with a level number that denotes the stage of routing that uses this link. The *i*-th level neighbor-links for some node *n* point at the 16 closest neighbors whose *id*s match the lowest *i*-1 nibbles of node *n*'s *id* and who have different combinations of the *i*-th nibble; If a link cannot be constructed because no such node meets the proper constraints, then the scheme chooses the node that matches the constraints as closely as possible. This process is repeated for all nodes and levels within a node.

The key mechanism of this approach is that links form a series of random embedded trees, with each node representing the root of one of these trees. As a result, the neighbor links can be used to route lookup requests from anywhere to a given node, simply by resolving the node's address one link at a time: first a level-one link, then a level-two link, etc. **Figure 3** shows how a lookup request for key 4958 can be routed in this way from node 0325 to node 4598.

This structure can be used to store objects in a structured manner, just generating an identifier for each object in the same shape of node's *id*s. Then each object is mapped to the single node whose *id* matches the object's identifier in the most bits (starting from the least significant); The improvements added by Tapestry to [15] are the ability to allow dynamic join and leave of nodes, and failure tolerance. Tapestry is part of the Oceanstore [9] global storage system.

2.2.3. *Pastry*

Pastry [2] is the third implementation of a distributed hash table we explore in this chapter. It actually mixes techniques seen both in Chord and in Tapestry.

Like Chord, also Pastry exploits a ring shaped abstract space for keys, but differently from it, Pastry can exploit a proximity metric to increase performance and even includes a mechanism to tolerate node failures. Each Pastry node maintains a *routing table*, a *neighborhood set* and a *leaf set*. A node's routing table R is organized into $\lceil \log_B N \rceil$ (with $B=2^b$) rows with 2^b-1 entries each. Entries at row n of R each refers to a node whose *id* shares the present node's *id* in the first n digits, but whose $n+1$th digit has one of the possible 2^b-1 values other than the $n+1$th digit in the present node's *id*. The *leaf set* is populated with the L nodes whose *id*s are the closest to n's *id* in the key ring, while the *neighborhood set* contains L nodes close to n with respect to a predefined proximity metric (L is a parameter of the system).

The *leaf set* is used by Pastry to ensure ring connectivity and correct behavior of *lookup* operation besides failure of $\lfloor L/2 \rfloor$ nodes with adjacent *id*s. The *neighborhood set* is instead used each time a node must be added to the routing table, in order to select it in a group containing only "close" nodes with respect to a predefined proximity metric.

The *lookup* function is realized in Pastry through an algorithm that is quite similar to the one employed by Tapestry. Even in this case request routing proceeds with consecutive approximations of the searched key with node *id*s: at each step the algorithm forwards the request to a node whose *id* matches the searched key for at least one more bit, with respect to the current node *id*. Through this mechanism Pastry is able to route messages in at most a logarithmic number of hops, with respect to the total number of nodes. The Pastry overlay network is used as a storage substrate by PAST [10].

2.2.4. *P-Grid*

P-Grid [12] philosophy slightly departs from what we have seen from Chord, Pastry and Tapestry. It implements a distributed binary search tree that can be built and maintained over any overlay communication infrastructure, either structured or unstructured.

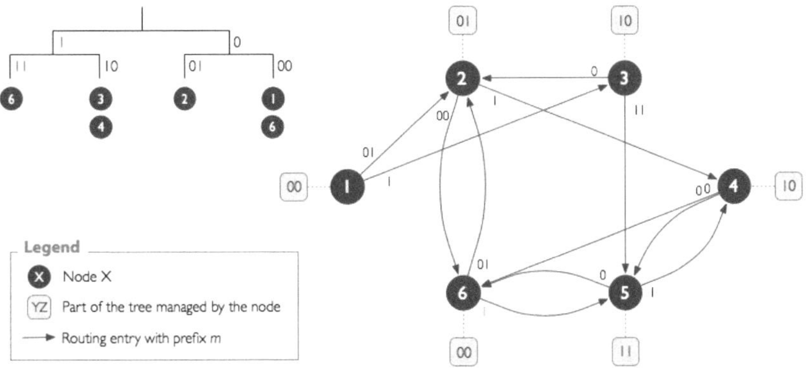

Figure 4. A binary search tree (left) along with its P-Grid implementation (right).

In P-Grid each node, identified as usual by a binary *id*, maintains only part of the overall tree, which comes into existence only through the cooperation of individual peers. Every node's position is determined by its path, that is, the binary string representing the subset of the tree's overall information that the node is responsible for. For example, the path of node 4 in **Figure 4** is 10, so it stores all data object items whose key begins with 10. The paths implicitly partition the search space and define the structure of the virtual binary search tree. As **Figure 4** shows, multiple nodes can be responsible for the same path. Node 1 and Node 6, for example, both store keys beginning with 00. Such replication improves P-Grid's robustness and responsiveness.

P-Grid's approach to routing is simple and efficient: for each bit in its path, a node stores the address of at least one other node that is responsible for the other side of the binary tree at that level. Thus, if a node receives a lookup request for a key it cannot directly satisfy, it must forward the request to a peer that is "closer" to the result. Suppose that node 6 in **Figure 4** executes *lookup(100)*. That node is not responsible for that key so it makes a lookup in its routing table for an entry related to keys starting with bit 1. The routing table in node 6 contains a pointer to node 5, thus the request is forwarded to this site (whose *id* is "closer" to the searched key). Node 5 looks at the next bit of the searched key and note that it is a 0, while its *id* is actually 11. This means that node 5 cannot handle the searched key. Looking in its routing table it finds a pointer to node 4 whose *id* starts with bits 10. The lookup request is then forwarded to node 4 that is actually the final destination.

The P-Grid construction algorithm, whose details can be found in [12], guarantees that node routing tables always provide at least one path from any node receiving a request to one of the nodes holding a replica so that any query can be satisfied regardless of the node queried.

3.   Data Object Storage Policies: Toward Availability and Load Balancing

As we pointed out in the previous section, global storage systems are built on top of overlay networks, which provide the fundamental primitives to store and retrieve objects. In this section, we will highlight which is the impact of different storage strategies on two properties of a system: *load balancing* and *availability*.

3.1.   Load Balancing

Balancing load among nodes is an important objective in data object storage infrastructures to avoid few nodes to become bottlenecks and possibly degrading system performance significantly. Load balance is expressed in terms of *storage requirements* and *data object requests*, i.e. a similar storage capacity should be requested from each node and data object requests should be spread among nodes such that serving load is uniformly distributed. In the next sections, *storage requirements* and *data object requests* are analyzed by pointing out the main orthogonal parameters that affect such load balancing metrics, that is the *size* of objects to be stored and their *popularity*.

3.1.1.   Storage requirements

In this section, we consider two different approaches to object storage whose aim is to leverage per-node storage capacity, in order to guarantee high global storage usage as the system approaches its maximal load. In detail, we investigate two data storage systems, PAST [10] and CFS [8], and their different way of satisfying the *even storage distribution* requirement among nodes. Specifically, in PAST the same storage space is required from every node, while in CFS storage space is required from each node proportionally to its storage capacity. Moreover, we point out the way these systems address the main possible causes of uneven load on nodes, that is:

1.   different storage capacity of individual nodes (for PAST);
2.   objects of different sizes;
3.   uneven assignment of node identifiers. This may lead to a skewed distribution of objects among nodes.

PAST tries to address these three issues through ad-hoc solutions. In particular, when a new node joins the system, it advertises its storage capacity; PAST controls the distribution of per-node storage capacities and asks the node, if it advertised a very large capacity, to split and join under multiple *nodeId*s. If a node advertises a small capacity, it is simply rejected. A node can, if it desires to, advertise only a fraction of its actual free disk space for use in PAST. Through this technique PAST is able to maintain at any given time storage capacities of different nodes within a range of no more than two orders of magnitude. Moreover, in order to address points 2 and 3, PAST introduces two mechanisms, namely *replica diversion* and *file diversion*. The aim of replica diversion is to balance remaining free storage space among nodes while file diversion purpose is to balance storage load among different portion of the keyspace handled by the underlying overlay network. Replica diversion and file diversion are detailed in section 3.2.1.4.

CFS ensures that storage load is balanced among nodes in rough proportion to their storage capacity. To reach this goal objects stored in CFS are split in a sequence of fixed-size blocks stored on several nodes. Moreover CFS exploits the so-called *virtual servers* mechanism, i.e. a real server (a node storing and serving data object) acts as multiple *virtual servers*. Each virtual server runs the CFS protocol and is identified by a *nodeId* calculated by hashing the IP address of the real server and the index arbitrarily assigned to the virtual server. The number of virtual servers created on each node depends on the node's storage capacity and can be adaptively modified to react to an evolving load. In this sense, a real server may delete or create some of its virtual servers in case of high or low load respectively. In this way, thanks to the uniform distribution of *nodeId*s and to CFS's block storage granularity, every virtual server is roughly in charge of the same amount of data.

Finally, it's worth noting that blocks' granularity may improve the usage of the global storage capacity available in the system. More specifically, those files, e.g. audio, video, software distributions etc., that can be larger than storage capacity of some nodes, are divided and stored in smaller blocks, thus allowing their storage as long as the global storage capacity is sufficient, even if per-node storage capacity is not.

3.1.2.　Data Object Requests

A node that stores a large and popular file is heavier loaded than a node storing an unpopular one. To overcome this problem many systems split each object in various blocks, allowing requests for that object to be managed by a set of nodes. In this way, nodes share evenly the requests and the corresponding serving load. Moreover, object fragmentation allows a single node to store blocks belonging to objects with different levels of popularity. In this way, low rate of requests due to unpopular blocks balances the heavy load caused by very popular ones. However, fragmentation comes at a cost: additional complexity in storage management and file look up. If files are stored as a whole one lookup per file is required rather than one per block. Moreover, in order to locate and retrieve individual blocks, additional information must be stored, and this information is proportional to the number of blocks an object is split into. Examples of systems using fragmentation are CFS [8], Glacier [11] and Oceanstore [9].

3.2.　Availability

An object is considered *available* if it is stored in the system and the time necessary to retrieve it is reasonable. According to this definition, the availability of an object can be evaluated through two orthogonal metrics: *fault tolerance* and *responsiveness*.

3.2.1.　Fault Tolerance

Redundancy is a key factor to ensure durable storage despite of node failures, and it is traditionally obtained through *data object replication*, i.e. various copies of each object are stored in the system. Fault tolerance can be obtained even through a more sophisticate technique called *erasure coding*, which tries to overcome the costs of traditional replication techniques, i.e. the increase in bandwidth usage and storage requirements.

It is important to note that, dealing with redundancy, it is often assumed that nodes share the same probability to fail and there is no correlation among failure probabilities. This assumption is generally not realistic since various nodes may be located in the same building, may share the same network link, may run the same software etc. For this reason, object placement policies can greatly impact the actual level of tolerance to faults of stored data.

3.2.1.1.　Data Object Replication
With data object replication redundancy is introduced in the system creating extra copies of any object (or block, as in CFS): given an object, S independent copies are created and stored on different nodes. The number S of replicas defines the *replication degree*, and its value can be decided *a priori* or adjusted dynamically according to

system evolution. In this sense, several global object storage systems, e.g. OceanStore, exploit an architectural paradigm, called *introspection,* which mimics adaptation in biological systems. More specifically, the set of nodes storing replicas of a specific data object share the responsibility of their own management. Each node monitors the requests it receives, in terms of the imposed load and their origin. Through an analysis of this information, a node can perceive the opportunity of moving or duplicating the replica it stores. According to information collected during previous interactions with clients (data consumers) and other nodes, the new host node is chosen. This node must pass a set of safety and minimum performance tests and finally it must agree to host the replica.

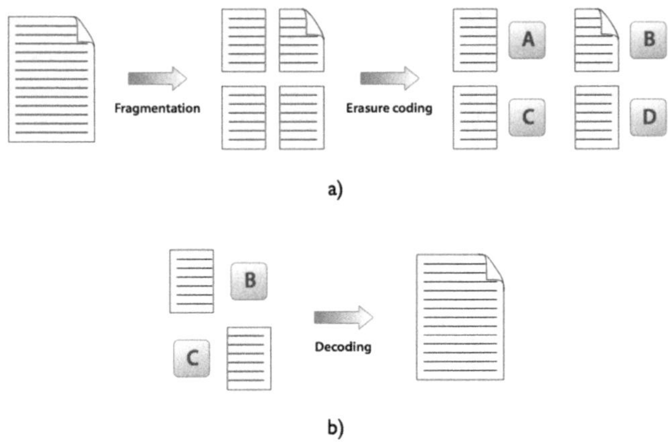

Figure 5. Erasure coding and decoding of a document.

3.2.1.2. Erasure Coding

Erasure coding provides redundancy without introducing the typical overhead associated to plain replication. As shown in **Figure 5** (a), each object is divided into m blocks that are then erasure coded to obtain n encoded blocks, with $n>m$. Encoded blocks have the same size of the original blocks and dependently on the coding scheme, may include or not the source blocks. The main property of erasure-coded objects is that the original object can be rebuilt starting from any m out of n encoded blocks, as shown in **Figure 5** (b). If $r=m/n$ is the *rate of encoding*, then the storage cost is incremented of $1/r$. For example, suppose we want to encode an object with a rate $r=1/4$. The object is first split in $m=16$ blocks that are then encoded in $n=64$ new blocks, increasing the storage cost by a factor of 4. It is worth noting that traditional replication can be seen as a particular case of erasure coding where $m=1$ and $n=1$.

In addition, in order to be useful, each block has to be retrieved correctly and completely. For this reason, erasure coding requires the precise identification of failed or corrupted blocks. OceanStore [9] exploits erasure coding to improve data durability. Moreover, in order to avoid corrupted blocks retrieval, it generates a hash over each block and recursively hashes over the concatenation of pairs of hashes to form a binary tree. Each block is stored along with the hashes neighboring its path to the root of this tree. When it is retrieved, the requesting machine can recalculate the hashes along the path and verify data integrity.

A widely used algorithm for erasure coding is the Reed-Solomon [26,27] code. OceanStore and Reperasure [25] are examples of systems using these codes. The Reed-Solomon code is based on the following property of polynomials. Let $A(x)= a_0 + a_1x + ... + a_{k-1}x^{k-1} + a_kx^k$ be a polynomial of degree k, then:

1. $A(x)$ is represented by its $k+1$ coefficients, that is $(a_0, a_1, ..., a_{k-1}, a_k)$,
2. $A(x)$ is represented by its evaluation at $k+1$ distinct points $x_0, x_1, ..., x_k$, i.e. it is represented with the following set of values $y_0=A(x_0)$, $y_1=A(x_1)$, ..., $y_k=A(x_k)$.

The coefficients of $A(x)$ can be retrieved by considering any $k+1$ evaluation of $A(x)$. If each coefficient represents a data object block and each encoded block is one of such evaluations, redundancy can be introduced in the system by evaluating A(x) in $n>k$ distinct points, that is by creating n encoded blocks, namely $y_0, y_1, ..., y_{n-1}$. In this way, given the following n linear equations:

$$y_0= a_0 + a_1x_0 + ...+ a_{k-1}\,x_0^{k-1} + a_k\,x_0^{k}$$
$$y_1= a_0 + a_1x_1 + ...+ a_{k-1}\,x_1^{k-1} + a_k\,x_1^{k}$$
$$...$$
$$y_{k+1}= a_0 + a_1x_{k+1} + ...+ a_{k-1}\,x_{k+1}^{k-1} + a_k\,x_{k+1}^{k}$$
$$...$$
$$y_{n-1}= a_0 + a_1x_{n-1} + ...+ a_{k-1}\,x_{n-1}^{k-1} + a_k\,x_{n-1}^{k}$$

A set of $k+1$ of such equations is sufficient to recalculate the $k+1$ original blocks.

In a more formal way, Reed-Solomon encoding is based on *Galois Field arithmetic* to ensure that all elements have multiplicative inverses. More specifically, data blocks are partitioned into *words* of fixed size; a collection of m words forms a vector $<d_1,d_2,...d_m>$. Then, each encoded block c_i is calculated from this vector through m dot products, i.e. $c_i=F_i(<d_1,d_2,...,d_m>)= d_1f_{i1}+ d_2f_{i2}... d_mf_{im}$. If n encoded blocks are created, we obtain a $m\cdot n$ *Vandermonde matrix* whose rows are tuples $(f_{i1}, f_{i2}, ..., f_{im})$ with $i\in[1..n]$. This matrix is defined as the *distribution matrix,* and denoted with F. To retrieve the original object, given any m blocks, a decoding matrix can be derived from the distribution matrix F and the original data blocks may be calculated again with dot products.

3.2.1.3. Techniques Comparison

In this section, we measure and compare data object availability in the case of traditional replication and erasure coding assuming failure independency [16]. Let μ be the availability of a node. If an object is replicated creating S copies that are subsequently spread over S different and independent nodes, the resulting availability of the object is:

$$A_{replication}(S) = \sum_{i=1}^{S} \binom{S}{i} \mu^i (1 - \mu)^{S-i}$$

Then consider the case in which an object is divided into b blocks that are then encoded in order to obtain $S\cdot b$ encoded blocks to be spread over different and independent nodes. Any b out of the $S\cdot b$ blocks are sufficient to rebuild the original object. Thus the object availability is:

$$A_{erasure}(b) = \sum_{i=b}^{Sb} \binom{Sb}{i} \mu^i (1-\mu)^{Sb-i}$$

Note that for $b=1$, $A_{replication}=A_{erasure}$.

From these two availability equations it is clear that, despite replication, erasure coding benefits from the combinatorial effect. In other words, with the same storage requirements, we can duplicate n blocks of an object or it is possible to code those blocks in order to obtain $2n$ erasure code blocks. If the blocks are distributed across $2n$ nodes, when using replication, at least one of the two replicated blocks has to be available in order to reconstruct such an object. With erasure coding any n out of $2n$ blocks can be used to rebuild the object and thus it is sufficient that any n nodes are available.

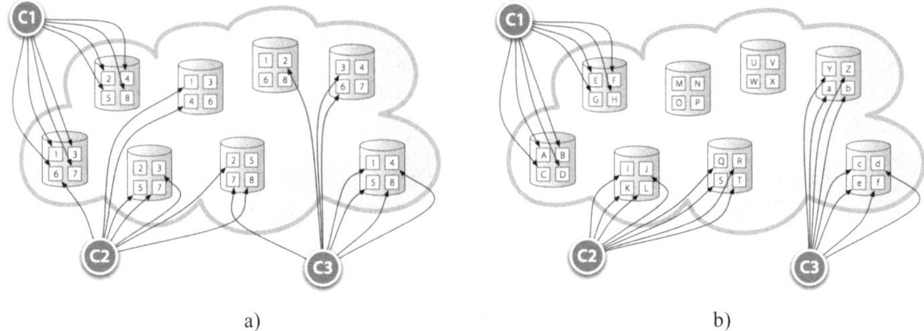

a)   b)

Figure 6. An example of redundancy obtained through replication (a) and erasure coding (b).

To clarify this point, let us consider the example of **Figure 6**. In this example an object is partitioned in 8 blocks that are replicated (**Figure 6** (a)) or encoded (**Figure 6** (b)). With replication each block is replicated 4 times obtaining a total of 32 blocks. With Reed-Solomon coding the original blocks are encoded to obtain again 32 blocks. When a client retrieves the object, in case of replication, it has to retrieve specific blocks (a copy of each original block), while with erasure coding any eight blocks are sufficient to recreate the original object. This means that, unlike erasure coding, in case of replication, object retrieval is possible only if there exists at least one replica of each original block. In this sense, erasure coding improves fault tolerance.

On the other hand, it has been proved [16] that the cost associated with using erasure codes increases more than linearly with the number of blocks to be encoded. Thus, at some point, this cost becomes overwhelming in comparison to the gain in availability.

3.2.1.4. Replica Placement

Due to the fact that data object reliability strongly depends on the likelihood of data object loss when concurrent nodes failures occur, block placement policy is a key factor in order to achieve a robust data object storage system. For example, when k random nodes fail concurrently in the system, the likelihood that some object has k replicas located on the k failed nodes strictly depends on the placement scheme used. In general, the higher is the probability that a concurrent node failure wipes out all replicas of an object, the less reliable the system is. In this sense, it is important to place object replicas or encoded blocks in such a way that the corresponding storage nodes fail independently. In the following, we analyze the most widely used placement policies: *sequential* and *symmetric*. For the sake of simplicity, policies are explained considering the case of multiple replicas but the same ideas can be applied to fragment distribution.

Sequential Placement

Sequential placement is simple in nature: one of the nodes acts as the lead node, or primary replica, and the k replicas are placed on itself and its k-1 successors according to a given order. The lead node is typically identified hashing the name of the object. This scheme is used in systems like CFS and PAST. The restrictive nature of this placement policy reduces the sensitivity to concurrent failures. If, and only if, k simultaneous failures occur on k consecutive nodes the object will be lost. This is unlikely when N is much larger than k. In general this approach is used in systems in which *nodeId* are generated by computing the hash function of the node IP address, since due to this assignment process nodes with adjacent *nodeId* are, with high probability, diverse in geography, ownership, jurisdiction etc. Thus sequential placement has a low likelihood of data object loss when concurrent failures occur, which improves data object reliability. Two widely used implementations of sequential placement exploit *successor-lists* and *leaf-sets*.

We explain the approach based on successor-lists through a case study: CFS. The core of CFS consists of two layers: (i) the DHash table layer that is responsible for storing keyed blocks, maintaining proper levels of replication as nodes come and go and caching popular blocks and (ii) the underlying Chord network (see Section 2.2.1). The DHash layer stores and retrieves uniquely identified blocks and handles distribution, replication and caching of those blocks. In particular, the DHash layer replicates each block on k CFS nodes and maintains the k replicas available as nodes come and go. A block is inserted in the CFS system using a hash of its content as its identifier. Moreover, DHash stores all replicas of a particular block at the k nodes immediately after the block successor in the Chord ring.

In order, to guarantee block availability, DHash layer ensures that if one of such successors fails, a new successor takes the responsibility to store the block's replica. The effectiveness of this replication scheme depends in part on the independence of failure and unreachability among the block's k replica nodes. Since the id of a node in the ring is obtained by hashing its IP address, nodes close to each other on the keyspace are not likely to be physically close. This provides the desired independence among failures.

The approach based on leaf-sets is used in PAST. More specifically, when an object is inserted in PAST, using the Pastry layer, the file is routed to the k nodes whose node identifiers are numerically closest to the 128 most significant bits of the file identifier (*fileId*). Each of these nodes then stores a copy of the file. The replication factor depends on the availability and persistence requirements of the file and may vary between files. An interesting aspect to point out is that not all the k closest nodes could accommodate a replica due to insufficient storage capacity. To solve this problem, PAST system introduces the *replica diversion* mechanism. In other words, if one of such a node , denoted A, cannot store a replica, it chooses a node B in its leaf set such that B is not among the k closest nodes and does not already accommodate a diverted replica. A asks B to store that replica on its behalf and it enters a pointer to B in order that the diverted replica is threaten as it was locally stored. This means that, if node B fails, a new node must be in charge of that replica and if A fails, the replica should remain accessible. To minimize the impact of extra-storage load due to replica diversion, PAST considers three relevant policies, respectively regarding, (i) acceptance of replicas into a node's local store, (ii) selection of node to which a replica should be diverted, and (iii) deciding when diverting the whole object in spite of diverting its replicas, that is choosing a different seed in the generation of *fileId*. This last policy is called *file diversion*.

It is worth to note that sequential placement may lead to frequently move object replicas due to new nodes arrival or departure in the system. Glacier and Pangaea storage systems try to overcome such a problem using non-sequential placement policies. In detail, Glacier considers an ad-hoc placement policy, i.e. an object is stored under a key k and its corresponding n blocks are placed in the $n+1$ equidistant points in the circular id space. Pangaea maintains a sparse strongly connected and randomized graph of replicas for each data object. Since this graph is sparse, adding or removing a replica involves only a constant cost in terms of displacement, regardless of the total number of replicas.

Finally, since requesting nodes have no information about the logical identifier of the replicas, when using sequential placement, each request must be routed to a specific node at first and then forwarded to replicas. This node thus constitutes both a unique point of failure and a bottleneck to serve requests. The policy placement explained in the next section, namely symmetric replication [34], solves this problem.

Symmetric Replication

The main idea behind symmetric replication is that each identifier in the system should be associated with f other identifiers. If an identifier i is associated to another identifier r, then each item has to be stored in nodes responsible for identifiers i and r. Specifically, the identifier space is partitioned into N/f equivalence classes such that identifiers in an equivalence class are all associated with each other. For the symmetry requirement to always remain true, it is required that the replication factor f divides the size of the identifier space N. A node responsible for identifier i also stores every item with an identifier belonging to the equivalence class of i. Accordingly, to find an item with identifier i, a different request can be made for any of the identifier associated with i. This increases responsiveness since the failure of a node along the path of one request does not require repeating the request as long as another concurrent request succeeds.

3.3.   *Responsiveness*

Another aspect of object availability concerns the time needed for a consumer (client) to retrieve an object, i.e. data availability does not only concern the actual presence of the object in the system but also the responsiveness of the system itself, since data objects stored in the system cannot be considered available if time necessary to retrieve them is excessive.

To improve responsiveness, objects should be stored in such a way that it will be cheap for a client to retrieve them, both in terms of lookup latency and time for download. More specifically, to retrieve and access an object, a client must first search it in the system, and then proceed with its download. In this sense, the physical position of an object in a wide-area network with respect to the client greatly affects the latency experienced by the client itself to access that object. At a first glance storing the object in the node nearest to the client, could seem the best solution to reduce network transmission latency. This strategy, in fact, could actually cause an overload of a specific node that consequently will introduce delays in the service. For this reason, objects should be placed in the vicinity of a majority of requesting clients while preserving load balancing. From this point of view, while sequential placement creates a bottleneck possibly increasing serving time, symmetric replication can be used to send out multiple concurrent requests and picking the first available response. In this sense, a very interesting approach is the one, based on *floating replicas*, introduced in OceanStore [9]: with this approach persistent objects are free to migrate throughout the infrastructure. This particular replica management is based on *introspection*, since observation and analysis of system information are necessary to conveniently move replicas through the system.

Another important aspect that affects responsiveness is data object granularity. As already said, the latency experienced by a node requesting an object is a combination between object lookup and download latencies. Obviously, retrieving an object stored in different blocks through sequential lookups, one for each block, can lead to a great increase of latency. If a set of lookups can be done in parallel, the latency experienced by the client is comparable with the latency of a single object lookup. Once all blocks are found they can be simultaneously downloaded reducing overall download time. In the case of a single object, the impacting factor in responsiveness is essentially the time needed to download the object.

In order to increase responsiveness, global data storage systems also exploit caching mechanisms. In PAST, for example, nodes use the *unused* portion of their disk space to cache objects. This cached data can be evicted and deleted at any time. In particular, cached objects can be deleted if necessary to allow the storage of other replicas. This implies that the increase in storage utilization of the system leads to cache performance degradation. Exploiting Chord's lookup properties, CFS caches objects in the paths traveled by client requests. When a CFS client looks up for a block with key k, it performs a Chord lookup passing for nodes whose identifier is successively closer to that of k's successor. At each step, the initiating node, i.e. the client, checks if the contacted node caches the block required. Eventually the client reaches k's successor or an intermediate node containing the object in its cache. In any case, once the block is found, it is sent to every nodes contacted during the lookup. Due to the fact that hops traveled by messages in the Chord ring become shorter and shorter, approaching the target key, clients looking for a same block are expected to traverse the same node in the last hops of the lookup. For this reason caching blocks in the path can effectively reduce the time necessary to find requested data. PAST and CFS use two different replacement policies for cached data objects. Specifically, CFS uses the *least-recently-used* policy in order to take in account data object popularity. On the contrary, PAST considers a more complex policy, the so-called *Greedy-Dual-Size*: upon caching, an object d is associated with a weight H_d calculated as the relation $c(d)/s(d)$, where $c(d)$ is a cost associated with d and $s(d)$ is the object size. When necessary, the object with the minimum H_d is evicted. It is important again to note the strong impact of objects' size in PAST.

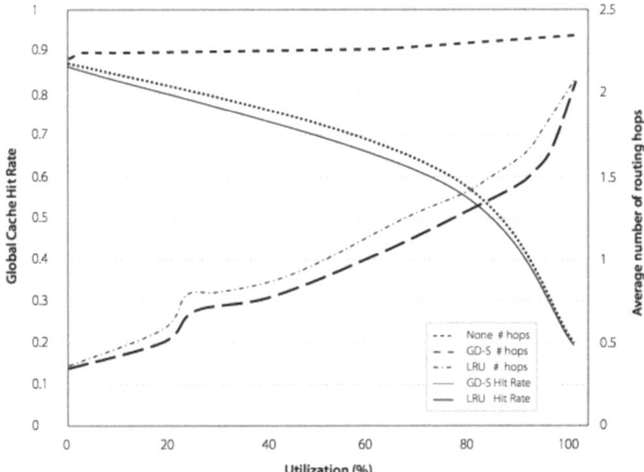

Figure 7. PAST simulation results [10]: global cache hit ratio and average number of message hops versus utilization using Least-Recently-Used (LRU), GreedyDual-Size (GD-S) and no caching.

In the following we resume simulation results presented in [10] about the impact of caching in PAST. In detail, the experiment uses 2250 PAST nodes. The storage space contributed by each PAST node was chosen from a truncated normal distribution with mean 27, standard deviation 10.8 and with upper and lower bound limits respectively at 51 and 2. Moreover, threshold for primary replica is t_{pri}=0.1, while threshold for diverted replica is t_{div}=0.05. Simulation measures the number of routing hops required to perform a successful lookup and the global cache hit ratio versus utilization. In detail, the average number of hops aims to capture the performance benefits of caching in terms of client latency and network traffic. The authors analyzed these parameters with and without caching enabled. As depicted in **Figure 7**, when caching is disabled, the number of routing hops required on average is constant to about 70% of storage utilization and then starts increasing slightly. The number of hops rises due to replica diversion. In fact, with high storage utilization it may be possible that several nodes do not have sufficient storage space to host a replica, and then the latter must be diverted to another hosting node. Exploiting caching the average number of hops for a successful lookup increases as usage raises. On the contrary, the global cache hit rate decreases when usage increases. When there is a low storage usage, objects are cached closer to where they are requested and thus few hops are necessary to retrieve the object. As the storage utilization increases, stored data objects increase and cache starts to replace some data objects. Thus hit ratio decreases and the number of hops consequently rises. Finally, the authors of [10] compared the above explained caching replacement policies, that is: GreedyDual-Size (DG-S) and Least-Recently-Used (LRU). Both policies have the same behavior, as shown in **Figure 7**, but DG-S has overall better performance than LRU.

4.　Data Object Updating

In most peer-to-peer systems [8,10,11] data object is assumed to be rather static and updates occur very infrequently. For this reason, facilities and support of most peer-to-peer systems focus on an efficient and robust access to data object in a read-only mode. A few systems supports data object update, and among those few, updates are supposed to be very rare. In these systems, the update of data object is handled as an exceptional event. This means that, for instance, it requires a complex coordination among data object's owners [9] or the updating follows only a best effort approach that does not guarantee the success of the data object update itself [18]. The issue of data object updating, however, has been becoming of primary importance for applications beyond file sharing, like trust management, peer commerce, bulletin-board systems, address books, project management information where data object updates may happen frequently. Only very recently some solutions for these applications have been proposed [19] but the problem is still far to be completely addressed. In the following, we survey solutions supported by current global data object storage systems.

4.1.　Toward a sustainable and meaningful level of consistency

A lot of work has been done for distributed read/write systems [20,21,22] but rethinking about old solutions and/or devising new solutions is mandatory due to the challenges related to the target environment, in particular:

- High replication factor
- Data object replicated over geographical areas on nodes which are online with very low probability
- Lack of global knowledge (a node holding a replica may not know where other replicas reside)

Data object replication imposes to solve the problem of replica consistency but the considered environment requires very scalable solutions able to deal with very unreliable data object's owners. In these systems, maintaining strong consistency could be impractical or even impossible, and for this reason weaker consistency criteria, like eventual consistency, are adopted.

4.1.1.　Eventual consistency

Maintaining the consistency of replicas means to rule the access of users to replicas and to synchronize replicas updates [23]. Traditionally, many systems working on LAN provide the so-called single copy semantics. Single copy semantics gives user the illusion of accessing a single, highly available copy of an object. In particular, the access to a replica is prohibited unless the replica content is up to date. Typical solutions require clients to access a quorum of replicas or to acquire exclusive locks on data they wish to update. Unfortunately, maintaining single-copy semantics in a global system worldwide deployed is practically and theoretically impossible [17]. For instance, as for partitionable networks, it can yield unacceptably low write availability.

Eventual consistency is a weaker consistency criterion than single-copy semantics, it is implementable in our targeted environment and current implementations are practical and efficient. In particular, eventual consistency allows data object presented to users to be stale. Differently from single-copy semantics implementations, which update all the replicas at once and possibly blocking read requests from users during the update application, eventual consistency implementations propagate updates in the background and allows any replica to be read directly most of the time. Eventual consistency guarantees that whatever the current state of replica is, if no new update is issued and the replicas can communicate freely for a long enough period, the contents of all the replicas become identical eventually.

From an implementation point of view, the issues to solve in order to guarantee eventual consistency are [23]:

1. update dissemination: each update must eventually reach all replicas.
2. update ordering: all updates must be eventually applied in the same order at each replica to assure that the last update is the same for all replicas.
3. update conflict resolution: concurrent updates that may semantically conflict should be detected and solved.

The first issue has been practically solved by epidemic dissemination as further discussed. The second and third are still open issues.

4.2.   Update Dissemination

Each update must eventually reach all replicas even though the update originator has gone off-line or is no more directly reachable. To this end, two types of dissemination have been proposed: *push based* or *pull based*. In the push based dissemination, each replica with an update sends or forwards the update to all (or to a subset of) replicas that are communicable. In the pull-based dissemination, each replica polls the state of others replicas periodically or on-demand in order to get missing updates. Fpr example, Ivy [13] is a multi-user read/write peer-to-peer file system using a pure pull approach. An Ivy file system consists of a set of logs, one log per participant. A log contains all of one participant's changes to the file system. Each participant finds data object by consulting all logs but performs modification only by appending on its log. This log exchange does not scale to systems with a huge number of writers.

The most favorable approach, indeed, is a hybrid approach that combines push and pull dissemination. The hybrid approach provides a first push phase followed by a pull phase. In the following, we analyze this hybrid approach adopted in P-Grid.

4.2.1.   P-Grid: a Hybrid Dissemination

The algorithm proposed in P-grid [12] for update dissemination uses an hybrid push/pull scheme that assures eventual delivery to all replicas with very high probability.

Push Phase - The push phase follows a constrained flooding scheme: a new update of an object is pushed by the initiator to a subset of peers, holding an object replica, that it knows, which in turn propagate it to other peers holding object replicas they know. The update is not blindly flooded to all nodes: a list, piggybacked with the update message, contains a partial set of peers to which the update has already been sent. A forwarder chooses nodes to which send the update message ignoring those in the list. The update is propagated with a probability that depends on how many times the update has been already forwarded.

Pull phase - In order to detect a missing update, each update is piggybacked with a version vector V, a vector of timestamps with dimension equal to the cardinality of the nodes holding an object replica. The timestamp is any number that increases monotonically, in this case each time a peer issues an update it computes locally its timestamp (by hashing the concatenated values of the current data object and time, the current IP address and a large random number) and piggybacks the vector version V with the computed timestamp as $V[i]$ element. Then, the $V[i]$ element on node i shows the time the last update was issued by i. Elements of $V[j]=v$ on node i indicate that i has received all updates issued at node j and with timestamps up to v. During the pull phase a node i polls the node j sending its version vector V_i. By the comparison of V_i with the version vector V_j, j can check if it has some update that i has missed. In particular if $V_j[k] > V_i[k]$ for some k, j sends to i all updates issued by k stored at j with timestamps greater than $V_i[k]$.

4.3.　Update Ordering and Conflict Resolution

To guarantee eventual consistency updates must be applied in the some order to each replica.

A widely used approach [25,9] lets clients (update issuers) to write their own copy without a preventive coordination with other replicas owners. These updates are *tentative* until the replicas' owners decide which is the global order in which they must be eventually applied. Once the update is globally ordered, the update is called *committed*. Then each committed update is spread in the system and eventually applied. This means that each replica's owner should be able to undo previous tentative updates it previously applied on the local replica when the committed update order differs from it. It is worth noting that tentative updates may conflict since different clients update concurrently their own copies without coordination. The types of conflicts are application dependent. For instance, in the bibliographic database of Bayou [25], there exist two types of conflicts: (i) the same bibliographic entry with two different keys and (ii) the same key associated with two different bibliographic entries. Mechanisms to detect and solve update conflicts depend on application semantics. In the following, we deepen how update ordering is performed in Oceanstore and what are the basic mechanisms for conflict resolution firstly proposed in Bayou and currently used in Oceanstore.

Another approach to implement eventual consistency is based on loosely synchronized clocks for updates ordering implemented by timestamping updates with the current clock value (P-grid [12], Pangaea [14]). This approach allows the detection of conflicts by comparing timestamps associated with updates. Usually the resolution of conflicts in these systems follows some deterministic rules (e.g. among two conflicts updates the tie is broken comparing update issuers identifiers). Section 4.3.2 describes how these mechanisms are implemented in Pangaea.

4.3.1.　A Two-Tier Approach for Update Ordering: Oceanstore

Oceanstore [9] is a global data object storage system providing access to persistent storage. The system is composed by a set of nodes (untrusted servers) spread over the Internet. Each client accesses the storage thanks to a specific server (provider).

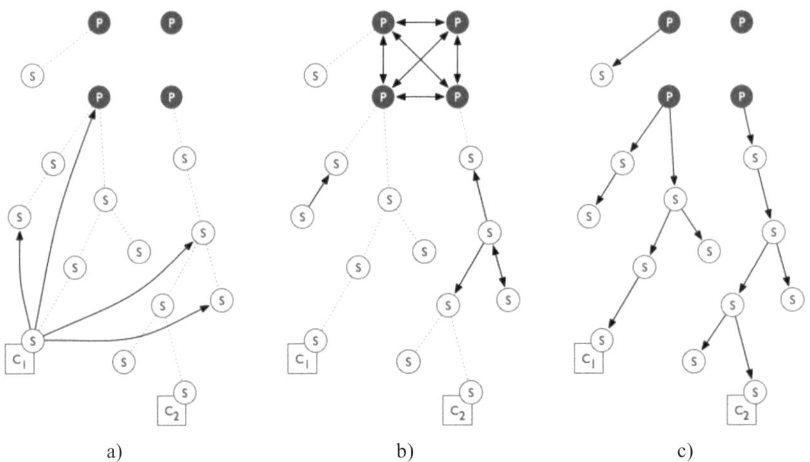

Figure 8. The update mechanism in Oceanstore: an example.

Object replication follows a two-tier approach. A specific small set of servers, called the *inner ring* of the object, are the primary owners of the object and store the primary replicas (primary tier). Other replicas, called secondary, are held by a large number of nodes mostly for caching reasons (secondary tier). Objects in Oceanstore are modified through *updates*. Every object in Oceanstore is read-only, so any update to an object creates a new version. The inner ring must be able to determine the last read-only version for consistency. In particular, a client sends the update by disseminating it in the system. The guarantee that the update eventually reaches all replicas of the inner ring is delegated to the underlying object location mechanism provided by Tapestry (see Section 2.2.2). The update sent by the client is called a *tentative update* until it is committed by the replicas forming the inner ring. These replicas, through a Byzantine agreement, decide the order, i.e. the version, of the update and then disseminate the committed update. This operation occurs through a dissemination tree that connects the inner ring with the secondary tier. Secondary replicas apply both tentative and committed update. An epidemic mechanism guarantees that every secondary replica eventually applies the last committed update: a first best-effort multicast down the dissemination tree pushes the update to the secondary tier. Then, secondary replicas pull missing information from parents and the primary tier.

As for update conflicts, they are detected by the inner ring and in many cases solved automatically; otherwise application-specific tasks may be pursued (see Section 4.3.2). In **Figure 8** it is shown the path of an update in Oceanstore: in **Figure 8** (a) the tentative update is sent toward the inner ring, then once the update reaches the inner ring it is ordered and committed (**Figure 8** (b)). The committed update is then sent to all nodes through a dissemination tree rooted at each inner ring node (**Figure 8** (c)). Note that Oceanstore provides single-copy semantics to each client always reading data object from the inner ring, it while provides eventual consistency to each client reading data object indifferently from the both primary and secondary tier.

As just said, the solution proposed by Oceanstore relies on a set of servers (the inner ring) to maintain replica consistency. These servers, even though untrusted, are special nodes capable of creating a sub-network with high bandwidth and a fixed infrastructure. These network characteristics are prerequisites to the convergence of the Byzantine agreement used for update commitment. However, in a pure peer-to-peer system, such special nodes are absent and no hierarchy there exists. Then, the solution proposed by Oceanstore is not straightforwardly applicable to a pure peer-to-peer system. Note that in Oceanstore the set of servers constituting the inner ring can tolerate up to f failures when the number of servers is equal or grater than $3f+1$.

4.3.2. Conflict Resolution in Bayou

Bayou [25] is a global data storage system designed for a mobile computing environment. Differently from all other systems discussed in this chapter, the topology of the network does not reflect logical relationships among nodes but is the very topology defined by physical connections among mobile nodes. Then, Bayou does not encompass the concept of an overlay network as defined in Section 2.1, however its mechanisms for maintaining eventual consistency are the basics for many global data storage systems like Oceanstore. As Oceanstore, Bayou is a system composed by a set of servers, a client is associated to one server each time it accesses the storage. An update is tentative until it is not committed, thanks to a pair-wise anti-entropy communication among servers. Clock synchronization is also exploited in order to make the ordering on committed updates as close as possible to the ordering on tentative updates. As for conflict detection and resolution, the originality of Bayou lies in detecting conflicts specified by the application and in resolving them automatically (when possible). In order to support arbitrary applications, the Bayou system provides two basic mechanisms, called, respectively, *dependency checks* and *merge procedures*. These mechanisms permit clients to indicate, for each individual update, how the system should detect conflicts involving the update and what steps should be taken to solve any detected conflicts based on the application's semantics.

Techniques for semantic-based conflict detection and resolution have previously been implemented into some systems to handle special cases such as file directory updates. For example, the Locus [26], Ficus [27], and Coda [28] distributed file systems all include mechanisms for automatically resolving certain classes of conflicting directory operations. Other systems, like Lotus Notes [29], do not provide application-specific mechanisms to handle conflicts, but rather create multiple versions of a document, file, or data object when conflicts arise. Bayou's dependency checks and merge procedures are more general than these previous techniques.

4.3.2.1. Dependency checks

Each update is associated with a dependency check: an application-supplied query and its expected results. A conflict arises when the query, once ran at some server against its local replica, returns a not expected result. If the dependency check fails the update is not applied and the server invokes a specific (application-dependent) procedure to solve the detected conflict.

Bayou's dependency checks, like the version vectors and timestamps traditionally used in other systems [e.g. Pangaea, P-Grid], can be used to detect when two users update the same data item without one of them first observing the other's update, i.e. it detects Write-Write conflicts. Detection of such conflicts is performed by querying the values of any data items being updated and ensuring that values have not changed since the update was submitted, as is done in Oracle's replicated database [30].

Bayou's dependency checking mechanism is more powerful than mechanisms based on version vectors, since it can detect Read-Write conflicts. Specifically, each update can explicitly specify the expected values of any data items on which the update depends, including data items that have been read but are not being updated. Thus, Bayou clients can emulate the optimistic style of concurrency control employed in some distributed database systems [31,32].

Moreover, given that dependency queries can read any data in the server's replica, dependency checks can enforce arbitrary, multi-item integrity constraints on the data. For example, suppose an update consists in transferring $100 from account A to account B. The application, before issuing the update, reads the balance of account A and discovers that it currently has $150. Traditional optimistic concurrency control would check that account A still had $150 before performing the requested update. The real requirement, however, is that the account have at least $100, and this can easily be specified in the update's dependency check. Thus, only if concurrent updates cause the balance in account A to drop below $100 a conflict arises.

4.3.2.2. Merge procedures

Once a conflict is detected, a *merge procedure* is run by the Bayou server in an attempt to solve the conflict. Merge procedures, associated with each update, are general programs written in a high-level, interpreted language. They can have embedded data, such as application-specific knowledge related to the update that was being attempted, and can perform arbitrary reads on the current state of the server's replica. The merge procedure associated with a Write is responsible for resolving any conflicts detected by its dependency check and for producing a revised update to apply. The complete process of detecting a conflict, running a merge procedure, and applying the revised update, is performed atomically at each server as part of the whole update.

The meeting room scheduling application provides good examples of conflict resolution procedures that are specific not only to a particular application but also to a particular update operation. This application allows users to reserve meeting rooms with the constraint that at most one person (or group) can reserve the room for any given period of time.

In this application users, well aware that their reservations may be invalidated by other concurrent users, can specify alternate scheduling choices as part of their original scheduling updates. These alternatives are encoded in a merge procedure that attempts to reserve one of the alternate meeting times if the original time is found to be in conflict with some other previously scheduled meeting. A different merge procedure altogether could search for the next available time slot to schedule the meeting, which is an option a user might choose if any time would be satisfactory.

In the case where automatic resolution is not possible, the merge procedure will still run to completion, but is expected to produce a revised update that logs the detected conflict in some fashion that will enable manual resolution later.

In contrast to systems like Coda [28] or Ficus [33] that lock individual files or complete file volumes when conflicts have been detected but not yet resolved, Bayou allows replicas to always remain accessible. This permits clients to continue to read previously written data and to continue to issue new updates. In the meeting room scheduling application, for example, a user who only cares about Monday meetings need not concern himself with scheduling conflicts on Wednesday. Of course, the potential drawback of this approach is that newly issued updates may depend on data that is in conflict and may lead to cascade conflict resolution.

4.3.3.　A Pure Peer-to-Peer Approach for Ordering and Conflict Detection: Pangaea

Pangaea [14] is a wide-area file system supporting data object sharing across a federation of up to thousands computers connected by dedicated or private networks. The infrastructure is decentralized and consists of commodity computers provided by end-users. Pangaea is a highly replicated system: whenever and wherever a file is accessed a new replica is created. The group of replicas is thus highly dynamic and potentially large. Pangaea addresses the challenges connected to these characteristics maintaining a sparse strongly connected and randomized graph of replicas for each file. Update dissemination uses a push approach by flooding the update (the entire file content) on this random graph. Pangaea assures eventual consistency, only if the replica graph is strongly connected. Updates are timestamped using loosely synchronized clock (each nodes goes roughly at the same speed). In particular, each update message is associated with a N-element vector of timestamps; these vectors are periodically exchanged among replicas [24] to learn about the status of other replicas. At receiver side all updates are sorted by their timestamps and applied. More in detail, it is assured that any replica i applies an update u only when all updates, applied at some other replica j before u, have been applied even at i. Concurrent updates have incomparable vectors, and vice-versa two updates with incomparable vectors are concurrent. Then, just checking the timestamp vectors of two nodes it is possible to detect conflicting updates. In this case Pangaea solves the conflict in two ways: one way is applying the last-writer-wins rule, i.e. applying the update coming from the node that issued the update at last. The alternative consists in concatenating the two versions in a single file and let the user fix the conflict manually.

Pangaea provides a pure peer-to-peer approach to data object updating as no server is needed, but the management of timestamp vectors and loosely synchronized clocks limit its applicability. In particular, clock synchronization is not always applicable or may be a bottleneck when millions of users need to be synchronized. The use of timestamp vectors allows updates' ordering at receiver side, but a missing update may block the application of successive updates. In this respect, Pangaea does not tolerate crashes of update initiators: update dissemination, initiated by a crashing process, may reach only a subset of replicas (it may then provokes a block).

References

[1]　I. Stoica, R. Morris, D. Karger, M. F. Kaashoek and H. Balakrishnan, *Chord: A Scalable Peer-to-Peer Lookup Service for Internet Applications*, Proceedings of ACM SIGCOMM, 2001.

[2]　A. Rowstron and P. Druschel, *Pastry: Scalable, Decentralized Object Location and Routing for Large-Scale Peer-to-Peer Systems*, Proceedings of International Conference on Distributed Systems Platforms (Middleware), 2001.

[3]　S. Ratnasamy, P. Francis, M. Handley, R. Karp and S. Shenker, *A scalable content-addressable network*, Proceedings of ACM SIGCOMM, 2001.

[4]　S. Q. Zhuang, B. Y. Zhao, A. D. Joseph, R. Katz and J. Kubiatowicz, *Tapestry: An Infrastructure for Fault-Tolerant Wide-Area Location and Routing*, Technical Report UCB/CSD-01-1141, University of California at Berkeley, Computer Science Division, 2001.

[5]　D. Malkhi, M. Naor and D. Ratajczak, *Viceroy: A scalable and dynamic emulation of the butterfly*, Proceedings of the 21st annual ACM symposium on Principles of distributed computing, 2002.

[6]　Moni Naor and Udi Wieder, *Novel Architectures for P2P Applications: the Continuous-Discrete Approach*, In ACM Symposium on Parallel Algorithms and Architectures, 2003.

[7]   D. Karger, E. Lehman, F. Leighton, M. Levine, D. Lewin and R. Panigrahy, *Consistent hashing and random trees: Distributed caching protocols for relieving hot spots on the world wide web*, Proceedings of the 29th Annual ACM Symposium on Theory of Computing, 1997.

[8]   F. Dabek, M. F. Kaashoek, D. Karger, R. Morris and Ion Stoica, *Wide-area cooperative storage with CFS*, Proceedings of the eighteenth ACM symposium on Operating systems principles, 2001.

[9]   D. Bindel, Y. Chen, P. Eaton, D. Geels, R. Gummadi, S. Rhea, H. Weatherspoon, W. Weimer, C. Wells, B. Zhao and J. Kubiatowicz, *OceanStore: An Extremely Wide-Area Storage System*, Technical Report UCB/CSD-00-1102, University of California at Berkeley, Computer Science Division, 2000.

[10] A. Rowstron and P. Druschel, *Storage management and caching in PAST, a large-scale, persistent peer-to-peer storage utility*, Proceedings of the eighteenth ACM symposium on Operating systems principles, 2001.

[11] A. Haeberlen, A. Mislove and Peter Druschel, *Glacier: Highly durable, decentralized storage despite massive correlated failures*, Proceedings of the 2ndt USENIX Symposium on NetworkedSystems Design and Implementation, 2005.

[12] K. Aberer, M. Punceva, M. Hauswirth and R. Schmidt, *Improving Data object Access in P2P Systems*, IEEE Internet Computing, vol. 6 issue 1 pp. 58-67, 2002.

[13] A. Muthitacharoen, R. Morris, T. M. Gil and B. Chen, *Ivy: A Read/Write Peer-to-Peer File System*, Proceedings of 5th Symposium on Operating Systems Design and Implementation, 2002.

[14] Y. Saito, C. Karamanolis, M. Karlsson and M. Mahalingam, *Taming aggressive replication in the Pangaea wide-area file system*, ACM SIGOPS Operating Systems Review, vol. 36 issue SI, 2002.

[15] C. Plaxton, R. Rajaraman and A. Richa, *Accessing nearby copies of replicated objects in a distributed environment*, Proceedings of ACM SPAA, pages 311-320, 1997

[16] W.K.Lin, D.M.Chiu and Y.B.Lee, *Erasure Code Replication Revisited*, pp. 90-97, Fourth International Conference on Peer-to-Peer Computing, 2004.

[17] M.J.Fischer, N.A.Lynch and M.S.Paterson, *Impossibility of Distributed Consensus with One Faulty Process*, Journal of the ACM, 32(2):374-382, 1985.

[18] I. Clarke, O. Sandberg, B. Wiley, and T. W. Hong, *Freenet: A Distributed Anonymous Information Storage and Retrieval System*, In Designing Privacy Enhancing Technologies: International Workshop on Design Issues in Anonymity and Unobservability, number 2009 in LNCS, 2001.

[19] A. Datta, M. Hauswirth, K. Aberer, *Updates in highly unreliable, replicated peer-to-peer systems*, Proceedings of the 23rd International Conference on Distributed Computing Systems, IEEE Computer Society , 2003

[20] D. B. Terry , Marvin M. Theimer, K. Petersen, A. J. Demers, M. J. Spreitzer, C. H. Hauser, *Managing Update Conflicts in Bayou, a Weakly Connected Replicated Storage System*, Proceedings of the 15th ACM Symposium on Operating Systems Principles, Dec. 1995.

[21] D.H. Ratner, *Roam: A Scalable Replication System for Mobile and Distributed Computing*, PhD thesis, UC Los Angeles, 1998. UCLA-CSD-970044.

[22] L.B. Mummert, M.R. Ebling, and M. Satyanarayanan, *Exploiting Weak Connectivity for Mobile File Access*, Proceedings of the 15th ACM Symposium on Operating Systems Principles, Dec. 1995.

[23] Y. Saito, M. Shapiro, *Optimistic replication*, ACM Computing Surveys, March 2005.

[24] R. A. Golding, D. D. E. Long, *Modeling replica divergence in a weak-consistency protocol for global-scale distributed data bases*, Technical report UCSC-CRL-93-09, Computer and Information Sciences Board, University of California, Santa Cruz, 1993.

[25] A. Demers, K. Petersen, M. Spreitzer, D. Terry, M.M. Theimer, and B. Welch, *The bayou architecture: Support for data sharing among mobile users*, In Proceedings Workshop on Mobile Computing Systems and Applications. IEEE, December 1994.

[26] B. Walker, G. Popek, R. English, C. Kline, and G. Thiel, *The LOCUS distributed operating system*, Proceedings Ninth Symposium on Operating Systems Principles, Bretton Woods, New Hampshire, October 1983, pages 49-70.

[27] R.G. Guy, J.S. Heidemann, W. Mak, T.W. Page, Jr., G.J. Popek, and D. Rothmeier, *Implementation of the Ficus replicated file system*, Proceedings Summer USENIX Conference, June 1990, pages 63-71.

[28] P. Kumar and M. Satyanarayanan, *Log-based directory resolution in the Coda file system*, Proceedings Second International Conference on Parallel and Distributed Information Systems, San Diego, California, January 1993.

[29] L. Kalwell Jr., S. Beckhardt, T. Halvorsen, R. Ozzie, and I. Greif, *Replicated document management in a group communication system*, In Groupware: Software for Computer-Supported Cooperative Work, edited by D. Marca and G. Bock, IEEE Computer Society Press, 1992, pages 226-235.

[30] A. Downing, *Conflict resolution in symmetric replication*, Proceedings European Oracle User Group Conference, Florence, Italy, April 1995, pages 167-175.

[31] M. J. Carey and M. Livny, *Conflict detection tradeoffs for replicated data*, ACM Transactions on Database Systems 16(4):703-746, December 1991.

[32] S. Davidson, H. Garcia-Molina, and D. Skeen, *Consistency in a partitioned network: A survey*, ACM Computing Surveys 17(3):341-370, September 1985.

[33] P. Reiher, J. Heidemann, D. Ratner, G. Skinner, and G. Popek, *Resolving file conflicts in the Ficus file system*, Proceedings Summer USENIX Conference, June 1994, pages 183-195.

[34] Ghodsi, Ali and Onana Alima, Luc and Haridi, Seif, *Symmetric Replication for Structured Peer-to-Peer Systems*, In proceedings of the 3rd International Workshop on Databases, Information Systems and Peer-to-Peer Computing, July 2005, Trondheim, Norway.

Global Data Management
R. Baldoni et al. (Eds.)
IOS Press, 2006

Towards Efficient Complex Data Management Services in Peer-to-Peer Networks[1]

Ioannis Aekaterinidis [a], Nikos Ntarmos [a], Theoni Pitoura [a], and Peter Triantafillou [a,2]

[a] *R.A. Computer Technology Institute and*
Department of Computer Engineering & Informatics
University of Patras, Greece

Abstract. Building efficient internet-scale data management services is the main focus of this chapter. In particular, we aim to show how to leverage DHT technology and extend it with novel algorithms and architectures in order to (i) improve efficiency and reliability for traditional DHT (exact-match) queries, particularly exploiting the abundance of altruism witnessed in real-life P2P networks, (ii) speedup range queries for data stored on DHTs, and (iii) support efficiently and scalably the publish/subscribe paradigm over DHTs, which crucially depends on algorithms for supporting rich queries on string-attribute data.

Keywords. DHT networks, data management services, publish-subscribe paradigm, altruistic and powerful peers, string-attribute and range queries over DHTs, efficient query processing, performance

1. Introduction

This chapter is concerned with offering complex data management services to applications built over a large-scale network infrastructure. The distinguishing characteristic and key challenge is that the presented solutions are founded on the harnessing of all distributed (data, processing, communication, and storage) resources available in the network in order to provide "traditional" data management functionalities. Related work has provided solutions for a large number of problems, from architectures and algorithms for searching for relevant data, to range query processing and data integration, and has started to examine how to support join and aggregate queries. This fact testifies to the importance our community is giving to being able to support data-intensive applications over large-scale network infrastructures.

---

[1] We warmly thank for major financial support the FP6 of the EU through the IST DELIS (IST-2004-001907), the PENED 2003 Programme of the EU and the General Secretariat for Research and Technology of the Helenic State, and the Programme Pythagoras of the European Social Fund (ESF) - Operational Program for Educational and Vocational Training II (EPEAEK II).

[2] Correspondence to: Peter Triantafillou, R.A. Computer Technology Institute and Department of Computer Engineering & Informatics, University of Patras, Greece. Tel.: +30 2610 996913; E-mail: peter@ceid.upatras.gr.

The envisaged network applications are to be built over all computational, networking, and storage resources available. Key to the success of such applications is thus their ability to effectively utilize all spare resources found in the network. The last few years, our community has witnessed a number of relevant techniques for creating efficient and scalable overlay networks: structured peer-to-peer networks (e.g. networks based on Distributed Hash Tables, or DHTs)[34,28,25,42] create a self-* infrastructure (i.e., self-repairable, self-managed) which facilitates the pooling together of various distributed resources, while guaranteeing efficient and scalable data access. Unfortunately, this data access is facilitated only for equality, exact-match queries, querying for a given resource identifier. The applications targeted by this work are required to offer a much richer interface and functionality, allowing the efficient processing of complex queries such as range queries, and continuous queries (involving a rich set of operators on numerical and string data types) such as subscriptions and the corresponding publications in the publish-subscribe paradigm. Efficiency is measured in a number of dimensions, including query response times, resource requirements (e.g., bandwidth) and scalability, fair processing load distribution among the network nodes, and resource utilization.

In this chapter we will specifically target the following problems which are central for the deployment of scalable data management solutions in large-scale peer-to-peer networks: the development of architectures and algorithms

- which can exploit the existence of altruistic and powerful peers, in order to speedup accesses to data,
- which can efficiently support range queries (and more complex query types, such as aggregation queries),
- which can support the publish/subscribe paradigm over p2p data networks. Typically, publish/subscribe systems depend on the efficient processing of predicates on string attributes involving operators such as prefix, suffix, and equality.

First, an architectural paradigm, coined PLANES, is discussed (first proposed in [23]), harnessing the characteristics of altruistic and selfish peers, weaving them into the structured network architecture. PLANES achieves significantly greater routing efficiency in such P2P networks for both the steady-state and highly-dynamic cases, without transferring routing overheads to other system functionalities, and introducing significant efficiency gains in terms of hop counts, routing state size and maintenance requirements, and robustness. Several architectures and algorithms are presented offering trade-offs between routing speedups vs the required number of altruists and their routing state and between routing path lengths in the steady-state case vs altruist-network connectivity requirements. The end result is that very small percentages of altruistic nodes are required, being burdened with small overheads, and introducing steady-state routing speedups by factors of up to 2-4 and by several orders of magnitude in the highly-dynamic case. At the same time, total routing state size is reduced by a factor of about 2, which leads to improved robustness. Furthermore, routing robustness is improved due to the smaller total routing state and the isolation of the ill-effects of selfish behaviour within small clusters of peers.

Next, we turn our attention to range queries and on how to efficiently support them. We overview an approach (first proposed in [40]) based on order-preserving (a.k.a locality-preserving) DHT networks, coined Locality-Preserving DHTs (LP-DHTs) and explain how it can speedup range queries and facilitate the support of aggregate queries.

Subsequently, we show how to exploit powerful nodes for even greater speedups. To this end, we present an architecture, coined RangeGuards[22], where a number of peers are charged with specific tasks for further significant speedups during range query processing. RangeGuards is based on: (i) a way to efficiently identify and collect those peers, and (ii) mechanisms to utilize them during range query processing. The performance results have shown that significant savings can be achieved by the proposed architecture. Perhaps most importantly, a key advantage of RangeGuards is that the dangers and inefficiencies of relying on weak nodes for range query processing, with respect to their processing, storage, and communication capacities, and their intermittent connectivity are avoided.

Finally, a complementary paradigm to employ for data access and storage is the publish/subscribe (pub/sub) paradigm. In a pub/sub environment users and applications "publish" data into the system. Similarly, users and applications define their interests in specific data items through "subscriptions". Subscriptions are in essence continuous queries involving a set of predicates to identify desired data. The system consists of a network of broker nodes whose functionality is to marry all incoming publications to the appropriate previously-stored subscriptions, passing the data to the users who have issued them. A particularly desirable characteristic is to utilize a DHT overlay for the broker network, leveraging thus the scalability, efficiency, and self-* benefits rendered by DHT-related research. Here we will overview our solutions which are based on extending the DHTs functionality to support the efficient processing of predicates on string [3] and numerical [37] typed attributes (which dominate in typical pub/sub services). These solutions are involving complex string predicates (such as prefix, suffix, and containment) in addition to simple exact-match string predicates, as well as range predicates on numerical attributes.

2. Altruism-Endowed Peer-to-Peer Data Management

2.1. Motivation

Large-scale studies of real-world peer-to-peer (mostly file-sharing) networks[2,30,31, 41], have testified to the fact that the P2P world consists of altruists, selfish peers, and of others with behavior ranging in between, with a non-negligible percentage of the last category showing altruistic behavior if given the incentives to do so. The bad news is that the great majority of peers (more than 70%[2,31]) were proven to be free riders. This is indeed very bad news for DHT-style overlays, since the great majority of peers may be joining the network and leaving very soon thereafter[30,41]. The good news are that a non-negligible percentage of the peers were proven to be altruistic[3]. Thus, we conjecture that, by giving incentives (to avoid the so-called tragedy of the commons), more network nodes will be willing to act altruistically.

Looking at related research in DHT-structured P2P networks, one notices that given a highly-dynamic environment in a N-Node network, routing performance degrades

---

[3]There is some disagreement whether this is true altruistic behaviour or a positive externality (i.e., a benefit to the community that results from peers acting in their own self- interest); Nonetheless, be it altruism or "altruism", the benefits to the community contributed by these peers are recognized by all! For this reason and for brevity in the remaining discussion we refer to altruistic nodes implying both altruistic and powerful nodes

to $O(N)$ hops (that is, if the network remains connected), mainly due to the difficulty in keeping up with the required updates to routing state. In order to guarantee in highly-dynamic cases $O(logN)$ routing performance, $O(log^2N)$ so-called stabilization "rounds"[19] need be ran by every node every half-life to update routing state (successors, predecessors, and fingers).

However, this solution transfers overhead from routing to the stabilization phases, while detecting the presence/absence of low-bandwidth nodes (which are the great majority) during stabilization is time-consuming and highly error prone (think of nodes behind modem lines). Hence, given the huge scales and the highly-dynamic nature of the vast majority of peers, current architectures fail to ensure $O(logN)$ routing in the highly-dynamic case. Furthermore, even $O(logN)$ hops, achieved in steady-state assuming "good node behavior", may not be good enough; after all, these are overlay hops with each being translated into multiple physical network hops. In addition, even $O(logN)$ hops over peers with low bandwidth will definitely create performance problems. Within the DHT world there is a complete lack of attention on exploiting powerful peers in order to improve performance.

Moreover, heterogeneity means more than a mere distinction between powerful and weak nodes; there is also heterogeneity with respect to their behavior, being altruistic or selfish. As of this, we advocate adding further structure to DHTs, leveraging altruistic peers. In this way, we can deliver definite performance guarantees for the steady-case and, perhaps more importantly, for the highly-dynamic cases. Over and above any hop-count improvements, we ensure a more stable infrastructure, especially during high churn[27]. We coin this architectural paradigm AESOP: Altruism-Endowed Self-Organizing Peers.

2.2. Position/Contributions

We intend to show how to leverage the coexistence of altruists and selfish peers found in real-life networks and harness them to improve routing performance. More specifically, our position is:

1. Weaving into the structured P2P network architectures the behavior and capability differences of peers, much-needed, quantifiable, and significant further routing speedups can be attained.
2. Routing speedups should refer to hop counts, routing state size and maintenance requirements, and robustness, and they should not be achieved by transferring overhead to other system operation phases (e.g., stabilization).
3. Routing speedups should pertain to the steady-state and highly-dynamic cases.
4. Altruistic and powerful nodes can be harnessed to offer these significant efficiency gains, while requiring that only a very small percentage of peers be altruistic, being burdened with only small overheads.

2.3. System Model

In general, we define altruistic peers to be the peers that (i) stay connected for significantly longer periods of time, and (ii) are willing and possess the necessary capacity to accept greater loads. With these characteristics in mind we revisit the "traditional" arguments about routing hot spots and about the overhead in dealing with the frequent topology changes inherent in P2P networks. Specifically, we advocate concentrating most routing chores at altruistic peers; these peers are willing to carry extra load and have the required capabilities to do so. This results in more efficient routing than forcing weaker nodes to partake heavily in the routing tasks.

The above decision will undoubtedly create greater routing tables at altruists. Traditionally, this causes greater reorganization overhead incurred when nodes enter and leave the network. However, the additional routing table entries of altruists will concern other altruistic peers. Because these stay connected for long periods of time, maintaining the freshness of this extra routing state does not result in prohibitively increased bandwidth overheads.

2.4. PLANES: Routing Optimization using Altruists

In PLANES, node and document identifiers (IDs) consist of m bits, allowing $N \leq 2^m$ nodes and documents. A small percentage of nodes (i.e. $A << N$) is altruistic.

2.4.1. Architecture and Algorithms

Our solution consists of partitioning the N nodes into DHT-structured clusters. For each cluster, a DHT-structured overlay network is created. (Note that any similar structure of choice can be used instead of DHTs, such as [21,1] yielding similar relative performance gains to that we show for DHTs). Given the desired cluster size, S, and the number of clusters, C, overall, $C = \frac{N}{S}$ clusters are formed. Each node requires minimal overhead for associating node IDs with cluster IDs (e.g. by hashing node IDs to cluster IDs). Due to the random placement of nodes around the DHT ring, within each cluster there exists at least one altruistic peer. Altruistic peers maintain greater routing state, with an entry for all other altruists, creating a completely connected altruistic overlay network. Thus, communication between altruistic nodes (and thus between clusters) requires 1 hop[4]. Later, we will do away with the complete connectivity requirement. Last, within every DHT cluster, all nodes maintain routing state for their neighbors, as required by the cluster's DHT. Thus, each node has $O(logS)$ neighbors. Also, all nodes keep routing state pointing to the altruistic node(s) in their cluster.

A node (altruistic or not) n_i joins the network, as usual, by finding the address of any member node, say of cluster c_s. Communicating with it, finds the address of the altruistic node for c_s. Then the id of the cluster to which it will belong, c_d, is determined. The altruistic node of the target cluster c_d is then found using the altruist for c_s. Finally, n_i joins the DHT structure of the target cluster, using the DHT join protocol and including an entry in its routing table for the cluster's altruist. Adding an altruist also involves communication within the altruist network to store the altruist network's routing table and update the other altruists' tables to include it. Further, all DHT-cluster nodes need to add an entry for it. A node leaving the network affects only the cluster's DHT structure, calling on the leave protocol of the DHT. Altruist deletion requires informing its cluster nodes and may require finding a replacement for it, e.g., if it is the last altruist for its cluster. This can be done examining its local routing table and selecting another altruist (typically one that is associated with a small number of clusters).

---

[4]In practice, we talk about a "highly-connected" altruistic network, and O(1) hops since complete connectivity is hard to achieve.

Routing is performed in two steps: (i) across clusters, from any node to a node in a different cluster, and (ii) within clusters, from any node (including an altruistic node) to another node in the same cluster. In the former case, given the completely-connected altruistic overlay network, routing to reach any cluster from outside the cluster requires two overlay hops: one hop from a node to its altruist and another from this altruist to the altruist of the target cluster. In the latter case routing is performed by sending the message over the cluster DHT network.

2.4.2. Extensions

In dynamic systems, the main concern is the overhead for maintaining freshness of routing state about altruists, which may become expensive or even impossible to maintain, breaking the complete-connectivity of the altruistic network. We first work in two dimensions: (i) reduce the required number of altruists and (ii) reduce their routing state. Then, we discuss an architecture without complete connectivity for the altruists network.

Using Fewer Altruists   We architect the network to consist of $C = \frac{N}{z \times logN}$ clusters, yielding a cluster size of $S = z \times logN$ for an appropriately-valued integer z. The key is to note that: (i) the required number of altruists (which is equal to C) decreases by a factor equal to z; and (ii) the routing hop count within each DHT cluster increases by $logz$, since $logS = log(z \times logN) = logz + log(logN)$.

Example: with one million nodes and $z = 6$, $C \approx 8335$ clusters, cutting the state and freshness overhead requirements by a factor of $6\times$ (going from a 50,000 altruistic-nodes network down to 8335 nodes). In return, instead of routing in <5 hops within the DHT cluster, we now require about <7 hops ($log120 \approx 7$). Taking this point further, using $z = 50$, results in 1000 clusters, each with 1000 nodes in it. Routing within each cluster now needs 10 hops; and the required number of altruists are now reduced by a factor of $50\times$.

Thus, we can still ensure significant speedups in routing (by a factor of about $2\times$ for the steady-state case and by orders of magnitude in the highly-dynamic case). At the same time, the overhead for maintaining high connectivity within the altruistic network, is dramatically reduced, since the number of altruists has been drastically reduced. Finally, we stress that requiring such a small percentage (0.1%) of altruistic nodes is not unrealistic [2,30,31,41].

Multi-level architectures   Alternatively (or complementarily) to the previous architecture, one can adopt the same layering principle recursively with respect now to the altruistic network. The motivation for this is twofold: (i) reduce further the overhead for maintaining complete/high connectivity between altruists, and (ii) exploit possible heterogeneities among altruists.

Fig. 1 outlines our approach for a three-layer P2P network. This network now includes a clustered altruistic P2P network with $A = 50,000$ altruistic nodes, partitioned in $C = 390$ clusters (AltNets), each of $S = 128$ altruistic nodes. This configuration is obtained by employing the $C = \frac{A}{z \times logA}$ configuration presented earlier and applied now for the altruistic network of A nodes, with $z = 8$.

Altruists belong in AltNet, or in Alt^{2}Net. In the network in Figure 3 the network has $N = 1,000,000$ nodes, with 5% (50,000) altruistic nodes being organized into two levels (of 390 altruistic clusters - AltNets - with 128 altruists each and an Alt^{2}Net network of 390 altruists, one for each AltNet cluster). Each DHT cluster (DHTNet) consists of 20

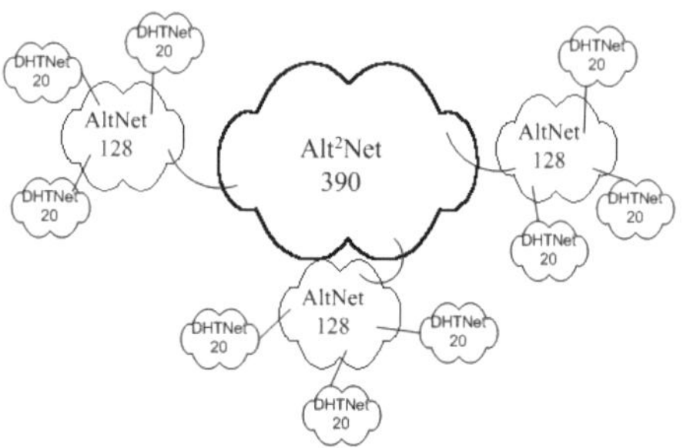

Figure 1. A Multilevel Altruism-based P2P Network.

nodes. Each DHTNet is served by an AltNet, with each AltNet serving 128 DHTNets. All AltNets and the Alt²Net are as before (almost) completely connected. The requirements in order to maintain this high connectivity are further drastically reduced: altruists within an AltNet (Alt²Net) need have 128 (390) neighbors. This represents a reduction by a factor of about 400 to 128, respectively.

At the same time, the significant routing speedups are maintained. For the example one-million-node network, instead of requiring two hops to reach the target DHT cluster, now two or four hops are required for this purpose (depending on whether the source and destination nodes are served by the same AltNet overlay, or not, respectively). So a total of about 6-8 hops are required: 2-4 to reach the target DHT cluster and about 4 to reach the target node within it. This gives a speedup of about 2.5 to $3\times$, compared to the 20 hops required in the steady-state case for the plain DHT architecture. Again, in the highly-dynamic case, the speedup is several orders of magnitude.

Note that, the more layers we deploy, the less the routing state powerful peers have to maintain. The latter, however, comes at the expense of routing hops. Whether more layers are suitable or not is highly dependent on the characteristics of the network and the actual application.

AltNets without Complete Connectivity   Altruistic networks can also be structured using a DHT, doing away with the completely-connected network; the altruists form a Chord [34] unit ring onto which altruistic node ids are placed, while cluster ids are mapped to the same ring (like document ids are mapped to Chord rings). Thus, altruists are responsible for clusters, as nodes are responsible for documents in Chord networks. Routing then at the top layer (i.e., from a source-cluster altruist to the destination cluster altruist) is done by routing through the altruists' Chord ring for the destination cluster id. The other steps remain the same.

This architecture also leverages the characteristics of altruists to yield high routing performance in the highly-dynamic case. Since we assume that the altruist routing state about their neighbors can be maintained even in the highly-dynamic case, routing within it requires $O(logC) = O(log\sqrt{N})$. But even in the unlikely case where this cannot be achieved, routing within the altruists' DHT will require $O(C) = O(\sqrt{N})$. Routing within the cluster DHTs requires in the highly-dynamic case $O(S) = O(\sqrt{N})$. Thus, overall, $O(\sqrt{N})$ hops are required, a drastic improvement compared to DHTs, making this architecture highly desirable.

3. Range Queries over DHTs

DHT-based data management systems (DHTs), built on distributed hash tables emerging by the way that peers define their neighbors, have become very popular providing efficient exact-match query capability. When dealing with range queries, however, the naive approach of individually querying each value in the range is greatly inefficient and thus infeasible in most cases. To support range queries, recent approaches use order-preserving (i.e. locality-preserving) hash functions for data placement in a DHT, which preserve the order of values by placing consecutive values on neighboring peers.

After the first wave of DHTs, the peer-to-peer research community started investigating structured overlays that would allow for more complex queries than simple equality, while achieving the same performance and scalability figures of early DHTs. This has lead to the design and implementation of several specially crafted DHTs, capable of efficient complex query processing: SkipNet[16], Skip Graphs[5], OP-Chord[40], PIER[17], Mercury[6], P-Trees[9], as well as the works by Ganesan et al.[12,13], Gupta et al.[14], and Sahin et al.[29], are examples of such systems.

Andrzejak and Xu ([4]) and Sahin, et al. ([29]) extended CAN ([25]) to allow for range query processing; however, performance is expected to be inferior compared to the other DHT-based solutions, since CAN lookups require $O(2 \cdot N^{1/2})$ hops, for a two-dimensional identifier space, whereas other solutions require logarithmic performance. Gupta et. al ([14]) propose an architecture based on Chord, and a hashing method based on a min-wise independent permutation hash function, but they provide only approximate answers to range queries. The system proposed in Ntarmos et al. ([22]) optimizes range queries by identifying and exploiting efficiently the powerful peers which have been found to exist in several environments.

The common idea behind these overlays with regard to range query processing, is that traditional DHTs destroy the locality of content, due to the randomizing (cryptographic) hash functions used to construct document IDs prior to insertion, but locality is a desired property when sequential access is sought, as is the case in range queries. Due to this, these overlays use the actual content (e.g. attribute values in a P2P-based RDBMS environment, file names in a file-sharing system, etc.) rather than the outcome of a (cryptographic) hash function to sort and store documents on the overlay. Thus document locality is preserved and range query processing consists of: (i) locating the node responsible for the start of the range, and (ii) following one-hop "successor" pointers until we reach the node responsible for the end of the range, gathering results in the meantime. If the desired range spans q nodes on the overlay, the above lead to a hop-count complexity of $O(\log N + q)$; $O(\log N)$ hops for phase (i), plus q more hops for phase (ii). We will use the term *LP-DHT ring* to refer to such a locality-preserving, range-queriable overlay in the rest of this paper.

3.1. OP-Chord: an Order-Preserving DHT over Chord

An approach based on an Order-Preserving DHT over Chord is presented in [40]. There, data objects are assumed to be the database tuples of a k-attribute relation $R(A_1, A_2,..., A_k)$, where A_i $(1 \leq i \leq k)$ are R's attributes. The attributes A_i are used as single-attribute indices of any tuple t in R. Their domain is DA_i, for any $1 \leq i \leq k$. Every tuple t in R is uniquely identified by a primary key, $key(t)$, which can be either one of its A_i attributes, or calculated by more than one A_i attributes.

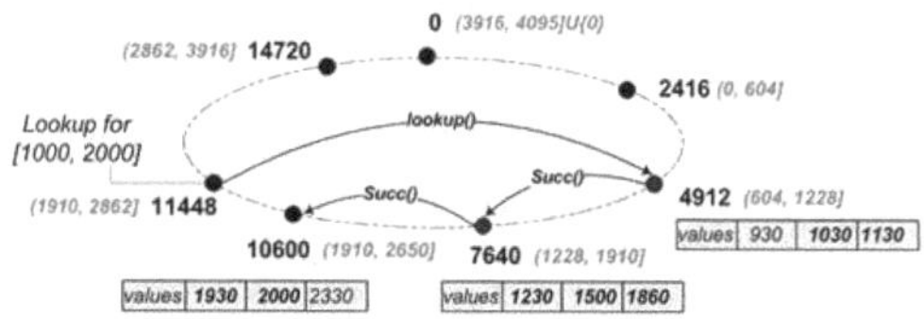

Figure 2. The substrate locality-preserving DHT. (a) A tuple with value v DA is stored on peer $succ(hash(v))$, (b) The range query [1000, 2000] is routed from peer $succ(hash(1000)) = 4912$, through the immediate successors, to peer $succ(hash(2000)) = 10600$.

In DHT-based networks, peers and data are assigned unique identifiers in an m-bit identifier space; here, we assume an identifier ring modulo 2^m. Traditional DHTs use secure hash functions to randomly and uniquely assign identifiers to peers and data, like Chord ([34]). A tuple's identifier is produced by hashing its attributes' values using k (at most [5]) order-preserving hash functions, $hash_i()$, to place tuples in range partitions over the identifier space. For fault tolerance reasons, a tuple is also stored at the peer mapped by securely hashing its $key(t)$. Thus, data placement requires $O((k + 1) \cdot \log N)$ hops, where N is the number of peers.

As most existing DHTs, tuples use consistent hashing ([18]): a tuple with identifier id is stored at the peer whose identifier is the "closest" to id in the identifier space (i.e. the successor function, $succ()$, of Chord ([34]). Peers also maintain routing information about peers that lie on the ring at logarithmically increasing distance (i.e. the finger tables of Chord ([34]). Using this information, routing a message from one peer to another requires $O(\log N)$ hops in the worst case, where N is the number of peers. For fault-tolerance reasons, each peer also maintains a maximum of $\log N$ successors.

Figure 2 illustrates data placement in a 14-bit order-preserving Chord-like ring, i.e. the id space is $[0, 16383]$. We assume single-attribute A tuples, $DA = [0, 4096)$. Let $N = 7$ peers inserted in the network with identifiers 0, 2416, 4912, 7640, 10600, 11448, and 14720. Each peer is responsible for storing a partition of the attribute domain DA, in an order-preserving way, as shown.

A range query is pipelined through those peers whose range of index entries stored at them overlaps with the query range. It needs $O(\log N + n')$ routing hops - n' is the number of these peers ([40]).

Figure 2 also illustrates how the range query [1000, 2000] initiated at peer 11448 is answered. Using the underlying DHT network look up operation, $lookup()$, we move to peer $succ(hash(1000))$, which is peer 4912. Peer 4912 retrieves all tuples whose values fall into the requested range, and forwards the query to its successor, peer 7640. The process is repeated until the query reaches peer 10600 (i.e. $succ(hash(2000))$), which is the last peer keeping the requested tuples.

Although it accelerates routing for range queries, this scheme cannot handle load balancing in the case of skewed data-access distributions. In another section below, an extension of this structure is presented, HotRoD, which deals with this problem while still attaining the efficiency of range query processing.

---

[5]Functions $hash_i()$ may be different for each one of the k different attributes A_i.

3.1.1. OP-Chord and Complex Queries

Handling multi-attribute queries in the standard Chord system is not efficiently supported. The best thing Chord can currently do is to issue one query for each of the attributes of the query, gather all results, and then process them to extract the desired result set. Two major categories of multi-attribute range queries are proposed: (i) queries whose predicates are connected with OR, and (ii) queries whose predicates are connected with AND. In the first case, any tuple matching any of the query constraints will be included in the final result set, while in the second case only tuples matching all query constraints will exist in the final result set.

Regarding join queries over two relations, OP-Chord ensures that nearby attribute values are hashed into the same (or near-by) peers, assuming that the attribute domains of the relations are the same. This means that transferring tuples from any of the two relations between different peers is not needed, since those tuples from one relation that may join with tuples from the other relation are stored at the same peer. Therefore, the join is performed at each peer locally, and results are transferred to the requestor (*hash join method*). However, all peers of the network should be accessed for a complete result set, which implies a cost of $O(N)$ routing hops which means high network bandwidth requirements and peer node processing loads.

Aggregation queries such as grouping, ordering, sum, count of, etc., can be easily handled, by combining multiple range queries with the corresponding functions over selected tuples. Since tuples are stored in the network in an ordered way, the calculation of a number of functions, such as min, max, average, etc. can be done using similar techniques from ordered lists in combination with the function $succ(n)$. However, cost is also high since all peers should be accessed. Both join and aggregation queries can be optimized by employing Range Guards.

3.2. RangeGuards: Range Queries over DHTs with a Twist of Altruism

Until now, the heterogeneity characterizing the peer population of real-world P2P networks has not been taken into account when architecting solutions for complex query processing, especially in DHT networks. Building on the above results, we attempt to fill this gap for optimizing the processing of range queries. Significant performance improvements are achieved due to (i) ensuring a much smaller hop count performance for range queries, and (ii) avoiding the dangers and inefficiencies of relying for range query processing on weak nodes, with respect to processing, storage, and communication capacities, and with intermittent connectivity.

Our intention is to form a second LP-DHT ring, the RangeGuard ring, above the LP-DHT ring, composed of powerful nodes – the RangeGuards or RGs – burdened with extra functionality chores. Each such node is responsible for storing the index tuples placed in nodes between its predecessor RangeGuard and itself. Thus, if there are M RGs in the system, they partition the normal LP-DHT ring into M continuous and disjoint ranges. Each RG maintains routing information for both the lower-level ring and the RangeGuard ring. Additionally, there is a direct link from each peer to the next RG in the upper-level ring (i.e. to the RG responsible for the peer). Nodes in the lower-level ring probe their RG (e.g. as part of the standard LP-DHT stabilization process), and automatically update the index tuples it stores.

Given the functionality offered by the vanilla LP-DHTs, *RG*s are identified and located as follows. The administrator of each node selects whether she wants her node to be a candidate for RangeGuard membership or not (much like it is done now with super-peers in most unstructured P2P sharing applications). A candidate node n, with id $n.id$, keeps track of the amount $n.\alpha$ of retrieval and/or just routing requests it serves. This information is updated periodically, every $\mathcal{E}$ seconds (also called an *epoch*). Thus, it keeps two *node performance counters* (or NPCs) – $n.\alpha_c$ and $n.\alpha_p$ – of requests served during the current and the previous epoch respectively.

This information is stored in the system as a four-attribute node performance relation $\mathcal{NPR} : \{n.id, n.\alpha_p, \mathcal{U}, status\}$, with primary key $n.id$, and indexed by $n.\alpha_p$. $status$ is a boolean variable, set to $true$ if the node is a member of the RangeGuard. $\mathcal{U}$ is a counter, incremented on every update of the tuple, and left-shifted (assuming a little-endian architecture) (i) on every update or (ii) every $\mathcal{E}+\delta$ seconds, with the timer being reset on every update. δ is a quantity depending on measurable characteristics (e.g. round-trip / ping time) of the end-to-end connection between node n and the node storing the index tuple with n's metadata. $\mathcal{U}$ encapsulates the amount of time a peer stays connected to the network. We believe that the network uptime of a peer and the number of requests it has served during this time, are enough evidence of a node's power and fitness for the RG ring. More elaborate metrics may be used instead, under the same intuition of storing these tuples on the lower LP-DHT ring; investigation of such metrics is an open issue and a subject of ongoing and future work. If a node wishes to cease being a candidate RG, it suffices to set a low value (e.g. 0) for its α_p and stop updating this information (so that its $\mathcal{U}$ value decays with inactivity). Also note that the $\mathcal{NPR}$ tuple of a node n is stored on this very node, since the primary key of the relation is the $n.id$ attribute.

3.2.1. Joining the RangeGuard

A node that is to join the RangeGuard uses its RG as the "bootstrap" node for the Range-Guard ring. The RG is responsible for retrieving the metadata of the candidate node and checking whether it is powerful enough (i.e. has served more requests than a predefined threshold) and has stayed online for long enough (based on the corresponding $\mathcal{U}$ value) to be allowed into the RangeGuard. If all prerequisites[6] are met, the standard LP-DHT join protocol is executed and the candidate node is promoted to the RG ring, otherwise the protocol terminates. After that, it updates the $status$ field in its entry in the $\mathcal{NPR}$ relation on the lower-level ring to reflect its promotion to RG status and notifies nodes in its arc of responsibility of its existence. Alternatively, this step may be left as part of the lower-level ring stabilization/maintenance process.

3.2.2. Admission into the RangeGuard

There are two ways for a node to be admitted into the RangeGuard: either (i) be promoted by a node already in the RangeGuard who wishes to shed some of its load, or (ii) volunteering to take up some region in the address space for which there exists no RG.

---

[6]These thresholds will probably vary depending on the semantics sought from the RangeGuard. Calculating crisp theoretical thresholds is an orthogonal issue and left as future work.

i. Promotion   Due to irregularities in the data or access distribution, a RangeGuard may get overloaded with incoming requests. Moreover, it is possible for a region in the Range-Guard to be underpopulated (e.g. imagine the RangeGuard ring in its setup phases). In such cases, a member of the RangeGuard can ask for support from candidate Range-Guards by promoting them to RG status.

With the infrastructure described earlier, when a RG wants to promote a node to RangeGuard status for a region around a point p – i.e. the id of a node in a distance of at most ϵ from a point p in the lower-level ring, with access count greater than a in the previous epoch, and a $\mathcal{U}$ value above u – it merely executes the range query:

select id **from** $\mathcal{NPR}$ **where** $\mathcal{U} > u$ **and** $\alpha_p > a$ **and** $0 \leq id - p < \epsilon$

The result set of this query will contain the IDs of candidate RGs in the region of interest. It is then up to the RG who originated the query to select the best candidate, inform it of its promotion, and initiate the *join* protocol to add it to the RG ring.

ii. Volunteering   Candidate RGs may lie in any region on the lower-level ring. For data/access distribution irregularity reasons similar to the ones urging RangeGuards to ask for support, it is possible for some regions to have such low data/access loads that the RangeGuard responsible for them has never been in need of support. This could result in large arcs/ranges on the lower-level ring being mapped to a single RangeGuard node, lo-cated many hops away on the lower-level ring from the first nodes on this arc. Although this is not an issue in the steady state, it may increase the time needed by a node on this arc to find a new RG, should the current RG leave the system abnormally.

We, thus, allow candidate RG nodes on the lower-level ring to volunteer for an RG position; if a candidate RG detects a situation as the one described earlier (i.e. a large distance between itself and its RG), it can contact the latter and ask to be promoted to RG status. The RG is responsible for going through the α_p and $\mathcal{U}$ checks and admitting the candidate to the RangeGuard or not.

3.2.3. Leaving the RangeGuard

Similarly, a RG may decide to leave the RangeGuard if it finds itself in a situation where its arc of responsibility becomes very small (due to candidate RGs being promoted to RG status in its vicinity), or the load it faces as an RG drops below some predefined threshold (e.g. an estimate of the load it should have, based on uniform data/access load). A RG that wishes to leave the RangeGuard ring, goes through the following steps: (1) it follows the LP-DHT ring "leave" protocol, transferring its RG-related stored data to the appropriate node(s) on the RG ring, (2) it updates the *status* field in its entry in the $\mathcal{NPR}$ relation on the lower-level ring, to denote that it is no longer a RangeGuard, and (3) optionally, it notifies the nodes that link to it on the RG ring to update their links, or leaves this to be done as a part of the RG ring stabilization/maintenance process.

Note that our approach uses standard LP-DHT ring operations to set up and maintain the RangeGuard ring. With the exception of the second step, the procedure described above is the standard LP-DHT *leave* protocol. Also note that the leaving RG does not need to notify nodes on its arc of responsibility of their new RG, since that will be achieved during the lower-level ring stabilization process. Consequently, the cost for a node to leave the RangeGuard is equal to the cost of executing the standard LP-DHT *leave* protocol for the RG ring, while data transfer is minimal due to the very small size of $\mathcal{NPR}$ tuples and the size of the RG ring. On the other hand, there is the requirement

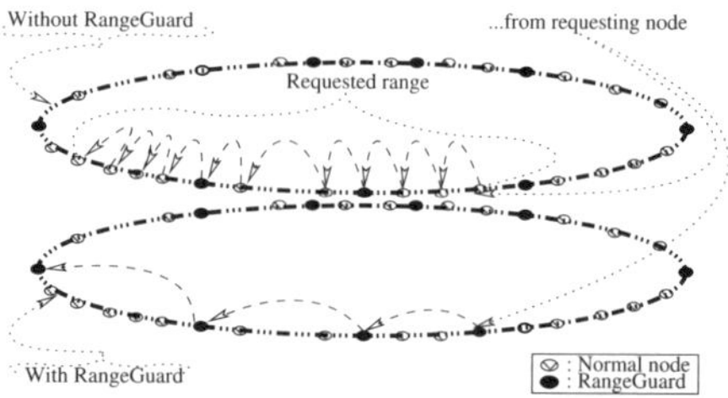

Figure 3. Range query processing with and without *RG*s.

for several RangeGuard peers with enhanced capabilities. This is not unrealistic, since many peers in real-life applications have proved to be more powerful. With the notion and exploitation of RangeGuards we can harness this power heterogeneity to achieve higher efficiency in range query processing.

3.2.4. Range Query Processing Using RGs

With RangeGuards in the scene, a query $(a_i.v_{low}, a_i.v_{high})$ on attribute a_i will be sent from the requesting node directly (1 hop) to the RG responsible for the requesting node's data. After this point the RangeGuards assume responsibility to gather the requested information, using the LP-DHT algorithm described earlier, except that now all operations take place on the RangeGuard ring (fig. 3). With data placement on the lower ring being reflected on the RangeGuard ring, the requested index tuples will reside between RG_l responsible for $a_i.v_{low}$ and RG_h responsible for $a_i.v_{high}$. This algorithm requires 1 routing hop to reach the RangeGuard ring, another $O(log(M))$ hops in the RG ring to reach RG_l, and as many routing hops as there are RangeGuards between RG_l and RG_h. Moreover, the $O(log(M))$ term can be further improved to $O(1)$, by using techniques similar to those presented in [15] or [23].

Since, there will probably be much fewer RGs in the system than there are nodes, and RangeGuards are more powerful (with respect to computing capacities, network bandwidth, and network uptime) than the average node in the system, this architecture is significantly more efficient that the one presented earlier. Specifically, for $5\% \times N$ RGs, although the worst-case hop-count efficiency remains in $O(N)$, it now has a rather significantly lower constant modifier (i.e. a 5% – or 20 times – lower hop-count). Note that we require a mere $5\% \times N$ nodes to be powerful and altruistic in our setting; as relevant research has pointed out [2,30,31], we can expect an average 5% of the node population in wide-scale peer-to-peer data sharing networks, such as Gnutella and Kazaa, to be powerful, altruistic nodes. Thus, by harnessing the full power of all these nodes, we can achieve even higher performance gains than those outlined above.

3.2.5. Performance Evaluation

We will be using our home-brewed LP-DHT, OP-Chord[40], as our overlay of choice. We have extended the basic Chord simulator[7], adding support for index tuples and range queries, and implementing our OP-Chord and RangeGuard architectures. We have chosen to test two aspects of the system: (i) the hop count efficiency of our range query processing algorithm, and (ii) the distribution of storage requirements and accesses on

---

[7]Available through http://www.pdos.lcs.mit.edu/chord/

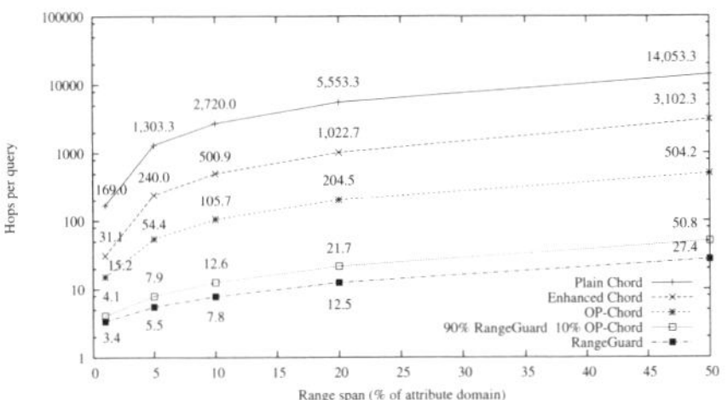

Figure 4. Hop count per range query (log-plot).

participating RG nodes during range query processing, under realistically skewed distributions.

Hop Count   The experiments used a single-index-attribute relation, with the index attribute taking $5,000$ integer values, following a Zipf distribution with θ=0.7 over $D[30]$. Range queries are generated using a separate Zipf distribution over the domain D (again with θ=0.7) for their lower bound, and a uniformly distributed range span S, ranging from 1% to 50% of the attribute domain. We report on a series of $50,000$-queries experiments for a system with N=1,000 nodes, M=50 ($\approx$5% $\times$ N) range guards, and $50,000$ tuples (the reported results are not sensitive to these values).

Performance Reference Points   We have compared the hop-count efficiency of the RG architecture against (i) plain Chord (PC), as a representative of traditional DHTs, (ii) an imaginary, enhanced Chord (EC), where for each range $\mathcal{R}$ the system knows the IDs of the n' nodes storing values in $\mathcal{R}a$, (iii) our OP-Chord architecture, and (iv) a hybrid system where 95% of queries are processed on the RG ring and the remaining 5% are dealt with on the OP-Chord ring. Assume we have an integer range query $r = <v_{low},$ $v_{high}>$. Further assume that the requested index tuples are stored on n' nodes, under Chord's hashing scheme, and on k nodes, managed by k' RangeGuards, under our OPHF (Order Preserving Hash Function) scheme. Then, in order to gather all possible results:

- PC: $|r|$ queries, or $O(|r|\log(N))$ hops, are needed.
- EC: $|n'|$ queries, or $O(|n'|\log(N))$ hops, must be executed.
- OP: we must first route to the node holding v_{low} and then follow k-1 successor pointers, for an $O(\log(N)+k)$ overall hop count.
- RG: we must route to the closest RG (1 hop), then to the RG holding v_{low} ($O(\log(M)$ hops) and follow $k' - 1$ successor pointers, for an $O(\log(M) + k')$ overall hop count.
- $OP + RG$: we flip a biased coin and choose among OP or RG processing, with the hop count complexities outlined above.

Fig. 4 summarizes the measured hop-counts per range query. Traditional DHTs were not designed with range queries in mind thus Chord performs poorly. The (unrealistically) enhanced Chord brings the required hop count down to $\approx$20% of the Chord figure. However, total global knowledge is required to implement this approach. On the other hand, by using the order-preserving hashing scheme and the RangeGuard architecture, the hop count is decreased by a factor of approx. 50 to 500 compared to PC, 10 to 110 compared to EC, and 5 to 20 compared to OP for different range spans, with the performance of $OP + RG$ following closely behind.

This improvement in hop counts, however, may come at the expense of fairness in load distribution; storing consecutive values on adjacent nodes on the network transforms any skewness in the value and access distributions to imbalances in the peer load distribution. For small networks and large datasets, this situation is somewhat "hidden" by the fact that highly popular data items/ranges overlap with less popular ones. For much larger networks, we shall either need a very large dataset to achieve a good load distribution and/or more elaborate load balancing mechanisms[24], to be discussed shortly.

4. Publish/Subscribe Systems over DHTs

Given the main functionality of locating and routing a $< data\ item, key >$ pair based on the key identifier, building an information exchange infrastructure based on the publish/subscribe paradigm while supporting a *'rich'* set of queries (queries involving prefix, suffix, and equality predicates on strings, and range and comparison predicates on numerical-typed attributes) is very challenging.

In this section we will overview how to support *rich* queries over string and numerical attributes on top of a DHT-based data network first presented in [37,3] under the scope of the publish/subscribe paradigm.

4.1. The Publish/Subscribe Paradigm and the Event/Subscription Schema

In the publish/subscribe paradigm (also known as information filtering) users express their interests with *subscriptions*. Whenever a certain *event* of interest appears, the user having issued the subscription is notified. Currently, there are two popular types of publish/ subscribe systems: i) *topic-based* and ii) *content-based*. *Topic-based* systems are much like newsgroups. *Content-based* systems are preferable as they give users the ability to express their interest by issuing *subscriptions*, specifying predicates over the values of a number of well defined attributes, and thus the matching of *publications* (a.k.a. *events*) to *subscriptions* (*interests*) is done based on the attributes' content.

The main challenge in a distributed pub/sub system is the development of an efficient infrastructure to expedite the distributed matching process. Distributed solutions have been provided for topic-based pub/sub systems [8,26,33]. More recently, some attempts on *distributed content-based pub/sub systems* use routing trees to disseminate the events to interested users based on multicast techniques [11,7,10,36,17,38]. Typically, processing subscriptions and/or events in these approaches requires one or both of the following: (i) setting up some type of broadcast tree and having the event traverse it in order to reach all possibly relevant subscriptions stored at all nodes, and/or (ii) multicasting the subscriptions to all nodes. Thus, invariably event and/or subscription processing requires $O(N)$ messages in N-node networks. However, there exist techniques for subscription summarization that may significantly reduce the constant in $O(N)$ complexity [39].

Some approaches have also considered the coupling of topic-based and content-based systems. The authors in [35] used a topic-based system (Scribe [8]) that is implemented in a decentralized manner using a DHT (Pastry [28]). In their approach the publications and the subscriptions are automatically classified in topics, using an appropriate application specific schema. A potential drawback of this approach is the design of the domain schema as it plays a fundamental role in the system's performance. Moreover, it is likely that false positives may occur. In [32] keyword searching is supported by applying a multi-level partitioning scheme with inverted indices on top of the SkipNet P2P infrastructure [16]. SkipNet uses a prefix scheme for node naming, but remains an open issue how this characteristic can be used for supporting prefix/suffix matching on string attributes. Some techniques found in the literature for string indexing may also be relevant to our goals. The most promising is the technique relying on n-grams [20] which can be applied for substring matching. However, they appear to have serious limitations that make them difficult to be applied in a highly dynamic and distributed environment.

4.1.1. The Event/Subscription Schema

The event/subscription schema is a set of A attributes ($a_i, 1 \leq i \leq A$). Each attribute a_i consists of a name, and a value $v(a_i)$. Under the case of a news feed system supporting stock market quotes, an event (news headlines or stock prices) is defined to be a set of $k < attribute, value >$ pairs ($k \leq A$), while a subscription (users' interests) is defined through an appropriate set of constraints on attributes' values over a subset of the A attributes of the schema. For string-typed attributes the allowable operators are: (i) prefix: the *NewsAgency* attribute in Sub1 bellow, (ii) suffix: the *Title* attribute in Sub1, and (iii) equality, while for numerical-typed the allowable operators are $\leq, \geq, \neq$ which in general may be expressed as any range in the attributes' domain defined by the minimum and maximum ($v_{min}(a_i), v_{max}(a_i)$) values and the attribute's precision $v_{pr}(a_i)$ (which in fact results in a finite number of distinct values). An event matches a subscription *if and only if* all the attribute predicates/constraints of the subscription are satisfied. For example Sub1, matches Event1. An event/subscription example follows:

$$\text{Sub1}=\{SubID_1:: \text{NewsAgency} :'\text{CNN}*', \text{Title} :'*\text{Debuts}'\}$$
$$\text{Sub2}=\{SubID_2:: \text{Label} :'\text{MSF}', \text{Price} :(12,20]'\}$$
$$\text{Event1} = \{\text{NewsAgency} : '\text{CNN}', \text{Title} : '\text{A380 Debuts}'\}$$

Each subscription is identified by the subscription identifier (SubID) which is the concatenation of three parts: c_1, c_2, and c_3. c_1 represents the id of the node where the subscription arrived (termed the origin or coordinator node) from a connected to that node client and keeps metadata information about the subscription, c_2 refers to the key of the subscription for identifying it among the stored ones at the origin node, and c_3 is the number of declared attributes in the subscription.

4.2. Subscription and Event Processing

4.2.1. Processing Subscriptions

The main idea in subscription processing is to store the subscription ids (SubIDs) at those nodes of the network that were selected by appropriately hashing the values of the attributes in the subscriptions. Then, the matching of an incoming event can be performed simply by asking those nodes for stored subscription ids.

Three lists (initially empty) are maintained for storing SubIDs in every node for every string attribute a_i of our schema. These are the $L_{ai-pref}$, $L_{ai-suff}$, and L_{ai} where we store the SubIDs of the subscriptions that contain prefix, suffix, or equality constraints, respectively, over the attribute a_i. The procedure of storing subscriptions starts by examining the operator defined in each attribute a_i of the subscription. Then if an equality is declared, SubID is stored in the L_{ai} list of the node with id equal or close the value returned by hashing the value of the attribute, $v(a_i)$. For prefix or suffix predicates, SubID is stored in the $L_{ai-pref}$ or $L_{ai-suff}$, of the appropriate node (as a result of hashing $v(a_i)$. For equality (regarding string or numerical attributes), prefix and suffix constraints, subscription storing requires $O(logN)$ hops in order to store the subscription id for each one of the defined attributes.

In the case of a numerical range constraint which is defined by $v_{low}(a_i)$ and $v_{high}(a_i)$ and since all values between $v_{low}(a_i)$ and $v_{high}(a_i)$ are finite (attribute's a_i domain), say n, we take advantage of a_i's specific precision $v_{pr}(a_i)$, and we follow n storage steps. At each step we store at an appropriate Chord [34] node, which is chosen by hashing the previous value incremented by the precision step, the SubID of the given subscription in the L_{ai} list. It is obvious that range processing requires $r \times O(logN)$hops, where r is defined to be $\frac{v_{high}(a_i)-v_{low}(a_i)}{v_{pr}(a_i)}$ for a given range constraint on attribute a_i. However, we can improve this performance by extending Chord's functionality to use an order preserving hash function (OPHF) in order to store the sequential values of a range interval in sequential nodes over the Chord ring. Under this environment we need to perform $O(logN)$ hops to locate the node which will store the minimum value of the range (that is $v_{low}(a_i)$ for the attribute a_i). Then, we have to perform r hops to store the remaining values in the range. This approach leads to $r+O(logN)$hops in total. More details regarding OPHF can be found in [40,37] .

4.2.2. Event Processing and Matching

Upon the arrival of a new event we start by processing each attribute separately. First we locate the node which stores SubIDs with equality constraints for the value $v(a_i)$ of the event's string or numerical attribute a_i (by hashing $v(a_i)$, locating the right node and looking at the L_{ai} list for stored SubIDs). Then the collected SubIDs are stored in the $L_{ai-EQUALITY}$ list for further processing.

In order to find the subscriptions that may have declared a prefix operation on the attribute a_i we should ask the nodes in the DHT in a way that is similar to that when dealing with equality constraints with the difference that we check all possible prefix strings of the value $v(a_i)$, by subtracting one character at a time from the end. Thus, given that the string-length of $v(a_i)$ is l, we have to check for l different string values. From those nodes we retrieve the $L_{ai-pref}$ lists. The same procedure is performed for the suffix operation, with the difference that we now check for the l suffixes of the value $v(a_i)$ and we finally collect the l $L_{ai-suff}$ lists. We then merge all the $L_{ai-suff}$ and $L_{ai-pref}$ into the $L_{ai-SUFFIX}$ and $L_{ai-PREFIX}$ lists respectively.

The event-subscriptions matching process starts by examining collected lists with subscription identifiers for each one of the a_i attribute defined in the event. Suppose, now, that a subscription $SubID_i$ is found to be in some collected list(s) and that this subscription involves $N_{a-sub-i}$ attributes. It can easily be shown that the subscription matches the event only if it appears in exactly $N_{a-sub-i}$ lists. The matched subscription identifiers are further processed in order to inform subscribers. For each attribute in the event the matching process requires in general $O(l \times logN)$ hops where l is the average length of string values.

4.3. Multi-dimensional Event Processing Optimizations

The optimizations that follow aim to reduce the processing cost during the matching phase at the origin node (the broker node where the incoming event arrived) in order

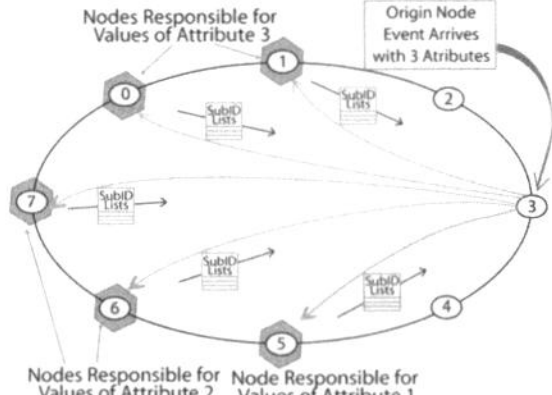

Figure 5. Coordinated matching.

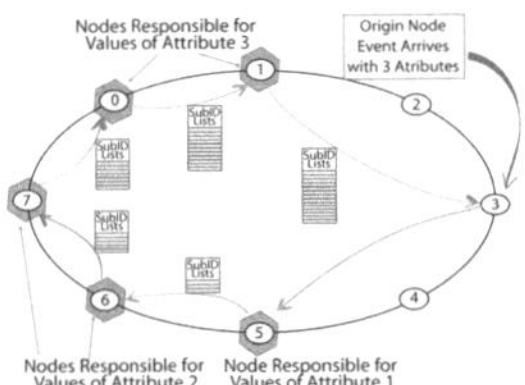

Figure 6. Distributed matching.

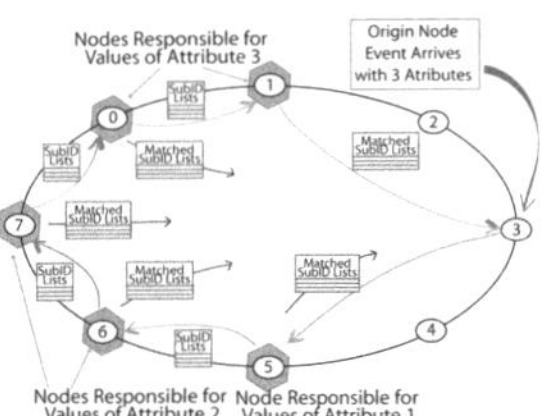

Figure 7. Hybrid matching.

to compute and deliver the matched events to interested users. Our motivation is to distribute when possible/profitable the matching phase to a number of involved nodes.

4.3.1. Coordinated Matching

The algorithm presented in the previous section starts by processing each attribute, a_i, of the event separately, by contacting a subset of nodes and retrieving the SubID lists as you can see in Figure 5. It is clear that the matching process is performed at the coordinator node (the broker where the event arrived).

Depending on the characteristics of the system (attribute and value popularities etc.) a significant number of the collected subscription ids are going to be dropped as the result of not matching the event. The propagation of those SubIDs, however, is responsible for overloading the network (and increasing the complexity of the matching algorithm at the coordinator node).

4.3.2. Distributed Matching

A first idea trying to ameliorate the above problem is to perform the matching process in a distributed, step-by-step way, as can be seen in Figure 6. The key idea is to order the events' attribute-values based on their expected selectivity[8]. This selectivity (i.e., the size of the SubID lists with SubIDs matching the event's attribute value) depends on the popularity of the attribute (i.e., how many subscriptions are involving this attribute) as well as on the attribute values' popularity.

This kind of ordering will lead to first processing the attributes that are likely to return a small result set and pass those relatively small lists to subsequent nodes in order to perform the matching. At each step i of *Distributed Matching* we ask a subset of nodes for the attribute/value under consideration and we merge all lists collected into the list $LocalList_i$. The lists of SubIDs that are sent from the previously examined node-subset are appropriately merged with $LocalList_i$ into $GlobalList_i$ and are sent to the next subset. Now, at each step i we examine $LocalList_i$ and $GlobalList_{i-1}$. From $LocalList_i$ we drop all those SubIDs that have defined[9] an attribute already examined and are not present in $GlobalList_{i-1}$. From $GlobalList_{i-1}$ we drop those SubIDs that have defined the current attribute and are not present in $LocalList_i$. The remaining SubIDs are merged

---

[8]The problem of identifying the selectivity of an event's attribute value is a formidable one in general. However, an extra communication phase between one node per each event attribute and the coordinator node, would allow the coordinator to know exactly all per-attribute result sizes.

[9]This can be achieved by replacing the c_3 field of the subscription identifier with an A-bit vector and mapping each defined attribute in the subscription with 1 in that vector.

into $GlobalList_i$ and are propagated to the next node. This process continues for the rest attributes.

4.3.3. Hybrid Matching

The weakness of *Distributing Matching* is that it is possible that many SubIDs, already matching the event, will be sent several times through the DHT network until they finally reach the origin node. Fortunately, often a node has enough information to determine whether it is at all possible that any SubID in a partial result set could possibly be sent back to the origin node and considered as matched. This is the case when the subscription does not declare any of the attributes that are going to be checked in later steps of the distributed matching process.

Hybrid Matching takes advantage of this fact. When we reach a point in the distributed matching where all the declared attributes of a subscription are already checked, the subscription matches the event and it is returned back directly to the origin node (Figure 7).

4.4. Experimentation and Performance Evaluation

4.4.1. Subscription Storing and Load Balancing

In most real-world environments, attribute value and access popularity distributions are not uniform. Such skewness may in general create storage and access load imbalances. The intuition behind our conjecture that load imbalances are not a significant problem is based on the following observation: even though a skewed value/access distribution of an attribute can create load imbalances, in real world applications there will be tens of attributes. Further, each pub/sub infrastructure is expected to support several applications (each with many attributes). As the total number of supported attributes increases, the load imbalances are disappearing (intuitively, nodes which are heavily hit for storing popular values for one attribute will be less hit for other attributes).

We performed a number of experiments in a simulated environment changing the number of attributes declared in each subscription/event as well as the skewness of the values' popularity (which follows the Zipfian popularity distribution with parameter θ). Our results have shown that as the number of attributes increases, the load imbalance ratio (i.e. maximum to minimum number of stored subscriptions among nodes) drops under the value of 5 even in the case of very skewed popularity distribution ($\theta=1.4$), which models a rather extreme case. It should be obvious that the same results will be obtained regardless of whether the skewed access distributions refer to value-occurrences (i.e., storage load) or value-accesses (i.e., access load).

4.4.2. Distributed Event Processing

Network bandwidth   Our specific performance metric here is the total number of SubIDs sent for the processing of each incoming event (when a SubID is sent r times, it is counted as r SubIDs). In order to find out how the system performs, we conducted a series of experiments varying the skewness of the popularity distributions of attributes (which controls which attributes an event involves). We also in parallel varied the skewness of the values' distributions. The value domain size of each attribute is large enough compared to the number of nodes. The popularities of attributes and the values of each attribute follow the Zipfian distribution.

By varying the skewness of attribute values' distribution we observed that the preferred algorithm is the *Coordinated Matching*, which is slightly better that *Hybrid Matching*, and considerably better than *Distributed Matching*. Note that, despite that the two best algorithms have similar performance, the matching phase is performed in a distributed manner under *Hybrid Matching*. This is expected to alleviate bottleneck problems related to performing the whole matching phase centrally at a broker in *Coordinated Matching*. *Distributed Matching* is the worst, in general, because, as we mentioned earlier, SubIDs that may already match the event, are repeatedly sent through the network until the last node.

In order to figure out under which circumstances the *Distributed* and *Hybrid Matching* algorithms can improve their performance compared to *Coordinated Matching* we tuned up our experimentation setup based on the following observation: the more uniform the distribution of an attribute's values is, the smaller the result set will be when merging a local result set with that sent by another node. This is because different SubIDs would, with a higher probability, have picked different values for common attributes. Thus, this is the best case for the filtering performed at each step of *Distributed* and *Hybrid Matching*, since they carry around fewer SubIDs at each step. We tuned the experimentation, so that popular attributes have uniform value distributions and less popular attributes have skewed value distributions.

Our results have shown that when many events and subscriptions involve a larger number of attributes, *Hybrid Matching* performs better compared to *Coordinated Matching* because there are many filtering steps and the popular attributes with small result sets seem to further help the filtering. A complementary explanation of the good performance of *Hybrid Matching* under the above setup is the fact that the overlap between the result sets of consecutive filtering steps is small and thus *Hybrid Matching* is capable of filtering as much as possible.

Event matching latency   During event matching, a key functionality is to merge all separate per-attribute result lists in order to identify the sudIDs that match all event attribute constraints. The *Distributed Matching* and *Hybrid Matching* algorithms appear to introduce processing-latency savings. We have studied this in detail, and concluded on the superiority of *Hybrid Matching* and *Distributed Matching* regarding their response time which drops below 20% of the response time of *Coordinated Matching* for 10% overlapping (overlapping factor controls the percentage of SubIDs found in both $LocalList_i$ and $GlobalList_{i-1}$ in each step i of the filtering process). As overlapping increases, meaning that filtering is less effective form step to step, as fewer SubIDs are dropped, *Distributed Matching* approaches the performance of *Coordinated Matching* while *Hybrid Matching* stays under 50% since the SubID lists at each step are expected to be smaller (recall that Hybrid sends back to the origin node, those SubIDs that are already matched and are not expected to be found in later steps)

5. Conclusions

In this chapter we presented both architectures and algorithms, aiming at providing complex data management services over internet-scale data networks. We assumed the data network is organized using a DHT overlay. The data management services we envision depend on effectively utilizing all available computational, networking, and storage resources in order to provide swiftly answers to traditional 'exact-match' (equality) queries as well as queries involving ranges of numerical values and queries with prefix/suffix/containment predicates on string-attributes.

Specifically, we discussed:

- *altruism-endowed peer-to-peer data management (AESOP and PLANES)* that exploits the heterogeneities in peer capabilities and behavior in order to expedite exact-match queries and offer more robust functionality.
- *range and complex query processing over DHT-based data management systems* by (i) employing order-preserving hashing (OP-Chord) which can expedite significantly such queries, and (ii) exploiting altruistic peers (RangeGuards), for the same goal;
- *an architecture and related algorithms that effectively supports the publish/subscribe paradigm over a DHT infrastructure*, extending DHTs so to enable support for string attributes and related predicates and then for subscription and event processing.

References

[1] K. Aberer, M. Hauswirth, M. Punceva, and R. Schmidt. Improving data access in P2P systems. *IEEE Internet Computing*, 6(1), Jan/Feb 2002.

[2] E. Adar and B.A. Huberman. Free Riding on Gnutella. *First Monday*, October 2000.

[3] I. Aekaterinidis and P. Triantafillou. Internet scale string attribute publish/subscribe data networks. In *14th ACM Conference on Information and Knowledge Management (CIKM05)*, 2005.

[4] A. Andrzejak and Z. Xu. Scalable, efficient range queries for grid information services. In *Proc. P2P*, 2002.

[5] J. Aspnes and G. Shah. Skip Graphs. In *Proc. SODA*, 2003.

[6] A. Bharambe, M. Agrawal, and S. Seshan. Mercury: Supporting scalable multi-attribute range queries. In *Proc. SIGCOMM*, 2004.

[7] A. Carzaniga and A. Wolf. Forwarding in a content-based network. In *Proc. SIGCOMM*, 2003.

[8] M. Castro, P. Druschel, A. Kermarrec, and A. Rowstron. Scribe: A large-scale and decentralized application-level multicast infrastructure. *Journal on Selected Areas in Communication*, 2002.

[9] A. Crainiceanu, P. Linga, J. Gehrke, and J. Shanmugasundaram. Querying peer-to-peer networks using P-trees. In *Proc. WebDB*, 2004.

[10] G. Cugola, E.D. Nitto, and A. Fuggetta. The jedi event-based infrastructure and its application to the development of the OPSS WFMS, 2001.

[11] G. Banavar, et.al. An efficient multicast protocol for content-based publish-subscribe systems. In *Proc. ICDCS*, 1999.

[12] P. Ganesan, M. Bawa, and H. Garcia-Molina. Online balancing of range-partitioned data with applications to peer-to-peer systems. In *Proc. VLDB*, 2004.

[13] P. Ganesan, B. Yang, and H. Garcia-Molina. Multi-dimensional indexing in peer-to-peer systems. In *Proc. WebDB*, 2004.

[14] A. Gupta, D. Agrawal, and A.E. Abbadi. Approximate range selection queries in peer-to-peer systems. In *Proc. CIDR*, 2003.

[15] A. Gupta, B. Liskov, and R. Rodrigues. One hop lookups for peer-to-peer overlays. In *Proc. HotOS IX*, 2003.

[16] N. Harvey, M. Jones, S. Saroiu, M. Theimer, and A. Wolman. Skipnet: A scalable overlay network with practical locality properties. In *Proc. USITS*, 2003.

[17] R. Huebsch, et al. Querying the internet with PIER. In *Proc. VLDB*, 2003.

[18] D. Karger, et al. Consistent hashing and random trees: Distributed caching protocols for relieving hot spots on the World Wide Web. In *Proc. ACM STOC '97*.

[19] D. Liben-Nowell, H. Balakrsihnan, and D. Karger. Observations on the dynamic evolution of peer-to-peer networks. In *Proc. IPTPS*, 2002.

[20] M. Harren, et al. Complex queries in DHT-based peer-to-peer networks. In *Proc. IPTPS*, 2002.

[21] D. Malkhi, M. Naor, and D. Ratajczak. Viceroy: A scalable and dynamic emulation of the butterfly. In *Proc. PODC*, 2002.

[22] N. Ntarmos, T. Pitoura, and P. Triantafillou. Range query optimization leveraging peer heterogeneity in dht data networks. In *Proc. DBISP2P*, 2005.

[23] N. Ntarmos and P. Triantafillou. AESOP: Altruism-Endowed Self-Organizing Peers. In *Proc. DBISP2P*, 2004.

[24] T. Pitoura, N. Ntarmos, and P. Triantafillou. HotRod: Range query processing and load balancing in peer-to-peer data networks. Technical Report TR 2004/12/05, R.A. Computer Technology Institute, 2004.

[25] S. Ratnasamy, P. Francis, M. Handley, R. Karp, and S. Shenker. A scalable content-addressable network. In *Proc. ACM SIGCOMM*, 2001.

[26] S. Ratnasamy, M. Handley, R. Karp, and S. Shenker. Application-level multicast using content-addressable networks. In *Proc Int. Workshop of NGC*, 2001.

[27] S. Rhea and D. Geels. Handling churn in a DHT. In *Proc. USENIX Technical Conference*, 2004.

[28] A. Rowstron and P. Druschel. Pastry: Scalable, distributed object location and routing for large-scale peer-to-peer systems. In *Proc. Middleware*, 2001.

[29] O.D. Sahin, A. Gupta, D. Agrawal, and A.E. Abbadi. A peer-to-peer framework for caching range queries. In *Proc. ICDE*, 2004.

[30] S. Saroiu, K. Gummadi, and S. Gribble. A measurement study of peer-to-peer file sharing systems. In *Proc. MMCN*, 2002.

[31] S. Sen and J. Wang. Analyzing peer-to-peer traffic accross large networks. *IEEE/ACM Transactions on Networking*, 12(2):219–232, 2004.

[32] S. Shi, G. Yang, D. Wang, J. Yu, S. Qu, and M. Chen. Making peer-to-peer keyword searching feasible using multi-level partitioning. In *Proc. IPTPS*, 2004.

[33] S.Q. Zhuang, et al. Bayeux: An architecture for scalable and fault-tolerant wide-area data dissemination. In *Proc. ACM NOSSDAV*, 2001.

[34] I. Stoica, et al. Chord: A scalable peer-to-peer lookup service for internet applications. In *Proc. ACM SIGCOMM*, 2001.

[35] D. Tam, R. Azimi, and H. Jacobsen. Building content-based publish/subscribe systems with distributed hash tables. In *Proc. DBISP2P*, 2003.

[36] W.W. Terpstra, S. Behnel, L. Fiege, A. Zeidler, and A.P. Buchmann. A peer-to-peer approach to content-based publish/subscribe. In *Proc. DEBS*, 2003.

[37] P. Triantafillou and I. Aekaterinidis. Content-based publish-subscribe over structured P2P networks. In *Proc. DEBS*, 2004.

[38] P. Triantafillou and A. Economides. Subscription summarization: A new paradigm for efficient publish/subscribe systems. In *Proc. IEEE ICDCS*, 2004.

[39] P. Triantafillou and A. Economides. Subscription summaries for scalability and efficiency in publish/subscribe systems. In *Proc. DEBS*, 2002.

[40] P. Triantafillou and T. Pitoura. Towards a unifying framework for complex query processing over structured peer-to-peer data networks. In *Proc. DBISP2P*, 2003.

[41] B. Wilcox-O'Hearn. Experiences deploying a large-scale emergent network. In *Proc. IPTPS*, 2002.
[42] B. Zhao, J. Kubiatowicz, and A. Joseph. Tapestry: An Infrastructure for Fault-Tolerant Wide-Area Location and Routing. Technical Report UCB/CSD-01-1141, UCBerkeley, 2001.

Global Data Management
R. Baldoni et al. (Eds.)
IOS Press, 2006

Data Aggregation in Large Scale Distributed Systems[1]

Giovanni Cortese[a], Federico Morabito[b], Fabrizio Davide [b],
Antonino Virgillito[c], Roberto Beraldi [c], Vivien Quema [c]
[a] *Interplay Software*
[b] *Telecom Italia Learning Services*
[c] *Università di Roma La Sapienza*

Abstract. Data aggregation, in its most basic definition, is the ability to summarize information. Data aggregation is highly relevant to distributed systems, which collect and process information from many sources, like Internet-scale information systems, and peer-to-peer data management systems. Several architectures and techniques have been recently explored (either in the context of Internet services, peer-to-peer, or wireless sensor networks research), aiming at the design of general purpose, highly scalable data aggregation services. In this chapter, we describe application scenarios, and review and compare several proposed designs for aggregation services. In the second part of the chapter, we present a complete case study for aggregation services, in the context of a DHT-based peer data management architecture. We argue that aggregation services would benefit for a design, which is consistent with and integrated into a general purpose data indexing functionality, and present GREG, an architecture which is based on this assumption.

Keywords. Peer-to-peer, data overlay, aggregation services, data indexing, DHT

1.   Introduction

Data aggregation has played an important role in data-centric applications since their inception. If we consider databases as the starting point of the research path towards future, large-scale, completely decentralized, pervasive data management infrastructures, we easily see that aggregation has deserved a prominent role from the beginning, with aggregation services implemented as a basic building block in database middleware.

A growing interest towards the realization of aggregation services, as a fundamental facility of distributed systems middleware, is clearly emerging. It is interesting to see that researchers in distributed systems, from different communities and with different objectives pushing their research (e.g. peer-to-peer overlays, sensor

---

[1] The work described in this chapter has been carried out as part of the IST Delis project in the Future Emerging Technologies – Complex Systems initiative. The work has been also partially supported by the Network of Excellence RESIST, funded by the IST program of the EU in the 7th framework program

networks, Internet services), are proposing architectures for distributed aggregation services.

The simplest definition of aggregation is simply "the ability to summarize information" [1]. In SQL databases, data across many tables can easily be aggregated. In a distributed system, data is originated on many nodes. Aggregation services allow for example averaging a value (e.g. system load) across a group of nodes, counting nodes having certain properties, finding the node with extremal values for some property etc.

Aggregation often leverages some hierarchical arrangement of the nodes in the distributed system; the aggregation service allows then each node to discover detailed views of *nearby* information, in addition to summary views of global information [2].

The work reported in this Chapter includes an extensive survey on research related to data aggregation, and describes how aggregation services are integrated into an XML-oriented, peer-to-peer data management middleware we are designing.

First, in Section 2 we describe application scenarios where data aggregation is important; we analyse the characteristics of applications and their requirements with respect to data aggregation. In the following part of the chapter (Section 3), we describe different techniques and designs which have been proposed so far, to address the requirements above. In the last section, we provide a complete case study in the design of an aggregation service, and describe a middleware architecture for self-managing, peer-to-peer data management which we are currently researching, and includes data aggregation facilities as an important feature.

2.   The Problem Space

2.1.Application Scenarios

This section presents the several different application areas that have motivated researchers looking at the problem of aggregation. Our aim is to create the proper background context for allowing the reader a better understanding, later in this chapter, of the techniques which have been proposed and researched. Each different perspective is closely associated with technological assumptions, constraints and requirements from one or more motivating applications. We also provide here a cross-reference to the works we review in section 3, and associate them (when applicable) to their main application area.

2.1.1.Systems Monitoring

One of the most important applications of aggregation services is distributed monitoring. Distributed monitoring is relevant to any application having many sensors collect data, to track some process or physical resource. Networks of routers, computing nodes (e.g. GRIDS), decentralised Internet applications (e.g. e-mail systems, process management infrastructures etc) are all examples of large, decentralized systems requiring monitoring.

In network and systems management applications, monitoring is mainly used to locate which host or application is using up most resources of the system, or anyway using resources in a way that deviates from expected patterns (often termed 'top-k monitoring' or the 'distributed heavy hitter' problem). The goal is to identify network sources, destinations, or protocols that account for significant or unusual amounts of traffic.

This functionality is required for system performance analysis, as well as for security enforcement (e.g. intrusion detection, DoS attack detection et al.).

Current systems which perform flow-level analysis are rather centralised and require to transfer data to a central datastore for analysis of data correlation (e.g. Cisco NetFlow [3] architecture). In order to implement distributed, flow-level top-k monitoring, several features are required.

First, nodes must be deployed in the system that collect and store packet traces. Such monitors also generate traffic summaries ('flow records') which aggregate information from packet traces. Summaries represent traffic as seen at the local monitor, at a level of detail which allows to analyse i.e. traffic originated from a particular customer or application, suspicious traffic flows. While techniques (i.e. high-performance stream-processing algorithms) for identifying heavy hitters (and other traffic summaries) at one router are well developed, applications may need aggregate views of the data. A distributed facility supporting complex queries must be available, to enable real-time processing of collected data without transferring all data to a central repository. Aggregation queries, supporting operators such as MAX, COUNT, AVG etc are the most important type of distributed query in this scenario.

In this scenario, queries are typically *continuous*. A query is issued once by a client, and runs for extended periods of time, reporting to the issuer a series of values at defined intervals, or as data becomes available.

Hierarchical scoping and aggregation, and administrative isolation, is a main concern in monitoring applications, since resources are most often structured according to some organizational hierarchy.

Related Work

Probably the most quoted research work on distributed data aggregation is Astrolabe [4] (section 3.2.1), which was designed in the first place to address distributed systems monitoring tasks. Astrolabe, as well as [2] (see 3.3.2), explicitly deal with administrative isolation and hierarchical scoping. However, for obvious reasons, many of the other reviewed contribution are also relevant to this application scenario.

2.1.2.Self-managing overlays

An overlay network is a computer network which is built on top of another network. Nodes in the overlay can be thought of as being connected by virtual or logical links, each of which corresponds to a path, perhaps through many physical links, in the underlying network. Overlay-based architectures are especially relevant to the design of large-scale (often Internet-based) applications with no clear point of centralized control.

The interest in overlay-based architectures is their potential as an enabler for the realization of 'autonomic' or self-managing services, running on many computing nodes, which are scalable with respect to the degree of required human intervention, as the number of nodes increases.

Critical to this goal is the ability for each node to obtain a (fairly) complete view of the other nodes' status. For example, in a distributed storage system, nodes may need to know statistics on data distribution or free space in the peer network (e.g. to optimize indexes, or to execute load balancing optimizations) There are however specific problems in gathering (in a way which is both efficient and reliable) information describing the overlay status. In fact, the large number of nodes which typically form a peer-to-peer overlay, and the high dynamics ('churn' of the members i.e. nodes joining and leaving the overlay), which are specific to the targeted systems, make the task very challenging.

An aggregation service consistent with this application should essentially be efficient in dealing with the large size and robust with respect to node failures. Other example applications, which are discussed in the works we surveyed, include finding lightly loaded nodes, discovering super-node candidates (i.e. nodes which exhibit better stability) and improving routing tables in peer-to-peer network.

Related Work

SOMO [5] (see 3.3.1) has been explicitly designed as an infrastructure for system metadata gathering and dissemination in structured overlay networks. Similarly, SDIMS has a strong applicability to this application scenario.

[6] (see 3.2.2) intends to develop robust and adaptive protocols for proactive aggregation, including the calculation of average, product and extremal values, building on the idea of anti-entropy aggregation (a scheme based on the anti-entropy epidemic communication model). It specifically deals with convergence of propagated values to their true value, and investigates techniques for coping with churn.

2.1.3.Sensor networks

Rather different motivations drive research on data aggregation in sensor networks.

Sensor networks consist of small computing devices capable of producing observations corresponding to real-world phenomena. Due to size and battery power limitations, these devices typically have limited storage capacity, limited energy resources, and limited network bandwidth. Data produced by nodes in the network propagates through the network via wireless links. When compared to local processing of data, wireless transmission is extremely expensive. The limited amount of energy, bandwidth, and storage capacity available to sensor nodes calls for specialized optimizations of queries injected into the network.

For this reason, researchers explored *in-network aggregation* as a power-efficient mechanism for collecting data in wireless sensor networks. In many sensor network scenarios, a large number of nodes produce data periodically which is consumed by a sink node. Such communication model is typical of physical monitoring scenarios, the primary application of sensor networks. Most techniques for in-network aggregation require the construction of a routing tree for propagating data from source nodes to the sink. Once established, each node utilizes the routing tree to find a path to the host node. The main idea behind in-network aggregation is that, rather than sending individual data items from sensors to sinks, multiple data items are aggregated as they are forwarded by the sensor network. Since typical queries, in sensor network applications, are interested to aggregates computed on the readings collected by the sensors (e.g. average), through intermediate aggregate processing important savings can be obtained in the size of transmitted data.

Related Work

In this chapter we will review extensively the TAG [7] approach (see 3.4 and 3.5). TAG's key feature is the adoption of the database concept of a generic query interface as the basis of an architecture for data collection in sensor networks. The idea behind TAG is to devise a *generic* as opposed to *application-specific* approach to aggregation in sensor networks. Several other works explore the algorithmic aspects of in-network aggregation e.g. [8, 9, 10] and many others.

2.1.4. Querying the Internet

A final, relevant application area is peer-to-peer databases, whether Internet-based as the title of this section evokes, or deployed in large enterprise networks.

It must be noted that peer-to-peer databases represent an 'horizontal' application, in the sense that results reported here might apply for example to system monitoring as well. In a peer-to-peer database, many nodes cooperate to implement storage, indexing and query processing facilities. Peer-to-peer databases should support complex queries, as their centralized counterparts, including range queries and aggregation queries.

Note that queries can be dispatched to many individual peers. As in sensor networks, if the query contains common relational operators such as COUNT, AVG, SUM etc. there may be an advantage in calculating the aggregations in-network rather than aggregating all query results at the peer issuing the query. While this would be the simplest option, if there are many individual nodes producing results (e.g. compute the average seconds from uptime on all network nodes), the one node receiving the data suffers from heavy inbound communication load. Mechanisms which allow to distribute the *in-bandwidth* load to multiple nodes are then desirable. For example, in a DHT-based design, one might think of aggregating intermediate results along the path implied by having all data producers routing query results to the client (or to another root node identifier specified in the query).

Related Work

PIER [11] is an early attempt to implement an Internet-scale, general-purpose relational query engine targeted at a peer-to-peer architecture of thousands or millions of participating nodes on the Internet. It supports massively distributed, database-style dataflows for both snapshot and continuous queries.

Note however that since PIER mechanisms for data aggregation are only briefly described in the paper, that rather focuses on efficient distributed joins, we do not cover it further in our review.

Our work, which we document in section 4, also falls in this category.

2.2. Types of aggregated data and aggregation functions

2.2.1. Taxonomy of aggregates

In this section we provide an informal taxonomy of aggregation functions, and show that different aggregates may pose different challenges to the designer of aggregation services.

Most of the presented systems support aggregation functions borrowed from the SQL language. In Section 3.5 we present more sophisticated solutions supported by a specific system, namely TAG. Until that point we basically consider the main aggregation functions, which are supported by most systems, as the classical summaries provided in SQL, that is: COUNT, COUNT DISTINCT, MIN, MAX, SUM, MEDIAN and AVERAGE.

However, the application of such functions in a distributed aggregation system presents some significant differences with their use in queries for database management systems. The first aspect is that a database query is typically pull-based, i.e. results are returned in response to the query, while a query in a distributed aggregation system can also be permanently stored and return results either periodically or each time the values change (*persistent query*). Persistent queries are typically used in monitoring applications.

As a second difference, data to be aggregated does not always follow a relational schema structure. Basically, all systems used data structured in attributes, though such attributes are not necessarily organized into tables and join operations are not permitted.

Finally, in a distributed aggregation system the data required for calculating aggregation is not entirely contained into a single server but it is spread in many nodes composing the distributed system. Obviously, this is the main difficulty behind distributed aggregation and will be widely discussed in the following of this chapter.

In this section we concentrate on a classification of the aggregation function, taken from [7], with the aim of identifying the main aspects characterizing the different aggregation functions as well as their implementation trade-offs in a distributed environment. The classification is structured into four dimensions, namely duplicate sensitivity, returned value, monotonicity, state requirements.

- **Duplicate Sensitivity**. Determines if the aggregate is affected by duplicate reading of a same value from a single node. For example, MAX, MIN and COUNT DISTINCT functions are *duplicate insensitive*, while COUNT, SUM, AVERAGE, MEDIAN are *duplicate sensitive*, because several readings of a same value change the value of the aggregate. The distributed computation of duplicate sensitive functions require then a duplicate detection mechanism in order to provide correct values. For example, if a gossiping protocol is used for the diffusion of readings, a node is likely to receive duplicate values from different nodes, then these values have to be detected and discarded.
- **Returned value**. This dimension defines the type of value returned by the aggregate function. An *exemplary* aggregate returns a specific value among the set of all values. Typical exemplary aggregates are MAX and MEDIAN. A *summary* aggregate returns a value that is not related to the set of readings, but is the result of a computation and in general does not either belong to the same domain as the aggregated values. Examples are COUNT, SUM, AVERAGE, COUNT DISTINCT. Exemplary aggregates are sensitive to loss of values and cannot be computed reliably by sampling. On the contrary, for summary aggregates, even in presence of value loss are able to return an approximation of the actual value, the more reliable it is, the less values are lost.
- **Monotonicity**. In a *monotonic* aggregate, given two partial values of the aggregate computed from two distinct subsets of the readings, the overall value obtained by considering all the readings is always greater than or lower than the partial values. This is the case for COUNT, MAX, SUM aggregates, while AVERAGE is not a monotonic aggregate.
- **State requirement**. The amount of state required for computing the aggregate, that has to be propagated toward the nodes that compute the aggregate. Obviously this is a critical issue with respect to the scalability of the aggregation. In a *distributive* aggregate, such as MAX, COUNT, SUM, the global aggregate of a set of partitioned values can be computed recursively by applying the function over the aggregates for each single partition. Hence, it is sufficient to compute and propagate only the partial result for each partition. In *algebraic* aggregates the partial results are not aggregates of a partition, but the state size required for computing the aggregate is constant. An example is the AVERAGE, that requires a constant-size state of two values (the partial sum and the partial count) to be propagated. In *holistic* aggregates the entire set of values is required in order to compute the aggregate, so no partial

aggregation is useful. Examples are MEDIAN and COUNT DISTINCT (where actually only the distinct values have to be propagated). Finally, in *content-sensitive* aggregates, the size of the partial state to be propagated is proportional to some statistical property of data values in the partition. This is the case for advanced statistical aggregates that will be discussed in Section 3.7.

2.2.2. Read vs write-dominated data

When designing a general-purpose aggregation service, we should keep into account that the type of data we are aggregating may be updated at very different rates. For example, in a network monitoring or GRID management application, some information changes very slowly (or does not change at all) like numInterfaces in a router or numCPUs in a GRID cluster. Other information such as avgLoad may change fast or very fast (e.g. numOctets observed on a router interface).

As a consequence, a propagation strategy that works well for a read-dominated attribute such as numCPU (for example, one that triggers a propagation to all nodes, upon a change in the value of the attribute), may not work for an attribute changing very quickly (such as a counter – in this case having on-demand update of the aggregated values, triggered by a user query is more bandwidth-effective).

Applications should then be able to adopt different propagation strategies for various aggregates. APIs for the aggregation service should then allow fine grain control on the different *aggregation processes* going on simultaneously in the distributed systems. SDIMS is apparently the first work addressing such fine-grained control over propagation strategies.

3.   The Solution Space

In this section we review existing research on data aggregation, trying to make the different possible characteristics (resulting from different choices taken by the designer of aggregation services) emerge from the analysis.

3.1. Design alternatives

The works we reviewed reveal the existence of several design alternatives, often due to the different goals and targeted applications.

Overlay architecture. A first alternative is related to the overlay architecture adopted. At a very coarse grain, two main alternative exist, that is unstructured overlays using probabilistic gossip protocols, and structured overlays. *Structured overlays* [22,23] have emerged mainly in an attempt to address the scalability issues that the first generation unstructured systems were originally faced with. These systems essentially provide a mapping between content and location, in the form of distributed routing indices, so that queries can be efficiently routed to the node hosting the desired content. Because of the fact they map a logical address to a physical one they are typically referred to as *Distributed Hash Tables* (DHTs). They offer a scalable and self-organising substrate for data dissemination and search-oriented applications such as the envisioned management platform. In *unstructured* peer-to-peer networks, the placement of content is completely unrelated to the overlay topology. The content needs to be located and the searching mechanisms range from flooding the network with propagating queries to more sophisticated solutions such as, gossiping, random walks and routing indices. This architecture is more appropriate for managing highly-transient node populations, while the search mechanisms have implications on the availability and scalability properties of the system.

Application Control. One important aspect is the level of control over the aggregation process that the design allows to the application designer. While some proposals make specific choices, other leave to the application the possibility (or responsibility) of tailoring the characteristics of the aggregation process with respect to:

- Protocol for propagation of aggregated information (e.g. timing, request-driven or data-driven)
- Topology of aggregation tree
- Type of aggregate functions supported

Declarative vs. programmatic approach. Also related to the issue of application control, several works provide a declarative language to applications for accessing the aggregation service. This in some sense may constrains the functionalities (for example, the set of aggregation functions) to those supported by the chosen language (often, SQL). Other proposals, by adopting a programmatic approach seem to allow a greater degree of freedom to application.

Administrative isolation: In several applications, peers in the system are naturally partitioned according to some administrative or organizational hierarchy. Administrative isolation ensures that queries within a domain are resolved locally, domain-scoped queries are resolved efficiently, and security policies can be applied effectively.

3.2.Information diffusion via gossiping

In the following, we describe two works, which use gossip to disseminate aggregate information in a decentralised system. Gossiping is a common technique in large-scale distributed systems for disseminating information when scalability is a major concern and flooding cannot be considered a feasible option. The idea is that each node in the system propagates the information only to a restricted subset of other nodes, typically chosen at random. Eventually all nodes will be aware of the information with a high probability regardless of events such as message losses and node failures.

3.2.1.Astrolabe

Astrolabe [4,12,13] is a gossip-based system, aimed at the collection of large-scale system state that can be reported to users in form of summaries. Astrolabe architecture is based on a set of hierarchically organized domains, called *zones*. Each zone is globally identified by a zone name, which corresponds to a path of zone identifiers from the root. Moreover, zones have an *attribute list*, called MIB (Management Information Base) that contains the information associated with the zone. These attributes are generated by *aggregation functions* deployed in each zone. An aggregation function is an SQL program taking a list of the MIBs of the zone's child zones and producing a summary of their attributes. Attributes in leaf zones are not generated by aggregation functions, but directly written by the application, starting from values extracted at the node. Astrolabe also provides security mechanisms for controlling the introduction of new aggregation functions. These security mechanisms take the form of certificates issued by each zone.

In practice, Astrolabe can be thought of as a form of decentralized hierarchical database, containing a table for each zone, with a row for each child zone and a column per attribute value (containing raw values in leaf zones and aggregated values in internal zones). Astrolabe defines an API that allows retrieving data from the tables using SQL operators. Typical utilisations of Astrolabe include counting the number of nodes that hold a copy of some particular file, building trees of TCP connections spanning zones in order to build scalable multicast primitives, implementing synchronization barriers by waiting until a minimum value is reached by each node in the system, etc.

Nodes running the Astrolabe system host an agent implementing the Astrolabe protocol. Each agent stores a local copy of a subset of the Astrolabe zone tree, composed of the zones on the path to the root, together with their sibling zones. Update of MIBs is performed via a gossip protocol ran among agents. Periodically, an agent first updates the MIB of the zone it manages. Then it randomly chooses other agents it will exchange information with. If the agents belong to the same zone, it exchanges information related to MIBs in that zone. If they are located in different zones, it exchanges state associated with the MIBs of their least common ancestor.

The Astrolabe system also defines mechanisms for handling joins and leaves of nodes. Failure detection is achieved by timestamping MIBs. When an agent does not receive updates from a particular agent during a certain amount of time, it removes the corresponding MIB from the subset of the tree it locally stores. Node joins are handled using a gossip mechanism: agents periodically send IP multicast messages (or a set of unicast messages) to discover other trees and merge.

It is important to point out that the gossip protocol only allows to achieve *eventual consistency*. That is, an update made to an attribute is certainly reflected on other attributes that depend on it only if updates cease. Otherwise, it is possible that an aggregation is updated with a value which is older than its previous one, i.e. updates are not monotonic. This weak notion of consistency directly stems from the probabilistic nature of the gossiping protocol and is adopted for the benefits it provokes in terms of scalability and fast dissemination.

3.2.2. Anti-entropy protocols for information aggregation

Jelasity et al. propose an aggregation protocol [6] that aims at providing access to the same global information, to all the components of a distributed system. This global information is built by aggregation functions that can compute a broad range of indicators: averages, sums, products, extremal values, etc.

The proposed protocol is based on gossiping. Its operating principle is very simple: each node p periodically initiates an exchange of its local estimate of the aggregate value with a random neighbor q returned by a GETNEIGHBOR function. Then, both nodes use an UPDATE function to update their estimate of the aggregate value using the remote value received during the exchange. The output of the UPDATE function and the remote value received during the exchange depend on the specific aggregation function being implemented by the protocol. Note that this protocol is *proactive* in the sense that it continuously provides the value of the aggregate function to all nodes in the system, contrary to *reactive* protocols that respond to specific queries issued by nodes in the network.

The main contribution of the paper is the theoretical analysis of the speed at which the value at each node converges to the true value (i.e. the variance tends to zero).

Authors define a metric, called convergence factor, defined as follows: being a cycle a set of calls to the UPDATE function by all the nodes in the system, the convergence factor is the ratio between the expected variance of values at each node in each two consecutive cycles. The lower it is, the faster the convergence of the aggregate function to its correct value. It is proved that, in the case of an aggregate function computing the average of values stored at each node, the convergence factor of the aggregate function only depends on the GETNEIGHBOR function: the more uniformly nodes are selected, the better the convergence factor. This result is interesting because it shows that the convergence factor does not depend on network size, time, or the initial distribution of the values. Moreover, a lower bound is provided on the reachable convergence factor and a GETNEIGHBOR function with a convergence factor (=0.303) close to the optimal (0.25). This GETNEIGHBOR function simply consists in picking a random permutation of the nodes and pairing each node with another random node. This function ensures that in each cycle, each node is guaranteed to be a member of at least one pair. The theoretical analysis is confirmed by both simulations and experiments carried out on the PlanetLab platform.

Finally, authors propose practical solutions to cope with nodes continuously joining and leaving the network. This phenomenon, referred to as *churn*, is typical in peer-to-peer systems and in this context harms convergence of the algorithm, causing estimates to be never up-to-date. The idea proposed is to periodically restart the protocol (say, each *x* cycles), which allows taking into account both the dynamicity in the network and the variability in values that are being aggregated. This restarting mechanism requires some synchronization between nodes, achieved by piggybacking *epoch* identifiers to messages exchanged between nodes. An epoch corresponds to the period (i.e. *x* cycles) of the restarting mechanism. Simulations and experiments on the PlanetLab platform show this idea to effectively work in practice, allowing to converge to an aggregate even in presence of churn.

3.3. Leveraging structured overlays

Several of the reviewed works leverage DHTs to support protocols for information aggregation in large-scale, dynamic systems. A DHT offers a permanent logical address space which is kept consistent though nodes continuously join and leave the system. An aggregation system generally exploits the DHT by building logical aggregation trees over the logical space. The main common difficulty is to maintain such hierarchical structures over the flat addressing space of a DHT. This is the point where the various proposals differ significantly. In describing such works, we analyse why it can be beneficial to leverage DHTs in aggregation services, and compare how each proposal integrate DHTs in its architecture.

3.3.1. SOMO: a Self-Organized Metadata Overlay

SOMO (which stands for Self-Organized Metadata Overlay) [5] is a DHT-based infrastructure for computing and disseminating aggregated information. Although the mechanism it proposes is fairly general, SOMO's motivating application is the gathering and dissemination of system and resource information in a DHT infrastructure.

SOMO is based on a tree-based logical structure, which is overlapped to the DHT abstraction. That is, a SOMO node is hosted by one physical node present in the DHT, while a DHT node can host more than one SOMO nodes.

A SOMO node is associated to an operation to be performed and to a report, which represents the result of the operation, as seen by the node. Operations supported by SOMO are not limited to aggregation operators but can be programmed (examples include sorting, filtering and so on). The computation of the operation starts either periodically or by a call from a node, and triggers a gathering phase in which each SOMO node requests reports from all its children. Finally, the gathered reports converge to the root, which is able to compute the final outcome of the operation, having gathered all the reports. The result is disseminated down in the SOMO hierarchy until reaching all the nodes.

SOMO is entirely self-organizing: the SOMO tree is built by local actions of DHT nodes and expands as long as the DHT grows. DHT nodes are leafs in the tree structure and to each group of k DHT nodes there is one SOMO node at the upper level. SOMO nodes aggregate in groups of k until reaching the root. Each SOMO node takes care of a subspace which is the union of the subspaces of all its children. The SOMO node is hosted by the DHT node that covers the central point of the subspace. Thanks to this mechanism, the SOMO tree has the property that it has more levels in regions of the DHT where more nodes are present. Finally, SOMO nodes are able to repair the tree when a DHT node leaves the system, thus making SOMO resilient to failures of nodes.

3.3.2.SDIMS: a Scalable Distributed Information Management System

SDIMS (acronym for Scalable Distributed Information Management System) [2] is a distributed application that manages data aggregation in large-scale distributed systems. The main principle behind SDIMS is borrowed from Astrolabe: SDIMS is also based on a hierarchical propagation protocol, allowing for scalable computation of aggregation functions. Moreover, the stored values are maintained in the form of MIBs, organized as in Astrolabe.

However, there are significant differences between the two approaches. The fundamental aspect is that SDIMS leverages an underlying DHT infrastructure when building the aggregation tree. While in Astrolabe, the organization of the aggregation hierarchy only follows administrative criteria, in SDIMS two dimensions are considered: firstly, one tree is present for each attribute type (while in Astrolabe a single hierarchy is considered for all attributes) and secondly, all nodes in a same administrative domain lies in a common aggregation subtree (this feature is referred to as *administrative isolation*). With respect to a single-tree approach, aggregation over multiple trees allows to better load balance node stress among several nodes acting as root.

Rather than considering the DHT as a black box, SDIMS utilizes the DHT by exposing its internal routing mechanism for building the aggregation tree in the following way: the tree for an attribute type is rooted at the node whose DHT address is the hash of the attribute type and name. The DHT routing tree is then considered, obtained by combining all the paths starting from all nodes and directed towards the root. The aggregation tree is built, where each node is responsible for aggregating as many subtrees in the logical tree as the depth of its subtree in the routing tree. For example, in a k level routing tree, the root contains *k-1* aggregation functions, while the leafs in the routing tree are also leafs in the aggregation tree (no aggregation functions).

An interesting and difficult problem is then how to achieve administrative isolation in this structure. In particular, the problem is to have routing paths for a key that entirely fall into a same administrative domain, which is the same of the target key. Since this usually is not guaranteed in common DHTs, the design choice made is

SDIMS was to implement a modification of a specific DHT (i.e., Pastry) in order to constraint routing to a single administrative domain.

Another characterizing aspect of SDIMS is that it permits a flexible choice of different strategies for computation and propagation of aggregates, allowing to tailor the system to various application requirements. A computation and propagation strategy in SDIMS is defined as a combination of three basic features: install of a function, update of an aggregate value and probe for an aggregate value. Under a lazy strategy, update is performed only locally. A probe is propagated in the tree, until it reaches the level of the desired aggregate. Only at this point the aggregate is computed in the corresponding subtree and returned above. This strategy is suited for write-dominated attributes, because it saves the overhead for propagating the updates, which are considered in the aggregates only when these are requested. On the other side of the spectrum, the aggressive strategy (more suited for read-dominated attributes) is such that all updates are immediately propagated up in the tree and the aggregates are always up-to-date, so that a probe can stop at the desired level without propagating down. Intermediate strategies are also possible.

Finally, SDIMS include several mechanisms for enhancing robustness in the face of reconfigurations of nodes. Specifically, SDIMS guarantees termination of probes and eventual consistency of updates by enforcing (i) persistent connectivity of the aggregation trees and (ii) data redundancy in the form of periodical re-aggregation activity and replication of data on different nodes.

3.3.3. Willow

Willow [14], a work by some of the Astrolabe proponents, is a generic distributed infrastructure providing, in addition to aggregation, also DHT-like functionality as well as publish/subscribe multicasting. Differently from all the above-cited works exploiting DHTs, Willow does not stack an aggregation protocol over a DHT, while it is rather a DHT augmented with aggregation capabilities.

Willow design is based on a logical binary tree. Each node in the tree is called a *domain* and has two children, corresponding to 1 and 0 bits. A physical node (*agent*) is associated to a 128-bit identifier and is a member of all the domains that have the same prefix as the agents' identifier. Then, all agents are members of the root domain and each agent is the only member of one leaf domain. Each domain the agent belongs to can be represented by a prefix d of the agents' identifier. If the agent is also in domain $d0$ it stores the references to some agents members of the child domain $d1$ or vice versa. In overall each agent stores such information for all the 128 domains it is in.

This structure is used to realize a unicast routing protocol which was first introduced in the Kademlia DHT [15]: given a target identifier, a message is routed by an agent to the agent it knows whose is closest to the target according to the XOR metric (i.e., the number of bits that differ in the two identifiers). This guarantees that the target agent is reached in a logarithmic number of steps.

Willow differs from Kademlia because it also supports multicast routing and attribute aggregation. Each domain can contain one or more attributes, whose value is given by an aggregate function computed over the same attributes in the child domain. Multicast starts from the root domain and propagates to all the children that satisfy a SQL predicate over the attributes, specified with the message. Differently from Astrolabe, attribute propagation among domains does not use gossiping: one agent is elected as contact for its domain and is responsible for sending attribute updates to its neighbors. Dissemination of the update within a domain exploits Willow multicast facility.

3.3.4.Using heap data structures to support max/min resource discovery

Several distributed applications are faced with the problem of discovering a resource above or below a given size (e.g. a powerful enough machine, or with enough free storage). This problem is best matched, in terms of abstract data structures, by a heap.

Cone [16] addresses the problem of having DHTs mimic other distributed data structures, in addition to hash tables; specifically, augmentation of DHTs to support heap operations is proposed. The main reason here for building on DHTs, rather than building a completely new architecture, seems to be the goal of preserving desirable DHT properties, such as the distributed lookup functionality, the ability to handle dynamic joins and leaves of nodes, and the load balancing properties.

A cone is a binary tree of nodes[2], with an aggregation key at the root of each subtree. Leaf nodes represent the set of values for the aggregation key; each interior node stores the maximum of the subtree rooted at the node, for the aggregation key (corresponding to an aggregation function over some attribute e.g. max freeSpace). Note that augmenting the DHT with a tree, as opposed to overlaying the tree on top of it, refers to the fact that cone tables use IP addresses to refer to parent and child nodes. Nodes in the distributed systems join first as DHT nodes, and then adjust their pointers to other nodes ('trickling' up or down in the tree) until they reach a position in the tree where the property for the aggregation key holds (i.e. the aggregation key is higher than nodes below and lower than node above).

Cone supports queries, such as finding resource of maximum size, or at least of a given size. Answering a query is implemented by searching the trie starting from any node, until the answer is found. Changing a key value causes the node trickling up or down in the tree until the order is restored.

While [16] does not elaborate the proposal to the extent of providing a comprehensive architecture, the Cone approach can be quite general. Different aggregation operators (other than MIN/MAX) can be implemented, according to authors. Cone can be used to implement several aggregations over possibly different attributes (this requires of course setting up independent trees).

3.4.Aggregates as stream of values: TAG

As cited in Section 2.1.3, sensor networks constitute an important application for aggregation techniques. Besides the peculiar technical characteristics of sensors, that were discussed above, this environment also presents a specific challenge for what concerns data themselves. The information to be aggregated flows from the sensors as a continuous stream of values. The aggregation system has to deal with such continuously streaming data with specific language and algorithmic solutions.

TAG (Tiny AGgregation Service) [7] is a service designed for aggregation in low-power, distributed, wireless environments. TAG is based on a hierarchical architecture where a single powered storage-rich base station plays the role of root node, and a set of wireless sensor devices (motes) is in charge of the query processing and aggregation operations. TAG allows users to express simple, declarative queries over streaming sensor data according to an SQL-like language, without joins.

With respect to standard SQL, TAG queries have different semantics: in particular, TAG supports persistent queries whose output is a stream of values, being more suited

---

[2] actually, a trie is built by the join procedure

for applications that monitor the trend of data measured by the sensors. TAG allows several aggregates to be included in queries, as well as grouping (GROUP BY clause).

Aggregation queries in TAG are executed *in network*: a sensor generally performs a partial computation of an aggregate whose result is a partial state record, which is propagated backwards to the querying node. Partial records are collected from children in the tree in response to a query and are used to compute a new partial record, which is forwarded to the parent. In network aggregation dramatically reduces the communication overhead required to compute an aggregate compared to a centralized approach, in which all sensor readings are sent to a central base station.

The service offered by TAG is structured into two phases: a distribution phase and a collection phase. The root node initiates the distribution phase. The goal of this phase is to propagate a query message into the network. TAG is agnostic wrt the routing algorithm used for this purpose. This means that in principle any algorithm allowing a root node to send a message to all sensors and to receive at least a copy of a message from any sensor could be used. The authors, however, propose the following technique for diffusing a query message into the sensor network.

The root node broadcasts a message asking the motes to form a routing tree. The message carries the id of the sending node and its distance (level) from the root, which is initialized to zero. On receiving a message for the first time, a mote sets its own level to the level heard from the message plus one, sets the sending node as its parent node and rebroadcasts a message containing its own level and id. This process continues until all nodes have processed a message, so that a tree is built. In order to deal with topological changes, i.e. due to mote faults, the root node triggers this process continuously over the time. During a collection phase sensor readings are aggregated and values are routed up from children to parents until the root is reached. The collection of data goes on continuously and is organized into epochs. Precisely, each aggregate values is made up from measurements referring to a same epoch.

3.5.Beyond average: more sophisticated aggregations

In Section 2.2 we presented and classified the most common types of aggregation function typically used in distributed aggregation system, pointing out that they are based on a straightforward SQL-like syntax. However, simple SQL queries may not be suited for specific applications that require more sophisticated ways for summarizing data distributions. In [17] three further types of aggregation are presented, that were implemented in the context of the TAG framework. Hence, such aggregate functions are specifically targeted for being used in sensor applications, though we believe they can be of general interest in the context of aggregation (in particular, multi-resolution summarization of data streams, which in this work is achieved through wavelets). We report in the following a general description of such aggregates, referring to [17] for a detailed description of their implementation.

Wavelet-based aggregation. The type of statistical data summaries that can be obtained through common SQL aggregation function is quite restricted. In particular, functions like AVERAGE, MAX and MIN do not allow to get a complete representation of the distribution of sensor readings. Hence, the TAG framework introduces summarization of statistical data distributions through wavelet-based aggregation. Wavelets allows to decompose a sequence of data (in this case, sensor readings) into multiple resolutions, where each resolution is associated to a frequency. That is, wavelets allow a frequency decomposition of a sequence similar to a Fourier series, but much more suited to represent non-periodic sequences [18]. Applying wavelet techniques to sensor-provided data introduces specific challenges: firstly, the complete set of data is not available, thus wavelet data has to be computed as long as readings flow through the aggregation tree; secondly, the processing power of sensor devices is limited and does not allow floating-point computation and complex mathematical primitives. Then, integer wavelets are considered as well as specific compact data representations, that permits at the same time fast, low-resource processing and low-bandwidth diffusion.

Distributed Map Construction. Many sensor-based applications require the construction of topographic maps of a zone populated with sensor, only starting from sensor readings. Maps should report both the distribution of sensors in space and the distribution of their value readings, highlighting the regions in space in which the sensor reading is (approximately) the same (*isobars*). More precisely, the set of possible sensor readings are partitioned and adjacent regions in the space that report readings in a same partition have to belong to a same isobar. The computation of isobars requires implementing geometric operators and primitive on sensors, in order to compute adjacency, merging and overlapping of polygons. [17] presents three algorithm for computation of isobars: a naïve, centralized algorithm, and two in network algorithms (leading respectively to exact and approximate computation), which allow to save a large amount of data transmitted for computation with respect to the centralized solution.

Object tracking. Tracking the path of moving objects through sensor readings is a classical problem for sensor-based applications. Though there are several research works specifically focusing on target tracking, the support for this feature in a distributed aggregation system allows to enhance tracking with ad-hoc aggregate functions, that can be applied on the data representing the paths followed by the moving objects. Regarding the support for object tracking included in the TAG framework, two algorithms are considered: the most efficient, in terms of energy consumption, exploits the "event" feature included in TAG, which allows to trigger a query when a specific event is detected by the sensor (which requires specific hardware generating interrupts to the device operating system).

4. GREGs: An Architecture for Integrated Data Indexing and Aggregation

At this stage, it should be clear that several designs suitable for aggregation services exist, and selection of best approach likely depends on the target application. We describe in the following a complete case study for aggregation services. We present an architecture, based on aggregation and indexing-capable objects named *GREGs*, that we are currently developing, which supports aggregation and is consistent with a broader scope peer-to-peer data management system which has been developed by some of the authors [19].

4.1.Background

In this section we provide a brief description of the peer-to-peer data management architecture which GREGs leverage.

System Overview

The system we consider consists of a large number of agents, which can be providers or consumers of data (or both). A comparably high number of peers cooperate to realize a distributed data management service, where each peer serves firstly as a place to store data, secondly as a helper to query processing, and finally as a forwarder of data (see "Figure 1 - System Overview").

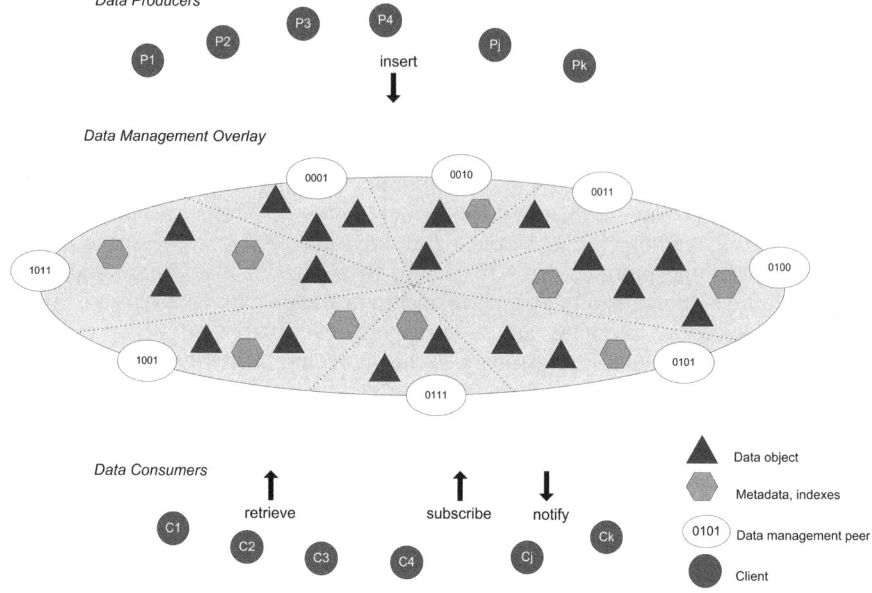

Figure 1 - System Overview

The common storage is used to store both application-level data, and metadata such as schema and index information, which will guide queries to find the data stored in the network of peers. Depending on requirements, application data can be better stored in a local storage at the provider node, and only the system's distributed indexing feature is exploited by applications in this case. Differently, applications can use the cooperative storage for both data and indexes. The former usage is associated either to data which change frequently (e.g. performance counters in a network monitoring agent), or that are generated on demand (e.g. via a Web Service).

Peers arrange in a self-organising structured overlay, for the purpose of communication and basic data indexing. The system implementation is built on top of a DHT-based self-organising communication overlay [23].

Producers interact with the system through one generalized *insert* primitive, which injects an object into the system. The object can be both dispatched to consumers which have declared an interest (through a subscription query), and stored in the common storage for the benefit of consumers which successively issue queries to which it may be relevant. The *insert* primitive allows the client to select between several alternative behaviors, including a desired persistency policy.

Consumers can access data using two primitives:

— *retrieve*: allows a client to pose an *ad-hoc query,* which is executed immediately and returns to the user a list of matching objects, among those persistently stored in the system
— *subscribe*: allows a client to post a long-running, continuous query. The client will be notified whenever an object has been inserted, or updated, which satisfies the subscription query

Data Storage

Applications store XML data in the network of peers. The unit of distribution is an XML fragment, as described by a '*storage type*' descriptor (we will use *type* for brevity in the following text). The system is oriented to storage and query of XML data; however in the remainder of this chapter we will refer more generically to objects, consisting of several attribute/ value pairs, and avoid dealing with XML specific issues.

A type descriptor is a collection of metadata, which provide directives to the distributed storage manager about the storage strategy for objects. Such directives include criteria for forming the primary key ('*id*') of the object, based on values of selected attributes; for indexing the fragment on alternate, secondary key attributes; for replication; and for selecting among different available strategies for mapping data to peers. With respect to the latter, supported mapping strategies include

- 'single': each object, as identified by its *id*, is individually stored in the peer having the closest node id,
- 'log': several instances of the object, having same *id,* are stored at the peer having the closest node id, and appended to a 'queue', as appropriate for example for a time series of observations reported by a sensor or network management agent,
- 'vector': multiple objects share the same primary id, and are stored in a vector at the responsible peer for id, while being individually addressable for selections or updates based on an instance key.

Data Replication

Storage type descriptors also provide hints on the desired replication level, which is applied to data objects. A leafset-based replication manager provides for replicating the data, and for maintaining the desired level of replication, in spite of events such as departure or failure of nodes.

Queries and Indexes

For both ad-hoc and subscription queries, selection of data to be retrieved is performed by specifying an XPath expression over the XML data stored in the repository. A query parser analyzes the query, and selects attributes for which an index exists; it then selects one or more indexes which will help processing the query. Query processing heavily relies on the index layer, which is layered atop the DHT.

While access based on primary key is mapped to DHT lookup operations, indexes are required for accessing data based on values other than primary key attributes/ elements, or for supporting complex queries. We support three index types: equality-predicate indexes, range-predicate indexes, and type-predicate indexes. Type-predicate makes it possible to process queries which do not include any condition on indexed attributes without broadcasting the query to all nodes (e.g. retrieve position information from all node providing such data).

Indexing will be further elaborated in the GREG-specific section, since they are heavily interrelated.

Storage Catalog

All metadata (type definitions, index definitions, long running queries etc.) is described in XML and stored in the DHT. The system Catalog is a dedicated storage to keep information describing the current configuration of the system.

Multicast

The system includes an application-level multicast facility, which leverages prefix routing of Plaxton trees (implemented as an extension of FreePastry and Scribe [24]). Although conceived as an internal mechanism (e.g. for disseminating management and metadata information), it can be used by applications if they need.

4.2.GREGs: aggregation-capable index objects

We now describe the design of a data indexing and aggregation service, based on the idea of *distributed indexing structures augmented with aggregation capabilities*, which support the processing of complex queries in a peer-to-peer environment.

4.2.1.Main Requirements and Assumptions

The primary application domain for the system we present is the management of large distributed IT infrastructure (such as networks, GRIDs, content distribution networks etc), a topic we investigate as part of the IST project DELIS in the FET Complex Systems initiative. The most important applications in decentralized network management are monitoring (e.g. performance and security), and information directories, to keep track of all resources in the system, and to locate resources which match specific requirements.

The system is designed both to support ad-hoc queries and long-running queries. However, we assume that techniques to improve aggregate processing are likely to be most important to a scenario, where a) a query runs continuously, over extended periods of time and b) many clients are interested to share the query results.

Several scenarios are possible; extreme scenarios range from a) few consumers, many producers (e.g. centralised network management) b) fully decentralized, unfiltered information dissemination between all nodes in the system (e.g. [6]).

Our architecture is designed for configurations where:

- an important number of nodes are consumers of aggregated information
- they are interested to aggregation calculated over filtered views of the data available in the system (e.g. temperature data for office rooms in a site, averaged based on grouping rooms by their floor)

In many cases, aggregation must be computed in a hierarchical fashion (e.g. find the average load in increasingly large portions on the network), at different resolutions, and should follow some criteria of proximity (e.g. find the least loaded node among those in my LAN).

4.2.2.Overview of the approach

In the approach we follow, supporting efficient aggregate[3] calculation requires a preliminary step, whose purpose is close to that of index creation in traditional data management.

The setup of an aggregation index involves instantiating several aggregation-capable index objects ('GREGs'), on different, randomly chosen, peers. As in traditional indexing schemes, GREGs work by partitioning the data space, according to

---

[3] Note that some of the following text applies equally well to non-aggregate query processing in our system, we talk from now on of aggregate processing without making any further distinction for sake of brevity

some application-defined scheme. This partitioning is reflected in two aspects of the index topology:

- *bounding predicates* of each index node
- *links* between index nodes

GREGs are responsible for calculating one or several aggregation function(s) over the covered partition.

The following is a summary of the characteristics of the design we are proposing, which will be expanded in the following sections:

- GREGs extend a data indexing framework with aggregation capabilities
- GREGs are programmatically created, either under responsibility of some user or of an autonomic system optimizer
- A set of GREGs, which collectively realize an index over some attribute, can be arranged in a graph, more often a hierarchy
- GREGs can use several strategies for controlling (re)calculation of the aggregate value (data-driven, query-driven, lazy etc), hence being able to best match the needs of application in terms of information quality vs. processing cost
- GREGs are DHT-addressable objects

4.2.3.System Design

Query Model and Aggregates in Queries

Before providing some details of GREG design, we describe the characteristics of the aggregate abstraction as seen by the clients of the system.

Logically, an aggregation query consists of the following.

- An aggregation clause consisting of a function over one or more aggregation attributes or some expression calculated on attributes. Arbitrary aggregation functions can be specified
- A *selection,* defining the set of data which should actually be input to aggregate calculation (e.g. compute aggregation function over all performance events from agents "where role = 'backbone_router'")
- An aggregation *dimension,* i.e. the attribute(s) used for grouping data into sets, over which intermediate aggregate is calculated, and the associated *partitioning* rules. In the simplest case, a 1-level partition of data values can be used, as in TAG (e.g. "compute the aggregate over all performance events from servers, grouped by cpu-type"). More complex, range-based or datacube style roll-up capabilities can be obtained by defining partitioning rules that yield respectively a range-based or a hierarchical decomposition of the data in the aggregating dimension.
- The cardinality in the time dimension of the aggregate. While in some cases the aggregate is a single value wrt time (i.e. it represent the 'current' MAX/ MIN/ AVG etc), in other cases its value must be a time series of values
- An update strategy – governing whether the update of the aggregate value is data driven or request driven

Evaluation of an aggregate query yields multiple values; individual values represent the value of the aggregate for different *partitions,* or ranges, of the data space, according to the *aggregation dimension,* and the value of the aggregate for the partition at different time instants i.e. for different *epochs.*

Aggregate computation is performed in a distributed style over several nodes (each associated to a partition of the data), as described below.

GREG functionalities

We start by covering the behavior of GREGs with respect to indexing. As introduced, each GREG is responsible for (or 'covers') some value range, of the indexed attributes. The interval is defined by a bounding predicate associated to the GREG.

GREGs have two fundamental behaviors. First, they support indexing and retrieval of persistent data by storing pointers to data objects. Second, they support data dissemination by acting as a rendez-vous point for data matching the their bounding predicate.

Leaf GREGs store a reference to each indexed object. In addition, they implement a cache which may store a set of attributes of the indexed object, for performance reasons. In addition to leaf index nodes, additional nodes ('interior' or 'root' nodes) can be created that cover increasingly larger portions of the attribute value range.

With respect to aggregation, GREGs provide several functionalities

- they maintain partial state needed to compute the aggregate;
- for epoch-based, continuous aggregation, they manage the required synchronization logic among children, before computing the aggregate;
- they support propagation logic as required in the aggregation query e.g. manage (upward) propagation of updates in the GREG tree as well as pushing downward requests of aggregate recalculation.

APIs

At the application level, system APIs allow to insert or query for data. At a lower level, APIs of the system provide a layer for interacting with GREG functionality, e.g. for creating and updating index objects, arranging them in some topology, propagating values, discovering and disseminating index-related metadata. Such APIs allow to extend the indexing and aggregation layer with specific strategies (such as algorithms for index creation and maintenance, query processing strategies etc).

We illustrate the main APIs by describing two collaborations in the system[4].

---

[4] Diagram notation is loosely reminiscent of UML communication diagrams but has been tailored to achieve a compact representation

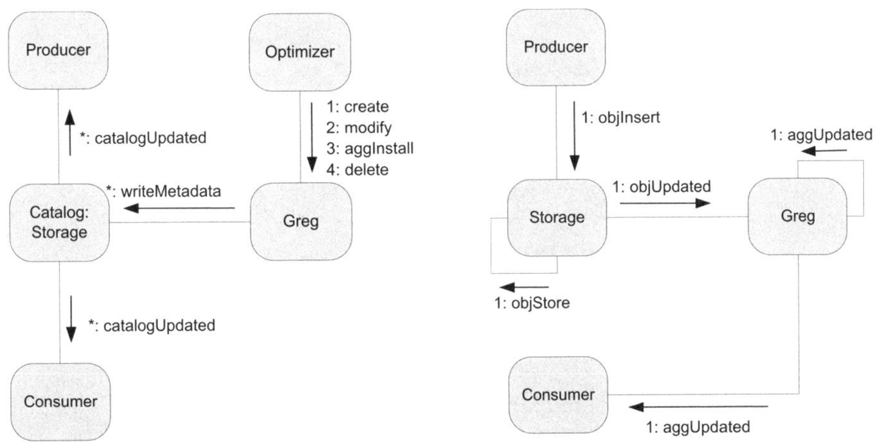

Figure 2 - Setup of Indexes and Aggregate Functions　　　Figure 3 - Updating Aggregates - Data Driven

"Figure 2 - Setup of Indexes and Aggregate Functions" lists the main APIs for accessing GREG functionality. A component having Optimizer role can create a GREG index, modify its attributes (including bounding predicates, topology e.g. parent/ child GREG pointers), install an aggregate function, delete the object (as a preliminary step, it likely reads metadata from the system Catalog Storage in the first place). GREGs then store their configuration information in the Catalog, and all components registered with the latter for update notification are informed of the action.

"Figure 3 - Updating Aggregates - Data Driven" shows a typical flow of messages in scenarios where producers inject data in the network. A producer asks a storage to store a data object (either new or update of an existing one), which takes care of the request. The storage also informs leaf GREGs, which cover the data object, of the new/ updated objects. Although not shown, even in this case Producers, Consumers and Storage get from the system Catalog Storage metadata describing existing indexes, replica factors for types etc.

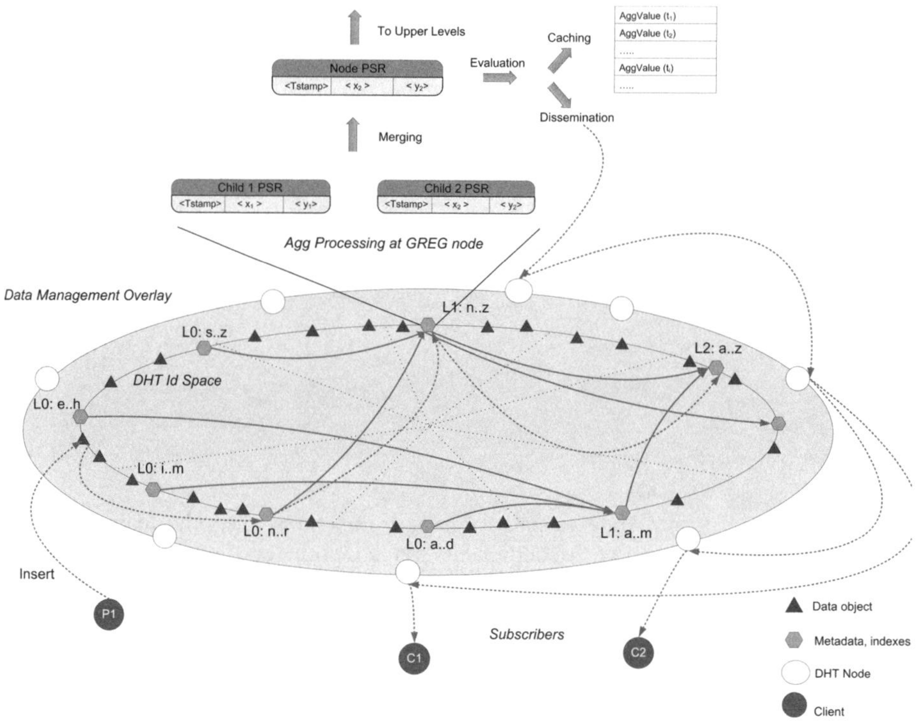

Figure 4 - Complete System View

"Figure 4 - Complete System View" aims at summarizing system operation in a single diagram. A producer (say, a management agent) injects an object periodically, in the network, which represents a resource utilization summary for the machine on which it runs. A 3-level hierarchical index exists in the DHT, on a "City" attribute of the object. An aggregation function is installed associated to the index, to compute the AverageDiskFree function. The attribute domain is partitioned as in figure (Level 0: a..d, e..h, i..m, n..r, s..z; Level 1: a..m; n..z; Level 2: a..z). Note that more interesting examples could result by creating hierarchies that group locations by city/ province/ state etc. The matching DHT node stores the object and notifies the responsible index. The value of the indexed attribute for the object is "Nantes" so level 0 index covering "n..r" is notified of the update. The node performs aggregate processing and passes the resulting Partial State Record (PSR) to its Level-1 parent GREG.

Level-1 GREG for n..z must aggregate PSRs from 2 children. The figure shows the processing that occurs at the node. Note that processing per aggregate function is described here; multiple aggregates can be associated to the same index, which is most often the case in realistic monitoring applications. PSR from child nodes are first merged to generate the PSR for the aggregating node. The PSR is passed along to GREGs higher in the hierarchy (L2: a..z). The computed aggregate value is then disseminated to consumers, who issued a long-running query matching AvgDiskFree(city=a..z); and is stored persistently in a local cache of the GREG, to allow answering ad-hoc queries from clients, asking for past data.

Dissemination

As highlighted by discussion above, dissemination of aggregate values to interested clients is a separate process from aggregation.

The process is similar to that used for normal queries. A query parser process a subscription query and recognizes the index object(s) which are candidate to support it. The client joins a multicast tree rooted at the index object, which acts as a rendez-vous point for all the data matching the bounding predicate of the index object. This is currently implemented by leveraging the Plaxton-tree based multicast features built into Pastry/ Scribe. Other techniques for dissemination may be used as well.

Update strategies – Triggering recalculations

By recognizing that a general-purpose aggregation service should operate on data which may be very diverse in terms of frequency of update (see section 2.2.2), our design aims at providing the needed flexibility over the way an aggregate is computed and propagated. In our aggregation architecture, we support several possible strategies for update of aggregate values:

- Update-driven: as soon as a value is updated by a producer, it is sent to index objects (which in turn recompute the aggregate; store a pointer to the producer, or disseminate the aggregate to interested consumers; finally, propagate the recomputed aggregate value to index objects higher in the hierarchy). A 'lazy' option allows to avoid propagation to non-leaf index objects in the tree;

- Epoch-based: a special case of update-driven strategy, in epoch-based strategy, time is partitioned over intervals, or *epochs* of duration t, and the aggregate value combines all the data generated by all producers (which are covered by the index object) during the time interval. When all data for the epoch has been received, the aggregate value is recomputed;

- Request-driven: as part of processing a client query, an index object can be probed for the aggregate value, for the covered interval. The node propagates the request to nodes down the hierarchy, and the aggregate value is recalculated possibly by probing the current values for all data in the system. A 'freshness' parameter allows to stop recalculation down the hierarchy as soon as an aggregate value having the desired quality is found. Updates triggered by this process to aggregate values at intermediate nodes may be disseminated to interested clients as usual.

4.2.4. Discussion and summary

The architecture we described aims at achieving load balancing benefits (i.e. limiting the in-bandwidth to the node issuing the aggregation query, and sharing the processing and communication effort among several nodes), while supporting the calculation of *intermediate aggregates which are meaningful in the application domain*.

Applications need to be able to select the appropriate aggregation attributes. In Astrolabe, the hierarchy was predefined. Other proposals [2,5] seem to use mechanisms which are either unaware of actual proximity of data in the application space when building the hierarchy, or use proximity in the identifier space as a criteria to organize the aggregation tree.

A characteristic of our approach is the close integration of aggregation with indexing and query processing similarly to PIER and TAG. Note that PIER however does not propose flexible indexing facilities in its architecture, and the aggregation facilities in the PIER paper are not well detailed. Also, given our approach we see very relevant to data aggregation techniques, which were originally developed for data indexing (e.g. [20]).

Another key characteristic of our approach is that it keeps distinct the aggregation phase from dissemination phase. While allowing efficient sharing of query results among several customers, it accounts for filtered information delivery. Several existing proposals (e.g. SDIMS and SOMO [2, 5]) concentrate on propagating information up and down a node of a tree, and do not support a clear separation of roles between providers, consumers, data management peers.

It must be clear, however, that our work does not aim at proposing novel algorithms for the individual components of an aggregation service (e.g. overlay maintenance, data indexing, information dissemination etc.); rather, its focus is on the architectural level and APIs.

On the other hand, it may benefit from and reuse algorithms for index creation and maintenance, or search that have been proposed elsewhere, such as Prefix Hash Trees (PHTs) [20], B+-Trees methods [21] and other. As a consequence, complexity considerations are of limited relevance here since they are instead inherited from the algorithm (all well known) that we use or can use.

Index maintenance and update

The strategy for construction and periodic reorganisation of GREGs is considered in our design an application-specific functionality.

In some settings, this would be a system administrator's task. The administrator would have control (e.g. through a command line interface) over the shape of the indexing and aggregation tree (including number of levels, number of index nodes and data partitions they should cover). To achieve load balancing, GREGs can be created by the application designer or system administrator, using her knowledge of the expected data distribution/query load to choose their number and granularity of the partitioning for domain data. We have implemented a simple tool for creating indexes which follows this strategy; the user provides a declarative description of GREGs and the ranges they cover.

Another strategy, which privileges a goal of achieving automatic load-balancing, would be to have GREGs created dynamically as in PHT or SOMO or B+Trees, where the tree grows or shrink based on the quantity of data in the system and their distribution. This approach however is not fully coherent with the goal of providing full application control of intermediate aggregation. Further work on our side aims at eventually attaining the two goals simultaneously.

On a similar direction, in [25], we discuss a preliminary work which uses clustering techniques for periodic reorganization of data space partitions.

5. Conclusions

Data aggregation is an important component of a distributed data management architecture. In this chapter we reviewed the current state of the art in distributed data aggregation, with a specific focus on peer-to-peer approaches. Existing research works were classified according to the general characteristics of the problem space and were extensively analyzed. No single design emerged as clearly superior; it is a fair and maybe obvious statement to say that each provided specific answers to the targeted application and architectural scenario.

In the second part of the chapter, we explored the design of data aggregation services in the context of a specific architecture, that is, a data overlay based on DHTs. Based on our own experience, we argued that aggregation services would benefit from an integrated design with a data indexing functionality, which in turn should be clearly layered on top of the base data management services (e.g. persistence, filtered data dissemination). We presented GREGs, a design which is consistent with this assumption, and yields a flexible package for handling complex queries in a peer-to-peer environment.

Future research should in the first place address self-optimization of the data overlay, having automated setup and maintenance of the distributed data structures which support indexing and aggregation as a primary goal.

References

[1]　Robbert van Renesse, The Importance of Aggregation. *Springer-Verlag Lecture Notes in Computer Science volume 2584 "Future Directions in Distributed Computing"*. A. Schiper, A. A. Shvartsman, H. Weatherspoon, and B. Y. Zhao, editors. Springer-Verlag, Heidelberg, April 2003.

[2]　P. Yalagandula and M. Dahlin. *A Scalable Distributed Information Management System*. In *Proceedings of ACM SIGCOMM*, August, 2004.

[3]　*Introduction to Cisco IOS NetFlow - A Technical Overview*, White Paper, CISCO Systems, 1February 2006.

[4]　R. van Renesse, K. P. Birman, and W. Vogels. Astrolabe: A Robust and Scalable Technology For Distributed Systems Monitoring, Management, and Data Mining. *ACM Transactions on Computer Systems*. vol. 21, no. 3, May 2003.

[5]　Z. Zhang, S.-M. Shi, and J. Zhu, SOMO: Self-Organized Metadata Overlay for resource management in p2p DHT, in *Proceedings of the Second Int. Workshop on Peer-to-Peer Systems (IPTPS'03)*, Berkeley, CA, Feb. 2003.

[6]　M. Jelasity and A. Montresor, Epidemic-style proactive aggregation in large overlay networks, in *Proceedings of the 24th International Conference on Distributed Computing Systems (ICDCS'04)*, pages 102-109, Tokyo, Japan, March 2004

[7]　S Madden, M. J. Franklin, J. M. Hellerstein, W. Hong, TAG: A Tiny AGgregation Service for Ad-Hoc Sensor Networks, *In Proceedings of the 5th Symposium on Operating System Design and Implementation (OSDI 2002)*, December 9-11, 2002, Boston, Massachusetts, USA.

[8]　B. Krishnamachari, D. Estrin, and S. B. Wicker. The impact of data aggregation in wireless sensor networks, In *Proceedings of the 22nd International Conference on Distributed Computing Systems*, pages 575–578, 2002.

[9]　S. Motegi, K. Yoshihara, Hiroki Horiuchi: DAG Based In-Network Aggregation for Sensor Network Monitoring. In *Proceedings of the 2006 International Symposium on Applications and the Internet (SAINT 2006)*, 23-27 January 2006, Phoenix, Arizona, USA

[10]　I. Solis and K. Obraczka, The Impact of Timing in Data Aggregation for Sensor Networks, In *Proceedings of ICC 2004*, 2004.

[11]　R. Huebsch, J. M. Hellerstein, N. Lanham, B. T. Loo, S. Shenker, and I. Stoica. Querying the Internet with PIER. In *Proceedings of 19th International Conference on Very Large Databases (VLDB)*, 2003.

[12]　R. van Renesse and K. P. Birman, Scalable Management and Data Mining using Astrolabe, in *Proceedings of the 1st International Workshop on Peer-to-Peer Systems*, March 2002, Cambridge, MA.

[13]　K. Birman, R. van Renesse, and W. Vogels, Scalable Data Fusion Using Astrolabe, in *Proceedings of the Fifth International Conference on Information Fusion 2002 (IF 2002)*, Annapolis, MA, July 2002.

[14]　Robbert van Renesse, Adrian Bozdog. Willow: DHT, Aggregation, and Publish/Subscribe in One Protocol, in *Proceedings of the International Workshop on Peer-to-Peer Systems (IPTPS '04)*, February 2004, San Diego, CA.

[15]　P. Maymounkov and D. Mazieres, Kademlia: A peer-to-peer information system based on the XOR metric, in *Proc. of the First International Workshop on Peer-to-Peer Systems (IPTPS'02)*, Cambridge, MA, Mar. 2002.

[16] R. Bhagwan, G. Varghese, and G.M. Voelker, "Cone: Augmenting DHTs to support distributed resource discovery," Tech. Rep. CS2003-0755, UC, San Diego, July 2003.

[17] J. M. Hellerstein, W. Hong, S. Madden, and K. Stanek. Beyond Average: Towards Sophisticated Sensing with Queries, in *Proceedings of the 2nd International Workshop on Information Processing in Sensor Networks (IPSN '03)*, March 2003.

[18] A. L. Graps, An Introduction to Wavelets, *IEEE Computational Sciences and Engineering*, Volume 2, Number 2, Summer 1995, pp 50-61.

[19] G. Cortese, F. Morabito et. al "Next-Generation Management Platform – Architecture, Algorithms and Prototypes" IST project Delis deliverable 2.3.2

[20] S. Ramabhadran, S. Ratnasamy, J. M. Hellerstein, S. Shenker, Brief Announcement: Prefix Hash Tree, In *Proceedings of ACM PODC*, St. Johns, Canada, July 2004.

[21] D. Comer, The Ubiquitous B-Tree, in *ACM Computing Surveys*, Vol. 11, No. 2, June 1979.

[22] I. Stoica, R. Morris, D. Karger, M. F. Kaashoek, and H. Balakrishnan, Chord: A Scalable Peer-to-peer Lookup Service for Internet Applications, in *Proceedings of ACM SIGCOMM 2001*, San Diego, CA, August 2001.

[23] A. Rowstron and P. Druschel, Pastry: Scalable, distributed object location and routing for large-scale peer-to-peer systems, in *Proceedings of Middleware 2001*, Germany, November 2001.

[24] M. Castro, P. Druschel, A-M. Kermarrec and A. Rowstron, SCRIBE: A large-scale and decentralised application-level multicast infrastructure, *IEEE Journal on Selected Areas in Communication (JSAC)*, Vol. 20, No, 8, October 2002

[25] E. Casalicchio, F. Morabito, G. Cortese and F. Davide "A novel approach to adaptive content-based subscription management in DHT-based overlay networks" To appear in *Global and P2P Computing*, special issue of Journal of Grid Computing (JoGC), 2006

Global Data Management
R. Baldoni et al. (Eds.)
IOS Press, 2006

Quality of Service in Publish/Subscribe Middleware[1]

Angelo Corsaro [b], Leonardo Querzoni [a,2], Sirio Scipioni [a], Sara Tucci Piergiovanni [a] and Antonino Virgillito [a]

[a] *Universitá di Roma La "Sapienza"*
[b] *Selex SI - Roma*

Abstract. During the last decade the publish/subscribe communication paradigm gained a central role in the design and development of a large class of applications ranging from stock exchange systems to news tickers, from air traffic control to defense systems. This success is mainly due to the capacity of publish/subscribe to completely decouple communication participants, thus allowing the development of applications that are more tolerant to communications asynchrony. This chapter introduces the publish/subscribe communication paradigm, stressing those characteristics that have a stronger impact on the quality of service provided to participants. The chapter also introduce the reader to two widely recognized industrial standards for publish/subscribe systems: the Java Message Service (JMS) and the Data Distribution Service (DDS).

Keywords. Publish/Subscribe, Event-based Systems

1. Introduction

Since the early nineties, anonymous and asynchronous dissemination of information has been a basic building block for many different distributed applications such as stock exchanges, news tickers, air-traffic control, industrial process control, etc.

Publish/Subscribe systems are nowadays considered a key technology for information diffusion. Each participant in a publish/subscribe communication system can play the role of a *publisher* or a *subscriber* of information. Publishers produce information in form of events, which are then consumed by subscribers. Subscribers can declare their interest on a subset of the whole information issuing subscriptions. Subscriptions are used to filter out part of the events produced by publishers.

The main semantical characterization of publish/subscribe is in the way events flow from publishers to subscribers: subscribers are not directly known by publishers, but rather they are indirectly addressed according to the content of events. This form of anonymity completely decouples publishers from subscribers, thus possibly allowing large scale deployments. Interactions between publishers and subscribers is mediated by

---

[1]This work was partially supported by a grant CINI-Finmeccanica on "QoS in information dissemination within network-centric architectures" and by the RESIST project, funded by the European Community.

[2]Correspondence to: Leonardo Querzoni, Via Salaria, 113 - 00198 Roma. Tel.: +39 06 4991 8480; Fax: +39 06 8530 0849; E-mail: querzoni@dis.uniroma1.it.

the publish/subscribe system, that, in general, is constituted by a set of nodes that coordinate among themselves in order to dispatch published events to all (and possibly only) interested subscribers.

Since publish/subscribe has been largely recognized as an effective approach for information diffusion, several publish/subscribe-based systems, both research contributions and commercial products have been presented and are actually used in many application contexts. From the research side, much work has been done in this field specifically by software engineering and distributed systems communities (focusing on scalability, efficient information delivery or efficient and expressive information matching). From the industrial side, relevant achievements are the widespread industrial standards that define semantics and interfaces for pub/sub middleware (Common Object Request Broker Architecture (CORBA) Event Service (CosEvent) [23], the CORBA Notification Service (CosNotification) [24], Java Message Service (JMS) [21] and, recently, Data Distribution Service (DDS) [19]). In both worlds, one important problem is related to the definition of quality of service (QoS) provision, defined as the guarantees that a pub/sub middleware can offer in terms of timeliness, reliability, availability etc. Market-ready solutions clearly must be able to provide QoS guarantees, for example in order to be deployed in mission critical applications. The definition and enforcement of QoS properties can be on the other hand a great inspiration for novel research contributions in this field.

The first part of this chapter gives the reader an overview of publish/subscribe systems, first introducing a general framework and then analyzing in details the models commonly used for subscriptions. Throughout this overview we focus on the definition of the very meaning of end-to-end QoS guarantees in a publish/subscribe system. Indeed, the complete decoupling between senders and receivers makes the exact semantics of the system not easily definable and subject to non-determinism. We identify the sources of such non-determinism and how to cope with it.

In the second part of the chapter the reader will be introduced to two important industrial standards for publish/subscribe middleware: the Java Message Service (JMS) [21] and the Data Distribution Service (DDS) [19]. JMS is a widely recognized standard for enterprise level messaging, targeted at applications such as application integration and large-scale data diffusion. Recently the Object Management Group (OMG) tried to sum up the characteristics of various proprietary publish/subscribe middleware products, to deliver a new standard for real-time oriented publish/subscribe; the result of this effort was the DDS specification. The two standards are presented by considering their general characteristics, their programming model and their QoS-related features. At the end of the chapter the reader should have gained an introductory knowledge about the ground where publish/subscribe middleware developers are today spending their efforts.

2. Framework

In this Section we define a general framework for publish/subscribe (pub/sub) systems. First we introduce the basic elements constituting a pub/sub system, then we discuss the semantics of the system.

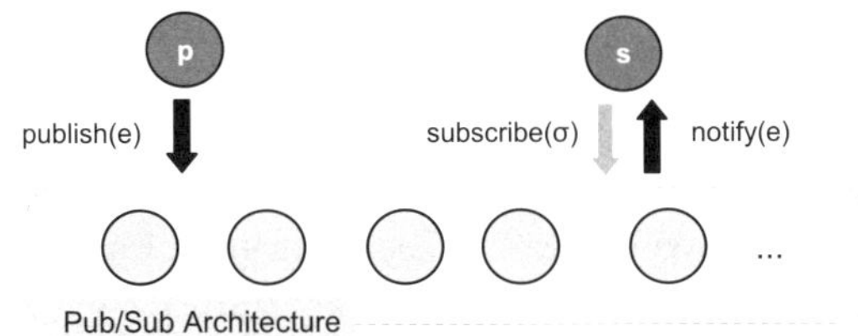

Figure 1. High-level interaction model of a publish/subscribe system with its clients (p and s indicate a generic publisher and a generic subscriber respectively).

2.1. Elements of a Publish/Subscribe System

A generic pub/sub communication system (often referred to in the literature as *Event Service* or *Notification Service*) is composed of a set of nodes distributed over a communication network. The clients of this system are divided according to their role into *publishers*, which act as producers of information, and *subscribers*, which act as consumers of information. Clients are not required to communicate directly among themselves but are rather *decoupled*: the interaction takes place through the nodes of the pub/sub system, that coordinate themselves in order to *route* information from publishers to subscribers. Participants' decoupling is a desirable characteristic in a communication system as applications can be easily developed just ingoring issues such as synchronization or direct addressing of subscribers.

Operationally, the interaction between client nodes and the pub/sub system takes place through a set of basic operations that can be executed by clients on the system and vice-versa (Figure 1). A publisher submits a piece of information e (i.e., an event) to the pub/sub system by executing the `publish(e)` operation. Commonly, an event is structured as a set of attribute-value pairs. Each attribute has a *name*, a simple character string, and a *type*. The type is generally one of the common primitive data types defined in programming languages or query languages (e.g. integer, real, string, etc.). On the subscribers' side, interest in specific events is expressed through *subscriptions*. A subscription σ is a filter over a portion of the event content (or the whole of it), expressed through a set of constraints that depend on the subscription language. A subscriber installs and removes a subscription σ from the pub/sub system by executing the `subscribe(σ)` and `unsubscribe(σ)` operations respectively.

We say that an event e *matches* a subscription σ if it satisfies all the declared constraints on the corresponding attributes. The task of verifying whenever an event e matches a subscription σ is called *matching*.

2.2. Subscription Models

Various ways for specifying the subscribers' interest led to distinct variants of the pub/sub paradigm. The subscription models that appeared in the literature are characterized by their expressive power: highly expressive models offer to subscribers the possibility to precisely match their interest, i.e. to receive only the events they are interested in. In this section we briefly review the most popular pub/sub subscription models.

Topic-based Model   Events are grouped in topics, i.e. a subscriber declares its interest for a particular topic to receive all events pertaining to that topic. Each topic corresponds to a logical channel ideally connecting each possible publisher to all interested subscribers. For the sake of completeness, the difference between channels and topics is that topics are carried within an event as a special attribute. Thanks to this coarse grain correspondence, either network multicast facilities or diffusion trees, one for each topic, can be used to disseminate events to interested subscribers.

The topic-based model has been the solution adopted in all early pub/sub incarnations. Examples of systems that fall under this category are TIB/RV [25], SCRIBE [8], Bayeux [31] and the CORBA Notification Service [24].

The main drawback of the topic-based model is the very limited expressiveness it offers to subscribers. A subscriber interested in a subset of events related to a specific topic receives also all the other events that belong to the same topic. To address problems related to low expressiveness of topics, several solutions are exploited in pub/sub implementations. For example, the topic-based model is often extended to provide hierarchical organization of the topic space, instead of a simple flat structure (such as in [1,25]). A topic B can be then defined as a sub-topic of an existing topic A. Events matching B will be received by all clients subscribed to both A and B. Implementations also often include convenience operators, such as wildcard characters, for subscribing to more than one topic with a single subscription[3]. Another method for enhancing expressiveness of the topic-based model is the *filtered-topic* variant [24,21], where a further filtering phase is performed once the message is received based on the content of the message. Messages that does not satisfy the filter are not delivered to the application.

Content-based Model   Subscribers express their interest by specifying conditions over the content of events they want to receive. In other words, a subscription is a query formed by a set of constraints composed through disjunction or conjunction operators. Possible constraints depend on the attribute type and on the subscription language. Most subscription languages comprise equality and comparison operators as well as regular expressions [7,28,16]. The complexity of the subscription language obviously influences the complexity of matching operation. For this reason it is not common to have subscription languages allowing queries more complex than those in conjunctive form (examples are [5,4]). A complete specification of content-based subscription models can be found in [22]. Examples of systems that fall under the content-based category are Gryphon [20], SIENA [29], JEDI [12], LeSubscribe [27], Hermes [26], Elvin [28].

In content-based publish/subscribe, events are not classified according to some predefined criterion (i.e., topic name), but rather according to properties of the events themselves. As a consequence, the correspondence between publishers and subscribers is on a per-event basis. The difference with a filtered-topic model is that events that not match a subscriber can be filtered out in any point in the system, not only on the receiver, thus possibly saving network resources. For these reasons, the higher expressive power of content-based pub/sub comes at the price of a higher resource consumption needed to calculate for each event the set of interested subscribers [6,14].

---

[3]For the sake of completeness, we point out that the word *subject* can be used to refer to hierarchical topics instead of being simply a synonymous for topic. Analogously, *channel-based* is sometimes [23] used to refer to a flat topic model where the topic name is not explicitly included in the event.

Type-based   In the type-based [15] pub/sub variant events are actually objects belonging to a specific type, which can thus encapsulate attributes as well as methods. With respect to simple, unstructured models, Types represent a more robust data model for application developer, enforcing type-safety at the pub/sub system, rather than inside the application. In a type-based subscription the declaration of a desired type is the main discriminating attribute. That is, with respect to the aforementioned models, type-based pub/sub sits itself somehow in the middle, by giving a coarse-grained structure on events (like in topic-based) on which fine-grained constraints can be expressed over attributes (like in content-based) or over methods (as a consequence of the object-oriented approach).

Concept-based   The underlying implicit assumptions within all the above-mentioned subscription models is that participants have to be aware of the structure of produced events, both under a syntactic (i.e., the number, name and type of attributes) and a semantic (i.e., the meaning of each attribute) point of view. Concept-based addressing [11] allows to describe event schema at a higher level of abstraction by using ontologies, that provide a knowledge base for an unambiguous interpretation of the event structure, by using metadata and mapping functions.

XML   Some research works [9,10,30] describe pub/sub systems supporting a semistructured data model, typically based on XML documents. XML is not merely a matter of representation but differs in the fact that introduces the possibility of hierarchies in the language, thus differentiating from a flat content-based model in terms of an added flexibility. Moreover, it provides natural advantages such as interoperability, independence from implementation and extensibility. As a main drawback, matching algorithms for XML-based language require heavier processing.

Location-awareness   Pub/Sub systems used in mobile environments typically require the support for location-aware subscriptions. For example, a mobile subscriber can query the system for receiving notifications when it is in the proximity of a specific location or service. Works describing various forms of location-aware subscriptions are [18,30]. The implementation of location-aware subscriptions requires the pub/sub system the ability to monitor the mobility of clients.

2.3. Semantics of a Publish/subscribe System

In the following we intend to characterize the general semantics of a pub/sub system in terms of three properties stating the exact behavior of any pub/sub implementation[4]. This is critical for understanding the subtleties hidden behind the definition of the expected QoS offered by a pub/sub system and for highlighting what are the aspects of the system that are influential for it. We first consider two parameters that respectively take into account (i) non-instantaneous effects of subscribe/unsubscribe operations and (ii) the non-instantaneous diffusion of an event to the interested subscribers after a publish operation executed by a publisher. These parameters model the time required for the internal processing in the system and the network delay elapsed to route subscriptions and notifications, in a distributed implementation.

Indeed, when a process issues a subscribe/unsubscribe operation, the pub/sub system is not immediately aware of the occurred event. In other words, at an abstract level, the

---

[4]The discussion is here presented informally. A formalization of the pub/sub semantics can be found in [3]

registration (resp. cancellation) of a subscription takes a certain amount of time, denoted as T_{sub}, to be stored into the system. This time encompasses for example the update of the internal data structures of the pub/sub system and the network delay due to the routing of the subscription among all the entities constituting the system. Analogously, as soon as a publication is issued, the pub/sub architecture performs a *diffusion* of the information in order to reach the set of interested subscribers. This operation takes a certain amount of time during which the system computes and issues notify operations to interested subscribers, i.e. diffusion of events takes a non-zero time and is represented by a parameter T_{pub}.

The characterization of the exact behavior of the system is actually not obvious as (i) the interest of a subscriber is a dynamic dimension and (ii) the notification of an event can be issued to a subscriber at any time during the diffusion interval of the event itself. Then, semantics of a pub/sub system can be expressed by the following three properties:

- *Safety (Legality)*: a subscriber cannot be notified for an information it is not interested in.
- *Safety (Validity)*: a subscriber cannot be notified for an event that has not been previously published.
- *Liveness*: The delivery of a notification for an event is guaranteed only for those subscribers that subscribed at a time at least T_{sub} before the event was published and maintain their subscriptions stable for the entire time T_{pub} taken by the event's dissemination.

Safety properties describe *facts* that cannot happen during system execution, while Liveness gives a precise definition of which subscribers must be surely notified about an event. Obviously the longer a subscription remains stable in the system (i.e., it is *durable*), the higher its probability of meeting all the events, despite T_{pub}. The Liveness property can be extended by considering the possibility for the pub/sub system to persistently store events for a finite, non-zero amount of time, denoted as Δ. Persistence is exploited in distributed pub/sub implementations to provide reliable delivery of events through retransmission, or to allow notification of an event also to subscribers that subscribe *after* the event has been published. A revised definition of Liveness that take into account event persistence is:

- *Liveness (with persistent events)*: The delivery of a notification is guaranteed only for those subscribers that subscribed at a time at most $\Delta - T_{sub}$ after the event is published and maintain their subscriptions stable in the interval $[T_s + T_{sub}, max(T_s + T_{sub} + T_{pub}, T_e + T_{pub})]$.

where T_s and T_e are the times at which the subscription and the event were issued respectively.

3. Quality of Service in Publish/Subscribe Systems

Given the above definitions we can easily see that when considering end-to-end QoS characteristics in a pub/sub system one cannot set aside the effect of decoupling between senders and receivers, which is the main peculiar feature of the pub/sub paradigm. The lack of a direct producer/consumer relationship makes the definition and enforcement of any end-to-end QoS policy very hard. Decoupling can introduce in several senses a *non-deterministic* behavior, meaning that the exact behavior of the system is difficult to specify, enforce and control. We give examples of how non-determinism can act over three fundamental aspects of QoS and security, namely reliable message delivery, timely delivery and trust relationship.

3.1. Reliable delivery

Reliable delivery of an event means determining the subscribers that have to receive a published event, as stated by the liveness property introduced in the previous section, and delivering the event to all of them. Event processing in the publish/subscribe infrastructure results in the event itself traveling several network hops, where each routing hop is potentially a source of non-determinism due to transmissions over asynchronous WAN channels or temporary node overloading. This can lead the value of T_{pub} to grow indefinitely, leading, from our definition of liveness, to a reduced probability of delivery of the notification to all the intended subscribers (*notification loss* [2]).

Persistence of events, durability of subscriptions and event retransmission can help to reduce the non-deterministic behavior, providing higher reliability in delivery. In general, the more an even remains in the system, the less non-determinism is experienced, at the price of a higher memory occupation. For example, the effect of runs between publications and subscriptions is limited and also the sensitivity to small delays in both subscription and publication dissemination. Reduction of non-determinism increases the probability that an intended receiver will get the information. If the information is stored in a permanently persistent way (i.e. with infinite memory) or it is infinitely retransmitted, non-determinism is completely absent and this probability raises to one.

3.2. Timeliness

Real-time applications often require strict control over the time elapsed by a piece of information to reach all its consumers. They are typically deployed over dedicated infrastructures or simply managed environments where synchronous message delivery can be safely assumed. Even in a completely managed environment, a pub/sub infrastructure which decouples publishers and subscribers, can introduce non-determinism through routing anomalies and unpredictable processing delays at each node. In overall, where timeliness constraints must be enforced, the design of the pub/sub system should privilege point-to-point communications where decoupling is limited or totally absent. The drawback of this choice lies in the main benefit introduced by the decoupling, that is the higher scalability obtainable by delegating the infrastructure, rather than the publishers, to know all the subscribers and determine the recipients for each event. Designing a QoS-driven pub/sub system which at the same time can scale to massive sizes is one major challenge in this area, particularly important for future implementations of the DDS specification (see Section 5).

3.3. Security and trust

Security issues represent one major problem in pub/sub systems, only marginally addressed at present by both researchers and industry. Aside from the obvious problem of granting access to the system only to authorized participants, an important aspect regards enforcing trust between publishers and subscribers. A subscriber wants to trust authenticity of the events it receives from the system, i.e. they has been generated by a trusty publisher and the information they contains have not been corrupted. On the system side, subscribers have to be trusted for what concerns the subscriptions they issue.

Since an event is in general delivered to several subscribers, the producer/consumer trust relationship that commonly occur in a point-to-point communication, in pub/sub system must involve multiple participants. Moreover, the fact that message traverses several infrastructure nodes during routing forces both publishers and subscribers to rely such intermediary nodes not to corrupt events, subscriptions or some of the participants' identities.

Designing trust measures implies knowing with certainty the identity of other participants and this is in clear contrasts with the anonymity which is at the base of pub/sub itself. Under the assumption of trust the decoupling can be preserved by using a solution like the one presented in [13], where trust between a publisher and each subscriber is enforced through a chain of trust relationships involving all the nodes in the infrastructure that are met on the event path. In other words, when forwarding a message (either an event or a subscription), an infrastructure node is also responsible for letting the trust relationship flow with the message.

In the most general case where one cannot assume the whole infrastructure to be trustworthy, the possibility of an event traveling potentially malicious networks or nodes should be taken into account. In [17] a solution to this scenario is proposed. The idea is to organize groups of trust in *scopes*, i.e. logical domains within the pub/sub infrastructure. The organization in scopes limits the visibility of publishers, subscribers, events and subscriptions within a single scope in order to allow each scope to be independent under the points of view of management, routing algorithm and so on. Since a scope isolates its participants from outside traffic it allows to relax the assumption of a fully trusted infrastructure to each single scope. [17] describes a method to add a new trusted node to an existing trusted scope, so that the assumption of completely trusted scope is preserved. If the node to be added can be reached only through one or more untrusted nodes the request is tunneled so that only encrypted information transits through the non-trusted part of the network.

4. Java Message Service

Java Message Service [21] is a standard promoted by Sun Microsystems to define a Java API, including a common set of interfaces and semantics, for the implementation of message-oriented middleware. It is part of the Java Enterprise Edition (J2EE) architecture since version 1.3. The compliance to the specification allows implementations from various vendors to be perfectly interoperable. In this way JMS guarantees a portable way for Java applications to exchange messages through products of different vendors.

Besides a message-centric publish-subscribe communication model, the JMS API also supports a *point-to-point* mode. With point-to-point, each application produces messages that are explicitly targeted toward a single receiver. A JMS implementation then represents a general-purpose *message oriented middleware* (MOM) that acts as an intermediary between heterogeneous applications, allowing to choose the communication mode that better suits the specific application needs.

JMS is specifically targeted at distributed enterprise systems, frequently presenting problems such as integration among heterogeneous components, management of complex workflows, dissemination of large-size data on a large scale and reliable data delivery. Those issues can be easily faced by means of a loosely coupled, flexible and standard communication mechanism such as a JMS MOM, that can effectively help in reducing development costs and time.

4.1. JMS Conceptual Model

The JMS conceptual model marks a clear separation between the point-to-point and the publish-subscribe models; nevertheless, in both cases, only non strongly typed messages are considered. Each message is characterized by a header (which includes message type, priority, etc.), by a set of extension of header metadata used to support, for example, compatibility with specific implementations and provider-specific properties, and a body which includes the application specific data core of the message. In the following we provide a characterization of entities that constitute the JMS conceptual model.

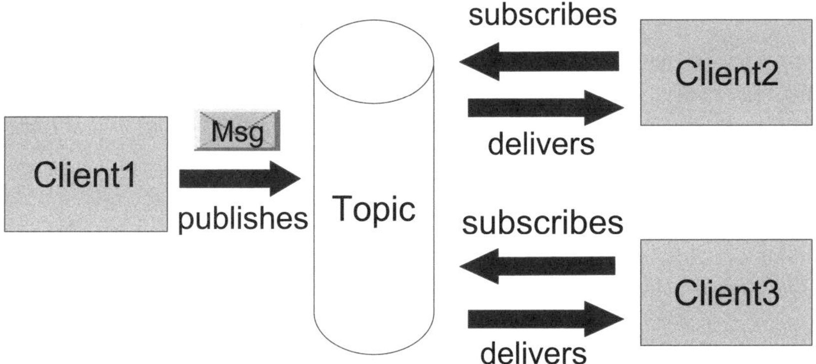

Figure 2. JMS Topic Model.

Topics. the JMS publish-subscribe API is based on *topics*. Publishers and Subscribers are anonymous and can dynamically publish and subscribe to various topics (see Figure 2). Applications can define reliability and QoS requirements for each topic.

Publishers and Subscribers. Publishers and Subscribers are the classes used for implementing producers and consumers for a topic. Multiple receivers can subscribe to the same topic and receive the same message. Topics, contrarily to queues, retain messages only as long as it takes to distribute them to current subscribers. The interaction is one-to-many and it has a timing dependency between senders and receivers: consumers receive only messages sent after their subscription and they must continue to be active in order to consume new messages (see Section 2.3). That is, events are not persistent. Non-determinism can be reduced by means of a *durable subscription*. Durable subscriptions provide the reliability of queues but nevertheless maintain the one-to-many interaction model. This aspect will be further analyzed in following section.

Subscriptions.   In the JMS API subscriptions are topic-based. Applications requiring higher expressiveness can exploit a form of filtered-topic model, as defined in the *Message Selector* API, where filters can be applied directly on receiver-side to received messages. A message selector is an expression whose syntax is based on SQL92. It is evaluated when an attempt is made to receive a message, and messages that do not match the selection criteria are discarded. Message selectors only work on header fields and properties: body and content of the message cannot be used for selection. Contrarily to a pure content-based model, message filtering in JMS is executed only on receiver-side.

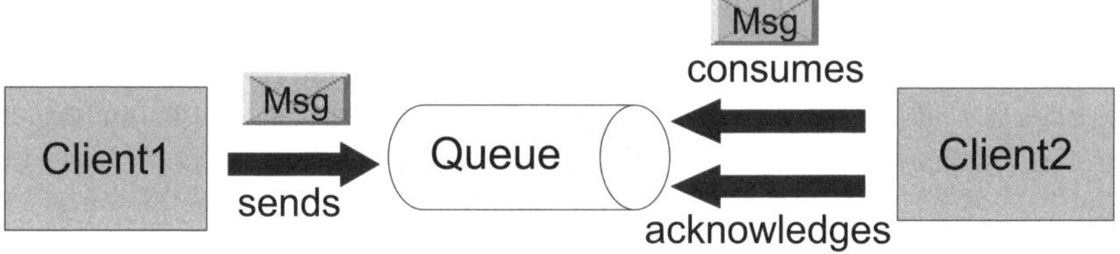

Figure 3. JMS Queue Model.

Point-to-point (Queues).   The point-to-point model of JMS exploit *queues*, where messages are stored until they are consumed or expire. Senders and receivers have to bind to a queue to use it and once they subscribe they can start sending and retrieving messages (see Figure 3).

Messages are explicitly addressed to a queue, and analogously receivers extract messages directly from a queue. There is no timing dependency between the execution of send and receive operations: the receiver can retrieve a message even if it was not running when the sender sent it. Finally the consumer of a message can send an acknowledgment as a result of the delivery of the message to queue.

Discovery   Another feature of JMS API is the ability to dynamically discover information related to topics: clients can explore topics and queues through a search on a centrally managed JNDI namespace.

4.2. JMS Programming model

A JMS application is composed from the following elements (Figure 4):

Administrated Objects. These are pre-configured objects that are created by administrators. They are of two types: `ConnectionFactory` and `Destination`. JMS clients access these objects through interfaces that have been standardized in the JMS specification, while the actual underlying technology strictly depends on the implementation. `ConnectionFactory` objects are used by clients to connect with a provider[5]. Each of these objects encapsulates a set of connection configuration parameters defined by an administrator. `Destination` objects are used by a sender to specify the target of a message it produces and by a re-

---

[5]JMS provider is a proprietary part of JMS application, which realizes the messaging system and provides administrative and control features.

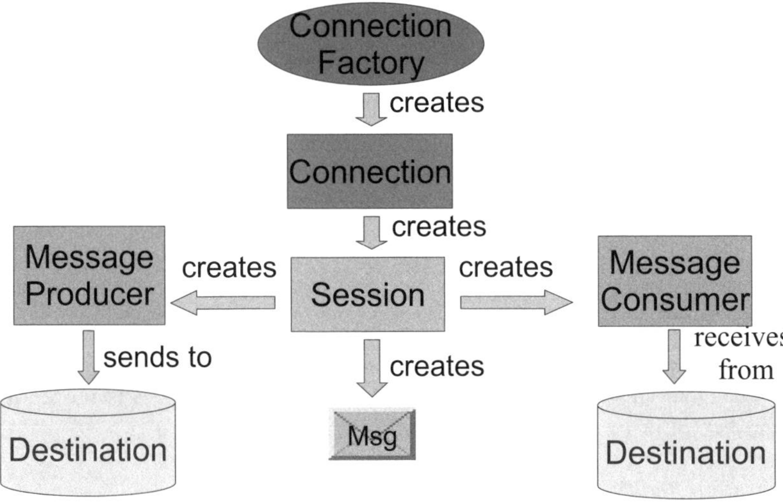

Figure 4. JMS Topic Model.

ceiver to specify the source of messages it consumes. In the point-to-point domain, `Destination` objects represent queues, while in the publish/subscribe domain they are called topics. Administrative and proprietary tools allow to create and to bind these two objects into a JNDI namespace. A JMS client can use JNDI to look up `ConnectionFactory` and `Destination` objects and establish a logical connection through the JMS provider.

Connections. Represent virtual connections to JMS providers. A connection is used to create sessions.

Sessions. Each `Session` object represents a single-threaded context for message producers, message consumers and messages. A session provides a transactional context where a set of sends and receives can be grouped in an atomic unit of work.

Message Producers and Consumers. Objects used for sending/receiving messages to/from destinations. Message production is asynchronous but JMS interface supplies two modality for message delivery: *synchronous* and *asynchronous*. Synchronous messages are delivered by calling the `receive` method. This method blocks the application until a message arrives or a timeout occurs. Asynchronous messages are consumed by creating a `message listener`. Its `onMessage` method is executed by the JMS provider when a message arrives at its destination.

4.3. Quality of Service

The only Quality of Service policy defined in the JMS specification is related to reliability. An application can require every message to be received once and only once or it rather can choose a more permissive (and generally more efficient) policy, allowing dropped and duplicated messages. JMS API specification provides various degree of reliability through various basic and advanced mechanisms.

4.3.1. Basic Reliability Mechanisms

The most interesting basic mechanisms are:

Specifying message persistence : a JMS application can specify that messages are persistent, thus ensuring that a message will not be lost in the event of a provider failure. Two delivery modes are defined in the JMS specification: *persistent* require JMS providers to log messages in a stable storage, while *non persistent* delivery mode does not require it.

Setting message priority levels : applications can set a message priority level; in this case the JMS provider will deliver urgent messages first. The JMS API provides methods to set priority levels for all messages sent by a producer, through the `setPriority` method of the `MessageProducer` interface, or to set priority level for specific messages, through *send* or *publish* methods of same interface.

Allowing messages to expire : in order to prevent duplicated messages an application can set an expiration time for a message. As in the previous case JMS API provides methods that allow to set a time to live counter for all messages produced from a publisher, or just a single one.

4.3.2. Advanced Reliability Mechanisms

The most advanced mechanism to provide reliable message delivery in the JMS specification is the creation of *durable subscriptions*. A durable topic subscription allows a subscriber to receive messages sent while it is not active. A durable subscription implements the reliability of queues in the publish/subscribe model. A durable subscription can have only one active subscriber at a time. When a durable subscriber registers a durable subscription, it specifies a unique identity by setting an ID for the connection and a topic and subscription name for the subscriber. Other subscriber objects that have the same identity resume the subscription in the state in which it was left by the preceding subscriber. The subscriber can be closed and reloaded, but the subscription continues to exist until the subscriber invokes the unsubscribe method. When the subscriber is reactivated the JMS provider sends it the stored messages.

Other features common in MOM products, like load balancing, resource usage control, and timeliness of messages, are not explicitly addressed in the JMS specification. Although recognized in the specification as fundamental for the development of robust messaging applications, they are considered provider-specific.

5. Data Distribution Service

The pub/sub paradigm is a natural match, and often a fundamental architectural building block, for a large class of real-time, mission, and safety critical application domains, such as industrial process control, air traffic control, defense systems, etc. These application domains are characterized by real-time information which flows from sensors to controllers and from controllers to actuators. The timeliness of data distribution is essential for maintaining the correctness and the safety of these systems, *i.e.*, failing in timely delivering data could lead to instability which might result in threats to either infrastructures of human lives.

Historically, most of the pub/sub middleware standards such as the CosEvent [23], the CosNotification [24], and JMS [21], etc., as well as most proprietary solutions, have lacked the support needed by real-time, mission, and safety critical systems. The main limitations are typically due to the limited or non-existent support for Quality of Service (QoS), and the lack of architectural properties which promote dependability and survivability, *e.g.*, lack of single point of failure.

Recently, in order to fill this gap, the OMG has standardized the DDS [19]. This standard gathers the experience of proprietary real-time pub/sub middleware solutions which had been independently engineered and evolved in niches, within the industrial process control, and in the defense systems applications domain. The resulting standard, which will be described in detail in the reminder of this Section, is based on a completely decentralized architecture, and provides an extremely rich set of configurable QoS.

Before proceeding with a detailed explanation of the DDS, it is worth mentioning that the standard defines two level of interfaces. At a lower level, it defines a Data Centric Publish Subscribe (DCPS) whose goal is to provide an efficient, scalable, predictable, and resource aware data distribution mechanism. Then, on top of the DCPS, it defines the Data Local Reconstruction Layer (DLRL), an optional interface which automates the reconstruction of data, locally, from updates received, and allows the application to access data as if it was local.

5.1. DDS Conceptual Model

The DDS conceptual model is based on the abstraction of a strongly typed Global Data Space (GDS) (see Figure 5), where publisher and subscriber respectively *write* (produce) and *read* (consume) data. In the reminder of this Section we will provide a precise characterization of the entities that constitute this global data space.

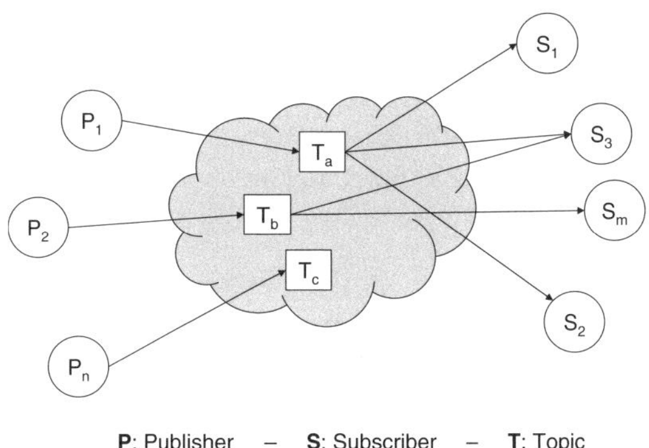

Figure 5. DDS Global Data Space.

Topic. A topic defines a type that can be legally written on the GDS. In the present standard, topics are restricted to be nonrecursive types defined by means of OMG Interface Definition Language (IDL). The DDS provides the ability to distinguish topics of the same type by relying on the use of a simple key. Finally, topics can be associated with specific QoS. From an applicative perspective, topics are the mean used by designer to define the application information model. The model supported by the DDS is not as powerful as that found in contemporary relational Data Base (DB)s, however it provides the ability to perform simple topic aggregation, as well as content based filtering.

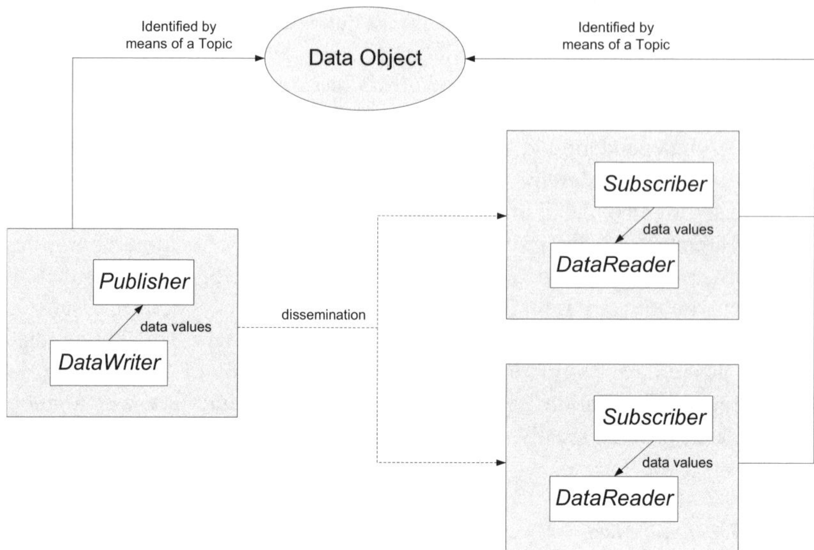

Figure 6. DDS ConceptualModel.

Publisher.   Topics allow the definition of the application data model, as well as the association of QoS properties with it. On the other hand, publishers provide a mean of defining data sources. A publisher, can declare the intent of generating data with an associated QoS, and to write the data in the GDS. The publisher declared QoS has to be compatible with that defined by the topic. More specifically, as depicted in Figure 6, the DDS relies on a topic specific `DataWriter` which serves as a typed writer to the GDS. On the other hand, the `Publisher` encapsulate the responsibility associated with the dissemination of data in agreement with the required QoS.

Subscriber.   Subscribers *r*ead topics in the global data space for which a matching subscription exist (the rules that define what represents a matching subscription are described below). The DDS relies on a topic specific `DataReader` which serves as a typed reader into the GDS. On the other hand, the `Subscriber` encapsulates the responsibility associated with the reception of data in agreement with the required QoS.

Subscription.   A subscription is the logical operation which glues together a subscriber to its matching publishers. In the DDS a matching subscription has to satisfy two different kind of conditions. One set of conditions relate to concrete features of the topic, such as its type, its name, its key, its actual content. The other set of conditions relate to the QoS. More specifically, the DDS provides a subscription scheme which is more general than the typical topic-based model described in Section 2.2 as it also allows for content based subscription – a subset of Structured Query Language (SQL) is used for specifying subscription filters. Regarding the QoS, the matching follows an requested/offered model in which the requested QoS has to be the same, or weaker, then the offered. As an example, a matching subscription for a topic which is distributed reliably, can be requesting the topic to be distributed either reliably or as best effort.

Discovery.　　Another key feature at the foundation of DDS is that all information needed to establish a subscription is discovered automatically, and, in a completely distributed manner. The DDS discovery service, finds-out and communicates the properties of the GDS's participants, by relying on special topics and on the data dissemination capability provided by the DDS.

Finally, for sake of completeness, it is worth pointing out that the DDS supports the concept of domains. A domain allows to administratively separate and confine the distribution of different data flows. A DDS entity can belong to different domains, however data cannot flow across domains.

5.2. DDS Programming Model

Now that we have seen what are the core concepts at the foundation of DDS, we are ready to move to its programming model. Figure 7, contains an Unified Modeling Language (UML) diagram which represents the core DDS Application Programming Interface (API) in terms of its key classes and their relationships.

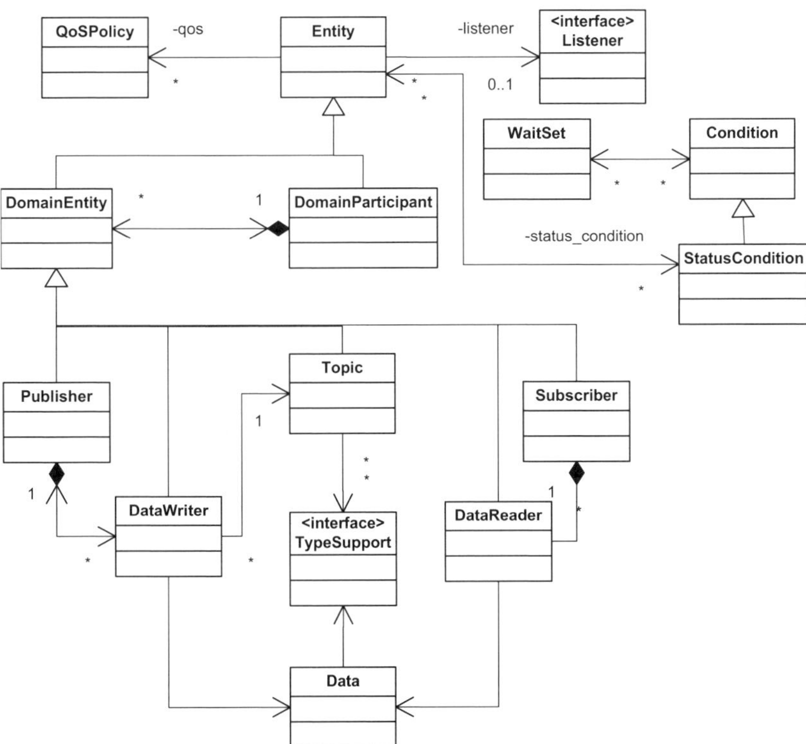

Figure 7. DDS Programming Model.

From Figure 7 it is worth noticing how the DDS API is mostly based on a rooted hierarchy at the base of which we find the `Entity` class. This class, by means of the association with the `QoSPolicy` class, defines the basic mechanisms for associating QoS with DDS entities. At the same time, with the association with the `Listener` and the `StatusCondition` classes define the two interaction model supported by the DDS API – the reactive and selective interaction model. The reactive model is supported by the `Listener` class. Instances of this class can be registered with any kind of DDS entity to receive callbacks on specific events, such as data being available for being read, etc. On the other hand, the selective model is supported by the `StatusCondition` class. Instances of this class can be used in a way similar to the UNIX `select` system call to poll or wait on specific conditions.

The `DomainParticipant` represents the local membership to a specific domain. Only publisher and subscribers belonging to the same domain can communicate. The `DomainEntity` exists essentially to enforce the fact that `DomainParticipant` cannot be nested. Finally, the diagram shows the classes defined by the DDS standard in order to write and read data from the GDS, *i.e.*, `Publisher`, `Subscriber`, `DataWriter`, etc.

5.3. Quality of Service

One of the key distinguishing features of the DDS when compared to other pub/sub middleware is its extremely rich QoS support. By relying on a rich set of QoS policies, the DDS gives the ability to control and limit (1) the use of resources, such as, network bandwidth, and memory, and (2) many non functional properties of the topics, such as, persistence, reliability, timeliness, etc. In the reminder of this Section we will provide an overview of the most interesting QoS defined by the DDS classifying them with respect to the aspect they allow to control.

Resources

The DDS defines a specific QoS policy to control the resources which can be used to meet requested QoS on data dissemination. Below are reported the most relevant QoS policies which allow to control computing and network resources.

- The `RESOURCE_LIMITS` policy allows to control the amount of message buffering performed by a DDS implementation.
- The `TIME_BASED_FILTER` allows applications to specify the minimum inter-arrival time between data samples. Samples which are produced at a faster pace are not delivered. This policy allows to control both network bandwidth as well as memory and processing power for those subscribers which are connected over limited bandwidth networks and which might also have limited computing capabilities.

The DDS provides other means to control the resources consumed, however, these will be presented below as they also have an impact on application visible properties of data.

Data Timeliness

The DDS provides a set of QoS policies which allow to control the timeliness properties of distributed data. Specifically, the supported QoS are described below.

- The `DEADLINE` QoS policy allows application to define the maximum inter-arrival time for data. Missed deadline can be notified by `Listeners` (see Figure 7).
- The `LATENCY_BUDGET` QoS policy provides a means for the application to communicate to the middleware the level of urgency associated with a data communication. Specifically, the latency budget specifies the maximum amount of time that should elapse from the instant in which the data is written to the instant in which the data is placed in the queue of the associated readers.

Data Availability

The DDS provides the following QoS policies which allow to control the data availability.

- The `DURABILITY` QoS policy provides control over the lifetime of the data written on the GDS. At one extreme it allows the data be configured to be volatile, at the other it allows to have data persistency. It is worth noticing that transient and persistent data enables time decoupling between the writer and the reader by making the data available for late joining reader, in the case of transient data, or even after the writer has left the GDS, for persistent data.
- The LIFESPAN QoS policy allows to control the interval of time for which a data sample will be valid. The default value is infinite.
- The `HISTORY` QoS policy provides a mean to control the number of data samples, *i.e.*, subsequent write of the same topic, have to be kept available for the readers. Possible values are the last, the last n samples, or all the samples.

Data Delivery

The DDS provides several QoS which allow to control how data is delivered and who is allowed to write a specific topic. More specifically the following QoS policies are defined.

- The `RELIABILITY` QoS policy allows application to control the level of reliability associated with data diffusion. The possible choices are reliable and best-effort distribution.
- The `DESTINATION_ORDER` QoS policy allows to control the order of changes made by publishers to some instance of a given topic. Specifically the DDS allows different changes to be ordered according to the source or the destination time-stamp.
- The `OWNERSHIP` QoS policy allows to control the number of writers permitted for a given topic. If configured as exclusive, then it indicates that a topic instance can be owned and thus written by a single writer. The ownership of a topic is controlled by means of another QoS policy, the `OWNERSHIP_STRENGTH`. This additional policy makes it possible to associate a numerical strength to writers, so that the owner of a topic is defined to be the one available with the highest strength. If the `OWNERSHIP` QoS policy is configured as shared then multiple writer can concurrently update a topic. The concurrent changes will be ordered according to the `DESTINATION_ORDER` policy.

In addition to the QoS policies defined above, the DDS provides some mean of defining and distributing bootstrapping information by means of the USER_DATA, TOPIC_DATA and GROUP_DATA. These policies apply at different level, as it can be guessed by the name, and are distributed by means of built-in topics.

References

[1] S. Baehni, P. Th. Eugster, and R. Guerraoui. Data-aware multicast. In *Proceedings of the 2004 International Conference on Dependable Systems and Networks (DSN 2004)*, pages 233–242, 2004.

[2] R. Baldoni, R. Beraldi, S. Tucci Piergiovanni, and A. Virgillito. Measuring notification loss in publish/subscribe communication systems. In *Proceedings of the 10th International Symposium Pacific Rim Dependable Computing (PRDC '05)*, 2004.

[3] R. Baldoni, R. Beraldi, S. Tucci Piergiovanni, and A. Virgillito. On the modelling of publish/subscribe communication systems. *Concurrency and Computation: Practice and Experience*, 17(12):1471–1495, 2005.

[4] S. Bittner and A. Hinze. On the benefits of non-canonical filtering in publish/subscribe systems. In *Proceedings of the International Workshop on Distributed Event-Based Systems (ICDCS/DEBS'05)*, 2005.

[5] A. Campailla, S. Chaki, E. M. Clarke, S. Jha, and H. Veith. Efficient filtering in publish-subscribe systems using binary decision diagrams. In *Proceedings of The International Conference on Software Engineering*, pages 443–452, 2001.

[6] A. Carzaniga, D.S. Rosenblum, and A.L. Wolf. Achieving Scalability and Expressiveness in an Internet-Scale Event Notification Service. In *Proceedings of the ACM Symposium on Principles of Distributed Computing*, pages 219–227, 2000.

[7] A. Carzaniga, D.S. Rosenblum, and A.L. Wolf. Design and Evaluation of a Wide-Area Notification Service. *ACM Transactions on Computer Systems*, 3(19):332–383, Aug 2001.

[8] M. Castro, P. Druschel, A. Kermarrec, and A. Rowston. Scribe: A large-scale and decentralized application-level multicast infrastructure. *IEEE Journal on Selected Areas in Communications*, 20(8), October 2002.

[9] R. Chand and P. Felber. Xnet: A reliable content-based publish/subscribe system. In *23rd International Symposium on Reliable Distributed Systems (SRDS 2004)*, pages 264–273, 2004.

[10] R. Chand and P. Felber. Semantic peer-to-peer overlays for publish/subscribe networks. In *Parallel Processing, 11th International Euro-Par Conference (Euro-par 2005)*, pages 1194–1204, 2005.

[11] M. Cilia. *An Active Functionality Service for Open Distributed Heterogeneous Environments.* PhD thesis, Department of Computer Science, Darmstadt University of Technology, August 2002.

[12] G. Cugola, E. Di Nitto, and A. Fuggetta. Exploiting an event-based infrastructure to develop complex distributed systems. In *Proceedings of the 10th International Conference on Software Engineering (ICSE '98)*, April 1998.

[13] I. Dionysiou, D. Frincke, D. E. Bakken, and C. Hauser. Actor-oriented trust. Technical Report EECS-GS-006, School of Electrical Engineering and Computer SCience, Washington State University, Pullman, WA, USA, 2005.

[14] P.Th. Eugster, P. Felber, R. Guerraoui, and S.B. Handurukande. Event Systems: How to Have Your Cake and Eat It Too. In *Proceedings of the International Workshop on Distributed Event-Based Systems (DEBS'02)*, 2002.

[15] P.Th. Eugster, R. Guerraoui, and Ch.H. Damm. On Objects and Events. In *Proceedings of the Conference on Object-Oriented Programming Systems, Languages and Applications (OOPSLA)*, 2001.

[16] F. Fabret, A. Jacobsen, F. Llirbat, J. Pereira, K. Ross, and D. Shasha. Filtering algorithms and implementation for very fast publish/subscribe. In *Proceedings of the 20th Intl. Conference on Management of Data (SIGMOD 2001)*, pages 115–126, 2001.

[17] L. Fiege, A. Zeidler, A. Buchmann, R. Kilian-Kehr, and G. Muhl. Security aspects in publish/subscribe systems. In *Proceedings of the 3rd International Workshop on Distributed Event-Based Systems*, 2004.

[18] Ludger Fiege, Felix C. Gärtner, Oliver Kasten, and Andreas Zeidler. Supporting mobility in content-based publish/subscribe middleware. In *ACM/IFIP/USENIX International Middleware Conference (Middleware 2003)*, pages 103–122, 2003.

[19] Object Management Group. Data distribution service for real-time systems specification, 2002.

[20] Gryphon Web Site. http://www.research.ibm.com/gryphon/.

[21] Sun Microsystems Inc. Java message service api rev 1.1, 2002.

[22] G. Muhl. Generic Constraints for Content-Based Publish/Subscribe. In *Proceedings of the 6th International Conference on Cooperative Information Systems (CoopIS)*, 2001.

[23] Object Management Group. CORBA event service specification, version 1.1. OMG Document formal/2000-03-01, 2001.

[24] Object Management Group. CORBA notification service specification, version 1.0.1. OMG Document formal/2002-08-04, 2002.

[25] B. Oki, M. Pfluegel, A. Siegel, and D. Skeen. The information bus - an architecture for extensive distributed systems. In *Proceedings of the 1993 ACM Symposium on Operating Systems Principles*, December 1993.

[26] P. Pietzuch and J. Bacon. Hermes: a distributed event-based middleware architecture. In *Proceedings of the International Workshop on Distributed Event-Based Systems (DEBS'02)*, 2003.

[27] R. Preotiuc-Pietro, J. Pereira, F. Llirbat, F. Fabret, K. Ross, and D. Shasha. Publish/subscribe on the web at extreme speed. In *Proc. of ACM SIGMOD Conf. on Management of Data*, Cairo, Egypt, 2000.

[28] B. Segall, D. Arnold, J. Boot, M. Henderson, and T. Phelps. Content Based Routing with Elvin4. In *Proceedings of AUUG2K, Canberra, Australia*, June 2000.

[29] SIENA Web Site. http://www.cs.colorado.edu/users/carzanig/siena/.

[30] T. Sivaharan, G. Blair, and G. Coulson. GREEN: A Configurable and Re-configurable Publish-Subscribe Middleware for Pervasive Computing. In *Proceedings of DOA 2005*, 2005.

[31] S. Q. Zhuang, B. Y. Zhao, A. D. Joseph, R. Katz, and J. Kubiatowicz. Bayeux: An architecture for scalable and fault-tolerant wide-area data dissemination. In *11th Int. Workshop on Network and Operating Systems Support for Digital Audio and Video*, 2001.

Global Data Management
R. Baldoni et al. (Eds.)
IOS Press, 2006

Design and Implementation of Atlas P2P Architecture[1]

Reza Akbarinia[1,3], Vidal Martins[1,2], Esther Pacitti[1], Patrick Valduriez[1]
[1]ATLAS group, INRIA and LINA, University of Nantes, France
[2]PPGIA/PUCPR – Pontifical Catholic University of Paraná, Brazil
[3]Shahid Bahonar University of Kerman, Iran
FirstName.LastName@univ-nantes.fr, Patrick.Valduriez@inria.fr

Abstract. Peer-to-peer (P2P) computing offers new opportunities for building highly distributed data systems. Unlike client-server computing, P2P is a very dynamic environment where peers can join and leave the network at any time and offers important advantages such as operation without central coordination, peers autonomy, and scale up to large number of peers. However, providing high-level data management services (schema, queries, replication, availability, etc.) in a P2P system implies revisiting distributed database technology in major ways. In this chapter, we discuss the design and implementation of high-level data management services in APPA (Atlas Peer-to-Peer Architecture). APPA has a network-independent architecture that can be implemented over various structured and super-peer P2P networks. It uses novel solutions for persistent data management with updates, data replication with semantic-based reconciliation and query processing. APPA's services are implemented using the JXTA framework.

Keywords. P2P data management, replication, persistence, update management, semantic-based data reconciliation, query processing, JXTA

1. Introduction

Data management in distributed systems has been traditionally achieved by distributed database systems [31] which enable users to transparently access and update several databases in a network using a high-level query language (*e.g.* SQL). Transparency is achieved through a global schema which hides the local databases' heterogeneity. In its simplest form, a *distributed database system* is a centralized server that supports a global schema and implements distributed database techniques (query processing, transaction management, consistency management, etc.). This approach has proved effective for applications that can benefit from centralized control and full-fledge database capabilities, *e.g.* information systems. However, it cannot scale up to more than tens of databases. Data integration systems [45][48] extend the distributed database approach to access data sources

---

[1] Work partially funded by the ARA Massive Data of the Agence Nationale de la Recherche.

on the Internet with a simpler query language in read-only mode. Parallel database systems [49] also extend the distributed database approach to improve performance (transaction throughput or query response time) by exploiting database partitioning using a multiprocessor or cluster system. Although data integration systems and parallel database systems can scale up to hundreds of data sources or database partitions, they still rely on a centralized global schema and strong assumptions about the network.

In contrast, peer-to-peer (P2P) systems adopt a completely decentralized approach to data sharing. By distributing data storage and processing across autonomous peers in the network, they can scale without the need for powerful servers. Popular examples of P2P systems such as Gnutella [12] and Freenet [10] have millions of users sharing petabytes of data over the Internet. Although very useful, these systems are quite simple (*e.g.* file sharing), support limited functions (*e.g.* keyword search) and use simple techniques (*e.g.* resource location by flooding) which have performance problems. To deal with the dynamic behavior of peers that can join and leave the system at any time, they rely on the fact that popular data get massively duplicated.

Initial research on P2P systems has focused on improving the performance of query routing in the unstructured systems which rely on flooding. This work led to structured solutions based on distributed hash tables (DHT), *e.g.* CAN [37] and CHORD [44], or hybrid solutions with super-peers that index subsets of peers [28]. Although these designs can give better performance guarantees, more research is needed to understand their trade-offs between fault-tolerance, scalability, self-organization, etc.

Recently, other work has concentrated on supporting advanced applications which must deal with semantically rich data (*e.g.* XML documents, relational tables, etc.) using a high-level SQL-like query language, *e.g.* ActiveXML [2], Edutella [28], Piazza [46], PIER [16]. As a potential example of advanced application that can benefit from a P2P system, consider the cooperation of scientists who are willing to share their private data (and programs) for the duration of a given experiment. For instance, medical doctors in a hospital may want to share some patient data for an epidemiological study. Medical doctors may have their own, independent data descriptions for patients and should be able to ask queries like "age and last weight of the male patients diagnosed with disease X between day1 and day2" over their own descriptions.

Such data management in P2P systems is quite challenging because of the scale of the network and the autonomy and unreliable nature of peers. Most techniques designed for distributed database systems which statically exploit schema and network information no longer apply. New techniques are needed which should be decentralized, dynamic and self-adaptive.

In this chapter, we discuss the design and implementation of high-level data management services in APPA (Atlas Peer-to-Peer Architecture), a P2P data management system which we are building. The main objectives of APPA are scalability, availability and performance for advanced applications [3]. APPA has a network-independent architecture that can be implemented over various structured and super-peer P2P networks. This allows us to exploit continuing progress in such systems. To deal with semantically rich data, APPA supports decentralized schema management and uses novel solutions for persistent data management with updates, data replication with semantic-based reconciliation and query processing. APPA's services are implemented using the JXTA framework.

The rest of the chapter is organized as follows. First, Section 2 discusses data management in P2P systems. Section 3 describes the APPA architecture. Section 4 introduces the APPA's solution to persistent data management and support for updates. Section 5 describes its solution to high level data replication and distributed semantic reconciliation. Section 6 introduces the query processing strategy in APPA. Section 7 discusses implementation issues using the JXTA framework. Section 8 discusses related work. Section 9 concludes.

2. Data Management in P2P Systems

In a P2P system, a large number of peers (*e.g.* PCs connected to the Internet) can potentially be pooled together to share their resources, information and services. These peers can both consume as well as provide data or services [43]. There are important features that distinguish P2P systems from distributed database systems (DDBS). First, in P2P systems, peers are very dynamic and can join and leave the system at anytime. Second, there is no centralized authority for managing the peers. Third, there is no global schema for the data that are shared by the peers. Finally, the answers to the queries are typically incomplete, because at each time some of the peers may be disconnected and their potential answers cannot appear in the final result. P2P systems are usually built to be used in *small worlds* [17], *i.e.* with millions of peers. However, we can use them for sharing data/service in *communities*, *i.e.* with hundreds or thousands of peers.

A P2P system has an *overlay* network built on the physical network, *i.e.* the Internet. There are three types of architecture for P2P networks. The first type is *unstructured, e.g.* Gnutella [12], where there is no predefined topology for linking the peers to each other. Query routing is done by flooding, *i.e.* each peer sends the query to its neighbors which then send it to their neighbors and so on. The second type is *super-peer, e.g.* Edutella [28], where some peers are responsible for indexing and locating the shared data. Each regular peer should be connected to at least one super-peer. The third type is *structured, e.g.* P-Grid [1], where there is a specific topology for peer linking. A main kind of structured networks is Distributed Hash Tables (DHTs), *e.g.* CAN [37], where each data is associated with a key and each peer is responsible for storing a range of keys and their associated data. DHTs support a routing mechanism that allows the users to find efficiently the peer responsible for a key.

For building advanced data management applications on top of P2P networks, we must deal with semantically rich data (*e.g.* XML documents, relational tables, etc.). To address these applications, we need functions similar to those of distributed database systems. In particular, users should be able to use a high-level query language to describe the desired data. But the characteristics of P2P systems create new issues. First, the dynamic and autonomous nature of peers makes it hard to give guarantees about result completeness and makes static query optimization impossible. Second, data management techniques need to scale up to high numbers of peers. Third, the lack of centralized authority makes global schema management and access control difficult. Finally, even when using replication, it is hard to achieve fault-tolerance and availability in the presence of unstable peers. Most of the work on sharing semantically rich data in P2P systems has focused on schema management, and query processing and optimization. However, there has been very little work on replication, transactions and access control.

Schema management and query processing are generally addressed together for a given class of P2P system. Peers should be able to express high-level queries over their own schema without relying on a centralized global schema. Thus the main problem is to support decentralized schema mapping so that a query on one peer's schema can be reformulated in a query on another peer's schema. In PeerDB [30], assuming an unstructured network, schema mapping is done on the fly during query processing using information retrieval techniques. Although flexible, this approach limits query expressiveness to keyword search. Furthermore, query routing relies on flooding which can be inefficient. In PIER [16], a DHT network, the focus is on scaling up query processing to very large configurations assuming that de-facto standard schemas exist. However, only exact-match and equijoin queries are supported. In Edutella [28], a hybrid system, RDF-based schema descriptions are provided by super-peers. Thus, SQL-like query processing can be done by super-peers using distributed database techniques. Piazza [46] proposes a more general, network-independent, solution to schema management that supports a graph of pair-wise mappings between heterogeneous schema peers. Algorithms are proposed to reformulate a query in Xquery on a peer's schema into equivalent queries on the other peers' schemas. ActiveXML [2] is a general P2P system based on active XML documents, *i.e.* XML documents with embedded Web service calls in XQuery. Query processing in ActiveXML relies on a cost model which helps evaluating distributed queries and deciding which data and services to replicate.

Data replication in the presence of updates and transactions remains an open issue. The data sharing P2P systems, like Gnutella, deal with static read-only files (*e.g.* music files) for which update is not an issue. Freenet [10] partially addresses updates which are propagated from the updating peer downward to close peers that are connected. However, peers that are disconnected do not get updated. ActiveXML [2] supports the definition of replicated XML fragments as Web service calls but does not address update propagation. Update is addressed in P-Grid [1], a structured network that supports self-organization. The update algorithm uses rumor spreading to scale and provides probabilistic guarantees for replica consistency. However, it only considers updates at the file level in a mono-master mode, *i.e.* only one (master) peer can update a file and changes are propagated to other (read-only) replicas.

Advanced applications are likely to need more general replication capabilities such as various levels of replication granularity and multi-master mode, *i.e.* whereby the same replica may be updated by several (master) peers. For instance, a patient record may be replicated at several medical doctors and updated by any of them during a visit of the patient, *e.g.* to reflect the patient's new weight. The advantage of multi-master replication is high-availability and high-performance since replicas can be updated in parallel at different peers. However, conflicting updates of the same data at different peers can introduce replica divergence. Then the main problem is to assure replica consistency. In distributed database systems [31], synchronous replication (*e.g.* Read-Once-Write-All) which updates all replicas within the same transaction enforces mutual consistency of replicas. However, it does not scale up because it makes use of distributed transactions, typically implemented by

2 phase commit. Preventive replication [34] can yield strong consistency, without the constraints of synchronous replication, and scale up to large configurations. However, it requires support for advanced distributed services and a high speed network with guaranteed maximum time for message reception as is the case in cluster systems. This assumption does not hold for P2P systems. A more practical solution is optimistic replication [33][41] which allows the independent updating of replicas and divergence until reconciliation. However, existing optimistic replication solutions do not address important properties of P2P systems such as peers' autonomy and dynamic behavior.

3. APPA Architecture

APPA has a layered service-based architecture. Besides the traditional advantages of using services (encapsulation, reuse, portability, etc.), this enables APPA to be network-independent so it can be implemented over different structured (*e.g.* DHT) and super-peer P2P networks. The main reason for this choice is to be able to exploit rapid and continuing progress in P2P networks. Another reason is that it is unlikely that a single P2P network design will be able to address the specific requirements of many different applications. Obviously, different implementations will yield different trade-offs between performance, fault-tolerance, scalability, quality of service, etc. For instance, fault-tolerance can be higher in DHTs because no peer is a single point of failure. On the other hand, through index servers, super-peer systems enable more efficient query processing. Furthermore, different P2P networks could be combined in order to exploit their relative advantages, *e.g.* DHT for key-based search and super-peer for more complex searching.

There are three layers of services in APPA: P2P network, basic services and advanced services.

P2P network. This layer provides network independence with services that are common to different P2P networks:

- **Peer id assignment:** assigns a unique id to a peer using a specific method, *e.g.* a combination of super-peer id and counter in a super-peer network.
- **Peer linking:** links a peer to some other peers, *e.g.* by locating a zone in CAN [37].
- **Key-based storage and retrieval (KSR):** stores and retrieves a *(key, data)* pair in the P2P network, *e.g.* through hashing over all peers in DHT networks or using super-peers in super-peer networks. An important aspect of KSR is that it allows managing data using object semantics (*i.e.* with KSR it is possible to get and set specific data attributes).
- **Key-based timestamping (KTS):** generates monotonically increasing timestamps which are used for ordering the events occurred in the P2P system. This service is useful to improve data availability.
- **Peer communication:** enables peers to exchange messages (*i.e.* service calls).

Basic services. This layer provides elementary services for the advanced services using the P2P network layer:

- **Persistent data management (PDM):** provides high availability for the *(key, data)* pairs which are stored in the P2P network.

- **Peer management:** provides support for peer joining, rejoining and for updating peer address (the peer ID is permanent but its address may be changed).
- **Group membership management:** allows peers to join an abstract *group*, become *members* of the group and send and receive membership notifications. This is similar to group communication [5][6][7][9][23][38].

Advanced services. This layer provides advanced services for semantically rich data sharing including schema management, replication, query processing, security, etc. using the basic services.

Figure 1 shows an APPA architecture based on a DHT network. In this case, the three service layers are completely distributed over all peers. Thus, each peer needs to manage P2P data in addition to its local data.

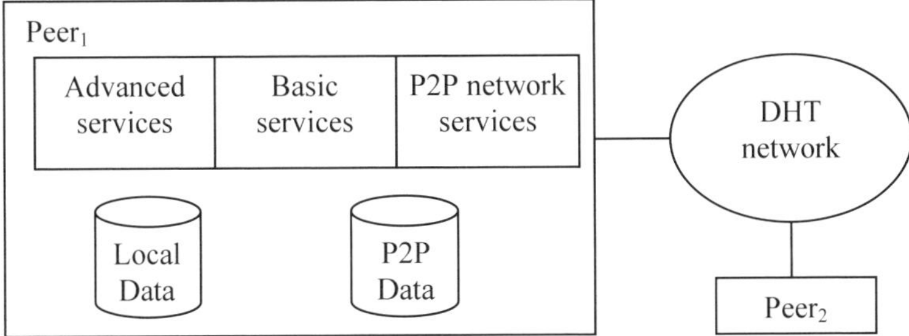

Figure 1 - APPA architecture with DHT

Figure 2 shows an APPA architecture based on a super-peer network. In this case, super-peers provide P2P network services and basic services while peers provide only the advanced services.

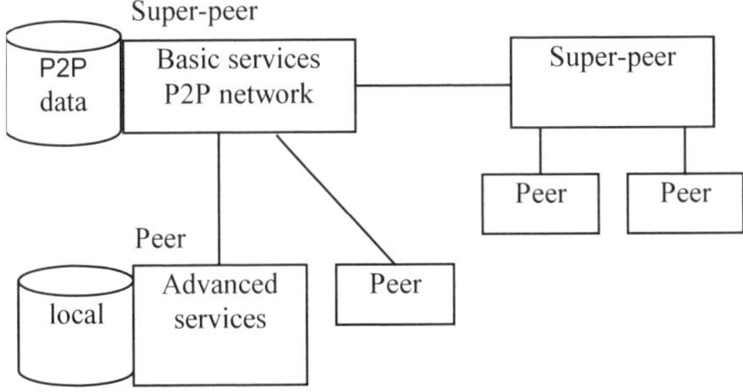

Figure 2 - APPA architecture with super-peer

4. Persistent Data Management

One of the main characteristics of P2P systems is the dynamic behavior of peers which can join and leave the system frequently, at anytime. When a peer gets offline, the data it stores becomes unavailable. To improve data persistence, we can rely on data replication by storing (*k, data*) pairs at several peers. If one peer is unavailable, the data can still be retrieved from the other peers that hold a replica. However, the mutual consistency of the replicas after updates can be compromised as a result of peers leaving the network or concurrent updates. Therefore, some of the replicas may not be *current, i.e.* they do not reflect the latest data stored with k in the P2P network. For some applications (*e.g.* agenda management, bulletin boards, cooperative auction management, reservation management, etc.) having the ability to get a current replica is very important.

In APPA, the PDM service provides data persistence through replication by using multiple hash functions. It also addresses efficiently the problem of retrieving current replicas based on timestamping. For doing its tasks, PDM takes advantage of KSR and KTS which are two services in the APPA's P2P network layer.

In this section, we first discuss how PDM provides data persistence, then we introduce the concept of timestamping, and finally we present the update operations which are the main operations of the PDM service.

4.1. Data Persistence Using Multiple Hash Functions

In APPA, a key k is mapped to a peer p using a hash function h. We call p the *responsible for k w.r.t. h*, and denote it by *rsp(k, h)*. A peer may be responsible for k w.r.t. a hash function h_1 but not responsible for k w.r.t. another hash function h_2. There is a set of hash functions H which can be used for mapping the keys to peers. The KSR service has an operation *put$_h$(k, data)* that, given a hash function $h \in H$, a data item *data* and its associated key k, stores the pair *(k, data)* at *rsp(k,h)*. This operation can be issued concurrently by several peers. There is another operation *get$_h$(k)* that retrieves the data associated with k stored at *rsp(k,h)*.

To improve data persistence, PDM stores each data and its associated key at several peers using a set of hash functions $H_r \subset H$. the set H_r is called the set of *replication hash functions*. The number of replication hash functions, *i.e.* $/H_r/$, can be different for different P2P networks. For instance, in a P2P network with low peer's availability, data availability can be increased using a high value of $/H_r/$ (*e.g.* 20).

Over time, some of the replicas stored with k at some peers may get stale, *e.g.* due to the absence of some peers at update time. To be able to return current replicas, before storing a data, PDM "stamps" it with a logical timestamp which is generated by KTS. Therefore, given a data item *data* and its associated key k, $\forall h \in H_r$, PDM replicates the pair *(k, {data, timestamp})* at *rsp(k,h)*. Upon a request for the data associated with a key, PDM returns one of the replicas which are stamped with the latest timestamp.

Timestamping

To generate timestamps, APPA uses KTS which is a distributed service. The main operation of KTS is *gen_ts(k)* which, given a key k, generates a real number as a *timestamp for k*. The timestamps generated by KTS have the *monotonicity* property, *i.e.* two timestamps generated for the same key are monotonically increasing. This property permits us to order the timestamps generated for the same key according to the time at which they have been generated.

Definition: Timestamp monotonicity. *For any two timestamps ts_1 and ts_2 generated for a key k respectively at times t_1 and t_2, if $t_1 < t_2$ then we have $ts_1 < ts_2$.*

KTS generates the timestamps in a completely distributed fashion, using local counters. At anytime, it generates at most one timestamp for a key k. Thus, regarding the monotonicity property, there is a total order on the set of timestamps generated for the same key. However, there is no total order on the timestamps generated for different keys.

In addition to *gen_ts*, KTS has another operation denoted by *last_ts(k)* which, given a key k, returns the last timestamp generated for k by KTS.

Update Operations

The main operations of the PDM service are *insert* and *retrieve* operations. The detail of these operations is as follows (see also Figure 3).

Insert(k, data): replicates a data and its associated key in the P2P network as follows. First, it uses KTS to generate a timestamp for k, *e.g. ts*. Then, for each $h \in H_r$ it stores the pair *(k, {data, ts})* at the peer that is *rsp(k,h)*. When a peer p, which is responsible for k w.r.t. one of the hash functions involved in H_r, receives the pair *(k, {data, ts})*, it compares *ts* with the timestamp, say ts_0, of its data (if any) associated with k. If $ts > ts_0$, p overwrites its data and timestamp with the new ones. Recall that, at anytime, *KTS.gen_ts (k)* generates at most one timestamp for k, and different timestamps for k have the monotonicity property. Thus, in the case of concurrent calls to *insert(k, data), i.e.* from different peers, only the one that obtains the latest timestamp will succeed to store its data in the P2P network.

Retrieve(k): retrieves the most recent replica associated with k in the P2P network as follows. First, it uses KTS to determine the latest timestamp generated for k, *e.g. ts_1*. Then, for each hash function $h \in H_r$, it uses the KSR operation *get$_h$(k)* to retrieve the pair *{data, timestamp}* stored along with k at *rsp(k,h)*. If *timestamp* is equal to ts_1, then the data is a current replica which is returned as output and the operation ends. Otherwise the retrieval process continues while saving in *data$_{mr}$* the most recent replica. If no replica with a timestamp equal to ts_1 is found (*i.e.* no current replica is found) then the operation returns the most recent replica available, *i.e. data$_{mr}$*.

```
insert(k, data)
begin
   ts := KTS.gen_ts (k);
       for  each  h∈Hr  do
           KSR.puth(k, {data, ts});
   end;

retrieve(k)
begin
   ts1 = KTS.last_ts(k);
   datamr = null;
   tsmr = - ∞;
   for  each  h∈Hr  do begin
      {data, ts} = KSR.geth(k);
      if (ts1 = ts) then begin
         return data; //one current replica is found
         exit;
      end;
      else if  (ts > tsmr) then  begin
         datamr = data;//keep the most recent replica
         tsmr = ts;   // and its timestamp
      end;
   end;
   return datamr
end;
```

Figure 3 - PDM update operations

5. Data Replication

Data replication is largely used to improve data availability and performance in distributed systems. In APPA, PDM is a low-level service that employs data replication to improve the availability of pairs (*key, data*) stored in the P2P network. For solving update conflicts by taking into account application semantics, APPA provides a higher-level replication service. This service is not based on a lazy master solution [32] for two reasons. First, whenever the master fails, updates on replicated data are blocked, because updates are done at a single node. Second, updates coming from far distant users may perform poorly due to unpredictable network delays. Thus, for developing an advanced replication service, we use a multi-master solution whereby any node may update replicated data. In particular, we are interested in optimistic solutions [33][41] which allow the asynchronous updating of replicas such that applications can progress even though some nodes are disconnected or have failed. This enables asynchronous collaboration among users. However, concurrent updates may cause replica divergence and conflicts, which should be reconciled.

In order to resolve conflicting updates [31], optimistic replication techniques use the following criteria [41]: (1) timestamp ordering, (2) sequencing of update arrivals at a primary node, or (3) application semantics. The latter is the most flexible approach because the user may specify reconciliation criteria. APPA's current solution exploits semantic reconciliation. Solutions for semantic reconciliation may be domain-specific or general-purpose. For instance, Ramsey and Csirmaz [36] deal with file system conflicting updates whereas IceCube [21][35] proposes a general method with reconciliation logic separated from application logic. IceCube is a sequential centralized solution where the central node may be a bottleneck. Moreover, if this node fails, the whole replication system may be blocked until recovery.

In this section, we present the DSR algorithm (Distributed Semantic Reconciliation Algorithm) [26], a dynamic distributed version of the semantic reconciliation provided by IceCube. Unlike IceCube, DSR is based on a distributed and parallel approach. With DSR, a subset of nodes, called reconcilers, are selected to concurrently reconcile conflicting updates.

The rest of this section is organized as follows. Section 5.1 introduces our replication model. Section 5.2 presents centralized reconciliation. Finally, Section 5.3 describes APPA's distributed semantic reconciliation.

5.1. Replication model

We define our replication model in the context of a virtual community which requires a high level of collaboration. A virtual community can be defined by the following properties [50]: (1) members have some shared goal, interest, need, or activity that provides the primary reason for belonging to the community; (2) members engage in repeated active participation and there are often intense interactions, strong ties and shared activities occurring between participants; (3) members have access to shared resources and there are policies for determining access to those resources; (4) members interchange information, support and services; (5) members share a context (social conventions, language, protocols). A virtual community typically has hundreds or even thousands of interacting users. It is greater than a group and smaller than a small world [17].

In our replication model, a *replica R* is a copy of a collection of objects (*e.g.* copy of a relational table, or an XML document). A *replica item* is an object belonging to a replica (*e.g.* a tuple in a relational table, or an element in an XML document). We assume *multi-master* replication, *i.e.* a replica R is stored in several nodes and all nodes may read or write R. Conflicting updates are expected, but with low frequency.

In APPA, we assume that a common schema description of R, noted *R-csd* (R common schema description) is defined by community members. Beyond this common description, it is possible that nodes already hold different local schema descriptions of R, noted *R-lsd* (R local schema description). In this case, each node n_i must also define mapping functions [46] among *R-lsd* and *R-csd*. As a result, local updates can be mapped into the common schema, and reconciled updates can be mapped to the local schema.

In order to update replicas, nodes produce *tentative* actions (henceforth actions) that are executed only if they conform to the application semantics. An *action* (noted a_n^i, where n indicates the node that has executed the action and i is the action identifier) is defined by the application programmer and represents an application-specific operation (*e.g.* a write operation on a file or document, or a database transaction). The application semantics is described by means of constraints between actions. A *constraint* is the formal representation of an application invariant (*e.g.* an update cannot follow a delete).

On the one hand, users and applications can create constraints between actions to make their intents explicit (they are called *user-defined constraints*). On the other hand, the reconciler node identifies conflicting actions, and asks the application if these actions may be executed together in any order (*commutative* actions) or if they are mutually dependent. New constraints are created to represent semantic dependencies between conflicting actions (they are called *system-defined constraints*).

Let us illustrate user- and system-defined constraints with the following example. Let *mutuallyExclusive*(a_1, a_2) be a constraint establishing that either a_1 or a_2 can be in a schedule, but not both. Let *parcel*(a_1, a_2) be a constraint defining an atomic (all-or-nothing) grouping, *i.e.* either all the constraint's actions execute successfully in any order, or none does. Let T be a replica copy, in our example, a relational table, K be the key attribute for T, and A and B be any two attributes of T. In addition, consider that the actions in Example 1 (with the associated constraints) are executed by nodes n_1, n_2 and n_3, and should be reconciled.

$a_1^{\,1}$: update T set A=a1 where K=k1

$a_2^{\,1}$: update T set A=a2 where K=k1

$a_3^{\,1}$: update T set B=b1 where K=k1

$a_3^{\,2}$: update T set A=a3 where K=k2

Parcel($a_3^{\,1}$, $a_3^{\,2}$)

Example 1 - Conflicting actions on T

In Example 1, actions $a_1^{\,1}$ and $a_2^{\,1}$ are semantically related, because they try to update the same replica item (*i.e.* T's tuple identified by *k1*) and the application finds a dependency between these actions (*i.e.* they manage the same attribute A). In this case, a *mutuallyExclusive*($a_1^{\,1}$, $a_2^{\,1}$) *system-defined constraint* is created to represent the semantic dependency. Similarly, $a_3^{\,1}$ and $a_3^{\,2}$ are semantically related because they are involved in a *parcel user-defined constraint*.

We define a *cluster* as set of actions related by constraints, and a *schedule* is a set of ordered actions that must be executed by all nodes in order to achieve eventual consistency.

5.2. Centralized Reconciliation

In this section, we describe the IceCube reconciliation solution which we will extend into a distributed solution in the next section. IceCube was built to manage data replication with semantic reconciliation for small/medium scale distributed systems in which nodes may connect and disconnect. Reconciliation is done in a single *reconciler* node; each node has its own replica of the shared data, and all replicas start in an identical initial state.

While disconnected, an application reads or writes its local replicas, and records update actions in a local log. Periodically, all computers reconnect and one node, namely the *reconciler node*, collects all the logs to perform reconciliation. The reconciler node then produces one or more schedules as a result of the combination of the actions stored in the logs. Afterwards, the reconciler node chooses one of the schedules based on some user criteria and propagates the chosen schedule to all involved nodes. Each node then applies the chosen schedule on its replica copy, leading to a new common state of all replicas. This approach ensures eventual consistency [35] among replicas. A system is eventually consistent if, when all nodes stop the production of new update actions, all nodes eventually reach the same value in their local replicas.

In order to produce a schedule, the reconciler node orders actions coming from different nodes based on application semantics. This is done in two sequential steps. First, the reconciler produces several *clusters* of actions (recall that each *cluster* contains a set of actions related by constraints). Next, the reconciler orders each cluster produced in the first step. Clusters are mutually-independent (*i.e.* there are no constraints involving actions of distinct clusters), and, as a result, they can be independently ordered.

To order a cluster, IceCube iteratively performs the following operations: i) select the action with the highest merit from the cluster and put it into the schedule (the merit of an action is a value that represents the estimated benefit of putting it into the schedule). If more than one action has the highest merit (different actions may have equal merits), the reconciler randomly selects one of them; ii) remove the selected action from the cluster; iii) remove from the cluster the remaining actions that conflict with the selected action. This iteration ends when the cluster becomes empty. As a result, cluster's actions are ordered. In fact, several alternative orderings may be produced until finding the best one. The *global schedule* is composed by the union of clusters' ordered actions.

5.3. Distributed Semantic Reconciliation

We now present DSR, a distributed algorithm to reconcile conflicting updates. Basically, data replication with DSR proceeds in three phases: (1) local action production, (2) action storage, and (3) distributed reconciliation. In the local action production phase, nodes execute local actions to update replicas while respecting user-defined constraints. Then, in the action storage phase, these actions (with the associated constraints) are stored in the P2P network using the PDM service. Finally, in the distributed reconciliation phase, reconciler nodes retrieve actions and constraints from the P2P network and produce a global schedule, by performing distributed conflict resolution based on the application semantics. This schedule is locally executed at each node.

In order to avoid communication overhead and due to dynamic connections and disconnections, we distinguish *replica nodes*, which are the nodes that hold replicas, from *reconciler nodes*, which is a subset of the replica nodes that participate in distributed reconciliation. Note that a node may be connected but does not participate in distributed reconciliation due to its limited computing power.

We now present DSR in more details. First, we introduce the reconciliation objects necessary to DSR. Then, we present the 5 steps of the DSR algorithm. Finally, we present how DSR manages disconnections and reconnections.

Reconciliation Objects

Data managed by DSR during reconciliation are held by *reconciliation objects* that are stored in the P2P network. The node where a reconciliation object is stored is called the *provider node* for that object. Reconciliation objects used by DSR are:

- **Action log R (noted L_R)**: it stores all tentative actions that update the replica R. In Example 1, T is a relational table, so all updates on T's tuples coming from any node are stored in L_T. Notice that an action is first stored locally in the replica node and then stored in the nodes that carry the involved action logs. In Example 1, only one action log is involved because a single replica is used, *i.e. T*. Action logs make up the input for reconciliation.

- **Action groups of R (noted G_R)**: in order to produce system-defined constraints, actions *suspect* of establishing semantic conflicts are gathered in action groups. A suspicion takes place when two actions try to update the same replica item. It is just a suspicion, because the application may judge safe to execute both actions. For instance, in Example 1, a_1^1 and a_3^1 try to update the same replica item, but they are *semantically independent*, because they change distinct independent attributes. Conversely, a_1^1 and a_2^1, which try to update the same replica item with conflicting values, are *semantically dependent*. Therefore, actions that try to update a common replica item are put together into the same action group, and for each replica R there may be a set of action groups (noted $G_R = \{G_1, G_2, \dots G_n\}$). The action groups associated with R are stored in the *action groups of R* reconciliation object. Action groups make up the input for clusters creation.

- **Clusters set (noted CS)**: recall that a cluster contains a set of actions related by constraints, and can be ordered independently from other clusters when producing the global schedule. A cluster is not associated with a replica. All clusters produced during reconciliation are stored in the *clusters set* reconciliation object.

- **Action summary (noted AS)**: it captures semantic dependencies among actions, which are described by means of constraints. In addition, the action summary holds relationships between actions and clusters, so that each relationship describes an action membership (an action is a *member* of one or more clusters). An action membership is a pair of values (a_n^i, C_j), where a_n^i represents an action to be reconciled, and C_j indicates a cluster which a_n^i belongs to.

- **Schedule (noted S)**: it contains a set of ordered actions, which is composed of the union of clusters' ordered actions. Thus, we denote a schedule reconciliation object as $S = S_1 \cup S_2 \dots \cup S_n$, where each S_i represents the subset of ordered actions coming from the cluster C_i.

- **Schedule history (noted H)**: it stores a chronological sequence of schedules' identifiers ($H = (S_{id1}, \dots, S_{idn})$). A replica node can check whether it is *up to date* by comparing the identifier of the last schedule it has locally executed with S_{idn}.

To enable the storage and retrieval of reconciliation objects in the P2P network, each reconciliation object receives a unique identifier of which application is aware. Thus, the application can provide these identifiers to reconciler nodes, so that any reconciler is able to access any reconciliation object stored in the P2P network.

DSR Algorithm

Here, we describe how DSR implements semantic reconciliation. As IceCube, DSR is a reconciliation engine which takes advantage of application semantics to solve action conflicts. However, unlike IceCube, DSR does not depend on a single reconciler node. It is completely distributed and exploits the processing power of connected nodes to improve system availability, scalability and fault-tolerance while providing good performance. Moreover, it is dynamic in the sense of selecting a subset of available replica nodes to proceed as reconciler nodes.

In order to provide parallel processing, DSR organizes distributed reconciliation in five steps, as shown in Figure 4. Any connected node can start reconciliation by inviting other available nodes to engage with it. A subset of engaged nodes is allocated to step 1, another subset is allocated to step 2, and so forth until the 5th step. Nodes at step 1 start reconciliation. The outputs produced at each step become the input to the next one. In the following, we describe the activities performed at each step, and we illustrate parallel processing by explaining how these activities could be executed simultaneously by two reconciler nodes, n_1 and n_2.

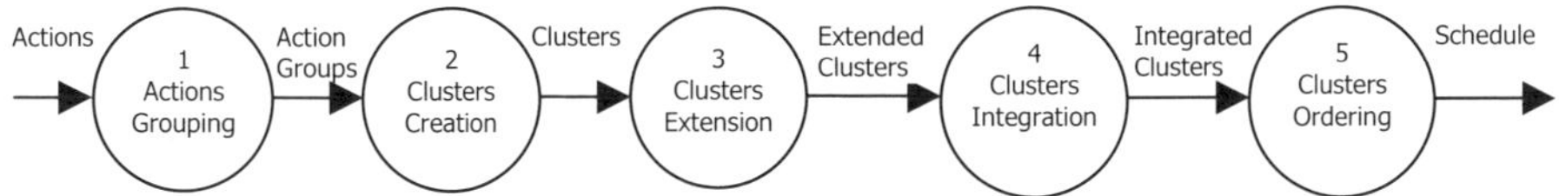

Figure 4 – DSR Steps

- **Step 1 – actions grouping**. For each replica R, this step takes actions related to R and put into the same group actions *suspect* of establishing semantic conflicts, thereby producing the *action groups of R* reconciliation object (G_R). In Example 1, suppose that n_1 takes $\{a_1^1, a_2^1\}$ and n_2, $\{a_3^1, a_3^2\}$ as input. By hashing the identifiers of replica items handled by these actions, n_1 put a_1^1 and a_2^1 into the group G_1 (a_1^1 and a_2^1 handle the same replica item) whereas n_2 put a_3^1 into G_1 and a_3^2 into G_2 (a_3^1 and a_3^2 handle distinct replica items). Thus, groups $G_1 = \{a_1^1, a_2^1, a_3^1\}$ and $G_2 = \{a_3^2\}$ are produced in parallel and are stored in the *action groups of T* reconciliation object (G_T).

- **Step 2 – clusters creation**. This step takes as input groups produced in the previous step in order to create clusters that are stored in the *clusters set* reconciliation object. For each group, semantic dependencies among actions are discovered, leading to the production of system-defined constraints, and the group is split into clusters of semantically dependent conflicting actions. In addition, this step updates actions' memberships in the action summary. In Example 1, consider that n_1 takes G_1 and n_2 takes G_2 as input. In this case, n_1 splits G_1 into clusters $C_1 = \{a_1^1, a_2^1\}$ and $C_2 = \{a_3^1\}$ (a_1^1 and a_2^1 are semantically dependent actions). At the same time, n_2 turn G_2 into cluster $C_3 = \{a_3^2\}$. All these clusters are stored in the *clusters set* reconciliation object (CS). In addition, n_1 and n_2 update the *action summary* reconciliation object (AS) with these action memberships, respectively: $\{(a_1^1, C_1), (a_2^1, C_1), (a_3^1, C_2)\}$ and $\{(a_3^2, C_3)\}$.

- **Step 3 – clusters extension**. User-defined constraints are not taken into account in clusters creation (*e.g.* although a_3^1 and a_3^2 belong to a *parcel*, the previous step does not put them into the same cluster, because they do not update common replica items). Hence, the third step extends clusters created in the second step by adding them new conflicting actions based on user-defined constraints (*extended clusters* are noted C_i^+). In addition, the third step updates actions' memberships in the action summary. In Example 1, assume that n_1 takes $C_1 = \{a_1^1, a_2^1\}$ as input whereas n_2 takes $C_2 = \{a_3^1\}$ and $C_3 = \{a_3^2\}$ (each node deal with 2 actions). Then, n_1 realizes that C_1 does not need extensions, because its actions are not involved in user-defined constraints; in parallel, due to the parcel constraint, n_2 extends C_2 and C_3 as follows: $C_2^+ = C_2 \cup \{a_3^2\}$, and $C_3^+ = C_3 \cup \{a_3^1\}$. In addition, n_2 updates the action summary with these action memberships: $\{(a_3^2, C_2), (a_3^1, C_3)\}$.

- **Step 4 – clusters integration**. Clusters extensions performed in the third step lead to the emergence of common actions among distinct clusters. The fourth step brings together extended clusters with common actions producing *integrated clusters* (an integrated cluster is noted C_i^{++}). In order to identify common actions, reconciler nodes analyze action memberships (*i.e.* if an action has m memberships, then it belongs to m extended clusters). In Example 1, consider that n_1 takes $\{(a_3^1, C_2^+), (a_3^1, C_3^+), (a_3^2, C_2^+), (a_3^2, C_3^+)\}$ as input whereas n_2 takes $\{(a_1^1, C_1), (a_2^1, C_1)\}$ (each node deals with the memberships of 2 actions). Thus, n_1 realizes that a_3^1 is a member of C_2^+ and C_3^+, so n_1 integrates them as follows: $C_4^{++} = C_2^+ \cup C_3^+ = \{a_3^1, a_3^2\}$; at the same time, n_2 realizes that a_1^1 and a_2^1 have just one membership, so n_2 does not perform integration. Recall that integrated clusters are mutually-independent.

- **Step 5 – clusters ordering**. This step takes integrated clusters as input and produces the global schedule that afterwards is executed by all replica nodes. As in IceCube, each cluster is independently ordered to produce a subset of ordered actions. The union of these subsets of ordered actions makes up the global schedule. In Example 1, suppose that n_1 takes C_1 as input whereas n_2 takes C_4^{++}. As a result, n_1 could produce the subset of ordered actions $S_1 = \{a_1^1\}$, because C_1 actions are mutually exclusive. In parallel, n_2 could produce the subset of ordered actions $S_4 = \{a_3^1, a_3^2\}$, because C_4^{++} actions are involved in a parcel constraint. The global schedule would be $S = S_1 \cup S_4 = \{a_1^1, a_3^1, a_3^2\}$.

At every step, the DSR algorithm takes advantage of data parallelism, *i.e.* several nodes perform simultaneously the same activity (*e.g.* clusters ordering) on a distinct subset of actions. No centralized criterion is applied to partition actions. In fact, whenever a set of reconciler nodes request data to a provider, the provider node naively supplies reconcilers with about the same amount of data.

Managing Dynamic Disconnections and Reconnections

Whenever distributed reconciliation takes place, a set of nodes N_d may be disconnected. As a result, the global schedule is not applied by nodes of N_d. Moreover, actions produced by N_d nodes and not yet stored in the P2P network are not reconciled. In order to assure eventual consistency despite disconnections, the replication service proceeds as follows.

Each node locally stores the identifier of the last schedule it has locally executed (noted S_{last}). In addition, the replication service stores in the P2P network a history of schedules produced by reconciliations ($H = (S_{id1}, S_{id2}, ..., S_{idn})$). As any reconciliation object, the schedule history has a unique identifier. The application knows this identifier and can provide it to the reconciler nodes. When a node n of N_d reconnects, it proceeds as follows: (1) n checks whether S_{last} is equal to S_{idn}, and, if not (*i.e.* n's replicas are out of date), n locally applies all schedules that follow S_{last} in the H history; (2) actions locally produced by n and not yet stored in the P2P network are put in the involved action logs for later reconciliation.

At the beginning of reconciliation, a set of connected replica nodes must be allocated to proceed as reconciler nodes. To minimize reconciliation time, such allocation should be dynamic, *i.e.* nodes should be allocated based on the reconciliation context (*e.g.* number of actions, number of replicas, network properties, etc.). Currently, we are elaborating a cost model and the associated algorithms for allocating reconciler nodes based on communication costs. These algorithms take into account cost changes due to dynamic disconnections and reconnections.

6. Query Processing

Query processing in APPA deals with schema-based queries and considers data replication. In this section, we first present schema mapping in APPA, and then we describe the main phases of query processing. We also introduce support for Top-k queries as a way to reduce network communication.

6.1. Schema Mapping

In order to support schema-based queries, APPA must deal with heterogeneous schema management. In a P2P system, peers should be able to express queries over their own schema without relying on a centralized global schema as in data integration systems [45]. Several solutions have been proposed to support decentralized schema mapping, *e.g.* [28][30][46]. For instance, Piazza [46] proposes a general, network-independent, solution that supports a graph of pair-wise mappings between heterogeneous schema peers. APPA uses a simpler solution that takes advantage of the collaborative nature of the applications. It assumes that peers that wish to cooperate, *e.g.* for the duration of an experiment, agree on a *Common Schema Description* (CSD). Given a CSD, a peer schema can be specified using views. This is similar to the local-as-view approach in data integration [24] except that, in APPA, queries at a peer are expressed against the views, not the CSD.

When a peer decides to share data, it needs to define a peer schema, only once, to map its local schema to the CSD. To simplify the discussion, we use the relational model (APPA uses XML) and the Datalog-like notation of [45] for mapping rules. Thus, a peer schema includes peer mappings, one per local relation. Given 2 CSD relation definitions r_1 and r_2, an example of peer mapping at peer p is:

$$p{:}r(A,B,D) \subseteq csd{:}r_1(A,B,C),\ csd{:}r_2(C,D,E)$$

In APPA, the mapped schemas are stored in the P2P network using the PDM service.

6.2. Query Processing Phases

Given a user query on a peer schema, the objective is to find the minimum set of relevant peers (query matching), route the query to these peers (query routing), collect the answers and return a (ranked) list of answers to the user. Since the relevant peers may be disconnected, the returned answers may be incomplete.

Query processing proceeds in four main phases: (1) query reformulation, (2) query matching, (3) query optimization and (4) query decomposition and execution.

Query reformulation. The user query (on the peer schema) is rewritten in a query on CSD relations. This is similar to query modification using views. For instance, the following query at peer p:

   select A,D from r where B=b

would be rewritten on the CSD relations as:

   select A,D from r_1,r_2 where B=b and $r_1.C=r_2.C$

Query matching. Given a reformulated query Q, it finds all the peers that have data relevant to the query. For simplicity, we assume conjunctive queries. Let P be the set of peers in the P2P system, the problem is to find $P' \subseteq P$ where each p in P' has relevant data, *i.e.* refers to relations of Q in its mapped schema. These peers can be iteratively (for each Q's relation) retrieved using the PDM service. Let R be the set of relations involved in Q, and $ms(p,r)$ denote that the mapped schema of peer p involves relation r, query matching produces:

   $P' = \{ p \mid (p \in P) \wedge (\exists r \in R \wedge ms(p,r)) \}$

Query optimization. Because of data replication, each relevant data may be replicated at some peers in P'. The optimization objective is to minimize the cost of query processing by selecting best candidate peer(s) for each relevant data based on a cost function. Selecting more than one candidate peer is necessary in a very dynamic environment since some candidate peers may have left the network. Thus, selecting several candidate peers increases the answer's completeness but at the expense of redundant work. This step produces a set $P'' \subseteq P'$ of best peers.

Query decomposition and execution. This phase is similar to that in data integration systems and APPA reuses well-known, yet sophisticated techniques. Since some peers in P" may have only subsets of Q's relations, query decomposition produces a number of subqueries (not necessarily different), one for each peer, together with a composition query to integrate, *e.g.* through join and union operations, the intermediate results [24]. Finally, the subqueries are sent to the peers in P", which reformulate it on their local schema (using the peer mappings), execute it, and send the results back to the sending peer, who integrates the results. Result composition can also exploit parallelism using intermediate peers. For instance, let us consider relations r_1 and r_2 defined over CSD r and relations s_1 and s_2

defined over CSD *s*, each stored at a different peer, and the query *select * from r, s where r.a=s.a and r.b=2 and s.c=5* issued by a peer *q*. A parallel execution strategy for *Q* is shown in Figure 5.

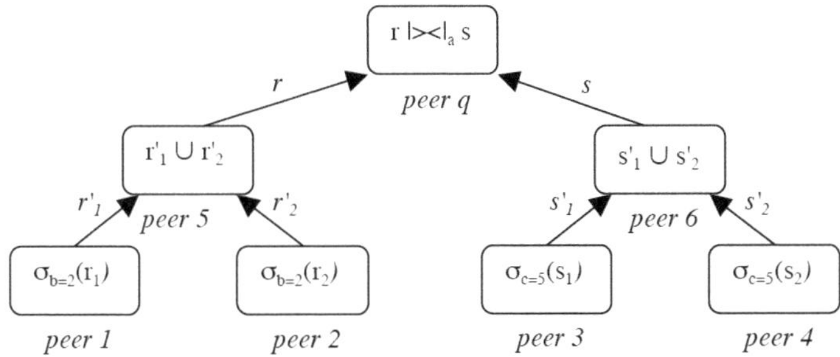

Figure 5 – Example of parallel execution using intermediate peers

This strategy exhibits independent parallelism between peers 1-4 (the select (σ) operations can all be done in parallel) and peers 5-6 (the union operations can be done in parallel). It can also yield pipelined parallelism. For instance, if the left-hand operand of an intermediate peer is smaller than the right-hand operand, then it would be entirely transferred first so the other operand could be pipelined thus yielding parallelism between peers 2-5-*q* and peers 4-6-*q*. Parallel execution strategies improve both the query response time and the global efficiency of the P2P system.

6.3. Top-k Queries

High-level queries over a large-scale P2P system may produce very large numbers of results that may overwhelm the users. To avoid such overwhelming, APPA uses Top-k queries whereby the user can specify a limited number (*k*) of the most relevant answers [4]. For example, consider a P2P system with medical doctors who want to share some (restricted) patient data for an epidemiological study. Then, one doctor may want to submit the following query over the P2P system to obtain the 10 top answers ranked by a scoring function over age and weight:

```
SELECT  *
FROM    Patient P
WHERE   (P.disease = "hepathitis") AND
        (P.age < 50) AND (P.weight > 70)
ORDER BY scoring-function(age, weight)
STOP AFTER 10
```

The scoring function specifies how closely each data item matches the conditions. For relational data, the most used scoring functions are *Min*, *Euclidean* and *Sum* functions [8]. For instance, in the query above, the scoring function could be *sum((age/10)*2,weight/20)* thus giving more importance to age.

Formally, let *Q* be a Top-k query and *P"* the set of peers that have relevant data to *Q*. Let *D* be the set of all relevant data items (*i.e.* tuples) that are owned by the peers involved in P''. Let $Sc(d, Q)$ be a scoring function that denotes the score of relevance of a data item $d \in D$ to Q. The goal is to find the set $T \subseteq D$, such that: $/T/ = k$ and $\forall d_1 \in T,\ \forall d_2 \in (D - T)$ then $Sc(d_1, Q) \geq Sc(d_2, Q)$

Efficient execution of Top-k queries in a large-scale distributed system is difficult. To process a Top-k query, a naïve solution is that the query originator sends the query to all nodes and merges all the results, which it gets back. This solution hurts response time as the central node is a bottleneck and does not scale up. APPA takes the advantage of P2P parallelism and executes Top-k queries by a tree-based algorithm, in which a lot of peers participate in merging the results and bubbling up the top results to the query originator.

7. APPA Implementation

To validate the design of APPA and perform experiments with collaborative applications, we have started the development of a prototype. Its implementation is done using JXTA (JuXTAposition), an open network computing platform designed for P2P computing [19]. JXTA provides various services and abstractions for implementing P2P applications. Furthermore, it can integrate with Web service standards to provide higher-level peer-to-peer communication. For implementing APPA's services, the programming language is Java, and common data structures are defined in XML (*e.g.* definitions of replicas and reconciliation objects).

7.1. JXTA Framework

JXTA is an open source application framework for P2P computing [19]. JXTA protocols aim to establish a network overlay on top of the Internet and non-IP networks, allowing peers to directly interact and self-organize independently of their physical network. JXTA technology leverages open standards like XML, Java technology, and key operating system concepts. By using existing, proven technologies and concepts, the objective is to yield a peer-to-peer system that is familiar to developers.

JXTA's architecture is organized in three layers (see Figure 6): JXTA core, JXTA services, and JXTA applications. The core layer provides minimal and essential primitives that are common to P2P networking. The services layer includes network services that may not be absolutely necessary for a P2P network to operate, but are common or desirable in the P2P environment. The applications layer provides integrated applications that aggregate services, and, usually, provide user interface. There is no rigid boundary between the applications layer and the services layer.

In JXTA, all shared resources are described by *advertisements*. Advertisements are language-neutral metadata structures defined as XML documents. Peers use advertisements to publish their resources. Some special super-peers, which are called *rendezvous* peers, are responsible for indexing and locating the advertisements.

7.2. APPA on top of JXTA

Figure 6 shows the architecture of the APPA prototype within JXTA. The functionality provided by APPA's peer id assignment service and peer linking service are already available in the JXTA core layer. Thus, APPA simply uses JXTA's corresponding functionality. In contrast, JXTA does not provide an equivalent service for key-based storage and retrieval (KSR). Thus, we implemented KSR on top of Meteor, an open-source JXTA service which implements the Chord and CAN protocols. APPA's advanced services, like replication and query processing, are provided as JXTA community services. The key advantage of APPA's implementation is that only its P2P network layer depends on the JXTA platform. Thus, APPA is portable and can be used over other platforms by replacing the services of the P2P network layer.

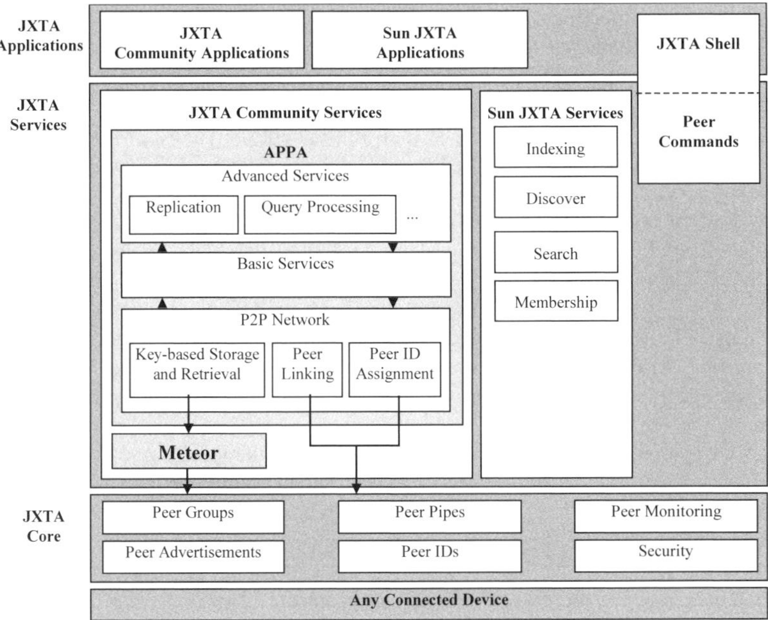

Figure 6: APPA Prototype within JXTA

Some of APPA's services (*e.g.* KSR, KTS, PDM and replication [25][26]) have been validated over the cluster of the Paris team at INRIA [15]. This cluster has 64 nodes connected by a 1-Gbps network. Each node has an Intel Pentium 2.4 GHz processor, and runs the Linux operating system. We make each node act as a peer in the P2P system. To have a topology close to real P2P overlay networks, we determine the peers' neighbors and we allow that every peer communicate only with its neighbors in the overlay network. Additionally, in order to study the scalability of these services with larger numbers of nodes, we implemented simulators using Java and SimJava [14] (a process based discrete event simulation package). Simulations were executed on an Intel Pentium IV with a 2.6 GHz processor, and 1 Gb of main memory, running the Windows XP operating system.

Although a cluster provides fast and reliable communication, which usually is not the case for P2P systems, it allows to validate the accuracy of APPA distributed algorithms and to evaluate the scalability of APPA services. We have deployed APPA over the cluster of Paris team because it was the largest network available to perform our experiments. In addition, this cluster is a member of the Grid'5000 project [13] which aims at building a highly reconfigurable, controlable and monitorable experimental Grid platform, gathering 9 sites geographically distributed in France featuring a total of 5000 CPUs. We intend to explore this powerful platform in future experiments.

The current version of the APPA prototype and its service simulators manage data using a Chord [44] DHT. Chord is a simple and well known DHT protocol that provides good properties (*e.g.* it is robust in the sense of supporting properly a large number of connections and disconnections). The experimental results showed that simulators are well calibrated and the implemented services have good performance and scale up.

Implementing on top of JXTA is relatively easy, since the JXTA framework provides several services with well-defined interfaces. However, the services of this framework are not easy to adapt. For instance, if one wishes to implement the Chord protocol over JXTA either she builds a completely new JXTA service (*e.g.* Meteor [27]) or she adapts the corresponding service on JXTA core (*e.g.* Théodoloz's master thesis [47]). The approach adopted by Meteor is easier to implement, but it has the inconvenience of making co-exist two independent lookup systems, namely Meteor and the original JXTA lookup system. On the other hand, adapting a JXTA core service is difficult as the JXTA framework does not provide variation points in its implementation. As a result, this approach requires understanding and changing of the entire associated source code. For simplicity reasons, in order to provide APPA prototype with Chord protocol, we adopted the Meteor service instead of changing JXTA core. However, Meteor is not a full-fledge product, and this causes some inconveniences too.

We also experienced small problems during the implementation of APPA because JXTA and its services are incomplete for large scale deployment. Thus, we used the JXTA Distributed Framework (JDF) [18] for deploying an instance of the APPA prototype on every cluster node. JDF simplifies the deployment process, but it is not compatible with the last version of JXTA. Thus, we installed two versions of the JXTA platform in the cluster and we switched between these versions depending on the context (*i.e.* for JDF, the oldest version; for the APPA prototype, the most recent version). In addition, JDF contains some errors that must be fixed through a script file. Notice that these problems do not affect final users as it concerns only the deployment for tests.

8. Related Work

P2P computing has attracted a lot of attention in the data management community. Many systems have been developed for managing shared data in P2P networks. However, they are typically dependent on the network (*i.e.* unstructured, structured or super-peer) for which they have been designed and cannot be easily used in other P2P networks.

Edutella [29] is a P2P system for data management in super-peer networks. In Edutella, a small percentage of nodes, *i.e.* super-peers, are responsible for indexing the shared data and routing the queries. The super-peers are assumed to be highly available with very good computing capacity. Super-peers are arranged in a hypercube topology, according to the HyperCuP protocol [42]. When a peer connects to Edutella, it should register at one of the super-peers. Upon registration, the peer provides to the super-peer its RDF-based metadata. The initial Edutella services are as follows: 1) query service for processing the queries based on RDF metadata; 2) replication service that provides data availability and workload balancing; 3) mapping service which is responsible for doing the mapping between the metadata of different peers to enable interoperability between them; and 4) annotation service which annotates materials stored anywhere within the Edutella network. The main difference between APPA and Edutella is that Edutella can only be implemented on top of a super-peer network, but APPA can be built on both super-peer and structured networks.

PeerDB [43] is a P2P system designed with the objective of high level data management in unstructured P2P networks. It exploits mobile agents for flooding the query to the peers such that their hop-distance from the query originator is less than a specified value, *i.e.* TTL (Time-To-Live). Then, the query answers are gathered by the mobile agents and returned back to the query originator. The architecture of PeerDB consists of three layers, namely the *P2P layer* that provides P2P capabilities (*e.g.* facilitates exchange of data and resource discovery), the *agent layer* that exploits agents as the workhorse, and the *object management layer* (which is also the application layer) that provides the data storage and processing capabilities.

PIER [16] is a massively distributed query engine built on top of a distributed hash table (DHT). It intends to bring database query processing facilities to widely distributed environments. PIER is a three-tier system organized as follows. Applications (at the higher-level) interact with PIER's Query Processor (at the middle-level) which utilizes an underlying DHT (at the lower-level) for data storage and retrieval. An instance of each DHT and PIER Query Processor component runs on every participating node. PIER currently implements a particular kind of DHTs, called Content Addressable Network (CAN) [37]. The main difference between PIER and APPA is that APPA's basic and advanced services run on top of any kind of super-peer and structured P2P network whereas PIER is dependent on DHTs.

OceanStore [22] is a utility infrastructure designed to span the globe and provide continuous access to persistent information. It envisions a cooperative utility model in which consumers pay a monthly fee in exchange for access to persistent storage. Such utility should be highly-available from anywhere in the network, employ automatic replication for disaster recovery, use strong security by default, and provide performance that is similar to that of existing LAN-based networked storage systems under many circumstances. Services should be provided by a confederation of companies. Users would pay their fee to one particular "utility provider", although they could consume storage and bandwidth resource from many different providers; providers would buy and sell capacity among themselves to make up the difference. Since this infrastructure is comprised of untrusted servers, data is protected through redundancy and cryptographic techniques. To improve performance, data is allowed to be cached anywhere, anytime. Additionally, monitoring of usage patterns allows adaptation to regional outages and denial of service attacks; monitoring also enhances performance through pro-active movement of data. OceanStore relies on Tapestry [51], an overlay location and routing infrastructure, such as DHTs, that provides location-independent routing of messages directly to the closest copy of an object or service using only point-to-point links and without centralized resources. There are two main differences between OceanStore and APPA. First, OceanStore depends on a specific overlay location and routing infrastructure (*i.e.* Tapestry) whereas the basic and advanced services of APPA may be deployed over any super-peer or structured overlay network. Second, the utility model of OceanStore assumes an infrastructure comprised of servers connected by high-speed links whereas APPA does not rely on servers or fast links.

P-Grid [1] is a peer-to-peer lookup system based on a virtual distributed search tree, similarly structured as standard distributed hash tables. In P-Grid, each peer holds part of the overall tree depending on its path, *i.e.* the binary bit string representing the subset of the tree's information that the peer is responsible for. A decentralized and self-organizing process builds the P-Grid's routing infrastructure which is adapted to a given distribution of data keys stored by peers. This process also addresses uniform load distribution of data storage and uniform replication of data to support uniform availability. On top of P-Grid's lookup system, other self-organizing services may be implemented (*e.g.* identity, adaptive media dissemination, trust management). Unlike APPA, that is independent of the overlay network, P-Grid relies on a specific virtual distributed search tree.

Like P-Grid, other structured P2P systems usually provide a basic lookup infrastructure on top of which other services and applications may be deployed. For instance, over Chord's lookup system, we find services as i3 [23], a large-scale reliable multicast, and applications such as CFS (Cooperative File System) [11], a peer-to-peer read-only storage system that provides provable guarantees for the efficiency, robustness, and load-balancing of file storage and retrieval. Likewise, on top of the Pastry object location and routing substrate [39] we find PAST [40], a large-scale peer-to-peer persistent storage utility that manages data storage and caching, and SCRIBE [6], an application-level implementation of anycast for highly dynamic groups.

9. Conclusion

In this chapter, we discussed the design and implementation of APPA (Atlas Peer-to-Peer Architecture), a P2P system for supporting advanced applications which must deal with semantically rich data (*e.g.* XML documents, relational tables, etc.). Such applications typically have a collaborative nature as in distributed scientific experimentation where scientists wish to share data and programs.

APPA has a network-independent architecture that can be implemented over various structured and super-peer P2P networks. It provides network services (peer id assignment, peer linking, peer communication, key-based storage and retrieval, etc), basic services (persistent data management, peer management, group membership) and advanced services such as schema management, replication and query processing. The main advantage of such architecture is to be able to exploit rapid and continuing progress in P2P networks.

APPA uses novel solutions for persistent data management, data replication and query processing. APPA provides data persistence with high availability through replication by using multiple hash functions. It also addresses efficiently the problem of retrieving current replicas based on timestamping. APPA also provides a higher-level replication service with multi-master replication. This service enables asynchronous collaboration among users. In order to resolve conflicting updates, we use a distributed semantic-based reconciliation algorithm which exploits parallelism. Query processing in APPA deals with schema-based queries and considers data replication. The main phases of query processing are query reformulation on a common schema description, query matching to find relevant peers, query optimization to select best peers, and query decomposition and execution. APPA also supports Top-k queries as a way to reduce network communication.

We have started the implementation of APPA using the JXTA framework. APPA's advanced services are provided as JXTA community services. Only the P2P network layer of the APPA implementation depends on the JXTA platform. Thus, APPA is portable and can be used over other platforms by replacing the services of the P2P network layer. We validated some of the APPA's services on the cluster of Paris team at INRIA, which has 64 nodes. Additionally, in order to study the scalability of these services with larger numbers of nodes, we implemented simulators using Java and SimJava. The current version of the APPA prototype and its service simulators manage data using a Chord DHT. Experimental results showed that simulators are well calibrated and the implemented services have good performance and scale up. Implementing on top of JXTA was relatively easy, but we faced some problems to adapt JXTA core services and to deploy the APPA prototype for tests using the JXTA framework.

References

[1] Aberer, K., Cudré-Mauroux, P., Datta, A., Despotovic, Z., Hauswirth, M., Punceva, M., and Schmidt, R. P-Grid: A Self-organizing Structured P2P System. *ACM SIGMOD Record, 32(3)*, 2003.

[2] Abiteboul, S., Bonifati, A., Cobena, G., Manolescu, I., and Milo, T. Dynamic XML documents with distribution and replication. *ACM SIGMOD Conf.*, 2003.

[3] Akbarinia, R., Martins, V., Pacitti, E., and Valduriez, P. Replication and query processing in the APPA data management system. *Distributed Data & Structures 6 (WDAS)*. Records of the 6th Int. Meeting (Lausanne, Switzerland), Waterloo. Carleton Scientific, 2004.

[4] Akbarinia, R., Martins, V., Pacitti, E., and Valduriez, P. Top-k Query Processing in the APPA P2P System. *Int. Conf. on High Performance Computing for Computational Science (VecPar -2006)*, 2006.

[5] Bhargava, A., Kothapalli, K., Riley, C., Scheideler, C., and Thober, M. Pagoda: A Dynamic Overlay Network for Routing, Data Management, and Multicasting. *Proc of ACM SPAA*, 2004.

[6] Castro, M., Druschel, P., Kermarrec, A-M., and Rowstron, A. SCRIBE: A large-scale and decentralized application-level multicast infrastructure. *IEEE Journal on Selected Areas in Communication (JSAC), 20(8)*, 2002.

[7] Castro, M., Jones, M. B., Kermarrec, A., Rowstron, A., Theimer, M., Wang, H., and Wolman, A. An Evaluation of Scalable Application-level Multicast Built Using Peer-to-peer Overlays. *IEEE Infocom*, 2003.

[8] Chaudhuri, S., and Gravano, L. Evaluating Top-k Selection queries. *VLDB Conf.*, 1999.

[9]   Chockler, G., Keidar, I., and Vitenberg, R. Group communication specifications: a comprehensive study. *ACM Computing Surveys*, 33(427-469), 2001.

[10] Clarke, I., Miller, S., Hong, T.W., Sandberg, O., and Wiley, B. Protecting Free Expression Online with Freenet. *IEEE Internet Computing, 6(1)*, 2002.

[11] Dabek, F. Kaashoek, M. F., Karger, D., Morris, R., and Stoica, I. Wide-area cooperative storage with CFS. *ACM Symp. on Operating Systems Principles (SOSP)*, 2001.

[12] Gnutella. http://www.gnutelliums.com/.

[13] Grid'5000 Project. http://www.grid5000.fr/.

[14] Howell, F. and McNab, R. SimJava: a discrete event simulation package for Java with applications in computer systems modeling. *Int. Conf. on Web-based Modeling and Simulation*, 1998.

[15] http://www.irisa.fr/paris/General/cluster.htm.

[16] Huebsch, R., Hellerstein, J., Lanham, N., Thau Loo, B., Shenker, S., and Stoica, I. Querying the Internet with PIER. *VLDB Conf.*, 2003.

[17] Iamnitchi, A., Ripeanu, M., and Foster, I. Locating data in (small world?) peer-to-peer scientific collaborations. *Int. Workshop on P2P Systems (IPTPS)*, 2002.

[18] JDF. http://jdf.jxta.org/.

[19] JXTA. http://www.jxta.org/.

[20] Kazaa. http://www.kazaa.com/.

[21] Kermarrec, A-M., Rowstron, A., Shapiro, M. and Druschel P. The IceCube approach to the reconciliation of diverging replicas. *ACM Symp. on Principles of Distributed Computing*, 2001.

[22] Kubiatowicz, J., Bindel, D., Chen, Y., Czerwinski, S., Eaton, P., Geels, D., Gummadi, R., Rhea, S., Weatherspoon, H., Weimer, W., Wells, C., and Zhao, B. OceanStore: An Architecture for Global-Scale Persistent Storage. *Int. Conf. on Architectural Support for Programming Languages and Operating Systems (ASPLOS)*, 2000.

[23] Lakshminarayanan, K., Rao, A., Stoica, I., and Shenker, S. Flexible and Robust Large Scale Multicast using i3. Tech. Rep. CS-02-1187, University of California – Berkeley, 2002.

[24] Levy, A., Rajaraman, A., and Ordille, J. Querying heterogeneous information sources using source descriptions. *VLDB Conf.*, 1996.

[25] Martins, V., Pacitti, E., and Valduriez, P. A Dynamic Distributed Algorithm for Semantic Reconciliation. *Distributed Data & Structures 7 (WDAS)*, 2006.

[26] Martins, V., Pacitti, E., and Valduriez, P. Distributed Semantic Reconciliation of Replicated Data. *Journées Francophones sur la Cohérence des Données en Univers Réparti (CDUR)*, 2005.

[27] Meteor. http://meteor.jxta.org/.

[28] Nejdl, W., Siberski, W., and Sintek, M. Design issues and challenges for RDF- and schema-based peer-to-peer systems. *ACM SIGMOD Record, 32(3)*, 2003.

[29] Nejdl, W., Wolf, B., Qu, C., Decker, S., Sintek, M., Naeve, A., Nilsson, M., Palmér, M., and Risch, T. EDUTELLA: a P2P networking infrastructure based on RDF. *Int. World Wide Web conf. (WWW)*, 2002.

[30] Ooi, B., Shu, Y., and Tan, K-L. Relational data sharing in peer-based data management systems. *ACM SIGMOD Record, 32(3)*, 2003.

[31] Özsu, T., and Valduriez, P. *Principles of Distributed Database Systems*. 2nd Edition, Prentice Hall, 1999.

[32] Pacitti, E. and Simon, E. Update propagation strategies to improve freshness in lazy master replicated databases. *The VLDB Journal, 8(3-4)*, 2000.

[33] Pacitti, E., and Dedieu, O. Algorithms for optimistic replication on the Web. *Journal of the Brazilian Computing Society, 8(2)*, 2002.

[34] Pacitti, E., Özsu, T., and Coulon, C. Preventive multi-master replication in a cluster of autonomous databases. *Euro-Par Conf.*, 2003.

[35] Preguiça, N., Shapiro, M. and Matheson, C. Semantics-based reconciliation for collaborative and mobile environments. *Int. Conf. on Cooperative Information Systems (CoopIS)*, 2003.

[36] Ramsey, N. and Csirmaz, E. An Algebraic Approach to File Synchronization. *ACM Int. Symp. on Foundations of Software Engineering*, 2001.

[37] Ratnasamy, S., Francis, P., Handley, M., Karp, R., and Shenker, S. A scalable content-addressable network. *Proc. of SIGCOMM*, 2001.

[38] Ratnasamy, S., Handley, M., Karp, R., and Shenker, S. Application-level Multicast using Content-Addressable Networks. *Proc of Networked Group Communication*, 2001.

[39] Rowstron, A. and Druschel, P. Pastry: Scalable, distributed object location and routing for large-scale peer-to-peer systems. *IFIP/ACM Int. Conf. on Distributed Systems Platforms (Middleware)*, 2001.

[40] Rowstron, A., and Druschel, P. Storage management and caching in PAST, a large-scale, persistent peer-to-peer storage utility. *ACM Symp. on Operating Systems Principles (SOSP)*, 2001.

[41] Saito, Y. and Shapiro, M. Optimistic Replication. *ACM Computing Surveys, 37(1)*, 2005.

[42] Schlosser, M., Sintek, M., Decker, S., and Nejdl, W. HyperCuP—Hypercubes, Ontologies and Efficient Search on P2P Networks. *Int. Workshop on Agents and Peer-to-Peer Computing*, 2002.

[43] Siong Ng, W., Ooi, B., Tan, k.L., and Zhou, A. PeerDB: A P2P-based System for Distributed Data Sharing. *Int. Conf. on Data Engineering (ICDE)*, 2003.

[44] Stoica, I., Morris, R., Karger, D. R., Kaashoek, M. F. and Balakrishnan, H. Chord: A scalable peer-to-peer lookup service for internet applications. *Proc. of ACM SIGCOMM*, 2001.

[45] Tanaka, A., and Valduriez, P. The Ecobase environmental information system: applications, architecture and open issues. *ACM SIGMOD Record, 3(5-6)*, 2000.

[46] Tatarinov, I., Ives, Z.G., Madhavan, J., Halevy, A., Suciu, D., Dalvi, N., Dong, X., Kadiyska, Y., Miklau, G., and Mork, P. The Piazza peer data management project. *ACM SIGMOD Record 32(3)*, 2003.

[47] Théodoloz, N. *DHT-based Routing and Discovery in JXTA*. Master Thesis, École Polytechnique Fédérale de Lausanne, 2004.

[48] Tomasic, A., Raschid, L., and Valduriez, P. Scaling access to heterogeneous data sources with DISCO. *IEEE Trans. on Knowledge and Data Engineering, 10(5)*, 1998.

[49] Valduriez, P. Parallel Database Systems: open problems and new issues. *Distributed and Parallel Databases, 1(2)*, 1993.

[50] Whittaker, S., Issacs, e., and O'Day, V. Widening the Net: Workshop report on the theory and practice of physical and network communities. *ACM SIGCHI Bulletin*, 29(3), 1997.

[51] Zhao, B. Y., Huang, L., Stribling, J., Rhea, S. C., Joseph, A. D., and Kubiatowicz, J. D. Tapestry: A Resilient Global-Scale Overlay for Service Deployment. *IEEE Journal on Selected Areas in Communications, 22(1)*, 2004.

Global Data Management
R. Baldoni et al. (Eds.)
IOS Press, 2006

Epidemic Dissemination for Probabilistic Data Storage

Hugo Miranda [a], Simone Leggio [b], Luís Rodrigues [a] and Kimmo Raatikainen [b]

[a] *Universidade de Lisboa*
Departamento de Informática
[b] *University of Helsinki*
Computer Science Department

Abstract. In Mobile Ad-Hoc Networks (MANETs) we are often faced with the problem of sharing information among a (potentially large) set of nodes. The replication of data items among different nodes of a MANET is an efficient technique to increase data availability and improve the latency of data access. However, an efficient replication scheme requires a scalable method to disseminate updates. The robustness and scalability of gossip (or epidemic) protocols make them an efficient tool for message dissemination in large scale wired and wireless networks. This chapter describes a novel algorithm to replicate and retrieve data items among nodes in a MANET that is based on a epidemic dissemination scheme. Our approach is tailored to the concrete network environment of MANETs and, while embedding several ideas from existing gossip protocols, takes into account the topology, scarcity of resources, and limited availability of both the devices and the network links in this sort of networks.

Keywords. Epidemic Algorithms, MANET, Distributed Data Storage

1. Introduction

Epidemic, or probabilistic, communication is a paradigm that mimics an efficient dissemination process found in the social and natural worlds. A virus makes use of each infected host as a new propagation agent, exponentially increasing the number of infected hosts. History has shown that epidemic dissemination is an effective way for spreading diseases, news and gossips.

In epidemic protocols, each process (node) acts as a message dissemination agent, propagating messages to other processes. Epidemic protocols are an interesting approach for message passing in large scale networks because they are decentralized. Nodes cooperate to deliver messages independently of the failure of other nodes and without the need of a complete or accurate view of the list of members. Due to their probabilistic nature, epidemic protocols cannot ensure (deterministic) reliable delivery. With small probability, a node may never be selected for infection and, therefore, may not receive one or more messages. Nevertheless, this sort of probabilistic guarantees are suitable for many large scale applications, with hundreds or thousands of participants, where ensuring a consistent state would be prohibitively hard and a resource consuming task. Good examples of target applications for epidemic protocols are network games, news feeds, etc.

Mobile Ad-hoc Networks (MANETs) constitute a challenging networking environment, due to the characteristics of the nodes, and to the dynamic nature of the network itself. In a MANET, the topology may be continuously changing, either because nodes join or leave the network, or simply because nodes move in the space. These events may result in temporary disruptions in the communication or network partitions.

The instability of the network is augmented by the fact that the wireless link often exhibits a low reliability, and that the nodes are powered with batteries, which have a limited lifetime. A node may therefore depart from the network abruptly and without notification. The network must be self-capable of performing maintenance operations and cope with the disappearance of a node or of a wireless link.

Changes in network topology affect a MANET especially from two points of view: first, the route between a given pair source-destination may become unavailable, and the network must be able to repair it. The later operation is performed by the routing protocols. Secondly, the failure of a node causes the unavailability of the services that the node was providing. One solution for avoiding that a service becomes unavailable in a MANET consists in replicating such a service among multiple nodes in the network.

The routing protocol tackles with the problem of route loss, by discovering and maintaining alternative routes to a destination. A data storage service may tackle the problem of data loss due to node departure, by keeping several copies of each data item in different nodes, such that each item can always be retrieved by other nodes with high probability. Note that. in general, centralized solutions must be avoided in MANETs, as they introduce a single point of failure in the network. Decentralized solutions are, therefore, favored.

Solutions for decentralized storage of data in MANETs must fulfill some requirements to comply with the characteristics of the networking environment where they are deployed. Data replication is the most important requirement. Efficient distribution is achieved if the items are replicated among nodes in the network, for reasons of availability, as describe above, but not only. MANETs are often characterized by conditions of poor connectivity among nodes. It is thus expensive that the request for a given data item is satisfied by a node that is several hops far away from the querying node. Returning the reply would involve building the route from source to destination; if the two nodes are far away, the probability that the route fails is higher. Moreover, processing the reply message drains the batteries of the intermediary hops along the path. Ideally, thus, data should be replicated to achieve a geographical even distribution of items in the MANET, so that all the queries are replied by the close neighbors of a querying node.

Data replication should not be over-redundant, as storage space is another limited resource in the nodes of a MANET. Unnecessarily storing a replica in a node's cache may prevent that node from storing a more useful item, in the context of the even distribution. In order to cope with the limited resources of the devices, such as batteries or processing power, the solution for efficient data spreading should not require an excessive amount of control messages, neither it should be computationally heavy.

Data replication algorithms for MANETs have several interesting applications. Research on ad-hoc networks has been initially targeted to support military applications; a battlefield scenario could benefit from an algorithm for replicating information among nodes, no matter the data source is a central point (like e.g., the command head quarters) or decentralized (e.g., measurements taken by soldiers on the field). Civil applications may also benefit from algorithms for cooperative data caching. For example, an ad-hoc wireless LAN could be formed in the campus of a university by the devices carried by students, professors or visitors. Information about e.g., campus services, could be requested on-demand without overloading the infrastructure of the campus network, and relayed by the nodes closest to the requesting one. An algorithm that takes care of efficiently replicating the data is very useful for the purpose; it could support a service discovery protocol so that also search for services is performed according to the algorithm logic.

PCache is an algorithm for efficiently replicating and retrieving data items in a MANET. PCache uses an epidemic approach to perform the data dissemination operation required for data replication. However, the probabilistic dissemination procedure is biased by a combination of semantic information (such as which items are replicated in each node) and topology information (collected at the link layer) to achieve an even geographical distribution of replicated data items in the MANET. As a result, PCache is typically able to satisfy requests for data items using a small number of messages. In favorable conditions, that depend on the number of nodes in the MANET, the size of their caches, and the total number of items present in the network, PCache is capable of placing a copy of most data items within the 1-hop neighborhood of any node.

This chapter presents recent results on the "data gathering" algorithm of PCache, used for retrieving all data items satisfying a given condition. Data gathering relies on a probabilistic broadcast algorithm for efficiently disseminating the query message. For completeness, the chapter briefly introduces the remaining components of PCache. An extensive description and evaluation of the replication and single item query algorithms for PCache can be found elsewhere [1].

The performance of probabilistic protocols in MANETs depends on factors not present in wired networks. The impact of these factors in the performance of probabilistic protocols in MANETs is exemplified by comparing two implementations of the query dissemination algorithm for data gathering: one where the decision to retransmit depends only of a random number generator local at each node and one taking in account the distance between the nodes.

The rest of the chapter is divided as follows: Section 2 describes the main concepts of gossiping and the parameters affecting a gossip protocol. Section 3 presents examples of cooperative caching algorithms, in a variety of networking environments. Section 4 illustrates the PCache algorithm, and how data items are disseminated in the network, providing a brief evaluation of the replication algorithm. Section 5 presents how PCache nodes are able to retrieve replicated items, distinguishing between retrieval of a single item by means of a key-value search filter and a conditional search where only items matching given conditions are returned. Finally, Section 6 summarizes the main issues addressed by this chapter.

2. Overview of Gossip Protocols

Gossip protocols are a scalable strategy to disseminate data in a large network. Figure 1 exemplifies the use of a gossip protocol to disseminate message m sent by the application running in node A. When the gossip protocol receives a message from the application, it

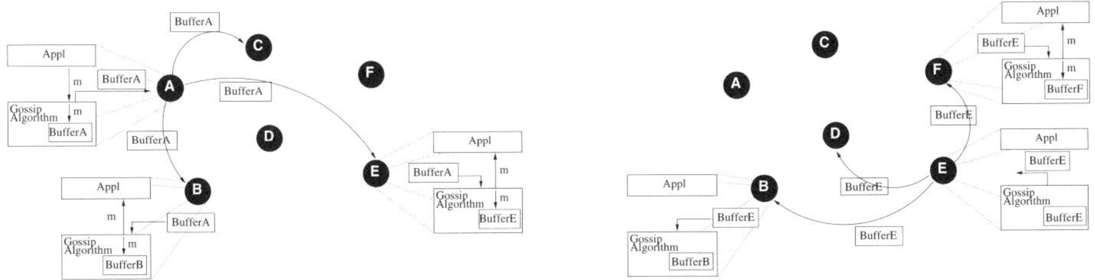

(a) Initial dissemination by the source   (b) Propagation of the message by node E

Figure 1. Dissemination of a message in a generic gossip system

adds the message to its buffer for dissemination. The protocol works in rounds. At every round, each node sends the content of its buffer to a predefined number of other participants. The number of nodes to whom the buffer is sent is called the *fanout*. Destinations of the buffer are randomly selected from a list kept locally at each node, hereafter named the *view* of the node.

After receiving a buffer, each node compares its content with the messages stored in its local buffer. A message not present in the local buffer is considered as a new message. New messages are passed (delivered) to the application and stored in the local buffer. In Figure 1(a), the buffer of node A was sent to nodes B, C and E. After inspecting the content of the buffer, the three nodes notice the presence of the new message m, deliver it to the application and store a copy in the local buffer. Similar steps are executed for any other message not present in the receiver's buffer. All nodes in the network execute the same procedure, i.e., they periodically gossip their buffers to a number of randomly selected targets. Figure 1(b) shows the case for node E. The node randomly selects three other participants, nodes B, D and F as targets for its buffer. The buffer will "infect" nodes D and F with m, that will deliver the message to the application. Since node B had previously stored m in its buffer, B does not deliver the message again to the application. Message m is kept in the buffer of node B.

2.1. Configurable Parameters

For simplicity, the previous example has omitted a number of particularities of different gossip protocols. In general, gossip protocols can be characterised by:

Message dissemination policy That dictates which, and what part of the messages in the buffer are sent on each round;

Buffer management Conditioning the size and the replacement of messages in the buffer;

Fanout or the number of nodes that will receive a buffer update at each round;

Membership That defines how nodes will enter and abandon the list of participants.

The implications of each of these factors on the performance of the gossip protocols are addressed below.

2.1.1. Message Dissemination Policy

Sending the entire content of the buffer can be an expensive operation consuming a large amount of bandwidth. An alternative is to use another unreliable but less costly mechanism (e.g. IP Multicast) to perform the initial deliver of each message and then use gossip to disseminate some unique ID of the messages stored at each buffer. A node could then compare the IDs of the messages on its buffer with those present in the buffer of other nodes to detect those that it did not receive. Requests and deliveries of the messages found to be missing may use some reliable delivery protocol like TCP. An example of this policy is bimodal multicast [2].

A second dimension of the message dissemination policy selects the messages to be sent on each round. In *unlimited gossiping*, all messages stored at the buffer are disseminated in each round. In *limited gossip* a bound is placed on the number of times that each node forwards a message. For example, lpbcast [3] handles differently new and old messages. Messages that entered the buffer during the last round are fully included in the gossip. On the contrary, only some unique identification of a random subset of older messages is included in the gossip. Nodes receiving the ID of a message that is not present in its buffers follow the algorithm of bimodal multicast and use some reliable protocol to request it to one of the participants.

In [4] message dissemination is further restricted by tagging each message with an integer, known as the *message age*. Prior to transmission, each node decrements the *message age*. The message ceases to be forwarded when its age reaches zero.

2.1.2. Buffer Management

In gossip protocols, the buffer performs two roles: it stores the messages to be disseminated in later rounds and detects message duplicates, preventing its delivery to the application. Optimizations can reduce the resources required for detecting duplicates for example by storing only a unique message ID or by keeping a list with the sequence number of the last message received from every other participant.

The buffer management must implement a policy to select the messages to be discarded when the buffer is full. It should be noted that, to be able to reply to requests for missing messages from other nodes, and independently of the policy, the buffer must be large enough to keep the messages for some time. A minimal buffer size will therefore, be dictated by the number of producers and the rate at which new messages are produced. Three policies have been proposed concerning the selection of messages to be discarded:

FIFO Purging The First-In-First-Out policy removes messages by the order of arrival at the buffer;

Random Purging Nodes randomly select some message for being discarded;

Semantic Purging The system preferably purges messages that have become obsolete by later messages.

Experimental comparisons suggest that FIFO provides better results than Random Purging [5,6]. In Semantic Purging [7] applications tag messages to indicate which of the past messages become obsolete. The gossip protocol uses this information to learn which messages are more adequate for removal. Applications of semantic purging are limited to specific cases where frequent updates render previous information obsolete. This is the case, for example, of the updates to the location of the players in distributed games or frequently updated quotes at the stock exchange market.

2.1.3. Fanout and Number of Rounds

The fanout is the number of destinations that will receive a node's buffer on each round. The higher the fanout, the more traffic is generated on the network and higher the load on the nodes in dispatching and inspecting incoming buffers. On the other hand, a small fanout may dictate a low probability of having a message delivered to all nodes.

To find an adequate proportion between the fanout and the number of nodes, [4] modeled a gossip protocol as a bins and balls problem. In the protocol presented in the paper, each message is forwarded only if received in the previous round. The age of the message is incremented on every transmission, until it exceeds a predefined limit, after which it is no longer retransmitted. The authors concluded that in this algorithm there is an high probability of having the message delivered to all nodes in a group of size n for a fanout greater or equal to $2e\frac{\ln n}{\ln \ln n}$ if the minimum age is $O(\log n)$. The same study also concluded that for a fixed fanout of 12, an adequate minimal age will depend on the number of nodes and is given by $O(\sqrt{n})$.

2.1.4. Membership

Until now, it was assumed that nodes know at least some of their neighbors, so that they can address messages to them. Two alternatives have been developed for managing the membership information in gossip systems.

In the *server-based model*, the list of participants is known in its entirety by one or more servers. These are responsible for the admission of new members and for distributing partial views of the membership to every node.

In decentralized approaches, joining nodes subscribe by contacting with any participant. In lpbcast [3], the contact node becomes responsible for disseminating the new subscription by advertising it in the following round. Nodes receiving the subscription will randomly select it to be included in its view and to advertise it.

2.2. Gossiping in MANETs

In wireless networks, the number of nodes listening to each broadcast is determined by the transmission power of the sender. Wireless networks have a significantly lower reliability and the broadcast nature of the media increases the probability of collisions and contention. The application of gossip protocols defined for wired, large scale networks, in the particular environment of wireless networks would result in weak performance and in the waste of the precious resources of the devices. Some recent research has been focused on finding adaptations of gossip protocols to fully exploit this particular environment.

Route Driven Gossip (RDG) [8] is an example of adaptation of gossip protocols to the particularities of MANETs. RDG exploits the topological information made available by routing protocols for ad-hoc networks like DSR [9] to reduce the number of messages required for maintaining a consistent membership and to reduce the overhead of the message delivery. In RDG, each node keeps a view that only includes nodes for which the routing protocol has a route in the cache. The view may be locally updated as a result of link failures or the adding of new routes, learned by the routing protocol. In the scope of MANETs, RDG is an interesting example of adaptation in the sense that it reduces to a minimum the number of route discoveries required for the nodes in a a view to communicate.

Many link layer protocols for ad-hoc networks lack the coordination mechanism to fully prevent collisions. Collisions may result in wasted bandwidth and battery power. The problem is addressed as a side-effect of a gossiping-based routing protocol for ad-hoc networks presented in [10]. The authors present several variations that make the decision to retransmit a route discovery message depend of factors like some probability or the number of nodes that have already retransmitted. The authors observe that gossiping is particularly affected by the gossiping probability and by the network topology. They find that a gossiping probability between 0.6 and 0.8 suffice for ensuring high reachability of nodes in the network and allows to reduce the number of messages sent to the network by 35%, when compared to basic flooding.

2.3. Using Gossip to Support Replication

PCache exploits the broadcast nature of the media to define for each node a trivial view composed by the nodes within its transmission range. Although for wireless networks, this approach follows the same principle proposed for wired networks in Directional Gossip [11]. In this protocol, members in the same local area network tend to participate in the views of each other. An interesting property of the implementation of the gossip protocol in PCache is that the entire view of each node can be reached by a single transmission. Therefore, PCache has a dynamic fanout given by the view size. Furthermore, the view exhibits locality, which has been identified as an advantageous property for views in wired networks for reducing the traffic (see for example [11,12]). However, this algorithm is more vulnerable to the creation of clusters, that emerge from the absence of distant nodes from the views.

PCache combines the mechanisms presented in [10,13,14] to define a fully decentralized broadcast algorithm that adapts the number of retransmissions to the number of nodes in the neighborhood. Furthermore, the broadcast algorithm privileges retransmissions from the nodes that are more distant to the source, thus providing higher coverage of the network with a smaller number of retransmissions. The performance of the PCache broadcast algorithm is evaluated in Section 5.

3. Cooperative Caching in MANETs

Distributing replicas of each data item is an effective way to achieve data availability and reduce latency in MANETs. However, the limited resources of the devices must be considered in the estimation of the number of replicas of each data item to be stored. Most of the research in distributed storage follows some deterministic algorithm for deciding the location of the replicas. In the majority of the cases, the goal is to store replicas of the data close to the nodes that are more likely to access it in the future. Estimation of future requirements is based for example on the history of previous accesses or by preferences indicated by the user.

The frequency of the accesses to the data items is used in [15] to define three deterministic algorithms for the allocation of replicas. Neighborhood awareness is taken into account as well, by eliminating replica duplication among neighboring nodes or group of nodes. The results show that neighbor awareness improves the accessibility of data item, at the expenses on more traffic in the network to maintain neighborhood information.

In autonomous gossiping[16] the data items themselves try to identify other hosts which may be interested in the item, based on the data item's own profile and host's profile, advertised during registration phase. This approach is in contrast to the traditional push model were data items are injected in the networks by the possessor nodes. Profiles are maintained in a distributed self-organizing way, and updated using gossiping techniques. When data items arrive at a node, the autonomous gossiping algorithm is applied to decide what the data item will do, in an autonomous and self-organizing fashion. Data items in a host decide whether continue to reside, migrate or replicate to another host.

The replication model presented in[17,18] assumes the presence of a single data source in the ad-hoc network. In[17], queries are unicast, addressed to the data source, and if a node in the path has either the data cached locally or the path to a node that holds the queried item, a reply is immediately returned to the querying node; otherwise, the request is forwarded to the data source. A hybrid approach combining the benefit of data and path caching is shown to be the best performing one. In[18] the querying scheme is broadcast; a four-way handshake is implemented to prevent nodes from receiving more than one reply to a given issued query. We deem that such a scheme is useful when the target data item is large in size. If the advertised items are small, it may be faster to send directly the queried item. The performance of both algorithms depends of the location of the querying node and of the previous queries for the same item.

Instead of using knowledge gathered from past experiences or user preferences, PCache relies on random distribution for (expectedly) placing a replica close to each node in the network. PCache is adequate for cases where it is not possible to infer future accesses to the data from past experiences or when the queries to a data item are uniformly distributed over the network. The randomness of the distribution is enhanced by having nodes to apply corrective measures based on partial advertisements of the state of neighboring nodes, piggybacked in replication and query messages.

A rationale similar to the one followed in PCache was applied for data forwarding in[19,20]. The authors propose to enhance data forwarding by having nodes to randomly distribute their cached contents to a random set of neighbors. If data received with a message does not fit into the cache of the node, then existing data are replaced by the new data. This shuffling ensures that an immediate neighbor gets a replica of the information being spread, and at the same time allows redistributing evenly the data among all the nodes of the networks. The algorithm is proactive, as dissemination is done in periodic gossiping rounds.

4. PCache: Probabilistic Storage in MANETs

This section gives an overview of the PCache replication algorithm. Contrary to usual applications of epidemic protocols, the algorithm does not aim at delivering every message to all participants. Instead, and taking into consideration the limited resources of the devices, the algorithm tries to geographically distribute the replicas of the stored items so that upon an application request, the item can be found in some node close to the source of the request, preferably in its view, defined by the nodes in its 1-hop neighborhood. Data items are replicated using a gossip algorithm requiring a small number of messages.

PCache is a reactive protocol in the sense that it only generates packets to satisfy the requests of applications. In the replication process, nodes cooperate to provide an adequate distribution of the replicas of new or updated versions of data items. The replication component of PCache makes use of three complementary mechanisms: an efficient best-effort probabilistic broadcast mechanism; a distributed algorithm for deciding which nodes replicate a given data item and a data shuffling mechanism to improve the distribution of data replicas. Nodes cooperate by replacing parts of the content of the gossip message with excerpts of the local cache to enhance distribution. Probabilities are used to remove determinism, increasing efficiency. The algorithm prevents broadcast storms by limiting the number of forwarding nodes. Furthermore, nodes are selected for forwarding depending on the expectations of the additional coverage that their transmission will provide. A more in depth description of the PCache algorithm for distributed data storage can be found elsewhere [1].

There are several interesting applications for our algorithm. For example, PCache can be used to implement a distributed name service (nodes would advertise their domain name and address), a service discovery protocol, or a directory service for a peer-to-peer file system.

This section begins by presenting the structure of the cache at each node and the content of PCache messages, and then provides a description and evaluation of the replication process.

4.1. Cache Structure

Each node in a PCache system has a cache (buffer) of a limited and predefined size. The cache is used to store replicas of a fraction of all the data items advertised. Each data item is composed of a key, a value, an expiration time and a version number with application dependent semantics. Data items are uniquely identified by its key. PCache stores at most one version of each data item in its cache. Because preference is given to the version with the highest number, it can be said that PCache implements a limited form of semantic purging.

Nodes continuously pursue a better distribution of the items, by varying the content of their caches. The goal of PCache is to provide an adequate distribution of data items so that each node is able to find a significant proportion of the total items in its cache or in the cache of the neighbors within its transmission range.

Nodes always try to keep their caches full, occupying all free space before beginning to overwrite cache entries. The system does not require the caches at all nodes to be of the same size but proposes a common format and cache update policy.

Each data item is stored in cache together with auxiliary information to support an adequate distribution of replicas . The popularity ranking counts the number of times that a node listened for the item in the messages it received. The *eraseCandidate* flag helps to leverage item distribution by suggesting the items that are more adequate for replacement.

A data item is said to be owned by the node who initiated its advertisement after an application request. To ensure that at least one copy of each item exists, nodes do not replace the items they own with items advertised by other nodes. It is assumed that owned items are stored in a separate region of the memory space of the devices so that the space available for caching third-party records is kept constant.

4.2. Message Content

PCache messages share a common header that describes the type of message (replication, query or reply), a *time to live* (TTL) field, decremented by each node that forwards the message, and additional information concerning the items it carries and their relation with the state of the cache of other nodes.

The fields *source*, containing the address of the node that created the message and *serial number*, containing a number local to each node and incremented at every message it creates, are used to uniquely identify a PCache message. To identify duplicates, nodes keep a record of the messages recently received. In PCache, it is common to have messages to be forwarded and edited by multiple hops. We define the source of a message as the node who created it and defined the value for the *source* and *serial number* fields. Messages are edited and forwarded by multiple *senders* which are not allowed to change the content of these fields.

Items are stored in an application dependent format, transparent for PCache. Similarly to some routing protocols ([9]), query messages accumulate the path to be used by a reply in a field, here identified as *route stack*. The header also carries information to help to leverage the distribution of items. This is the case of a field named *time from storage* (TFS).

4.3. Broadcast Algorithm

A probabilistic broadcast algorithm is used for forwarding replication and query messages, although with some differences, highlighted in the respective sections. It should be noted that the algorithm does not intend to deliver the messages to all nodes with high probability. Instead, the retrieval of a data item from the network is guaranteed by the combination of both the replication and retrieval procedures and by the replication of the data items. This allows to use an unreliable broadcast algorithm, focused on the reduction of the number of messages. The broadcast algorithm puts together a mechanism to limit the number of retransmissions when compared to flooding (similar to those in [10,13]) and a protocol that uses the receiving power of messages to optimize the propagation of the message [13,14] and adapts them to an environment where the expectations of delivery are lower. It is assumed that the reception power of a message can be provided by the network card driver of the devices.

The algorithm tries to reach the largest number of nodes with the lowest number of transmissions. Therefore, the algorithm privileges retransmissions performed by nodes located farther away from the previous sender, which have an higher probability of reaching a bigger number of the nodes that have not yet received the message. To limit the resource consumption of the nodes, the algorithm also prevents from retransmitting nodes whose contribution to the number of nodes covered is believed to be small.

For each message m, the broadcast algorithm works as follows. Each node receiving for the first time a copy of m will place it on hold. The hold time is proportional to the power with which the message was received. Disregarding any fading effects in the wireless media, it is expected that nodes more distant to the sender of m have a lower holding period. During the hold period, each node counts the number of duplicates of m it receives. Preliminary simulations showed that when nodes are uniformly distributed, a node listening to at least two retransmissions can discard the message without negatively influencing the coverage of the message dissemination procedure. Therefore, a node will retransmit m if it has listened to less than two retransmissions of the message at the end of the message holding period. The message will be marked for dropping otherwise. The handling of a message is dependent of its type (replication or query).

4.4. Replication Process

The rationale for the replication process is better explained assuming a configuration where nodes do not move and that nodes have unlimited cache size (so that entries in the cache are never replaced). In this scenario, the replication process provides a reasonable probability that all items are found within the transmission range of every node. However, even in situations of limited cache size and nodes mobility, the algorithm provides a reasonably even distribution of data items, as Section 4.6 will show. The replication algorithm mandates that, starting at the last storage, every third node propagating a replication message stores the advertised items. Complete determinism is removed from the algorithm by permitting other intermediary nodes to store the record, although with a small probability. In principle, this approach allows any intermediary node to have a copy within its 1-hop neighborhood; the copy would be located either in the node from which a message was received, or in the next hop (if it exists).

Replication of data items is triggered by the source node with the broadcast of a replication message. In replication messages, the *time from storage* (TFS) field indicates the distance (in number of hops) from the sender to the closest node that is known to have stored the items. Therefore, the source node sets the TFS field to zero to indicate that the records are stored in its local cache.

Each node receiving a replication message places it on hold for a period of time proportional to the reception power, as described in Section 4.3. During the hold period, the node counts the number of retransmissions listened and calculates *mintfs*, which is the lowest value of the TFS from the original message and of all retransmissions. At the end of the hold period, *mintfs* will indicate the distance in hops to the closest node(s) that stored a copy of the item.

When the hold period expires, the node uses the number of retransmissions listened, *mintfs* and a random number generator to decide for one of three possible actions:

- If a node listens to two or more retransmissions and *mintfs* < 2, following the rationale of the broadcast algorithm, it can safely discard the message. Listening to two or more retransmissions suggests that the propagation of the message in the neighborhood is being assured through some of the neighbors, so there is no need to further forward the message. A low value of *mintfs* (0 or 1) indicates that a close neighbor has stored the message, so it is advisable to reserve space in the cache for items carried in another message.

- The data item is stored in the node's cache and the message is retransmitted. This will be the action to execute with probability $e^{mintfs-2}$ if the first criteria did not apply. The probability of storing an item increases with the distance to the closest copy. In particular, if the closest copy is three hops away (signaled by a *mintfs* of two) a copy will always be stored in the node. Nodes executing this alternative will forward the replication message with the TFS field set to 0. As a consequence, the *mintfs* of neighbor nodes that did not terminated the hold period will be set to the lowest possible value and will have their probability of storing the item re-

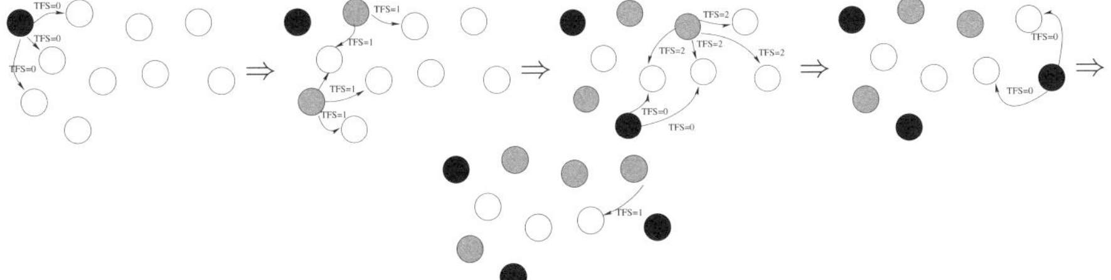

Figure 2. Progress in replication of an item

duced. From the above, it can also be concluded that TFS and *mintfs* are always bound between 0 and 2. PCache benefits from having some randomization associated with the decision of storing an item. $e^{mintfs-2}$ has shown to be adequate because it presents an exponential grow with the distance to the closest copy. The probability of storage for nodes with *mintfs* of zero or one is respectively 0.14 and 0.36.

- A message will be forwarded but the data will not be stored in the cache if none of the previous conditions applied. The TFS of the retransmission will be set to *mintfs*+1 to inform the listening nodes of the additional hop to the closest node that stored the item.

Figure 2 exemplifies a replication where all nodes are able to retrieve the item in its 1-hop neighborhood. Nodes that forwarded the message are represented in gray and nodes that stored and forwarded the item in black. Three copies of the item were stored. The first at the source node, the second due to randomness and the third because the node had a *mintfs* of two at the end of the holding period. For clarity, only a subset of the message receptions are represented.

4.5. Complementary Items

In complement to the information relevant for the action in progress, in PCache, all messages carry as many *Complementary items* as possible, without exceeding a predefined maximum message size. The role of Complementary items is to leverage an even geographical distribution of the information by mixing fractions of the cache of different nodes that have been forwarding the message and by letting neighbor nodes learn relevant information about the state of each other caches, without requiring a membership protocol. These items are not relevant for the operation taking place, but help in propagating data throughout the network. Complementary items are handled similarly regardless of the type of the message that carries them.

4.6. Performance of the Replication Algorithm

This section provides a brief overview of how the replication algorithm of PCache adapts to different networking environments. More detailed results, addressing other metrics and scenarios can be found in [1].

A prototype of PCache was implemented in the *ns-2* network simulator v 2.28. The simulated network is composed of 100 nodes uniformly disposed over a region with

1500mx500m. 10 different deployments of the nodes were randomly defined. The simulated network is an IEEE 802.11 at 2Mb/s. Network interfaces have a range of 250m using the Free Space propagation model.

Each run consists of 100 replications each performed by a different node in a time instant selected uniformly from the time interval between 1s and 290s. No warm up period is defined. 10 traffic files were generated.

The sensitivity of PCache to different parameters is evaluated by testing the parameter with different values while keeping the remaining consistent with the baseline configuration. In the baseline configuration, the cache of the nodes was defined for accepting at most 10 items, excluding owned items, which are stored in a separate region of the memory. Each data item has a size of 250 bytes (50 for the key and 200 for the value). In this configuration, a full cache occupies about 3KBytes, which is a small value. Bigger values of cache size improve the performance of PCache, as there is more storage space available in the network. The message size was limited to 1300 bytes. After removing the space required for the PCache header (estimated to be 13 bytes for the fixed part), a PCache message will carry at most 5 data items. All values presented below average 10 independent runs, combining one different random deployment of the nodes and one traffic file.

To reduce query traffic, PCache aims at storing a significant proportion of the data items in the 1-hop neighborhood of every node. Relevant for this analysis is the ratio between the size of the cache in the 1-hop neighborhood of each node and the total number of items. This ratio, hereafter named Relative Neighborhood Cache Size ($RNCS$), is given by $RNCS = \dfrac{\sum_{i \in \text{neigh}} CS_i}{\#items}$ where CS_i is the cache size of node i in a neighborhood and *# items* is the total number of advertised items. Assuming that the number of 1-hop neighbors is n and that all nodes have an equal cache size, the equation can be simplified to $RNCS = n\dfrac{CS}{\#items}$. The effect of the variation of each of these parameters in PCache was evaluated individually keeping the remaining parameters according to the baseline configuration described in the beginning of the section.

The main metric used for evaluation is the *Average nodes without an item in 1-hop neighborhood (N1)*: at the end of the simulation, and for each data item d, N1 accounts the number of nodes that do not have a replica of d in its 1-hop neighborhood. The value is the average of this count for the 100 data items.

Figure 3 shows how the efficiency of the data distribution is affected with the variation of each of the parameters in $RNCS$. Each point in the figure is the average of the N1 metric for 10 runs in similar conditions but with different deployments of the nodes and moments of registration. The variations of $RNCS$ by changing the cache size of each node and of the total number of items are labeled respectively as "Cache Size" and "Items". For the variation of the cache size, the results were computed using sizes between 3 and 17 items at intervals of two. The number of items varied in the interval between 50 and 400 at intervals of 50.

To vary the number of neighbors, the baseline configuration was tested with the nodes configured with different transmission power while keeping the size of the simulated space constant. The tests were performed for transmission ranges between 150 and 325 meters at intervals of 25 meters.[1] The number of neighbors was estimated by averaging the number of nodes that received every broadcast message on every simulation

---

[1]Transmission ranges below 150m do not provide accurate results due to the large number of isolated nodes.

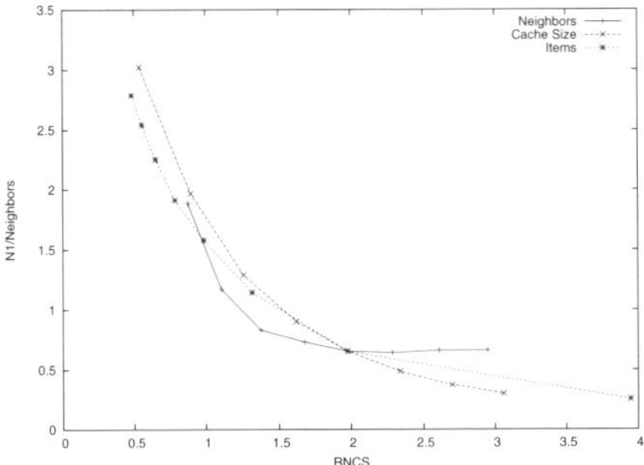

Figure 3. N1 metric for variations of RNCS

with the same transmission range. The figures identify the results of these tests with the label "Neighbors".

Because one of the criteria used to change RNCS makes the number of neighbors vary, the results for the N1 metric can not be compared directly for the three varying factors. Therefore, Figure 3 presents N1 after an harmonization which consisted in dividing N1 by the average number of neighbors. The figure shows that the average number of nodes without some data item stored in its neighborhood decays rapidly as the storage capacity of the neighborhood increases. PCache can handle better a reduced number of neighbors but the benefit of adding new nodes has a limit when the total capacity of the neighborhood reaches twice the number of advertised items. On the contrary, with the increase of the size of the cache or the reduction of the number of items, PCache is capable of further improving its performance.

5. Data Retrieval

Besides efficiently replicating data, a distributed data storage algorithm must also provide the means to efficiently retrieve it. In some applications, queries will be performed to retrieve a single value. This is the case, for example, of a Name service, where the query item would be the common name of the resource and the reply its current address. We call this process "retrieval of a single item".

However, in other applications, it may be necessary to perform queries where the number of values satisfying the conditions is unknown *a priori*. For example, users may find interesting to learn about all available printers, or devices satisfying some constraints. PCache can also be used to assist a communication application, where some users want to communicate with people in the ad-hoc network matching a specified profile. A query for all the people interested, e.g., in sports, can be issued, and PCache can return to the querying node a list of users and the necessary contact information. In practice, instead of a key value, queries will be performed specifying a condition that must be satisfied by the key of the data item. Conditional queries operations will be referred to as "data gathering" operations.

5.1. Single Item Retrieval

To retrieve some value from the network, a node begins by looking for the key in its local cache. If the value is not found, the node broadcasts a *query message* containing the key. An expanding ring search is performed due to the expectations that the replication process was able to store the value in the 1-hop neighborhood of the node. The message is first broadcast with TTL equal to one. The query is reissued with a large TTL if no reply is received within some predefined time limit. The protocol imposes a limit on the number of retries to be performed, which occur at growing time intervals. If a node receiving a query message finds the requested key in its cache, it sends a point to point reply to the source of the query. Otherwise, it will enter the broadcast algorithm described in Section 4.3. Here, we do no longer concentrate on the single item retrieval, and discuss in more details the operations of gathering. For more details on the retrieval process, refer to [1].

5.2. Data Gathering

In *Data Gathering* operations, the number of keys and items satisfying the query is unknown. The query is performed by specifying some condition that must be satisfied by the keys. Because the number of items satisfying the query is unknown, the query is always broadcasted to the network.

Data gathering has some similarities with the problem of data aggregation, extensively investigated in the scope of sensor networks (see for example [21,22,23,24,25]). However, contrary to sensor networks, in MANETs the network topology is expected to change frequently, due to the movement of the nodes. Therefore, routes between communicating devices are assumed to be unstable and to change frequently. Furthermore, PCache does not assume a single data source or sink.

Data gathering operations may produce a large number of redundant messages in both the dissemination of the query and on the forwarding of the replies with obvious implications in the resource consumption of the devices. As a preliminary step to decrease redundancy, PCache relies on the efficient replication of data items to impose a limit on the distance (in number of hops) that the query travels by performing a ring-search. The radius of the ring is defined at the source of the query in a field commonly identified as Time-To-Live (TTL). Each node forwarding the message decrements the value in this field. The message ceases to be forwarded when TTL reaches zero.

The nodes in the ring are dynamically partitioned in clusters. Each cluster head is responsible for decreasing redundancy by aggregating replies from the remaining cluster members. Redundancy is reduced by preventing nodes from sending replies containing data items already known by the cluster heads. The main characteristic of our clustering approach is that it is stateless and message-driven, that is, clusters are formed based only on the content of received messages. There is no need to implement a dedicated membership protocol, or for the cluster heads, to keep state information on the nodes belonging to their cluster. The algorithm works as follows.

A gathering query message is broadcasted by a source node S containing a description of the query and the records present in its cache that satisfy it. These records are used to prevent redundant replies.

All nodes become members of the cluster headed by the node from which they first received the query message. Therefore, all nodes in the transmission range of S become members of S's cluster. A node creates and becomes head of another cluster if the TTL of the message permits its retransmission and if it decides to retransmit the message. The decision can follow two alternative algorithms described in the following subsection.

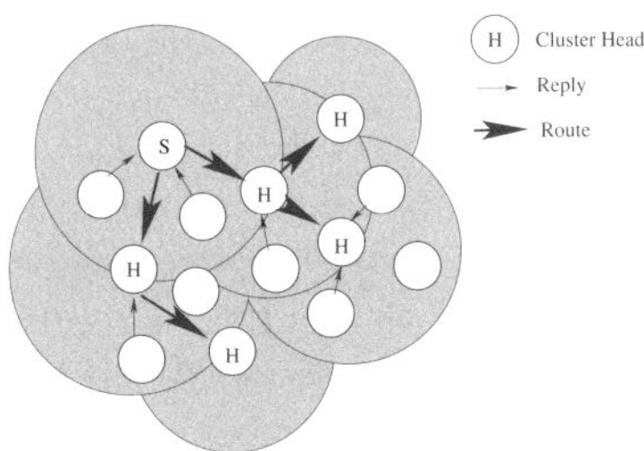

Figure 4. Propagation of gathering messages and replies

Before retransmitting, the cluster head decrements the TTL and appends its address to the list of forwarders in the message. The chain of cluster heads that is formed defines the route to be followed by the reply messages. The node also searches its cache for data items satisfying the query but that were not present in the incoming message. These records are appended to the gathering query message up to the message maximum size and to a reply message, that is placed on hold for a period of time proportional to the value of the TTL field in the message. A node deciding not to become a cluster head sends a reply with the data items in its cache satisfying the query and that were not present in the gathering message. No message is transmitted if the node does not have any data item satisfying the above conditions in its cache. The reply message is addressed to S and follows the route advertised in the query. Therefore, it is first delivered to its cluster head. The reply may consist in several messages if the data items satisfying the condition do not fit the maximum message size for the network. It should be noted that since messages follow an hop-by-hop route determined at the PCache level, the gathering algorithm does not depend of a routing protocol.

A cluster head receiving a reply addressed to S and that is still on its hold period aggregates the data by appending the non-redundant data items to its reply. When the timer expires and if the reply is not empty, it is sent, again addressed to S but delivered to the previous cluster head in the chain started at S. Eventually, all replies reach node S. To save resources, cluster heads discard all state concerning the query after sending the replies. Therefore, all replies received after the expiration of its timer are forwarded by the node without further processing. The reply may be aggregated on one of the other cluster heads in the path to node S if its timer has not expired or be delivered to S. A run of the algorithm is exemplified in Figure 4.

5.3. Cluster Formation Algorithm

This section describes two alternative distributed methods for the election of the cluster heads of the gathering algorithm. The *Probabilistic Clustering Algorithm* (PCA) is a plain implementation of probabilistic protocols in MANETs. In PCA each node receiving a gathering query decides to forward it with an independent and uniform probability Pf. In the *Distance-Aware PCache Clustering Algorithm* (DACA), nodes apply the broadcast algorithm described in Section 4.3 to decide if the message should be forwarded. Recall that in this algorithm, before retransmitting, nodes monitor the network listening for retransmissions of the message. The network is monitored by a period of time proportional to the reception power of the first copy of the message. In DACA, only nodes listening to less than two retransmissions of a gathering query retransmit it and become cluster heads.

Given that, in MANETs, the location of the nodes is expected to change frequently and can not be predicted, it can also be said that DACA is a probabilistic algorithm. The next section shows that DACA can cover a larger region of the space with a lower number of messages. In addition, it shows that DACA is self-adaptable to network conditions, in particular, to the density of the nodes. It should be noted that an adequate choice of Pf depends, for example, of the number of nodes in the neighborhood. The comparison of DACA and PCA in different networking environments emphasizes how the particularities of MANETs can affect the performance of gossip protocols.

5.4. Comparison

The simulation test-bed used for comparing PCA and DACA algorithms extends the one used in Section 4.6 to evaluate the efficiency of the replication algorithm. Here, nodes move accordingly to the random way-point model [9] using three different speed models: 0m/s, 3-7m/s and 5-15m/s. For simplicity, each of the three speed models is identified by its intermediate value, respectively 0m/s, 5m/s and 10m/s. In the latter cases, pause times are randomly selected between 0 and 20s. Runs are executed for 900s of simulated time. Evaluation of data gathering is preceded by the replication of the records, that takes place between 1s and 290s. Each run consists of 300 queries starting at 300s and uniformly distributed until the 890s of simulated time. The nodes performing the queries and the queried items are randomly selected and the distribution of the nodes over the simulated space and the instant of data item replication varies on each run. In the following, each data point averages 10 runs in similar conditions. The efficiency of the gathering algorithm is evaluated using two metrics.

Coverage Gives the proportion of data items satisfying a given gathering operation that are effectively delivered to the querying nodes. Only data items present in the node's local cache or delivered to it in the first 10 seconds after the query has been issued are accounted.

Traffic A second metric accounts with the number of gathering query and reply packets forwarded by the nodes. It should be noted that each forwarding of a query or reply is accounted individually.

In the baseline configuration used in this section, each operation tries to collect 10% of the total number of advertised items. Message and record sizes are unchanged from the scenario used for evaluating the replication algorithm. A gathering query message accommodates the query description and up to four items. The reply message can carry up to five data items.

Selection of Pf In the probabilistic algorithm, the number of forwarding's of the data gathering query message depends of the probability of forwarding (Pf), the number of nodes and of the radius of the ring (the TTL). Figure 5 shows the performance of the algorithm for different values of TTL as a function of Pf. These results were obtained with 0m/s.

Figure 5(a) shows that coverage does not vary significantly for TTL values greater or equal to three. However, the redundancy introduced by an increment of the TTL results in the transmission of additional messages as can be observed in Figure 5(b).

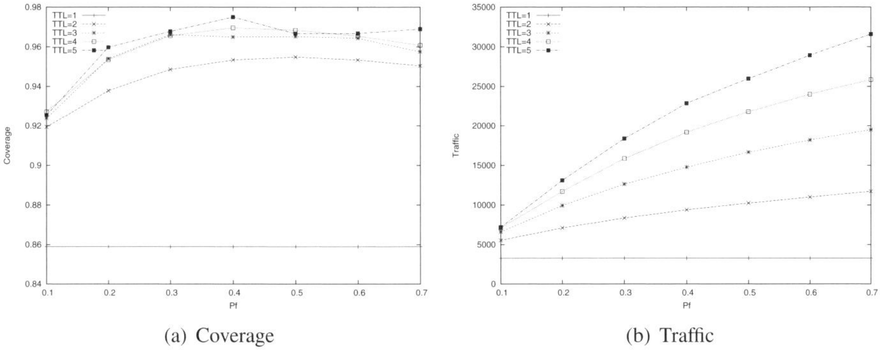

(a) Coverage   (b) Traffic

Figure 5. Performance of PCA

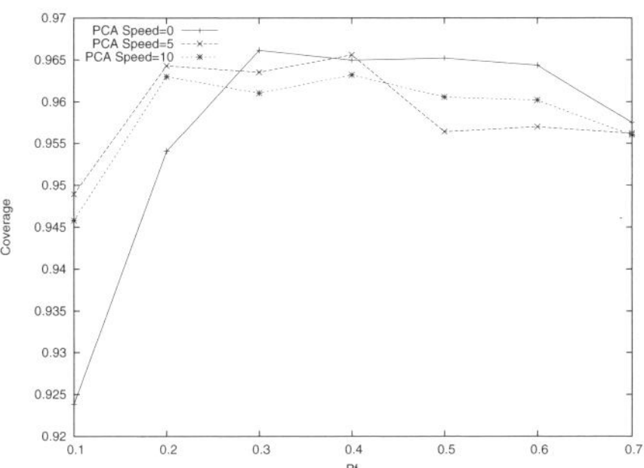

Figure 6. Coverage of PCA for different speeds and Pf when TTL=3

It should be noted that even when the gathering message is broadcast only by the querying node (TTL=1), gathering operations are able to retrieve on average 86% of the values satisfying the query, what suggests that the replication algorithm is providing a reasonable distribution of the records.

An interesting aspect of Figure 5(a) is that for a combination of high probabilities and TTL, coverage may even decline in an effect attributed to the contention resulting from the excessive traffic generated.

Influence of Speed   The failure of the links resulting from the movement of the nodes is a well-known problem for long-term connections in ad hoc networks [9,26]. Figure 6 confirms that the decoupled nature of PCache makes the protocol weekly affected by node movement when TTL is three. The improvements of the coverage when Pf is low and nodes move are attributed to the tendency of the nodes to concentrate at the center of the simulated space. This is an effect that has been previously identified in the random way-point movement model [27].

Adaptation   This paragraph evaluates the capability of both algorithms to adapt to different network conditions. Again, we use the Relative Neighbor Cache Size (RNCS) formula to unify the different changes to the networking environment. In the graphics below, RNCS was evaluated using the same parameters and constants described in Section 4.6. In all simulations presented, gathering query messages were initialized with TTL=3. PCA was run with Pf=0.3.

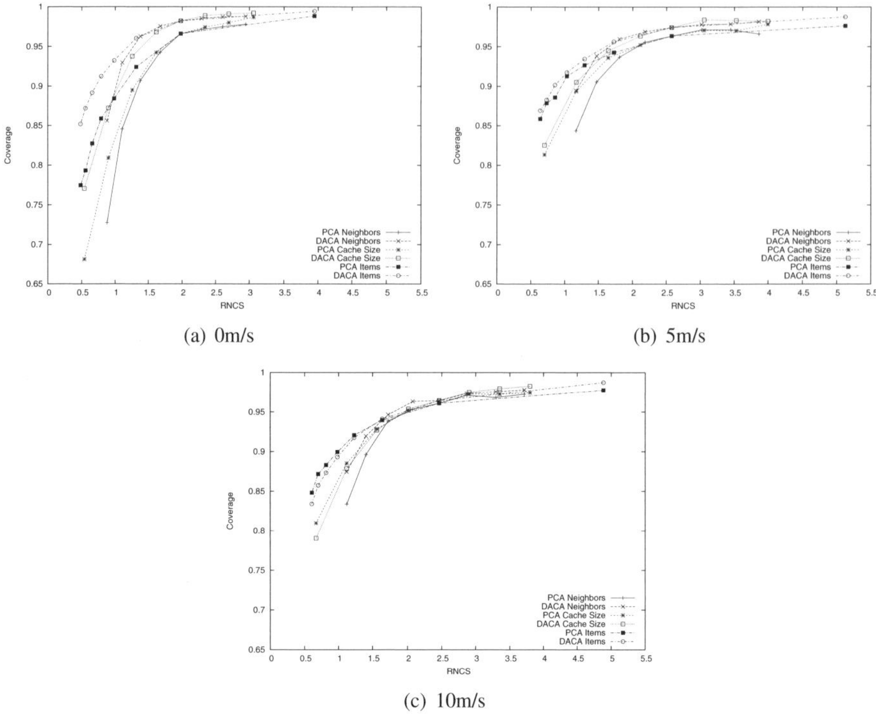

Figure 7. Coverage of PCA and DACA for different speeds

Figure 7 shows that the performance of PCache is differently affected by variations in cache size, number of data items and number of neighbors. The slight shift of the plots relatively to the x axis is justified by the use of the random way-point movement model. As described before, the use of this movement model increases the number of neighbors by concentrating nodes at the center of the simulated space and consequently, affects the estimation of the values of RNCS.[2]

Both PCA and DACA improve their performance when nodes move and, as expected, when the availability of storage in the neighborhood (the RNCS) increases. For the same conditions, DACA generally performs better than PCA but the difference between the algorithms is attenuated as the speed increases. Only in some specific conditions presented in Figure 7(c) the performance of PCA is slightly better than the performance of DACA.

To evaluate the adaptation capabilities of both algorithms, Figure 8(a) presents the traffic in the simulations where the transmission range varies, keeping the number of data items and the cache size of the nodes stable. As a result of the application of Pf to each neighbor, in PCA, the number of messages increases almost linearly with the number of neighbors. Instead, DACA adapts the number of query messages to the size of the neighborhood, presenting a lower growing rate.

---

[2]Recall from Section 4.6 that the number of neighbors is estimated by averaging the number of receptions of every message transmitted during the simulations.

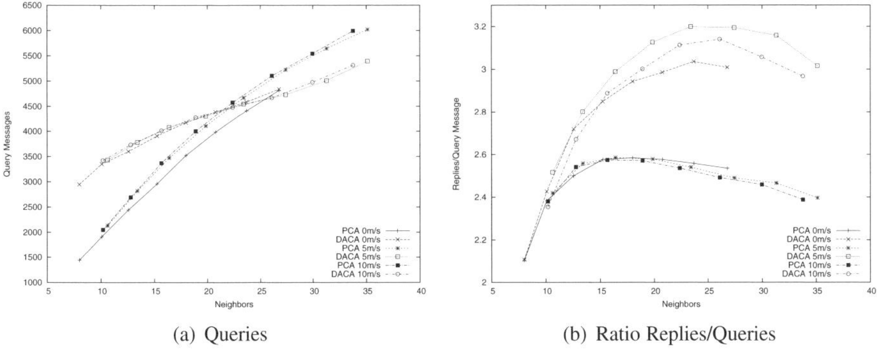

(a) Queries   (b) Ratio Replies/Queries

Figure 8. Messages sent for the variation of the number of neighbors

Figure 7 has already shown that, in the general case, DACA provides a better coverage than PCA. This behavior is partially explained by Figure 8(b) where the y axis divides reply by query messages, exposing the "efficiency" of each query message on reaching other nodes. For the same conditions, DACA presents a ratio substantially higher than PCA. This effect is attributed to the proportional delay imposed to the devices in the broadcast algorithm that privileges retransmissions from nodes more distant to the source. Therefore, for the same TTL, DACA is capable of covering a larger area and, consequently, additional nodes.

The additional coverage of DACA comes from the probability of the nodes in the additional region covered, to store records that are not present in the region covered by PCA. As a result, DACA has an higher probability of retrieving data items that had not been sufficiently spread by the replication algorithm.

6. Conclusions

This chapter addressed the issue of data replication in an unstructured environment, such as mobile ad-hoc networks (MANET). Particularly, we discussed replication strategies based on epidemic data dissemination and distribute data storage in MANETs.

We first traced some basic concepts of epidemic, or gossip-based, algorithms, underlining the fundamental parameters and giving pointers to the related work. We then gave a panoramic on algorithms for distributed data storage among nodes. They differ in a number of features, e.g., in the target networking environment, which ranges from sensor networks to world-scaled networks or in the policy of replacements of cached items.

The core part of the chapter has described novel algorithms allowing nodes in a MANET to distribute and retrieve replicated data items. The algorithms leverage on the characteristics of the transmission medium where it meant to be deployed, by using the inherent broadcast nature of wireless links. The decentralized philosophy, which we deem being the most suitable in MANETs, is fully exploited by the algorithm, which does not require any centralized entity to function. Instead, nodes acquire information on the state of the caches of the neighboring nodes by inspecting the received messages. This approach allows building an efficient distribution of data items, and it is stateless, as state information is mostly carried by the messages and not locally stored. A stateless approach is very suited to the limited resources of the devices that may presumably form a MANET.

Acknowledgments

The work presented in this chapter was partially supported by the European Science Foundation (ESF) programme Middleware for Network Eccentric and Mobile Applications (MiNEMA) and by project Probabilistically-Structured Overlay Networks (P-SON), POSC/EIA/60941/2004 through Fundação para a Ciência e Tecnologia (FCT) and FEDER.

References

[1] Hugo Miranda, Simone Leggio, Luís Rodrigues, and Kimmo Raatikainen. A stateless neighbour-aware cooperative caching protocol for ad-hoc networks. DI/FCUL TR 05–23, Department of Informatics, University of Lisbon, December 2005. Also as Technical Report Number C–2005–76. Computer Science Department, University of Helsinki.

[2] Kenneth P. Birman, Mark Hayden, Oznur Ozkasap, Zhen Xiao, Mihai Budiu, and Yaron Minsky. Bimodal multicast. *ACM Transactions on Computer Systems*, 17(2):41–88, 1999.

[3] P.T. Eugster, R. Guerraoui, S.B. Handurukande, A.-M. Kermarrec, and P. Kouznetsov. Lightweight probabilistic broadcast. In *Proceedings of the International Conference on Dependable Systems and Networks*, pages 443–452, Goteborg, July 1–4 2001.

[4] Boris Koldehofe. Simple gossiping with balls and bins. In *Proceedings of the 6th Annual International Conference on Principles of Distributed Systems (OPODIS '02)*, pages 109–117, December 2002.

[5] P. Kouznetsov, R. Guerraoui, S.B. Handurukande, and A.-M. Kermarrec. Reducing noise in gossip-based reliable broadcast. In *Proceedings of the 20th IEEE Symposium on Reliable Distributed Systems (SRDS'2001)*, pages 186–189, New Orleans, LA, October 28–31 2001.

[6] Boris Koldehofe. Buffer management in probabilistic peer-to-peer communication protocols. In *Proceedings of the 22nd International Symposium on Reliable Distributed Systems (SRDS'2003)*, pages 76–85, October 6–18 2003.

[7] José Pereira, Luís Rodrigues, and Rui Oliveira. Semantically reliable multicast: Definition, implementation and performance evaluation. *IEEE Transactions on Computers, Special Issue on Reliable Distributed Systems*, 52(2):150–165, February 2003.

[8] Jun Luo, Patrick Th. Eugster, and Jean-Pierre Hubaux. Route driven gossip: probabilistic reliable multicast in ad hoc networks. In *Proceedings of the 22nd Annual Joint Conference of the IEEE Computer and Communications Societies (INFOCOM 2003)*, volume 3, pages 2229–2239. IEEE, March 2003.

[9] David B. Johnson and David A. Maltz. *Mobile Computing*, chapter Dynamic Source Routing in Ad Hoc Wireless Networks, pages 153–181. Kluwer Academic Publishers, 1996.

[10] Zygmunt J. Haas, Joseph Y. Halpern, and Li Li. Gossip-based ad hoc routing. In *Proceedings of the 21st Annual Joint Conference of the IEEE Computer and Communications Societies (INFOCOM 2002)*, volume 3, pages 1707–1716. IEEE, June 23–27 2002.

[11] Meng-Jang Lin and Keith Marzullo. Directional gossip: gossip in a wide area network. In *Proceedings of the 3rd European Dependable Computing Conference (EDDC-3)*, volume 1667 of *Lecture Notes in Computer Science*, pages 364–379, Berlin, Germany, 1999. Springer-Verlag.

[12] Laurent Massoulié, Anne-Marie Kermarrec, and Ayalvadi J. Ganesh. Network awareness and failure resilience in self-organizing overlay networks. In *Proceedings of the 22nd In-

ternational Symposium on Reliable Distributed Systems (SRDS), pages 47–55, October 6–18 2003.

[13] Yu-Chee Tseng, Sze-Yao Ni, Yuh-Shyan Chen, and Jang-Ping Sheu. The broadcast storm problem in a mobile ad hoc network. *Wireless Networks*, 8(2/3):153–167, 2002.

[14] Philip Levis, Neil Patel, David Culler, and Scott Shenker. Trickle: A self-regulating algorithm for code propagation and maintenance in wireless sensor networks. In *Proceedings of the 1st USENIX/ACM Symposium on Networked Systems Design and Implementation (NSDI 2004)*, 2004.

[15] Takahiro Hara. Effective replica allocation in ad hoc networks for improving data accessibility. In *Proceedings of the 20th Annual Joint Conference of the IEEE Computer and Communications Societies (INFOCOM 2001)*, volume 3, pages 1568–1576, Anchorage, AK, April 22–26 2001. IEEE.

[16] Anwitaman Datta, Silvia Quarteroni, and Karl Aberer. Autonomous gossiping: A self-organizing epidemic algorithm for selective information dissemination in mobile ad-hoc networks. In Mokrane Bouzeghoub, Carole Goble, Vipul Kashyap, et al., editors, *Proceedings of the International Conference on Semantics of a Networked World (IC-SNW'04)*, volume 3226 / 2004 of *Lecture Notes in Computer Science*, pages 126–143, Paris, France, June 17–19 2004. Springer-Verlag Heidelberg.

[17] Liangzhong Yin and Guohong Cao. Supporting cooperative caching in ad hoc networks. *IEEE Transactions on Mobile Computing*, 5(1):77–89, Jan.-Feb. 2006.

[18] Sunho Lim, Wang-Chien Lee, Guohong Cao, and Chita R. Das. A novel caching scheme for improving internet-based mobile ad hoc networks performance. *Elsevier Journal on Ad-Hoc Networks*, 4(2):225–239, March 2006.

[19] Daniela Gavidia, Spyros Voulgaris, and Maarten van Steen. Epidemic-style monitoring in large-scale wireless sensor networks. Technical Report IR-CS-012, Vrije Universiteit Amsterdam, Vrije Universiteit Amsterdam. Faculty of Science. Department of Computer Science. De Boelelaan 1081a, 1081 HV. Amsterdam, The Netherlands, March 2005.

[20] Daniela Gavidia, Spyros Voulgaris, and Maarten van Steen. A gossip-based distributed news service for wireless mesh networks. In *Proceedings of the 3rd IEEE Conference on Wireless On demand Network Systems and Services (WONS)*, Les Menuires, France, January 2006.

[21] Tian He, Brian M. Blum, John A. Stankovic, and Tarek Abdelzaher. AIDA: Adaptive application-independent data aggregation in wireless sensor networks. *Transactions on Embedded Computing Systems*, 3(2):426–457, 2004.

[22] Samuel Madden, Michael J. Franklin, Joseph M. Hellerstein, and Wei Hong. TAG: a Tiny AGgregation service for ad-hoc sensor networks. *SIGOPS Operating Systems Review*, 36(SI):131–146, 2002.

[23] Bartosz Przydatek, Dawn Song, and Adrian Perrig. SIA: secure information aggregation in sensor networks. In *Proceedings of the 1st International Conference on Embedded Networked Sensor Systems (SenSys '03)*, pages 255–265, New York, NY, USA, 2003. ACM Press.

[24] Mohamed A. Sharaf, Jonathan Beaver, Alexandros Labrinidis, and Panos K. Chrysanthis. Balancing energy efficiency and quality of aggregate data in sensor networks. *The VLDB Journal*, 13(4):384–403, 2004.

[25] Nisheeth Shrivastava, Chiranjeeb Buragohain, Divyakant Agrawal, and Subhash Suri. Medians and beyond: new aggregation techniques for sensor networks. In *Proceedings of the 2nd International Conference on Embedded Networked Sensor Systems (SenSys '04)*, pages 239–249, New York, NY, USA, 2004. ACM Press.

[26] Charles E. Perkins and Elizabeth M. Royer. Ad-hoc on-demand distance vector routing. In *Proceedings of the 2nd IEEE Workshop on Mobile Computing Systems and Applications*, pages 90–100, New Orleans, LA, February 1999.

[27] Christian Bettstetter, Giovanni Resta, and Paolo Santi. The node distribution of the random waypoint mobility model for wireless ad hoc networks. *IEEE Transactions on Mobile Computing*, 2(3):257–269, Jul/Sep 2003.

Global Data Management
R. Baldoni et al. (Eds.)
IOS Press, 2006

Data Management
in Wireless Sensor Networks

Iacopo Carreras, Francesco De Pellegrini, Csaba Kiraly, and Imrich Chlamtac [1]
CREATE-NET, *Via Solteri 38/A, 38100 Trento, Italy*

Abstract. Wireless Sensor Networks are emerging as one of the most promising research directions, due to the possibility of sensing the physical world with a granularity unimaginable before. In this chapter, we address some of the major challenges related to the collection and elaboration of data sourcing from such networks of distributed devices. In particular, we describe the concepts of data storage, data retrieval and data processing. We discuss how such data management techniques will be able to sustain a novel class of data-intensive applications, which use the network as an interface to the physical world. Then, we identify some threats to the deployment of such networks on a large scale basis. In particular, we argue that even if appealing, the underlying composition of very large and heterogeneous wireless sensor networks poses enormous engineering challenges, calling for innovative design paradigms. Finally, we discuss an alternative solution, and the related data management mechanism, for the provisioning of sensor-based services in future pervasive environments.

Keywords. Wireless Sensor Network, scalability, data aggregation, distributed data storage

1. Introduction

Sensors have been applied in systems for more than a century, with the aim of providing feedback to human operators and implementing control feedback loops. The common notion of a sensor network, however, arose quite recently, when conveying and processing the information delivered by spatially distributed sensors became feasible. A sensor network is generally composed by an ensemble of network nodes with computation, sensing and communication capabilities. These nodes are distributed over a region to be monitored and are capable of sensing the environmental conditions and conveying information to the final end-user.

One of the earlier applications of sensor networks, where monitoring was obviously of strategical importance, was location detection and tracking. In fact, early sensor networks were developed for military reasons and one of the first example of a sensor network was the SOSUS (Sound Surveillance System) [1]. The SOSUS, in particular, was developed during the early 50's in order to detect and localize enemy submarines.

Later on, in the 70's, under the Distributed Sensor Networks (DSN) DARPA project, the research on sensor networks started focusing on a network composed of a large num-

[1]This work was partially funded by the EU under the BIONETS project EU-IST-FETSAC-FP6-027748

ber of low-cost sensor nodes. At that time, most studies were concerned with sensing technology, communication issues, processing techniques and how to compose a distributed software architecture.

Anyway, it was certainly during the last decades that major advances were achieved in all these areas. Sensing (and actuating) technology benefited largely from the advent of MEMS (Micro Electro-Mechanical Systems) technologies. In particular, low-cost and low-energy wireless communication protocols have been developed, and Wireless Sensors Networks (WSNs) [2,3] are emerging as one of the most promising research directions for the next decades. As a consequence, recent protocols have been standardized in the IEEE family in order to match the requirements of WSNs. Examples are the IEEE 802.15.1, which embodies mostly the Bluetooth standard, and the IEEE 802.15.4, which implements part of the communication stack of the popular ZigBee sensor technology. RFID and active RFID are also technologies discussed in research papers and widely deployed in industrial applications.

It is worth mentioning, though, that besides RF technology, research has been carried out on alternate propagation techniques, suitable for specific media and application scenarios. It is the case of acoustic waves, used for underwater communications [4], and infrared, employed for short range communications [5], or even magnetic induction or capacitive coupling for proximity communications.

Meanwhile, several hardware/software solutions appeared in mass production, the most popular being the Mote open-source hardware and software platform developed at U.C. Berkeley. Nowadays, several enhanced versions of the Mote exist, the de-facto worldwide standard being the Crossbow MICA Mote [6], which can be found in almost any WSN lab. Other HW platforms try to compete with the MICAs in size, price and performance. The processing capabilities can range from simple 8-bit microcontrollers to general purpose 400 MHz processors. Platform-independent operating systems and middleware softwares are also being developed to support energy-aware sensing, communication and processing capabilities.

Besides all these technical efforts and all the papers showing the widespread diffusion of sensor networks, expected to change the way we interact with our environment with major advantages on our everyday life, such forecasts are far from reality. In fact, the cost of sensor nodes is still far from the estimated price of some cents per unit which would permit massive deployment of sensors. Available solutions, in practice, are mostly custom made sensor devices, built with multiple sensing elements, long lasting battery and proper casing. In the end, including deployment into the figure, their cost is in the order of tenths of dollars. In the last part of this chapter we will present recent results in the WSN research field aimed at solve the cost issue and pave the way for massive sensor deployment.

1.1. Typology of sensor networks

Many types of sensor networks exist. In some cases wired energy supply and/or communication is not feasible, and this forces the adoption of wireless sensor networks (WSNs). Other settings require nodes to be small, cheap or densely deployed. In general, we find convenient to define what sensor networks are by characterizing them based on the type of nodes, the network, the communication and processing techniques applied [7,8]:

a) *Node constraints.* Nodes of a sensor network differ in size, energy and cost constraints. The *size* of sensor nodes ranges from huge radar stations to coin sized sensor nodes and cubic millimeter sensor nodes are under development [9,10]. Size, as well as *cost* and *deployment*, pose constraints to the sensor processing capability, onboard memory size and available energy sources. Energy sources, for example, can range from batteries through solar panels to mains supply.

b) *Network architecture.* The *number of nodes* in a sensor network varies from dozens to thousands, or theoretically even to millions [9] of devices. Sensor networks differ also in their *spatial coverage* and *node density* since some of them should be aimed at monitoring very large areas (e.g. woods or oceans), whereas others could be spread on the surface of a mug [10]. A sensor network can be *homogeneous*, consisting of identical nodes, or not homogeneous, where sensors differ in their physical sensing devices or in their computation/communication capabilities. Sensor networks need also to be *deployed* and organized into a network: self-organizing structures for randomly deployed nodes or a planned deployment are two possible options; *mobility* of devices has also to be accounted for.

c) *Communications.* The range of foreseen applications pose different requirements on the way the communication stack is implemented. Some applications require simple event notifications with very low *bandwidth*, while others transmit continuous streams of measurement data (e.g. video streams). *QoS* constraints are also different, ranging from high delay best-effort to delay-constrained services (e.g. high speed control for industrial plants). Different physical *media*, including RF, optical/infrared, and acoustic waves are possible.

d) *Processing architecture.* Sensor networks can implement a centralized or a distributed *processing architecture*, depending on node capabilities, processing, communications and energy constraints and the targeted applications. *Processing capabilities* of nodes can range from dumb ADCs through image processing DSPs to general purpose processors.

Due to the broad variability of sensor networks and the various application domains, it is not surprising that sensor networks are custom made, specialized solutions, even if some standard components are already available. In what follows, we will focus on how data are managed in one of the most promising field, namely Wireless Sensors Networks (WSNs). In particular, in the next section we describe existing data management solutions for WSNs. In a further section, we investigate on a WSN scenario where sensor nodes can be deployed on a very large scale and we describe what the challenges are for data management in such an environment. In the end, we describe possible solutions and research directions.

2. Wireless Sensor Networks

As we mentioned before, the advances in embedded systems, sensors and miniaturized radios, made wireless sensors networks (WSNs) emerge as one of the most promising research directions for the next decades [2,3]. With a WSN we mean a large number of cheap, self-organizing network nodes able to autonomously perform sensing operations, to communicate and/or store data. A WSN is typically *immerse* in the phenomenon to be observed and, after a start-up phase, it is able to convey the information generated from sensors to a remote end-user. For several applications, moreover, we expect that WSNs are deployed in hostile environments. Other types of applications will require that sensors are embedded into structures where maintenance is simply not feasible. The general assumption is then that, someday, the cost of nodes will be low enough that they can be simply discarded rather than recharged. Clearly, prolonging network lifetime for these nodes is a critical issue, and it has to be taken into account in the design of each part of a WSN.

The intimate connection with its immediate physical environment allows each sensor to provide localized measurements and detailed information that is hard to obtain through traditional instrumentation, thus paving the way for new classes of applications, which are currently raising the interest of the research community.

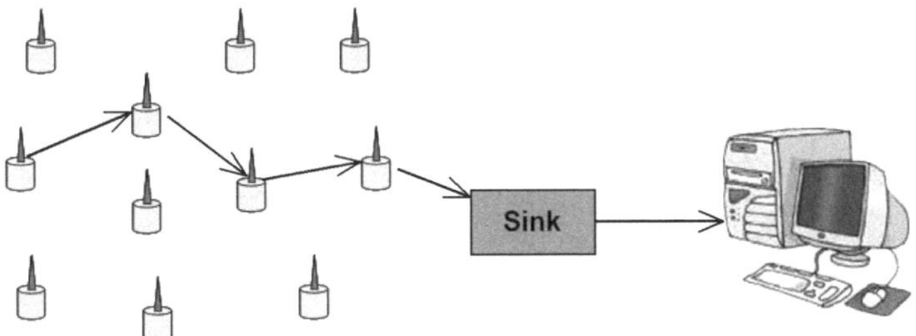

Figure 1. Wireless Sensor Network architecture.

2.1. Data Management in Wireless Sensor Networks

A typical WSN architecture is the one shown in Fig. 1, where densely deployed sensor nodes monitor some phenomenon trough their sensing capabilities and, once useful information is available, data is sent back to the sink node, which acts as the gateway between the WSN and a standard communication network such as the Internet. The *usefulness* of the information can not be determined a-priori, since it depends on the kind of application (e.g., tracking, monitoring, alerting, etc.), the physical phenomenon to be observed (e.g., the redundancy of the phenomenon) and the expected lifetime of the sensor networks. As two extreme cases, we can think of an application reporting the temperature in a remote region, and a fire alarm application, which detects the fire in a public office. In both application scenarios, the temperature is the phenomenon to be measured. However, in the first case the end-user is mostly interested in collecting a large number of sensor readings for a long period of time. This first case is characterized by large volumes of data collected for an extremely long period of time, but without the need for an extreme accuracy on the collected information (missing data can be eventually extrapolated). Conversely, the fire alarm application will be in a stand-by state for most of the time, but it needs to be extremely reliable and accurate when fire is detected. All these considerations are reflected in the way a WSN is programmed and the data circulating in the sensor network are processed and managed. Data management in WSNs deals with the challenging task of defining how sensor-originated data are efficiently managed, stored and conveyed outside a WSN.

Existing sensor networks assume that the sensors are preprogrammed and send data to a central front end where the data is aggregated and stored for offline querying and analysis. This approach has two major drawbacks. First, the user cannot change the behavior of the system dynamically. Second, communication in today's networks is orders of magnitude more expensive than local computation; thus in-network storage and processing can vastly reduce resource usage and extend the lifetime of a sensor network.

2.2. WSN as a Distributed Database

Typically, a WSN is *immerse* around the phenomenon to be monitored. The expected mode of usage of a WSN is that users program the sensors through *queries* [11,12,13], using a query-like declarative specification (such as SQL) of the information to be collected. This is an efficient way of abstracting the system details, and relies on a user-friendly interface for programming the sensors. As an example, in Alg. 1 the remote user is querying the WSN for light and temperature information from those sensors measuring a temperature value above a given threshold (10 in this specific case). The queried information is collected with a sampling period of 2 seconds.

A *query layer* [14] is in charge of translating the declarative language of the query into execution plans, taking into account the different constraints deriving from the specific application and sensor networks deployment.

Algorithm 1 Example of a query injected in a Wireless Sensor Network

---

```
SELECT nodes id, light, temp
FROM sensors
WHERE temp > 10
SAMPLE PERIOD 2 s
```

The main differences between a WSN and a traditional database system can be listed as follows:

- delivers a stream of data: the sensor networks, when receiving the query, answers sending data at constant predefined time intervals;
- communication errors: the data generated by the sensor nodes are delivered back to the sink through a multi-hop communication, where the communication links may be extremely unreliable and affected by errors. This means that data is reaching the sink with an extremely variable delay and reliability;
- real-time processing: since the energy spent in processing operations is several orders of magnitude lower then the one spent for communicating, it is usually preferable to process the information in real-time, in order to avoid unnecessary transmissions. This will be further explained in the following.

There are several implementations of query processors, which translate the SQL-like syntax into system operations. TinyDB [15] is a query processor implementation running on top the TinyOS [16] operating system. By taking advantage of a user-friendly interface, remote users are able to easily query the WSN using the appropriate SQL syntax. The COUGAR sensor database [13] is another implementation of a query processing layer. There COUGAR platform implementations for Mica Mote and Sensorial demos.

2.3. Distributed storage in WSN

Storage is an extremely limited resource in WSNs, since data generated from sensors can easily saturate the memory available on sensor nodes. In general, the data generated from a sensor network can be stored in a centralized or distributed fashion. When applying a centralized paradigm, all the information generated from sensors are collected from the remote end-user and stored in a centralized repository with unlimited power and storage resources [11]. This highly facilitates the querying of information, but strongly impacts the energy consumption related to conveying every single sensor reading outside the WSN. As a consequence, a centralized storage approach is considered to be appropriate only for low-data rate application scenarios.

An alternative approach consists in storing the information inside the network, according to a distributed paradigm [17,18]. This differs from traditional distributed storage systems because of the stringent energy and storage limitations imposed by the sensor nodes, and because of the spatial/temporal dependence of the stored data that allows the use of compression techniques. even in this case, the application scenario defines the constraints of the mechanism to be applied. There is a vast class of applications where data is first collected and then analyzed offline. Hence, data is generated continuously, but read only once. As an example, we can think of a military application where sensors are scattered in the battlefield and read from airplanes flying over the sensor networks [19]. Another example can be found in [20], where a sensor networks for wildlife tracking was deployed in order to monitor the migration of zebras. In this application, sensors were attached to animals and scientists collected information as zebras were coming in range with them. Information was therefore stored on zebras's sensor node until a new data collection point (sink) was reached.

In these application scenarios, distributed data storage defines how data is collaboratively stored, queried and managed in order to meet the sensor nodes memory limitations and the application requirements. The fundamental questions to be answered are in this case are: how information is *queried/searched* and how information is *stored/managed*.

There are different approaches to the search problem. One possibility is to store all the information locally on each sensor node. The injected query is then propagated until the interested nodes are reached. The nodes start to send back the requested information. The most popular protocol implementing the described paradigm is Directed Diffusion [21], where a sensing task is disseminated in the sensor networks from the sink in the form of an interest for *named data*. Data is named using attribute-value pairs. A path is then set up to the sensor nodes matching the interest, and the detected events matching the interest start to flow toward the sink following the established path. The drawback of this approach is that it could be extremely expensive to forward the interest to all he nodes of the network in the case of large deployments. Moreover, the limited capacity of the memory of sensor nodes is not explicitly addressed.

Distributed indexing addresses the problems highlighted before utilizing structured replication and distributed search techniques. The fundamental idea is to group the events together and map them to a precise spatial location. A node detecting an event stores this event to the mirror nearest to its location. This allows the construction of hierarchical search trees, thus reducing the cost for reaching the nodes with useful information. Data-centric storage (DCS) [22] is an example of the described indexing schemes, where a hash function is defined for mapping a detected event to a geographical location. As opposed to traditional database systems where latency is the optimization criteria adopted in most of the indexing schemes, in DCS the indexing of data is targeting the minimization of the communication cost required for extracting data from the sensor network. Through the described techniques information is *searched* more efficiently, but problems still subsist in the case of long-term storage. In this case, in order not to exceed the storage capabilities of sensor nodes, a mechanism is needed that defines the lifetime of the gathered information. A typical approach consists in varying the resolution of the stored information, depending on its age. The most recent information is stored with the maximum resolution, while of older information only summaries are kept. In [17], the use of wavelets is explored for creating information summaries with a different resolution. The fidelity of the information is sacrificed for guaranteeing a long-term storage.

2.4. In-network Processing

In-network processing [23,24], often referred as data aggregation, is one of the most common approaches to reduce the communication overhead. It is well understood that, for short-range communications, local computation is much cheaper than radio communications. The cost of 1 single bit over 100 m. costs as much as 3000 instructions [25]. Starting from this consideration, in-network aggregation tries to maximally exploit the correlations in data in order to minimize the size of data and, correspondingly the communication cost. Correlation can be expected along multiple axes: spatial, temporal, among different sensors. Besides the possibility of reducing the volume of bits transmitted, in a vast class of application scenarios the end-user is not interested in the complete historical data of the sensor network, but rather in detecting some specific events (e.g., the trigger of an alarm) or in a "condensed" view of the observed phenomenon (e.g, the maximum temperature in the monitored region).

In-network processing assumes store-and forward processing of messages, where a message is a meaningful unit of data that a node can process. On each node of the sensor network, an in-network processing layer is in charge of handling the incoming messages, process them and decide the next messages to be sent.

In [26], a generic aggregation service for a network of TinyOS sensor nodes is defined, namely the Tiny Aggregation Service (TAG). The service is based on a declarative interface, similar to the one described in Sec. 2.2, that allows the distribution of the operators among the nodes of the network in order to minimize the power consumption. TAG operates over the data as it flows through the sensor nodes, applying aggregation operators and combining different readings into compact ones, where possible.

Aggregation operators are typically supported by query layers, where a declarative approach is adopted for describing the data to be retrieved.

2.5. Discussion

The techniques introduced before have the potential to widen the services applicable on WSN networks. In fact data management over WSN will be critical to enable user-situated applications with direct interface to the surrounding environment. It is easily understood that such services and their related applications will be far from those of existing networks. For example, even simple applications as navigation systems might change compared to their current implementation. Currently, navigation systems use the Global Positioning System GPS to support navigation applications: the position of the GPS device is determined and then localized on a map. In the customary solution, the road-map data collection is fixed and does not change over time and route decisions are taken independent of the environmental conditions (time, date, presence of traffic jams, accidents, deviations etc.): using a WSN with the specific task of measuring traffic conditions on the surrounding area novel metrics such as delay or "crowdness" of a path could be introduced in the search for the optimal path.

Along this line, a novel class of applications and services are arising soon, with a major impact on the way we conceive today any technology-aided operation. But, we identify a fundamental catch: such applications will require a massive deployment of sensors, which is not a simple technical task. In fact, either deployed on large areas, or concentrated in a small area with a high density of sensors per square meter, such networks configure naturally as *large scale* networks. This is especially true for certain types of applications, such as location detection [27], where increasing the sensor density means finer resolution and also more robustness against devices failures. It is likely that the concept of large-scale network, which so far have been confined to a purely theoretical exercise, will become of paramount practical relevance. Thus, the common paradigm of a WSN would be a distributed communication/computing environment characterized by an extremely large number of devices [28,9][2]. Anyway, the more fine-grid data are required by applications to such WSN networks, the larger the number of data sources, i.e. sensors, and this means a potentially tremendous increase of the number of data flows. The injection of huge quantity of environmental data is then bound to raise strong scalability issues for the underlying networking infrastructure. Further, these scenarios will be populated by very different devices, ranging from small embedded sensors, TAGs and RFIDs to complex and powerful mobile phones and laptops. As described before, the information will be gathered from the surrounding ambient through sensing/identifying devices, but it might be consumed by user devices located very far from the source.

3. An Architecture for Large Scale WSNs

As we mentioned before, we can foresee that these upcoming pervasive communication/computing environments pose three main challenges to the conventional networking approaches: *heterogeneity, scalability and complexity* [29].

Heterogeneity stems from the ongoing differentiation in the devices which will form the future ubiquitous network. In practice, we can devise at least two opposite trends. On one hand, portable devices (e.g., laptops, PDAs, smart-phones etc.) are becoming more and more performing, with a large amount of processing power. They usually carry satisfactory communication capabilities even for intense data transfers and are enforced with energy aware software and hardware design aimed to much longer lasting communication and computations than before. In the opposite direction, there is a technological trend toward miniaturized devices with sensing/identifying and basic communication capabilities. Such devices could be embedded in the objects surrounding us in our ev-

---

[2]These kind of networks are sometimes described by the term pervasive, in order to underline that we expect a true *continuum* of such devices embedded in the environment.

eryday life and represent the ideal interface to the variables describing the surrounding environment.

We notice that according to the Internet philosophy, any application running on such devices would require a full communication protocol stack such as a TCP/IP pile plus a network interface, a link layer, a MAC and PHY layer, and all this severely impairs the possibility of sizing the hardware and software complexity on their true communication requirements.

As concerns *scalability*, the end-to-end paradigm typical of Internet-based communications, suffers from insurmountable scalability problems when applied to large-scale wireless environments. The first concrete concerns on the feasibility of a flat ad-hoc sensor network can be traced back to the seminal work of Gupta and Kumar on the capacity of wireless networks [30]. Subsequent works have dig further into such topic, finding the conclusion that imposing strict connectivity requirements may negatively impact network capacity [31,32]. In the case of pervasive environments the problem is further exacerbated by the fact that a massive sensor deployment will introduce a huge number of data sources in the network, so that several flows sourcing from the same spots would congestion further the available paths.

The third issue is *complexity*, related to the need of controlling and maintaining network functionalities. On one hand, in the pervasive environment, one challenging issue is the matter of numbers, since the system may potentially comprise several millions of interacting nodes. This has a huge impact on the complexity and on the scalability of the control mechanisms: in large-scale systems the amount of regulation needed increases as a superlinear function of the number of nodes, and with the orders of magnitude considered here this is per-se a serious threat.

We conclude that in the case of heterogeneous and large-scale sensor networks, conventional centralized solutions cannot easily be adapted to such networks, and we need to resort to a (rather efficient) distributed management paradigm. This is a direct consequence of the fact that, as we already stressed, in such environments, full connectivity cannot be grated apriori. Anyway, in order to organize the complexity of such environments into a purposeful system, it is needed a framework for providing stable operations and service management functionalities (i.e., configuration, performance, accounting, fault and security) in a fully distributed and decentralized way. In the following we describe the main features of a design solution able to jointly solve these problems for certain delay tolerant applications.

3.1. A Two Tier Architecture

Instead of coping against the unavoidable heterogeneity of devices, the Nomadic Sensor Network solution described in [29,33,34] leverages heterogeneity and splits the nodes of the future pervasive communication environment into two categories. The split is made following the different logical role and the different technical features of the nodes in the network. This split into a two-tier architecture represents the main functional hierarchy of the nomadic wireless networking paradigm [29,33,34]. In the end, this functional hierarchy based on the role of network devices ends up in a precise separation of the requirements of processing/communication/storage capabilities of the devices. As depicted in Fig 2, in particular we expect two kind of nodes:

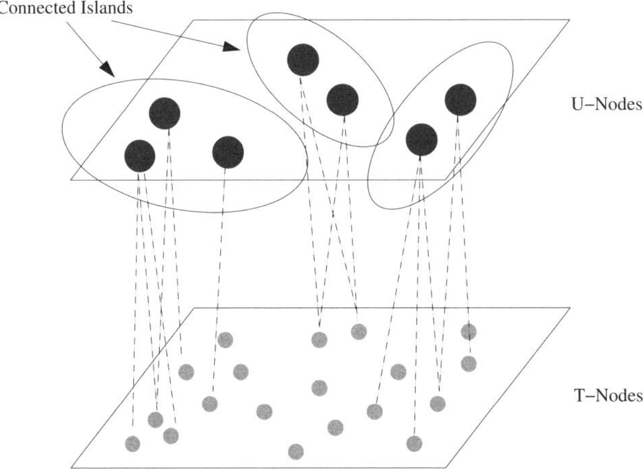

Figure 2. The 2-tier hierarchy of Nomadic Sensor Networks.

- *T-Nodes*, which will be simple tiny devices deployed in the environment, with sensing and basic communication functionalities. These nodes should be low-power and as simple as possible, in order to minimize costs for repair or maintenance. The unique role of T-nodes is to act as *source of information* on the status of the environment: the term pervasivity should be in this context interpreted as the need for fine-grained environmental data. We expect T-nodes to run a minimal protocol with no need to store and forward. The only communication requirements are short-range exchange of raw data, obtained from measurements, to U-nodes in proximity.

- *U-nodes*, which correspond to users' devices (e.g., PDAs, cell phones etc.). Their role will be to both gather information from T-Nodes deployed in the environment, and diffuse information to other U-Nodes in proximity. Clearly, U-nodes perform more complex operations on raw data and run complex information exchange protocols. U-nodes will be moving in the environment as a consequence of the physical movement of the users carrying them around, and will collect information from T-Nodes and store this information in their local memory.

The effect of such a hierarchical split is apparent because no communication among T-Nodes is encompassed and, compared to the conventional sensor network approach, T-nodes are freed from the overhead caused by store-and-forward operations. This is expected to allow for smaller, cheaper and longer-lasting devices [35]. U-Nodes can "poll" the nearby T-Nodes and communicate among them when they get into mutual communication range. Based on the distinction, all the information available to U-nodes will be available either from proximity T-Nodes or from other U-Nodes. Notice that this relaxes the need for the network to be always connected, since T-nodes will generate data when interrogated by U-nodes, and this will heavily reduce the required number of links.

The Nomadic Sensor Network overcomes the scalability issues of large scale sensor networks, since no end-to-end communication is employed. In fact, under an end-to-end paradigm, the scalability issues of a large scale ad-hoc sensor network are due to two key features: the exponential growth of the end to end traffic along with the number of sensors and the concurrent decrease of the capacity at the increase of the number of communicating nodes.

The key is to adopt an infrastructure-less networking paradigm tailored to pervasive computing environments, based on the 2-tier hierarchy devised before and a suitable data management mechanisms. The term nomadic , in particular, refers to the mechanism to spread the information once raw data are collected by T-nodes: as it has been shown by Grossglauser and Tse, it is possible to obtain a scalable network by dropping the connectivity requirement and exploiting nodes mobility to convey information [36]. Thus, the first mechanism used to cope with scalability issues is related to the role of U-Nodes where we exploit the mobility of devices in order to let information flow. In this way network connectivity is not required *a priori*, so that, in principle, the topology of the nomadic network can and up into an archipelago of connected islands of nodes (see Fig 2). We notice that in the case of the pervasive environment, the relevant key feature is that a huge fraction of the information should be exchanged locally. Thus, we let U-nodes exchange information in a peer-to-peer fashion through single-hop broadcasting: to some extent, our model may somehow resemble Delay Tolerant Networking [37]. But, Delay Tolerant Networking aims at maintaining the end-to-end semantics (typical of the Internet protocols) in a disconnected environment, thus applying store-and-forward policies for the delivery of data to the end user.

Differently, in this framework, the information comes locally from the environment, and it is limited both in space and time, so that end-to-end communications are replaced by localized peer-to-peer exchanges.

In the end, and depending on the trade offs of density and mobility of devices, information is diffused by either multihopping among U-nodes, and this is the conventional way MANETs [38] work, or just through opportunistic exchanges when U-nodes come into communication range [39]. Thus, most of the communications are restricted to fraction of the overall network, i.e. they are local. We remark that the peer-to-peer exchange described above is completely different from the end-to-end conventional communication approach and addressing and routing are not an issue. Conversely, the trigger to U-nodes to require information and process information, will be dictated by the services mounted on the U-nodes, and, so to speak, driven locally by the services.

3.1.1. Data Management in Nomadic Sensor Networks: Information Filtering

We can then exploit the locality (in both space and time) of information coming from the environment: the basic concept is that data originating from sensors loose their usefulness (i.e., information content) as soon as they spread (in both time and space domain). In other words: assume that we transmit sensors-gathered information in an end-to-end fashion, then it is quite understood that we would overload the network with data carrying a potentially low information content. Then, a further mechanism is introduced, called Information Filtering [29]. The Information Filtering mechanism aims at reducing the overhead of data with low information content, by filtering the packet flows based on their age and traveled distance. A first technique is clearly to act on a threshold basis, i.e. dropping information older than a given age or information which traveled more than a certain distance. In general, the problem is to determine the optimal policy for a node, i.e. if a U-node should drop the information or continue the diffusion of the received information: larger thresholds will impact negatively network capacity and overload U-node memory, small thresholds will cancel a large fraction of sensor information.

Putting together the structure outlined above, from the communication point of view, the net result is a quite simple system, which relies on two layers, i.e. the U-Nodes layer the T-Nodes layer, U-nodes communicate among them when they get within radio range, the information spreads according to the user mobility pattern and it is filtered to preserve the system from overflowing.

Of course, since we do not assume a priori any backbone support, the information flow is generated solely by the physical movement of users, together with the opportunistic exchange of data. Contextual information, which is generated from sensors, is also diffused by means of the users' physical mobility: clearly, this means that, for efficiently running services based on this mechanism, an adequate level of users mobility is needed in order to provide a sufficient flow of information in the environment [29].

4. Conclusions

Wireless Sensor Networks are emerging as one of the most promising technologies for bringing the pervasive computing vision into reality. Due to the possibility of sensing the physical world with a granularity unimaginable before, a vast class of innovative applications becomes possible.
However, WSNs come at the cost of totally new technological challenges to be faced. Sensor nodes need to work in an extremely frugal energy budget, since they are often deployed in remote locations where the replacement of batteries is not an option, and this calls for innovative techniques capable of prolonging the network lifetime. Data management in WSN deals with the challenging task of *exploiting* the relevance of the information in order to reduce the communication needed for conveying the data outside the network. In this chapter, we have briefly reviewed the reference WSN data management techniques adopted, with a particular attention to distributed storage, distributed querying and data aggregation.
The proposed techniques, while reducing the communication overhead, thus alleviating the constraints on the sensor nodes, do not solve the communication problems deriving from a a network composed by thousands of nodes applying a multi-hop communication paradigm for delivering data. This is the major result of the seminal work of Gupta-Kumar [30], where it is shown the throughput of a large-scale network is O of the inverse of the number of nodes. Hence, as the number of nodes increases, alternative solutions has to be considered. In the second part of this chapter, we have reviewed a 2-tier network architecture tailored to the provisioning of pervasive services in urban environments. The proposed architecture, by assuming mobile users as nodes of the network, leverages on their movement and on the opportunistic relaying of data for relaxing the constraints on the sensor nodes. The proposed network architecture has been described, together with the principles of a suitable data management technique, called Information Filtering.

5. Acknowledgements

The architecture of Nomadic Sensor Networks was conceived and developed under the support of the EU within the framework of the BIONETS project EU-IST-FETSAC-FP6-027748 [40].

References

[1] E. C. Whitman, "Sosus: The "secret weapon" of undersee surveillance," *UnderseeWarfare*, vol. 7, no. 2, Winter 2005.

[2] D. Culler, D. Estrin, and M. Srivastava, "Guest editors' introduction overview of sensor networks," *Computer*, vol. 37, no. 8, pp. 41–49, August 2004.

[3] I. F. Akyildiz, W. Su, Y. Sankarasubramaniam, and E. Cayirci, "Wireless sensor networks: a survey," *Computer Networks*, vol. 38, pp. 393–422, 2002.

[4] I. F. Akyildiz, D. Pompili, and T. Melodia, "Underwater acoustic sensor networks: Research challenges," *Ad Hoc Networks (Elsevier)*, vol. 3, no. 3, pp. 257–279, May 2005.

[5] J. Lifton, D. Seetharam, M. Broxton, and J. A. Paradiso, "Pushpin computing system overview: A platform for distributed, embedded, ubiquitous sensor networks," in *Pervasive '02: Proceedings of the First International Conference on Pervasive Computing*.   London, UK: Springer-Verlag, 2002, pp. 139–151.

[6] "Crossbow technology inc." [Online]. Available: http://www.xbow.com/

[7] C.-Y. Chong and S. P. Kumar, "Sensor networks:evolution, opportunities, and challenges," *Proceedings of the IEEE*, vol. 91, no. 8, pp. 1247–1256, August 2003.

[8] K. Romer and F. Mattern, "The design space of wireless sensor networks," *Wireless Communications, IEEE*, vol. 11, no. 6, pp. 54–61, Dec 2004.

[9] J. M. Kahn, R. H. Katz, and K. S. J. Pister, "Next century challenges: Mobile networking for "smart dust"," in *Proc. of ACM MobiCom*, Seattle, 1999, pp. 271–278.

[10] D. Arvind and K. Wong, "Speckled computing: Disruptive technology for networked information appliances," in *in Proceedings of the IEEE International Symposium on Consumer Electronics (ISCE'04)*, September 2004, pp. 219–223.

[11] P. S. Philippe Bonnet, Johannes Gehrke, "Towards sensor database systems," *Lecture Notes in Computer Science*, vol. 1987, p. 3, 2001.

[12] A. Deshpande, C. Guestrin, S. Madden, J. M. Hellerstein, and W. Hong, "Model-driven data acquisition in sensor networks." in *VLDB*, 2004, pp. 588–599.

[13] Y. Yao and J. Gehrke, "The cougar approach to in-network query processing in sensor networks," 2002. [Online]. Available: citeseer.ist.psu.edu/yao02cougar.html

[14] ——, "Query processing for sensor networks." in *In Proc. Conf. on Innovative Data Syst. Res*, 2003, pp. 233–244.

[15] S. Madden, M. J. Franklin, J. M. Hellerstein, and W. Hong, "Tinydb: an acquisitional query processing system for sensor networks." *ACM Trans. Database Syst.*, vol. 30, no. 1, pp. 122–173, 2005.

[16] V. Handziski, J.Polastre, J.H.Hauer, C.Sharp, A.Wolisz, and D.Culler, "Flexible hardware abstraction for wireless sensor networks." in *In Proc. Conf. on EWSN*, 2005.

[17] D. Ganesan, B. Greenstein, D. Estrin, J. Heidemann, and R. Govindan, "Multiresolution storage and search in sensor networks," *j-TOS*, vol. 1, no. 3, pp. 277–315, Aug. 2005.

[18] S. Tilak, N. B. Abu-Ghazaleh, and W. R. Heinzelman, "Collaborative storage management in sensor networks," *CoRR*, vol. cs.NI/0408020, 2004.

[19] L. Tong, Q. Zhao, and S. Adireddy, "Sensor networks with mobile agents," in *MILCOM 2003 - IEEE Military Communications Conference*, October 2003, pp. 688–693.

[20] T. Liu, C. M. Sadler, P. Zhang, and M. Martonosi, "Implementing software on resource-constrained mobile sensors: Experiences with impala and zebranet." in *MobiSys*, 2004.

[21] C. Intanagonwiwat, R. Govindan, D. Estrin, J. Heidemann, and F. Silva, "Directed diffusion for wireless sensor networking," *IEEE/ACM Trans. Netw.*, vol. 11, no. 1, pp. 2–16, 2003.

[22] S. Shenker, S. Ratnasamy, B. Karp, R. Govindan, and D. Estrin, "Data-centric storage in sensornets," October 2002. [Online]. Available: citeseer.ist.psu.edu/shenker02datacentric.html

[23] T. He, B. M. Blum, J. A. Stankovic, and T. F. Abdelzaher, "Aida: Adaptive application-independent data aggregation in wireless sensor networks." *ACM Trans. Embedded Comput. Syst.*, vol. 3, no. 2, pp. 426–457, 2004.

[24] B. Krishnamachari, D. Estrin, and S. B. Wicker, "The impact of data aggregation in wireless sensor networks," in *ICDCSW '02: Proceedings of the 22nd International Conference on Distributed Computing Systems.* Washington, DC, USA: IEEE Computer Society, 2002, pp. 575–578.

[25] G. J. Pottie and W. J. Kaiser, "Wireless integrated network sensors," *Commun. ACM*, vol. 43, no. 5, pp. 51–58, 2000.

[26] S. Madden, M. J. Franklin, J. M. Hellerstein, and W. Hong, "Tag: a tiny aggregation service for ad-hoc sensor networks," *SIGOPS Oper. Syst. Rev.*, vol. 36, no. SI, pp. 131–146, 2002.

[27] S. Ray, R. Ungrangsi, F. D. Pellegrini, A. Trachtenberg, and D. Starobinski, "Robust location detection in emergency sensor networks," in *Proceedings of INFOCOM 2003*, San Francisco, 2003.

[28] M. Weiser, "The computer for the 21st century," *ACM Mob. Comput. Commun. Rev.*, vol. 3, no. 3, pp. 3–11, 1999.

[29] I. Carreras, I. Chlamtac, F. D. Pellegrini, and D. Miorandi, "Bionets: Bio-inspired networking for pervasive communication environments," *IEEE Transactions on Vehicular Technology*, to appear.

[30] P. Gupta and P. R. Kumar, "The capacity of wireless networks," *IEEE Trans. on Inf. Th.*, vol. 46, no. 2, pp. 388–404, Mar. 2000.

[31] O. Dousse and P. Thiran, "Connectivity vs capacity in dense ad hoc networks," in *Proc. of IEEE INFOCOM*, Hong Kong, 2004.

[32] O. Dousse, M. Franceschetti, and P. Thiran, "The costly path from percolation to full connectivity," in *Proc. of Allerton Conf.*, Urbana Champaign, US, 2004.

[33] I. Carreras, I. Chlamtac, H. Woesner, and H. Zhang, "Nomadic sensor networks," in *Proceedings of the Second European Workshop on Wireless Sensor Networks (EWSN).* Istanbul, Turkey: Springer-Verlag, Jan. 2005, pp. 166–176.

[34] I. Chlamtac, I. Carreras, and H. Woesner, "From internets to bionets: Biological kinetic service oriented networks," in *Advances in Pervasive Computing and Networking*, B. Szymanski and B. Yener, Eds. Springer Science, 2005, pp. 75–95.

[35] I. Carreras, I. Chlamtac, H. Woesner, and H. Zhang, "Nomadic sensor networks," in *Proc. of EWSN*, Istanbul, Turkey, 2005.

[36] M. Grossglauser and D. Tse, "Mobility increases the capacity of ad hoc wireless networks," *IEEE/ACM Trans. on Netw.*, vol. 10, no. 4, pp. 477–486, Aug. 2002.

[37] K. Fall, "A delay-tolerant network architecture for challenged internets," in *Proc. of ACM SIGCOMM*, Karlsruhe, DE, 2003.

[38] I. Chlamtac, M. Conti, and J. Liu, "Mobile ad hoc networking: imperatives and challenges," *Ad-Hoc Networks Journal*, vol. 1, pp. 13–64, Jul. 2003.

[39] A. Chaintreau, P. Hui, J. Crowcroft, C. Diot, R. Gass, and J. Scott, "Pocket switched networks: Real-world mobility and its consequences for opportunistic forwarding," Univ. of Cambridge, Tech. Rep. UCAM-CL-TR-617, 2005.

[40] The BIONETS IP Project. [Online]. Available: http://www.bionets.org

Global Data Management
R. Baldoni et al. (Eds.)
IOS Press, 2006

Systematic Design of P2P Technologies for Distributed Systems

Indranil Gupta

Dept. of Computer Science
University of Illinois at Urbana-Champaign, Urbana IL 61801
Ph: 1-217-265-5517. Fax: 1-217-265-6494.
indy@cs.uiuc.edu

Abstract. While several peer-to-peer (p2p) schemes have emerged for distributed data storage, there has also been a growing undercurrent towards the invention of *design methodologies* underlying these peer-to-peer systems. A design methodology is a *systematic technique* that helps us to not only design and create new p2p systems (e.g., for data storage) in a quick and predictable manner, but also increases our understanding of existing systems. This chapter brings together in one place previous and existing work by several authors on design methodologies that are intended to augment the activity of p2p algorithms, keeping our focus centered around (but not restricted to) data storage systems. As design methodologies grow in number and in power, researchers are increasingly likely to rely on them to design new p2p systems.

Keywords. Distributed Protocols, Design, Methodologies, Declarative Programming, Differential Equations, Composable Methodologies

1. Introduction

Today, researchers design large-scale distributed systems (such as p2p data stores) mostly by using an ad-hoc approach, with literature, experience, and education as the only available aids. This has arguably resulted in very complex distributed systems [20] and great difficulty in understanding the properties of these systems. Worse still, this has caused increased unreliability in today's systems [6], and a phenomenon that Tanenbaum calls "software bloat" [22].

However, in the past few years, a new series of techniques has emerged to both (1) simplify our understanding of existing distributed systems, as well as to (2) help us to design new distributed systems in a systematic manner. We refer to these two uses above as [12]: (1) retroactive and (2) progressive uses respectively.

A design methodology for a distributed protocol (or distributed system) can be loosely characterized as [12] "an organized, documented set of building blocks, rules and/or guidelines for design of a class of distributed protocols. It is possibly amenable to automated code generation."

To start off, let us briefly look at two examples of very power design methodologies.

For instance, Loo et al recently designed a system called P2 [15]. P2 is generally speaking a declarative language that can be used to specify the topologies of p2p overlays such as Chord and multicast overlays such as Narada. In effect, the researcher designing a system can not only formally specify the rules for the overlay topology, but also potentially formally (and automatically) verify properties of the system, as well as generate code for the system! One argument goes that had Chord been originally designed using P2, the entire system would have taken but half a day to design and code up, not the several months that it took its human designers! Further, as the authors of P2 showed, this automatically designed system would have performance that is quite close to that of the hand-designed Chord.

The second methodology we wish to point to is one that translates certain classes of differential equations into *equivalent* distributed protocols [11]. The derived protocols are replicated state machines with local and simple actions and transition rules, but most importantly, the globally emergent behavior of the protocol is equivalent to the behavior of the original differential equations. Differential equations have been used by several scientists (especially non-Computer Scientists) to represent ideas and results - this design methodology now allows protocols to be systematically derived from these natural models *predictably and without any side effects.* Article [11] then goes on to show how endemic disease models can be used to build distributed storage systems, and how other models (all represented as differential equations), e.g., ecological models, can be translated into protocols for important distributed computing problems.

The above methodologies are only indicative of the power of design methodologies. The rest of this chapter will expand on the details of some of these methodologies, and the reasons why they are good starting grounds to invent both new methodologies as well as new distributed systems.

In Section 2, we present a taxonomy of design methodologies, not necessarily restricted to distributed systems only. Section 3 discusses declarative programming models for distributed system design, and Section 4 describes the translation of differential equations into distributed protocols. Section 5 briefly outlines several other emergent and mature methodologies for p2p systems. We summarize the chapter in Section 6.

A note is due on the material in this chapter - all the material covered in this chpater has already been presented by researchers previously, hence in a sense, this chapter is akin to a survey paper on this new topic, albeit with hints at future directions. Thus, it is unavoidable and inevitable that this chapter reuses and in some cases reproduces, certain defintions, tables, descriptions of algorithms from the original publication. This is done mainly to ensure that the algorithms and designs proposed by the original authors of the respective paper(s) are presented faithfully. Wherever such reproduction occurs, we reference the original text, even if it is a reference to one of our own prior papers. Nevertheless, the reader will find that this reproduction is not a mere cut-and-paste: the material has been sufficiently edited to make it fit into the flow of the chapter and tie it to additional discussion. It is hoped that this approach of ours will preserve both the context and yet present the referenced authors' work in the best light.

Methodology Types	Innovative	Composable
Formal	Protocols from Differential Equations [11]; Bluespec for hardware synthesis [1]; P2 language for P2P systems [15]; RAML language for routing design [9].	TCP/IP layered architecture; Extensible router and OS designs (e.g., Click [14], SPIN, x-kernel [4,25]); Routing [28]; Probabilistic I/O automata [26]; Strategy Design Patterns [8]; Stacked architectures (e.g., Horus [24]).
Informal	Design Patterns [7].	DHT design methodologies [13,18]; Protocol family for survivable storage [27]; Probabilistic protocols [23].

Table 1. **How Existing Methodologies Fit into the Proposed Taxonomy (part of table borrowed from [12]).**

2. Taxonomy of Methodologies

In order to motivate an understanding of the features of methodologies, in this section, we first discuss a taxonomy of classification for them. This taxonomy first appeared in article [12]. In order to define our taxonomy, we have to define several terms - our definitions for these terms thus require unavoidable borrowing from the article [12].

Formal vs. Informal: A methodology that is specified using precise rules or a stringent framework is called a *formal* methodology. Otherwise the methodology is said to be *informal.* These "rules" for a formal methodology could either be mathematical or logical notation, or the grammar of a high level programming language. Respective examples are the probabilistic I/O automata [26], and the methodology of [11] that takes as input a set of differential equations (satisfying certain conditions), and generates code for a distributed protocol that is equivalent. Previous methodologies for DHT design [13,18] have been informal. We will discuss all these methodologies at different points during this chapter.

Due to their rigor (either through a formal framework or a compiler), formal methodologies can be used to create protocols with predictable or provable properties, and also to generate protocol code automatically. For example, the distributed protocols generated from differential equations in [11] are provably equivalent to the original differential equation, and can be generated by a toolkit called DiffGen [11]. On the other hand, informal methodologies are less rigorous and more flexible, but can have multiple possible interpretations. An informal methodology could be converted into a formal one through implementation of a specific interpretation. For example, an informal probabilistic protocol composable methodology can be instantiated through a high level language called Proactive Protocol Composition Language (PPCL) [10,23], thus making it formal. Once again, we will discuss each of these methodologies at different points during this chapter.

Innovative vs. Composable: Design methodologies must be capable of assisting in innovation of new protocols, as well as in the ability to reuse and adapt existing protocols. These are achieved respectively through innovative methodologies and composable methodologies. An innovative methodology describes how completely novel protocols can be created, e.g., [7,11]. A composable methodology typically describes *building blocks* and *composition rules or guidelines.* Building blocks are either standalone protocols or strategies, and composition rules help combine the blocks to create new protocols with enhanced properties. For example, the informal methodology for DHT design in [13] uses four types of building blocks - overlay, membership, routing, and preprocessing. Strategy design patterns are another example of a composable methodology [8].

Table 1 summarizes the above discussion.

Discovery of Methodologies: Different approaches are possible for the *discovery* of these methodologies:

1. **Retroactive**: A methodology is discovered for an existing system or class of protocols. Ex: methodologies for routing [28] and probabilistic protocols [10].

2. **Progressive**: A methodology is invented that creates a novel class of protocols. Ex: the design of protocols from differential equations can generate new protocols for dynamic replication and majority voting [11].

3. **Auxiliary**: A methodology is discovered to assist and complement an existing methodology. Ex: protocol families for survivable storage architectures [27] combine several auxiliary methodologies for differing system models.

3. Declarative Languages for Protocol Design

Recently, there has been emergence of several declarative paradigms for specifying the design of distributed systems. As opposed to imperative programming languages (such as C or Java) that explicitly describe the detailed actions of a distributed protocol (i.e., the *how*), a declarative approach to programming instead specifies the low-level *goals* of the distributed protocol (i.e., the *what*), leaving the translation of this specification into actual code to a separate compiler or interpreter (which in turn can perhaps be changed by the user).

Declarative programming can be achieved by either a functional programming language (ML-like) or by a logic programming language (Prolog-like) or a constraint language. Below, we first describe P2 a declarative logic programming that can be used to design peer to peer systems (and eventually in distributed data stores). Then, we briefly describe RAML, a language that can be used to design routing protocols. Although the second case study is not directly related to storage, it is related to routing, an important component in any distributed store.

Notice that both the methodologies presented below are formal and innovative methodologies, although the second methodology (Section 3.2) is also amenable to composition. Both these methodologies have both retroactive and progressive uses.

3.1. P2: Declarative Design of P2P Overlays

B.T. Loo et al's P2 is a declarative logic language intended for the design of overlays as well as multicast protocols [15]. Since overlays are directly applicable in designing distributed stores, below, we describe the application of P2 to design of a simple, canonical overlay. P2 is based on Datalog, a general declarative query language that is a "pure" subset of Prolog that is free of imperative constructs.

Consider a peer to peer system that is structured as a logical ring - each node lies at some point in this ring and has a successor and a predecessor. This ring overlay is the most canonical form of the Chord peer to peer system [21], and we will describe the use of P2 in designing the ring overlay. Article [15] details the design of the entire Chord system (which has several non-successor neighbors for each node in order to speed up search).

P2 uses several rules to specify what the system needs to achieve. Each of these rules applies at each node that is participating in the overlay. Below, we describe some of the rules:

- $materialize(succ, 120, infinity, keys(2))$

This rule specifies that each node in the system will maintain a table called *succ* (successor) whose tuples will be retained for 120 seconds and have unbounded size, while *keys()* specifies the position of tuple field that is the primary key of the table.

- $stabilize(X) : -periodic(X, E, 3)$

Here, canonically, *stabilize* is a table with row that has value (X) for an X, if table *periodic* has a row with value $(X, E, 3)$ for some E. Specifically in P2 though, *periodic* is not a table – instead it is a built-in *stream* that periodically produces a tuple with a unique identifier E at node X (in the distributed system), in this case once every 3 seconds. This also means that *stabilize* itself is not a table maintained at a node, but instead an event generated at the node. As we will see below, this *stabilize* event further causes the node to refresh the successor tables of its neighbors, as well as to increment its own successor table version number.

- $lookupResults@R(R, K, S, SI, E) : -node@NI(NI, N),$
  $lookup@NI(NI, K, R, E), succ@NI(NI, S, SI), Kin(N, S]$

Each object in this peer to peer system has a unique identifier that lies somewhere along the ring overlay. When a query or an insert request is generated by some node in the system for a given object (with the object id), it needs to be *routed* to the appropriate node in the ring overlay, i.e., the node that lies right after the object id's location in the logical ring.

The above described rule returns a succesful lookup result if the received lookup seeks a key K found between the receiving node's identifier and that of its successor.

- $sendSuccessor@SI(SI, NI) : -stabilize@NI(NI,\_), succ@NI(NI,\_, SI)$
- $succ@PI(PI, S, SI) : -sendSuccessors@NI(NI, PI), succ@NI(NI, S, SI)$

Finally, the above two rules come into play when the node (periodically) needs to refresh its successor table (and that of its table). In the first rule above, a node asks its successors (all if there are multiple successors) to send it their own successors, whenever the *stabilize* event is issued at that node. The second rule above then installs the returned successor at the original node.

In summary, we have taken only five rules above to specify the design of the entire ring overlay - from basic tables to lookup to stabilization. Article [15] describes the design of the entire Chord protocol (substantially more complex than the above ring overlay) in merely 47 rules!

Some advantages of such a declarative approach to design are evident; other benefits are not so obvious:

1. Ease of Protocol Specification: A protocol designer no longer has to write a C/C++/Java program several thousand lines long to design a new system. Design is a matter of writing only a few rules.
2. Formal Verification: Any such declarative design can potentially be run by specially-built verification engines that find bugs in the design, or better still, analyze the scalability and fault-tolerance of the protocol.
3. On-line distributed debugging: Execution history can be exported as a set of relational tables, distributed debugging of a deployed distributed system can be achieved by writing the appropriate P2 rules.
4. Breadth: The same language P2 can be used to design other p2p overlays beyond Chord (e.g., the Narada overlay) - this makes possible quantitative comparisons among these systems that are much more believable than mere simulation-based comparisons. In addition, hybrid designs can be explored.

Clearly, the downside to this approach is the learning curve associated with "yet another new language". Yet, if the results of article [15] are to be believed, the performance obtained by a system designed using P2 is comparable to the original hand-coded system. In view of the above benefits, many researchers might consider it worth to learn another programming language, especially if it makes the difficult job of system design a little bit easier.

3.2. RAML: Declarative Design of Routing Protocols

Routing protocols for the Internet are difficult to design and much more difficult to verify for correctness. There has been a lack of design methodologies for routing protocol design, leading to the over-use of fairly well-understood protocols, e.g., BGP is not intended as an IGP, yet is being pressed into service as IGP in several parts of the Internet - this is a problem since BGP convergence properties are not well-known. A different IGP protocol would need to be designed.

In [9], Griffin and Sobrinho present a new programming language called the *Routing Algebra Metalanguage (RAML)* which enables protocol designers to specify classes of *routing algebras* and manipulate the algebras, as well as verify several convergence and correctness properties about such algebras.

Below, we briefly give an overview of the Metarouting framework of [9], mentioning the authors' findings. For more details, the reader should refer to [9].

RAML Overview: The design of any routing protocol consists of both policies and mechanisms. Policy defines how the attributes of a route are described, what defines a route as a "best" route, etc. The mechanism defines how routing messages are exchanged, what route selection algorithms are exchanged etc. Clearly, in any routing protocol, there is an inter-play between the corresponding parts of policy and mechanism.

The RAML language is based on a metarouting framework that defines a tuple:

$RP = < A, M, \ldots >$,

where A is a routing algebra (the policy part) and M is a set of mechanisms that can be associated with a routing adjacency. Several mechanisms can be used for the same protocol. We will ignore the rest of the above tuple for the purposes of simplicity in this chapter. The algebra is represented as:

$A = (\Sigma, <=, L, \oplus, \ldots)$

In the above description of a routing algebra A, Σ is a path signature and $<=$ is a preference relation over Σ that is both complete (i.e., defined for all pairs of elements from Σ) and also transitive. Finally, L is a set of link labels and $\oplus$ is a relation from $L \times \Sigma \to \Sigma$.

This algebra now allows us to specify in place of $\oplus$ simple operators such as ADD, MULT, MAX, MIN, etc., so that we can now reason about paths. For instance, shortest path routing can be reasoned about by using $\oplus = ADD$ above and using the normal $<=$ relation to compare different paths in Σ.

More importantly though, for a given class of algebras, one can define important path properties. The main properties explored in [9] are: Monotonicity, Strict Monotonicity and Isotonicity - all these properties apply to pairs in $L \times L$ w.r.t. the operation $\oplus$. For instance, ADD satisfies all the above three properties.

The authors then go on to define operations among entire pairs of algebras, i.e., given two different routing algebras A_1 and A_2, one can define composite routing protocols based on, say, the lexical product of the two algebras. The authors also explore scoped product and disjunction-based composition. *Notice that this makes the RAML methodology in a sense both innovative and composable.*

Finally, the authors show how RAML can be used to define "better" IGP protocols than BGP - one description they present involves merely a 1-line specification (for A)! Yet, this algebra has provable convergence and correctness properties. Then, the authors go on to reason about BGP itself and specify it in their RAML framework. They show that the policy component of BGP is in fact a scoped product of the EBGP policy component's algebra and the IBGP's policy component's algebra. Here both EBGP and IBGP can each be represented as a RAML algebra.

This is an extremely powerful methodology - not merely for design (one can specify entire routing policies within just 1 line), but also for reasoning about the convergence and correctness properties of these policies. It is likely that RAML or RAML-like languages will be increasingly used by the networking community both retroactively as well as progressively, over the coming few years.

4. Methodologies for Nature-Based Design of Distributed Systems

Several fields of science including Biology, Chemistry, Physics, and several non-engineering fields such as sociology, etc. use differential equations to represent ideas and results. Translating ideas and results from these fields into distributed protocols in a systematic manner requires a design methodology. Several nature-inspired distributed systems have been designed, e.g., [2]. However, without a *systematic* design methodology being used for the translation, there is the risk that a protocol derived from a natural phenomenon may not be an accurate translation, or worse still have side-effects in distributed computer systems that are otherwise not seen in nature.

Here, we briefly present previously published results for an innovative methodology that translates sets of differential equations into *equivalent* distributed protocols - some of the discussion is inevitably borrowed from the article [11]. An equation set generates a state machine, with each variable mapped to a state, and terms mapped to protocol actions. Stable equilibrium points in the original equations map to self-stabilizing behavior (fractions of nodes in respective states), and simplicity of terms maps to scalable communication.

In brief, consider a system of differential equations in the form $\dot{\bar{X}} = \frac{d\bar{X}}{dt} = \bar{f}(\bar{X})$, where $\bar{X}$ is a vector of variables, f is a vector of $|X|$ functions, and the left hand sides denote each of the variables differentiated with respect to time t. An example with $X = \{x, y, z\}$ is:

$$\dot{x} = -\beta xy + \alpha z$$

$$\dot{y} = \beta xy - \gamma y$$

$$\dot{z} = \gamma y - \alpha z \tag{1}$$

Here, α, β, γ are parameters lying in the interval $[0, 1]$. When the methodology of [11] is applied to the above equation, the protocol generated is *equivalent* to the original equation system, viz., *the fractions of processes in different states in the distributed system, at equilibrium, is the same as the values of the variables when the original equations are in equilibrium.*

Below, we describe in brief the protocol derived from the above differential equation system, as well as the general methodology. For more details on the details of the translation methodology, the reader is encouraged to refer to the original paper [11].

Endemic Protocol: Equations (1) above in fact represent the survival of endemic diseases (such as the flu) in a fixed-size human population, with x, y, z respectively the fractions of receptives, infected, and immune individuals. The protocol derived from it is a new *dynamic and migratory replication model.* In this dynamic and migratory replication scheme, once a given file is inserted into a distributed group of computer hosts connected in an overlay, the emergent behavior of the protocol ensures that the file has a small number of replicas moving continuously among the hosts in the distributed system (only "infected" hosts store a replica). Without using too much network bandwidth, this scheme ensures *attacker-resilience* – an attacker cannot accurately guess the current set of replica nodes for a given file.

Effectively, the protocol derived from equations (1) above can be represented as a replicated state machine that runs independently at each process in the distributed system. This replicated state machine is represented below. Here, (1) an "infected" host is labelled as being in a "Stash" state since it is storing the file, and (2) an "immune" host is labelled as an "averse" host for historical reasons.

The state machine derived has three states - x (susceptible or *receptive*), y (infected or *stash*), z (immune or *averse*). *A process is responsible if and only if it is in the stash state.* The actions are as follows.

Assume that $\beta \in (0, 1]$. State actions can be defined to be executed periodically, as discussed earlier in the methodology. (i) (γy term) A process p in the stash state tosses a coin with a biased heads probability γ - if the coin falls heads, process p changes its state to averse. This transition is accompanied by a deletion of the object replica at p. (ii) (αz term) A process p in the averse state tosses a coin with heads probability α, and changes state to receptive if this coin falls heads up. (iii) (βxy term) A process p in the receptive state chooses 1 target uniformly at random, and if the target is in the stash state, and a locally flipped coin (with heads probability β) falls heads simultaneously, process p changes its state to stash (after an object transfer).

The analysis of this protocol reveals that this distributed system has two equilibria:

$$(x_\infty, y_\infty, z_\infty) = (1, 0, 0), \text{ and}$$

$$(x_\infty, y_\infty, z_\infty) = (\gamma/\beta, \frac{1 - \gamma/\beta}{1 + \gamma/\alpha}, \frac{1 - \gamma/\beta}{1 + \alpha/\gamma})$$

$$(2)$$

We call these respectively as the *first equilibrium point* and the *second equilibrium point*. The first equilibrium results in all copies of the object disappearing; all processes eventually turn receptive. The second equilibrium is more desirable, since it guarantees a stable number of stashers in the system.

Surprisingly, the analysis in [11] shows that *starting the distributed system initially at any point <u>other</u> than the line $y = 0$ (includes the first equilibrium point) causes it to eventually (and quickly) converge towards the second equilibrium.* This leads the protocol to have the following properties: (1) Self-Stabilization: the system always tends to converge back to a stable (small) number of stashers, (2) Untraceability: it is probabilistically difficult for an attacker to guess who all the stashers are (the window until this set changes is very short), (3) Fault-tolerance: due to the properties (1) and (2) above, massive failures and churn are tolerated by the protocol, (4) Scale: the above properties are guaranteed by basically using constant bandwidth at each host, independent of the system size.

This dynamic and migratory replication model is currently being used to design a new distributed file system called "Folklore" [19].

The Translation Methogology: In order to clearly classify the differential equation classes that can be converted into distributed protocols, we first describe a taxonomy of differential equation systems. We focus only on equation systems that have a single differential per component equation, and are of order and degree 1. Such an equation is canonically $\dot{\bar{X}} = \bar{f}(\bar{X})$. We also denote the equation for variable $x \in X$ as $f_x(\bar{X})$. Further, each $x \in X$ lies in $[0,1]$ with differentials at the interval end-points being either zero or pointing in towards the other direction.

We define a *term* as an elementary unit of f_x. In other words, we express each $f_x(\bar{X})$ as a sum of elementary terms, where each term could be either positive or negative. Our translation methodology works on equation systems that are both *restricted polynomial* and *completely partitionable*.

An equation system $\dot{\bar{X}} = \bar{f}(\bar{X})$ is *restricted polynomial* if (i) it has only polynomial terms, and (ii) for each $f_x(X)$, it is true that each negative term $-T = -c_T \Pi^{y \in X} y^{i_{y,f_x,T}}$ that occurs in it ($c_T \in [0,1]$) has $i_{x,f_x,T} >= 1$. Equation system (1) is an example of a restricted polynomial system.

An equation system $\dot{\bar{X}} = \bar{f}(\bar{X})$ is said to be *completely partitionable* if and only if (i) it is completethe sum of all right hand sides of all the equations sum to zero, and (ii) the multi-set consisting of all terms in $\bar{f}(\bar{X})$ can be written as a union of mutually disjoint subsets, where each subset contains exactly two terms, and the two terms in each subset add up to zero (i.e., one term is the negative of the other in the pair). For example, equation system (1) is completely partitionable.

Now we describe two translation techniques for certain term pairs in the differential equation system. Consider a polynomial term of the form $-T = -c.\Pi^{y \in X} y^{i_{y,f_x,T}}$, occurring in f_x, with the corresponding $+T$ term occurring in f_y. If $-T = -c.x$, it can be translated into a *Flipping* action, otherwise it is translated into a *One-time-sampling* action. Each of these actions are executed periodically, with the time to the next action determined by a memoryless distribution with an average of $\frac{1}{k_x}$ time unit, where k_x is the number of negative terms on the right hand side of f_x - each next action is selected at random from among the k_x possibilities. Needless to say, the definitions of these terms are also borrowed from [11].

- *Flipping:* A term of the type $-c.x$ ($c \in [0,1]$) occurring on the right hand side (henceforth "r.h.s.") of $\dot{x} = f_x(\bar{X})$ is mapped to a flipping action. A process in state x *locally* tosses ("flips") a biased coin that has heads probability c. Only if the coin turns up heads, does the process transition out of state x; the new state is y, where $\dot{y} = f_y(\bar{X})$ contains the corresponding $+c.x$ term, and $y \neq x$. Notice that for one execution of the flipping action at a given process, the probability of success, and thus state transition, is c.

- *One-time-sampling:* A term $-T$ of the type $-T = -c.x^{i_{x,f_x,T}}.\Pi^{y \in X - \{x\}} y^{i_{y,f_x,T}}$ ($c \in [0,1]$) that occurs on the r.h.s. of $\dot{x} = f_x(\bar{X})$ with $i_{x,f_x,T} >= 1$ is mapped into the following action. A process in state x samples $(i_{x,f_x,T} - 1 + \Sigma^{y \in X - \{x\}}(i_{y,f_x,T}))$ other processes, each such target process selected uniformly at random from across the group. In addition, the process also flips *locally* a biased coin that has heads probability c. Let the variables $y \in X$ be ordered lexicographically. Then the process makes a transition out of state x (and into the corresponding state with the $+T$ term) if and only if (i) each of the first $i_{x,f_x,T} - 1$ target choices happen to be in state x; and (ii) for each $j : 1 \leq j \leq)$, we have $\Sigma^{y \in X - \{x\}} i_{y,f_x,T}$, the jth

process sampled is in the same state as the jth variable in $\Pi^{y \in X - \{x\}} y^{i_y, f_x, T}$ (when ordered lexicographically); and (iii) the flipped local coin falls heads [1]. Notice that for one execution of this one-time-sampling action at a given process, the probability of success, and thus state transition, is $c.x^{i_x, f_x, T-1}.\Pi^{y \in X - \{x\}} y^{i_y, f_x, T}$.

The article [11] then goes on to show that the above two translation techniques are sufficient to translate *any differential equation system that is both completely partitionable and restricted polynomial.* This class is not small at all - it contains a large number of very useful differential equations, including the endemic process shown earlier in this section. In addition, this methodology can also be used to design a new protocol for majority voting in large-scale distributed systems (derived from a model of biological competition among ecosystem species), and a protocol from adaptive Grid Computing (derived from coordination models for honeybees). The reader is encouraged to see details in [11].

This methodology can be automated to generate code at the protocol designer's desk. The differential equation translation methodology has been incorporated into a design toolkit called *DiffGen*, which enables a designer to input differential equations (in a Mathematica-like format), and outputs compilable and deployable C code for the equivalent protocol.

The methodology just presented is extremely powerful in designing new distributed storage systems. The Folklore file system [19] creates an untraceable data store by building on top of the core endemic protocol described above. Article [11] also describes how differential equations representing certain ecosystem behaviors (the Lotka-Volterra model of competition) can be translated into a distributed protocol for majority voting, with potential use in distributed digital archives that need to ensure that the "good" copies of articles survive in spite of bit-rot and malicious attacks [17].

Intuitively, the protocols generated by this methodology are similar to Complex Adaptive Systems, and can be considered as a type of "Emergent Thinker" [5]. The methodology avoids any of the side-effects of informal translation mechanisms. Besides it revealing that natural phenomena can indeed be translated systematically into distributed protocols, the more surprising aspect of this direction of research has been that the generated protocols in fact (1) solve useful and practical problems, and (2) have many (and more!) characteristics that distributed systems designers consider important for large-scale distributed systems.

5. Other Methodologies

In the previous sections in this chapter, we have focused on a select set of recent developments in the field of design methodologies for distributed systems and distributed stores. In this section, we focus on some not-so-recent and some classical design methodologies for distributed systems. This section will wrap up our discussion on the topic.

---

[1] The idea behind this condition is of course similar to that behind the well-known *Law of Mass Action.* Flipping is in fact a special case of One-time-sampling.

5.1. Other Theoretical Methodologies

Probabilistic I/O automata and Composition: Lynch and Tuttle [16] originally defined a model of an I/O automaton that contains states, as well as transition rules defined among state pairs. The transition rules are based on *actions* possible in those states, where each action could be either one of the following three types – input, output, or internal actions.

Wu et al then extended this I/O automaton and were able to define a probabilistic I/O automaton in [26]. In this variant, for each state and each action that the state can receive, the specification defines probabilities of transition to all possible next-states. In addition, a delay function is defined, determining how long the system will wait in this state before moving to the selected next-state.

Most importantly though, Wu et al go on to describe how entire automata can be composed with each other. Then, they detail how automaton properties such as equivalence and other properties such as full abstraction.

In a sense, the probabilistic I/O automaton model is an advanced version of the differential equation-based automata derived in Section 4. It should be possible to further develop the translation mechanisms described for differential equations in Section 4 so as to enable the design of more complex (and thus more powerful) probabilistic I/O automata.

Automatic Discovery of Mutual Exclusion Protocols: In any distributed storage system, the ability to access resources (e.g., files) in a mutually exclusive manner (i.e., at most one process accesses the file at any time, with deadlock-freedom and starvation-freedom) is very important. Bar-David and Taubenfeld have described a methodology in [3] which allows the protocol designer to specify (via a new high-level programming language) several parameters that they require from a mutual exclusion algorithm. With these parameters, their tool then goes off and explores all possible programs (in pseudo-code) that satisfy the constraints specified, yet are correct solutions to the mutual exclusion problem.

The constraints that can be specified by the designer include: (1) number of processes (2) number of lines of code (3) number, size and type of variables (4) type of conditions: simple or complex. Complex conditions are composed of two simple conditions (terms) related by and, or, xor. The design of their tool contains three basic components – an internal algorithm generator, an algorithm verifier, and an optimizer.

The authors explore the feasibility of their design for small-scale distributed systems (up to a few processes only), yet this yields interesting results. For instance, the authors found that with a constraint of two shared bits among processes and simple conditions, any mutual exclusion protocol has to have at least 7 entry commands and at least 1 exit command. The author's tool also managed to find a mutual exclusion protocol that was shorter than a classical mutual exclusion algorithm previously proposed by Dekker - the new algorithm has merely 6 entry and 1 exit commands while Dekker's algorithm had 9 entry and 2 exit commands.

The benefits of using similar tools lies not merely in being able to generate simpler programs that solve the given problem correctly (although this has clear benefits such as reduction of code complexity, ease of debugging and maintenance). The benefit lies more in being able to make the protocol designer's job easier without taking away any of the flexibility or stifling the creativity involved in the protocol design process.

5.2. Other Informal Methodologies

Informal Methodology for P2P systems: Iamnitchi and Foster presented an informal methodology for the design of p2p resource discovery schemes in [13]. This composable methodology requires the design of four components:

1. Membership Protocol: Specifies how hosts maintain their neighbors, in spite of node join, leave and failure.
2. Overlay Construction: Specifies how neighbors are selected from among all possible candidates. Usually based on a set of invariants and rules.
3. Request Processing: Routing, through the overlay, of lookup and insert and delete requests to the appropriate responsible node in the system.
4. Preprocessing: Includes prefetching and usage-based and other optimizations.

In addition, nodes in a p2p overlay for resource discovery typically have unique (logical) nodeID's assigned to them. Manku [18] explores several techniques for flexible nodeID assignment and maintenance in p2p systems. He uses balanced binary trees for nodeID management and assignment. This adds a fifth component to the above design informal methodology.

Adaptive Data Stores: There is a wide variety of system designs and protocols for survivable storage infrastructures. Each design point addresses a particular fault model (e.g., crash-stop or Byzantine, repairable or non-repairable, synchronous or asynchronous). Thus the fault model assumption is typically incorporated in at the protocol design time.

Wylie et al [27] describe work on a mechanism that allows a distributed store to address a wide variety of fault models by making the fault-model decision at run-time, rather than at design-time. This is achieved by developing a framework where multiple protocols, each addressing a separate fault model, can be incorporated. Then, at run-time, the appropriate fault-models can be selected, either explicitly, or dynamically and automatically by detecting the most prevalent types of faults (through a separate detector).

This is an informal composable methodology that helps design an adaptive distributed storage system; one that can tolerate a wide variety of faults. This approach has the potential of being able to reuse the existing plethora of protocols for different fault-models and pull them into a single system design that gets the best-of-all-worlds performance.

6. Summary

This chapter has studied several design methodologies for the design of distributed systems, with focus on distributed storage structures. We first saw a taxonomy of design methodologies. Then we saw how declarative programming models can be used for the design of distributed p2p systems. Then, we have seen how natural phenomena and results and ideas from other fields of Science can be translated in a systematic manner into useful and practical distributed protocols. We also saw a few other design methodologies - both formal and informal.

The number and power of design methodologies for distributed systems is growing, and is reaching critical mass. Design methodologies have the potential to speed up the process of protocol design without stifling the creativity of this activity, and will likely play an increasing role in the next few years. Some methodologies are informal, others can be tied to automated code generation engines that allow a designer to go from idea to system implementation and experiments within the matter of a few seconds! If some of these methodologies (e.g., P2 being a case in point) had been invented a few years ago, the p2p research field would have had a much more accelerated development! Yet, like most research in this area, we end with an open-ended observation that the discovery of methodologies itself is a difficult task - there is, as yet, no "methodology to discover or reason about methodologies".

References

[1] Arvind. Bluespec: A language for hardware design, simulation, synthesis and verification. In *Proc. MEMOCODE*, page 249, Jun. 2003.

[2] O. Babaoglu, H. Meling, and A. Montresor. Anthill: A framework for the development of agent-based peer-to-peer systems. In *Proc. 22nd ICDCS*, 2002.

[3] Y. Bar-David and G. Taubenfeld. Automatic discovery of mutual exclusion algorithms. In *Proc. ACM PODC*, 2003.

[4] B. Bershad and S. Savage et al. Extensibility, safety and performance in the SPIN operating system,. In *Proc. ACM SOSP*, pages 267–284, Dec. 1995.

[5] S. Camorlinga and K. Barker. The emergent thinker. In *Proc. SELF-STAR*, May-Jun. 2004.

[6] Computing Research Association (CRA). Grand Research Challenges in Distributed Systems. http://www.cra.org/reports/gc.systems.pdf.

[7] E. Gamma, R. Helm, R. Johnson, and Vlissides J. *Design Patterns: elements of reusable object-oriented software*. Addison-Wesley, 1st edition, 1995.

[8] B. Garbinato and R. Guerraoui. Using the strategy design pattern to compose reliable distributed protocols. In *Proc. USENIX Conf. Obj.-Or. Tech. and Sys.*, pages 221–232, Jun. 1997.

[9] T.G. Griffin and J.L. Sobrinho. Metarouting. In *Proc. ACM SIGCOMM*, 2005.

[10] I. Gupta. *Building Scalable Solutions to Distributed Computing Problems using Probabilistic Components*. PhD Thesis, Dept. of Computer Science, Cornell University, Jan. 2004.

[11] I. Gupta. On the design of distributed protocols from differential equations. In *Proc. ACM PODC*, pages 216–225, 2004.

[12] I. Gupta and et al. A case for methodology research in self-* distributed systems. *LNCS 3460, Self-Star Properties in Complex Information Systems*, pages 260–272, 2005.

[13] A. Iamnitchi and I. Foster. Peer-to-peer approach to resource location in Grid environments. *Grid Resource Management*, 2003.

[14] E. Kohler and R. Morris et al. The Click modular router. *ACM TOCS*, 18(3), Aug. 2000.

[15] B.T. Loo, T. Condie, J. Hellerstein, and et al. Implementing declarative overlays. In *Proc. ACM SOSP*, 2005.

[16] Nancy Lynch and Mark Tuttle. An introduction to input/output automata. *CWI-Quarterly*, 2(3):219–246, Sep. 1989.

[17] P. Maniatis, M. Roussopoulos, T. J. Giuli, D. S. H. Rosenthal, Mary Baker, and Yanto Muliadi. Preserving peer replicas by rate-limited sampled voting. In *Proc. ACM SOSP*, pages 44–59, 2003.

[18] G. S. Manku. Balanced binary trees for id management and load balance in distributed hash tables. In *Proc. ACM PODC*, pages 197–205, 2004.

[19] R. V. Morales and I. Gupta. Providing both scale and security through a single core probabilistic protocol. In *Proc. 1st StoDiS*, 2005.

[20] A. Spector. Plenary Talk. ACM SOSP, 2003.

[21] I. Stoica, R. Morris, D. Karger, F. Kaashoek, and H. Balakrishnan. Chord: A Scalable Peer-To-Peer Lookup Service for Internet Applications. In *Proc. ACM SIGCOMM*, pages 149–160, 2001.

[22] A. Tanenbaum. Plenary Talk. ACM SOSP, 2005.

[23] N. Thompson and I. Gupta. A composable methodology for proactive distributed protocols, Sept. 2004. TR UIUCDCS-R-2004-2490.

[24] R. van Renesse, S. Maffeis, and K. P. Birman. Horus: a flexible group communications system. *CACM*, 39(4):76–83, April 1996.

[25] J. Ventura, J. Rodrigues, and L. Rodrigues. Response time analysis of composable micro-protocols. In *Proc. 4th IEEE OORTDC*, pages 335–342, 2001.

[26] S.-H. Wu and S. A. Smolka et al. Composition and behaviors of probabilistic I/O automata. *TCS*, 176(1-2):1–38, Apr. 1997.

[27] J. Wylie and G.R. Goodson et al. A protocol family approach to survivable storage infrastructures. In *Proc. FUDICO*, 2004.

[28] G. Xie and J. Zhan et al. Routing design in operational networks: a look from the inside. In *Proc. ACM SIGCOMM*, pages 27–40, 2004.

Section 2

Semantic Interoperability in the Large

Global Data Management
R. Baldoni et al. (Eds.)
IOS Press, 2006

177

Data Management in Peer-to-Peer Data Integration Systems

Diego Calvanese [a], Giuseppe De Giacomo [b], Domenico Lembo [b,1],
Maurizio Lenzerini [b], and Riccardo Rosati [b]

[a] *Faculty of Computer Science, Free University of Bozen-Bolzano*
[b] *Dipartimento di Informatica e Sistemistica, Università di Roma "La Sapienza"*

Abstract. Decentralized data management has been addressed during the years by means of several technical solutions, ranging from distributed DBMSs, to mediator-based data integration systems. Recently, such an issue has been investigated in the context of Peer-to-Peer (P2P) architectures. In this chapter we focus on P2P data integration systems, which are characterized by various autonomous peers, each peer being essentially an autonomous information system that holds data and is linked to other peers by means of P2P mappings. P2P data integration does not rely on the notion of global schema, as in traditional mediator-based data integration. Rather, it computes answers to users' queries, posed to any peer of the system, on the basis of both local data and the P2P mappings, thus overcoming the main drawbacks of centralized mediator-based data integration systems and providing the foundations of effective data management in virtual organizations.

In this chapter we first survey the most significant approaches proposed in the literature for both mediator-based data integration and P2P data management. Then, we focus on advanced schema-based P2P systems for which the aim is semantic integration of data, and analyze the commonly adopted approach of interpreting such systems using a first-order semantics. We show some weaknesses of this approach, and compare it with an alternative approach, based on multi-modal epistemic semantics, which reflects the idea that each peer is conceived as a rational agent that exchanges knowledge/belief with other peers. We consider several central properties of P2P data integration systems: modularity, generality, and decidability. We argue that the approach based on epistemic logic is superior with respect to all the above properties.

Keywords. Peer-to-Peer Data Integration, Logic-based Framework, Semantics

1. Introduction

Data management systems have been continuously evolving during the years to respond to customer demand and the new market requirements. Starting from the late 80s, centralized systems, which had often produced huge, monolithic, and generally inefficient databases, have been replaced by decentralized systems in which data are maintained in different sites with autonomous storage and computation capabilities. All such systems

---

[1]Correspondence to: Domenico Lembo, Dipartimento di Informatica e Sistemistica, Università di Roma "La Sapienza", Via Salaria 113, 00198 Roma, Italy. Tel.: +39 06 4991 8339; Fax: +39 06 8530 0849; E-mail: lembo@dis.uniroma1.it.

are characterized by an architecture in which data returned to a user query might not be physically stored at the site queried by the user. In distributed databases, decentralization of data is generally achieved to enhance system performance, and is precisely designed and controlled. However, such an architecture is not able to support the integration of previously existing systems, where data dispersed over several sources are required to be accessed in a centralized and uniform way. Database federation tools enable data from multiple heterogeneous data sources to appear as if it was contained in a single federated database. Such tools provide mechanisms which mask the native characteristics of each source and represent it in a common format, thus enabling a centralized and transparent data access. Mediator-based data integration systems (schematized in Figure 1) provide in addition the capability of defining a (virtual) global schema representing the unified view of the application domain, which is related to the sources through a suitable mapping establishing a semantic relationship between them. Here, the integration can be performed in a declarative way, and query answering, i.e., the problem of providing answers to users' queries posed on the virtual global schema, is in general a form of reasoning with incomplete information, and is achieved by means of powerful mechanisms and advanced techniques. More recently, the issue of cooperation, integration, and coordination

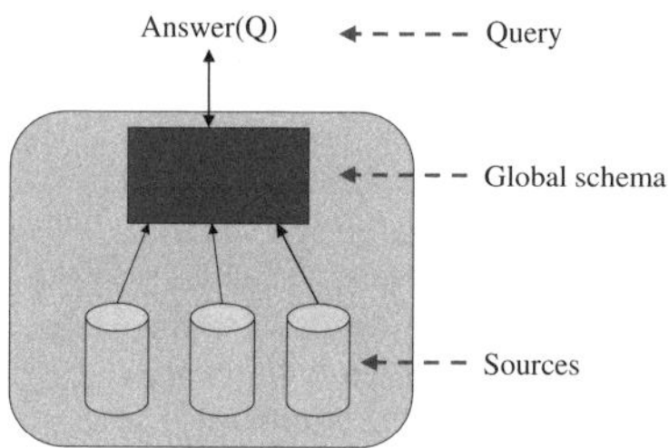

Figure 1. Mediator-based Data Integration System

between data nodes in open distributed systems has been investigated in the context of Peer-to-Peer (P2P) data management [50]. In short, a P2P system is characterized by a structure constituted by various autonomous nodes (called sources, sites, agents, or peers, depending on the context in which such systems are studied) that hold data and that are linked to other nodes by means of mappings. Differently from all the above mentioned architectures, P2P systems do not require a centralized management and are not developed under the control of central authority. Each peer provides part of the overall information available from a distributed environment, and acts both as a client and as a server in the system. The result is a completely decentralized architecture, flexible and able to handle dynamic changes in the system, which peers can join or leave at run-time. Then, favored by its characteristics, P2P computing is expected to soon penetrate the world of information technology, leveraging the growth of virtual organizations willing to share information on the network, as well as supporting the electronic business. As for this last kind of applications, new forms of electronic brokerage are emerging, where each broker is a peer offering goods or services either directly on behalf of a producer, or through another broker, i.e., through a peer to which a percentage fee is due in case of a transaction. In many cases, for example, in the electronic commerce for the tourism domain, such P2P applications are very data intensive as each peer must store large amounts of travel and hotel data or query such data across a heterogeneous P2P network. Furthermore, they are characterized by a potentially huge number of peers willing to access to such a business. At the same time, mobile end consumer devices such as cell phones and PDAs are becoming more powerful as their processing power and data storage capacities approach the speed and memory of workstations. This opens a perspective of data intensive P2P applications for participants in mobile networks.

Nowadays, apart from the basic structure and algorithms for P2P information integration systems, research and technology on advanced data integration is at an embryonic state, and an in-depth investigation on the field is still needed in order to achieve powerful, human level P2P data integration. Recent research is devoted to provide techniques for evolving from basic P2P networks supporting only file exchanges using simple filenames as metadata [32,68], to more complex systems like schema-based P2P networks [50,6,37,20]. In particular, in a *P2P data integration system* [50] each peer is essentially a mediator-based data integration system, i.e., it manages a set of local data sources semantically connected, via a *local mapping*, to a (virtual) global schema called the *peer schema*. In addition, the specification of a peer includes a set of *P2P mappings* that specify the relationships with the data exported by other peers, as shown in Figure 2. Information in such systems can be *queried* to any peer (by external users or other peers). The queried peer, by exploiting its P2P mappings, can make use of the data in the other peers for providing the answer.

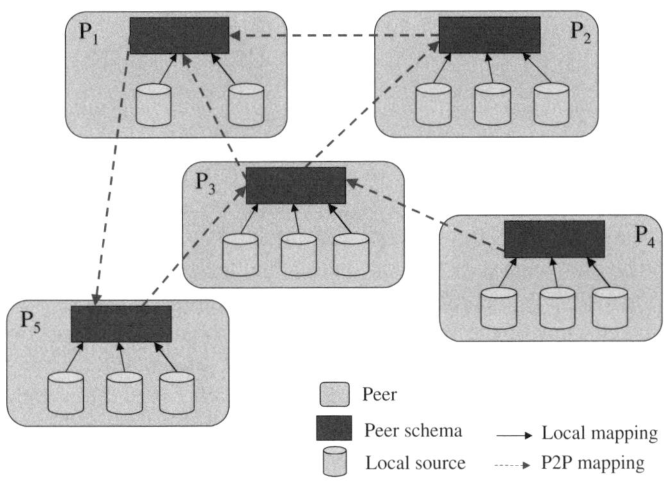

Figure 2. Peer-to-Peer Data Integration System

In this chapter, we survey the most significant approaches proposed in the literature for both mediator-based data integration and P2P data management. In particular, our analysis on P2P data management ranges from first systems developed for content sharing in a networking environment, to advanced schema-based P2P data integration systems. Then, focusing on P2P data integration, we analyze the commonly adopted approach for interpreting P2P systems using a first-order (FOL) semantics. We show some weaknesses of this approach, and compare it with an alternative approach, based on epistemic semantics. We consider several central properties of P2P data integration systems: modularity, generality, and decidability. We show that the approach based on epistemic logic is clearly superior to the usual approaches based on first-order logic with respect to all the above properties. In particular, we show that, in systems in which peers have decidable schemas and conjunctive mappings, but are arbitrarily interconnected, possibly presenting cycles in the network of peers, the first-order approach may lead to undecidability of query answering, while the epistemic approach always preserves decidability. This is a fundamental property, since the actual interconnections among peers are not under the control of any actor in the system. In this respect, our formalization nicely models the modularity of P2P architectures, i.e., the fact that each peer is autonomous, without resorting to any assumptions such as acyclicity, on the topology of the P2P systems. To this aim, we formalize a P2P data integration system in terms of the multi-modal epistemic logic $S5_n$, according to which each peer is modeled as a rational agent that exchanges knowledge/belief with other peers. This is in line with the idea of modeling a distributed information system in terms of multi-agent modal logic [34].

The rest of this chapter is organized as follows. In Section 2 we review approaches to both mediator-based data integration and P2P data management. In Section 3 we provide a formal framework for P2P data integration, and in Section 4 we describe classical FOL semantics for interpreting such a framework. Then, in Section 5 we discuss the main limitations of FOL approaches and motivate the need of a different semantic characterization based on epistemic logic, which is then precisely described in Section 6. In Section 7 we discuss the issues of modularity, generality and decidability under the two semantics. Finally, in Section 8 we highlight some open issues and challenging research directions.

2. State of the art

The main scientific base for P2P data integration is in traditional mediator-based data integration. The goal of mediator-based data integration systems is to provide clients with the access to data stored in heterogeneous and autonomous sources, without the need to know the physical characteristics of such sources and the precise location of the data.

As shown in Figure 1, a mediator-based data integration system exports to the user a global reconciled view of the data, called *global schema*, in terms of which the user formulates his/her queries, and the system maintains a declarative specification (i.e., a *mapping*) of the interrelationships between the global schema and the sources, often in turn represented through a *source schema* [67,58,55]. Two basic approaches for specifying the mapping have been proposed in the literature. The first approach, called *global-as-view* (GAV), requires that a view, i.e., a query, over the sources is associated with every element of the global schema, so that its meaning is specified in terms of the data residing at the sources. This is, for example the approach followed in [41,66,44,11]. Conversely, the second approach, called *local-as-view* (LAV), requires the sources to be defined as views over the global schema, i.e., it requires that a query over the global schema is associated to every source element. Examples of proposals following such an approach are [53,33,19]. More recently, a further approach has been considered, which allows for specifying mapping assertions in which a query over the global schema is put in correspondence with a query over the source schema [55]. Such an approach, which is called *global-local-as-view* (GLAV), since it generalizes both the LAV and the GAV approach [55], as so far received little attention in mediator-based data integration (whereas it has been recently investigated in P2P data integration, as we will see in the following sections).

Among the various problems related to data integration, the problem of answering queries posed over the global schema is the one that has been addressed most intensively. First proposals, developed in the middle 90s, faced such a problem in a procedural way, thus not providing the users with any declarative support to data integration. Systems like TSIMMIS (The Stanford-IBM Manager of Multiple Information Sources) [28], or Garlic [24] can be essentially considered as (simple) hierarchies of wrappers and mediators (and therefore can be both considered a primitive form of GAV systems). Wrappers are modules that hide the real nature of a data source, and present it and its data in a suitable format adopted within the system. Each wrapper manages the access to a single source and is in charge of translating queries over such a source in the specific language it uses, taking the answer the source returns, and providing them to the mediators. Each mediator is in charge of performing actual integration, by triggering the right wrappers, putting together the data that they return, and providing the final answer to users' requests (or feeding in turn other mediators). It has to be stressed that in TSIMMIS and Garlic no global integration is ever performed, since each mediator works in an independent manner.

Systems like Information Manifold (IM) [59,60], or INFOMASTER [43,2,33] follow instead a more declarative approach. Such systems allow for the specification of a global schema, a source schema (both schemas are assumed to be relational), and a mapping between them, which for both systems is specified according to the LAV approach, whereas both queries in the mapping and user's queries posed over the global schema are conjunctive queries, i.e., SQL select-project-join queries. For query processing, the Information Manifold system makes use of a procedure called the *bucket algorithm*, whereas the INFOMASTER system uses the *inverse rules algorithm*. Both algorithms solve query answering via query rewriting: a user query posed over the global schema is first suitably reformulated in a new query specified over the source schema, and then evaluated over the source extension in order to obtain the final answers. Several extensions have been proposed for both the algorithms. For example, in [33] the inverse rules algorithm is extended in order to handle users' queries specified in recursive Datalog, the presence of functional dependencies over the global schema, and the presence of limitations in accessing the sources (binding patterns), whereas in [64] an interesting optimization of the bucket algorithm has been proposed which significantly speeds up query processing.

A recent intensive investigation has been addressed the query answering problem for those cases in which integrity constraints (ICs) are specified over relational global schemas. ICs allow for enriching the representation of the integration domain, therefore constitute a powerful feature from a modeling point of view. However, they strongly affect the query answering process, since data stored at the sources may be in general incomplete or inconsistent with respect to such constraints. As for the first issue, query answering turns out to be a form of reasoning in the presence of incomplete information, suitably supported by a first-order interpretation of the system. This is the case of [49], which considers (limited combinations of) inclusion and functional dependencies in LAV data integration systems, or [10], where an algorithm for query answering in GAV systems, in the presence of key and foreign key constraints is provided, or [13] where a completely intensional procedure based on query rewriting is defined for all decidable cases in which key and inclusion dependencies are specified over the global schema. However, in those cases in which data may contradict global integrity constraints, the problem arises of how to obtain significative answers from inconsistent systems. Traditionally, the approach adopted to remedy to this problem has been through data cleaning [7]. This approach is procedural in nature, and is based on domain-specific transformation mechanisms applied to the data retrieved from the sources. Only very recently first academic prototype implementations have appeared, which provide declarative approaches to the treatment of inconsistency of data, in the line of the studies on consistent query answering [4]. In such approaches the common basic idea is that the inconsistency might be eliminated by modifying the database representing the extension of the system, and reasoning on the "repaired" database. Depending on the semantic assumption adopted for the system, several forms of repairing may be possible. Recently, several approaches to formalize repair semantics by using logic programs have been proposed [46,13,8]. The common idea is to encode the constraints of the global schema into a logic program, using unstratified negation or disjunction, such that the stable models of this program [42] yield the repairs of the global database. Among the most interesting proposals for managing inconsistency in data integration, we mention the INFOMIX system [56]. INFOMIX provides solutions for GAV data integration of heterogeneous data sources (e.g., relational, XML, HTML) accessed through relational global schemas over which powerful forms of integrity constraints can be issued (e.g., key, inclusion, and exclusion dependencies), and user queries are specified in a powerful query language (e.g., Datalog). The query answering technique proposed in such a system is based on query rewriting in Datalog enriched with negation and disjunction, under stable model semantics [13,48].

A setting similar to the one considered in INFOMIX is the one at the basis of the DIS@DIS system [14]. Even if limited in its capability of integrating sources with different data formats (the system actually considers only relational data sources), DIS@DIS however provides mechanisms also for integration of inconsistent data in LAV. In [9,8] an approach similar to the one followed in INFOMIX is followed, but a different repair semantics is adopted, which, to some extent, does not seem adequate to capture also incompleteness of data. Other interesting proposals on consistent query answering are the Hippo system [31,30], and the ConQuer system [38,40]. However, such proposals have been essentially developed in the context of a single database system, and therefore do not deal with all aspects of a complex data integration environment. Furthermore, w.r.t. classes of constraints and query language considered, the Hippo and the ConQuer systems are to some extent orthogonal to the INFOMIX and the DIS@DIS systems. They are geared towards highly efficient query answering for specific, polynomial-time classes of queries, whereas INFOMIX and DIS@DIS, instead, aim at supporting more general, highly expressive classes of queries (including also queries intractable under worst case complexity).

Many other studies have considered the query answering problem in data integration systems in various settings. For example, in [45,58] the relational setting under various assumptions on the languages used for the mapping and the queries has been analyzed, whereas in [18,19] query answering has been studied for the setting in which the global schema is formulated in an expressive conceptual data model. Also, query answering in the presence of semistructured data sources and global schemas has been the subject of [21,23,22], and is still the subject of intensive investigations.

A different approach in mediator-based semantic interoperability looks at data management under the perspective of exchanging data between the sources and the global schema. Sources are again connected by means of mappings to the global schema, but in this case, the focus is on materializing the data flowing from the sources to the global schema. This problem is addressed in particular by the studies on Data Exchange. In short, Data Exchange is the problem of taking data structured under a source schema and creating an instance of a target schema (called solution) that reflects the source data as accurately as possible. Among several papers produced in the field, we mention [35,36,3], where data exchange is considered also in the presence of expressive constraints specified over the target schema, and powerful forms of mappings between the source and the target schema.

More recently, the issue of data integration, has been investigated in the more dynamic context of Peer-to-Peer (P2P) data management [50]. In the last years, the P2P paradigm has been imposing in different contexts where the issue of cooperation, integration, and coordination between information nodes in a networked environment assumes a crucial role, including the Semantic Web [51], Grid computing, service oriented computing and distributed agent systems [63,52]. In all these systems, the problem of interoperability still needs deep investigation. In the following we review the main approaches proposed so far in the literature.

P2P systems have recently become popular for content sharing, and a number of different approaches have been studied to perform content retrieval in such networks (e.g., adaptation, deterministic placement of contents) [32,68]. In particular, the P2P paradigm was made popular by Napster, which employed a centralized database with references to the information items (files) on the peers. Gnutella, another well-known P2P system, has no central database, and is based on a communication-intensive search mechanism. More recently, a Gnutella-compatible P2P system, called Gridella [1], has been proposed, which follows the so-called Peer-Grid (P-Grid) approach. A P-Grid is a virtual binary tree that distributes replication over community of peers and supports efficient search. P-Grid's search structure is completely decentralized, supports local interactions between peers, uses randomized algorithms for access and search, and ensures robustness of search against node failures. As pointed out in [47], current P2P systems focus strictly on handling semantic-free, large-granularity requests for objects by identifier, which both limits their utility and restricts the techniques that might be employed to distribute the data. These current sharing systems are largely limited to applications in which objects are described by their name, and exhibit strong limitations in establishing complex links between peers. To overcome these limitations, data-oriented approaches to P2P have been proposed recently [5,50,6,47]. Some of them, see e.g., [69,5], are developed according to a super-peer based topology. A super-peer is a special node which manages a subset of client nodes. Such nodes interact only with the super-peer to which they are connected and receive results from it, whereas super-peers are also connected one another and communicate with other super-peers on behalf of their clients. In such systems, P2P computing is actually performed at the super-peer level, whereas communication between the super-peer and its clients is managed according to more traditional mediator-based techniques.

Conversely, other schema-based P2P systems do not require the presence of a super-peer. This is for example the case of the Piazza system [47], in which data origins serve original content, peer nodes cooperate to store materialized views and answer queries, nodes are connected by bandwidth-constrained links and advertise their materialized views to share resources with other peers. On the other hand, strong limitations on the topology of the mappings among peers are imposed by the system in order to allow for effective query answering.

However, apart from basic structure and algorithms, there is still a fundamental lack of understanding behind the basic issues of data integration in P2P systems, both from the point of view of modeling the system and characterizing its semantics, and from the point of view of computing answers to queries posed to a peer.

As for the modeling problem, it needs to be investigated whether the usual approach of resorting to a first-order logic interpretation of P2P mappings (followed, e.g., by [26, 50,6]), is still appropriate in the presence of an arbitrary structure of the system, possibly involving cycles among various nodes, or whether alternative semantic characterizations should be adopted [15]. As for the computational perspective, the basic task of computing query answers in P2P systems is still largely uninvestigated. Difficulties arise from the necessity of distributing the overall computation to the single nodes, exploiting their local processing capabilities and the underlying technological framework. Furthermore, query answering is in general related to the problem of finding a way to obtain answers relying only on the query answering services available at the peers. Each peer of the P2P system provides the service of answering queries expressed over its exported schema, and in general such services are the only basic services that we can rely upon in order to answer queries.

The problem is even more complex when peers export an ontology (rather than a simple relational schema) [65,16]. Here, the problem of how to exploit the mappings between peers in order to answer queries posed to one peer is in general hard to solve, even in very simple settings (e.g., when the whole system is constituted by two interoperating peers as in [16]). Indeed, query answering in this setting is actually a complex form of query reformulation. Notice that this problem is crucial in several contexts, as, for example mediator-based data integration, in particular in the case where the global schema is expressed as an ontology. Also, recent studies on query rewriting under integrity constraints, some of that [13,10] we discussed before, are strictly related to such a form of query rewriting. Then, this problem is of clear relevance for the Semantic Web, even if research on the Semantic Web has focused more on the problem of ontology matching (i.e., finding the mapping between peers).

Analogously to the case of mediator-based data integration, in the P2P architecture a different approach to achieve cooperation between different peers can be the one of exchanging data between peers. Peers are again interconnected by means of mappings, but in this case, the focus is on materializing the data flowing from one peer to another. Whereas traditional Data Exchange has been the subject of several recent investigations, P2P Data Exchange has so far received little attention. In [39] the problem of deciding the existence of a solution and establishing computational complexity of such a decision process is addressed in Peer Data Exchange, a setting in which only two peers interact that have different roles and capabilities. However, Data Exchange in a full-fledged P2P setting remains still unexplored.

3. Formal framework for peer-to-peer data integration systems

In our work, we use the framework for P2P data integration presented in [20], which is briefly described in this section.

We refer to a fixed, infinite, denumerable set Γ of constants. Such constants are shared by all peers, and denote the data items managed by the Peer-to-Peer Data Integration System (P2PDIS). Moreover, given a relational alphabet A, we denote with $\mathcal{L}_A$ the set of function-free first-order logic formulas whose relation symbols are in A and whose constants are in Γ.

We also consider conjunctive queries, i.e., SQL select-project-join queries. Formally, a *conjunctive query* (CQ) of arity n over A is a query written in the form

$$\{\mathbf{x} \mid \exists \mathbf{y}.\, body_{cq}(\mathbf{x}, \mathbf{y})\}$$

where $body_{cq}(\mathbf{x}, \mathbf{y})$ is a conjunction of atoms of $\mathcal{L}_A$ involving the free variables (also called the *distinguished* variables of the query) $\mathbf{x} = x_1, \ldots, x_n$, the existentially quantified variables (also called the *non-distinguished* variables of the query) $\mathbf{y} = y_1, \ldots, y_m$, and constants from Γ.

A *P2P data integration system* $\mathcal{P} = \{P_1, \ldots, P_n\}$ is constituted by a set of n peers. Each peer $P_i \in \mathcal{P}$ (cf. [50]) is defined as a tuple $P_i = (id, G, S, L, M, \mathcal{L})$, where:

- id is a symbol that identifies the peer P_i within $\mathcal{P}$, called the identifier of P_i.
- G is the *schema* of P_i, which is a finite set of formulas of $\mathcal{L}_{A_G}$ (representing local integrity constraints), where A_G is a relational alphabet (disjoint from the other alphabets in $\mathcal{P}$) called the *alphabet* of P_i. Intuitively, the peer schema provides an intensional view of the information managed by the peer.
- S is the *(local) source schema* of P_i, which is simply a finite relational alphabet (again disjoint from the other alphabets in $\mathcal{P}$), called the *local alphabet* of P_i. Intuitively, the source schema describes the structure of the data sources of the peer (possibly obtained by wrapping physical sources), i.e., the sources where the real data managed by the peer are stored.
- L is a set of *(local) mapping assertions* between G and S. Each local mapping assertion is an expression of the form

  $$cq_S \rightsquigarrow cq_G,$$

  where cq_S and cq_G are two conjunctive queries of the same arity, respectively over the source schema S and over the peer schema G. The local mapping assertions establish the connection between the elements of the source schema and those of the peer schema in P_i. In particular, an assertion of the form $cq_S \rightsquigarrow cq_G$ specifies that all the data satisfying the query cq_S over the sources also satisfy the concept in the peer schema represented by the query cq_G. In the terminology used in data integration, the combination of peer schema, source schema, and local mapping assertions constitutes a GLAV *data integration system* [55] managing a set of sound data sources S defined in terms of a (virtual) global schema G.
- M is a set of *P2P mapping assertions*, which specify the semantic relationships that the peer P_i has with the other peers. Each assertion in M is an expression of the form

  $$cq' \rightsquigarrow cq,$$

  where cq, called the *head* of the assertion, is a conjunctive query over the peer (schema of) P_i, while cq', called the *tail* of the assertion, is a conjunctive query of the same arity as cq over (the schema of) one of the other peers in $\mathcal{P}$. A P2P mapping assertion $cq' \rightsquigarrow cq$ from peer P_j to peer P_i expresses the fact that the P_j-concept represented by cq' is mapped to the P_i-concept represented by cq.

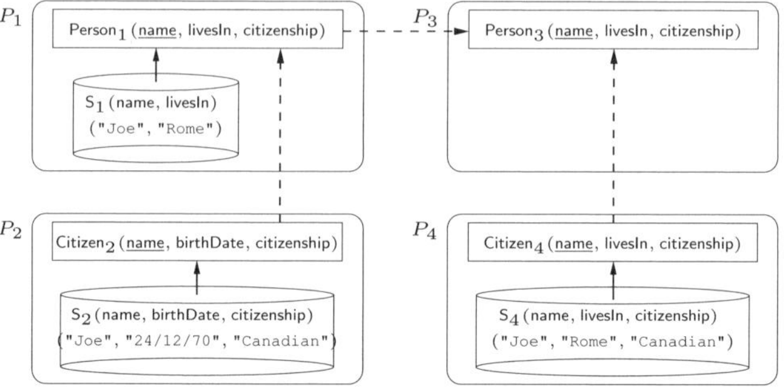

Figure 3. The P2P Data Integration System of Example 3.1

From an extensional point of view, the assertion specifies that every tuple that can be retrieved from P_j by issuing query cq' satisfies cq in P_i. Observe that no limitation is imposed on the topology of the whole set of P2P mapping assertions in the system $\mathcal{P}$, and hence, as in [20], the set of all P2P mappings may be cyclic.

- $\mathcal{L}$ is a relational query language specifying the class of queries that the peer P_i can process. We assume that $\mathcal{L}$ is some fragment of FOL that accepts at least conjunctive queries. We say that the queries in $\mathcal{L}$ are those *accepted by* P_i. Notice that this implies that, for each P2P mapping assertion $cq' \rightsquigarrow cq$ from another peer P_j to peer P_i in M, we have that cq' is accepted by P_j.

An *extension* for a P2PDIS $\mathcal{P} = \{P_1, \ldots, P_n\}$ is a set $\mathcal{D} = \{D_1, \ldots, D_n\}$, where each D_i is an extension of the predicates in the local source schema of peer P_i.

A P2PDIS, together with an extension, is intended to be queried by external users. A user enquires the whole system by accessing any peer P of $\mathcal{P}$, and by issuing a *query* q to P. The query q is processed by P if and only if q is expressed over the schema of P and is accepted by P.

Example 3.1 Let us consider the P2PDIS in Figure 3, in which we have 4 peers P_1, P_2, P_3, and P_4 (in the following, we assume that each peer P_i is identified by i).

The global schema of peer P_1 is formed by a relation schema $\mathsf{Person}_1(\underline{\mathsf{name}}, \mathsf{livesIn}, \mathsf{citizenship})$, where name is the key (we underline the key of a relation). P_1 contains a local source $\mathsf{S}_1(\mathsf{name}, \mathsf{livesIn})$, mapped to the global view by the assertion $\{x, y \mid \mathsf{S}_1(x, y)\} \rightsquigarrow \{x, y \mid \exists z. \mathsf{Person}_1(x, y, z)\}$. Moreover, it has a P2P mapping assertion $\{x, z \mid \exists y. \mathsf{Citizen}_2(x, y, z)\} \rightsquigarrow \{x, z \mid \exists y. \mathsf{Person}_1(x, y, z)\}$ relating information in peer P_2 to those in peer P_1.

P_2 has $\mathsf{Citizen}_2(\underline{\mathsf{name}}, \mathsf{birthDate}, \mathsf{citizenship})$ as global schema, and a local source $\mathsf{S}_2(\mathsf{name}, \mathsf{birthDate}, \mathsf{citizenship})$ mapped to the global schema through the local mapping $\{x, y, z \mid \mathsf{S}_2(x, y, z)\} \rightsquigarrow \{x, y, z \mid \mathsf{Citizen}_2(x, y, z)\}$. P_2 has no P2P mappings.

P_3 has $\mathsf{Person}_3(\underline{\mathsf{name}}, \mathsf{livesIn}, \mathsf{citizenship})$ as global schema, contains no local sources, and has a P2P mapping $\{x, y, z \mid \mathsf{Person}_1(x, y, z)\} \rightsquigarrow \{x, y, z \mid \mathsf{Person}_3(x, y, z)\}$ with P_1, and a P2P mapping $\{x, y, z \mid \mathsf{Citizen}_4(x, y, z)\} \rightsquigarrow \{x, y, z \mid \mathsf{Person}_3(x, y, z)\}$ with P_4.

P_4 has $\mathsf{Citizen}_4(\underline{\mathsf{name}}, \mathsf{livesIn}, \mathsf{citizenship})$ as global schema, and a local source $\mathsf{S}_4(\mathsf{name}, \mathsf{livesIn}, \mathsf{citizenship})$ mapped to the global schema through the local mapping $\{x, y, z \mid \mathsf{S}_4(x, y, z)\} \rightsquigarrow \{x, y, z \mid \mathsf{Citizen}_4(x, y, z)\}$. P_4 has no P2P mappings.

Finally, Figure 1 shows also an extension of the P2P data integration system, which includes $S_1($`"Joe"`, `"Rome"`$)$, $S_2($`"Joe"`, `"24/12/70"`, `"Canadian"`$)$, and $S_4($`"Joe"`, `"Rome"`, `"Canadian"`$)$. ∎

4. Classical semantics for P2P data integration systems

In this section we present a logical formalization of P2P data integration systems based on classical first-order logic. Such a formalization is the first one that has been proposed for P2P data integration [26,54,50].

We assume that the peers are interpreted over a fixed infinite domain Δ. We also fix the interpretation of the constants in Γ (cf. previous section) so that: (i) each $c \in \Gamma$ denotes an element $d \in \Delta$; (ii) different constants in Γ denote different elements of Δ; (iii) each element in Δ is denoted by a constant in Γ.[2] It follows that Γ is actually isomorphic to Δ, so that we can use (with some abuse of notation) constants in Γ whenever we want to denote domain elements.

4.1. Semantics of one peer

We focus first on the semantics of a single peer $P = (id, G, S, L, M, \mathcal{L})$. Let us call *peer theory of P* the FOL theory T_P defined as follows. The alphabet of T_P is obtained as union of the alphabet A_G of G and the alphabet of the local sources S of P. The axioms of T_P are the formulas in G plus one formula of the form

$$\forall \mathbf{x}. (\exists \mathbf{y}. \, body_{cq_S}(\mathbf{x}, \mathbf{y}) \supset \exists \mathbf{z}. \, body_{cq_G}(\mathbf{x}, \mathbf{z}))$$

for each local mapping assertion $cq_S \rightsquigarrow cq_G$ in L.

Observe that the P2P mapping assertions of P are not considered in T_P, and that T_P is an "open theory", since for the sources in P we only have the schema, S, and not the extension. We call *local source database* for P, a database D for the source schema S, i.e., a finite relational interpretation of the relation symbols in S. An interpretation $\mathcal{I}$ of T_P is a *model of P based on D* if it is a model of the FOL theory T_P such that for each relational symbol $s \in S$, we have that $s^{\mathcal{I}} = s^D$.

Finally, consider a query q of arity n, expressed in the query language $\mathcal{L}$ accepted by P. Given an interpretation $\mathcal{I}$ of T_P, we denote with $q^{\mathcal{I}}$ the set of n-tuples of constants in Γ obtained by evaluating q in $\mathcal{I}$ (viewed as a database over the relations in G), according to the semantics of $\mathcal{L}$. We define the *certain answers $ANS(q, P, D)$* to q (accepted by P) based on a local source database D for P, as the set of tuples $\mathbf{t}$ of constants in Γ such that for all models $\mathcal{I}$ of P based on D, we have that $\mathbf{t} \in q^{\mathcal{I}}$.

4.2. Semantics for P2P data integration systems

Based on the above logical formalization of a peer, we now present the "classical" approach to providing a semantics to the whole P2P data integration system. The classical approach is what we may call the FOL approach, followed by [26,54,50]. In this ap-

---

[2]In other words the constants in Γ act as *standard names* [57].

proach, one associates to a P2P data integration system $\mathcal{P}$ a *single* (open) FOL theory $T_{\mathcal{P}}$, obtained as the disjoint union of the various peer theories (P2P mappings are not considered in $T_{\mathcal{P}}$).

By following the approach used for a single peer, we consider a *source database $\mathcal{D}$ for $\mathcal{P}$*, simply as the (disjoint) union of one local source database D for each peer P in $\mathcal{P}$. We call *FOL model of $T_{\mathcal{P}}$ based on $\mathcal{D}$* an interpretation $\mathcal{I}$ of the FOL theory $T_{\mathcal{P}}$ such that for each relational symbol s of the source schemas in the peers of $\mathcal{P}$, we have that $s^{\mathcal{I}} = s^{\mathcal{D}}$. Then we call *FOL model of $\mathcal{P}$ based on $\mathcal{D}$* a model $\mathcal{I}$ of $T_{\mathcal{P}}$ based on $\mathcal{D}$ that is also a model of the formula

$$\forall \mathbf{x}. \, (\exists \mathbf{y}. \, body_{cq_1}(\mathbf{x}, \mathbf{y}) \supset \exists \mathbf{z}. \, body_{cq_2}(\mathbf{x}, \mathbf{z}))$$

for each P2P mapping assertion $cq_1 \rightsquigarrow cq_2$ in the peers of $\mathcal{P}$.

Finally, given a query q over one of the peers P in $\mathcal{P}$ (assuming that the identifier of P is id) and a source database $\mathcal{D}$ for $\mathcal{P}$, we define the *certain answers* $ANS_{fol}(q, id, \mathcal{P}, \mathcal{D})$ to q in $\mathcal{P}$ based on $\mathcal{D}$ under FOL semantics, as the set of tuples $\mathbf{t}$ of constants in Γ such that for every FOL model $\mathcal{I}$ of $\mathcal{P}$ based on $\mathcal{D}$, we have that $\mathbf{t} \in q^{\mathcal{I}}$.

5. Limitations of first-order approaches

Although correct from a formal point of view, the usual approach of resorting to a first-order logic interpretation of P2P mappings, which we have described in the above section, has several drawbacks, both from the modeling and from the computational perspective. Consider, for example, three central desirable properties of P2P systems:

- *Modularity*: i.e., how autonomous are the various peers in a P2P system with respect to the semantics. Indeed, since each peer is autonomously built and managed, it should be clearly interpretable both alone and when involved in interconnections with other peers. In particular, interconnections with other peers should not radically change the interpretation of the concepts expressed in the peer.
- *Generality*: i.e., how free we are in placing connections (P2P mappings) between peers. This is a fundamental property, since actual interconnections among peers are not under the control of any actor in the system.
- *Decidability*: i.e., are sound, complete and terminating query answering mechanisms available? If not, it becomes critical to establish basic quality assurance of the answers returned by the system.

Actually, these desirable properties are weakly supported by approaches based directly on FOL semantics. Indeed, such approaches essentially consider the P2P system as a single flat logical theory. As a result, the structure of the system in terms of peers is lost and remote interconnections may propagate constraints that have a deep impact on the semantics of a peer. Moreover, under arbitrary P2P interconnections, query answering under the first-order semantics is undecidable, even when the single peers have an extremely restricted structure. Motivated by these observations, several authors proposed suitable limitations to the form of P2P mappings, such as acyclicity, thus giving up generality to retain decidability [50,54,35].

To overcome the above drawbacks, we propose a new semantics for P2P systems, with the following aims:

- We want to take into account that peers in our context are to be considered autonomous sites that exchange information. In other words, peers are modules, and the modular structure of the system should be explicitly reflected in the definition of its semantics.
- We do not want to limit a-priori the topology of the mapping assertions among the peers in the system. In particular, we do not want to impose acyclicity of assertions.
- We seek for a semantic characterization that leads to a setting where query answering is decidable, and possibly, polynomially tractable.

We base our proposal of a new semantics for P2P systems on epistemic logic, and we show that the new semantics is clearly superior to the usual FOL semantics with respect to all three properties mentioned above.

6. Multi-modal epistemic formalization

In this section we present a logical formalization of P2P data integration systems. Although one possible choice for formalizing such systems is classical first order logic, it was argued in [20] that using epistemic logic brings several advantages. In particular, we adopt a *multi-modal* epistemic logic, based on the premise that each peer in the system can be seen as a rational agent. More precisely, the formalization we provide in this section is based on $S5_n$, the multi-modal version of the modal logic S5 [29,57].

6.1. The logic $S5_n$

The language $\mathcal{L}(S5_n)$ of $S5_n$ is obtained from first-order logic by adding a set $\mathbf{K_1}, \ldots, \mathbf{K_n}$ of modal operators, for the forming rule: if ϕ is a (possibly open) formula, then also $\mathbf{K_i}\phi$ is so, for $1 \leq i \leq n$ for a fixed n. In $S5_n$, each modal operator is used to formalize the epistemic state of a different agent. Informally, the formula $\mathbf{K_i}\phi$ should be read as "ϕ is known to hold by the agent i". The semantics of $S5_n$ is such that what is known by an agent must hold in the real world: in other words, the agent cannot have inaccurate knowledge of what is true, i.e., believe something to be true although in reality it is false. Moreover, $S5_n$ states that the agent has complete information on what it knows, i.e., if agent i knows ϕ then it knows of knowing ϕ, and if agent i does not know ϕ, then it knows that it does not know ϕ. In other words, the following assertions hold for every $S5_n$ formula ϕ:

$$\mathbf{K_i}\phi \supset \phi \qquad \text{known as the axiom schema T}$$
$$\mathbf{K_i}\phi \supset \mathbf{K_i}(\mathbf{K_i}\phi) \qquad \text{known as the axiom schema 4}$$
$$\neg\mathbf{K_i}\phi \supset \mathbf{K_i}(\neg\mathbf{K_i}\phi) \qquad \text{known as the axiom schema 5}$$

To define the semantics of $S5_n$, we start from first-order interpretations. As done in Section 4, we restrict our attention to first-order interpretations that share a fixed infinite domain Δ and assume that constants of the set Γ act as standard names for Δ.

Formulas of $S5_n$ are interpreted over $S5_n$-structures. A $S5_n$-*structure* is a Kripke structure E of the form $(W, \{R_1, \ldots R_n\}, V)$, where: W is a set whose elements are called *possible worlds*; V is a function assigning to each $w \in W$ a first-order interpretation $V(w)$; and each R_i, called the *accessibility relation* for the modality $\mathbf{K_i}$, is a binary relation over W, with the following constraints:

if $w \in W$ then $(w, w) \in R_i$, i.e., R_i is reflexive

if $(w_1, w_2) \in R_i$ and $(w_2, w_3) \in R_i$ then $(w_1, w_3) \in R_i$, i.e., R_i is transitive

if $(w_1, w_2) \in R_i$ and $(w_1, w_3) \in R_i$ then $(w_2, w_3) \in R_i$, i.e., R_i is euclidean

An $S5_n$-*interpretation* is a pair E, w, where $E = (W, \{R_1, \ldots R_n\}, V)$ is an $S5_n$-structure, and w is a world in W. We inductively define when a sentence (i.e., a closed formula) ϕ *is true in an interpretation* E, w (or, is true on world $w \in W$ in E), written $E, w \models \phi$, as follows:[3]

$$
\begin{aligned}
E, w \models P(c_1, \ldots, c_n) \quad &\text{iff} \quad V(w) \models P(c_1, \ldots, c_n) \\
E, w \models \phi_1 \wedge \phi_2 \quad &\text{iff} \quad E, w \models \phi_1 \text{ and } E, w \models \phi_2 \\
E, w \models \neg\phi \quad &\text{iff} \quad E, w \not\models \phi \\
E, w \models \exists x.\, \psi \quad &\text{iff} \quad E, w \models \psi_c^x \text{ for some constant } c \\
E, w \models \mathbf{K_i}\phi \quad &\text{iff} \quad E, w' \models \phi \text{ for every } w' \text{ such that } (w, w') \in R_i
\end{aligned}
$$

We say that a sentence ϕ is *satisfiable* if there exists an $S5_n$-*model* for ϕ, i.e., an $S5_n$-interpretation E, w such that $E, w \models \phi$, *unsatisfiable* otherwise. A *model* for a set Σ of sentences is a model for every sentence in Σ. A sentence ϕ is *logically implied* by a set Σ of sentences, written $\Sigma \models_{S5_n} \phi$, if and only if in every $S5_n$-model E, w of Σ, we have that $E, w \models \phi$.

Notice that, since each accessibility relation of a $S5_n$-structure is reflexive, transitive and Euclidean, all instances of axiom schemas T, 4 and 5 are satisfied in every $S5_n$-interpretation.

6.2. Epistemic semantics for P2P data integration systems

Due to the characteristics mentioned above, $S5_n$ is well-suited to formalize P2PDISs of the kind presented in Section 3. Let $\mathcal{P} = \{P_1, \ldots, P_n\}$ be a P2PDIS in which each peer P_i has identifier i. For each peer $P_i = (i, G, S, L, M, \mathcal{L})$ we define the theory $\mathcal{T}_K(P_i)$ in $S5_n$ as the union of the following sentences:

- Global schema G of P_i: for each sentence ϕ in G, we have

$$\mathbf{K_i}\phi$$

  Observe that ϕ is a first-order sentence expressed in the alphabet of P_i, which is disjoint from the alphabets of all the other peers in $\mathcal{P}$.

- Local mapping assertions L between G and the local source schema S: for each mapping assertion $\{\mathbf{x} \mid \exists \mathbf{y}.\, body_{cq_S}(\mathbf{x}, \mathbf{y})\} \rightsquigarrow \{\mathbf{x} \mid \exists \mathbf{z}.\, body_{cq_G}(\mathbf{x}, \mathbf{z})\}$ in L, we have

$$\mathbf{K_i}(\forall \mathbf{x}.\, \exists \mathbf{y}.\, body_{cq_S}(\mathbf{x}, \mathbf{y}) \supset \exists \mathbf{z}.\, body_{cq_G}(\mathbf{x}, \mathbf{z}))$$

- P2P mapping assertions M: for each P2P mapping assertion $\{\mathbf{x} \mid \exists \mathbf{y}.\, body_{cq_j}(\mathbf{x}, \mathbf{y})\} \rightsquigarrow \{\mathbf{x} \mid \exists \mathbf{z}.\, body_{cq_i}(\mathbf{x}, \mathbf{z})\}$ between the peer j and the peer i in M, we have

$$\forall \mathbf{x}.\, \mathbf{K_j}(\exists \mathbf{y}.\, body_{cq_j}(\mathbf{x}, \mathbf{y})) \supset \mathbf{K_i}(\exists \mathbf{z}.\, body_{cq_i}(\mathbf{x}, \mathbf{z})) \tag{1}$$

---

[3] We have used ψ_c^x to denote the formula obtained from ψ by substituting each free occurrence of the variable x with the constant c.

In words, this sentence specifies the following rule: for each tuple of values $\mathbf{t}$, if peer j knows the sentence $\exists \mathbf{y}.\, body_{cq_j}(\mathbf{t}, \mathbf{y})$, then peer i knows the sentence $\exists \mathbf{z}.\, body_{cq_i}(\mathbf{t}, \mathbf{z})$ holds.

We denote by $\mathcal{T}_K(\mathcal{P})$ the theory corresponding to the P2PDIS $\mathcal{P}$, i.e., $\mathcal{T}_K(\mathcal{P}) = \bigcup_{i=1,\ldots,n} \mathcal{T}_K(P_i)$.

Example 6.1 We provide now the formalization of the P2PDIS of Example 3.1. The theory $\mathcal{T}_K(P_1)$ modeling peer P_1 is the conjunction of:

$$\mathbf{K_1}(\forall x, y, y', z, z'.\, \mathsf{Person}_1(x, y, z) \wedge \mathsf{Person}_1(x, y', z') \supset y = y' \wedge z = z')$$
$$\mathbf{K_1}(\forall x, y.\, \mathsf{S}_1(x, y) \supset \exists z.\, \mathsf{Person}_1(x, y, z))$$
$$\forall x, z.\, \mathbf{K_2}(\exists y.\, \mathsf{Citizen}_2(x, y, z)) \supset \mathbf{K_1}(\exists y.\, \mathsf{Person}_1(x, y, z))$$

The theory $\mathcal{T}_K(P_2)$ modeling peer P_2 is the conjunction of:

$$\mathbf{K_2}(\forall x, y, y', z, z'.\, \mathsf{Citizen}_2(x, y, z) \wedge \mathsf{Citizen}_2(x, y', z') \supset y = y' \wedge z = z')$$
$$\mathbf{K_2}(\forall x, y, z.\, \mathsf{S}_2(x, y, z) \supset \mathsf{Citizen}_2(x, y, z))$$

The theory $\mathcal{T}_K(P_3)$ modeling peer P_3 is the conjunction of:

$$\mathbf{K_3}(\forall x, y, y', z, z'.\, \mathsf{Person}_3(x, y, z) \wedge \mathsf{Person}_3(x, y', z') \supset y = y' \wedge z = z')$$
$$\forall x, y.\, \mathbf{K_1}(\exists z.\, \mathsf{Person}_1(x, z, y)) \supset \mathbf{K_3}\exists z.\, \mathsf{Person}_3(x, z, y)$$
$$\forall x, y, z.\, \mathbf{K_4}(\mathsf{Citizen}_4(x, y, z)) \supset \mathbf{K_3}\mathsf{Person}_3(x, y, z)$$

The theory $\mathcal{T}_K(P_4)$ modeling peer P_4 is the conjunction of:

$$\mathbf{K_4}(\forall x, y, y', z, z'.\, \mathsf{Citizen}_4(x, y, z) \wedge \mathsf{Citizen}_4(x, y', z') \supset y = y' \wedge z = z')$$
$$\mathbf{K_4}(\forall x, y, z.\, \mathsf{S}_4(x, y, z) \supset \mathsf{Citizen}_4(x, y, z))$$

∎

The extension $\mathcal{D} = \{D_1, \ldots, D_n\}$ of a P2PDIS $\mathcal{P}$ is modeled as a sentence constituted by the conjunction of all facts corresponding to the tuples stored in the sources, i.e., $DB(\mathcal{D}) = \bigwedge_{i=1}^{n} DB(D_i)$ where $DB(D_i) = \mathbf{K_i}(\bigwedge_{t \in r^{D_i}} r(t))$.

A client of the P2PDIS interacts with one of the peers, say peer P_i, posing a *query* to it. A query q is an open formula $q(\mathbf{x})$ with free variables $\mathbf{x}$ expressed in the language accepted by the peer P_i (we recall that such a language is a subset of first-order logic). The semantics of a query $q \in \mathcal{L}$ posed to a peer $P_i = (i, G, S, L, M, \mathcal{L})$ of $\mathcal{P}$ with respect to an extension $\mathcal{D}$ is defined as the set of tuples

$$ANS_{\mathsf{S5}_n}(q, i, \mathcal{P}, \mathcal{D}) = \{\mathbf{t} \mid \mathcal{T}_K(\mathcal{P}) \cup DB(\mathcal{D}) \models_{\mathsf{S5}_n} \mathbf{K_i}q(\mathbf{t})\}$$

where $q(\mathbf{t})$ denotes the sentence obtained from the open formula $q(\mathbf{x})$ by replacing all occurrences of the free variables in $\mathbf{x}$ with the corresponding constants in $\mathbf{t}$.

6.3. Query answering in P2PDISs under the epistemic semantics

Finally, we point out that query answering in P2P data integration systems under the epistemic semantics described above has been studied in [15,20]. In particular, it has

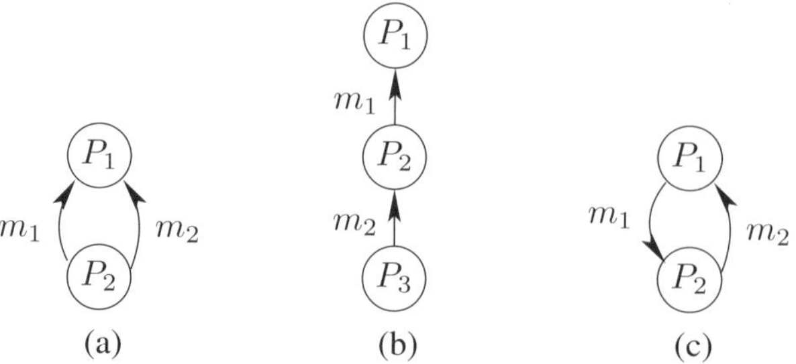

Figure 4. Interactions between two mappings

been proved that, under very general assumptions about the structure of the single peers and the query language, query answering in a P2PDIS under the epistemic semantics is decidable and, in many cases, tractable in data complexity, i.e., queries can be answered in polynomial time with respect to the size of the data stored at the peers.

In the above epistemic setting, two different query answering strategies have been explored. In the first one, described in [15], a bottom-up algorithm has been defined, which is able to answer a query by incrementally collecting the certain answers to suitable queries that are iteratively computed at the various peers, following the topology of the mappings among the peers. The second approach, presented in [20], adopts a top-down technique that is heavily based on query reformulation: in particular, the peer to which the initial query is posed incrementally collects the global reformulation of the query, which is computed by a distributed algorithm that exploits both the mappings among the peers and a local query reformulation ability of each peer. We refer the interested reader to [15,20] for more details.

7. Comparison between the two semantics

In this section, we compare the epistemic and FOL semantics for P2P systems presented above. The comparison is guided by three principles, namely modularity, generality, and decidability of query answering. To highlight the differences between the two semantics, we will consider the simplest setting in which interactions may occur, namely systems containing only two P2P mappings. The three types of systems we discuss in the following are depicted in Figure 4, and represent respectively the case of parallel, sequential, and cyclic composition, where each circle represents a peer, and an arrow from a peer P' to a peer P represents a mapping assertion whose head is a CQ over P and whose tail is a CQ over P'.

We first need to provide some definitions. For the sake of simplicity, in the following we slightly simplify the formalization, and denote a peer P_i by a quadruple $P_i = (G, S, L, M)$, i.e., with respect to the notation used above, we omit the first component id (the identifier of P), and the last component $\mathcal{L}$ (the class of queries that the peer P can process), and assume that: (i) the identifier of peer P_i is the subscript i of the peer symbol; (ii) all peers accept the same query language $\mathcal{L}$, and such an $\mathcal{L}$ is the language of conjunctive queries.

Given a peer $P = (G, S, L, M)$, we denote as $\tau(P)$ the peer (G, S', L', M) such that:

1. S' is obtained from S by adding a new source predicate symbol r, of the same arity as cq', for each P2P mapping assertion $cq' \rightsquigarrow cq$ in M between a peer P' and P. We also denote as $Q(r)$ the query cq' in the tail of the corresponding P2P mapping assertion, and denote as $P(r)$ the peer P', i.e., the peer over which the query $Q(r)$ is expressed.
2. L' is obtained from L by adding the local mapping assertion $\{\mathbf{x} \mid r(\mathbf{x})\} \rightsquigarrow cq$ for each P2P mapping assertion $cq' \rightsquigarrow cq$ in M.

Furthermore, for a P2P system $\mathcal{P}$, we denote as $\tau(\mathcal{P})$ the P2P system $\{\tau(P) \mid P \in \mathcal{P}\}$. For each peer P, we call *auxiliary alphabet* of P, denoted as *AuxAlph*(P), the set of new source predicate symbols thus defined. Informally, in each peer the additional sources corresponding to the predicates in the auxiliary alphabet are used to "simulate" the effect of the P2P mapping assertions with respect to contributing to the data of the peer.

7.1. Modularity: Parallel composition

We consider a P2P system $\mathcal{P}_{par}$ with the structure depicted in Figure 4(a), and to highlight the interdependence between mappings, we further assume that P_1 does not contain local sources (and local mappings). Hence, $\mathcal{P}_{par}$ is constituted by two peers $P_1 = (G_1, \emptyset, \emptyset, \{m_1, m_2\})$, and $P_2 = (G_2, S_2, L_2, \emptyset)$.

Informally, in the context of parallel composition, we can consider a semantics for P2P systems as modular, if for every query q over P_1, and for every source database D_2 for P_2, the certain answers to q in $\mathcal{P}_{par}$ with respect to D_2 under the considered semantics can be computed by first populating P_1 with the data retrieved by independently applying the two mappings and then evaluating q over such data. Formally, let m_1 be $cq'_1 \rightsquigarrow cq_1$, let m_2 be $cq'_2 \rightsquigarrow cq_2$, and consider the peer $\tau(P_1) = (G_1, \{r_1, r_2\}, \{m'_1, m'_2\}, \{m_1, m_2\})$, where m'_1 is $\{\mathbf{x} \mid r_1(\mathbf{x})\} \rightsquigarrow cq_1$ and m'_2 is $\{\mathbf{x} \mid r_2(\mathbf{x})\} \rightsquigarrow cq_2$. For a local source database D_2 for P_2, let $\delta(P_1, D_2)$ be the local source database for $\tau(P_1)$ such that $r_1^{\delta(P_1, D_2)}$ coincides with the certain answers $ANS(cq'_1, P_2, D_2)$ over the single peer P_2, and $r_2^{\delta(P_1, D_2)}$ coincides with the certain answers $ANS(cq'_2, P_2, D_2)$ over P_2. Now, semantics X is modular if for every query q to P_1 and for every source database D_2 for P_2, we have that $ANS_X(q, 1, \mathcal{P}, \{D_2\})$ coincides with the certain answers $ANS(q, \tau(P_1), \delta(P_1, D_2))$ over $\tau(P_1)$. The following theorems show that a P2P system as simple as $\mathcal{P}_{par}$ is sufficient to separate the epistemic and the FOL semantics with respect to modularity.

Theorem 7.1 *There is a P2P system* $\mathcal{P}_{par} = \{P_1, P_2\}$ *of the form as above, a source database* D_2 *for* P_2, *and a query* q *to* P_1 *such that* $ANS_{fol}(q, 1, \mathcal{P}, \{D_2\}) \neq ANS(q, \tau(P_1), \delta(P_1, D_2))$.

Proof (sketch). We exhibit $\mathcal{P}_{par} = \{P_1, P_2\}$, D_2, and q such that the claim holds. Let $P_1 = (\{u/1\}, \emptyset, \emptyset, \{m_1, m_2\})$ and $P_2 = (G_2, \{s/1\}, \{\ell_2\}, \emptyset)$, with $G_2 = \{\forall x\, (u_3(x) \supset u_1(x) \vee u_2(x))\}$, and

$$\ell_2 = \{x \mid s(x)\} \rightsquigarrow \{x \mid u_3(x)\}$$
$$m_1 = \{x \mid u_1(x)\} \rightsquigarrow \{x \mid u(x)\}$$
$$m_2 = \{x \mid u_2(x)\} \rightsquigarrow \{x \mid u(x)\}$$

Consider the source database $D_2 = \{s(a)\}$ for P_2. It is easy to see that for the query $q = \{x \mid u(x)\}$ we have that $ANS_{fol}(q, 1, \mathcal{P}, \{D_2\}) = \{a\}$, while $\delta(P_1, D_2) = \emptyset$, and hence $ANS(q, \tau(P_1), \delta(P_1, D_2)) = \emptyset$. $\square$

For the epistemic semantics, from the results in [20], we get the following theorem.

Theorem 7.2 *Let $\mathcal{P}_{par}$ and D_2 be as above. Then, for every query q over P_1 we have that $ANS_{S5_n}(q, 1, \mathcal{P}, \{D_2\}) = ANS(q, \tau(P_1), \delta(P_1, D_2))$.*

7.2. Modularity: Sequential composition

We consider a P2P system $\mathcal{P}_{seq}$ with the structure depicted in Figure 4(b). Again, to highlight the interaction between the mappings, we assume that both P_1 and P_2 do not contain local sources. Hence, $\mathcal{P}_{seq}$ is constituted by three peers $P_1 = (G_1, \emptyset, \emptyset, \{m_1\})$, $P_2 = (G_2, \emptyset, \emptyset, \{m_2\})$, and $P_3 = (G_3, S_3, L_3, \emptyset)$.

Informally, in the context of sequential composition, we can consider a semantics for P2P systems as modular, if for every query q_1 over P_1, and for every source database D_3 for P_3, the certain answers to q in $\mathcal{P}_{seq}$ with respect to D_3 under the considered semantics can be computed by (i) populating P_2 with the data retrieved by applying the mapping m_2, (ii) using such data to populate P_1 by applying the mapping m_1, and (iii) evaluating q over P_1. Formally, let m_1 be $cq_2 \rightsquigarrow cq_1$, let m_2 be $cq_3 \rightsquigarrow cq'_2$, and consider the peers $\tau(P_1) = (G_1, \{r_1\}, \{m'_1\}, \{m_1\})$ with $m'_1 = \{\mathbf{x} \mid r_1(\mathbf{x})\} \rightsquigarrow cq_1$ and $\tau(P_2) = (G_2, \{r_2\}, \{m'_2\}, \{m_2\})$ with $m'_2 = \{\mathbf{x} \mid r_2(\mathbf{x})\} \rightsquigarrow cq'_2$. For a local source database D_3 for P_3, let $\delta(P_2, D_3)$ be the local source database for $\tau(P_2)$ such that $r_2^{\delta(P_2, D_3)} = ANS(cq_3, P_3, D_3)$ and let $\delta(P_1, P_2, D_3)$ be the local source database for $\tau(P_1)$ such that $r_1^{\delta(P_1, P_2, D_3)} = ANS(cq_2, P_2, \delta(P_2, D_3))$. Now, semantics X is modular if for every query q to P_1 and for every source database D_3 for P_3, we have that $ANS_X(q, 1, \mathcal{P}, \{D_3\}) = ANS(q, \tau(P_1), \delta(P_1, P_2, D_3))$.

We show that also in the context of sequential composition, while the epistemic semantics for P2P systems is modular, the FOL semantics is not so.

Theorem 7.3 *There is a P2P system $\mathcal{P}_{seq} = \{P_1, P_2, P_3\}$ of the form as above, a source database D_3 for P_3, and a query q over P_1 such that $ANS_{fol}(q, 1, \mathcal{P}, \{D_3\}) \neq ANS(q, \tau(P_1), \delta(P_1, P_2, D_3))$.*

Proof (sketch). Exploiting a result in [61], we exhibit $\mathcal{P}_{seq} = \{P_1, P_2, P_3\}$, D_3, and q such that the claim holds. Let $P_1 = (\{u/2\}, \emptyset, \emptyset, \{m_1\})$, $P_2 = (\{v/2\}, \emptyset, \emptyset, \{m_2\})$, and $P_3 = (\{w/2\}, \{s/2\}, \{\ell_2\}, \emptyset)$, with

$$m_1 = \{x, y \mid \exists z_1, z_2 \, (v(x, z_1) \wedge v(z_1, z_2) \wedge v(z_2, y))\} \rightsquigarrow \{x, y \mid u(x, y)\}$$
$$m_2 = \{x, y \mid w(x, y)\} \rightsquigarrow \{x, y \mid \exists z \, (v(x, z) \wedge v(z, y))\}$$
$$\ell_2 = \{x, y \mid s(x, y)\} \rightsquigarrow \{x, y \mid w(x, y)\}$$

Consider the source database $D_3 = \{s(a_i, a_{i+1}) \mid 1 \leq i \leq 7\}$ for P_2. It is easy to see that for the query $q = \{x, y \mid \exists z \, (u(x, z) \wedge u(z, y))\}$ we have that $ANS_{fol}(q, 1, \mathcal{P}, \{D_3\}) = \{(a_1, a_7)\}$, while $ANS(q, \tau(P_1), \delta(P_1, P_2, D_3)) = \emptyset$. $\square$

For the epistemic semantics, from the results in [20], we get the following theorem.

Theorem 7.4 *Let $\mathcal{P}_{seq}$ and D_3 be as above. Then, for every query q over P_1 we have that $ANS_{S5_n}(q, 1, \mathcal{P}, \{D_3\}) = ANS(q, \tau(P_1), \delta(P_1, P_2, D_3))$.*

7.3. Decidability: Cycle between two peers

We consider a P2P system $\mathcal{P}_{cyc}$ with the structure depicted in Figure 4(c). The presence of a cycle between two peers suffices to make query answering undecidable under the FOL semantics.

Theorem 7.5 *There is a P2P system $\mathcal{P}_{cyc} = \{P_1, P_2\}$ of the form as above, a source database $\mathcal{D}$ for $\mathcal{P}_{cyc}$, such that computing the certain answers to queries over the single peers P_1 and P_2 is decidable, while computing the certain answers to queries in $\mathcal{P}_{cyc}$ based on $\mathcal{D}$ under the FOL semantics is undecidable.*

Proof (sketch). The undecidability result follows by a reduction from undecidability of query answering under inclusion and functional dependencies [62,27,12].

Consider a relational schema $\mathcal{R}$ with inclusion and functional dependencies. We construct the peer $P_1 = (G_1, S_1, L_1, M_1)$ as follows: G_1 contains the relations of $\mathcal{R}$, plus two additional relations inc and fun, both containing one attribute $r.A$ for each attribute A in a relation r of $\mathcal{R}$. G_1 contains all inclusion assertion of $\mathcal{R}$, plus one inclusion assertion $r[\mathbf{A}, \mathbf{B}] \subseteq inc[r.\mathbf{A}, r.\mathbf{B}]$ and one functional dependency $fun : r.\mathbf{A} \to r.\mathbf{B}$, for each functional dependency $r : \mathbf{A} \to \mathbf{B}$ in $\mathcal{R}$ (we have denoted by $r.\mathbf{A}$ the tuple of attributes corresponding to $\mathbf{A}$). S_1 contains a source relation s_r for each relation r in $\mathcal{R}$, and L_1 maps such relations to the corresponding relations in G_1. M_1 contains a single P2P mapping assertion $\{\mathbf{x} \mid inc(\mathbf{x})\} \rightsquigarrow \{\mathbf{x} \mid rem(\mathbf{x})\}$.

Then we construct the peer $P_2 = (G_2, \emptyset, \emptyset, M_2)$, where G_2 contains only the relation rem (of the same arity as inc and fun), and M_2 contains a single P2P mapping assertion $\{\mathbf{x} \mid rem(\mathbf{x})\} \rightsquigarrow \{\mathbf{x} \mid fun(\mathbf{x})\}$.

Notice that query answering in P_1 is decidable, since all functional dependencies are on the relation fun, which is not related through inclusion dependencies to the other relations in G_1, and the implication problems and query answering problems for inclusion and functional dependencies separately are decidable [25,12]. Also, P_2 is trivially decidable. On the other hand, under the FOL semantics, the P2P mappings propagate the functional dependencies on fun to inc, and hence in turn to the relations in G_1. Therefore, the whole set of dependencies in $\mathcal{R}$ are reflected in G_1, thus making query answering in the P2P system as a whole undecidable.   □

Notice that, since P_1 and P_2 are in general designed independently of each other, even if care is taken to retain decidability of query answering for each of them separately, when interconnected in a P2P system, under the FOL semantics there is no way to ensure decidability of query answering in the whole system, since no single actor has the control on all the P2P mappings. This is a further indication of the lack of modularity in systems based on the FOL semantics. Observe also that the only way to retain decidability would be to trade it with generality, by restricting the topology of the P2P mappings [50,54,35]. In practice this may even be unfeasible, again since no actor is in control of all P2P mappings.

On the other hand, under the epistemic semantics we can retain both generality and decidability for P2P systems with *arbitrary* structure, as shown in [15,20].

Theorem 7.6 *For each P2P system $\mathcal{P}$ of the form as above and a source database $\mathcal{D}$ for $\mathcal{P}$ such that computing the certain answers to queries over the single peers is decidable, computing the certain answers to queries in $\mathcal{P}$ based on $\mathcal{D}$ under the epistemic semantics is decidable.*

8. Future research directions and conclusions

In this chapter we have provided a formal framework for P2P data integration, and we have proposed a new semantics for such a framework based on epistemic logic. We have compared such a semantics with the commonly adopted semantics based on first-order logic, and we have shown that the epistemic approach is superior to the first-order one with respect to three central properties for P2P systems, namely, modularity, generality, and decidability. We have also devised polynomial time query answering algorithms that are sound and complete for the problem of computing certain answers to user queries accepted by peers in the system (i.e., computing the set ANS_{S5_n}). The details of the algorithms are described in [15] and in [20] .

We point out that our formalization and our query answering algorithm are among the first results on advanced P2P data integration, and that research and technology on such field is still at an embryonic state. Actually, a number of issues need to be investigated and resolved in order to facilitate powerful, human level P2P information integration. Among them, we consider the following ones the most challenging and important:

- Inconsistency tolerance, i.e., developing suitable mechanisms for the management of data inconsistency. Inconsistency in P2P data integration systems may arise for different reasons: a peer may be locally inconsistent because its data (possibly coming from local sources) violate integrity constraints specified on its schema; data coming into a peer from other peers may contradict constraints when combined with data locally managed by the peer; data coming into a peer from different peers may result mutually inconsistent, i.e., combined together may violate integrity constraints of the peer schema. Hence, the main issue is to deal appropriately with inconsistencies, in order to avoid trivialized query results. First results on this issue recently appeared in [17].

- Preferences and trust management, i.e., choosing from data coming from different peers on the basis of preferences/trust specifications. In P2P data integration systems, each peer may want to specify information on how it trusts peers, with respect to certain kind of data, to which it is connected, e.g., by assigning different quality values (e.g., reliability, availability, etc.) to data coming from different peers. Obviously, the "best" data should be preferred to the others. Preference/trust specifications can be used both to solve data inconsistencies and to rank data belonging to query answers. Indeed, when dealing with mutually inconsistent data coming from different peers, a peer may choose to trust only those data coming from the preferred peer (e.g., the most reliable one). Furthermore, a peer may choose to select which data have to be first returned in the answer to a query, on the basis of preference/trust assertions, in order to speed up query processing. Also, preference specifications can be used during the query answering process to avoid or delay access to peers that have a low preference degree.

- Authorization and privacy management, i.e., controlling the accessibility of the data in the peers. In general, each peer in the system wants to allow only controlled accesses to its data, i.e., the peer needs the ability of specifying privacy or confidentiality for (a portion of) its data, or guaranteeing disclosure of certain information from particular users. An interesting approach which follows a logical perspective has been recently proposed in [70] in the context of a single database. The proposed method is based on the idea of specifying, for each user, a set of authorized views, representing the information that the user is allowed to access. We think that this idea nicely captures the logical essence of access control, and might be somehow transferred in the context of P2P data integration, where it is crucial that each peer is able to specify data privacy policy in a declarative way.

- Model management, i.e., methods for dealing with the dynamics of a P2P data integration system, in which peers may join and leave at any time, or be temporarily unavailable. This requests for both advanced meta-data management and handling partial and incomplete information.

- Data exchange, i.e., dealing with the materialization of data flowing from one peer to another. Materialized data can be profitably used in P2P data management in several ways, e.g., can be exploited to reduce the number of accesses to remote peers during query processing. Notice that whereas traditional data exchange has been the subject of several recent investigations (see Section 2 for a brief description), P2P data exchange has so far received little attention, and it still remains largely unexplored.

All these issues are unresolved to date and require major efforts and advances in future research in the field.

9. Acknowledgments

This research has been partially supported by the FET project INFOMIX: Boosting Information Integration, funded by EU under contract number IST-2001-33570, the project SEWASIE: SEmantic Webs and AgentS in Integrated Economies, funded by the EU under contract number IST-2001-34825, and the FET project TONES: Thinking ONtologiES, funded by the EU under contract number FP6-7603.

References

[1] K. Aberer, M. Punceva, M. Hauswirth, and R. Schmidt. Improving data access in P2P systems. *IEEE Internet Computing*, 2002.

[2] S. Abiteboul and O. Duschka. Complexity of answering queries using materialized views. In *Proc. of the 17th ACM SIGACT SIGMOD SIGART Symp. on Principles of Database Systems (PODS'98)*, pages 254–265, 1998.

[3] M. Arenas, P. Barcelo, R. Fagin, and L. Libkin. Locally consistent transformations and query answering in data exchange. In *Proc. of the 23rd ACM SIGACT SIGMOD SIGART Symp. on Principles of Database Systems (PODS 2004)*, pages 229–240, 2004.

[4] M. Arenas, L. E. Bertossi, and J. Chomicki. Consistent query answers in inconsistent databases. In *Proc. of the 18th ACM SIGACT SIGMOD SIGART Symp. on Principles of Database Systems (PODS'99)*, pages 68–79, 1999.

[5] D. Beneventano, S. Bergamaschi, F. Guerra, and M. Vincini. Querying a super-peer in a schema-based super-peer network. In *Proc. of the 3rd VLDB Int. Workshop on Databases, Information Systems and Peer-to-Peer Computing (DBISP2P 2005)*, 2005.

[6] P. A. Bernstein, F. Giunchiglia, A. Kementsietsidis, J. Mylopoulos, L. Serafini, and I. Zaihrayeu. Data management for peer-to-peer computing: A vision. In *Proc. of the 5th Int. Workshop on the Web and Databases (WebDB 2002)*, 2002.

[7] M. Bouzeghoub and M. Lenzerini. Introduction to the special issue on data extraction, cleaning, and reconciliation. *Information Systems*, 26(8):535–536, 2001.

[8] L. Bravo and L. Bertossi. Logic programming for consistently querying data integration systems. In *Proc. of the 18th Int. Joint Conf. on Artificial Intelligence (IJCAI 2003)*, pages 10–15, 2003.

[9] L. Bravo and L. Bertossi. Disjunctive deductive databases for computing certain and consistent answers to queries from mediated data integration systems. *Journal of Applied Logic – Special Issue on Logic-based Methods for Information Integration*, 3(2):329–367, 2005.

[10] A. Calì, D. Calvanese, G. De Giacomo, and M. Lenzerini. Data integration under integrity constraints. *Information Systems*, 29:147–163, 2004.

[11] A. Calì, D. Calvanese, G. De Giacomo, M. Lenzerini, P. Naggar, and F. Vernacotola. IBIS: Semantic data integration at work. In *Proc. of the 15th Int. Conf. on Advanced Information Systems Engineering (CAiSE 2003)*, pages 79–94, 2003.

[12] A. Calì, D. Lembo, and R. Rosati. On the decidability and complexity of query answering over inconsistent and incomplete databases. In *Proc. of the 22nd ACM SIGACT SIGMOD SIGART Symp. on Principles of Database Systems (PODS 2003)*, pages 260–271, 2003.

[13] A. Calì, D. Lembo, and R. Rosati. Query rewriting and answering under constraints in data integration systems. In *Proc. of the 18th Int. Joint Conf. on Artificial Intelligence (IJCAI 2003)*, pages 16–21, 2003.

[14] A. Calì, D. Lembo, R. Rosati, and M. Ruzzi. Experimenting data integration with DIS@DIS. In *Proc. of the 16th Int. Conf. on Advanced Information Systems Engineering (CAiSE 2004)*, volume 3084 of *Lecture Notes in Computer Science*, pages 51–56. Springer, 2004.

[15] D. Calvanese, E. Damaggio, G. De Giacomo, M. Lenzerini, and R. Rosati. Semantic data integration in P2P systems. In *Proc. of the Int. Workshop on Databases, Information Systems and Peer-to-Peer Computing (DBISP2P 2003)*, 2003.

[16] D. Calvanese, G. De Giacomo, D. Lembo, M. Lenzerini, and R. Rosati. What to ask to a peer: Ontology-based query reformulation. In *Proc. of the 9th Int. Conf. on Principles of Knowledge Representation and Reasoning (KR 2004)*, pages 469–478, 2004.

[17] D. Calvanese, G. De Giacomo, D. Lembo, M. Lenzerini, and R. Rosati. DL-Lite: Tractable description logics for ontologies. In *Proc. of the 20th Nat. Conf. on Artificial Intelligence (AAAI 2005)*, pages 602–607, 2005.

[18] D. Calvanese, G. De Giacomo, M. Lenzerini, D. Nardi, and R. Rosati. Description logic framework for information integration. In *Proc. of the 6th Int. Conf. on Principles of Knowledge Representation and Reasoning (KR'98)*, pages 2–13, 1998.

[19] D. Calvanese, G. De Giacomo, M. Lenzerini, D. Nardi, and R. Rosati. Data integration in data warehousing. *Int. J. of Cooperative Information Systems*, 10(3):237–271, 2001.

[20] D. Calvanese, G. De Giacomo, M. Lenzerini, and R. Rosati. Logical foundations of peer-to-peer data integration. In *Proc. of the 23rd ACM SIGACT SIGMOD SIGART Symp. on Principles of Database Systems (PODS 2004)*, pages 241–251, 2004.

[21] D. Calvanese, G. De Giacomo, M. Lenzerini, and M. Y. Vardi. Rewriting of regular expressions and regular path queries. *J. of Computer and System Sciences*, 64(3):443–465, 2002.

[22] D. Calvanese, G. De Giacomo, M. Lenzerini, and M. Y. Vardi. View-based query processing: On the relationship between rewriting, answering and losslessness. In *Proc. of the 10th Int. Conf. on Database Theory (ICDT 2005)*, volume 3363 of *Lecture Notes in Computer Science*, pages 321–336. Springer, 2005.

[23] D. Calvanese, G. De Giacomo, and M. Y. Vardi. Decidable containment of recursive queries.

Theoretical Computer Science, 336(1):33–56, 2005.

[24] M. J. Carey, L. M. Haas, P. M. Schwarz, M. Arya, W. F. Cody, R. Fagin, M. Flickner, A. Luniewski, W. Niblack, D. Petkovic, J. Thomas, J. H. Williams, and E. L. Wimmers. Towards heterogeneous multimedia information systems: The Garlic approach. In *Proc. of the 5th Int. Workshop on Research Issues in Data Engineering – Distributed Object Management (RIDE-DOM'95)*, pages 124–131. IEEE Computer Society Press, 1995.

[25] M. A. Casanova, R. Fagin, and C. H. Papadimitriou. Inclusion dependencies and their interaction with functional dependencies. *J. of Computer and System Sciences*, 28(1):29–59, 1984.

[26] T. Catarci and M. Lenzerini. Representing and using interschema knowledge in cooperative information systems. *J. of Intelligent and Cooperative Information Systems*, 2(4):375–398, 1993.

[27] A. K. Chandra and M. Y. Vardi. The implication problem for functional and inclusion dependencies is undecidable. *SIAM J. on Computing*, 14(3):671–677, 1985.

[28] S. S. Chawathe, H. Garcia-Molina, J. Hammer, K. Ireland, Y. Papakonstantinou, J. D. Ullman, and J. Widom. The TSIMMIS project: Integration of heterogeneous information sources. In *Proc. of the 10th Meeting of the Information Processing Society of Japan (IPSJ'94)*, pages 7–18, 1994.

[29] B. F. Chellas. *Modal Logic: An introduction*. Cambridge University Press, 1980.

[30] J. Chomicki, J. Marcinkowski, and S. Staworko. Computing consistent query answers using conflict hypergraphs. In *Proc. of the 13th Int. Conf. on Information and Knowledge Management (CIKM 2004)*, pages 417–426, 2004.

[31] J. Chomicki, J. Marcinkowski, and S. Staworko. Hippo: a system for computing consistent query answers to a class of SQL queries. In *Proc. of the 9th Int. Conf. on Extending Database Technology (EDBT 2004)*, pages 841–844. Springer, 2004.

[32] I. Clarke, S. G. Miller, T. W. Hong, O. Sandberg, and B. Wiley. Freenet: A distributed anonymous information storage and retrieval system. In *Proc. of the Int. Workshop on Design Issues in Anonymity and Unobservability (DIAU 2000)*, 2000.

[33] O. M. Duschka, M. R. Genesereth, and A. Y. Levy. Recursive query plans for data integration. *J. of Logic Programming*, 43(1):49–73, 2000.

[34] R. Fagin, J. Y. Halpern, Y. Moses, and M. Y. Vardi. *Reasoning about Knowledge*. The MIT Press, 1995.

[35] R. Fagin, P. G. Kolaitis, R. J. Miller, and L. Popa. Data exchange: Semantics and query answering. In *Proc. of the 9th Int. Conf. on Database Theory (ICDT 2003)*, pages 207–224, 2003.

[36] R. Fagin, P. G. Kolaitis, and L. Popa. Data exchange: Getting to the core. In *Proc. of the 22nd ACM SIGACT SIGMOD SIGART Symp. on Principles of Database Systems (PODS 2003)*, pages 90–101, 2003.

[37] E. Franconi, G. Kuper, A. Lopatenko, and L. Serafini. A robust logical and computational characterisation of peer-to-peer database systems. In *Proc. of the VLDB International Workshop On Databases, Information Systems and Peer-to-Peer Computing (DBISP2P 2003)*, 2003.

[38] A. Fuxman, E. Fazli, and R. J. Miller. ConQuer: Efficient management of inconsistent databases. In *Proc. of the ACM SIGMOD Int. Conf. on Management of Data*, pages 155–166, 2005.

[39] A. Fuxman, P. G. Kolaitis, R. Miller, and W. C. Tan. Peer data exchange. In *Proc. of the 24rd ACM SIGACT SIGMOD SIGART Symp. on Principles of Database Systems (PODS 2005)*, pages 160–171, 2005.

[40] A. Fuxman and R. J. Miller. First-order query rewriting for inconsistent databases. In *Proc. of the 10th Int. Conf. on Database Theory (ICDT 2005)*, volume 3363 of *LNCS*, pages 337–351. Springer, 2005.

[41] H. Garcia-Molina, Y. Papakonstantinou, D. Quass, A. Rajaraman, Y. Sagiv, J. D. Ullman,

V. Vassalos, and J. Widom. The TSIMMIS approach to mediation: Data models and languages. *J. of Intelligent Information Systems*, 8(2):117–132, 1997.

[42] M. Gelfond and V. Lifschitz. The stable model semantics for logic programming. In *Proc. of the 5th Logic Programming Symposium*, pages 1070–1080. The MIT Press, 1988.

[43] M. R. Genereseth, A. M. Keller, and O. M. Duschka. Infomaster: An information integration system. In *Proc. of the ACM SIGMOD Int. Conf. on Management of Data*, pages 539–542, 1997.

[44] C. H. Goh, S. Bressan, S. E. Madnick, and M. D. Siegel. Context interchange: New features and formalisms for the intelligent integration of information. *ACM Trans. on Information Systems*, 17(3):270–293, 1999.

[45] G. Grahne and A. O. Mendelzon. Tableau techniques for querying information sources through global schemas. In *Proc. of the 7th Int. Conf. on Database Theory (ICDT'99)*, volume 1540 of *Lecture Notes in Computer Science*, pages 332–347. Springer, 1999.

[46] G. Greco, S. Greco, and E. Zumpano. A logical framework for querying and repairing inconsistent databases. *IEEE Trans. on Knowledge and Data Engineering*, 15(6):1389–1408, 2003.

[47] S. Gribble, A. Halevy, Z. Ives, M. Rodrig, and D. Suciu. What can databases do for peer-to-peer? In *Proc. of the 4th Int. Workshop on the Web and Databases (WebDB 2001)*, 2001.

[48] L. Grieco, D. Lembo, M. Ruzzi, and R. Rosati. Consistent query answering under key and exclusion dependencies: Algorithms and experiments. In *Proc. of the 14th Int. Conf. on Information and Knowledge Management (CIKM 2005)*, pages 792–799, 2005.

[49] J. Gryz. Query rewriting using views in the presence of functional and inclusion dependencies. *Information Systems*, 24(7):597–612, 1999.

[50] A. Halevy, Z. Ives, D. Suciu, and I. Tatarinov. Schema mediation in peer data management systems. In *Proc. of the 19th IEEE Int. Conf. on Data Engineering (ICDE 2003)*, pages 505–516, 2003.

[51] J. Heflin and J. Hendler. A portrait of the Semantic Web in action. *IEEE Intelligent Systems*, 16(2):54–59, 2001.

[52] R. Hull, M. Benedikt, V. Christophides, and J. Su. E-services: a look behind the curtain. In *Proc. of the 22nd ACM SIGACT SIGMOD SIGART Symp. on Principles of Database Systems (PODS 2003)*, pages 1–14. ACM Press and Addison Wesley, 2003.

[53] T. Kirk, A. Y. Levy, Y. Sagiv, and D. Srivastava. The Information Manifold. In *Proceedings of the AAAI 1995 Spring Symp. on Information Gathering from Heterogeneous, Distributed Enviroments*, pages 85–91, 1995.

[54] C. Koch. Query rewriting with symmetric constraints. In *Proc. of the 2nd Int. Symp. on Foundations of Information and Knowledge Systems (FoIKS 2002)*, volume 2284 of *Lecture Notes in Computer Science*, pages 130–147. Springer, 2002.

[55] M. Lenzerini. Data integration: A theoretical perspective. In *Proc. of the 21st ACM SIGACT SIGMOD SIGART Symp. on Principles of Database Systems (PODS 2002)*, pages 233–246, 2002.

[56] N. Leone, T. Eiter, W. Faber, M. Fink, G. Gottlob, G. Greco, E. Kalka, G. Ianni, D. Lembo, M. Lenzerini, V. Lio, B. Nowicki, R. Rosati, M. Ruzzi, W. Staniszkis, and G. Terracina. The INFOMIX system for advanced integration of incomplete and inconsistent data. In *Proc. of the ACM SIGMOD Int. Conf. on Management of Data*, pages 915–917, 2005.

[57] H. J. Levesque and G. Lakemeyer. *The Logic of Knowledge Bases*. The MIT Press, 2001.

[58] A. Y. Levy. Logic-based techniques in data integration. In J. Minker, editor, *Logic Based Artificial Intelligence*. Kluwer Academic Publisher, 2000.

[59] A. Y. Levy, A. Rajaraman, and J. J. Ordille. Querying heterogenous information sources using source descriptions. In *Proc. of the 22nd Int. Conf. on Very Large Data Bases (VLDB'96)*, 1996.

[60] A. Y. Levy, D. Srivastava, and T. Kirk. Data model and query evaluation in global information systems. *J. of Intelligent Information Systems*, 5:121–143, 1995.

[61] J. Madhavan and A. Y. Halevy. Composing mappings among data sources. In *Proc. of the 29th Int. Conf. on Very Large Data Bases (VLDB 2003)*, pages 572–583, 2003.

[62] J. C. Mitchell. The implication problem for functional and inclusion dependencies. *Information and Control*, 56:154–173, 1983.

[63] M. P. Papazoglou, B. J. Kramer, and J. Yang. Leveraging Web-services and peer-to-peer networks. In *Proc. of the 15th Int. Conf. on Advanced Information Systems Engineering (CAiSE 2003)*, pages 485–501, 2003.

[64] R. Pottinger and A. Y. Levy. A scalable algorithm for answering queries using views. In *Proc. of the 26th Int. Conf. on Very Large Data Bases (VLDB 2000)*, pages 484–495, 2000.

[65] L. Serafini and C. Ghidini. Using wrapper agents to answer queries in distributed information systems. In *Proc. of the 1st Int. Conf. on Advances in Information Systems (ADVIS-2000)*, volume 1909 of *Lecture Notes in Computer Science*. Springer, 2000.

[66] A. Tomasic, L. Raschid, and P. Valduriez. Scaling access to heterogeneous data sources with DISCO. *IEEE Trans. on Knowledge and Data Engineering*, 10(5):808–823, 1998.

[67] J. D. Ullman. Information integration using logical views. *Theoretical Computer Science*, 239(2):189–210, 2000.

[68] S. R. Waterhouse, D. M. Doolin, G. Kan, and Y. Faybishenko. Distributed search in P2P networks. *IEEE Internet Computing*, 6(1):68–72, 2002.

[69] B. Yang and H. Garcia-Molina. Designing a super-peer network. In *Proc. of the 19th IEEE Int. Conf. on Data Engineering (ICDE 2003)*, 2003.

[70] Z. Zhang and A. Mendelzon. Authorization views and conditional query containment. In *Proc. of the 10th Int. Conf. on Database Theory (ICDT 2005)*, volume 3363 of *Lecture Notes in Computer Science*, pages 259–273. Springer, 2005.

Global Data Management
R. Baldoni et al. (Eds.)
IOS Press, 2006

Belief Propagation on Uncertain Schema Mappings in Peer Data Management Systems [1]

Philippe Cudré-Mauroux [2], and Karl Aberer
School Of Computer and Communication Sciences
EPFL – Switzerland

Abstract. Until recently, most data integration techniques involved central components, e.g., global schemas, to enable transparent access to heterogeneous databases. Today, however, with the democratization of tools facilitating knowledge elicitation in machine-processable formats, one cannot rely on global, centralized schemas anymore as knowledge creation and consumption are getting more and more dynamic and decentralized. Peer Data Management Systems (PDMS) provide an answer to this problem by eliminating the central semantic component and considering instead compositions of local, pair-wise mappings to propagate queries from one database to the others.

In the following, we give an overview of various PDMS approaches; all the approaches proposed so far make the implicit assumption that all schema mappings used to reformulate a query are correct. This obviously cannot be taken as granted in typical PDMS settings where mappings can be created (semi) automatically by independent parties. Thus, we propose a totally decentralized, efficient message passing scheme to automatically detect erroneous schema mappings in a PDMS. Our scheme is based on a probabilistic model where we take advantage of transitive closures of mapping operations to confront local belief on the correctness of a mapping against evidences gathered around the network. We show that our scheme can be efficiently embedded in any PDMS and provide an evaluation of our techniques on large sets of automatically-generated schemas.

Keywords. Data Integration, Peer Data Management Systems, Belief Propagation

1. Introduction

Data integration techniques have traditionally revolved around global schemas to query heterogeneous databases in a transparent way: popular techniques such as LAV (Local-

---

[1]The work presented in this chapter was carried out in the framework of the EPFL Center for Global Computing and supported by the Swiss National Funding Agency OFES as part of the IST European project Evergrow No 001935, and was supported (in part) by the National Competence Center in Research on Mobile Information and Communication Systems (NCCR-MICS), a center supported by the Swiss National Science Foundation under grant number 5005-67322.

[2]Correspondence to: Philippe Cudré-Mauroux, School Of Computer and Communication Sciences, Station 14, EPFL, 1010 Lausanne, Switzerland. Tel.: +41 21 693 6787; Fax: +41 21 693 8115; E-mail: philippe.cudre-mauroux@epfl.ch.

As-View) or GAV (Global-As-View) drew considerable attention as they permit deterministic reformulations of queries over various data sources. These centralized approaches, however, require the definition of an integrated schema supposedly subsuming all local schemas. This requirement is particularly stringent in highly heterogeneous, dynamic and decentralized environments such as the Web or Peer-to-Peer overlay networks. In these settings, largely autonomous and heterogeneous data sources coexist without any central coordination. Keeping a global schema up-to-date or defining a schema general enough to encompass all information sources is thus unmanageable in practice in this context. This evolution motivated the research community to imagine new paradigms for handling heterogeneous data in decentralized environments. In this chapter, we focus on the Peer Data Management Systems (PDMS) approach, which recently drew considerable attention in this context [1,2].

PDMS take advantage of local, pairwise schema mappings between pairs of databases to propagate queries posed against a local schema to the rest of the network in an iterative and cooperative manner. No global semantic coordination is needed as peers only need to define local mappings to a small set of related databases to be part of the global network of databases. Once a database sends a query to its immediate neighbors through local mapping links, its neighbors (after processing the query) in turn propagate the query to their own neighbors, and so on and so forth until the query reaches all (or a predefined number of) databases. The way the query spreads around the network mimics the way messages are routed in a Peer-to-Peer (P2P) system, thus the appellation *Peer Data Management Systems.*

The vast majority of PDMS approaches, however, propagate queries without concern on the validity or quality of the mappings. This obviously represents a severe limitation, as one cannot expect any level of consistency or quality on PDMS mappings for several reasons: first, remember that PDMS target large-scale, decentralized and heterogeneous environments where autonomous parties have full control on schema designs. As a result, we can expect irreconcilable differences on conceptualizations (e.g., epistemic or metaphysical differences on a given modelization problem, see also [3]) among the databases. Also, the limited expressivity of the mappings, usually defined as queries or using an ontology definition language like OWL [4], precludes the creation of correct mappings in many situations (e.g., mapping an attribute onto a relation). Finally, given the vibrant activity on (semi-) automatic alignment techniques (see [5] for a recent overview), we can expect some (most?) of the mappings to be generated automatically in large-scale settings, with all the evident quality problems associated.

In the following, we propose a probabilistic technique to determine the quality of schema mappings in PDMS settings in a totally automated way and without any form of central coordination. As peers do not always share common data, mapping errors are typically difficult to discover from a local perspective in PDMS. Our methods are based on the analysis of cycles and parallels paths in the graph of schema mappings: after detecting mapping inconsistencies by comparing transitive closures of mapping operations, we build a global probabilistic inference model spanning the entire PDMS system. We show how to construct this model in a totally decentralized way by involving local information only. We describe a decentralized and efficient method to derive mapping quality measures from our model. Our approach is based on a decentralized version of iterative sum-product message passing techniques (loopy belief propagation). We show how to embed our approach in PDMS systems with a very modest communication overhead by piggybacking on normal query processing operations. Finally, we present an evaluation of our techniques applied on large corpuses of automatically-generated schemas.

2. Peer Data Management Systems

Integration systems traditionally adopted the Federated Databases model (see Figure 1 a). This model provides a uniform access to multiple heterogeneous data sources through a centralized Federated Database Server. Wrappers deal with syntactic heterogeneity by converting each local database to a common representation. In this way, data can be stored using various data models (e.g., semi-structured, text files) at the local databases, while the Federated Database only deals with a unique – typically relational – representation. A mediator integrates data with the same meaning but stored using different schemas. It can for example define correspondences (mappings) between various schemas to reformulate a query posed against the integrated schema to queries posed against each local database. The Local As View (LAV) approach defines each local database as a view on an federated, centralized schema. In the Global As View approach, on the other hand, the federated schema is defined in terms of the local schemas. Clients can thus query the Federated Database Server, typically through a SQL interface, which is able to reformulate the query thanks to the mediator, query the local databases and collect results through the wrappers to finally return all answers to the clients.

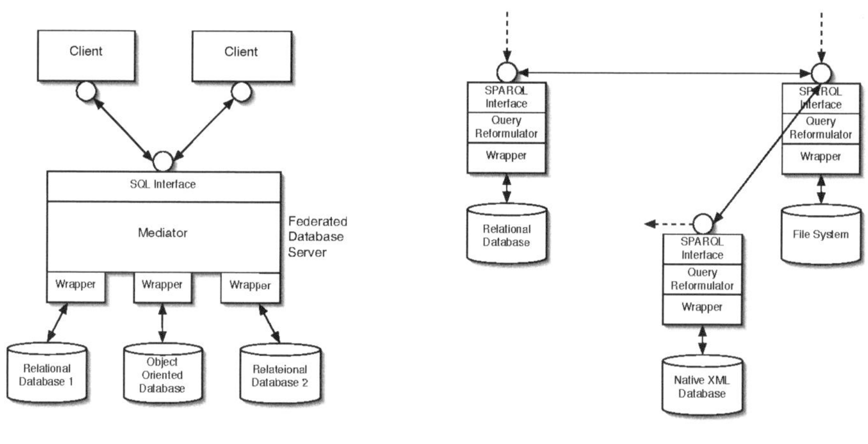

Figure 1. Two data integration models: Federated Databases (a) based on a central federated schema and Peer Data Management Systems (b) based on peer-to-peer mappings between the databases

One of the main limitations of this model lies in its centralization: the Federated Database Server represents a single point of failure and is responsible for integrating *all* databases taking advantage of a *global* schema. The server severely hampers the scalability of the approach and violates the autonomy of the local sources. Aware of these limitations, the research community recently explored new techniques to manage and integrate data in large scale, decentralized or Peer-to-Peer settings (see [1] for a recent tutorial on Semantic Overlay Networks). In Peer Data Management Systems settings (see Figure 1 b), the centralized mediator disappears and is replaced by an unstructured collection of peer-to-peer mappings between the databases. PDMS take advantage of these local, pair-wise schema mappings between pairs of databases to propagate queries posed against a local schema to the rest of the network in an iterative and cooperative manner. No global semantic coordination is needed as peers only need to define local mappings to a small set of related databases to be part of the global network of databases. Once a database sends a query to its immediate neighbors, its neighbors (after processing the query) can reformulate the query against their local databases, and propagate the query to their own neighbors, and so on and so forth until the query reaches all (or a predefined number of) databases.

Mappings in a PDMS can be defined as views, or by taking advantage of an on-tology language such as OWL. Note that in practice, the way the various schemas and schema mappings are organized might be independent of the physical organization of the databases: Figure 2 depicts a Semantic Overlay Network where the organization of the peer at the overlay layer is uncorrelated with the organization of the schemas and schema mappings at the mediation layer. In this way, peers can create or share schemas irrespective of their location in the overlay network.

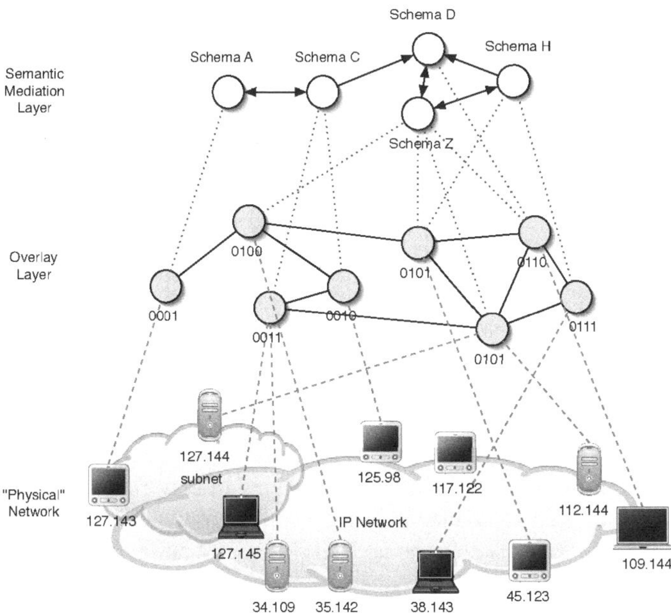

Figure 2. A three-layered representation of a Semantic Overlay Network: machines (bottom layer) organize themselves into a peer-to-peer overlay (intermediate layer) and communicate through a Semantic Mediation Layer (top layer) defining mappings between the various schemas used in the network

In the following, we concentrate on a probabilistic analysis of the Semantic Media-tion Layer in order to detect inconsistent schema mappings. Our approach is quite naturally based on some of our previous ideas [6,7] for analyzing the network of mappings. Others have also focused on PDMS settings recently: in [8], Bernstein et al. formulated requirements for P2P databases in terms of local mappings and semi-automatic solutions for data integration. Edutella [9], based on a super-peer topology, was one of the early PDMS systems deployed. Piazza [10,11] is a PDMS system which provides efficient query reformulations algorithms for relational and semi-structured data models. The Hyperion [12] project relies on rules to propagate data in a PDMS network according to mapping tables. PeerDB [13] examines the problem of sharing relational data in P2P networks from an information retrieval perspective. One of our earlier systems, GridVine [14], is based on a structured overlay layers and thus supports three uncorrelated layers as depicted in Figure 2.

3. Problem Definition

For the sake of clarity, we consider in the following only simple PDMS settings where each peer represents a separate database (i.e., there is a direct correlation between the overlay layer and the semantic mediation layer). Our methods work in an identical manner in more complex settings.

We model PDMS as collections of peers; Each individual peer p represents a database storing data according to a distinct structured schema. As we wish to present an approach as generic as possible, we do not make any assumption on the exact data model used by the databases in the following but illustrate some of our claims with examples in XML and RDF. We only require the databases to store information with respect to some concepts we call *attributes* a (e.g., attributes in a relational schema, elements or attributes in XML and classes or properties in RDF). Additionally, we suppose that each peer can be identified and contacted by a unique identifier (e.g., an IP address or a peer ID in a P2P network).

Peers are connected one another through (un)directed edges representing (un)directed pairwise schema mappings. A schema mapping m allows a query posed against a local schema to be evaluated against another schema. This operation is uni or bi-directional depending on the language used to express the mappings. Again, we do not make assumptions on that language, except that it should allow to connect pairs of semantically similar attributes. Note that this language may for example allow for syntactic transformations (e.g., transforming a date from one format to another) or complex mappings (e.g., mapping an attribute to part of another attribute). Finally, remember that our fundamental assumption is that some mappings might be incorrect, i.e., mappings might map an attribute from one database to a semantically irrelevant attribute in another database.

We consider queries posed locally against the schema of a given peer. Queries are composed of generic selection / projection operations op on attributes. For each attribute a_i appearing in the query, the system (or the expert user) defines a semantic threshold θ_{a_i} under which the query should not be propagated any further: as the query gets propagated throughout the network of peer databases, each intermediate peer checks the probability $P(a_i = correct)$ of each attribute in the query being semantically preserved by a mapping operation. The query is forwarded through a mapping link to another peer database only if all attributes are preserved, that is if for all a_i, $P(a_i = correct) > \theta_{a_i}$ for the given mapping. Note that other per-hop forwarding behaviors could easily be implemented with our techniques (see [7]) but we stick to the given scheme for simplicity.

Given this setting, our goal is to provide probabilistic guarantees on the correctness of a mapping operation, i.e., to determine $P(a_i = correct)$. As any processing in a PDMS, we wish our methods to operate without any global coordination in a purely decentralized manner. Also, we would like our methods to be totally automated, as precise as possible and fast enough to be applied on large schemas or ontologies.

3.1. An Introductory Example

Before delving into technicalities, we start with a high-level, introductory example of our approach. Let us consider the simple PDMS network depicted in Figure 3. This network is composed of four databases $p_1, \ldots, p_4$. All databases store a collection of XML documents related to pieces of art, but structured according to four different schemas (one per database). Each database supports XQuery as query language. Various pairwise XQuery schema mappings have been created (both manually and automatically) to link the databases; Figure 4 below shows an example of mapping between two schemas and how one can take advantage of this mapping to resolve a query posed against two different schemas.

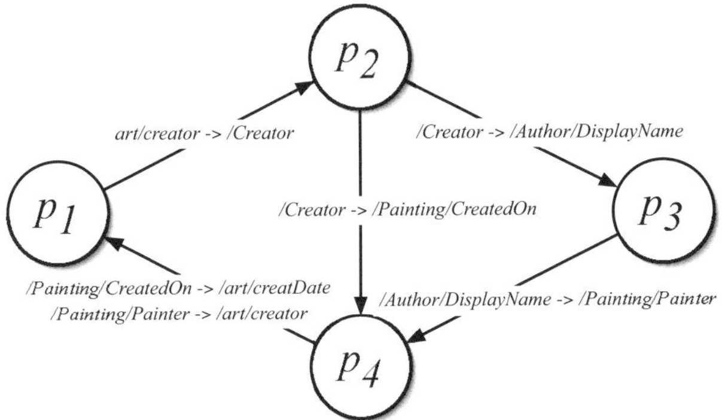

Figure 3. A simple directed PDMS network of four peers and five schema mappings, here depicted for the attribute *Creator*

Let us suppose that a user in p_2 wishes to retrieve the names of all artists having created a piece of work related to some river. The user could locally pose an XQuery like the following:

```
q_1 =
FOR $c IN distinct-values (ArtDatabank//Creator)
WHERE $c/..//Item LIKE "%river%"
RETURN <myArtist> $c </myArtist>
```

This query basically boils down to a projection on the attribute *Creator*: $op_1 = \pi_{Creator}$ and a selection on the title: $op_2 = \sigma_{Item=\%river\%}$. The user issues the query and patiently awaits for answers, both from his local database and the rest of the network.

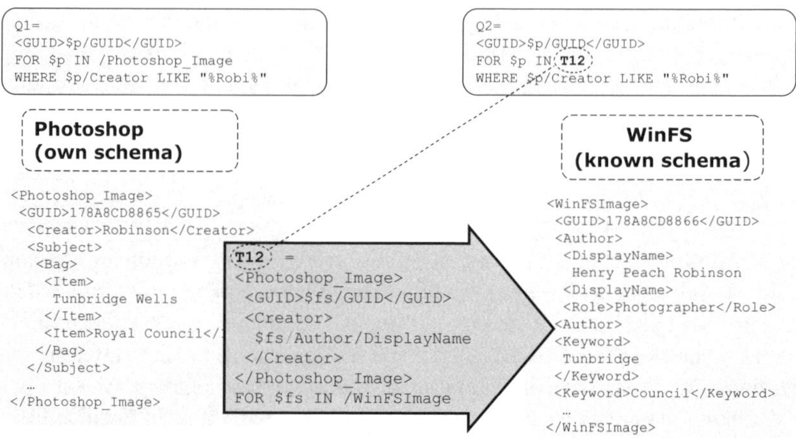

Figure 4. An example of schema mapping (here between peers p_2 and p_3) expressed as an XQuery

In a standard PDMS, the query would be forwarded through both outgoing mappings of p_2, generating a fair proportion of false positives as one of these two mappings (the one between p_2 and p_4) is incorrect for the attribute *Creator* (the mapping erroneously maps *Creator* in p_2 onto *CreatedOn* in p_4, see Figure 3). Luckily for our user, the PDMS system he is using implements our belief propagation techniques. Without any prior information on the mappings, the system detects inconsistencies for the mappings on *Creator* by analyzing the cycles $p_1 \rightarrow p_2 \rightarrow p_4 \rightarrow p_1$ and $p_1 \rightarrow p_2 \rightarrow p_3 \rightarrow p_4 \rightarrow p_1$, as well as the parallel paths $p_2 \rightarrow p_4$ and $p_2 \rightarrow p_3 \rightarrow p_4$ in the mapping network. In a decentralized process, the PDMS constructs a probabilistic network and determines that the semantics of the attribute *Creator* will most likely be preserved by all mappings, except by the mapping between p_2 and p_4 which is more likely to be faulty. Thus, this specific query will be routed through mapping $p_2 \rightarrow p_3$, and then iteratively to p_4 and p_1. In the end, the user will retrieve all artist names as specified, without any false-positive since the mapping $p_2 \rightarrow p_4$ was ignored in the query resolution process.

4. Modeling PDMS as Factor-Graphs

In the following, we take advantage of query messages being forwarded from one peer to another to detect inconsistencies in the network of mappings. We represent individual mappings and network information as related random variables in a probabilistic graphical model. We will then efficiently evaluate marginal probabilities, i.e., mapping quality, using these models.

4.1. A Quick Reminder on Factor-Graphs and Message Passing Schemes

We give below a brief overview of message passing techniques. For a more in-depth coverage, we refer the interested reader to one of the many overviews on this domain, such as [15]. Note that Belief Propagation as introduced by Judea Pearl [16] is actually a specialized case of a standard message passing sum-product algorithm.

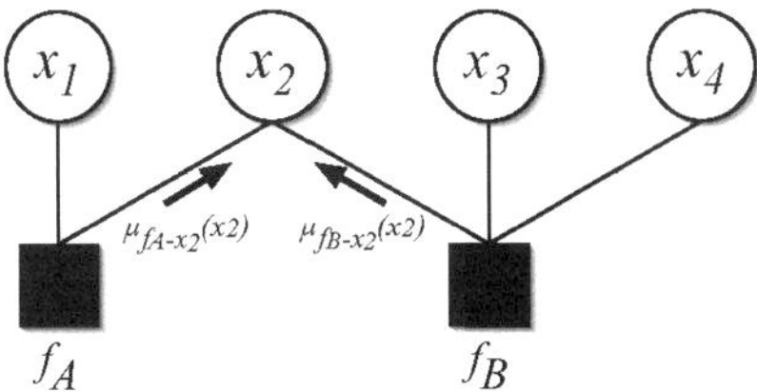

Figure 5. A simple factor-graph of four variables and two factors

Probabilistic graphical models are a marriage between probability theory and graph theory. In many situations, one can deal with a complicated global problem by viewing it as a factorization of several local functions, each depending on a subset of the variables appearing in the global problem. As an example, suppose that a global function $g(x_1, x_2, x_3, x_4)$ factors into a product of two local functions f_A and f_B: $g(x_1, x_2, x_3, x_4) = f_A(x_1, x_2)f_B(x_2, x_3, x_4)$. This factorization can be represented in a graphical form by the *factor-graph* depicted in Figure 5, where variables (circles) are linked to their respective factors (black squares). Often, one is interested in computing a *marginal* of this global function, e.g.,

$$g_2(x_2) = \sum_{x_1}\sum_{x_3}\sum_{x_4} g(x_1, x_2, x_3, x_4) = \sum_{\sim\{x_2\}} g(x_1, x_2, x_3, x_4)$$

where we introduce the summary operator $\sum_{\sim\{x_i\}}$ to sum over all variables but x_i. Such marginals can be derived in an efficient way by a series of *sum-product* operations on the local function, such as:

$$g_2(x_2) = \left(\sum_{x_1} f_A(x_1, x_2)\right)\left(\sum_{x_3}\sum_{x_4} f_B(x_2, x_3, x_4)\right).$$

Interestingly, the above computation can be seen as the product of two messages $\mu_{f_A \to x_2}(x_2)$ and $\mu_{f_B \to x_2}(x_2)$ sent respectively by f_A and f_B to x_2 (see Figure 5). The *sum-product* algorithm exploits this observation to compute all marginal functions of a factor-graph in a concurrent and efficient manner. Message passing algorithms traditionally compute marginals by sending two messages — one in each direction — for every edge in the factor-graph:

variable x to local factor f:

$$\mu_{x \to f}(x) = \prod_{h \in n(x)\setminus\{f\}} \mu_{h \to x}(x)$$

local factor f to variable x

$$\mu_{f \to x}(x) = \sum_{\sim\{x\}}\left(f(X)\prod_{y \in n(f)\setminus\{x\}} \mu_{y \to f}(y)\right)$$

where $n(\cdot)$ stands for the neighbors of a variable / function node in the graph.

These computations are known to be exact for cycle-free factor-graphs; in contrast, applications of the sum-product algorithm in a factor-graph with cycles only result in approximate computations for the marginals [17]. However, some of the most exciting applications of the sum-product algorithms (e.g., decoding of turbo or LDPC codes) arise precisely in such situations. We show below that this is also the case for factor-graphs modelling Peer Data Management Systems.

4.2. On Factor-Graphs in Undirected PDMS

In the following, we explain how to model a network of mapping as a factor-graph. These factor-graphs will in turn be used in Section 5 to derive quality measures for the various mappings in the network.

4.2.1. Cyclic Mappings

Semantic overlay network topologies are not generated at random. On the contrary, they are constructed by (computerized or human) agents aiming at interconnecting partially overlapping information sources. We can expect very high clustering coefficients in these networks, since similar sources will tend to bond together and create cluster of sources. As an example, a study of an online network of related biologic schemas (in the the the SRS system, http://www.lionbioscience.com) shows an exponential degree distribution and an unusually high clustering coefficient of 0.54 (as of May 2005). Consequently, we can expect semantic schema graphs to exhibit *scale-free* properties and an unusually high number of loops [18].

Let us assume we have detected a cycle of mappings $m_0, m_1, \ldots, m_{n-1}$ connecting n peers $p_0, p_1, \ldots, p_{(n-1)}, p_0$ in a circle. Cycles of mappings can be easily discovered by the peers in the PDMS network, either by proactively flooding their neighborhood with probe messages with a certain Time-To-Live (TTL) or by examining the trace of routed queries in the network. We take advantage of transitive closures of mapping operations in the cycle to compare a query q posed against the schema of p_0 to the corresponding query q' forwarded through all n mappings along the cycle: $q' = m_{n-1}(m_{n-2}(\ldots(m_0)(q))))$. q and q' can be compared on an equal basis since they are both expressed in terms of the schema of p_0. In an ideal world, $q' \equiv q$ since the transformed query q' is the result of n identity mappings applied on the original query q. In a distributed setting, however, this might not always be the case, both because of the lack of expressiveness of the mappings and of the fact that mappings can be created in (semi-) automatic ways.

When comparing an attribute a_i in an operation $op_q(a_i)$ appearing in the original query q to the attribute a_j from the corresponding operation $op'(a_j)$ in the transformed query q', three subcases may occur in practice:

$a_j = a_i$: this occurs when the attribute, after having been transformed n times through the mappings, still maps to the original attribute when returning to the semantic domain of p_0. Since this indicates a high level of semantic agreement along the cycle for this particular attribute, we say that this represents positive feedback f^+ on the mappings constituting the cycles.

$a_j \neq a_i$: this occurs when the attribute, after having been transformed n times through the mappings, maps to a different attribute when returning to the semantic domain of p_0. As this indicates some disagreement on the semantics of a_i along the cycle of mappings, we say that this represents negative feedback f^- on the mappings constituting the cycles.

$a_j = \perp$: this occurs when some intermediary schema does not have a representation for the attribute in question, i.e., cannot map the attribute onto one of its own attributes. This does not give us any additional (feedback) information on the level of semantic agreement along the cycle, but can still represent some valuable information in other contexts, for example when analyzing query forwarding on a syntactic level (see also [7]). In the current case, we consider that the probability on the correctness of a mapping drops to zero for a specific attribute if the mapping does not provide any mapping for the attribute.

We focus here on single-attribute operations for simplicity, but our results can be extended to multi-attribute operations as well.

Also, we take into account the fact that series of erroneous mappings on a_i can accidentally *compensate* their respective errors and actually create a correct composite mapping $m_{n-1} \circ m_{n-2} \ldots \circ m_0$ in the end. Assuming a probability Δ of two or more mapping errors being compensated along a cycle in this way, we can determine the conditional probability of a cycle producing positive feedback $f_{\circlearrowleft}^+$ given the correctness of its constituting mappings $m_0, \ldots, m_{n-1}$:

$$P(f_{\circlearrowleft}^+|m_0, \ldots, m_{n-1}) = \begin{cases} 1 & \text{if all mappings correct} \\ 0 & \text{if one mapping incorrect} \\ \Delta & \text{if two or more} \\ & \text{mappings incorrect} \end{cases}$$

This conditional probability function allows us to create a factor-graph from a network of interconnected mappings. We create a global factor-graph as follows:

```
for all mapping m in PDMS
   add m.factor to global factor-graph;
   add m.variable to m.factor;
for all mapping cycle c in PDMS
   add c.feedback.factor to global factor-graph;
   add c.feedback.variable to c.feedback.factor;
   for all mapping m in mapping cycle c
      link c.feedback.factor to m.variable;
```

Figure 6 illustrates the derivation of a factor-graph from a simple semantic network of four peers $p_1, \ldots, p_4$ (left-hand side of Figure 6). The peers are interconnected through five mappings $m_{12}, m_{23}, m_{34}, m_{41}$ and m_{24}. One may attempt to obtain feedback from three different mapping cycles in this network:

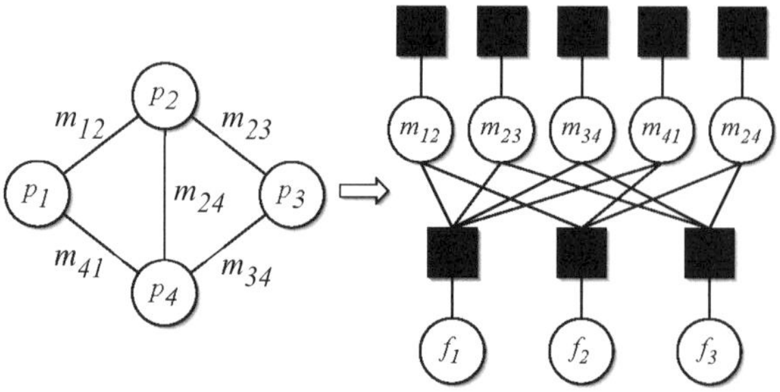

Figure 6. Modeling an undirected network of mappings as a factor-graph

$$f_\circlearrowleft^1 : m_{12} - m_{23} - m_{34} - m_{41}$$
$$f_\circlearrowleft^2 : m_{12} - m_{24} - m_{41}$$
$$f_\circlearrowleft^3 : m_{23} - m_{34} - m_{24}.$$

The right-hand side of Figure 6 depicts the resulting factor-graph, containing from top to bottom: five one-variable factors for the prior probability functions on the mappings, five mappings variables m_{ij}, three factors linking feedback variables to mapping variables through conditional probability functions (defined as explained above), and finally three feedback variables f_k. Note that feedback variables are usually not independent: two feedback variables are correlated as soon as the two mapping cycles they represent have at least one mapping in common (e.g., in Figure 6, where all three feedbacks are correlated).

4.3. On Factor-Graphs in Directed PDMS

One may derive similar factor-graphs in directed PDMS networks, focusing this time on directed mapping cycles and parallel mapping paths. Parallel mapping paths occur when two different series of mappings m' and m'' share the same source and destination. The conditional probability function for receiving positive feedback $f_\rightrightarrows^+$ through two parallel paths m' and m'' is as follows (see [19] for details):

$$P(f_\rightrightarrows^+ | \{m'\}, \{m''\}) = \begin{cases} 1 & \text{if all mappings correct} \\ 0 & \text{if one mapping incorrect} \\ \Delta & \text{if two or more} \\ & \quad \text{mappings incorrect} \end{cases}$$

Figure 7 shows an example of a directed mapping network with four peers and six mappings. Feedback from two directed cycles and three pairs of parallel paths might be gathered from the network:

$$f_\circlearrowleft^1 : m_{12} \rightarrow m_{23} \rightarrow m_{34} \rightarrow m_{41}$$
$$f_\circlearrowleft^2 : m_{12} \rightarrow m_{24} \rightarrow m_{41}$$
$$f_\rightrightarrows^3 : m_{21} \| m_{24} \rightarrow m_{41}$$
$$f_\rightrightarrows^4 : m_{24} \| m_{23} \rightarrow m_{34}$$
$$f_\rightrightarrows^5 : m_{21} \| m_{23} \rightarrow m_{34} \rightarrow m_{41}.$$

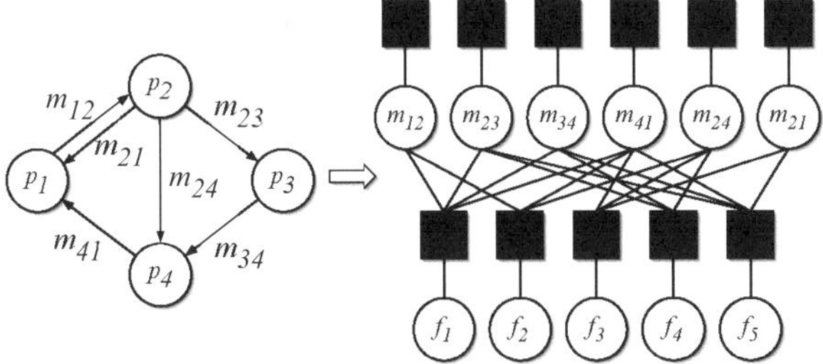

Figure 7. Modeling a directed network of mappings as a factor-graph

As for the undirected case, the right-hand side of Figure 7 represents the factor-graph derived from the directed mapping network of the left-hand side.

Since undirected mapping networks and directed mapping networks result in structurally similar factor-graphs in the end, we treat them on the same basis in the following. We only include two versions of our derivations when some noticeable difference between the undirected and the directed case surfaces.

5. Embedded Message Passing

So far, we have developed a graphical probabilistic model capturing the relations between mappings and network feedback in a PDMS. To take advantage of these models, one would have to gather *all* information pertaining to *all* mappings, cycles and parallel paths in a system. However, adopting this centralized approach makes no sense in our context, as PDMS were precisely invented to avoid such centralization. Instead, we devise below a method to embed message passing into normal operations of a Peer Data Management System. Thus, we are able to get globally consistent mapping quality measures in a scalable, decentralized and efficient manner while respecting the autonomy of the peers.

Looking back at the factor-graphs introduced in Section 4.2 and 4.3, we make two observations: i) some (but not all) nodes appearing in the factor-graphs can be mapped back onto the original PDMS graph, and ii) the factor-graphs contain cycles.

5.1. On Feedback Variables in PDMS Factor-Graphs

Going through one of the figures representing a PDMS factor-graph from top to bottom, one may identify four different kinds of nodes: factors for the prior probability functions on the mappings, variable nodes for the correctness of the mappings, factors for the probability functions linking mapping and feedback variables, and finally variable nodes for the feedback information. Going one step further, one can make a distinction between nodes representing local information, i.e., mapping factors and mapping variables, and nodes pertaining to global information, i.e., feedback factors and feedback variables.

Mapping back local information nodes onto the PDMS is easy, as only the nodes from which a mapping is departing need to store information about that mapping (see per hop routing behavior in Section 3). Luckily, we can also map the other nodes rather easily, as they either contain global but *static* information (density function in feedback factors), or information gathered around the local *neighborhood* of a node (Δ, observed

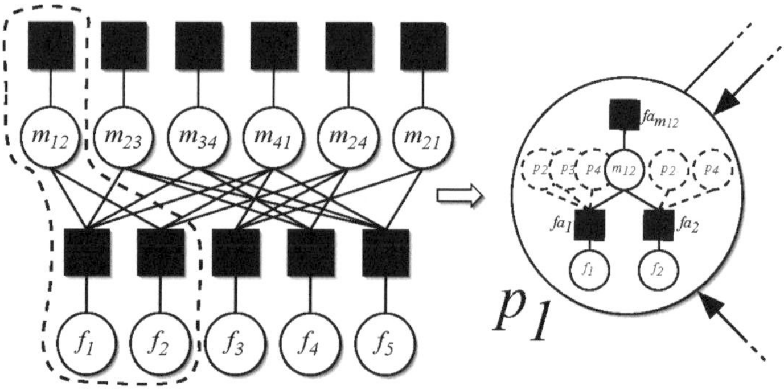

Figure 8. Creating a local factor-graph in the PDMS (here for peer p_1)

values for $f_{\circlearrowright}^i$ and $f_{\Rightarrow}^j$). Hence, each peer p only needs to store a fraction of the global factor-graph, fraction selected as follows:

```
for all outgoing mapping m
   add m.factor to local factor-graph;
   add m.variable to m.factor;
   for all feedbackMessage f containing m
      add f.factor to m.variable;
   if f.isPositive
      add f.variable(+) to f.factor;
   else if feedback.isNegative
      add f.variable(-) to f.factor;
   for all mapping m' in feedback except m
      add virtual peer m'.peer to f.factor;
```

where $feedbackMessage$ stands for all feedback messages received from neighboring peers (resulting from probes flooded within a certain TTL throughout the neighborhood or from analyzing standard forwarded queries). Figure 8 shows how p_1 from Figure 7 would store its local factor-graph.

Note that, depending on the PDMS, one can choose between two levels of granularity for storing factor-graphs and computing related probabilistic value: coarse granularity – where peers only store one factor-graph per mapping and where they derive only one global value on the correctness of the mapping – and fine granularity – where peers store one instance of the local factor-graph per attribute in the mapping, and where they derive one probabilistic quality value per attribute. We suppose we are in the latter situation but show derivations for one attribute only. Values for other attributes can be derived in a similar fashion.

5.2. On Cycles in PDMS Factor-Graphs

Cycles appear in PDMS factor-graphs as soon as two mappings belong to two identical cycles or parallel paths in the PDMS. See for example the PDMS in Figure 6, where m_{12}

and m_{41} both appear in cycles $p_1 - p_2 - p_4 - p_1$ and $p_1 - p_2 - p_3 - p_4 - p_1$, hence creating a cycle $m_{12} - factor(f_1) - m_{41} - factor(f_2) - m_{12}$ in the factor-graph. As mentioned above, the results of the sum-product algorithm operating in a factor-graph with cycles cannot (in general) be interpreted as exact function summaries.

One well-known approach to circumvent this problem is to transform the factor-graph by regrouping nodes (*clustering* or *stretching* transformations) to produce a factor tree. In our case, this would result in regrouping all mappings having more than one cycle or parallel path in common; this is obviously inapplicable in practice, as this would imply introducing central components in the PDMS to regroup (potentially large) sets of independent peers. Instead, we rely on iterative, decentralized message passing schedules (see below) to estimate marginal functions in a concurrent and efficient way. We show in Section 6 that those evaluations are sufficiently accurate to make sensible decisions on the mappings in practice.

5.3. Embedded Message Passing Schedules

Given its local factor-graph and messages received from its neighborhood, a peer can locally update its belief on the mappings by reformulating the sum-product algorithm (Section 4.1) as follows:

local message from factor fa_j to mapping variable m_i:

$$\mu_{fa_j \to m_i}(m_i) =$$
$$\sum_{\sim\{m_i\}} \left(fa_j(X) \prod_{p_k \in n(fa_j)} \mu_{p_k \to fa_j}(p_k) \prod_{m_l \in n(fa_j)\setminus\{m_i\}} \mu_{m_l \to fa_j}(m_l) \right)$$

local message from mapping m_i to factor $fa_j \in n(m_i)$:

$$\mu_{m_i \to fa_j}(m_i) = \prod_{fa \in n(m_i)\setminus\{fa_j\}} \mu_{fa \to m_i}(m_i)$$

remote message for factor fa_k from peer p_0 to peer $p_j \in n(fa_k)$:

$$\mu_{p_0 \to fa_k}(m_i) = \prod_{fa \in n(m_i)\setminus\{fa_k\}} \mu_{fa \to m_i}(m_i)$$

Posterior correctness of local mapping m_i:

$$P(m_i|\{\mathcal{F}\}) = \alpha \left(\prod_{fa \in n(m_i)} \mu_{fa \to m_i}(m_i)) \right)$$

where $alpha$ is a normalizing factor ensuring that the probabilities of all events sum to one (i.e., making sure that $P(m_i = correct) + P(m_i = incorrect) = 1$).

In cycle-free PDMS factor-graphs (i.e., trees), exact messages can be propagated from mapping variables to the rest of the network in at most two iterations (due to the specific topology of our factor-graph). Thus, all inference results will be exact in two iterations.

For the more general case of PDMS factor-graph with cycles, we are stuck at the beginning of computation since every peer has to wait for messages from other peers.

We resolve this problem in a standard manner by considering that all peers virtually received a unit message (i.e., a message representing the unit function) from all other peers appearing in their local factor-graphs prior to starting the algorithm. From there on, peers derive probabilities on the correctness of their local mappings and send messages to other peers as described above. We show in Section 6 that for PDMS factor-graphs with cycles, the algorithm converges to very good approximations of the exact values obtained by a standard global inference process. Peers can decide to send messages according to different schedules depending on the PDMS; we detail below two possible schedules with quite different performance in terms of communication overhead and convergence speed.

5.3.1. Periodic Message Passing Schedule

In highly dynamic environments where databases, schemas and schema mappings are constantly evolving, appearing or disappearing, peers might wish to act proactively in order to get results on the correctness of their mappings in a timely fashion. In a Periodic Message Passing Schedule, peers send remote messages to all peers p_i appearing in their local factor-graph every time period τ. This corresponds to a new round of the iterative sum-product algorithm. This periodic schedule induces some communication overhead (a maximum of $\sum_{c_i}(l_{c_i} - 1)$ messages per peer every τ, where c_i represent all mapping cycles passing through the peer and l_{c_i} the length of the cycles) but guarantees our methods to converge within a given time-frame dependent on the topology of the network (see also Section 6). Note that τ should be chosen according to the network churn in order to guarantee convergence in highly dynamic networks. Its exact value may range from a couple of seconds to weeks or months depending on the exact situation.

5.3.2. Lazy Message Passing Schedule

A very nice property of the iterative message passing algorithm is that it is tolerant to delayed or lost messages. Hence, we do not actually require any kind of synchronization for the message passing schedule; Peers can decide to send a remote message whenever they want without endangering the global convergence of the algorithm (the algorithm will still converge to the same point, simply slower, see next section). We may thus take advantage of this property to totally eliminate any communication overhead (i.e., number of additional messages sent) induced by our method by piggybacking on query messages. The idea is as follows: every time a query message is sent from one peer to another through a mapping link m_i, we append to this query message all messages $\mu(m_i)$ pertaining to the mapping being used. In this case, the convergence speed or our algorithm is proportional to the query load of the system. This may be the ideal schedule for query-intensive or relatively static systems.

5.4. Prior Belief Updates

Our computations always take into account the mapping factors (top layer of a PDMS factor-graph). These factors represent any local, prior knowledge the peers might possess on their mappings. For example, if the mappings were carefully checked and validated by a domain expert, the peer might want to set all prior probabilities on the correctness of the mappings to one to ensure that these mappings will always be treated as correct.

In most cases, however, the peers only have a vague idea (e.g., presupposed quality of the alignment technique used to create the mappings) on the priors related to their surrounding mappings initially. As the network of mappings evolves and time passes, however, the peers start to accumulate various posterior probabilities on the correctness of their mappings thanks to the iterative message passing techniques described above. Actually, the peers get new posterior probabilities on the correctness of the mappings as long as the network of mappings continues to evolve (e.g., as mappings get created, modified or deleted). Thus, peers can decide to modify their prior belief by taking into account the evidences accumulated in order to get more accurate results in the future. This corresponds to learning parameters in a probabilistic graphical model when some of the observations are missing. Several techniques might be applied to this type of problem (e.g., Monte Carlo methods, Gaussian approximations). We propose in the following a simple Expectation-Maximization [20] process which looks as follows:

- Initialize the prior probability on the correctness of the mapping taking into account any prior information on the mapping. If no information is available for a given mapping, start with $P(m = correct) = P(m = incorrect) = 0.5$ (maximum entropy principle).
- Gather posterior evidences $P_k(m = correct|\{\mathcal{F}_k\})$ on the correctness of the mapping thanks to cycle analyses and message passing techniques. Treat these evidences as new observations for every change of the local factor-graphs (i.e., new feedback information, new, modified or lost cycle or parallel path)
- After each change of the local factor-graph, update the prior belief on the correctness of the mapping m given previous evidences $P_k(m = correct|\{\mathcal{F}_k\})$ in the following way:

$$P(m = correct) = \sum_{i=1}^{k} P_i(m = correct|\{\mathcal{F}_i\})k^{-1}$$

Hence, we can make the prior values slowly converge to a local maximum likelihood to reflect the fact that more and more evidences are being gathered about the mappings as the mapping network evolves.

5.5. *Introductory Example Revisited*

Let us now come back to our introductory example and describe in more detail what happened. Imagine that the network of databases was just created and that the peers have no prior information on their mappings. By sending probe queries with $TTL \geq 4$ through its two mapping links, p_2 detects two cycles and one parallel path, and gets all related feedback information. For the attribute *Creator*:

$$f_{\circlearrowright}^{1+} : m_{12} \rightarrow m_{23} \rightarrow m_{34} \rightarrow m_{41}$$
$$f_{\circlearrowright}^{2-} : m_{12} \rightarrow m_{24} \rightarrow m_{41}$$
$$f_{\rightrightarrows}^{3-} : m_{24} \| m_{23} \rightarrow m_{34}$$

p_2 constructs a local factor-graph based on this information and starts sending remote messages and calculating posterior probabilities on its mappings according to the

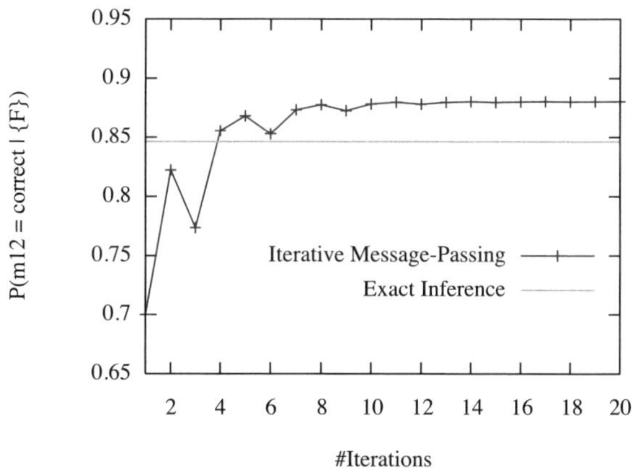

Figure 9. Convergence of the iterative message passing algorithm compared to exact inference (example graph, priors at 0.7, $\Delta = 0.1$, f_1^+, f_2^-, f_3^-)

schedule in place in the PDMS. Δ, the probability that two or more mapping errors get compensated along a cycle, is here approximated to 1/10: if we consider that the schema of p_2 contains eleven attributes, and that mapping errors map to a randomly chosen attribute (but obviously not the correct one), the probability of the last mapping error compensating any previous error is 1/10, thus explaining our choice. After a handful of iterations, the posterior probabilities on the correctness of p_2's mappings towards p_3 and p_4 converge to 0.59 and 0.3 respectively. The second mapping has been successfully detected as faulty for the given attribute, and will thus not be used to forward query q_1 ($\theta_i = 0.5$). The query will however reach all other databases by being correctly forwarded through $p_2 \rightarrow p_3$, $p_3 \rightarrow p_4$ and finally $p_4 \rightarrow p_1$. As the PDMS network evolves, p_2 will update its prior probabilities on the mapping toward p_3 and p_4 to 0.55 and 0.4 respectively to reflect the knowledge gathered on the mappings so far.

6. Performance Evaluation

We present below series of results related to the performance of our approach. We start by giving a couple of results pertaining to simple PDMS networks before analyzing larger sets of automatically generated networks.

6.1. Performance Evaluation on the Example Graph

6.1.1. Convergence

As previously mentioned, our inference method is exact for cycle-free PDMS factor-graphs. For PDMS factor-graphs with cycles, our embedded message passing scheme converges to approximate results in ten iterations usually. Figure 9 illustrates a typical convergence process for the example PDMS factor-graph of Figure 6 for schemas of about ten attributes (i.e., Δ set to 0.1), prior beliefs at 0.7 and cycle feedback as follows: f_1^+, f_2^-, f_3^- .

6.1.2. Fault-Tolerance

As mentioned earlier for the lazy message passing schedule, our scheme does not requires peers to be synchronized to send their messages. To simulate this property, we randomly discard messages during the iterative message passing schedule and observe the resulting effects. Figure 10 shows the results if we consider, for every message to be sent, a probability $P(send)$ to send it only (example network, $\Delta = 0.1$, priors at 0.8, f_1^+, f_2^-, f_3^-). We observe that our method always converges, even for cases where 90% of the messages get discarded, and that the number of iterations required in order for our algorithm to converge grows linearly with the rate of discarded messages.

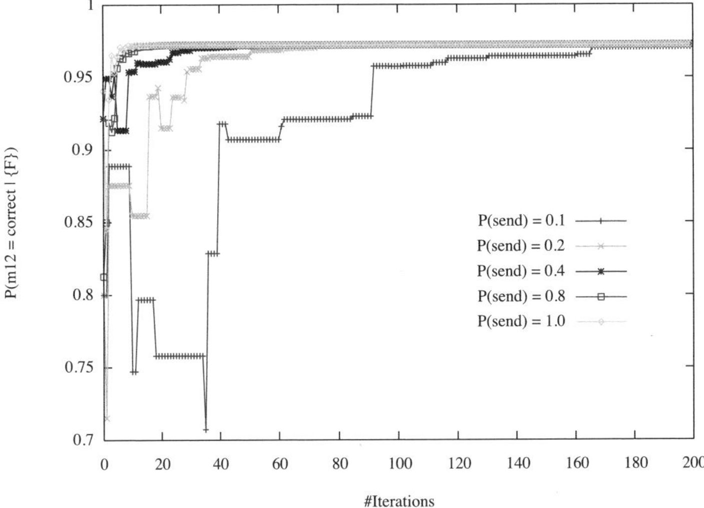

Figure 10. Robustness against faulty links, with probabilities of correctly sending a message ranging from 10% to 100% (example graph, priors at 0.8, $\Delta = 0.1$, f_1^+, f_2^-, f_3^-)

6.2. Performance Evaluation on Random PDMS Networks

To test our heuristics on larger networks, we create schema nodes and add edges by randomly choosing a distinct pair of nodes for each undirected mapping we wish to include. We obtain irreflexive, non redundant and undirected Poisson-distributed graphs in this manner. We randomly pick a certain proportion of mappings and create erroneous links. Also, we randomly select a given percentage of cycle feedback for which two or more errors get compensated. Finally, we run our iterative message passing heuristics on the resulting graphs and determine for each mapping whether it is correct or not (most probable value of $P(m_i = correct|\{\mathcal{F}\})$). The results are given in terms of *precision* values, where precision is defined as the ratio of the number of correctly evaluated mappings over the total number of mappings evaluated. Each result is given as an average value calculated over twenty consecutive rounds, with a confidence interval corresponding to a confidence level of 95%.

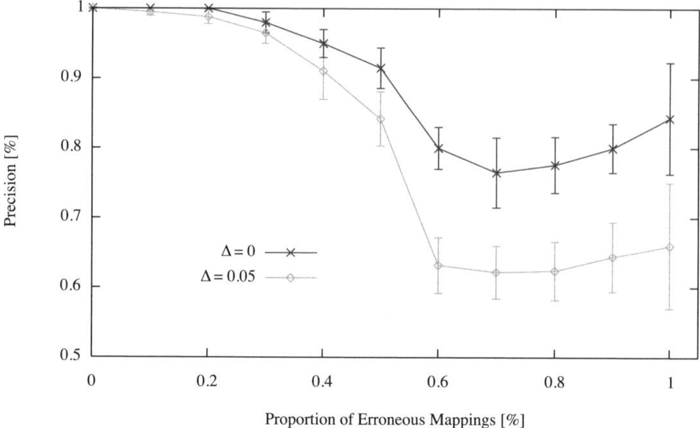

Figure 11. Precision of erroneous mapping detection on random networks of 50 schemas and 200 mappings, with a varying proportion of erroneous mappings, two values of Δ, TTL = 5 to detect cycles and without any a priori information

6.2.1. Performance with an Increasing Proportion of Erroneous Mappings

Figure 11 provides results corresponding to networks of 50 schemas and 200 mappings, with an increasing percentage of erroneous mappings and for relatively small schemas ($\Delta = 5\%$). Our methods work surprisingly well for low densities of incorrect mappings, with 98% or more of correct decisions for networks with less than 30% of erroneous mappings. For networks with a larger proportions of incorrect mappings, the results are less spectacular but still satisfying with precision values above 60%. Note that these values are obtained automatically, via a totally decentralized process and without any prior information on the mappings. Compensating errors make it difficult to detect all errors in networks with many erroneous mappings (cycles which should be treated as negative are in fact seen as positive). This fact is highlighted by a second curve in Figure 11 ($\Delta = 0$), corresponding to very large schemas, where compensating errors can be neglected and where it is much easier to make sensible decisions on networks with very high proportions of incorrect mappings.

6.2.2. Precision with an Increasing Number of Mappings

Figure 12 provides results corresponding to networks of 50 schemas and an increasing number of mappings between the schemas. For sparse networks (e.g., 50 mapping links, corresponding to one mapping per schema on average), few cycles can be detected and thus little feedback information is available. As more and more mappings are created, more feedback information gets available thus making it easier to take sensible decisions on the correctness of the mappings. Dense networks have a very high number of long cycles (e.g., in scale-free networks, where the number of large loops grows exponentially with the size of the loops considered [18]); the longer the cycle, however, the less interesting it is from an inference point of view as it is related to a higher number of mapping variables (and hence represents less precise information). Thus, peers should always be cautious to analyze the most pertinent feedback information only, pertaining to cycles or parallel paths as small as possible, and to keep their TTL for detecting cycles and parallel

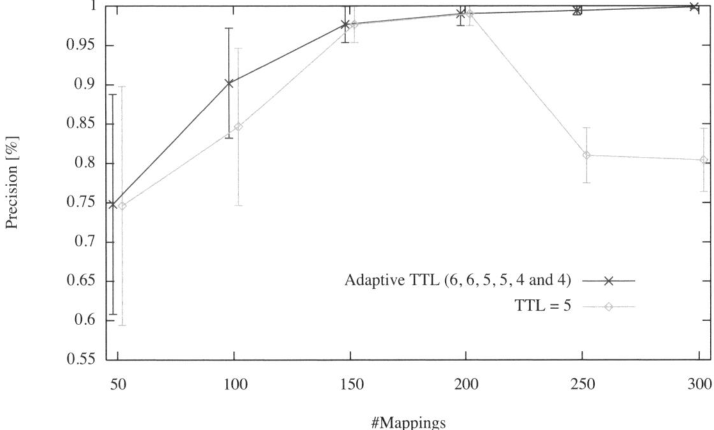

Figure 12. Precision of erroneous mapping detection on random networks of 50 schemas and a varying number of mappings, with a proportion of 20% of erroneous mappings, $\Delta = 0.05$, without any a priori information but with different TTL values for detecting the cycles

paths relatively small; to highlight this fact, Figure 12 shows two curves: one for a fixed TTL of 5 and one with an adaptive TTL (6 for 50 to 100 mappings, 5 for 150 to 200 mappings and 4 from 250 mappings). Adapting the TTL value is important in two situations: first, in sparse networks where peers should try to detect longer cycles in order to get more feedback information (e.g. for 100 mappings in Figure 12, where a TTL of 6 leads to better results than a TTL of 5). In very sparse networks, however, there are simply too few mappings to detect a sufficient number of cycles, even for large TTL values (e.g., for 50 mappings in Figure 12). Second, in dense networks, where precious information given by short cycles can rapidly be diluted by taking into account longer cycles (e.g., for 300 mappings in Figure 12, where more than 20000 cycles of length 5 can be discovered, leading to poorer results if all taken into account). From a local perspective, peers should thus start with low TTL values and increase their TTL only when very few cycles are discovered. This also ensures the scalability of our approach: peers can concentrate on their direct vicinity and do not need to analyze the network as a whole.

7. Conclusions and Future Work

As distributed database systems move from static, controlled environments to highly dynamic, decentralized settings, we are convinced that correctly handling uncertainty and erroneous information will become a key challenge for improving the overall quality of query answering schemes. The vast majority of approaches are today centered around global and deductive methods, which seem quite inappropriate to maximize the performance of systems that operate without any form of central coordination. Contrary to these approaches, we consider an abductive, non-monotonic reasoning scheme, which reacts to observations and inconsistencies by propagating belief in a decentralized way. Our approach is computationally efficient as it is solely based on sum-products operations. Also, we have shown its high effectiveness by evaluating it on sets of randomly generated database networks. We are currently implementing our approach in our Semantic Overlay Network called GridVine [14] and plan to analyze the computational overhead and scalability properties of our iterative message passing approach in dynamic environments. Furthermore, we are currently interested in testing other inference techniques (e.g., generalized belief propagation [21], or techniques constructing a junction tree in a distributed way [22]) in order to determine the most efficient way of performing inference in our decentralized database setting.

References

[1] K. Aberer and P. Cudré-Mauroux. Semantic Overlay Networks. In *International Conference on Very Large Data Bases (VLDB)*, 2005.

[2] K. Aberer (ed.). Special issue on peer to peer data management. *ACM SIGMOD Record*, 32(3), 2003.

[3] P. Bouquet et al. Specification of a common framework for characterizing alignment. In *KnowledgeWeb Deliverable 2.2.1*, *http://knowledgeweb.semanticweb.org*.

[4] D. L. McGuinness and F. van Harmelen (eds). Owl web ontology language overview. W3C Recommendation, 2004.

[5] J. Euzenat et al. State of the art on current alignment techniques. In *KnowledgeWeb Deliverable 2.2.3*, *http://knowledgeweb.semanticweb.org*.

[6] K. Aberer, P. Cudré-Mauroux, and M. Hauswirth. Start making sense: The Chatty Web approach for global semantic agreements. *Journal of Web Semantics*, 1(1), 2003.

[7] K. Aberer, P. Cudré-Mauroux, and M. Hauswirth. The Chatty Web: Emergent Semantics Through Gossiping. In *International World Wide Web Conference (WWW)*, 2003.

[8] P. A. Bernstein, F. Giunchiglia, A. Kementsietsidis, J. Mylopoulos, L. Serafini, and I. Zaihrayeu. Data management for peer-to-peer computing: A vision. In *Workshop on the Web and Databases (WebDB)*, 2002.

[9] W. Nejdl, B. Wolf, C. Qu, S. Decker, M. Sintek, A. Naeve, M. Nilsson, M. Palmér, and T. Risch. EDUTELLA: a P2P networking infrastructure based on RDF. In *International World Wide Web Conference (WWW)*, 2002.

[10] I. Tatarinov and A. Halevy. Efficient Query Reformulation in Peer-Data Management Systems. In *SIGMOD Conference*, 2004.

[11] I. Tatarinov, Z. Ives, J. Madhavan amd A. Halevy, D. Suciu, N. Dalvi, X. Dong, Y. Kadiyaska, G. Miklau, and P. Mork. The Piazza Peer Data Management Project. *ACM SIGMOD Record*, 32(3), 2003.

[12] M. Arenas, V. Kantere, A. Kementsietsidis, I. Kiringa, R. J. Miller, and J. Mylopoulos. The Hyperion Project: From Data Integration to Data Coordination. *SIGMOD Record*, 32(3), 2003.

[13] B. C. Ooi, Y. Shu, and K.-L. Tan. Relational Data Sharing in Peer-based Data Management Systems. *ACM SIGMOD Record*, 32(3), 2003.

[14] K. Aberer, P. Cudré-Mauroux, M. Hauswirth, and T. van Pelt. Gridvine: Building internet-scale semantic overlay networks. In *International Semantic Web Conference*, 2004.

[15] F.R. Kschischang, B.J. Frey, and H.-A. Loeliger. Factor graphs and the sum-product algorithm. *IEEE Transactions on Information Theory*, 47(2), 2001.

[16] J. Pearl. *Probabilistic Reasoning in Intelligent Systems : Networks of Plausible Inference*. Morgan Kaufmann, 1988.

[17] K. M. Murphy, Y. Weiss, and M. I Jordan. Loopy belief propagation for approximate inference: An empirical study. In *Uncertainty in Artificial Intelligence (UAI)*, 1999.

[18] G. Bianconi and M. Marsili. Loops of any size and hamilton cycles in random scale-free networks. In *cond-mat/0502552 v2*, 2005.

[19] P. Cudré-Mauroux, K. Aberer, and Andras Feher. Probabilistic message passing in peer data managemen systems. In *International Conference on Data Engineering (ICDE)*, 2006.

[20] A. Dempster, N. Laird, and D. Rubin. Maximum likelihood from incomplete data via the em algorithm. *Journal of the Royal Statistical Society*, 39, 1977.

[21] J.S. Yedidia, W.T. Freeman, and Y Weiss. Generalized belief propagation. *Advances in Neural Information Processing Systems (NIPS)*, 13, 2000.

[22] M.A. Paskin and C.E. Guestrin. A robust architecture for distributed inference in sensor networks. In *Intel Research Technical Report IRB-TR-03-039*, 2004.

Global Data Management
R. Baldoni et al. (Eds.)
IOS Press, 2006

Emergent Schema Management
for P2P-based Applications

Challenges, Approaches, and Open Issues

Felix Heine [a,1]

[a] *Paderborn Center for Parallel Computing, Paderborn University*

Abstract. In p2p based data mangement applications, it is unrealistic to rely upon a centralized schema or ontology. The p2p paradigm is more than a new underlying infrastructure. It supports an emergent approach to data management where the data is generated and inserted into the network in a decentralized fashion. Thus, each peer or group of peers will have its own schema to store the data. Moreover, the user querying the data will use yet another schema to formulate the request.

The vision of emergent schema management is to resolve these heterogeneities automatically in a self-organizing, emergent way by taking advantage of overlaps and mediators scattered over the network. The emerging schema information can be used in various ways, i.e. to drive the construction of an overlay network, and to route queries through the network.

In this article, we start by explaining the various challenges. We look at the problem both from the viewpoint of the database community describing schemas as entity-relationship models, and from the viewpoint of the knowledge representation community using logic-based formalisms. We then survey existing p2p based approaches dealing with semantics, schemas, and mediation. After describing our own approach to p2p schema management, we conclude with an outlook to open problems in the field.

Keywords. Schema Management, Ontologies, Information Integration, P2P, Data Management, Emergence

1. Introduction

Large scale data management is a challenging task. Through modern information technologies, more and more data and information is available online. However, it is often difficult to find the relevant information, and to efficiently combine the pieces found in various data sources. The problems lie both in the sheer amount of data and in syntactic and semantic heterogeneities.

Even within single organizations, sometimes a large number of different data sources is available. The need to process this data collection as a whole and to draw conclusions from the aggregated information residing in the sources lead to the field of data warehousing. The typical approach is to copy every relevant piece of information into a large,

---

[1]Correspondence to: Felix Heine, PC[2], Fürstenallee 11, 33102 Paderborn, Germany. Tel.: +49 5251 60 6322; Fax: +49 5251 60 6297; E-mail: fh@upb.de.

centrally managed data warehouse (DWH), which is then used for evaluating queries, e.g. in so called decision support systems. See [35] for a deeper discussion of DHW concepts.

However, in many cases the relevant data sources span multiple organizations. In the collaboration of multiple companies, or when mining the information contained in the world wide web, it is necessary to combine multiple heterogenous information sources which are decentrally controlled. The Semantic Web initiative [11] aims at this goal.

To face these challenges, a system needs to be capable of integrating *a huge number* of information sources which are *syntactically and semantically heterogenous, decentrally managed*, and which may be *highly dynamic*. Two important aspects have to be regarded. First, the underlying infrastructure must be scalable and flexible. Second, the system must handle the heterogeneities of the data sources.

With respect to *infrastructure*, p2p systems [53] have gained much attention of the research community in recent years. They provide a good basis for large-scale data management systems. Compared to traditional approaches, p2p systems offer good scalability features, combined with decentralized control and flexibility. Within this chapter, we focus on p2p based systems. The *integration aspect* has attracted researchers both from the database community and from the knowledge representation community, with results ranging from approaches based on entity-relationship models [39] to Ontology-based systems [17] using formal logic. Recently, the strong connection between these issues has been realized and systems turned up [43,30,4,13] which apply the methods of information integration on top of a p2p based infrastructure.

An important idea behind modern p2p systems is the notion of *emergence* [38]. Typical p2p systems consist of a huge number of relatively small entities, which might be unreliable. They are neither centrally controlled, nor do they have to be professionally managed and supervised. However, the network as a whole provides reliability and other properties which *emerge* from the collective behavior of the peers. Following this notion of emergence, we expect from such a system that *global knowledge emerges from the individual pieces of information* which are contributed to the network by the peers.

From the lack of central control we can deduce that there will not be a lingua franca which each peer uses to describe its own data. Even if the p2p network is restricted to a certain domain of knowledge, we cannot assume a fixed standard which suffices to describe any data a peer might want to insert into the network. Additionally, data already stored in legacy databases or knowledge representation systems has to be integrated into p2p systems. Thus the networks require efficient methods to manage heterogeneities in the description of information. Efficiency comprises both low consumption of technical as well as human resources. We consider this aspect crucial for the success of data oriented p2p systems.

Throughout this chapter, we use the term *schema* for a collection of meta-data used to describe the structure of data stored at some point. We use it in a broad manner subsuming aspects ranging from entity-relationship models to Ontologies based on formal logics [27]. By *schema management*, we mean any activity related to the storage, exchange, comparison, translation, querying, or other uses of schema information. We further use the terms *data, information, and knowledge* interchangeably.

Even before the advent of p2p systems, integration issues where important in the fields of knowledge management, data warehousing, and distributed databases; see e.g.

[39,23,49,17,19,20]. However, the existing approaches are not directly applicable to p2p schema management, as p2p systems pose additional challenges.

In the next section, we dive into the problem details of p2p schema management and develop criteria to distinguish and categorize existing approaches. In the following section we survey and classify the work already published in this area. Anticipating the summary, no currently existing approach is a full-fledged solution to all problems in p2p schema management. Finally, we describe a new, scalable way to schema management based on Semantic Web technologies. We end the chapter with a summary and conclusion.

2. Challenges for Emergent Schema Management

Before heading towards the details, we define the term *schema* in the context of this chapter, and explain *schema management* by describing the various usages of schemas in data management systems.

First of all, a schema *defines the structure* of valid data. It defines which entities, attributes, relations, etc. can be used to insert data, and it may impose integrity constraints on the values of certain instances. However, there are two more important use-cases for schema information. The user needs schema information in order to be able to browse the data or to *formulate meaningful queries*. Furthermore, the schema information enables query optimization in the *query processor* [36].

Especially for the query processor, also summary information about existing data like histograms is highly useful. Although not schema information in the strict sense, we also regard this type of meta information within this chapter.

We can envision multiple levels of schema-handling p2p systems. A basic schema awareness requires each peer to commit to a global schema. The next level allows multiple schemas. Each peer's schema is registered and communicated. However, queries are only routed to peers which share the query's schema. Further elaborated systems allow to specify mediators which are used to translate either queries or the data in order to answer queries with differing schemas. The final step is the integration of mechanisms for automatic schema matching, in order to reduce human interaction during the design of mediators.

In this section, we describe the basic design choices for emergent semantic systems, followed by a discussion of the types of heterogeneities to be resolved. Different schema integration approaches are mentioned in the subsection 2.3. The origin of the schema and the mediators is discussed in the following subsection, and finally information quality and updates are reviewed.

2.1. Basic Design Choices

When talking about schema management, we first have to talk about the **data model**. In current p2p solutions, a broad variety of data models is used. We classify the data models in the categories relational, object-oriented, and semi-structured [25]. We further call a data model if it is build using logic-based knowledge representation systems *deductive*. Examples of the latter are description logics (DL) systems [5]. Relational and object-oriented data models have their origins in traditional database research. Semi-structured approaches like XML do not expect the schema to be fixed before storing data. Deductive approaches are mostly motivated from the recent development of the Semantic Web which is based on knowledge representation frameworks using formal logic and deduction. However, also the database community has exploited the use of logics for data storage and querying, which has lead to the field of deductive databases. There are no sharp boundaries between these categories, and hybrid models like the object-relational model [25] are possible.

When integrating a web-scale number of different data sources, one also has to think of *heterogeneities in the data model*. However, no current approach takes this fully into account, as it leads to an enormous complexity. Typically, a system assumes to use an a priori fixed data model. If there are multiple data models allowed, they typically have to be wrapped locally, resulting in a system-wide homogenous data model. Enhancements in the data model are typically out of scope. So it is unclear how to develop the capabilities of a system which is deployed in large scales.

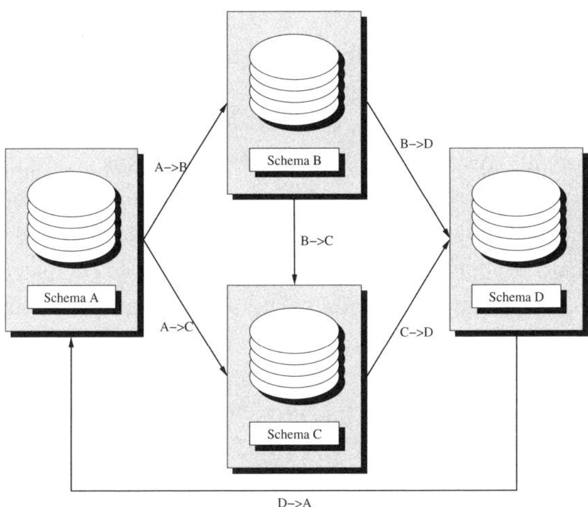

Figure 1. Local data system model.

Closely related to the data model is the **system model**. By this, we mean the degree up to which a system integrates the various data sources. Systems can have individual units consisting of a single data source or a collection of data sources. Each unit has a schema subsuming the individual schemas of the sources. In these systems, individual query results are typically generated by the data stored on a single unit. We coin this model the *local data system model*, cf. figure 1. The system knows some rules, which allow to translate a query from the schema of one unit to the schema of another unit. With these translations, the query can also be answered by other data sources.

Other approaches look at the entire data scattered over the whole system, and try to answer queries by reasoning with *all entries*. This approach is shown in figure 2. It mirrors the behavior of a centralized system where each source contributes its local data. We thus call it *global data system model*. However, the query processing is done in a decentralized fashion. An intermediate approaches is to treat schema information globally, while the instance data is managed locally.

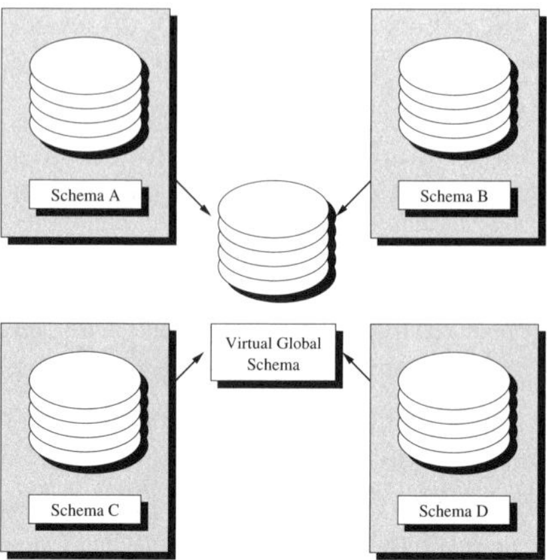

Figure 2. Global data system model.

A system supports one or more **query semantics**. Typical semantics are relational algebra, datalog semantics [25], RDF queries [46], RDF-Schema [14] aware queries, or instance checking in description logics systems. Each of these query semantics can be combined with a specific system model. In the local data system model, it is relatively easy to support different query semantics as the system can rely on the local query processors. In the global data system model, more sophisticated query semantics are difficult to achieve as it its hard to identify the data relevant to the current query.

When talking about the data model and the system model, we have to discuss the *closed world assumption* (CWA) and the *open world assumption* (OWA), i.e. the question whether missing information is assumed to be negative, or whether they it is assumed to be unknown. The OWA is a typical characteristic of description logics systems, while relational databases typically use the CWA [5]. For the global data system model, the OWA seems to be appropriate. For the local data system model, we can envision either an OWA or a CWA local to a specific data source.

The system model is closely related to the underlying **infrastructure**. Roughly speaking, there are currently two competing approaches: structured p2p networks and unstructured p2p networks [54]. Unstructured p2p networks follow the idea of the gnutella network. They have been enhanced in various ways, typically by switching from a flat topology to an hierarchical approach like super-peer networks (e.g. [45]), or by introducing semantic overlay networks (e.g. [18]). However, a central problem in these networks remains the question how to find peers which have relevant information for the query without flooding the whole network.

Structured p2p networks are mostly based on the abstraction of distributed hash tables (DHTs) [7]. They are designed to find key-based entries in an efficient and scalable way. Properly used, they can enhance the efficiency and flexibility of query answering. However, as the indices are founded on fixed keys, it is difficult to answer range queries, although there are approaches to solve this problem [3,44]. Also the load balancing might be a problem if there are highly popular keys which either generate a huge storage load or a huge query load, see e.g. [16]. A further disadvantage is a constant network load needed to maintain the DHT itself and the entries in the hash table.

2.2. Heterogeneities

Heterogeneity is a very broad term. Different systems support various types of heterogeneities. In this section, we classify and define the types of heterogeneities relevant for this discussion.

First of all, data sources can have *syntactic heterogeneities*, e.g. different RDF [41] representations like RDF/XML [9] or N3 [10], or syntactic variants of a query language with the same query semantics. Although important in practice, we ignore these heterogeneities as they are easily resolvable by appropriate conversion tools. *Data heterogeneities* are differently assigned values for attributes which are otherwise identical. Examples are different keys or different scales for numeric values. The next type are *schema heterogeneities*, which means that – e.g. in the relational data model – the data is organized in different tables, the attributes have different names, etc. In knowledge representation systems, this means that the knowledge bases use different ontologies. The worst kind of differences of the data sources are *heterogeneities in the semantics of data storage or querying*. An example is a user who expects the query evaluator to respect transitivity of certain properties, while the answering peer does not support transitive semantics.

2.3. Types of Schema Integration

The possible types of schema management are tightly connected to the different system models. The database community has developed data integration systems [39]. These systems use a *mediated schema* to provide a uniform interface to various data sources. Additionally, translation rules have to be stored which encode the relationship between the source schemas and the mediated schema.

The central component is the *query reformulation algorithm*. It takes a query formulated using the mediated schema and translates it into a query using the schemas of the data sources. We call this approach *mediator based*, as each set of translation rules serves as a mediator between two schemas.

Various formalisms exist to encode the mediators. The basic approaches are LAV (local as view), GAV (global as view), or a combined approach coined GLAV. In the GAV approach, the mediated schema is represented as a set of views over the data sources. The LAV approach is opposite: the contents of the data sources are described as views over the mediated schema.

This type of integration is especially well suited for unstructured p2p networks where each peer can maintain mappings to the schemas used by its direct neighbors in the network. When routing a query via multiple hops through such a network, we build implicitly chains of mappings, thereby generating new mappings which exploit the transitivity of mappings. Piazza [30] and Hyperion [4] are examples for such systems. However, in general a mapping between two schemas is lossy. Thus in long chains of mappings the losses will add up and lead to a highly reduced view of the original data. If we take the possibility of errors in the mediators into account, also the errors might add up in long chains. The Chatty Web approach [1] tries to deal with these problems.

Another way to integrate the data is more relevant to the deductive data model. Here, no individual mappings between two schemas are described. The schemas as well as the instance data is considered to be knowledge, to which deductive algorithms can be applied. These algorithms infer new knowledge which follows logically from the existing, exploiting so-called *intermodel assertions* [17]. Thus the schema information is broken down into individual pieces of knowledge, and the mappings themselves are small pieces of mapping information for individual entities. For each situation, the logical calculus tries to find the relevant pieces to construct an answer.

This approach leads to a much higher flexibility in describing, obtaining, and applying mapping information. However, reasoning procedures are typically computationally expensive and difficult to apply in a p2p environment, when combined with the global data system model.

An important aspect when talking about the type of integration is the underlying formalism used to describe the mappings, which determines both the *flexibility and expressiveness* of the mappings, and the *complexity of query answering*. Query answering might even be undecidable in generale for some formalisms [49,39].

2.4. Origin of the Schema

Within a relational or an object oriented data model, the existence of a schema is typically a mandatory prerequisite to store data. The schema might include integrity constraints which define which kind of data is valid. We can directly access this schema and publish it to the network.

The other data models, notably the semi-structured and the deductive, do not mandatorily require a schema. Thus there can be data without a schema. However, due to the data model, this data is always up to some extend self-describing. Thus there is a possibility to generate a schema from the data. However, in contrast to an a priori existing schema, this schema will not impose integrity constraints over the data, it will merely describe which types of data are available. Such a generated schema is known as a Data Guide [26] and serves as a structural summary of the information contained in a database.

In the context of p2p networks, a combination of both approaches can be useful. In case a schema exists, this schema is used and published, else the Data Guide can replace the schema up to a certain extend. Both the existing schema as well as the Data Guide can finally be annotated with statistical information about the data to support query routing and answering.

2.5. Origin of the Mediators

Today, the mediators are typically handcrafted by human experts who have to understand both the semantics of the mediator language and the schema domains. As this is an error-prone and time-consuming procedure, the automatic or semi-automatic generation of mediators is desirable.

There are approaches to automatic schema matching or ontology matching [47,22]. These approaches exploit various techniques like text mining using natural language descriptions of the relevant concepts, structural comparison, key-word detection, etc. Another way is to use the existing mediators to generate new ones, e.g. by chaining, see [30].

2.6. Information Quality

In p2p networks, the maintenance of information quality is a huge challenge. As there is no central authority or control, any peer can push arbitrary information to the network. Thus the network has to cope both with unintentional errors and with malicious attacks and spamming.

This problem exists for the data as well as for schema information. However, malicious schema information might be a much worse problem, because it can lead to wrong interpretation of correct data. Thus a relative small amount of wrong information might cause a huge number of queries to return faulty results.

If the expressivity of the data model is high enough, the network could try to detect contradictions. By this, it is not clear which information is faulty, however it can be detected that there is a problem.

2.7. Updates

Updates in general are an important challenge for p2p data management. In the presence of schema heterogeneities, this becomes even more difficult. First of all, we have to look at the system model and decide who is allowed to update which data. Second, we have to decide whether data can be updated only via their original schema or via arbitrary views.

A simple solution is to leave the update process to the individual peers. So each peer is only responsible for its own data, and nobody else is allowed to update this peer's data. However, according to the application it might be desirable to allow peers to update also foreign data. Besides consistency problems (see e.g. [8]), this opens new challenges in the schema management field.

We then have to assume that the updating peer uses a different schema than the updated peer. Thus we have to apply mappings during the update process. As with the query process, this can involve multiple steps via different peers.

3. Survey of existing Approaches

Within this section, we survey existing approaches related to the field of p2p based data management which have schema management components. The survey does not aim to be exhaustive; we rather describe selected works which represent different approaches to the problem.

We start with two systems having their roots in traditional database research: Hyperion [4] and Piazza [31,30]. Their basic assumption is quite similar: each peer holds a collection of physical relations, and associated schema information. It has furthermore a mediated schema, which represents a homogenous view including the peer's own relations and the mediated schema of the neighbors of this peer. Both systems assume the existence of mapping information. They differ in the types of supported mappings.

Next, we describe the Chatty-Web approach [1], which is a specific solution to the problem of errors and losses during the mediation between different schemas.

Furthermore, we describe some of the systems stemming from the Semantic Web research. GridVine [2], the ICS/Forth RDF Suite [37], and Edutella [43,42,15] are systems based on RDF which employ RDF Schema information. Finally, we mention Bibster [29] as an example of a domain-specific application of schema based p2p systems focussing on the exchange of bibliographic meta-data.

3.1. Hyperion and Piazza

The origins of Hyperion and Piazza are stand-alone data integration systems for relational or XML-based data. Hyperion and Piazza can be seen as a natural evolution step of these systems, moving from a single, centralized mediated schema towards an arbitrary number of peers where each peer runs a local data integration system which integrates both its own data and data from the other peers.

The basic architecture of both systems is similar, see figure 3. Each system consists of peers holding *stored relations*, which are connected via an unstructured p2p network. In Hyperion, the *peer schema* is the schema of the stored relations, while in Piazza the peer schema is a mediated schema which spans both over its own stored relations and the peer schemas of other peers.

The relationships between the different schemas are represented through mappings. In Hyperion, the mappings use a GLAV [39] formalism at the schema level, which is supplemented with data mappings at the instance level. Thus, also the relationship between individual entities can be expressed.

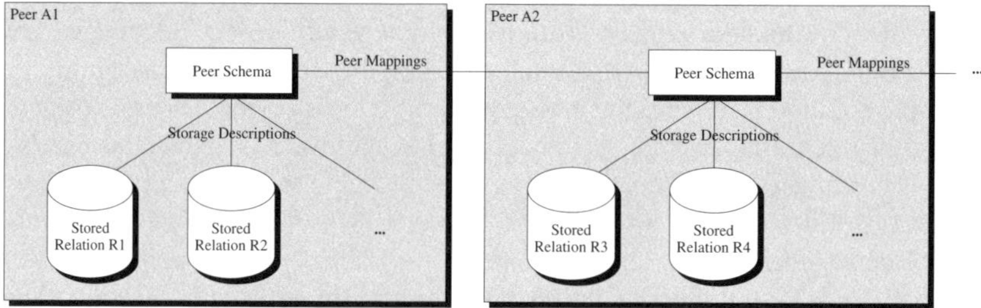

Figure 3. Piazza architecture.

Piazza focuses on the schema level. Two types of mappings are used. First, mappings between the stored relations and the peer relations; second, between the peer schemas. In Piazza, mappings are defined in a language called $\mathcal{PPL}$ (Piazza Peer Language). It allows for the following mapping descriptions:

Storage descriptions relate the stored relations of a peer A to its peer schema. They are of the form $A : R = Q$, where Q is a conjunctive query over the peer schema, and R is a relation stored at peer A. Thus the content of the relation R is formulated in terms of a view definition over the peer schema, resulting in a LAV formalism. In case the peer relation does not contain every tuple expected in the view, Piazza allows descriptions using inclusion: $A : R \subseteq Q$.

The second type of mappings are *peer mappings*, which link the schemas of different peers. They can be of different forms. The first form expresses facts about results of queries. They are of the form $Q_1(\mathcal{A}_1) = Q_2(\mathcal{A}_2)$ or $Q_1(\mathcal{A}_1) \subseteq Q_2(\mathcal{A}_2)$, where Q_1 and Q_2 are queries over the peer schemas from a set of peers $\mathcal{A}_1$ or $\mathcal{A}_2$, respectively. Their meaning is that the evaluation of these queries will always have the same result, or the result of the evaluation of Q_1 over $\mathcal{A}_1$ will always be a subset of the result of Q_2 over $\mathcal{A}_2$. Thus they are called *equality* and *inclusion mappings*. The second form of peer mappings is a *definitional mapping* which is a datalog rule over the peer relations.

Both systems use an unstructured p2p network. Thus each peer has a limited set of connections to neighboring peers, and might store some peer mappings relating its data to the neighbors data. A peer which receives a query formulated using its peer schema, will reformulate the query using the available mappings, and forward it to the other peers.

In Piazza, a global system catalog containing all mappings is assumed during the query reformulation. The authors have identified this flaw and are working towards a distributed version of the query reformulation algorithm. They plan to use DHT techniques to store a distributed system catalogue.

3.2. Chatty Web

As said in section 2.3, new mappings between different schemas can be generated by exploiting a transitive relationship between existing mappings. However, as translations may be lossy or may have errors, the quality of these new mappings might be poor.

The Chatty Web approach [1] is a way to detect these problems, and to steer the routing decisions in the network according to the observed quality. The underlying system model is the local data system model, typically combined with an unstructured p2p network. Thus each peer or group of peers has its own schema and maintains links together with schema translations to other peers.

The whole network can be seen as a graph, where each group of peers with a common schema are represented by a vertex, while the known translations are the edges. A query which is routed through this graph is continiously translated in order to match the target schema.

An important feature of this graph is the existence of cycles. This means that a node, which routes a query toward another semantic domain, might receive the same query again later. However, the query will have been modified multiple times through various mappings. As the original peer knows also the original version of the query, it is able to compare these two versions and draw conclusions about the quality of the mappings on the used path.

Consider a source node S and a target node T. The source node receives a query using its schema, and forwards the query towards T. Node T expects to receive a query in its own schema. The mappings are on the attribute level and specify how the attributes of S can be expressed as functions over the attributes of T. These mappings are applied to the query, so that it can be evaluated over T's database.

When a peer receives a query, it detects whether the query has passed a cycle. In this case, the similarity between the original version and the new version is measured with different indicators:

- *Syntactic Similiarity*: Here, attributes are counted which are missing in the target query. However, as not all attributes share the same importance for a query, they are weighted with both a user defined weight and a system-supplied weight in the case of selection-relevant attributes. The system weight reflects the selectivity of the attribute.
- *Cycle analysis*: Here, the correctness of the resulting query is measured. Each attribute may be preserved (positive score), may have vanished (neutral score), or it may have been replaced by a wrong attribute (negative score). Furthermore, the probability of compensating errors is calculated and taken into account.
- *Result analysis*: This analysis checks to which degree a known functional dependency is respected by the query results returned from peers on the cycle that don't share the same schema.

Subsequently, these measures are used in routing decisions. The user is requested to supply lower bounds for the similarities. Queries are only routed to neighbors where the iteratively updated measures are above these bounds. This ensures that queries will be routed into domains where they are likely to produce valid answers, and prevents flooding.

3.3. GridVine and ICS/Forth RDF Suite

GridVine [2] is an DHT based RDF [41] repository. RDF triples in the network are indexed by subject, predicate, and object. Thus, GridVine can retrieve matches for a triple pattern with a single lookup as long as there is at least one element of the triple known. Based upon this basic lookup primitive, more complex queries are available. GridVine supports the RDQL query language [51].

RDFS [14] is the schema language for RDF and provides the basis for semantic interoperability of RDF based knowledge bases. In RDFS, properties and classes can be defined, and hierarchies can be built. However, as RDFS lacks a way to describe equality between concepts, GridVine borrows the semantics for equivalent properties from OWL [52] to translate queries into other semantic domains. This translation information is also stored using the DHT.

For each query which is received by a peer, this peer looks up translations in the network and can thus reformulate the query to other semantic domains. A translated query is either forwarded to a target peer which then executes the translated query and recursively translates and forwards the query, or the original node stays responsible for the query and iteratively applies multiple translations.

To steer the translation decision and to measure the quality of multiple chained translations, GridVine applies methods from the Chatty Web approach.

The ICS/Forth RDF Suite [37] is also a p2p based RDF store which is aware of RDF Schema. In contrast to GridVine, the RDF triples themselves are not distributed but rather stay at the original node. Thus for an exhaustive answer to a query the system needs to execute the query on each peer which might have answers to the query.

RDF Schema information is used to identify peers which may hold matches for the given query. For this, so-called RVL views are defined which represent parts of the schema graph. A query graph is broken down into multiple sub-graphs; for each sub-graph peers are searched which have matching RVL [2] views. By this, both the RDF Schema inheritance (called vertical subsumption) and sub-graph relationships (called horizontal subsumption) are respected. The main focus of the work is the query planning and execution, driving the breakdown of the query graph and the forwarding of the sub-queries to the target nodes.

3.4. Edutella

The Edutella project [42,15] implements a schema-based p2p system. By this, the authors mean a system which is aware of schema information and uses it in query optimization and routing. Multiple schemas are allowed, but currently no translation is applied to mediate between different schemas. It is up to the user to produce queries which match the schema used to describe the data. However, Edutella is work in progress and aims

---

[2]RDF View Language

to fill this gap. In the Edutella white paper [43] a meditator architecture is described in which so-called *query hubs* present views spanning over the data of multiple peers which can be queried using the hub's schema.

Edutella is based on a super-peer architecture. A small number well-equipped nodes are selected to form the super-peer network, while the other peers connect in a star-like fashion to the super-peers. The super-peers are connected in a so-called HyperCuP [3] topology. In this structure, each super-peer can be seen as the root of a spanning tree which is used for query routing, updates of indices, and broadcasting.

Each peer sends indices of its data to its super-peer. This information can be stored in different granularities, like schema, property, property value range, or property value. However, the index never points to individual data entries but to peers. This kind of index is called an SP-P (super-peer - peer) index.

The super-peers share their index information along the spanning tree structures. Thus each SP also holds several SP-SP (super-peer - super-peer) indices which guide the peer when forwarding the query or parts of it to other super-peers.

Based upon this infrastructure, a query processor and optimizer tries to split the query into multiple parts and to ship the query to target peers which are likely to have results for these parts. The same part of a query might also be shipped to multiple super-peers and peers. The queries may carry code for user-defined operators, so that the operators can be executed on the peer which holds the relevant data.

In order to cope with different query semantics, Edutella defines the *Edutella Common Data and Query Exchange Model* (ECDM). It is based on RDF and is used internally to represent queries and their results. The query language is called RDF query exchange language (RDF-QEL)[4]. In the most general form, RDF-QEL queries are datalog queries, with several built-in predicates suited for the evaluation of RDF-based data. In order to cope with peers with limited query processors the query language has different levels, from rule-less queries over conjunctive, disjunctive, up to linear recursive and finally general recursive queries.

3.5. Bibster

The Bibster system [29] is an example application of the SWAP[5] project [21]. It is an unstructured p2p system based on JXTA [40] which targets the exchange of bibliographic meta-data like (e.g. BibTeX entries) in academic communities. It is schema aware in the sense that two different schemas are supported. One is the ACM topic hierarchy, the other one is Semantic Web for Research Communities (SWRC) [6].

The information sources are integrated into these schemas a priori by a local component which supports a fixed set of mappings. Thus, no query reformulation is necessary. The classification of the database entries according to the ACM topic hierarchy is used to measure the expertise of a peer. A similarity measure between a query and the expertise of a peer is calculated and used in the routing decisions of the network.

An important aspect of Bibster is the removal of duplicate results. In the field of bibliographic databases, it is likely that numerous peers have overlapping sets of entries.

---

[3]Hypercube P2P
[4]The specification can be found under `http://edutella.jxta.org/spec/qel.html`
[5]Semantic Web and Peer-to-Peer, `http://swap.semanticweb.org`
[6]`http://ontoware.org/projects/swrc`

However, these entries are not 100 percent identical, but rather similar. Thus, an important task of Bibster is to detect similar entries in the result set of a query and to remove them.

4. RDF Schema based P2P Data Management

Within this section, we describe our own approach, which is motivated from Grid research [24]. In large Grids, resource discovery is a challenging problem. First of all, the size of Grids will grow making scalability an issue. Second, Grids evolve beyond pure networks providing CPU cycles and storage space towards ubiquitous devices integrating any kind of services [6]. Thus the heterogeneity of resource descriptions will increase. No standard will be able to follow the rapid development of new hardware, software, and services and their integration into the Grid.

Thus, we assume that providers will need to extend the resource description schema to suit their needs. Further, resource matchers for Grids need additional information about the resources like compatibility information and dependencies between e.g. a certain program and a licence server.

Although the origins of this work lie in Grid computing, we stress that the developed system is general purpose and can be used also in other scenarios like Semantic Web or management of networks.

Our goal is to realize the global data system model. From the users point of view, the system behaves the same way as a centralized system. It integrates knowledge from all providers and reasons about it. As a small example, we would like the system to integrate compatibility information from node X (*Itanium is compatible to Pentium*) with resource descriptions from node Y (*I have a cluster with Itanium CPUs*) to answer a query (*I need a cluster with Pentium CPUs or compatible*).

In the following subsection, we introduce basic design decision of the system and underlying assumptions. After that, we define the problem in a formal way. The last two parts of this section consider the knowledge distribution in the network and the query processing algorithm.

4.1. Introduction

We chose to build our system upon DHTs as they provide a scalable and efficient way to realize the global data system model. Additionally, we chose RDF and RDF Schema as a knowledge representation framework. We think that more sophisticated Ontology languages like OWL would also be attractive for our work; however, the scalability of OWL reasoners is limited [5].

The important point in the previous section was that the schema knowledge and the knowledge about the resources can be located on different nodes, so that the query answer can only be computed by combining these distributed RDF graphs.

In general, we assume to have n nodes participating in the p2p network. All of them have some local knowledge stored as RDF triples. They also have local schema knowledge stored as RDF Schema triples. The schema knowledge does not need to be the same for every node. In fact, we are convinced that it is impossible to ensure synchronization of schema knowledge in large world-wide distributed environments or to restrict the schema to a single common standard. Moreover, it is desirable to allow each node to add locally needed schema information on the fly. If new entities need to be described, new classifications may become necessary. Waiting for a new version of some standard schema does not solve this problem.

However, we assume that there is an ontology which serves as a common schema, at least for some subsets of the nodes. This ontology will be the basis which can be extended locally. Additional schema knowledge may be stored to allow translation from one ontology to the other. Without such common understanding, no interoperability would be possible.

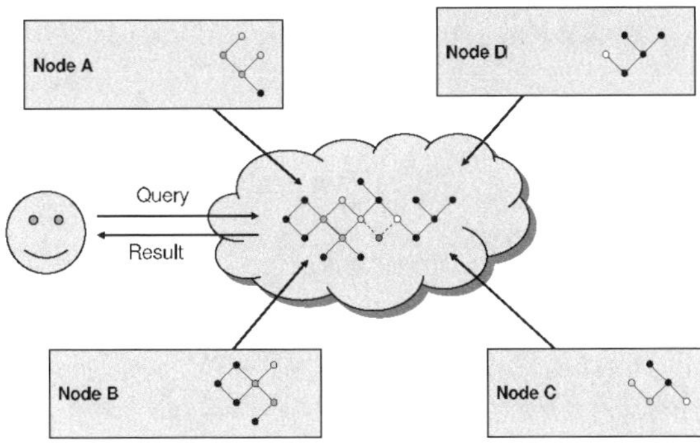

Figure 4. Virtual pool of knowledge.

Our desired result is to put all this knowledge from all the nodes virtually in one pool, apply RDFS entailment rules to this pool and evaluate queries with respect to the union of the knowledge, see figure 4. This approach is very beneficial, as overlaps in the schema knowledge are used to build bridges between different schemas used by different nodes. A query is formulated as a pattern consisting of multiple triples where parts of the URI references and labels are replaced by variables. We call the RDF graph resulting from the union of the local knowledge and appliance of the entailment rules the *model graph*, while we call the query pattern the *query graph*.

4.2. Formal Problem Definition

Now we define the foundations more formally. Both the model and the query graph are directed graphs. The labels of the model graph can be URI references or XML literal values, or blank node labels. For the following discussion, we do not have to differentiate between URI references and XML literals, so we define the set of labels to be $\mathcal{L}$ which contains both types of entities. The set of blank node labels is denoted by $\mathcal{B}$. Thus each vertex is labelled with an element of either $\mathcal{L}$ or $\mathcal{B}$. An edge of an RDF graph cannot have a blank label, so only elements of $\mathcal{L}$ are allowed here. RDF permits multi-edges, i.e. more than one edge between a pair of nodes, and no stand-alone vertices are allowed, so the graph can be described as a triple set

$$T_M \subseteq (\mathcal{L} \cup \mathcal{B}) \times \mathcal{L} \times (\mathcal{L} \cup \mathcal{B})$$

The query graph is defined analogously. However, instead of blank node labels, we use variables from a set $\mathcal{V}$ of variables, and we allow edges to be labelled with variables. Thus the query graph in triple representation is

$$T_Q \subseteq (\mathcal{L} \cup \mathcal{V}) \times (\mathcal{L} \cup \mathcal{V}) \times (\mathcal{L} \cup \mathcal{V})$$

For convenience, we denote the set of variables occurring in T_Q by $\mathcal{V}_Q$, and the set of literals occurring in T_Q by $\mathcal{L}_Q$. The sets $\mathcal{L}_M$ and $\mathcal{B}_M$ are defined analogously.

The desired semantics for our query evaluation are as follows: given a model graph T_M and a query graph T_Q, find every mapping for the variables occurring in T_Q to the set of blank nodes and literals occurring in T_M, such that for each triple in T_Q there is a matching triple in T_M. Thus we search for mappings

$$R : \mathcal{V}_Q \to \mathcal{L}_M \cup \mathcal{B}_M$$

such that for every triple $\langle s, p, o \rangle \in T_Q$ there is a triple $\langle s', p', o' \rangle \in T_M$ such that:

$$s \in \mathcal{V}_Q \Rightarrow s' = R(s) \quad s \in \mathcal{L}_Q \Rightarrow s' = s$$

$$p \in \mathcal{V}_Q \Rightarrow p' = R(p) \quad p \in \mathcal{L}_Q \Rightarrow p' = p$$

$$o \in \mathcal{V}_Q \Rightarrow o' = R(o) \quad o \in \mathcal{L}_Q \Rightarrow o' = o$$

Note that this definition includes the possibility to match two different variables to the same value, as we do not insist on R being an injective function, which makes the problem a bit different to the subgraph isomorphism problem (see [56]). We impose two restrictions upon T_Q. First, we expect it to be connected (not strongly connected). This is natural, as we can break the query evaluation of an unconnected query graph in multiple evaluations of the connected components. The result set for the whole query is determined by enumerating every combination of the results for the connected components. Second, we expect that there exists at least one triple in T_Q having at least one labelled element. One of these labels will serve as a starting point for the query evaluation.

4.3. Knowledge Distribution

In order to query the knowledge, we have to pre-distribute the RDF triples to well-defined nodes in the network to prevent flooding. We also pre-evaluate the RDFS rules and distribute the resulting triples. By this, the query evaluation does not have to regard the reasoning any more. In this section, we describe these mechanisms.

4.3.1. Triple Distribution

The general architecture is shown in figure 5. Each node i has initially stored a set of RDF triples, which contains both schema knowledge SK_i and local knowledge LK_i.

In order to be able to query the knowledge, we have to have a way to find relevant triples for the query, as we do not want to query every node in the triple. For this purpose, we connect the nodes via a structured peer-2-peer network which implements a distributed hash table [7].

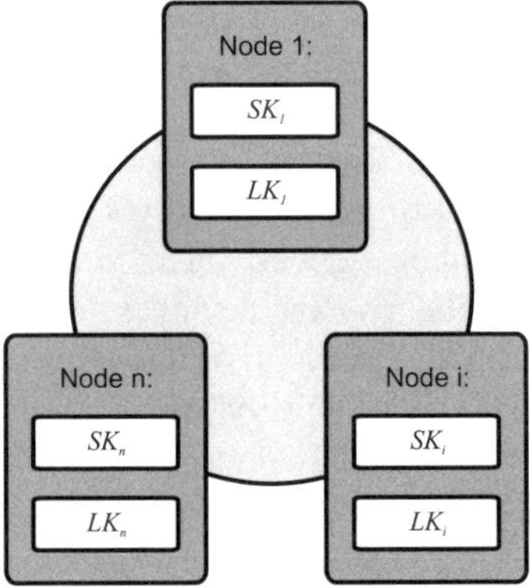

Figure 5. DHT-based p2p network.

There are different DHT approaches available like Chord [55], Pastry [50], or CAN [48]. All have some kind of lookup mechanism in common. This lookup mechanism enables the user to determine a specific node which is responsible to store data for a certain key.

In our scenario, we use the URI references respectively the XML literals as keys. We store each triple three times, indexing by the subject, predicate, and object. Thus each node sends out its own triples to the responsible nodes. The target nodes store the triples for later retrieval. Note that we assume blank node labels to be unique in the network. This can simply be achieved by adding a node identifier to the label. Thus we can assure that we can join the triple-sets without caring about the blank node labels.

Thus, after finishing this process, the whole model graph is accessible in a well-defined way over the DHT network. There are several ways to retrieve triples from the network. To retrieve a set of triples, at least one part of the triples must be fixed. We use this part as a key to the DHT network, retrieving all triples with this value.

We define three functions, *getBySubject*, *getByPredicate* and *getByObject*, which we use to retrieve sets of triples. As an example we describe the *getBySubject* function. It takes a label as input and retrieves all triples from the network where the subject equals this label. It calls the lookup operation of the DHT network to retrieve the network node which stores these triples. So the execution time of these functions is determined by the time the lookup operation takes plus the transfer time of the result set. It will be a central goal of the query algorithm to minimize both the number of calls to these functions and the size of the returned triple sets.

4.3.2. RDFS rules

The RDF semantics document [32] describes how RDFS entailment can be viewed as a set of rules which generate new RDF triples from existing ones. For our scenario, the taxonomy-related rules are most important. First, they ensure that the subClassOf and subPropertyOf relationships are transitive. Second, they propagate instances of classes and properties towards more generic classes and properties. As an example, the class-related rule states:

If X is a sub-class of Y,

> *and A is an instance of X,*
> *then A is also an instance of Y.*

The pre-conditions of all rules share at least one URI in common. Thus, there is always at least one node were all triples are locally known. This means that all RDFS rules can be evaluated locally without network interaction. However, the resulting triples have to be further distributed to the responsible nodes.

See [33] for a discussion about the length of this process and the message load generated by it. Although this discussion focussed on taxonomies generated from DL reasoners, it applies as well to the RDFS taxonomies we are using here.

The the transitivity of the subClassOf and subPropertyOf predicates is supported implicitly. The triples are not generated, but the taxonomy rules implicitly propagate instances or pairs of instances to every class / property in the transitive closure of the subClassOf / subPropertyOf relation.

4.4. Query evaluation

Our algorithm for evaluating the queries works in two phases. In the first phase, we determine candidate sets for each of the triples in the query graph, as well as for the variables. The candidate sets for the variables and for the triples are mutually dependent, thus we have a refinement procedure which successively removes candidates from both sets which are not suitable. In the second phase, matching combinations of triple candidates are searched locally.

Thus, the first phase collects a subgraph of the model graph distributed over the network which is large enough to contain every result for the query. The second phase is a subgraph matching in this smaller, local model graph which reveals the final results of the query.

4.4.1. Determination of Candidate Sets

The task of this phase is to identify parts of the model graph which are relevant for the query. The main focus of the algorithm is to reduce network load during this phase. This means, that we want to contact as less nodes as possible, and to transfer a minimal amount of data. We present different strategies, which are compared in the following section.

The main idea behind the algorithm is to determine how much candidates are expected for each triple and to iteratively choose the triple with the smallest expected candidate set. At each time, the algorithm maintains a set of candidates for each triple, denoted $C_T(t)$, $t \in T_Q$ and a set of candidates for each variable denoted $C_V(v)$, $v \in \mathcal{V}_Q$. Candidate sets may be undefined. As a short-cut, we will write $C_V(v) = \Delta$ iff the candidate set for v is not defined. We furthermore define $|C_V(v)| := \infty$ iff $C_V(v) = \Delta$. As it will simplify the algorithms presented later, we further define the candidate set of a fixed value (either literal or URI reference) to be the one-element set containing that value: $C_V(x) = \{x\}$ iff $x \in \mathcal{L}$.

Then some network communication will be used to retrieve the candidate sets, leading to new estimates for the other triples. We use the notion of the *specification grade* of a triple to see where we expect the smallest communication overhead. If you look at the way we distribute the triples, we can either use the subject, the predicate, or the object to retrieve the candidates. Each of these can either be a variable or a fixed value. If it is a fixed value, we have to do a single lookup to retrieve the candidate set. If it is a variable, the number of lookups is determined by the current number of candidates for this variable. If there are no candidates for the variable so far, we cannot use it to retrieve a candidate set.

Thus we define the specification grade of a triple's element as follows:

$$sg1(x) = \begin{cases} |C_V(x)| & : & C_V(x) \neq \Delta \\ \infty & : & C_V(x) = \Delta \end{cases}$$

Due to our above definition, this can be written short-hand as $sg1(x) = |C_V(x)|$. The specification grade for a triple is the minimum specification grade of its elements:

$$sg1(\langle s, p, o \rangle) = \min(sg1(s), sg1(p), sg1(o))$$

The idea behind this definition is that the specification grade determines the number of lookup operations needed. Thus we can write down the algorithm:

function candidates(T_Q, T_M)
    set each $C_T(t)$ and $C_V(v)$ to Δ
    while there is an undefined $C_T(t)$
        determine a triple $t = \langle s, p, o \rangle$ where
            • $C_T(t) = \Delta$, and
            • $sg1(t) \leq sg1(t') \, \forall t'$ with $C_T(t') = \Delta$
        if $sg1(t) = sg1(s)$
            $C_T(t) := \bigcup_{x \in C_V(s)} getBySubject(x)$
            $C_T(t) := \{\langle s, p, o \rangle \in C_T(t) : p \in C_V(p), o \in C_V(o)\}$
        else
            similar code for predicate and object
        end if
        if refine($C_T, C_V, \{t\}, \emptyset$) = error
            return error
        end if
    end while
    return ok
end function

The heart of the algorithm is the refinement procedure. There are two ways of refinement. First, we can look at a variable's candidate set. We compare it with the candidate sets for each triple where this variable occurs. If a candidate does not occur within the triple candidate set, it has to be removed from the variable candidate set. The other way around, we look at the candidate set for a triple and remove any candidates where there is some value not within the matching variable's candidate set. We always keep track of the set of changed variables V and changed triples T, so that we do not have to check every set.

function refine(C_T, C_V, T, V)
    while $V \neq \emptyset$ **or** $T \neq \emptyset$
        for each $t = \langle s, p, o \rangle \in T$

if $s \in \mathcal{V}$
$\quad C_V(s) := C_V(s) \cap \mathrm{subject}(C_T(t))$
$\quad$ **if** $C_V(s)$ has been changed
$\quad\quad V := V \cup \{s\}$
$\quad$ **end if**
end if
similar code for predicate and object
$T := T - \{t\}$
end for
for each $v \in V$
$\quad$ **for each** $t \in T_Q$
$\quad\quad$ **if** $\mathrm{subject}(t) = v$
$\quad\quad\quad C_T(t) := \{\langle s', p', o' \rangle \in C_T(t) : s' \in C_V(v)\}$
$\quad\quad\quad$ **if** $C_T(t)$ has been changed
$\quad\quad\quad\quad T := T \cup \{t\}$
$\quad\quad\quad$ **end if**
$\quad\quad$ **end if**
$\quad\quad$ *similar code for predicate and object*
$\quad$ **end for**
$\quad V := V - \{v\}$
end for
if some $C_V(v)$ or $C_T(t)$ is empty
$\quad$ **return** error
end if
end while
return ok
end function

The crucial question is how we can further reduce the network load. The refinement procedure is uncritical, as it works completely local. Thus we have to look at the order in which the triple candidates are retrieved from the network. The definition of the specification grade as given above ensures a minimal number of lookup operations in the current step. However, it can lead to a large number of candidates for the triple, leading to both a high bandwidth consumption and a large number of lookups in further steps. Furthermore, if we already have candidates for other variables in the triple, we can use these candidates to reduce the size of the returned candidate set. In the following two subsections, we introduce methods to benefit from these ideas.

4.4.2. Look-Ahead

The first enhancement is to introduce a look-ahead for the candidate set size in order to choose the next triple during the first phase of the query evaluation. We implement this look-ahead by summing up the result set sizes for each lookup instead of only counting the number of lookups. This is a trade-off, as it results in further lookups during the calculation of the sg value, however, it might lead to a better path trough the query graph with fewer candidates to transfer.

We define the following functions to retrieve the needed statistical information: *cntBySubject*, *cntByPredicate*, and *cntByObject*, respectively. They work similar to the *getBySubject* etc. functions, however, instead of returning the triple set, they only return its size.

The new definition of the specification grade is as follows. We have to define three different functions, referencing to the three elements of a triple. We only describe the subject function *sgs*; *sgp* and *sgo* are analogous.

$$sgs(x) = \begin{cases} \sum_{s \in C_V(x)} cntBySubject(s) & : \quad C_V(x) \neq \Delta \\ \infty & : \quad C_V(x) = \Delta \end{cases}$$

The specification grade of a triple is now defined as

$$sg2(\langle s, p, o \rangle) = \min(sgs(s), sgp(p), sgo(o))$$

During the collection of the candidate sets, we retrieve the sg of a triple multiple times. Thus we defined a further version *sg3* which implements a cache which is valid during the evaluation of a single query. Thereby, we can reduce the overhead introduced by the additional lookup-operations.

4.4.3. Bloom Filters

When we retrieve candidates for a triple $\langle v_1, v_2, v_3 \rangle$, we have to choose an element whose candidates we use as a key for the DHT lookup. Assume we choose v_1 which has the candidate set $\{x, y, z\}$. Then we contact three nodes by using lookup(x), lookup(y), and lookup(z). These nodes return all triples where the subject is either x, y, or z.

We might also have candidates for the other two variables. If we further transfer the known candidates for v_2 and v_3 during the *getBySubject* function, the target nodes could reduce the result sets. However, also the candidate sets for the other variables might be large, so that the reduction of the result set is outweighed by the additional transfer of the candidate sets.

Bloom filters [12] are ideal for this situation. A bloom filter is a compact representation of a set using an array of bits of a fixed size. Each element which is stored in the filter is hashed multiple times using different hash functions. The bits corresponding with the hash values are set in the filter. Membership test is done in the same way. Thus, each element of the set is reliably detected. However, so-called false positives are possible. This means, that an element is detected to be a member of the set which is in fact a non-member.

Thus we can encode the candidate sets for the other variables as bloom filters and send these filters to the target node. This node locally sorts out non-matching results and sends back the reduced candidate set. Due to the false positives of the bloom filter, there may be too many candidates, however, they are removed by the refinement procedure. As each set member is reliably detected, no candidate will be lost, which ensures the correctness of the query results.

The bloom filters can be used both in the *getBySubject* etc. functions and the *cntBySubject* functions. The former can be combined with all versions of the specification grade; the latter results in a new definition of *sg4*, which results in a better look-ahead as the already known candidates for the other elements of the triple are included. We combine the *sg4* version with the caching mechanism of *sg3*. The cache is filled as soon as a *sg4* value is calculated. This means, that we might later loose better estimates when we have received candidates for more variables. However, the caching effect reduces the number of lookups dramatically.

4.4.4. Final Evaluation

After having retrieved candidate sets for all triples and variables, we have to do the final evaluation to retrieve matches for the query. This is done completely local. However, it can be computationally expensive. In general, every combination of candidates for the triples has to be considered and tested, which are exponentially many. In fact, the query complexity version of RDF querying is NP complete. However, the data complexity version is in P, see [28].

We employ a backtracking algorithm. In each step, it chooses a triple which has more than one candidate, and fixes each of the candidates in a loop. By fixing a triple candidate, we also fix values for the variables. Triple candidates are only chosen if they don't contradict with previous variable assignments. For a full description of the algorithm, see [34].

5. Conclusion and Open Problems

In this chapter, we have given an overview of the field of *Emergent Schema Management*. With an ever increasing number of online-available information sources, the need for integration of these sources rises. The main challenge in this integration is to automatically overcome heterogeneities on different levels while maintaining scalability.

We have provided a classification of the basic design choices, of the types of heterogeneities, and of the types of schema integration. We have further discussed the origins of schema information and mediators, and briefly touched the topics of information quality and distributed updates to the information sources.

A number of case studies shed some light on a selection of current research in this field, including our own work. Each of these projects focusses on a specific subset of the problem; none of them is a full fledged solution resolving all main challenges.

In the remainder of this section, we list what we feel are the most challenging open problems to be resolved by future research.

- *Sophisticated logics*: To integrate arbitrary pieces of information scattered over the globe, expressive logics such as the various flavors of Description Logics are desirable. They are expected to play an important role in the forthcoming Semantic Web. However, complex reasoning procedures hinder scalability. In such scenarios, it is difficult to identify the pieces of information relevant for a given query.
- *Global data system model*: To detect arbitrary connections between seemingly unrelated information sources, and to take full advantage of the stored datasets, we feel that the global data system model is superior to any local approach. However, it typically needs a kind of virtual global catalog, which is then distributed over a DHT network. The maintenance of this catalog becomes increasingly difficult in the light of an highly dynamic environment.

- *Automated construction of schema and mappings*: The success of any integration system relies on the existence of schema information and mappings between these schemas. A typical assumption is that this information is human supplied. However, the larger the whole system grows, the more important it will be to generate reliable mappings automatically, either by combining existent mappings or by automated approaches of schema or Ontology mapping.
- *Trust and Security*: The assumption that each peer in the network behaves well will not hold in larger, open scenarios. Malicious peers will try to influence the behavior of the system to gain advantages. Thus we think that trust and security will be important aspects of practical systems which are deployed beyond small research communities.
- *Dynamics*: Information is not static. Thus also the systems integrating various sources need to respect the dynamics of the underlying data. A system will be the more useful the more recent the results are. However, as caching and replication are basic elements of most systems, this poses additional challenges resolving the pay-off between freshness and performance.

Concluding, we believe that the research activity in this area already has achieved highly useful results forming a stable basis for further work to resolve the remaining issues.

Acknowledgements

Partially supported by the EU within the 6th Framework Programme under contract 001907 "Dynamically Evolving, Large Scale Information Systems" (DELIS).

References

[1] Karl Aberer, Philippe Cudré-Mauroux, and Manfred Hauswirth. Start making sense: The Chatty Web approach for global semantic agreements. *Journal of Web Semantics*, 1(1), December 2003.

[2] Karl Aberer, Philippe Cudré-Mauroux, Manfred Hauswirth, and Tim Van Pelt. GridVine: Building Internet-Scale Semantic Overlay Networks. In *The Semantic Web - ISWC 2004: Third International Semantic Web Conference, Hiroshima, Japan.*, pages 107–121, 2004.

[3] Artur Andrzejak and Zhichen Xu. Scalable, Efficient Range Queries for Grid Information Services. In *2nd IEEE International Conference on Peer-to-Peer Computing (P2P2002)*, September 2002.

[4] Marcelo Arenas, Vasiliki Kantere, Anastasios Kementsietsidis, Iluju Kiringa, Renée J. Miller, and John Mylopoulos. The hyperion project: from data integration to data coordination. *SIGMOD Record*, 32(3):53–58, 2003.

[5] Franz Baader, Diego Calvanese, Deborah McGuinness, Daniele Nardi, and Peter Patel-Schneider, editors. *The Description Logic Handbook*. Cambridge University Press, 2003.

[6] Henri Bal et al. Next Generation Grids 2: Requirements and Options for European Grids Research 2005-2010 and Beyond. `ftp://ftp.cordis.lu/pub/ist/docs/ngg2_eg_final.pdf`, 2004.

[7] Hari Balakrishnan, M. Frans Kaashoek, David Karger, Robert Morris, and Ion Stoica. Looking Up Data in P2P Systems. *Communications of the ACM*, 46(2):43 – 48, February 2003.

[8] Roberto Baldoni, Ricardo Jiménez-Peris, Marta Patiño-Martínez, Leonardo Querzoni, and Antonino Virgillito. Dynamic Quorums for DHT-based P2P Networks. In *4th IEEE Int. Symp. on Network Computing and Applications (NCA)*, 2005.

[9] Dave Beckett. RDF/XML Syntax Specification (Revised). `http://www.w3.org/TR/rdf-syntax-grammar`, 2004.

[10] Tim Berners-Lee. Primer: Getting into RDF & Semantic Web using N3. `http://www.w3.org/2000/10/swap/Primer.html`, 2000.

[11] Tim Berners-Lee, James Hendler, and Ora Lassila. The Semantic Web. *Scientific American*, May 2001.

[12] Burton H. Bloom. Space/Time Trade-offs in Hash Coding with Allowable Errors. *Commun. ACM*, 13(7):422–426, 1970.

[13] Matteo Bonifacio, Roberta Cuel, Gianluca Mameli, and Michele Nori. A peer-to-peer architecture for distributed knowledge management. In *Proceedings of the 3rd International Symposium on Multi-Agent Systems, Large Complex Systems, and E-Businesses MALCEB '2002*, 2002.

[14] Dan Brickley and Ramanathan V. Guha. RDF Vocabulary Description Language 1.0: RDF Schema. `http://www.w3.org/TR/rdf-schema`, 2004.

[15] Ingo Brunkhorst, Hadhami Dhraief, Alfons Kemper, Wolfgang Nejdl, and Christian Wiesner. Distributed queries and query optimization in schema-based p2p-systems. In *Databases, Information Systems, and Peer-to-Peer Computing, First International Workshop, DBISP2P, Berlin Germany, September 7-8, 2003, Revised Papers*, pages 184–199, 2003.

[16] Min Cai, Martin Frank, Baoshi Pan, and Robert MacGregor. A Subscribable Peer-to-Peer RDF Repository for Distributed Metadata Management. *Journal of Web Semantics: Science, Services and Agents on the World Wide Web, Vol. 2, Issue 2*, 2005.

[17] Diego Calvanese, Giuseppe De Giacomo, Maurizio Lenzerini, Daniele Nardi, and Riccardo Rosati. Knowledge representation approach to information integration. In *In Proc. of AAAI Workshop on AI and Information Integration, pages 58-65. AAAI Press/The MIT Press, 1998.*, 1998.

[18] Arturo Crespo and Hector Garcia-Molina. Semantic Overlay Networks for P2P Systems. In *Agents and Peer-to-Peer Computing, Third International Workshop, AP2PC 2004, New York, NY, USA, July 19, 2004, Revised and Invited Papers*, pages 1–13, 2004.

[19] AnHai Doan, Jayant Madhavan, Robin Dhamankar, Pedro Domingos, and Alon Halevy. Learning to match ontologies on the Semantic Web. *The VLDB Journal*, 12(4):303–319, 2003.

[20] Dejing Dou, Drew McDermott, and Peishen Qi. Ontology Translation on the Semantic Web. In *Lecture Notes in Computer Science*, volume 2888, pages 952 – 969. Springer-Verlag, 2003.

[21] Marc Ehrig, Peter Haase, Ronny Siebes, Steffen Staab, Heiner Stuckenschmidt, Rudi Studer, and Christoph Tempich. The SWAP Data and Metadata Model for Semantics-Based Peer-to-Peer Systems. In *Multiagent System Technologies, First German Conference, MATES 2003, Erfurt, Germany, September 22-25, 2003, Proceedings*, pages 144–155, 2003.

[22] Marc Ehrig and York Sure. Ontology mapping - an integrated approach. In *The Semantic Web: Research and Applications, First European Semantic Web Symposium, ESWS 2004, Heraklion, Crete, Greece, May 10-12, 2004, Proceedings*, pages 76–91, 2004.

[23] Ronald Fagin, Phokion G. Kolaitis, Renée J. Miller, and Lucian Popa. Data Exchange: Semantics and Query Answering, 2002.

[24] Ian Foster and Carl Kesselman, editors. *The Grid2: Blueprint for a New Computing Infrastructure*. Morgan Kaufmann, 2004.

[25] Hector Garcia-Molina, Jeffrey D. Ullman, and Jennifer D. Widom. *Database Systems. The Complete Book*. Prentice Hall, 2003.

[26] Roy Goldman and Jennifer Widom. DataGuides: Enabling Query Formulation and Optimization in Semistructured Databases. In *Proceedings of the Twenty-Third International Conference on Very Large Data Bases, Athens, Greece*, pages 436–445, August 1997.

[27] Nicola Guarino. Formal Ontology in Information Systems. In *Proceedings of the 1st International Conference on Formal Ontologies in Information Systems, FOIS'98*, 1998.

[28] Claudio Gutierrez, Carlos Hurtado, and Alberto Mendelzon. Formal aspects of querying RDF databases. In *First International Workshop on Semantic Web and Databases*, 2003.

[29] Peter Haase, Jeen Broekstra, Marc Ehrig, Maarten Menken, Peter Mika, Mariusz Olko, Michal Plechawski, Pawel Pyszlak, Björn Schnizler, Ronny Siebes, Steffen Staab, and Christoph Tempich. Bibster - A Semantics-Based Bibliographic Peer-to-Peer System. In *The Semantic Web - ISWC 2004: Third International Semantic Web Conference,Hiroshima, Japan, November 7-11, 2004. Proceedings*, pages 122–136, 2004.

[30] Alon Y. Halevy, Zachary G. Ives, Jayant Madhavan, Peter Mork, Dan Suciu, and Igor Tatarinov. The Piazza Peer Data Management System. *IEEE Trans. on Knowledge and Data Eng.*, 16(7), 2004.

[31] Alon Y. Halevy, Zachary G. Ives, Dan Suciu, and Igor Tatarinov. Schema Mediation in Peer Data Management Systems. In *19th International Conference on Data Engineering (ICDE)*, 2003.

[32] Patrick Hayes. RDF Semantics. `http://www.w3.org/TR/rdf-mt`, 2004.

[33] Felix Heine, Matthias Hovestadt, and Odej Kao. Towards Ontology-Driven P2P Grid Resource Discovery. In *5th International Workshop on Grid Computing (GRID 2004), Pittsburgh, PA, USA.*, pages 76–83, 2004.

[34] Felix Heine, Matthias Hovestadt, and Odej Kao. Processing complex RDF queries over P2P networks. In *P2PIR'05: Proceedings of the 2005 ACM workshop on Information retrieval in peer-to-peer networks*, pages 41–48, New York, NY, USA, 2005. ACM Press.

[35] William H. Inmon. *Building the Data Warehouse*. John Wiley & Sons, 2005.

[36] Michael Kifer, Arthur Bernstein, and Philip M. Lewis. *Database Systems. An Application-Oriented Approach*. Addison Wesley, 2005.

[37] George Kokkinidis, Lefteris Sidirourgos, and Vassilis Christophides. Query Processing in RDF/S-based P2P Database Systems. *Semantic Web and Peer to Peer*, November 2005.

[38] John Kubiatowicz. Extracting guarantees from chaos. *Communications of the ACM*, 46(2):33 – 38, February 2003.

[39] Maurizio Lenzerini. Data integration: a theoretical perspective. In *PODS '02: Proceedings of the twenty-first ACM SIGMOD-SIGACT-SIGART symposium on Principles of database systems*, pages 233–246, New York, NY, USA, 2002. ACM Press.

[40] Qusay H. Mahmoud, editor. *Middleware for Communications*. John Wiley & Sons, Ltd, 2004.

[41] Frank Manola and Eric Miller. RDF Primer. `http://www.w3.org/TR/rdf-primer`, 2004.

[42] Wolfgang Nejdl, Wolf Siberski, and Michael Sintek. Design Issues and Challenges for RDF- and Schema-Based Peer-to-Peer Systems. *SIGMOD Record, Special Issue on Peer-to-Peer Data Management*, September 2003.

[43] Wolfgang Nejdl, Boris Wolf, Changtao Qu, Stefan Decker, Michael Sintek, Ambjörn Naeve, Mikael Nilsson, Matthias Palmér, and Tore Risch. EDUTELLA: a P2P networking infrastructure based on RDF. In *WWW2002, May 7-11, 2002, Honolulu, Hawaii, USA*, pages 604–615, 2002.

[44] Nikos Ntarmos, Theoni Pitoura, and Peter Triantafillou. Range query optimization leveraging peer heterogeneity in DHT data networks. In *3rd International Workshop on Databases, Information Systems and Peer-to-Peer Computing (DBISP2P 2005)*, August 2005.

[45] Vassilis Papadimos, David Maier, and Kristin Tufte. Distributed Query Processing and Catalogs for Peer-to-Peer Systems. In *Proceedings of the 2003 CIDR Conference*, 2003.

[46] Eric Prud'hommeaux and Andy Seaborne (eds.). SPARQL Query Language for RDF. `http://www.w3.org/TR/rdf-sparql-query`, 2005.

[47] Erhard Rahm and Philip A. Bernstein. A survey of approaches to automatic schema matching. *VLDB J.*, 10(4):334–350, 2001.

[48] Sylvia Ratnasamy, Paul Francis, Mark Handley, Richard M. Karp, and Scott Shenker. A scalable content-addressable network. In *SIGCOMM*, pages 161–172, 2001.

[49] Marie-Christine Rousset and Chantal Reynaud. Knowledge representation for information integration. *Inf. Syst.*, 29(1):3–22, 2004.

[50] Antony Rowstron and Peter Druschel. Pastry: Scalable, decentralized object location and routing for large-scale peer-to-peer systems. In *Proc. of the 18th IFIP/ACM International Conference on Distributed Systems Platforms (Middleware 2001)*, 2001.

[51] Andy Seaborne. RDQL - A Query Language for RDF. `http://www.w3.org/Submission/2004/SUBM-RDQL-20040109`, 2004.

[52] Michael K. Smith, Chris Welty, and Deborah L. McGuinness. OWL Web Ontology Language Guide. `http://www.w3c.org/TR/owl-guide`, 2004.

[53] Ralf Steinmetz and Klaus Wehrle, editors. *Peer-to-Peer Systems and Applications*. Springer, 2005. LNCS 3485.

[54] Ralf Steinmetz and Klaus Wehrle. What Is This "Peer-to-Peer" About? *Peer-to-Peer Systems and Applications, LNCS 3485*, 2005.

[55] Ion Stoica, Robert Morris, David Liben-Nowell, David Karger, M. Frans Kaashoek, Frank Dabek, and Hari Balakrishnan. Chord: A Scalable Peer-to-peer Lookup Service for Internet Applications. *IEEE Transactions on Networking*, 11, 2003.

[56] Julian R. Ullmann. An Algorithm for Subgraph Isomorphism. *J. ACM*, 23(1):31–42, 1976.

Global Data Management
R. Baldoni et al. (Eds.)
IOS Press, 2006

249

Pragmatic Distributed Type Interoperability[1]

Philippe Altherr [a], Sébastien Baehni [b], Valéry Bezençon [c], Patrick Eugster [d],
Rachid Guerraoui [b] and Maxime Monod [b]

[a] *EPFL, LAMP*
[b] *EPFL, LPD*
[c] *UNINE, Enterprise Institute*
[d] *Purdue University, Dept. of Computer Sciences*

Abstract. It is appealing, yet challenging, to provide a set of geographically separated users with the same computing environment despite differences in underlying hardware or software.

This paper addresses the question of how to provide *type interoperability*: namely, the ability for types representing the same software module, but possibly defined by different programmers, in different languages and running on different distributed platforms, to be treated as one single type.

We present a pragmatic approach to deal with type interoperability in a dynamic distributed environment. Our approach is based on an optimistic transport protocol for passing objects by value (or by reference) between remote sites and a set of implicit type interoperability rules. We experiment the approach over the .NET platform which we indirectly evaluate.

Keywords. Distributed Programming, Types, Objects, Interoperability, Serialization, Middleware, Dynamic Proxies, .NET

1. Introduction

There are different forms of interoperability and these differ according to their abstraction level. *Interoperability at the hardware level* is typically about devising an operating system, e.g., Linux, that runs on different machines, e.g., PCs, Laptops, PDAs. *Interoperability at the operating system level* ensures that the programming language, e.g., Java through its byte code and virtual machine, is independent from the underlying operating system, e.g., Linux, Unix, Windows, Mac OS. *Interoperability at the programming language level* guarantees that a class written in a specific language, e.g., C++, can be used in another language, e.g., Java, transparently. This is for instance what .NET aims at offering.

This paper focuses on an even higher level of interoperability: *type interoperability*. The goal is to make transparent for the programmer the use of one type for another,

---

[1]The work presented in this paper was supported by the National Competence Center in Research on Mobile Information and Communication Systems (NCCR-MICS), a center supported by the Swiss National Science Foundation under grant number 5005-67322.

even if these types do not exactly have the same methods or names, as long as they aim at representing the same software module. These types might be written in the same language but by different programmers, they might be written in different languages, or even running on different platforms.

We address the issue of type interoperability in a distributed environment where objects of new types are introduced and passed by value in the system (or by reference). Typically this issue arises whenever different software modules might need to be assembled in a distributed application. Some of these modules represent a single logical entity.

Type interoperability has been studied in centralized applications (e.g., [11]). However, as we discuss in Section 2, the proposed solutions are too rigid for a dynamic distributed environment. In short, such solutions assume a priori global knowledge of the type hierarchy. Our aim is to provide a transparent solution to this problem in a distributed environment. Basically, we are interested in devising a flexible scheme to allow objects of different types, that aim at representing the same logical entity, to be remotely exchanged (not only passed by reference, but especially also passed by value) as if they were of the same type, even if these types (a) have different methods or names, (b) are written in different languages or (c) are running on different platforms. The challenge here is to provide this transparency with acceptable performance.

This paper presents our approach to distributed type interoperability based on an optimistic transport protocol. To experiment our approach in a concrete setting, we have implemented it over a popular object-oriented platform: .NET[2]. This platform has been chosen because it provides the highest level of interoperability "underneath" type interoperability: language interoperability. We extend .NET to allow for type interoperability and we provide associated structural interoperability rules, themselves implemented via .NET dynamic proxies. Our approach requires a small overhead for invoking an interoperable typed object received from a remote host, and we precisely measure this overhead through our prototype implementation.

Section 2 puts our work in the perspective of general approaches to language and type interoperability. Section 3 overviews the problem of type interoperability in a distributed environment and our approach to address it. Section 4 details the protocol we use to test if two types are interoperable. Section 5 describes how types are represented and Section 6 presents our type interoperable rules. Section 7 overviews the implementation of our prototype and Section 8 gives some performance measurements over it. Finally, Section 9 draws some conclusions.

2. Related Work

We present here several works that point closest to our type interoperability approach.

2.1. Subtyping in Static Typed Languages

Subtyping rules, as in languages like Java [8], C# [4], somehow define a kind of type interoperability. Indeed, once a type T is considered as a subtype of a type T', instances

---

[2]Of course the choice of the .NET platform implicitly fixes the operating system (Windows) and runtime environment (*common language runtime*–CLR) respectively, while the set of programming languages is fixed through our choice of supporting only those supported by .NET. However, our approach could be implemented on another platform like CORBA or Java RMI.

of T can be used as instances of T' transparently. Even if the verification of our type interoperability rules use similar techniques as those performed during subtyping tests (like covariance and contravariance, c.f., [2]), we aim at interoperability at another level. Actually, in the static typed languages we aimed at, types are subtypes of other types if they are declared as such by the programmer. Furthermore, the compiler takes care of checking if the types do not violate the subtyping rules defined by the considered languages. These rules can be based on the features of the types only (e.g., type name, signature of the methods, signature of the constructors) or even on the actual behavior of the types, like in [14].

In this paper, we try to address the problem of determining if a type is interoperable with another one with neither imposing any assumptions on who wrote these types nor on the types themselves. The types can hence be written by different programmers who do not know each other and who do not know each other's respective type hierarchies. Furthermore, we do not want the programmer to rewrite its own types to make them interoperable with new ones received through the wire (we want the interoperability to be transparent for the programmer) and as a consequence, the tests for interoperability will be done only at runtime in contrast with the type checking tests performed at compilation.

2.2. Safe Structural Conformance for Java

Type interoperability was addressed for a centralized context in [11] through the notion of *structural conformance*. The structural conformance rules are expressed for the Java type hierarchy (a type is structurally conformant with another type if it implements each method of the second type) which narrows the scope of structural conformance. Moreover only types that are tagged as being structural conformant can pretend to do so, meaning that legacy interfaces can never be used with structural conformance. Our approach has the aim to extend the structural approach in a decentralized environment such that interoperable types do not need to share the same type hierarchy, neither to be tagged as being interoperable.

2.3. Compound Types for Java

The idea of providing compound types for Java [3] aims at simplifying the composition and re-usability of Java types without having to change them or agree on a common design. A new way to express a type was introduced: *[TypeA,TypeB,...,TypeN]*. This new notation defines all the types declared to implement *TypeA*, *TypeB*,..., *TypeN*. With compound types the programmer can express a "kind" of interoperability as the implemented methods of a type are taken into account instead of only its name. This approach can be considered as a composition of nominal and pure structural subtyping. As presented upper, we aim at having type interoperability at a higher level.

2.4. Interoperability in CORBA

CORBA [16] addresses the language interoperability problem through an *interface definition language* (IDL). This IDL provides support for pass by reference semantics which make it possible to call a specific method from one language to another. Pass by value semantics for object types have been added to CORBA through *value types* to enable the passing of invocation arguments. The adopted solution is rather tedious to use, as developers are required to implement such types in all potentially involved languages. In particular, this makes it hard to add value (sub)types with new behavior at runtime. Note that CORBA implementations provide various mechanisms, such as the *dynamic skeleton interface* and *dynamic invocation interface*, as well as the concept of *smart proxies* found in many ORB implementations, which enable to some extent the realization of type interoperability. Pass by value semantics with object types would however be strongly limited because of the lack of a general protocol for transferring efficiently objects as well as type interoperability rules.

2.5. Interoperability in Java RMI

Java RMI enables the transfer of objects by value as arguments of remote invocations, thanks to its built-in serialization mechanism. By virtue of subtyping, an instance of a new class can be used as invocation argument, provided that it conforms to the type of the corresponding formal argument. By transmitting the corresponding class (byte code) to an invoked object previously unaware of that class, one can implement a scheme where new event classes are automatically propagated. The underlying dynamic code loading and linking ensured by the Java virtual machine would also make it possible to extend/alter the behavior of existing classes at runtime. Though the Java virtual machine has been used to run code written in various languages, the exploitation of its type safe dynamic code loading and linking [13,17] is problematic outside of Java. Like CORBA, this dynamic linking mechanism could be used for implementing type interoperability, but again, to our knowledge, no efficient protocol and type interoperability rules have never been proposed.

2.6. Microsoft .NET

Just like CORBA, .NET aims at unifying several object-oriented languages, in the case of .NET through a *common type system* (CTS). The advantage here is that the programmer does not need to reimplement the type of interest in all programming languages in order to use the pass by value semantics. Nevertheless, .NET does not address the issue of transparently unifying types that are not identical but that aim at representing the same logical entity, i.e., interoperable types.

2.7. Renaissance

The *Renaissance* system [15] implements an interesting RPC scheme where types with different methods or names can be invoked as if they were the same type, as long as they interoperate between each other. The idea is based on structural conformance rules as means to compare such types. The approach is however limited in that it relies on an explicit type definition language called *lingua franca* (even though mainly for the purpose of generating typed proxies), and does not support pass by value semantics with object types. Our approach for type interoperability is not bound to any intermediate language but rather to the type system of the platform itself. Moreover, our approach encompasses pass by value semantics as well as pass by reference semantics.

3. Overview

This section overviews the problem of type interoperability in a distributed environment and our approach to address it.

3.1. Problem

Consider the well-known and illustrative case of Java, C#. Types are defined explicitly through interfaces, or implicitly through classes. Consider a type `Person` with a field `name` of type `Name` as shown in Figure 1. A first programmer can implement this type by declaring a class with a setter method named `setName()` and a getter method named `getName()`. Another programmer can implement the same type with the following setter and getter respectively: `Set_Name()` and `Get_Name()`. Clearly, even if the two implementations provide the same functionalities, they are not compatible, i.e. the programmers cannot interchange instances of the two implementations transparently. In "static" environments (where all the types of objects are known at the start of the system) this problem is "easy" to solve because the translation rules can be hard-coded into the system.

```
public interface IPerson {
  public void setName(Name newName);
  public Name getName();
}
public class Person : IPerson {
  private Name name;
  public Person(Name name) {...}
  public void setName(Name newName) {...}
  public Name getName() {...}
}
public class Name {
  private string firstName, lastName;
  public Name(string firstName, string lastName) {...}
}
```

Figure 1. Type `Person` and `Name`

However, when the system is distributed and "dynamic", i.e. where new objects of new types can be put into the system through remote locations at runtime, this problem is not trivially solved. A set of general rules that can be compatible with every type must be created and implemented into the system. This implementation must be compatible with the pass by reference and the pass by value semantics in order to achieve full distribution interoperability.

3.2. Our Approach

We implement (1) the general rules needed for ensuring type interoperability as well as (2) a protocol that can be used in order to receive and use objects of interoperable types. A distributed and "dynamic" environment is assumed. We do not tackle the problem in a local setting, because it raises type safety issues that are difficult to resolve without proving the type soundness of the solution (as in a local setting all the required types are available at hand upon compilation which is the not necessary the case in a dynamic distributed setting). Our general protocol to achieve type interoperability in a distributed environment is depicted in Figure 2 and explained in more details in Section 4.

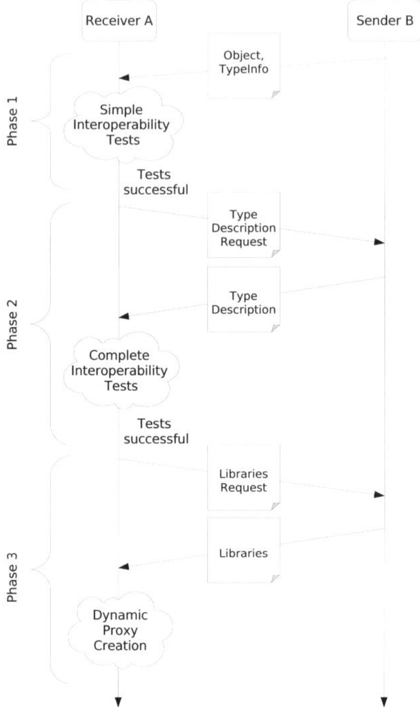

Figure 2. Pragmatic type interoperability protocol

Our protocol can be decomposed in three phases: (1) reception of an object and execution of simple interoperability tests, (2) if those tests succeed, the complete interoperability tests are performed and (3) upon the success of the complete interoperability tests, the object is deserialized and a dynamic proxy is created for it. At the end of the third phase, the received object is usable through the created dynamic proxy as if it were an object of another type (i.e., the type impersonated by the dynamic proxy).

4. Protocol

As presented in Section 3, our protocol can be decomposed in three phases: (1) simple interoperability tests, (2) complete interoperability tests and (3) dynamic proxy creation. We present in the following all the different phases in more details for the pass by value case and finally present the pass by reference case.

4.1. Simple Interoperability Tests

Let us assume without loss of generality, an object being transferred to one receiver A, by one sender B, as depicted in Figure 2. When B wants to send an object to A, it encapsulates it inside a message containing the object together with its minimal type information (i.e., `TypeInfo`, see Section 5.2).

When A receives such a message, it first checks if it has already received an object of the same type. If this is the case, it can directly know if the object is of interest or not (thanks to the previously results stored into its memory). If A is not interested in the object, it simply drops it. Otherwise, this means that it has already downloaded the code of the object and consequently it creates a new dynamic proxy of the type of interest for the received object and deserializes the object.

In the case where A receives such an object for the first time, it first tests if the type of the received object is equal to the type of its interest. This test is easily performed in checking the different attributes of the minimal type information. If it happens that the type of the received object is the same than the type of interest of A then the object can be deserialized and used just as is, without needing any dynamic proxy. However, if the types are not the same, A checks if the name of the types and the modifiers of the types are interoperable according to the rules given in Section 6.

If the types are not interoperable then the object is dropped, otherwise the second phase of the protocol takes place, namely the complete interoperability tests.

4.2. Complete Interoperability Tests

In this phase, once the simple interoperability tests have successfully completed, the receiver A asks the sender B for a more complete description (i.e., `TypeDescription`, see Section 5) of the type of the object it has just received. When receiving such a request, B sends what we call the type description of the type of the object. This type description contains all the different elements needed to perform the tests described in Section 6, namely, testing the interoperability of the types over their respective: (1) name, (2) fields, (3) methods' signatures, (4) constructors' signatures and (5) supertypes.

If one of the tests fails, the object is dropped by A. Otherwise, if the type of the object appears to be interoperable with the type of interest of A, A creates a mapping between the methods, constructors and the fields of the type of interest and the type of the received object. This mapping will be needed in the third phase to generate the dynamic proxy. Indeed, when a method is called on the instance of the dynamic proxy of the type of interest, this call must be transformed to a call to the method of the type of the received object. Once the mapping is created (in our prototype this is done on the fly during the complete interoperability tests), the protocol goes in its last phase, namely the dynamic proxy creation.

4.3. Dynamic Proxy Creation

Once the complete interoperability tests have been achieved successfully, the receiver asks for the code of the object it received. Upon this request, B sends the code of the object to receiver A. When A receives the code of the object it deserializes it and creates a dynamic proxy for it (see Section 7.5). This dynamic proxy is of the type of interest such that A can manipulate the received object as if it were an object of its type of interest. When A makes a method call on the instance of the dynamic proxy, this call is caught by the dynamic proxy and forwarded accordingly to the received object. The forwarding of the method call is done as specified by the mapping created during the second phase.

4.4. Pass by Reference Alternative

It is possible to use the very same protocol presented above for dealing with pass by reference semantics, e.g., when a potential client attempts to narrow an object reference obtained through a lookup service, with three minor differences. First, no object needs to be sent anymore between the sender and the receiver but only the minimal type information. This is due to the fact that the object will be accessed remotely and not locally. Next, during the third phase, when the sender receives the request for the code of the object (in this specific case the code corresponding to the `TypeInfo`), instead of sending the code of the object that must be accessed remotely, he must send the code of a specific "client" object that is a subtype of the type of the remote object and which aim is to retrieve a reference to the remote object and to dispatch the method calls to it. For instance, if a sender wants to give remote access to an object of type `IPerson` (see Figure 1), he must provide the "client" code depicted in Figure 3 (we do not catch in this code any possibly raised exceptions for brevity).

```
public class ClientPerson : IPerson {
  IPerson remote;
  public ClientPerson() {
    TcpClientChannel chan = new TcpClientChannel();
    ChannelServices.RegisterChannel(chan);
    remote = (IPerson)Activator.GetObject(typeof(IPerson),
                          "tcp://192.168.34.2:1002/Person");
  }
  public void setName(Name newName) {remote.setName(newName);}
  public Name getName() {return remote.getName();}
}
```

Figure 3. Specific client class for the `IPerson` remote object

Finally, when receiving such code, instead of deserializing the object received in the first phase, the receiver must create a new instance of the "client" type and method calls must be dispatched to it, via the dynamic proxy.

5. Type Representation

This section discusses the representation of types. Our objective is to make the comparison between two types possible, according to the rules we will describe in Section 6, without having to transfer their respective implementations. To achieve this goal, we rely on introspection mechanisms (that are provided in platforms like Java or .NET).

5.1. Overview

Once the object, and its minimal type information (denoted by `TypeInfo`, see Section 5.2), are received on a given receiver A, a test must be performed to check if this object is of interest for A. In other words, this means that the type of the received object must be interoperable with the type of interest of A. Downloading directly the package/assembly containing the type of the received object is not an option, because this would consume too many network and memory resources, especially if it appears that the type of the received object and the type of interest are not interoperable. For that reason, as presented in Section 4, only a type description (denoted by `TypeDescription`) is downloaded.

To create the `TypeInfo` and the `TypeDescription`, the reflective capabilities of the object-oriented platform are used as a basis, as they provide some useful mechanisms that help us to get information about a type, like its variables, its methods and their attributes.

5.2. Type Information

The minimal type information needed to characterize a type is determined by what we call its type information, i.e., `TypeInfo`. This data structure contains the modifiers of the type, its name as well as the filename containing its code (e.g., assembly name in .NET or class name in Java) and the path where we can download its code. As presented in Section 4, when an object is sent through the wire, its type information is attached to it. For instance, Figure 4 depicts the type information for the type `Int32`.

```
modifiers:       AutoLayout, AnsiClass, NotPublic, Public, SequentialLayout,
                 Sealed, Serializable, BeforeFieldInit
typeName:        Int32
assemblyName:    mscorlib, Version=1.0.3300.0, Culture=neutral,
                 PublicKeyToken=b77a5c561934e089
downloadPath:    80.238.35.226:c:\windows\microsoft.net\
                 framework\v1.0.3705\mscorlib.dll
```

Figure 4. `TypeInfo` for the `Int32` type

5.3. Type Description

In order to test for the interoperability between two types, we need more than just the `TypeInfo`. Indeed, we need for each type: its *identity*[3], information about its attributes, the signature of its methods, constructors and information regarding its supertypes. All these information can be obtained by means of introspection.

However, recall that the serialization mechanisms of the main object-oriented platforms we think of (.NET or Java) are not able to serialize/deserialize an object without knowing in advance its type. For that reason, our own introspection objects for representing fields, methods, constructors, interfaces and the superclass of an object need to be created and serialized. To create and initialize such instances of our introspection classes, the native introspection classes of the chosen object-oriented platform are used.

All instances of our introspections objects will be regrouped together into one special type called `TypeDescription`. In Section 7 we make this type implement the `ITypeDescription` interface. This interface, depicted in Figure 5, defines the necessary methods to to acquire the information about the type of an object.

Please note that even if the `TypeDescription` type gives a way to describe the type it reflects (i.e., its fields, methods including the arguments of the methods, construc-

---

[3]We rely on the concept of type identity provided by the underlying platform. As a matter of example, .NET provides globally unique identifiers (GUIDs) of 128 bits long for types.

```
public interface ITypeDescription
{
  ClassInfo[] GetClassInfo();
  ConstructorInfo[] GetConstructorsInfo();
  MethodInfo[] GetMethodsInfo();
  SuperClassInfo[] GetSuperClassesInfo();
  InterfaceInfo[] GetInterfacesInfo();
  FieldInfo[] GetFieldsInfo();
}
```

Figure 5. `ITypeDescription` interface

tors, etc), it however does not describe the fields or the methods of the types of the formal *arguments* of the methods or of the fields themselves. There is no recursion in the type description for two main reasons, namely (1) for saving time during the creation of the type description and (2) for keeping the serialized `TypeDescription` instances small because a subtype description might already be available at the receiver side, so there is no need to transport redundant information.

6. Type Interoperability

This section presents our type interoperability rules. We first make a classification of the different categories of interoperability before giving our specific rules.

6.1. Interoperable Categories

Hardware interoperability aims at devising an operating system to work on different computers. *Operating system interoperability* ensures that the programming language is independent from the underlying operating system. Another category, now provided by the .NET platform allows to use a type described in one programming language (C# for example) in another language (VB.NET). We call this category *language* interoperability.

Type interoperability focuses on the interoperability between types. This category gathers two subsets: *implicit structural* type interoperability and *implicit behavioral* type interoperability. Implicit structural type interoperability encompasses what we call *explicit* type interoperability. Namely, explicit type interoperability takes into account the type hierarchy to which a type belongs, i.e. subtyping issues. The combination of the implicit structural type interoperability and the implicit behavioral type interoperability results in a "strong" *implicit* type interoperability.

The implicit behavioral type interoperability is based on the behavior of the type, i.e., based on the result of its methods. This type of interoperability is very difficult to analyze in the sense that the body of the methods cannot just be compared but these methods must also be executed in order to compare their results for corresponding inputs. Another less restrictive possibility would be to enforce pre- and post-conditions on the methods and check that these conditions are satisfied. This has been done in [14] and could be achieved using Aspect-Oriented Programming [10] at another level than the type declaration, though with severe limitations [1]. Moreover, even if behavioral type interoperability should be feasible for types dealing only with primitive types it would become rather tricky for more complex types. Finally, the implicit structural interoperability strictly relies on the structure of the type. By structure, we mean the type name, the name of its supertypes, the name and the type of its fields and the signature of its methods[4].

In this paper we focus on implicit structural type interoperability only. For presentation simplicity, we say implicit structural interoperability instead of implicit structural type interoperability.

6.2. Type Interoperability Rules

We first introduce here several basic notations and definitions that will help us explain the different aspects of interoperability. Finally we present the implicit structural interoperability rules.

6.2.1. General Definitions and Notations

To make things clearer, and in order to be able to describe the different aspects making all together the implicit structural interoperability rules, several terms are defined. Figure 6 presents those terms, notations and the implicit structural interoperability rules. First some notations that are used in the rules are defined. Then a definition of the general interoperability rules is given[5]. The second definition describes the equality of two types. The third definition explains the equivalence between two types. The fourth and the fifth definitions denote the notation for the superclass and the interfaces of a certain type. The sixth definition defines the $name()$ method used in the interoperability rules. Finally Figure 6 presents the implicit structural rules.

6.2.2. Decomposing Implicit Structural Interoperability

We define different aspects of interoperability as follows:

Name (i): This aspect takes into account the name of the different types, methods and constructors to compare to. A name of a type T (respectively of a method $m()$ or of a constructor $cons()$) is said be interoperable with the name of a type T' (respectively of a method $m'()$ or of a constructor $cons'()$) if the result of the `NameInterop()` method is equal to true. The implementation of this method is left to the programmer. As an example, our prototype makes use of the Levenshtein distance [12] (which can be set) together with a synonym dictionary (we could moreover use wildcards).

Fields (ii): A field f of type T_f ($f : T_f$) defined in a type T is said to be interoperable with a field f' of type $T_{f'}$, defined in a type T', if T_f and $T_{f'}$ are implicit structurally interoperable.

Supertypes (iii): This aspect takes into account the supertypes of the type and its interfaces (if any)[6]. A type T is said to be interoperable to a type T', with respect to T''s type hierarchy (i.e., supertypes), if the supertype and the interfaces of T are interop-

---

[4]Structural interoperability has been studied in [11] and is in between what we call explicit type interoperability and implicit structural type interoperability.

[5]Implicit interoperability is noted $\leq_I$, while explicit interoperability is noted $\leq_E$, and the implicit structural interoperability is noted: $\leq_{Is}$. Finally, $T \leq T'$ denotes the fact that instances of T can be used safely whenever an instance of T' is expected.

[6]The distinction between the type and its supertypes is done in order to make things clearer.

Notations:
  T denotes a type
  T_{GUID} denotes the globally unique identifier of type T
  $m()$ denotes a method
  $cons()$ denotes a constructor
Interoperability:
  $T \leq_E T' \Rightarrow T \leq T'$
  $T \leq_I T' \Rightarrow T \leq T'$
  $T \leq_{Is} T' \Rightarrow T \leq_I T'$
Equality:
  $T == T'$ iif $T_{GUID} == T'_{GUID}$
Equivalence:
  $T \leq T' \wedge T' \leq T \Rightarrow T \equiv T'$ (case for $\leq_E$ iif T'==T)
Superclass:
  $T^{super} \equiv (T' \mid T'\ superclass of\ T)$
Interfaces:
  $T^{inter} \equiv (\{T' \mid T'\ interfaceof\ T\})$
Name:
  $(name(x) \mid x \in \{T, m(), cons()\}) \equiv name\ of\ x$

Name Interoperability (i):
  $(x \leq_{Is}^{name} x' \mid x, x' \in \{T, m(), cons()\}) \Rightarrow$
  $NameInterop(name(x), name(x')) == true$

Field Interoperability (ii):
  $T \leq_{Is}^{field} T' \Rightarrow \forall f' : T_{f'} \in T' \ \exists f : T_f \in T \mid T_f \leq_{Is} T_{f'}$

Supertypes Interoperability (iii):
  $T \leq_{Is}^{hier} T' \Rightarrow (T^{super} \leq_{Is} T'^{super} \wedge T^{inter} \leq_{Is} T'^{inter})$

Method Interoperability (iv):
  $T \leq_{Is}^{meth} T' \Rightarrow \forall m'(Perm(a_{1'} : T_{1'}, ..., a_{n'} : T_{n'})) : T_{r'} \in T'$
  $\exists m(Perm(a_1 : T_1, ..., a_n : T_n)) : T_r \in T \mid m() \leq_{Is}^{name} m'() \wedge$
  $\forall i \in [1, n](T_{i'} \leq_{Is} T_i) \wedge T_r \leq_{Is} T_{r'}$

Constructor Interoperability (v):
  $T \leq_{Is}^{cons} T' \Rightarrow \forall cons(Perm(a_1 : T_1, ..., a_n : T_n)) \in T$
  $\exists cons(Perm(a_{1'} : T_{1'}, ..., a_{n'} : T_{n'})) \in T' \mid$
  $cons() \leq_{Is}^{name} cons'() \wedge \forall i \in [1, n](T_{i'} \leq_{Is} T_i)$

Implicit Structural Interoperability (vi):
  $T \leq_{Is} T' \Leftrightarrow (T \leq_{Is}^{name} T' \wedge T \leq_{Is}^{hier} T' \wedge T \leq_{Is}^{field} T' \wedge$
  $T \leq_{Is}^{meth} T' \wedge T \leq_{Is}^{cons} T') \vee T == T' \vee T \leq_E T'$

Figure 6. Interoperability rules

erable respectively, in the implicit structural sense, to the supertype and the interfaces of a type T'. T^{super} and T^{inter} denote the supertype and the set of interfaces of type T respectively.

Methods (iv): Interoperability between two methods $m()$ and $m'()$ is a bit more tricky. First, the modifiers of the methods are supposed to be the same (this assumption is implicitly made in the rule) and the name of the methods $m()$ and $m'()$ must be interoperable. Then both (1) the return value type of the methods and (2) the arguments of the methods are considered. To understand the rule presented in Figure 6, one must think which makes use of (1) the return value and (2) the arguments of the method: the instance of the type expected to be received (depicted as the "real" object) or the object received that must implicitly structurally interoperate (depicted as the implicitly structurally interoperable object). In (1) the "real" object uses the return value of type T_r of the method $m()$, meaning that T_r must implicitly structurally interoperate with the return value of type $T_{r'}$ of the method $m'()$. In (2), the implicit structurally interoperable object (received through the wire) must deal with the instances, given as arguments of its methods, by the "real" object. Consequently, the argument $T_{i'}$ of the method $m'()$ must implicitly structurally interoperate with the argument T_i of the method $m()$. Note that the permutations of the arguments of the methods (denoted by $Perm(a_1, a_2, ..., a_n)$) are taken into account.

In other words, contravariance is acceptable for the arguments of the methods and covariance is acceptable for the return values of the methods of a type T that must implicitly structurally interoperate with a type T'.

Constructor (v): The final step before defining the implicit structural interoperability rule is to describe the interoperability rule for the constructors. This rule is the same as the one for the methods except that the return values are not considered.

6.2.3. Implicit Structural Interoperability (vi)

A type T implicitly structurally interoperates with a type T' if T interoperates with type T' in all the aspects defined before or if T and T' are equivalent or if T interoperates explicitly with T'.

Please note that we do not impose any guidelines if a field, a method or a constructor of a type T matches several fields, methods or constructors of a type T' of which it implicitly interoperate with (e.g., a method with a single argument x_1 of type T_1 in T can match an arbitrary number of methods with a single argument $x_{1'}$ for as long as $T_1 \leq T_{1'}$). Consequently during the implementation of the rules, it is up to the programmer to decide what is more suitable.

6.3. Limitations of the Implicit Structural Interoperability

Type interoperability enables to receive and use an object as if its type is equivalent to the type of interest. In this sense, type interoperability broadens the scope of objects a receiver party can handle.

However, it should be clear for the receiver that if the types of the objects it receives are implicit structurally interoperable with its type of interest, it has no way to know the actual implementation of the types of the received objects. Our hypothesis is that two types that represent the same software entity should have somehow the same structure. This assumption might not be the case at all. Indeed, let us assume that we have the following methods: (1) `setName(String firstName, String lastName)` and (2) `setName(String lastName, String firstName)`. In this case, the methods are interoperable even if clearly the results will not be the same.

The same limitation goes for the implementation of the `NameInterop()` method if we decide not to restrict the Levensthein distance. For instance, if we take even a Levensthein distance of 1, a `car` type could be interoperable with a `bar` type (however without taking into account the methods which most likely should be different and make the complete interoperability tests fail).

7. Implementation

Our pragmatic type interoperability protocol, together with the type interoperability rules presented respectively in Section 4 and in Section 6 have been implemented on the .NET platform.[7]

We have chosen this platform mainly because it provides language interoperability. However, relying on such a platform brings a limitation in terms of operating system interoperability (.NET has been designed to run on Windows). Concerning this issue, an open-source project, called *mono* (www.mono-project.com) has been launched to port the essential libraries of .NET to other operating systems like Linux, Mac OS X, Windows and Unix. This allows .NET to be interoperable at the operating system level.

In this section, we first present how to use our prototype, then we describe its design and we finally give more details on the implementation of: (1) the protocol, (2) the type interoperability rules and (3) the dynamic proxies.

7.1. Using our APIs

Our prototype can be used via the following lines:

```
IProtoCallback ipc = new MyCallback();
ISerializer is = new BinarySerializer();
Type subscribedType = typeof(Person);
PtiProtocol ptip = new PtiProtocol(ipc, is, subscribedType);
```

To use our protocol we only need to instantiate a `PtiProtocol`. For this we have to provide: (1) an instance of a `IProtoCallback`, (2) an instance of a `ISerializer` as well as (3) the type we are interested in.

1. The `IProtoCallback` instance is used to be notified by the protocol with new objects which types are interoperable with the type of interest. These objects are delivered as dynamic proxy instances (i.e., instance of `ProxyMsg`). The programmer can then handle those instances through the `Handle()` method as presented below:

   ```
   public class MyCallback: IProtoCallback {
     public void Handle(IMessage msg) {
       ProxyMsg pm = (ProxyMsg)msg;
       Person p = (Person)pm.Proxy;
       Console.WriteLine("New instance of type Person: "+p);
     }
   }
   ```

   A `ProxyMsg` instance contains a getter method (i.e., `.Proxy`) to retrieve the instance of the dynamic proxy of the received object. The programmer can then type-cast the proxified object into the type of its interest.

2. The `ISerializer` instance gives the choice to the programmer to decide which kind of serialization mechanisms the prototype will use. This can be either a `BinarySerializer`, a `XMLSerializer` or a `SOAPSerializer`.

---

[7]Our prototype has been designed for dealing with pass by value objects but could be easily enhanced, as presented in Section 4, to support pass by reference objects.

3. The last parameter of the `PtiProtocol` constructor symbolizes the receiver interest, which is represented as a `Type`.[8]

Finally, if a sender wants to send an object to a specified set of receivers (denoted by their IP addresses), it uses the `BroadCastToSubscribers()` method as presented below.

```
Person p = new Person(new Name("John","Doe"));
String[] ips = {"192.168.73.2","192.168.73.3"};
ptip.BroadCastToSubscribers(p,ips);
```

7.2. Design

Figure 7 depicts the design of our prototype. Currently our prototype supports only the TCP communication layer, but it could also be possible to use a reliable UDP communication layer.

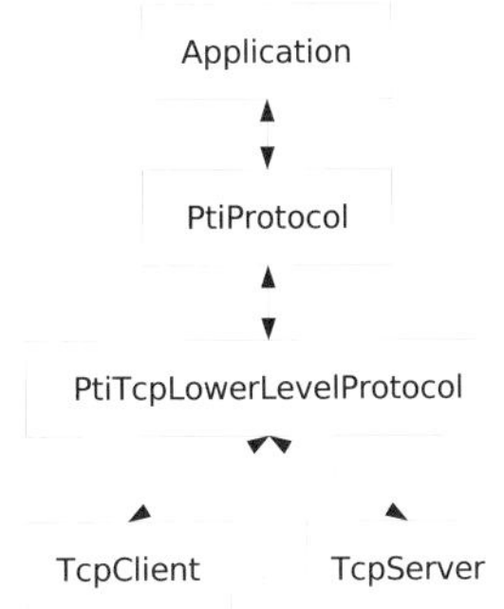

Figure 7. Design of our prototype

The `PtiProtocol` class contains the state machine of the protocol presented in Figure 2 and is explained in more details in Section 7.3. As presented above, it is possible for the application to receive objects in specifying a callback during the instantiation of the `PtiProtocol`.

The `PtiTcpLowerLevelProtocol` class is responsible for making the interface between the TCP communication layer and the `PtiProtocol`. This implies transforming byte arrays into messages (i.e., `IMessage`) understandable by the `PtiProtocol` and vice versa. To that end the `PtiTcpLowerLevelProtocol` uses the serializer specified during the instantiation of the `PtiProtocol`. This can be either a `BinarySerializer`, a `XMLSerializer` or a `SOAPSerializer`. We explain here briefly the characteristics of each serializer:

Binary serialization: This form of serialization has the advantages of preserving type fidelity, meaning that the *entire* state of an object is serialized/deserialized (i.e., including non-public fields), and being efficient. Its implementation is comparable to serialization in Java.

---

[8] In the current implementation of our prototype, the receiver can express interest in one type only. Moreover, another limitation is that the same piece of code is used to initialize a sender or a receiver, which means that even if a sender is not interested in any type, it has to provide one to the `PtiProtocol` constructor.

XML serialization: The XML serialization, in contrast, neither preserves type fidelity (only public fields are considered) nor is efficient. However this mechanism is very useful for applications which are not to be restricted by the data types they use, because it enables the use of objects without being forced to have the type describing it. Indeed, as the XML serialization serializes the object in a human-readable format, it is not necessary to know at runtime the type of the serialized object received in order to take benefit of its public fields. With access to public fields without deserialization, objects can consequently be efficiently (pre)filtered while in transit [6]. However, on the other hand, in order to take advantage of those fields, one must provide its own deserialization mechanisms.

SOAP serialization: This third serialization mechanism combines the benefits of both previously presented mechanisms, by being essentially an XML serialization, yet providing the possibility of exploiting the .NET advanced serialization mechanisms, i.e, *customizable* serialization and deserialization. Moreover, the SOAP serialization allows to serialize an object and its fields without imposing any design guidelines (special constructor, etc).

These serialization mechanisms are used to transform the different type of messages our protocol deals with, namely: (1) `ObjectMsg`, (2) `TDMsg`, (3) `AssemblyMsg`, (4) `RequestMsg` and (5) `UnderlyingTIsMsg`. The `ObjectMsg` represents the type of the message that is sent when a sender wants to send an object through the wire. It contains the serialized object together with the `TypeInfo` of the type of the object. The `TDMsg` is used to carry the type description of a type whereas the `AssemblyMsg` carries the assembly (i.e., code) of the type of an object. The `RequestMsg` is sent when the receiver needs either an assembly (at the end of the complete interoperable tests) or a type description (at the end of a simple interoperable test). Finally the `UnderlyingTIsMsg` is not sent through the wire, like the other messages, but is a state machine internal message.

7.3. Protocol

The `PtiProtocol` class can be split in two other main classes: the `PtiDispatcher` and the `PtiStateMachine`. The first class is used to store the different received messages and to dispatch them to the state machine or to send a request for the missing data (i.e., either for downloading the type descriptions or the assemblies). Moreover, the `PtiDispatcher` is responsible for storing the different instances of the running state machines. Indeed, for each instance of a protocol, a state machine is initialized. Each instance of a protocol is assigned an identifier which lets the `PtiDispatcher` choose the corresponding state machine according to the protocol message it received. This architecture allows for the instances of the protocol to be independent and consequently the receiver is not blocked by a sender if the latter one does not respond anymore and can therefore receive objects from other senders. Figure 8 depicts the general behavior of the `PtiDispatcher`.

Our protocol state machine uses the "state pattern" in which each state corresponds to a specific class. The state machine stores the different states and runs the current state up to the final one. The current state of the state machine is updated by the states themselves, i.e., at the end of its execution, a state specifies to the state machine the new

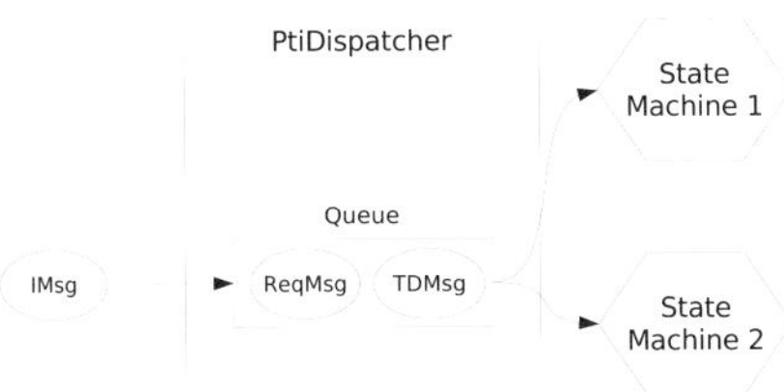

Figure 8. Behavior of the `PtiDispatcher`

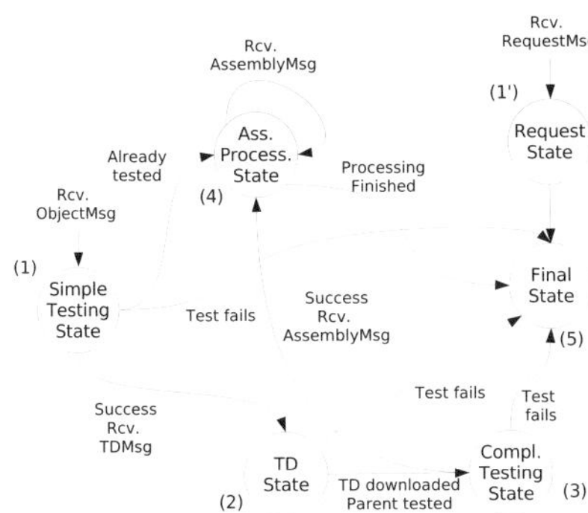

Figure 9. State machine of our protocol

state to execute. Figure 9 illustrates our state machine and details our protocol presented in Figure 2.

You can notice that our state machine contains six main different states.[9] We briefly describe each of them in the following:

Simple Testing State: Upon reception of an object together with its `TypeInfo` we can distinguish three cases: (1) the tests over the `TypeInfo` fail, (2) the tests have already been done on an object of the same type and the type of the received object is interoperable with the type of interest and (3) the `TypeInfo` of the type of the object interoperates with the `TypeInfo` of the type of interest, but it is the first time that such an object (and `TypeInfo`) is received. In the first case, the state machine switches into the *Final State* and the object is dropped. In the second case, the state machine switches into the *Assembly Processing State*. In the last case, the state machine switches into the *TD State*.

Request State: Upon reception of a request message, the requested data (i.e., `TypeDescription` or `Assembly`) are transferred back to the requesting node and the state machine switches into the *Final State*.

TD State: During this state, the type descriptions of the type as well as its supertypes are downloaded (if needed) but before downloading the type descriptions, the

---

[9]In our prototype, the *TD State* is furthermore split in three different states, but for sake of simplicity, we describe them all here without distinction.

`TypeInfo` of the supertypes are downloaded (if necessary) in order to apply simple interoperable tests over them. If the simple tests succeed the complete type descriptions are downloaded, stored into a `Repository`, together with the `TypeInfo` (to prevent downloading multiple times the same `TypeInfo` and `TypeDescription`) and the state machine switches into the *Complete Testing State*, otherwise the type descriptions do not need to be downloaded, the object is dropped and the state machine switches into the *Final State*.

Complete Testing State: During this state, the complete interoperability tests are performed. If the tests fail, the object is dropped and the state machine switches into the *Final State*. Otherwise, the state machine switches into the *Assembly Processing State*. During the complete interoperability tests, a mapping is dynamically created between the methods and fields of the type of interest and the methods and fields of the type of the object. This mapping is stored in a `MappingTable` and will be used by the dynamic proxy for dispatching the calls to the right methods.

Assembly Processing State: In this state, the assemblies of the type (and supertypes) of the received object are downloaded, the object is deserialized and the dynamic proxy is created. Finally, the state machine switches into the *Final State*.

Final State: In this state, all the resources that the state machine uses are garbage collected.

7.4. Type Interoperability Rules

In .NET (and also in Java), one can only create a dynamic proxy for an abstract type (i.e., and interface). This basically means that our prototype can only deal with abstract types as type of interest. Consequently, the rules described in Section 6 must be rewritten. Most of them remain the same (with some minor modifications), except the constructors rule that is removed and the supertypes rule that is changed. The .NET specific rules are presented in Figure 10.

Name: This aspect remains the same. Please see Figure 6 for its description.

Fields: This rule remains the same. The only modification is that now fields refer to either `Property`, `Event`, `Indexer` types as only those fields are acceptable in a .NET interface.

Method (i): This rule remains quite the same. But a particular care must be taken for the arguments of methods as well as their return types. Indeed, if the arguments/return type of a method interoperates "only" implicitly, those arguments then must be interface type, because in this case, dynamic proxies have to be used (and only interfaces are usable with dynamic proxies). T_i *isinterface* denotes that T_i is an interface.

It might be possible that the arguments (or the return type) are equivalent or interoperate explicitly. In this case they do not need to be interfaces. To take into account this property without changing all the different rules, the tests of equivalence ($T == T'$) and explicit interoperability ($T \leq_E T'$) have been added. Those tests are already present in the implicit structural interoperability rule, but as they are combined, in the method interoperability rule (i), with the test of being an interface or not, they cannot cover the equivalent and explicit interoperability cases, why the redundancy.

Supertypes (ii): This rule changes slightly as there is no need anymore to care about the superclass of a type.

> Method interoperability (.NET version) (i):
> $$T \leq_{Is}^{meth} T' \Rightarrow \forall m'(Perm(a_{1'} : T_{1'}, ..., a_{n'} : T_{n'})) : T_{r'} \in T'$$
> $$\exists m(Perm(a_1 : T_1, ..., a_n : T_n)) : T_r \in T \mid m() \leq_{Is}^{name} m'() \wedge \forall i \in [1, n](T_{i'} == T_i \vee$$
> $$T_{i'} \leq_E T_i \vee (T_{i'} \leq_{Is} T_i \wedge T_{i'} \; isinterface)) \wedge$$
> $$(T_r == T_{r'} \vee T_r \leq_E T_{r'} \vee (T_r \leq_{Is} T_{r'} \wedge T_r \; isinterface))$$
> Supertypes interoperability (.NET version) (ii):
> $$T \leq_{Is}^{hier} T' \Rightarrow (T^{inter} \leq_{Is} T'^{inter})$$
> Strong implicit structural interoperability (.NET version):
> $$T \leq_{Is} T' \Leftrightarrow (T \leq_{Is}^{name} T' \wedge T \leq_{Is}^{hier} T' \wedge T \leq_{Is}^{field} T' \wedge$$
> $$T \leq_{Is}^{meth} T') \vee T == T' \vee T \leq_E T'$$

Figure 10. .NET compliant rules

7.5. Dynamic Proxies

In this section, we first give a brief overview of the concept of dynamic proxies and how they are implemented in .NET and finally present how we use them in our prototype.

7.5.1. Overview

A *dynamic proxy* class is a class that implements a list of interfaces specified at runtime such that a method invocation through one of the interfaces on an instance of the class can be encoded and dispatched to another object through a uniform interface. Thus, a dynamic proxy class can be instantiated to create a typed proxy object for a list of interfaces without requiring any code pre-generation, such as with compile-time tools.

This mechanism is available in the .NET platform [9] under the `RealProxy` abstract class and the `TransparentProxy` class. Extending the `RealProxy` class lets the programmer define a new dynamic proxy class. To do so, a subclass of the `RealProxy` class must define a special constructor and implement a specific `Invoke()` method. The constructor to implement takes only one parameter which is the type to impersonate. The `Invoke()` method takes and returns an `IMessage` object.[10] This method is performed every time a method is called on the dynamic proxy. The return type contains the expected return value (which is type-cast to the real type the invoker expects to receive, that implies the returned value must be an instance of the expected return type). With the help of the `Invoke()` method arguments, it is possible to retrieve the name and the arguments of the real method the caller invoked. Figure 11 shows an implementation of such a dynamic proxy class.

To obtain a dynamic proxy, the `getTransparentProxy()` method is called on an instance of a `RealProxy`. This method returns an instance of a `TransparentProxy` which can be type-cast into the type provided to the constructor of the dynamic proxy class. Figure 12 shows a class that uses such a dynamic proxy. Please note that the `Person` type (Figure 1) is a subtype of the `IPerson` interface (as we can only use interfaces with dynamic proxies in .NET).

7.5.2. .NET Dynamic Proxies in our Protocol

In all the cases (methods, fields, supertypes), a dynamic proxy for the type of interest is created and the `Invoke()` method dispatches the calls to the received object. The

---

[10] The `IMessage` type of the `Invoke()` method is .NET specific and must not be confused with the `IMessage` type that is used by our `PtiProtocol`.

```
public class MyProxy : RealProxy {
 public Object o;
 public MyProxy(Type t, Object o): base(t) {this.o = o;}
 public override IMessage Invoke(IMessage msg) {
  IMethodMessage m = (IMethodMessage)msg;
  MethodInfo method = o.GetType().GetMethod(m.MethodName);
  Object retValue = method.Invoke(o,m.Args);
  return new ReturnMessage(retValue,null,0,
         m.LogicalCallContext, (IMethodCallMessage)m);
 }
}
```

Figure 11. Example of a dynamic proxy

```
public class TestProxy {
 public static void Main(String[] argv) {
   MyProxy mp = new MyProxy(typeof(IPerson),
             new Person(new Name("Bob","Morane")));
   IPerson ip = (IPerson)mp.GetTransparentProxy();
   Console.WriteLine(ip.getName());
 }
}
```

Figure 12. Class using a dynamic proxy

mapping between the method call of the dynamic proxy and the method call of the received object is done via the help of the `IMessage` of the `Invoke()` method as well as with the `MappingTable` built during the complete interoperability tests. The implementation of the `Invoke` method must take a special care of the return types, methods arguments types, and fields types as presented below.

Implicitly structurally interoperable methods: Here, two cases must be taken into account: (1) The return types are implicitly structurally interoperable, (2) the arguments are implicitly structurally interoperable. For these two cases, one must keep in mind that the programmer is interested in a specific type he designed. So he must expect to deal only with instances of this type.

Return types: The programmer expects to receive an instance of a specific type in return of his method call, but instead he receives an instance of a type that is "only" implicitly structurally interoperable. In order to give him what he requests, a specific dynamic proxy must be created for the expected type. The `Invoke()` method of this new dynamic proxy is designed to dispatch the calls of the returned object to the implicitly structurally interoperable one.

Argument types: The types of the arguments, provided upon invocation, of the received object do not match. In that case, a dynamic proxy is created for each argument of the received object. The `Invoke()` method in this case dispatches the calls to the arguments the programmer provided.

Recursion: In the above two cases, specific dynamic proxies to impersonate a specific type are defined. But what if the impersonating type has also methods that have arguments and/or return types that only implicitly structurally interoperable to the impersonated type, i.e. if the implicit structural interoperability has several levels?

In that case, the rules must be applied recursively up to the point where the different types are equivalent or interoperate explicitly.

Due to this recursion, it might happen that the final call to a `simpleMethod()` method of a type T ends up with the following call (in this example T is interoperable with T'): `Proxy`$_T$`(Proxy`$_{T'}$`(obj`$_T$`)).simpleMethod()`[11] which is equivalent to the following call: `obj`$_T$`.simpleMethod()`. This last call is of course much less time consuming than the first one and our prototype has been optimized to deal with such recursive problems (see Section 8).

Implicitly structurally interoperable fields: Let us focus here on either properties, events or indexers (called here "fields"). All these fields can in turn declare methods. This implies, for example, that `a.myProperty` calls the `get()` method of the property (the same applies for indexers) and if the following `a.myProperty += aValue` call is done, the `set()` method is in turn called. For that reason, special care must be taken about the return type of the `get()` method and of the value given to the `set()` method, because there could exist "only" implicit interoperability between the fields of the objects of interest and the ones of the interoperable object. To achieve "complete" transparency, the same mechanisms described above for the methods are used.

Implicitly structurally interoperable supertypes: This case does not imply any special care as if two types have super-abstract types that are implicitly structurally interoperable it implies, according to the rules, that they have methods or fields which are implicitly structurally interoperable. We fall back then into the above two cases, i.e. dealing with several dynamic proxies.

8. Performance

We present here some performance results of our prototype implementation. We first measure the time taken to create the `TypeInfo` of a given type together with its `TypeDescription`. We then present the time taken between the reception of an object up to when it is usable by the application (i.e., the time taken to perform the complete protocol with the simple and complete interoperability tests together with the creation of the dynamic proxy). Next, we compare the invocation time of a method call with the invocation time of the same method call but through a dynamic proxy. We finally present performance measurements on the time taken to call a method through recursive dynamic proxies.

The measurements for the creation of the `TypeInfo` and `TypeDescription` were done on an AMD Athlon XP 1800+, 1GB Ram running on Windows XP Professional whereas all the other performance measurements were done on two Pentiums 3, 1Ghz, 512 MB Ram, Windows 2000 SP2, the network was a 100 Mb/s LAN. All measurements uses the Microsoft .NET Framework 1.0 version 1.0.3705.

---

[11]Where `Proxy`$_T$`(obj`$_{T'}$`)` symbolizes a proxy of type T which targets the object of type T', `obj`$_{T'}$.

8.1. `TypeInfo` and `TypeDescription` *Creation Time*

We have conducted the creation of the `TypeInfo` and `TypeDescription` over all the types of the `mscorlib.dll` (which contains all the core type of the .NET framework).

The mean time to create a `TypeInfo` is equal to 1.09 [ms] whereas the time taken to create a `TypeDescription` is equal to 3.17 [ms].

8.2. *Interoperability Testing*

We measure now the time from the reception of an object until its possible use by the application. This basically means that the object must go through the simple and complete interoperability tests and a dynamic proxy must be created in order for it to be usable by the application layer. The type that the receiver subscribes to is `IA3` and the object received through the wire is `IB3` as presented in Figure 13.

```
Interface IA3 {IA m1(IA2, IA);}
Interface IA2 {int m1(); double m2(float, int, long , double);}
Interface IA: IA2 {IA m3(IA, double, int);}
Interface IB3 {IB m1(IB2, IB);}
Interface IB2 {int m1(); double m2(double, float, long , int);}
Interface IB: IB2 {IB m3(IB, double, int);}
```

Figure 13. Subscribed (`IA3`) and remote (`IB3`) type

According to the rules presented in Section 6, if we want `IB3` to be interoperable with `IA3`, `IA2` must be interoperable with `IB2`, `IA` must be interoperable with `IB` (and vice-versa) and `IB2` must be interoperable with `IA2`.

We measure now the time from the reception of the object until the creation of the dynamic proxy. The very same object is sent by the sender hundred times but before each reception of an object, all the variables at the receiver side are reset (i.e., the simple and complete interoperable tests are performed each time). Moreover, each experiment is averaged five times for each different serializer (i.e., binary serializer, soap serializer and XML serializer). These averages are shown in Figure 14 together with the time taken to check the interoperability of type `IB3` with `IA3` as if the code of those types were available locally (i.e., such that no information is sent through the network).

We can notice that, for every serializer, the first test takes more time than the other ones. This is due to the initialization of the different classes of our protocol (e.g., class loading, heap allocation). Once the first test is performed, the local tests take around 75 [ms] to perform whereas the binary, soap and XML serializers take 120 [ms], 150 [ms] and 160 [ms] respectively. The binary serializer is faster than the other serializers and also create smaller messages.

Figure 15 depicts the very same tests except that now the variables that are used to store the results of the interoperable tests are not reset. Consequently the results obtained are much faster as the state machine only goes through the *Simple Testing State* and *Assembly Processing State* (without having to download the code). We can notice that the interoperable tests for types that have already been tested are more than 100 times faster than the time for taken to test a new type for interoperability. These times are quite the same for every serializers and is around 0.6-0.7 [ms].

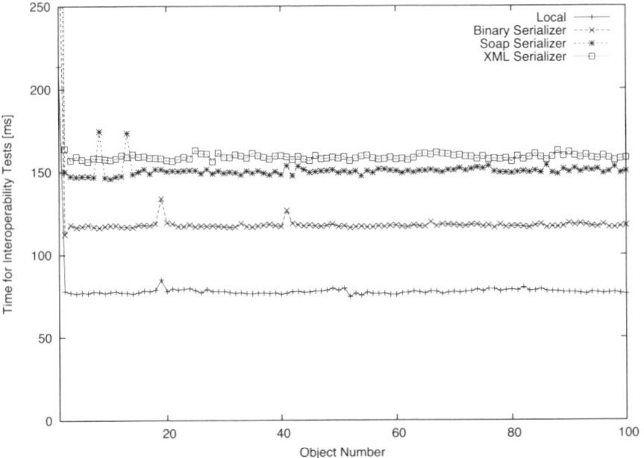

Figure 14. Time taken for the tests of interoperability without memory

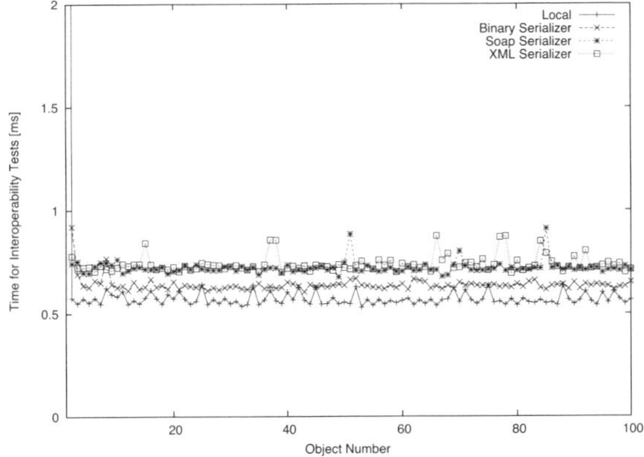

Figure 15. Time taken for the tests of interoperability with memory

8.3. Dynamic Proxy

We now present in Figure 16 the invocation time (averaged over 100 computations) of a Fibonacci method for different parameter values. We measure this invocation time for a direct method call and for a call through a dynamic proxy. We can observe that the overhead due to the use of the dynamic proxy is constant for any value of the parameter. This overhead corresponds to 7-9 [ms].

In the second test, we measured the efficiency of our recursion optimization (see Section 7). To that end, we consider the following recursive method:

```
public IA1 a1(IA1 object, int recursion) {
   if (recursion <= 0) return new IA1();
   else return object.a1(object, recursion -1);
}
```

Consider also the following declaration (where `recObj` is of type `IB1` interoperable with type `IA1`):

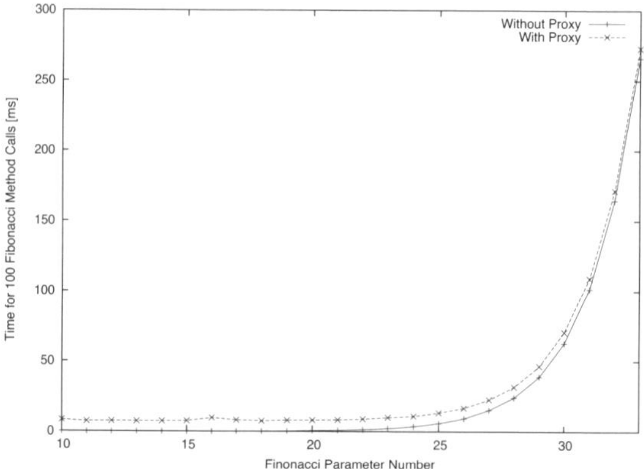

Figure 16. Invocation time on a Fibonacci method with variable parameter n

```
AProxy proxy = new AProxy(typeof(IA1), recObj);
IA1 tpA = (IA1)proxy.GetTransparentProxy();
IA1 paramA = new A1();
IA1 res = tpA.a1(paramA, anInt);
```

The value of `anInt` determines the number of recursive proxy calls (see Table 1).

Table 1. Total number of proxy calls with respect to the value of `anInt`

`anInt == 0`	one call on `tpA`
`anInt == 1`	one call on `tpA`, one call on $\text{Proxy}_{IB1}(\text{paramA})$
`anInt == 2`	one call on `tpA`, two calls on $\text{Proxy}_{IB1}(\text{paramA})$, one call on $\text{Proxy}_{IA1}(\text{Proxy}_{IB1}(\text{paramA}))$
...	...
`anInt == n`	total number of proxy calls $== \frac{n(n+1)}{2} + 1$

Consequently, the order of proxy calls is $O(n^2)$, where n is equal to the recursion level. This means that without optimization, the performance will drop quickly. This is exemplified by Figure 17 where we measure the invocation time for 1000 recursive method calls either directly or through a proxy (with our optimization or not).

We can see that for a 0 level recursion, it takes 8 [s] to perform all the invocations through a dynamic proxy whereas it is instantaneous without a proxy (this is due to the 8 [ms] overhead shown before). What it is interesting to see is that without optimization the invocation time through dynamic proxies increases quadratically, as expected. On the contrary, with optimization, the overhead of one method call is constant and is at most equal to two times the overhead of a call through a dynamic proxy, no matter the number of recursions.

9. Concluding Remarks

This paper addresses the issue of type interoperability in a distributed environment. We make transparent for the programmer the use of one type for another, even if these types

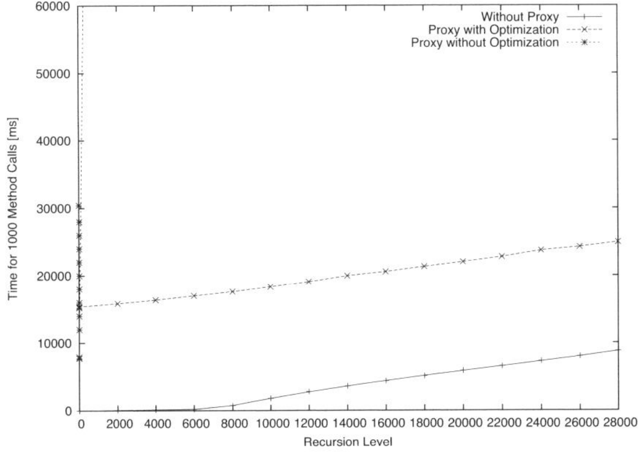

Figure 17. Invocation time for 1000 method calls

do not exactly have the same methods or names, as long as they aim at representing the same software module. We believe this form of interoperability to be crucial in modern distributed computing where several software modules, possibly developed by different programmers, on different languages and systems, need to be unified. Our approach can also be used to extend CORBA or Java RMI with type interoperability capabilities.

One obvious application of type interoperability is type-based publish/subscribe (TPS) [7]. With TPS, subscribers express their interests in events of a given type and publishers produce events of specific types. The main issue with TPS is that the subscribers and the publishers must agree a priori on the types they want to transfer/receive. Enhancing TPS with type interoperability would simply alleviate this problem. Another possible application of this form of interoperability is the borrow/lend (BL) abstraction [5]. In this application *lenders* can lend *resources* to *borrowers* via specific criteria. A possible criterion is *type interoperability*, for a type T_B with which the lent resource's type T_L must interoperate.

In general, combining type interoperability with language interoperability makes the use of object-oriented middleware systems more attractive. One of the main issues in such systems is indeed that the different programmers must agree on a common type system or, at least, on a common way of describing types. This kind of assumption is far from being trivial in distributed dynamic systems where new types can be defined and exchanged on the fly, which changes the type hierarchy continuously.

Our approach is based on implicit structural type interoperability rules and relies on an optimistic transport protocol. The implicit structural type interoperability we have defined relaxes the strong assumptions of a type system. However, even if our rules have been written in a general way, we are aware that we cannot ensure complete interoperability for all the possible cases and that it might happen that two types are considered to interoperate when they are not.

Finally, we have pointed out that the price for having type interoperability in a distributed system is not so high in comparison with the possibilities offered by such an enhanced system.

References

[1] S. Balzer, P. Th. Eugster, and B. Meyer. Can Aspects implement Contracts. In *The 2nd International Workshop on Rapid Integration of Software Engineering Techniques (RISE 2005)*, 2005.

[2] A.P. Black, N. Hutchinson, E. Jul, H.M. Levy, and L. Carter. Distribution and Abstract Types in EMERALD. *IEEE Transactions on Software Engineering*, SE-13(1):65–76, January 1987.

[3] M. Büchi and W. Weck. Compound Types for Java. In *Proceedings of the 13th ACM Conference on Object-Oriented Programming Systems, Languages and Applications*, pages 362–373, October 1998.

[4] *C# Language Specification*. http://www.ecma-international.org/publications/standards/Ecma-334.htm, 2005.

[5] P.Th. Eugster and S. Baehni. Abstracting Remote Object Interaction in a Peer-2-Peer Environment. In *2002 Joint ACM Java Grande - ISCOPE Conference*, November 2002.

[6] P.Th. Eugster, P. Felber, R. Guerraoui, and S.B. Handurukande. Event Systems: How to Have Ones Cake and Eat It Too. In *Proceedings of the IEEE International Workshop on Distributed Event-Based Systems*, pages 625–630, July 2002.

[7] P.Th. Eugster, R. Guerraoui, and C.H. Damm. On Objects and Events. In *Proceedings of the 16th ACM Conference on Object-Oriented Programming Systems, Languages and Applications*, pages 131–146, October 2001.

[8] J. Gosling, B. Joy, G. Steele, and G. Bracha. *The Java Language Specification*. Addison-Wesley, 2005.

[9] K. M. Hussain. *Microsoft .NET Programming Tutorial*. Dotnetrox web site, 2001.

[10] G. Kiczales, J. Lamping, A. Menhdhekar, Ch. Maeda, C. Lopes, J.-M. Loingtier, and J. Irwin. Aspect-oriented programming. In *Proceedings of the 11th European Conference on Object-Oriented Programming (ECOOP '97)*, pages 220–242, June 1997.

[11] K. Läufer, G. Baumgartner, and V.F. Russo. Safe Structural Conformance for Java. Technical Report CSD-TR-96-077, Department of Computer Sciences, Purdue University and West Lafayette, December 1996.

[12] V. I. Levenshtein. *Binary Codes Capable of Correcting Deletions, Insertions and Reversals*, volume 163, chapter 4. Doklady Akademii Nauk SSSR, 1965.

[13] S. Liang and G. Bracha. Dynamic Class Loading in the Java Virtual Machine. In *Proceedings of the 13th ACM Conference on Object-Oriented Programming Systems, Languages and Applications*, pages 36–44, October 1998.

[14] B. Liskov and J. M. Wing. A Behavioral Notion of Subtyping. *ACM Transactions on Programming Languages and Systems*, 16(6):1811–1841, November 1994.

[15] P. A. Muckelbauer and V. F. Russo. Lingua Franca: An IDL for Structural Subtyping Distributed Object Systems. In *Proceedings of the USENIX Conference on Object-Oriented Technologies (COOTS'95)*, pages 117–133, June 1995.

[16] OMG. *The Common Object Request Broker: Architecture and Specification*, 2001.

[17] Sun. *Java Core Reflection API and Specification*, 1999.

Section 3

Applications

Global Data Management
R. Baldoni et al. (Eds.)
IOS Press, 2006

Towards Scalability
of Similarity Searching

Pavel Zezula, Vlastislav Dohnal, David Novak
Faculty of Informatics, Masaryk University, Brno, Czech Republic

Abstract. With the increasing number of applications that base searching on similarity rather than on exact matching, novel index structures are needed to speedup execution of similarity queries. An important stream of research in this direction uses the metric space as a model of similarity. We explain the principles and survey the most important representatives of index structures. We put most emphasis on distributed similarity search architectures which try to solve the difficult problem of scalability of similarity searching. The actual achievements are demonstrated by practical experiments. Future research directions are outlined in the conclusions.

Keywords. similarity search, scalability, distributed index structure, metric space, peer-to-peer network

1. Introduction

There is no doubt that the proliferation of new data types will lead to change or dramatic extension of one of the most fundamental data processing paradigms, namely searching. It seems that the binary YES or NO classification for the data entities retrieved and not desired will be substituted by a gradual assessment of relevance, which naturally implies a sort of ranking with respect to a user-defined reference, model, or other idealized specification of desired data. Though other possibilities are expected in the future, such a search paradigm is typically designated as the *similarity search*.

In this chapter, we summarize the latest efforts in similarity searching using *metric space* as a theoretical abstraction. We briefly summarize ideas and principles, as well as generic partitioning and search strategies which have been developed for similarity search in metric spaces. The wide spectrum of existing methods is illustrated by a short description of two orthogonal approaches to design of index structures: the M-tree, based on a hierarchical dynamic decomposition of metric data, and the D-index that applies a multilevel hashing.

The second part of the chapter concentrates on scalable and distributed techniques for similarity search. Specifically, we describe four methods of metric space indexing developed recently. The first two structures follow the basic *ball* and *generalized hyperplane* partitioning principles, respectively. The other two apply transformation strategies – the metric similarity search problem is transformed into a series of range queries executed on existing distributed structures for exact matching. Each of the structures is able to execute similarity queries for any metric and they all exploit parallelism during query processing. A concise summary of extensive performance trials is also reported.

2. Foundations of Metric Space Searching

The area of similarity searching is a hot topic for both research and commercial applications. Current data processing applications cope with considerably less structured data and with much less precise queries than traditional database systems. Examples are multimedia data like images or videos that offer query-by-example search, product catalogs that provide users with preference-based search, scientific data records from observations or experimental analyses such as biochemical and medical data, or XML documents that come from heterogeneous data sources on the Web or in intranets and thus do not exhibit a global schema. Such data can neither be ordered in a canonical manner nor meaningfully searched by precise database queries that would return exact matches. A useful abstraction for nearness is provided by the mathematical notion of *metric space* [1].

Treating data collections as metric objects brings a great advantage in generality, because many data classes and information-seeking strategies conform to the metric point of view. Accordingly, a single metric indexing technique can be applied to many specific search problems quite different in nature. In this way, the important *extensibility* property of access structures is automatically satisfied. An indexing schema that allows various forms of queries, or which can be modified to provide additional functionality, is of more value than a schema otherwise equivalent in power or even better in certain respects, but which cannot be extended.

In general, the search problem can be described as follows:

Problem 1 *Let $\mathcal{D}$ be a domain, d a distance measure on $\mathcal{D}$, and $(\mathcal{D}, d)$ a metric space. Given a set $X \subseteq \mathcal{D}$ of n elements, preprocess or structure the data in X so that proximity queries are answered efficiently.*

From a practical point of view, X can be seen as a file (a dataset or a collection) of objects from the domain $\mathcal{D}$ along with d as the proximity measure, i.e., the distance function defined for an arbitrary pair of objects from $\mathcal{D}$. Though several types of similarity queries exist and others are expected to appear in the future, the basic types are known as the *similarity range* and the *nearest neighbor(s)* queries.

2.1. Metric Spaces

Suppose a metric space $\mathcal{M} = (\mathcal{D}, d)$ defined for a domain of objects (or the objects' *keys* or *indexed features*) $\mathcal{D}$ and a total (distance) function d. In this metric space, the properties of the function $d : \mathcal{D} \times \mathcal{D} \mapsto \mathbb{R}$, sometimes called the metric space postulates, are typically characterized as:

$$\forall x, y \in \mathcal{D}, d(x, y) \geq 0 \qquad\qquad \text{non-negativity,}$$

$$\forall x, y \in \mathcal{D}, d(x, y) = d(y, x) \qquad\qquad \text{symmetry,}$$

$$\forall x, y \in \mathcal{D}, x = y \Leftrightarrow d(x, y) = 0 \qquad\qquad \text{identity,}$$

$$\forall x, y, z \in \mathcal{D}, d(x, z) \leq d(x, y) + d(y, z) \qquad\qquad \text{triangle inequality.}$$

For brevity, some authors call the *metric function* simply the *metric*. All indexing techniques described in this article work for an arbitrary metric, e.g., the *Minkowski distance* (L_p metrics), the *quadratic form distance* functions [2,3], the *edit distance*, also called the *Levenshtein distance* [4], the *Jaccard's coefficient*, or the *Hausdorff distance* [5], to name a few of them.

2.2. Similarity Queries

A similarity query is defined by a query object q and a constraint on the form and extent of proximity required, typically expressed as a distance. The response to a query returns all objects that satisfy the selection conditions, presumed to be those objects close to the given query object.

Probably the most common type of similarity query is the *similarity range query* $R(q, r)$. The query is specified by a query object $q \in \mathcal{D}$, with some query radius r as the distance constraint. The query retrieves all objects found within the distance r of q, formally:

$$R(q, r) = \{o \in X \mid d(o, q) \leq r\}.$$

If needed, individual objects in the response set can be ranked according to their distance with respect to q. Observe that the query object q does not necessarily exist in the collection $X \subseteq \mathcal{D}$ to be searched, and the only restriction on q is that it belongs to the metric domain $\mathcal{D}$. For convenience, Figure 1a shows an example of a range query. In a geographic application, a range query can formulate the requirement: *Give me all French restaurants within a distance of three kilometers from my hotel.*

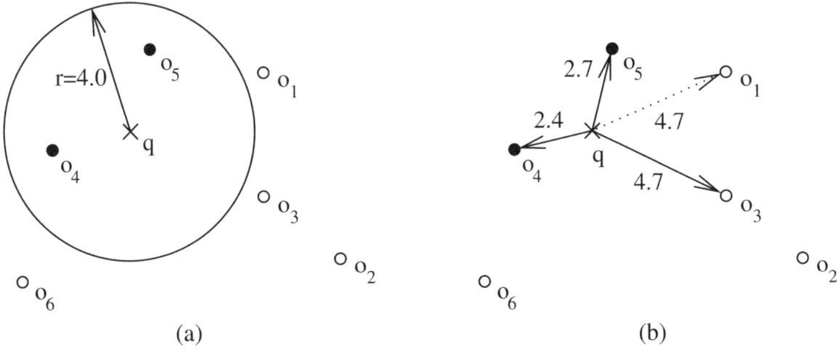

Figure 1. (a) Range query $R(q, 4.0)$ and (b) nearest neighbor query $3NN(q)$.

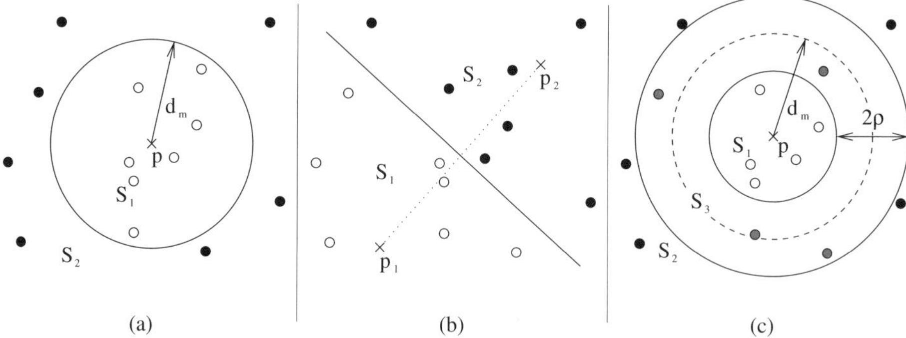

Figure 2. Examples of partitioning: (a) the ball partitioning, (b) the generalized hyperplane partitioning, and (c) the excluded middle partitioning.

An alternative way to search for similar objects is to use *nearest neighbor queries*. The elementary version of this query finds the closest object to the given query object, that is the nearest neighbor of q. The concept can be generalized to the case where we look for the k nearest neighbors. Specifically, $kNN(q)$ query retrieves the k nearest neighbors of the object q. If the collection to be searched consists of fewer than k objects, the query returns the whole database. Formally, the response set can be defined as follows:

$$kNN(q) = \{R \subseteq X, |R| = k \wedge \forall x \in R, y \in X \setminus R : d(q, x) \leq d(q, y)\}.$$

When several objects lie at the same distance from q as the k-th nearest neighbor, the ties are solved arbitrarily. Figure 1b illustrates the situation for a $3NN(q)$ query. Here the objects o_1, o_3 are both at distance 4.7 and the object o_3 is chosen as the third nearest neighbor (at random), instead of o_1. If we continue with our geographic application, we can pose a query: *Tell me which two French restaurants are the closest to my hotel.*

2.3. Partitioning Principles

Partitioning, in general, is one of the most fundamental principles of any storage structure, aiming at dividing the search space into sub-groups, so that once a query is given, only some of these groups are examined when evaluating the query. Given a set $S \subseteq \mathcal{D}$ of objects in metric space $\mathcal{M} = (\mathcal{D}, d)$, Uhlmann [6] defines *ball partitioning* and *generalized hyperplane partitioning*, while Yianilos [7] suggests *excluded middle partitioning*. In the following, we briefly characterize these techniques.

Ball partitioning breaks the set S into subsets S_1 and S_2 using a spherical cut with respect to $p \in \mathcal{D}$, where p is the *pivot*, chosen arbitrarily. Let d_m be the median of $\{d(o, p), \forall o \in S\}$. Then all $o \in S$ are distributed to S_1 or S_2 according to the following rules:

- $S_1 \leftarrow \{o \mid d(o, p) \leq d_m\}$,
- $S_2 \leftarrow \{o \mid d(o, p) \geq d_m\}$.

The redundant conditions $\leq$ and $\geq$ assure balance when the median value is not unique. This is accomplished by assigning each element at the median distance to one of the subsets in an arbitrary, but balanced, fashion. An example of a data space containing fourteen objects is depicted in Figure 2a. The selected pivot p and the median distance d_m establish the ball partitioning.

Generalized hyperplane partitioning can be considered as an orthogonal principle to ball partitioning. This schema also breaks the set S into subsets S_1 and S_2. This time, though, two reference objects (pivots) $p_1, p_2 \in \mathcal{D}$ are arbitrarily chosen. All other objects $o \in S$ are assigned to S_1 or S_2 depending upon their distances from the selected pivots as follows:

- $S_1 \leftarrow \{o \mid d(p_1, o) \leq d(p_2, o)\}$,
- $S_2 \leftarrow \{o \mid d(p_1, o) \geq d(p_2, o)\}$.

In contrast to ball partitioning, the generalized hyperplane does not guarantee a balanced split, and a suitable choice of reference points to achieve this objective is an interesting challenge. An example of a balanced split of a hypothetical dataset is given in Figure 2b.

Excluded middle partitioning [7] divides S into three subsets S_1, S_2 and S_3. In principle, it is an extension of ball partitioning which has been motivated by the following fact: Though similarity queries search for objects lying within a small vicinity of the query object, whenever a query object appears near the partitioning threshold, the search process typically requires accessing both of the ball-partitioned subsets. The central idea of excluded middle partitioning is therefore to leave out points near the threshold d_m in defining the two subsets S_1 and S_2. The excluded points form the third subset S_3. An illustration of excluded middle partitioning can be seen in Figure 2c, where the shaded objects fall into the exclusion zone. With such an arrangement, the search for similar objects always ignores at least one of the subsets S_1 or S_2, provided that the search selectivity is smaller than the *thickness* of the exclusion zone. Naturally, the excluded points cannot be lost, so they can either be considered to form a third subset or, if the set is large, the basis of a new partitioning process. Given the thickness of the exclusion zone 2ρ, the partitioning can be defined as follows:

- $S_1 \leftarrow \{o \mid d(o, p) \leq d_m - \rho\}$,
- $S_2 \leftarrow \{o \mid d(o, p) > d_m + \rho\}$,
- $S_3 \leftarrow$ otherwise.

Figure 2c also depicts a situation where the split is balanced, i.e., the cardinalities of S_1 and S_2 are the same. However, this is not always guaranteed.

2.4. Filtering Principles

Since the performance of similarity search in metric spaces is not only I/O-bounded, but also CPU-bounded, it is very important to limit the number of evaluations of expensive distance function as much as possible. To this aim, pruning conditions must be applied not only to avoid accessing irrelevant sets of objects, but also to minimize the number of distances computed. The rationale behind such strategies is to use already-evaluated distances between some objects, while

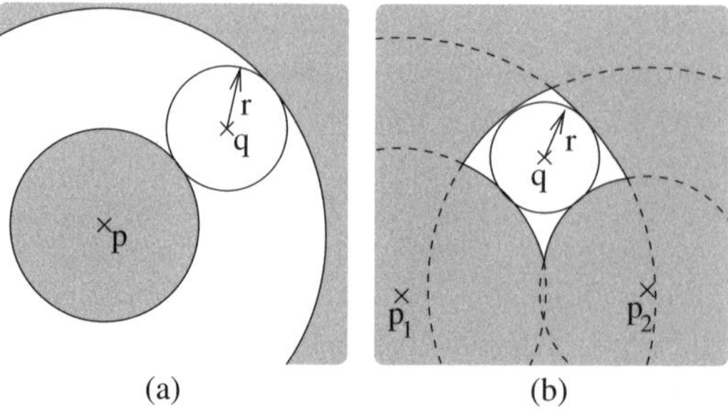

(a)   (b)

Figure 3. Illustration of filtering technique: (a) using a single pivot, (b) using a combination of pivots.

properly applying the metric space postulates – namely the triangle inequality, symmetry, and non-negativity – to determine bounds on distances between other objects.

Given a range query $R(q, r)$, we can eliminate database objects by applying the following lemma, provided we know the distance between p and all database objects.

Lemma 1 *Given a metric space* $\mathcal{M} = (\mathcal{D}, d)$ *and three arbitrary objects* $q, p, o \in \mathcal{D}$, *it is always guaranteed:*

$$|d(q, p) - d(p, o)| \leq d(q, o) \leq d(q, p) + d(p, o).$$

Consequently, the distance $d(q, o)$ *can be bounded from below and from above, provided the distances* $d(q, p)$ *and* $d(p, o)$ *are known.*

This constraint called the *Object-Pivot Distance Constraint* [8,9] helps estimate the distance between the query object q and any database object o, knowing the distances $d(q, p)$ and $d(p, o)$. If the lower bound on distance $d(q, o)$ is greater than the query radius, the object o can be eliminated immediately. This situation is demonstrated in Figure 3a, where the white area contains objects that cannot be eliminated under such a distance criterion. After elimination, a search algorithm would proceed by inspecting all remaining objects and comparing them against the query object using the distance function d, i.e., for all non-discarded objects o, verify the query condition $d(q, o) \leq r$.

To achieve a greater degree of pruning, several pivots can be combined into a single *pivot filtering* technique [10]. The underlying idea is shown in Figure 3b where the reader can observe the improved filtering effect for two pivots. We formalize this concept in the following lemma.

Lemma 2 *Assume a metric space* $\mathcal{M} = (\mathcal{D}, d)$ *and a set of pivots* $P = \{p_1, \ldots, p_n\}$. *We define a mapping function* $\Psi \colon (\mathcal{D}, d) \to (\mathbb{R}^n, L_\infty)$ *as follows:*

$$\Psi(o) = (d(o, p_1), d(o, p_2), \ldots, d(o, p_n)).$$

Then, we can bound the distance $d(q, o)$ *from below:*

$$L_\infty(\Psi(q), \Psi(o)) = \max_{i=1}^{n} |d(q, p_i) - d(o, p_i)| \le d(q, o).$$

The mapping function Ψ returns a vector of distances from an object o to all pivots in P. For a database object, the vector actually contains the pre-computed distances to pivots. On the other hand, the application of Ψ on a query object q requires computation of distances from the query object to all pivots in P. Once we have the vectors $\Psi(q)$ and $\Psi(o)$, the lower bound criterion can be applied to eliminate the object o if $|d(q, p_i) - d(o, p_i)| > r$ for any $p_i \in P$. The white area in Figure 3b represents the objects that cannot be eliminated from the search using two pivots. These objects will still have to be tested directly against the query object q with the original metric function d. Notice that the mapping Ψ is *contractive*, that is the distance $L_\infty(\Psi(o_1), \Psi(o_2))$ is never greater than the distance $d(o_1, o_2)$ in the original metric space.

3. Centralized Index Structures for Large Databases

Many metric index structures are described in recent surveys [11,8,9], some of them defined as main memory structures. In the following, we concentrate on two typical disk-oriented representatives able to manage large collections of data.

3.1. Metric Tree Family

A dynamic structure called the Metric Tree (M-tree) is proposed in [12]. It can handle data files that change size dynamically, which becomes an advantage when insertions and deletions of objects are frequent. In contrast to other metric trees, the M-tree is built bottom-up like B-trees by splitting its fixed-size nodes. Each node is constrained by a sphere-like (ball) region of the metric space. In Figure 4a, ball regions around the pivots o_1, o_2, o_4, o_7 and o_{10} are shown. Notice that pivots can even be repeated in the M-tree several times, e.g., the objects o_1 and o_2. A leaf node entry contains a data object and its distance from the pivot kept in the parent node. Each internal node entry keeps a child node pointer, the pivot and the covering radius of the ball region that bounds all objects indexed below, and the distance from this pivot to its parent pivot. An example of M-tree is presented in Figure 4b. Obviously, the distance to the parent pivot has no meaning for the root, which is expressed by '-.-' in the figure. The pruning effect of search algorithms is achieved by respecting the covering radii and the distances from objects to their pivots in parent nodes.

Dynamic properties in storage structures are highly desirable but typically have a negative effect on performance. Furthermore, the insertion algorithm of the M-tree is not deterministic and inserting objects in different order results in different trees. That is why the *bulk-loading* algorithm has been proposed in [13]. The basic idea of this algorithm works as follows: Given a set of objects, the initial clustering produces l sets of relatively close objects. This is done by choosing l distant objects from the set and promoting them to pivots. The remaining objects get assigned to the nearest pivot. Then, the bulk-loading algorithm is invoked for

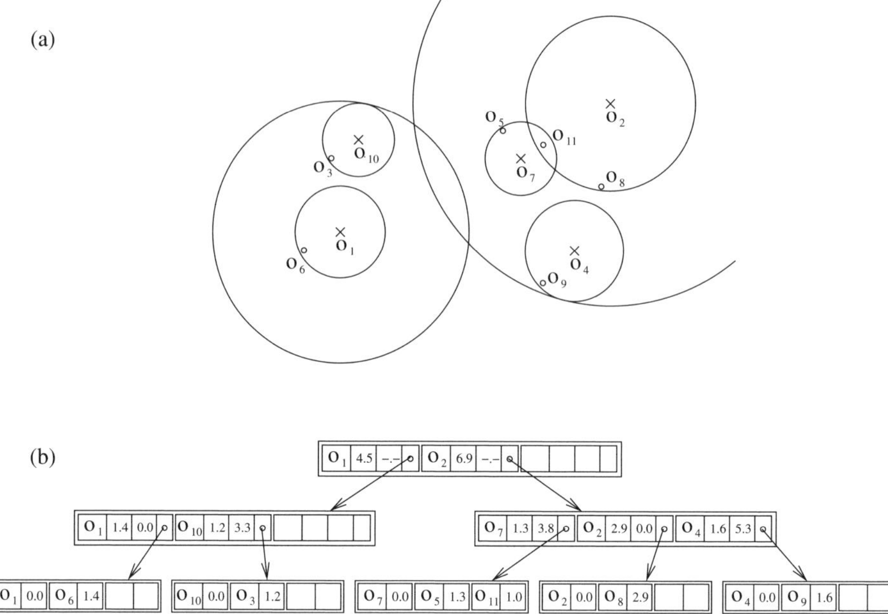

Figure 4. Example of an M-tree: (a) a 2-D representation of partitioning; pivots are denoted by crosses and the circles around pivots correspond to values of covering radii; (b) a tree structure consisting of three levels.

each of these l sets, resulting in an unbalanced tree. Special refinement steps are applied to make the tree balanced.

The idea of the M-tree was later extended in [14] to a metric tree structure called the Slim-tree. In order to gain control over the overlap among metric regions, the *fat-factor* is defined and systematically used. The Slim-tree also uses new insertion and split algorithms, which results in improved performance. Another extension of the M-tree insertion algorithm with the objective of building more compact trees was proposed in [15]. Very recently, Skopal [16] has proposed a variant which combines the M-tree with principles of pivot filtering (see Section 2.4) to develop the Pivoting M-tree (PM-tree).

3.2. Distance Index

Similarity Hashing (SH), as proposed in [17], is built upon a completely different principle than the M-tree. It is a multi-tier hashing structure, consisting of search-separable sets on each tier, organized in buckets. The structure supports easy insertion and bounded search costs, because at most one bucket need to be accessed at each level for range queries up to a pre-defined value of the search radius. At the same time, the number of distance computations is always significantly reduced by the use of pre-computed distances obtained at insertion time, as defined in Lemma 2. Buckets of static files can be arranged in such a way that I/O costs never exceed the cost of scanning a compressed sequential file.

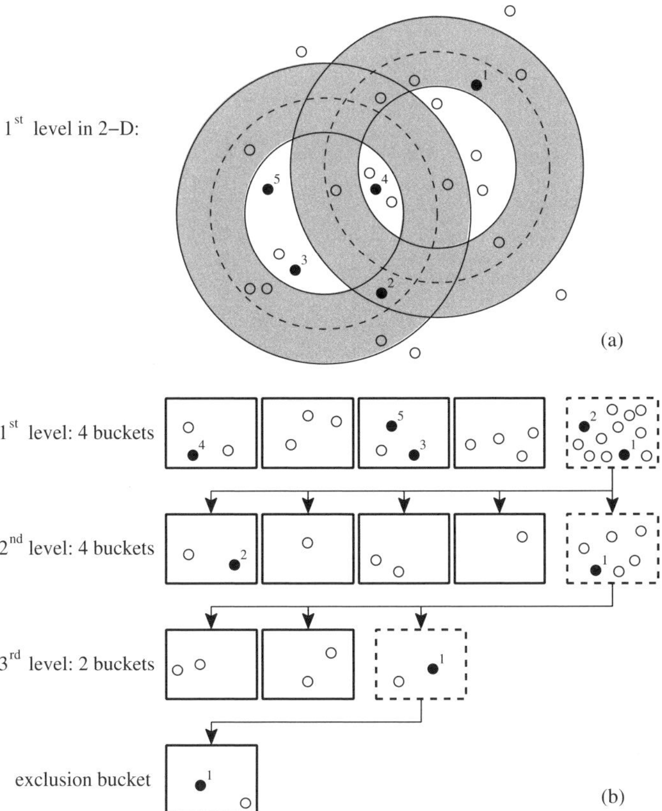

Figure 5. Example of D-index structure: (a) a combination of excluded middle partitioning functions and (b) a resulting three-level structure.

Experimental results demonstrate that the performance of SH is superior to other available tree-based structures.

The similarity hashing approach is exploited in a structure called the Distance Index (D-index) [18]. The D-index applies excluded middle partitioning to hashed organizations. To obtain more than two sets as this partitioning does, the D-index allows combinations of several excluded middle partitioning functions. An example of a combination of two functions is presented in Figure 5a. The combination of more functions still forms the single exclusion zone which is then recursively partitioned on the next level. This procedure creates a multilevel access structure as depicted in Figure 5b. The structure in the example consists of three levels and one exclusion zone stored in the exclusion bucket of the whole structure. In contradistinction to tree-based structures, navigation along the tree branches is unnecessary, and each storage bucket is accessible directly.

In principle, the concept of similarity hashing is not necessarily restricted to the excluded middle partitioning principle. The authors of [19] define another three split functions that are able to achieve the same effect, i.e., to produce sets separable up to a pre-defined distance radius ρ. Based on well-known geometric

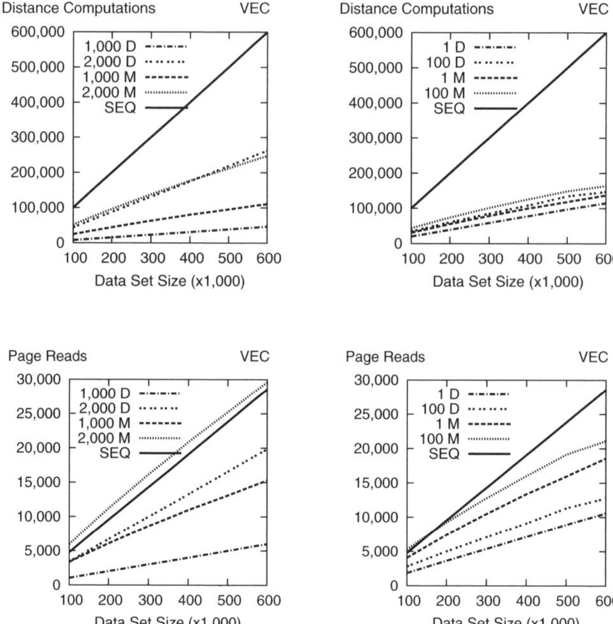

Figure 6. Scalability of range (left) and nearest neighbor queries (right) for the VEC dataset.

concepts, these methods are called the *elliptic, hyperbolic,* and *pseudo-elliptic ρ-split* functions.

3.3. Performance Trials

Extensive performance evaluation published in [10] shows that, depending on the query type and the distance distribution of searched datasets, index structures can speedup search time significantly. However, considering the amount of available data on the web, scalability of search structures with respect to data volume is probably the most important issue to investigate.

Figure 6 presents scalability of range and nearest neighbor queries in terms of distance computations and memory block accesses. In these experiments, the VEC dataset (45-dimensional color vectors compared by the quadratic form distance function) is used and the amount of data grows from 100,000 up to 600,000 objects. Apart from the SEQ (sequential) organization, individual curves are labeled by a number indicating either the count of nearest neighbors or the search radius, and a letter, where 'D' stands for the D-index and 'M' for the M-tree. The basic lessons learned from these experiments are twofold:

- similarity search is expensive;
- in terms of scalability, the behavior of centralized indexes is practically linear.

Of course, there are differences in search costs among individual techniques, but the global outcome is that the search costs grow linearly with the dataset size. This property makes their applicability to huge data archives more difficult, because, after a certain point, centralized indexes become inefficient for users' needs.

Suitable solutions arise from two possibilities. First, increased performance may be obtained by sacrificing some precision in search results. This technique is called *approximate similarity search* and many suitable solutions can be found in [20,21]. Second, more storage and computational resources may be used to speed up executions of queries. The main idea here is to modify centralized solutions by considering parallel environments and to develop distributed structures. We elaborate on this issue in the following section.

4. Scalable and Distributed Index Structures

The huge amounts of digital data that are produced nowadays make heavy demands on scalability of the data-oriented applications. The previous section indicates that the similarity search is inherently expensive and even though sophisticated dynamic disk-oriented index structures can reduce both computational and I/O costs, the similarity indexing approach would require some radical changes if a swift processing of large datasets is requested.

A way to achieve this goal is to shift from centralized data structures towards distributed environment. This step provides not only easily enlargeable and practically unlimited storage capacity, but especially significant potentiation of the system computational power and the possibility of exploiting parallelism during the query processing.

In this section, we provide descriptions of four specific approaches to the design of distributed structures for similarity search based on the metric space model. They form overlay structures based on the *Peer-to-Peer* (P2P) paradigm which inherently provides extensibility, fault tolerance, and self-organization of the *peers*, i.e., autonomous and equivalent nodes composing the system. The introduced architectures can also be considered to be *Scalable and Distributed Data Structures* (SDDS) [22] since they meet the following requirements:

- Data expands to new nodes gracefully, and only when the nodes already used are efficiently loaded.
- There is no master site to be accessed when searching for objects, e.g., there is no centralized directory.
- The data access and maintenance primitives, e.g., search, insertion, split, etc., never require atomic updates to multiple nodes.

The fundamental idea of the first two approaches, GHT* and VPT* [23,24], is to base the structure purely on the principles of metric indexing, namely on the *generalized hyperplane partitioning* and *ball partitioning* schemas, respectively (see Section 2.3). The other two, MCAN [25] and M-Chord [26], adopt an orthogonal approach and use transformation strategies – the metric similarity search problem is converted into the issue of range queries, which has already been addressed in the Peer-to-Peer environment. Consequently, existing distributed structures may be exploited, namely the CAN [27] in order to resolve multi-dimensional range queries for the MCAN and the Chord [28] for answering one-dimensional range queries in the case of the M-Chord structure.

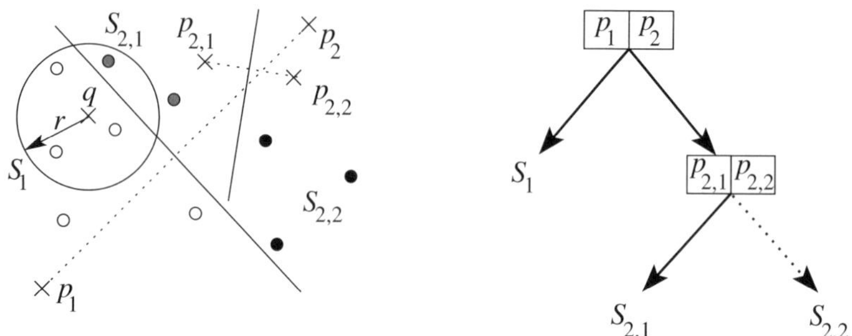

Figure 7. Example of a Generalized Hyperplane Tree, tree branches accessed by the query are emphasized.

4.1. Distributed Generalized Hyperplane Tree

The *Distributed Generalized Hyperplane Tree* (GHT*) [23,24] is the first distributed data structure published and is based on the metric indexing principles. It exploits generalized hyperplane partitioning (see Figure 2b on Page 4) in order to build up a distributed binary tree [29].

Let us briefly introduce the Generalized Hyperplane Tree (GHT) [6] as one of the basic metric index structures and as the foundation of the GHT*. The GHT is a binary tree that is built by a recursive selection of two pivots and partitioning of the set of objects by the generalized hyperplane schema. The process of partitioning starts with the whole dataset and proceeds until the size of the sets gets below a predefined limit. Figure 7 depicts an example of a two level GHT built over a set of fourteen objects with the leaf size limit of six objects. As well as the partitioning schema, the tree is not necessarily balanced.

Given a range similarity query $R(q, r)$, the GHT search algorithm traverses the tree from the root to leaves. In each internal node with pivots p_1, p_2, the distances $d(q, p_1)$ and $d(q, p_2)$ are computed. These values are used in the following step in order to skip accessing the subtree that certainly does not contain any object from the query scope. The distances between object q and any object in the subtree may be estimated by means of the *Double-Pivot Distance Constraint* [8,9] based on the triangle inequality property of metric function d.

Lemma 3 *Assume a metric space* $\mathcal{M} = (\mathcal{D}, d)$ *and objects* $o, p_1, p_2 \in \mathcal{D}$ *such that* $d(p_1, o) \le d(p_2, o)$. *Given a query object* $q \in \mathcal{D}$ *and the distances* $d(p_1, q)$, $d(p_2, q)$, *the distance* $d(q, o)$ *is lower-bounded as follows:*

$$max\left\{ \frac{d(p_1, q) - d(p_2, q)}{2}, 0 \right\} \le d(q, o).$$

The GHT search algorithm does not access a subtree if this lower bound is greater than the search radius r. Please, note that both subtrees can be accessed – see an example in Figure 7 in which both branches are followed from the root node and finally the leaves S_1 and $S_{2,1}$ are visited. Reaching a leaf node, the distance

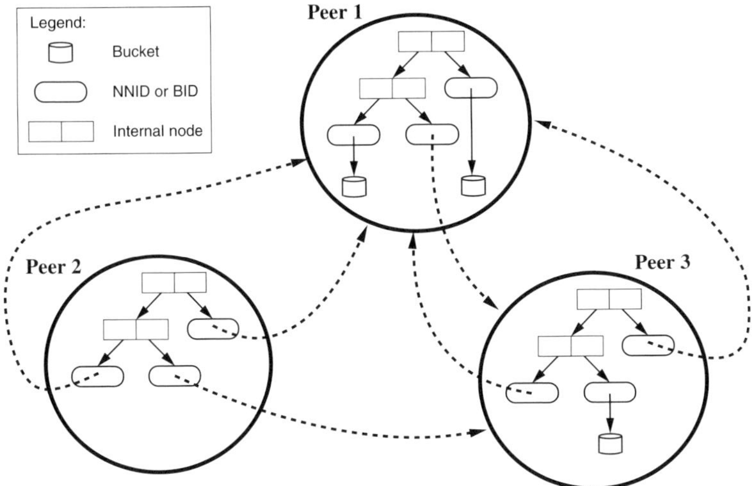

Figure 8. Architecture of the GHT* system – the Address Search Tree.

$d(q, o)$ is evaluated for every object o stored in this node and the objects that fulfill the query are returned.

Every peer in the GHT* system provides a set of storage areas of limited capacity that are called *buckets*. Buckets are labeled uniquely within the peer by *BID* identifiers. The peers themselves are globally identified by labels denoted as *NNID* (Network Node ID). The architecture of the system and its navigation schema are determined by a binary *Address Search Tree* (AST) based on the GHT principles. Internal nodes consist of two pivots in the GHT manner and leaf nodes point either to a local bucket (BID) or to another peer (NNID). Figure 8 provides an example of the overall GHT* structure.

In a dynamic distributed structure it would be inappropriate to keep full up-to-date replicas of the AST in all peers. Therefore, every peer maintains only those root-leaf branches that lead to one of its local buckets and the remaining pointers are substituted by NNIDs of peers responsible for the respective parts of the AST. Therefore, only a limited number of peers are contacted and updated when the system structure changes.

Any peer of the system may initiate an *insert* operation. This peer traverses its local AST part using generalized hyperplane partitioning in the internal nodes and possibly follows the NNID pointer by forwarding the operation to the respective peer until a bucket is reached and the new object is stored. An overfilled bucket is split by selecting two pivots, creating an AST internal node, and allocating a new bucket either on the local peer or on another peer if necessary.

The processing of a range query follows the original GHT algorithm. The search algorithm ends up in a set of buckets on several peers. Next, the buckets are fully searched and the partial answers are returned to the peer that initiated the query. During an insertion process, distances between the inserted object and all pivots on the root-bucket path are evaluated. These precomputed values are stored together with the object and are exploited at query time for further filtering

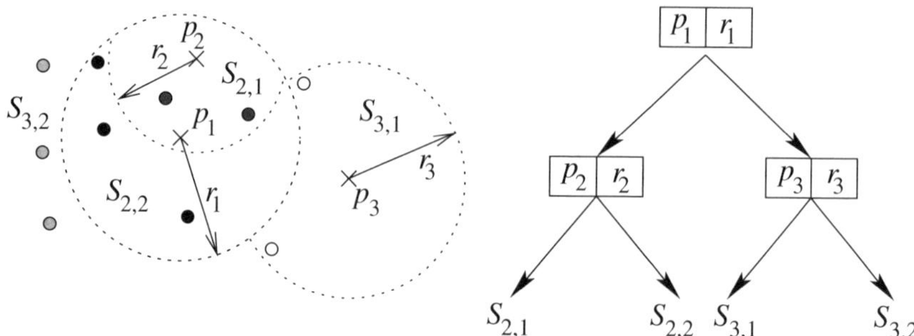

Figure 9. Example of a Vantage Point Tree.

by virtue of the triangle inequality property of the metric distance function (for details refer to Section 2.4).

Please note that we have achieved the desired property of performing the computational intensive operations on multiple peers in a parallel manner. There is a price to be paid for the communication costs of sending operation requests and returning replies.

The algorithm for $kNN(q)$ is also defined on the GHT* structure. The queries are resolved in two consecutive phases:

1. Search the bucket that would store q and find the k nearest objects within this bucket. Measure the distance d_k from q to the k-th nearest object found.
2. Execute the range query $R(q, d_k)$ and return the k nearest objects from the query result (skip the bucket already visited).

If less than k objects are stored in the bucket examined in the first phase then some other radius-estimation techniques are employed [24] possibly resulting in multiple range queries with growing radius.

4.2. Distributed Vantage Point Tree

The VPT* is the twin structure of the GHT* sharing the system architecture. The only difference is in the partitioning schema used and respective space pruning principles since the VPT* employs ball partitioning and builds a distributed version of the *Vantage Point Tree* (VPT) [30].

Figure 9 provides an example of a VPT structure which recursively applies ball partitioning (see Figure 2a on Page 4) to the indexed set until a predefined storage size limit for leaves is reached. Since in every step the set is split equally according to the median of distances between the pivot and objects, the static VPT is balanced. But the structure dynamism – in the sense of gradual object insertions and leaf-node splitting – makes the tree potentially unbalanced.

The VPT* search algorithm follows the same general strategy as the GHT* and differs in the tree branches pruning schema. The ball partitioning provides the lower and upper bounds on the distances between a pivot and objects in the outer and inner subset, respectively. Thus, the *Range-Pivot Distance Constraint* [8,9], described in the following lemma, is used to prune the search space.

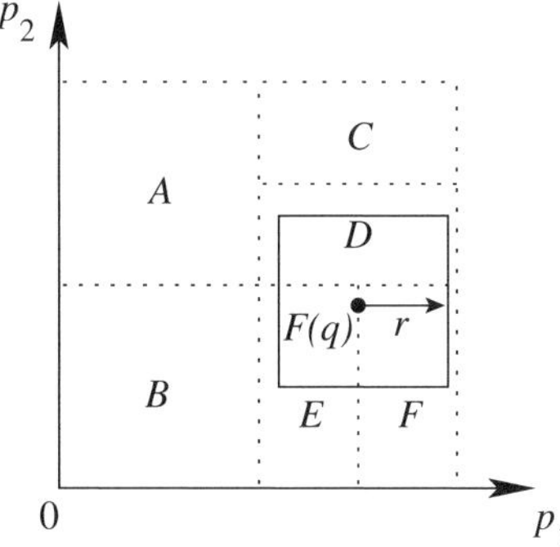

Figure 10. Logical structure of the Metric CAN.

Lemma 4 *Given a metric space* $\mathcal{M} = (\mathcal{D}, d)$ *and objects* $o, p \in \mathcal{D}$ *such that* $r_l \leq d(p, o) \leq r_h$, *and given some* $q \in \mathcal{D}$ *and an associated distance* $d(q, p)$, *the distance* $d(q, o)$ *can be restricted by the range:*

$$max\{d(p, q) - r_h, r_l - d(p, q), 0\} \leq d(q, o) \leq d(p, q) + r_h.$$

Having a range query $R(q, r)$, this lemma is employed and the actual lower bounds on the distances from q to objects in the left and right branches are obtained. If one of these bounds is greater than r, the respective branch is not accessed.

4.3. Metric Content Addressable Network

As mentioned above, the Metric CAN (MCAN) [25] is a transformation technique which employs an existing solution in order to build a distributed data structure for metric space indexing. It defines a mapping from the general metric space into an n-dimensional vector space which is then used for data partitioning and navigation by means of the P2P protocol CAN (*Content Addressable Network*) [27].

Having a set of n pivots $p_1, p_2, \ldots, p_n$ preselected from a sample dataset, the mapping $\Psi \colon \mathcal{D} \to \mathbb{R}^n$ is defined as follows:

$$\Psi(o) = (d(o, p_1), d(o, p_2), \ldots, d(o, p_n)), \forall o \in \mathcal{D}. \tag{1}$$

Every peer takes over responsibility for a *zone* (hypercuboid) of the n-dimensional space and stores data objects having Ψ-values within this zone. See an example of such a zoning of two-dimensional space in Figure 10. This partitioning as well as the routing algorithm follow the CAN protocol. Every peer maintains a routing table that contains the network identifiers and the coordinates of its neighbors in the vector space. In order to locate the peer responsible for a given key $k \in \mathbb{R}^n$, the routing algorithm recursively passes the query to the neighboring peer that is geometrically the closest to the target point k in the space. The average number of neighbors per peer is proportional to the space's dimension n while the average number of hops to reach a peer is inversely proportional to this value.

When inserting a new object o into the MCAN structure, the peer that initiates the operation first computes the $\Psi(o)$ coordinates using Eq. 1. The pivots $p_1, \ldots, p_n$ needed in the mapping are selected by a specialized algorithm from a sample dataset on the first peer startup and they are common to all peers. The insertion request is forwarded (using the CAN navigation) to the peer responsible for the n-dimensional $\Psi(o)$ key. The target peer stores the object o. When a peer reaches its storage size limit it performs a split operation if there is a free peer available. The peer's zone is split into two hypercuboid parts dividing the storage equally. One of the new zones is assigned to the new active peer and the routing tables of the neighboring nodes are eventually updated.

Because the mapping Ψ is contractive, a range query $R(q, r)$ can be transformed into an n-dimensional range query – the hypercube with side $2r$ centered in $\Psi(q)$. In Figure 10, a two-dimensional example is presented. All peers intersecting this hypercube have to be visited in order to finish processing of the range query $R(q, r)$ (the peers D, E, and F in the example). These relevant peers are identified by a CAN-based *multicast algorithm* [31,32]. Next, the peers are examined to find qualifying objects. This process is accelerated by applying the filtering technique in Lemma 2 on Page 7. Any object o for which the inequality $\exists i : |d(p_i, q) - d(p_i, o)| > r$ holds can be directly discarded without evaluating $d(q, o)$. The efficiency of this filtering can be further improved by using additional pivots $p_{n+1}, p_{n+2}, \ldots, p_m$ regardless of the CAN dimensionality n. The distances between these pivots and database objects have to be evaluated and stored during insertion. The filtering technique is utilized in the GHT* and VPT* in a similar way.

The algorithm for $kNN(q)$ similarity queries adopts analogous two-phase approach as the GHT* (see Section 4.1). The first phase finds the upper bound on the distance from q to its k-th nearest neighbor by exploring the peer that would store q. The second phase executes the range query that covers the detected upper bound.

4.4. Metric Chord

Analogously to the MCAN approach, the M-Chord [26] defines a transformation of the original metric data space. The fundamental idea is to map the space into a one-dimensional domain and to link up this domain with the P2P routing protocol Chord [28].

The mapping is defined using the vector indexing method *iDistance* [33,34], but generalized to metric spaces. This technique partitions the vector space into n clusters $(C_0, C_1, \ldots, C_{n-1})$, identifies reference points within the clusters $(p_0, p_1, \ldots, p_{n-1})$, and maps the data objects according to their distances from the cluster's reference point. Having a separation constant c that avoids clusters' overlaps, the *iDistance* value for an object $o \in C_i$ is

$$idist(o) = d(p_i, o) + i \cdot c.$$

This mapping schema is visualized in Figure 11a. When a range query $R(q, r)$ is to be processed, several *iDistance* intervals are specified for the clusters that intersect the query sphere – see an example in Figure 11b.

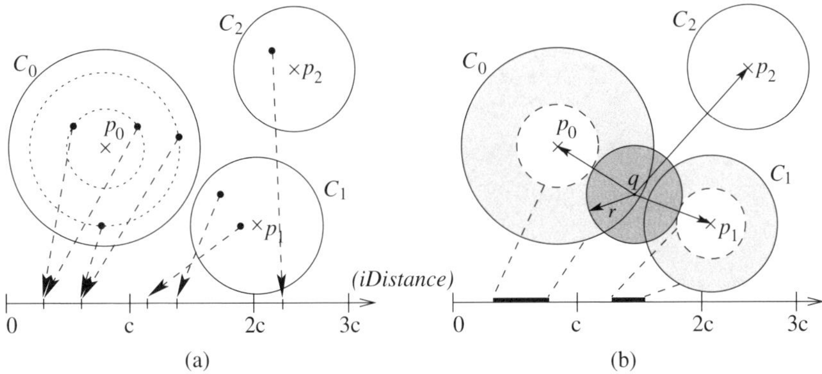

Figure 11. The principles of the *iDistance* method.

Since there is no coordinate system in general metric space, the *iDistance* space partitioning and selection of reference points are not applicable to the metric space generalization of the method. Therefore, a set of n pivots $p_0, p_1, \ldots, p_{n-1}$ is selected in order to maximize the filtering effect and the space is partitioned according to these pivots. Specifically, the Voronoi-like partitioning is applied, i.e., every object is assigned to its closest pivot.

Because the *iDistance* domain is to be used as the key space for the Chord protocol (described in detail below), the domain has to be *normalized* by an order-preserving hash function h into the M-Chord domain of size 2^m. The parameter m should be large enough to make the probability of hash collisions negligible. In the ideal case, the resulting domain would have a uniform distribution in order to fully preserve the routing performance of the Chord. The function h is defined so that it is uniform with respect to the distribution of a given sample dataset. If the distribution of the indexed dataset significantly differs from the sample set, the Chord performance is damaged. Applying the function h, the M-Chord key-assignment formula becomes, for an object $o \in C_i$, $0 \leq i < n$:

$$m\text{-}chord(o) = h(d(p_i, o) + i \cdot c). \tag{2}$$

Once the data space is mapped into the one-dimensional M-Chord domain, the responsibility for intervals of this domain is divided between active peers of the system. The navigation within the system is supplied by the P2P routing protocol Chord [28]. This protocol presumes that each of the participating peers is assigned a key from the indexed domain. The peers are shaped into a virtual circle (modulo the domain size 2^m) and every peer is responsible for the keys between the key of its predecessor on the circle and its own key. The peers maintain information about two neighbors on the circle and about up to m long-distance peers which ensure the localization of the peer responsible for a given key through, with high probability, logarithmic number of forward messages.

Figure 12 shows the logical architecture of the system. The part (a) of the figure provides a schema of the insert operation of an object $o \in \mathcal{D}$ into the structure. First, the initiating peer N_{ins} computes the $m\text{-}chord(o)$ key using Eq. 2

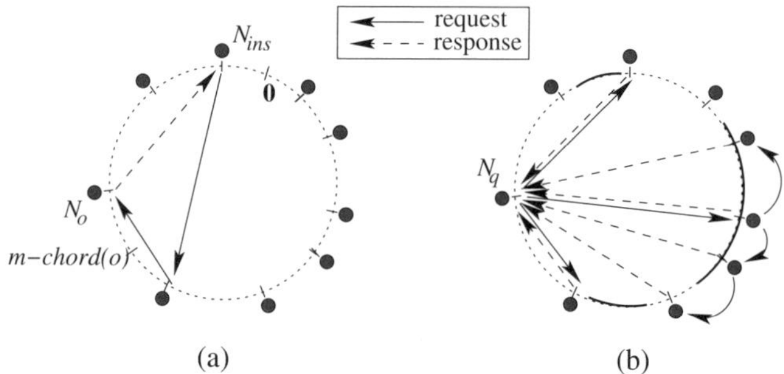

Figure 12. The schema of (a) the insert and (b) range operation for the M-Chord structure.

and then employs the Chord to forward a store request to the peer N_o responsible for the computed key. Peers store data objects in a B^+-tree according to their M-Chord keys. When a peer reaches its storage size limit it executes a split. A new peer is placed on the M-Chord circle, so that the requester's storage is split evenly.

Since the data mapping is based on the *iDistance* technique, several M-Chord intervals of interest may be determined for a range query $R(q, r)$. The peer N_q that initiates the query identifies these intervals and the Chord protocol is then employed in order to reach the peers responsible for the midpoints of the intervals. Finally, the request is spread to all peers covering the particular interval (refer to Figure 12b).

Through the *iDistance* pruning technique, the objects $o \in C_i$ that fulfill condition $|d(o, p_i) - d(q, p_i)| > r$ for any p_i are filtered out. Such a filtering can be performed with respect to all n pivots in the sense of Lemma 2 on Page 7. When inserting an object o into the M-Chord and evaluating Eq. (2), the distances $d(o, p_i)$ are computed $\forall i : 0 \leq i < n$. These values get stored along with the object o and the improved filtering using all pivots is applied at query time in order to avoid unnecessary distance evaluations.

The general strategy for a $kNN(q)$ query processing is similar to the strategy adopted by the distributed structures introduced above. The first phase goes through the leaf level of the B^+-tree on the peer that is responsible for the key m-chord(q). After finding k objects "near" q and setting an upper bound on the distance from q to its k-th nearest neighbor, the second phase executes a range query that ensures an efficient completion of the query processing.

5. Experience from Performance Trials

The step towards distributed data structures for similarity searching was motivated by insufficient scalability of centralized structures. The inherently heavy computational demands of similarity query processing, as the most critical aspect, are reduced due to parallelism. The number of computations of the distance function is considered as the most important indicator of efficiency of centralized index structures (see Section 3.3). The equivalent of this quantity in distributed and parallel environment is the *parallel number of distance computations* – the maximum number of distance evaluations performed in a serial manner during query processing.

The price to be paid for the utilization of parallelism are the costs of communication among the nodes of a distributed system. The relative importance of the communication costs depends on the implementation area of the structure. Since all the systems introduced in the previous section are described on the level of principles, they can be implemented, e.g., within a cluster of computers, over a dedicated set of workstations connected into a high-speed LAN, or as a world-wide peer-to-peer overlay network. Because all the presented approaches expect the intra-system communication via a message passing protocol, the following two criteria can be considered in order to measure the communication costs:

- *total number of messages* – the number of all messages (requests and responses) sent during a query processing,
- *maximum hop count* – the maximum number of messages sent in a serial way in order to complete a query.

The results presented in this section have been obtained from performance experiments conducted on prototype implementations of the four structures described above. The detailed analysis of the experiments is provided in [35]. The systems grow dynamically as the volume of stored data increases – provided that there is sufficiency of resources to enlarge the system. In the described experiments, the storage capacity of individual peers is 5,000 data objects for all the systems (five buckets with capacity 1,000 in the case of the GHT* and the VPT*). The average storage load ratio was about 66%, which results in approximately 300 active peers for the dataset size of 1,000,000 objects which is the maximum file size tested.

Figure 13 depicts the scalability trends of processing of range queries $R(q; 1,500)$ for the four structures while increasing the dataset size. The dataset and the distance function used are identical to the dataset VEC introduced in Section 3.3, i.e. the 45-dimensional vectors of color images features compared by the quadratic form distance function.

The graph in Figure 13a exhibits a quite stable trend of the parallel number of distance computations for all structures. The noticeable fluctuations of the MCAN are caused by cumulations of splits of multiple overloaded peers. All four algorithms for range queries are designed in such a way that no peer performs significant computations before forwarding requests to other peers. Therefore, the upper limit on the parallel number of distance computations is the maximum number of data objects stored in a single peer which is 5,000 in this setting. The two native approaches, the GHT* and the VPT*, have lower parallel costs than the transformation techniques. The reason is that the usage of buckets spreads the "near" data more widely over the peers while the transformation techniques inherently try to preserve the locality of data. The other side of the coin is the number of peers involved in the query processing. The native techniques demonstrate noticeably higher percentage of visited peers (the GHT* almost all peers even for smaller query radii).

Figures 13b and 13c show the communication costs in the terms of the total number of messages sent and the maximum hop count, respectively. The total

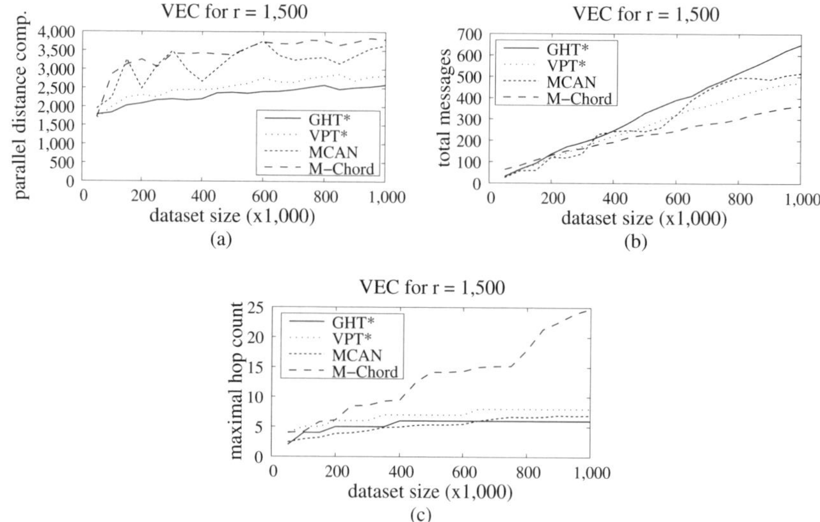

Figure 13. The scalability trends for the range query $R(q, 1,500)$: (a) parallel number of distance computations, (b) total number of messages, and (c) maximum hop count.

messaging grows with the size of the structure because the space area relevant to the range query is covered by more peers. This indicator grows faster for the GHT* because it contacts higher percentage of peers while processing a query. The graphs for M-Chord indicate that the total message costs grow slowly but the major increase is in a serial way of message passing which negatively influences the hop count. This is caused by the, currently sequential, algorithm for message distribution within M-Chord clusters (see Section 4.4). The parallel number of distance computations together with the maximum hop count can be considered as the characterization of the actual response time of the query.

Another positive effect brought by the distributive nature of the structures is the ability to receive and process multiple queries simultaneously if posted from various peers of the system. Then, the so-called *interquery parallelism* can be considered as the level of capability of accepting multiple simultaneous queries. In the following experiment, groups of 10–100 queries were executed at the same moment – each from a different peer. The *overall parallel costs* of the set of queries were measured as the maximum number of distance computations performed on a single peer of the system. This value can be considered as a characterization of the overall response time of the set of queries. The query objects have been selected at random from the dataset and the size of the stored data volume has been fixed at 500,000 objects. Figure 14a shows the overall parallel costs and it can be seen that the actual values are similar for all the structures.

In order to measure the improvement gained from the simultaneous processing of queries, a baseline for the overall parallel costs has been established as the *sum of the parallel costs* of individual queries. The ratio of this sum to the *overall parallel costs* characterizes the improvement achieved by the interquery parallelism and we refer to this ratio as the *interquery improvement ratio*. This value can also be interpreted as the number of queries that can be handled by

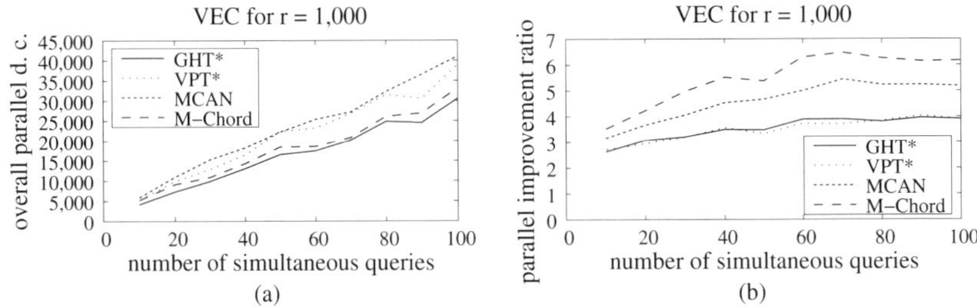

Figure 14. (a) The overall parallel costs and (b) the interquery improvement ratio.

a system simultaneously without slowing down. The graph in Figure 14b shows this ratio and we can see that the improvement is better for the transformation techniques than for the native ones which is mainly caused by different parallel costs of processing of the individual queries.

Our findings can be summarized as follows. The desired scalability of the similarity search has been reached by distributing of query processing over a set of cooperating peers. We introduced and compared four different distributed data structures – two of them based purely on the principles native for the metric indexing (the GHT* and the VPT*) and two techniques that transform the problem of the similarity indexing and take advantage of some existing solutions (the M-Chord and the MCAN).

The native structures spread data and computations more uniformly over the set of peers and, thus, reach shorter response times. On the other hand, the transformation techniques preserve the locality of data and involve fewer peers while answering a query and they gain more from the simultaneous processing of queries. Depending on the amount of resources available, the behavior of the structures, e.g., the upper bound on the response time, can be efficiently tuned by setting the storage capacity of individual peers.

6. Conclusions and Future Research Directions

The notion of similarity has been studied extensively in the field of psychology. In The MIT Encyclopedia of the Cognitive Sciences [36], Robert L. Goldstone says the following about similarity: "An ability to assess similarity lies close to the core of cognition. The sense of sameness is the very keel and backbone of our thinking. An understanding of problem solving, categorization, memory retrieval, inductive reasoning, and other cognitive processes require that we understand how humans assess similarity." With the increasing diversity of digital data types covering practically all forms of fact representation, computerized data processing must respect these natural principles and provide adequate tools for similarity searching.

By assuming the metric space model of similarity, we have surveyed the recent achievements in developing index structures that would speedup execution of similarity queries in large collections of data. We have defined the principles of metric searching and shortly explained functionality of two orthogonal indexing principles based on tree decomposition and hashing, respectively. We have also reported on recent developments in distributed similarity search architectures, the scalability of which has been demonstrated by real-life experiments on prototype systems.

In spite of the impressive number and variety of exiting computerized search structures, they are all based on the "divide and conquer" paradigm. In other words, given a collection of data, the structure divides objects into buckets (partitions or even computer nodes in a network) so that once a query is posed, only some of them need to be searched. The idea is simple and pragmatic because, in general, a job can finish earlier if there is less work to be done.

Scalable and distributed structures use centralized entities neither for search nor for maintenance transactions while dynamically adding new computational and storage resources. Provided that enough reliable computational power is available, this approach solves the problem of scalability, and the performance can even be tuned to the needs of specific applications. However, it is still the organization which decides where to store data – the "divide and conquer" paradigm is still applied – which naturally implies a lot of data transfer among participating nodes.

However, many autonomous information resources (digital libraries, databases, Web servers) already exist in current computer networks. They maintain their own data which can be searched and answers can be passed even to the outside world. But they want to retain a total control over their own data resources. Unless explicitly required, they also do not accept somebody else's data for storage. Such a situation calls for a radical change of the underlying search paradigm. The biggest challenge is to find self-organized solutions that would evolve in time and still scale to the expected data volumes. Such an initiative must be based on new solid theoretical grounds to avoid a possibly quick but ad hock solutions which sooner or later fail due to their not rigorous definitions and unpredictable behavior. Such a future research challenge should certainly go beyond capabilities of the traditional computer science and should try to find inspiration in other scientific areas, such as social sciences, biology, or mathematical theories of epidemic diseases.

References

[1] J. L. Kelly. *General Topology.* D. Van Nostrand, New York, 1955.

[2] J. L. Hafner, H. S. Sawhney, W. Equitz, M. Flickner, and W. Niblack. Efficient color histogram indexing for quadratic form distance functions. *IEEE Transactions on Pattern Analysis and Machine Intelligence (TPAMI 1995)*, 17(7):729–736, 1995.

[3] T. Seidl and H.-P. Kriegel. Efficient user-adaptable similarity search in large multimedia databases. In *Proceedings of the 23rd International Conference on Very Large Data Bases (VLDB 1997), Athens, Greece, 1997*, pages 506–515. Morgan Kaufmann, 1997.

[4] V. I. Levenshtein. Binary codes capable of correcting spurious insertions and deletions of ones. *Problems of Information Transmission*, 1:8–17, 1965.

[5] D. P. Huttenlocher, G. A. Klanderman, and W. J. Rucklidge. Comparing images using the Hausdorff distance. *IEEE Transactions on Pattern Analysis and Machine Intelligence (TPAMI 1993)*, 15(9):850–863, 1993.

[6] J. K. Uhlmann. Satisfying general proximity/similarity queries with metric trees. *Information Processing Letters*, 40(4):175–179, 1991.

[7] P. N. Yianilos. Excluded middle vantage point forests for nearest neighbor search. In *Proceedings of the 6th DIMACS Implementation Challenge: Near Neighbor Searches (ALENEX 1999), Baltimore, Maryland, 1999*, 1999.

[8] G. R. Hjaltason and H. Samet. Index-driven similarity search in metric spaces. *ACM Transactions on Database Systems (TODS 2003)*, 28(4):517–580, 2003.

[9] P. Zezula, G. Amato, V. Dohnal, and M. Batko. *Similarity Search: The Metric Space Approach.* Springer, 2005.

[10] V. Dohnal. *Indexing Structures fro Searching in Metric Spaces.* PhD thesis, Faculty of Informatics, Masaryk University in Brno, Czech Republic, 2004. http://www.fi.muni.cz/~xdohnal/phd-thesis.pdf.

[11] E. Chávez, G. Navarro, R. A. Baeza-Yates, and J. L. Marroquín. Searching in metric spaces. *ACM Computing Surveys (CSUR 2001)*, 33(3):273–321, September 2001.

[12] P. Ciaccia, M. Patella, and P. Zezula. M-tree: An efficient access method for similarity search in metric spaces. In *Proceedings of the 23rd International Conference on Very Large Data Bases (VLDB 1997), Athens, Greece, 1997*, pages 426–435. Morgan Kaufmann, 1997.

[13] P. Ciaccia and M. Patella. Bulk loading the M-tree. In *Proceedings of the 9th Australasian Database Conference (ADC 1998), Perth, Australia, 1998*, volume 20(2) of *Australian Computer Science Communications*, pages 15–26. Springer, 1998.

[14] C. Traina, Jr., A. J. M. Traina, B. Seeger, and C. Faloutsos. Slim-Trees: High performance metric trees minimizing overlap between nodes. In *Proceedings of the 7th International Conference on Extending Database Technology (EDBT 2000), Konstanz, Germany, 2000*, volume 1777 of *Lecture Notes in Computer Science*, pages 51–65. Springer, 2000.

[15] T. Skopal, J. Pokorný, M. Krátký, and V. Snášel. Revisiting M-Tree building principles. In *Proceedings of the 7th East European Conference on Advances in Databases and Information Systems (ADBIS 2003), Dresden, Germany, 2003*, volume 2798 of *Lecture Notes in Computer Science*. Springer, 2003.

[16] T. Skopal. Pivoting M-tree: A metric access method for efficient similarity search. In *Proceedings of the Annual International Workshop on DAtabases, TExts, Specifications and Objects (DATESO 2004), Desna, Czech Republic, 2004*, volume 98 of *CEUR Workshop Proceedings*. Technical University of Aachen (RWTH), 2004.

[17] C. Gennaro, P. Savino, and P. Zezula. Similarity search in metric databases through hashing. In *Proceedings of the 3rd ACM Multimedia 2001 Workshop on Multimedia Information Retrieval (MIR 2001), Ottawa, Ontario, Canada, 2001*, pages 1–5. ACM Press, 2001.

[18] V. Dohnal, C. Gennaro, P. Savino, and P. Zezula. D-Index: Distance searching index for metric data sets. *Multimedia Tools and Applications*, 21(1):9–33, 2003.

[19] V. Dohnal, C. Gennaro, P. Savino, and P. Zezula. Separable splits in metric data sets. In *Proceedings of the 9th Italian Symposium on Advanced Database Systems (SEBD 2001), Venezia, Italy, 2001*, pages 45–62. LCM Selecta Group, Milano, 2001.

[20] P. Zezula, P. Savino, G. Amato, and F. Rabitti. Approximate similarity retrieval with M-Trees. *The VLDB Journal*, 7(4):275–293, 1998.

[21] G. Amato, F. Rabitti, P. Savino, and P. Zezula. Region proximity in metric spaces and its use for approximate similarity search. *ACM Transactions on Information Systems (TOIS 2003)*, 21(2):192–227, April 2003.

[22] W. Litwin, M.-A. Neimat, and D. A. Schneider. LH* – a scalable, distributed data structure. *ACM Transactions on Database Systems (TODS 1996)*, 21(4):480–525, 1996.

[23] M. Batko, C. Gennaro, and P. Zezula. Similarity grid for searching in metric spaces. In *DELOS Workshop: Digital Library Architectures, Lecture Notes in Computer Science*, volume 3664/2005, pages 25–44. Springer, 2005.

[24] M. Batko, C. Gennaro, and P. Zezula. A scalable nearest neighbor search in P2P systems. In *Proceedings of the 2nd International Workshop on Databases, Information Systems, and Peer-to-Peer Computing (DBISP2P 2004), Toronto, Canada, 2004, Revised Selected Papers*, volume 3367 of *Lecture Notes in Computer Science*, pages 79–92. Springer, 2004.

[25] F. Falchi, C. Gennaro, and P. Zezula. A content-addressable network for similarity search in metric spaces. In *Proceedings of the 3rd International Workshop on Databases, Information Systems, and Peer-to-Peer Computing (DBISP2P 2005), Trondheim, Norway, 2005*, pages 126–137, 2005.

[26] D. Novak and P. Zezula. M-chord: A scalable distributed similarity search structure. Will appear in *Proceedings of First International Conference on Scalable Information Systems (INFOSCALE 2006), Hong Kong, 2006*. IEEE Computer Society, 2006.

[27] S. Ratnasamy, P. Francis, M. Handley, R. Karp, and S. Schenker. A scalable content-addressable network. In *Proceedings of the 2001 Conference on Applications, Technologies, Architectures, and Protocols for Computer Communications (SIGCOMM 2001), San Diego, California, 2001*, pages 161–172. ACM Press, 2001.

[28] I. Stoica, R. Morris, D. Karger, M. F. Kaashoek, and H. Balakrishnan. Chord: A scalable peer-to-peer lookup service for internet applications. In *Proceedings of the 2001 Conference on Applications, Technologies, Architectures, and Protocols for Computer Communications (SIGCOMM 2001), San Diego, California, 2001*, pages 149–160. ACM Press, 2001.

[29] B. Kröll and P. Widmayer. Distributing a search tree among a growing number of processors. In *Proceedings of the 1994 ACM SIGMOD International Conference on Management of Data (SIGMOD 1994), Minneapolis, Minnesota, 1994*, pages 265–276, 1994.

[30] P. N. Yianilos. Data structures and algorithms for nearest neighbor search in general metric spaces. In *Proceedings of the 4th Annual ACM Symposium on Discrete Algorithms (SODA 1993), Austin, Texas, 1993*, pages 311–321. ACM Press, 1993.

[31] M. B. Jones, M. Theimer, H. Wang, and A. Wolman. Unexpected complexity: Experiences tuning and extending can. Technical Report MSR-TR-2002-118, Microsoft Research, 2002.

[32] S. Ratnasamy, M. Handley, R. Karp, and S. Shenker. Application-level multicast using content-addressable networks. In *Proceedings of the 3rd International COST264 Workshop on Networked Group Communication, London, UK, 2001*, volume 2233 of *Lecture Notes in Computer Science*. Springer, 2001.

[33] C. Yu, B. C. Ooi, K.-L. Tan, and H. V. Jagadish. Indexing the distance: An efficient method to knn processing. In *VLDB 2001, Proceedings of the 27th International Conference on Very Large Data Bases, 2001, Roma, Italy*, pages 421–430. Morgan Kaufmann, 2001.

[34] H. V. Jagadish, B. C. Ooi, K.-L. Tan, C. Yu, and R. Zhang. iDistance: An adaptive B^+-tree based indexing method for nearest neighbor search. *ACM Transactions on Database Systems (TODS 2005)*, 30(2):364–397, 2005.

[35] M. Batko, D. Novak, F. Falchi, and P. Zezula. On scalability of the similarity search in the world of peers. Will appear in *Proceedings of First International Conference on Scalable Information Systems (INFOSCALE 2006), Hong Kong, 2006*. IEEE Computer Society, 2006.

[36] Robert L. Goldstone. *The MIT Encyclopedia of the Cognitive Sciences*, chapter Similarity, pages 763–765. MIT Press, 2001.

Global Data Management
R. Baldoni et al. (Eds.)
IOS Press, 2006

"To Infinity and Beyond"[1]: P2P Web Search with Minerva and Minerva∞[2,3]

Matthias Bender[a], Sebastian Michel[a], Peter Triantafillou[b], Gerhard Weikum[a],
Christian Zimmer[a]

[a] *Max-Planck Institute for Informatics, Saarbrücken, Germany*
[b] *RACTI and University of Patras, Rio, Greece*

Abstract. Peer-to-peer (P2P) computing is an intriguing paradigm for Web search for several reasons: 1) the computational resources of a huge computer network can facilitate richer mathematical and linguistic models for ranked retrieval, 2) the network provides a collaborative infrastructure where recommendations of many users and the community behavior can be leveraged for better search result quality, and 3) the decentralized architecture of a P2P search engine is a great alternative to the de-facto monopoly of the few large-scale commercial search services with the potential risk of information bias or even censorship. The challenges of implementing this visionary approach lie in coping with the huge scale and high dynamics of P2P networks. This paper discusses the architectural design space for a scalable P2P Web search engine and presents two specific architectures in more detail. The paper's focus is on query routing and query execution and their performance as the network grows to larger scales.

Keywords. Peer-to-peer system, Web search, distributed information retrieval

1. Introduction

1.1. Motivation

The peer-to-peer (P2P) approach facilitates the sharing of huge amounts of data in a distributed and self-organizing way. These characteristics offer enormous potential benefit for search capabilities powerful in terms of scalability, efficiency, and resilience to failures and dynamics. Additionally, such a search engine can potentially benefit from the intellectual input (e.g., bookmarks, query logs, click streams, etc.) of a large user community participating in the data sharing network. Finally, but perhaps even more importantly, a P2P web search engine can also facilitate pluralism in informing users about internet content, which is crucial in order to preclude the formation of information-resource monopolies and the biased visibility of content from economically powerful sources.

---

[1] From the movie "Toy Story".

[2] This research has been partly funded by the EU Integrated Projects DELIS and AEOLUS.

[3] Correspondence to: Matthias Bender, Max-Planck Institute for Informatics, Stuhlsatzenhausweg 85, D-66123 Saarbrücken, Germany. Tel.: +49 681 9325 500; Fax: +49 681 9325 599; E-mail: mbender@mpi-inf.mpg.de.

Our challenge therefore is to exploit P2P technology's powerful tools for efficient, reliable, large-scale content sharing and delivery to build P2P web search engines. We wish to leverage distributed hash table (DHT) technology and build highly distributed algorithms and data infrastructures that can render P2P web search feasible.

The original architectures of DHT-based P2P networks are typically limited to exact-match queries on keys. More recently, the data management community has focused on extending such architectures to support more complex queries. All this related work, however, is insufficient for text queries that consist of a variable number of keywords, and it is absolutely inappropriate for full-fledged Web search where keyword queries should return a ranked result list of the most relevant approximate matches [18].

The crucial challenge in developing successful P2P Web search engines is based on reconciling the following high-level, conflicting goals: on the one hand, delivering high quality results with respect to precision/recall, and, on the other hand, providing scalability in the presence of a very large peer population and the very large amounts of data that must be communicated in order to meet the first goal. We put forward Minerva and Minerva∞, whose architectures, designs, and implementations offer solutions to these conflicting goals, striking appropriate, albeit different compromises.

1.2. Problem Definition

Our targeted system consists of a number N of peers, P_j, $j = 1, ..., N$, forming a network G. In general, peers are assumed to be independently performing web crawls. A peer P_j at the end of such a crawl constructs and stores one (or more) *index lists*, $I_j(t)$, over a term t (aka. "attribute" or "keyword") of interest. Index lists are essentially inverted indices, one per term, associating the term with the documents which contain it and with numeric scores that capture the relevance of the document for the given term based on statistical models. Thus, the peers store, share, and are used to deliver index lists contents. Each $I_j(t)$ consists of a number of *(docID, score)*-pairs, where score is a real number in $(0, 1]$ reflecting the significance of the document with docID for term t. Each index list is assumed to be sorted in descending order according to score.

Search requests in our P2P web search engine, initiated at a peer P_{init}, have the form of a top-k query, $q(T, k)$, which consists of a nonempty set of terms, $T = \{t_1, t_2, ..., t_m\}$, and an integer k. Assuming the existence of a set of peers storing the data of the most relevant index lists for the terms in T, the fundamental functionality our P2P web search engine must provide is twofold:

1. Identify the appropriate peers that should be accessed.
2. Devise efficient methods for P_{init} to access this distributed index lists' information so to produce the list of (the IDs of) the top-k documents for the term set T. The top-k result list is defined as the sorted list in descending order of $total score$ which consists of pairs $(docID, total score)$, where $total score$ for a document with ID $docID$ is the sum of the scores of this document in all m index lists.

With respect to the first task, we stress that it is more challenging than it may appear at first sight. Note that the set of peers to be contacted is not simply the set of all peers that store relevant index list data. Such a set could contain a very large number of peers and contacting all of them may be prohibitive. Moreover, the choice of target peers in a network with highly autonomous peers must be overlap-aware, as many peers may have highly overlapping local data contents gathered and indexed from their crawls. The querying peer P_{init} benefits from forwarding the query to a specific remote peer only if that peer can provide high-quality answers that are complementary to the results that P_{init} already knows from executing the query locally or from other peers that were already chosen. So the key challenges here are to (i) define appropriate metrics, measuring the expected utility/value that the inclusion of each peer will bring into the result set, and (ii) weigh this expected peer utility against the cost of contacting it, since our goal is not simply to produce a high quality result, but also to do so efficiently.

The second functionality is essentially that of a top-k query processing engine. With respect to this task, we stress that efficient distributed top-k query processing engines is a subject which has been largely overlooked, with the first promising approaches appearing very recently [17,37].

1.3. Outline

This paper is an overview of our recent and ongoing research on P2P systems for scalable, efficient, and effective Web search. More details can be found in our publications [5,6,37,38,36,43,7].

The rest of the paper is organized as follows. Section 2 briefly discusses related work. Section 3 discusses the architectural design space for P2P Web search. Section 4 gives an overview of the Minerva prototype system, which emphasizes the autonomy of peers. Section 5 goes into depth on the query routing and processing in Minerva. Section 6 gives an overview of the Minerva∞ approach, which emphasizes unlimited scalability (hence the name). We conclude with an outlook on future work.

2. Related Work

2.1. Peer-to-Peer Architectures

The efficient location of nodes and data keys (e.g., file names) in a P2P architecture is a fundamental problem that has been tackled from various directions. Early (but nevertheless popular) systems like Gnutella rely on unstructured architectures in which a peer forwards messages to all known neighbors. Typically, these messages include a *Time-to-live (TTL)* tag that is decreased whenever the message is forwarded to another peer. Even though studies show that this *message flooding* (or *gossiping*) works remarkably well in most cases, there are no guarantees that all relevant nodes will eventually be reached. Additionally, the fact that numerous unnecessary messages are sent interferes with our goal of a highly scalable architecture.

Recent research on P2P systems, thus, favors structured overlay networks with guarantees about message routing path lengths as well as lookup efficiency, and strong behavior regarding scale and dynamics (i.e., failures and churn) which can be guaranteed with high probability. Systems such as Chord [51], CAN [45], Pastry [47], P2P-Net [13], or P-Grid [3] are typically based on various forms of distributed hash tables (DHTs) and support mappings from keys, e.g., titles or authors, to locations in a decentralized manner such that routing scales well with N, the number of peers in the system. Typically, an exact-match key lookup can be routed to the proper peer(s) in at most $O(log\ N)$ hops, and no peer needs to maintain more than $O(log\ N)$ routing information. These architectures can also cope well with failures and the high dynamics of a P2P system as peers join or leave the system at a high rate and in an unpredictable manner. However, the approaches are limited to exact-match, single keyword queries on keys. This is insufficient when queries should return a ranked result list of the most relevant approximate matches in the spirit of IR models.

2.2. Distributed IR and Web Search

Many approaches have been proposed for distributed IR, most notably, CORI [16], the decision-theoretic framework [40], GlOSS [25], and methods based on statistical language models [49]. In principle, these methods could be applied to a P2P setting, but they fall short of various critical aspects: they incur major overhead in their statistical models, they do not scale up to large numbers of peers with high dynamics, and they disregard the crucial issue of collection overlap.

[57] considers a centralized metadata directory that stores metadata of a rather small and static set of search engines. The authors propose metadata pruning, invoked by the centralized directory, to decrease the directory's load by considering only the top-r peers for each query term. However, this technique does not prevent the single search engines to register their full set of metadata at the directory and it is unclear how the directory can adapt to changes in the peers collection if it does not periodically retrieve the full metadata from each peer. In parallel to our work, [2] very recently proposed a P2P index structure that is optimized to contain only the most discriminative keys, e.g., terms with high peer-specific frequencies. However, in contrast to our approach that index maintains entries with document granularity, whereas we keep only peer-granularity entries thus making the P2P index much more light-weight.

Galanx [56] is a P2P search engine implemented using the Apache HTTP server and BerkeleyDB. A site's Web servers are the peers of this architecture; pages are stored only where they originate from, thus forming an overlap-free network. PlanetP [19] is a publish-subscribe service for P2P communities, supporting content ranking search. The global index is replicated using a gossiping algorithm. Odissea [52] assumes a two-layered search engine architecture with a global index structure distributed over the nodes in the system. It actually advocates using a limited number of nodes, in the spirit of a server farm. GridVine [1] addresses the problem of building scalable semantic overlay networks and identifies strategies for their traversal using P-Grid [3]. P2P-Diet [30] consists of super-peers and client-peers and aims to support both ad-hoc and continues queries. Pepper [39] is a hierarchical peer-to-peer system that supports searching and browsing. In Pepper, super-peers use the decision-theoretic framework [23] for resource selection.

2.3. Chord - A Scalable P2P Lookup Service

Chord [51] is a distributed lookup protocol that provides the functionality of a distributed hash table (DHT) by supporting the following *lookup* operation: given a key, it maps the key onto a node. For this purpose, Chord uses consistent hashing [31]. Consistent hashing tends to balance load, since each node receives roughly the same number of keys. Moreover, this load balancing works even in the presence of a dynamically changing hash range, i.e., when nodes fail or leave the system or when new nodes join.

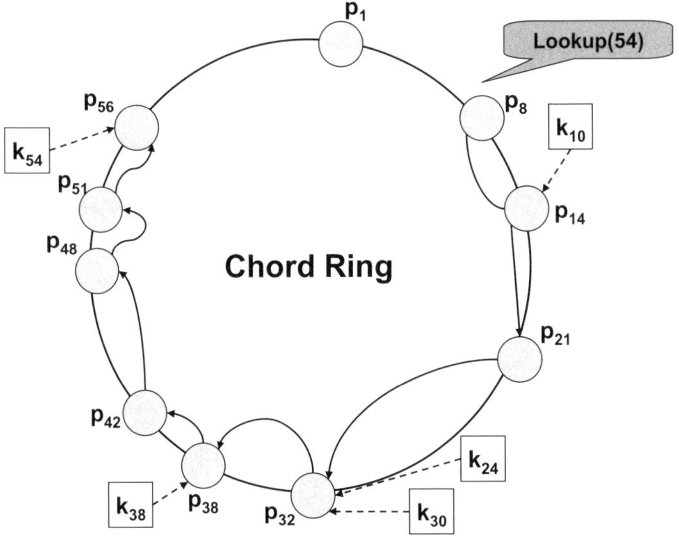

Figure 1. Chord Architecture

The idea behind Chord is as follows: all nodes P_i and all keys k_j are mapped onto the same cyclic ID space. In the following, we use keys and peer numbers as if the hash function had already been applied, but we do not explicitly show the hash function for simpler presentation. Every key k_j is assigned to its closest successor P_i in the ID space, i.e., every node is responsible for all keys with identifiers between the ID of its predecessor node and its own ID. For example, consider Figure 1. Ten nodes are distributed across the ID space. Key k_{54}, for example, is assigned to node P_{56} as its closest successor node.

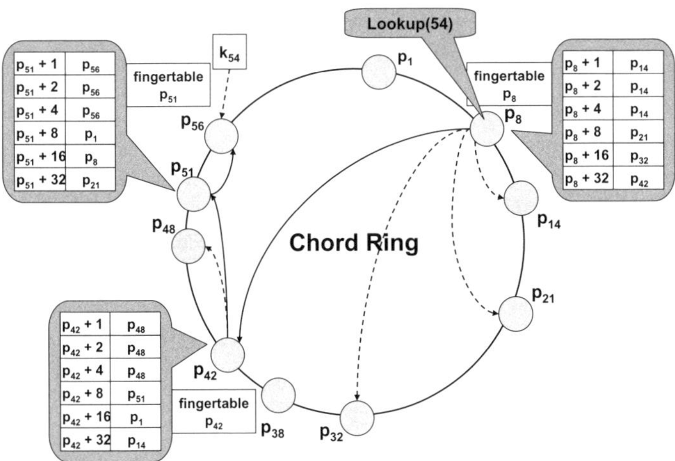

Figure 2. Chord Lookups Using Finger Tables

A naive approach of locating the peer responsible for a key would be to follow the successor pointers on the ID circle. To accelerate lookups, Chord maintains additional routing information: each peer P_i maintains a routing table called *finger table*. The m-

th entry in the table of node P_i contains a pointer to the first node P_j that succeeds P_i by at least 2^{m-1} on the identifier circle. This scheme has two important characteristics. First, each node stores information about only a small number of other nodes, and knows more about nodes closely following it on the identifier circle than about nodes farther away. Secondly, a node's finger table does not necessarily contain enough information to *directly* determine the node responsible for an arbitrary key k_i. However, since each peer has finger entries at power of two intervals around the identifier circle, each node can forward a query at least halfway along the remaining distance between itself and the target node. This property is illustrated in Figure 2 for node P_8. It follows that the number of nodes to be contacted (and, thus, the number of messages to be sent) to find a target node in an N-node system is $O(\log N)$.

Chord implements a stabilization protocol that each peer runs periodically in the background and which updates finger tables and successor pointers in order to ensure that lookups execute correctly as the set of participating peers changes. But even with routing information becoming stale, system performance degrades gracefully.

Chord can provide lookup services for various applications, such as distributed file systems or cooperative mirroring. However, Chord by itself is not a search engine, as it only supports single-term exact-match queries and does not support any form of ranking.

3. Architectural Design Space

We identify the following key environment characteristics and desirable performance features, which can greatly influence the design choices for a P2P web search engine.

1. *Peer Autonomy*: As mentioned, peers work independently, possibly performing web crawls. There are two specific aspects of autonomy of concern. First, whether a peer is willing to relinquish the storage/maintenance of its index lists, agreeing that they be stored at other peers. For instance, a peer may insist on storing/maintaining its own index lists, worrying about possible problems, (e.g., index-list data integrity, availability, etc). Second, a peer may not be willing to store index lists produced by other peers.
2. *Sharing Granule*: Influenced by the autonomy levels as above and performance concerns, the shared data can be at the level of complete index lists, portions of index lists, or even simply index list metadata appropriately defined.
3. *Ultra Scalability*: For the most popular terms, there may be a very large number of peers storing index lists. Accessing all such peers may not be an option. Hence, designing with ultra scalability in mind must foresee the development of mechanisms that can select the best possible subset of relevant peers, in a sense that the efficiency of operation and result quality remain at acceptable levels. Complementarily, peers storing popular index lists may form bottlenecks hurting scalability. Hence, designing for ultra scalability also involves a novel strategy for distributing index list information that facilitates a large number of peers pulling together their resources during query execution, forming in essence large-capacity, "virtual" peers.
4. *Short Latency*: Short Latency may conflict with scalability. For example when, for scalability reasons, query processing is forced to visit a number of peers which

collectively form a large-capacity "virtual" peer, query execution time may be adversely impacted, even at light loads or smaller scales.

5. *Exact vs Approximate Results*: Approximate results may very well be justified at large scales. Recently, research results on high-quality approximate top-k algorithms have started emerging [37]. Beyond approximate top-k algorithms, when forced, for scalability and efficiency reasons, to contact a subset of the peers storing relevant index list data, like Minerva does, exact answers become unrealizable.

Table 1 summarizes the design space occupied by Minerva and Minerva∞. Minerva assumes largely autonomous peers, storing locally data at the level of complete index lists. In addition, compact metadata regarding index list data are widely shared via a special, DHT-based directory. Minerva is designed for autonomy and short query response times. Minerva∞, on the other hand, occupies a totally different space. It assumes an environment of more open, highly collaborative peers. Peers are willing to relinquish control of their own index lists, distributing their contents throughout the nodes of G and are willing to store index list contents from index lists of other peers. The granule of sharable data and data distribution are (collections of) index list entries of the form *(docID, score)*. Finally, Minerva∞ is designed for ultra scalability.

Design Dimension	Minerva	Minerva∞
High Autonomy	+	
Controllable Sharing Granule Size		+
Ultra Scalability		+
Short Latency	+	
Exact Results		+

Table 1. Design Space

4. The Minerva System

We envision that each peer has a full-fledged Web search engine, including a crawler and an index manager. The crawler may be thematically focused or crawl results may be postprocessed so that the local index contents reflect the corresponding user's interest profile. With such a highly specialized and personalized "power search engine" most queries should be executed locally, but once in a while the user may not be satisfied with the local results and would then want to contact other peers. A "good" peer to which the user's query should be forwarded (aka. query routing) would have thematically relevant index contents, which could be measured by statistical notions of similarity between peers. Both query routing and the formation of "statistically semantic" overlay networks could greatly benefit from collective human inputs in addition to standard statistics about terms, links, etc.: knowing the bookmarks and query logs of thousands of users would be a great resource to build on. Note that this notion of Web search includes ranked retrieval and, thus, is fundamentally much more difficult than Gnutella-style file sharing or simple key lookups via overlay networks such as distributed hash tables. Further note that, although query routing in P2P Web search resembles earlier work on metasearch engines and distributed information retrieval [35], it is much more challenging because of the large scale and the high dynamics of the envisioned P2P system with thousands or millions of computers and users.

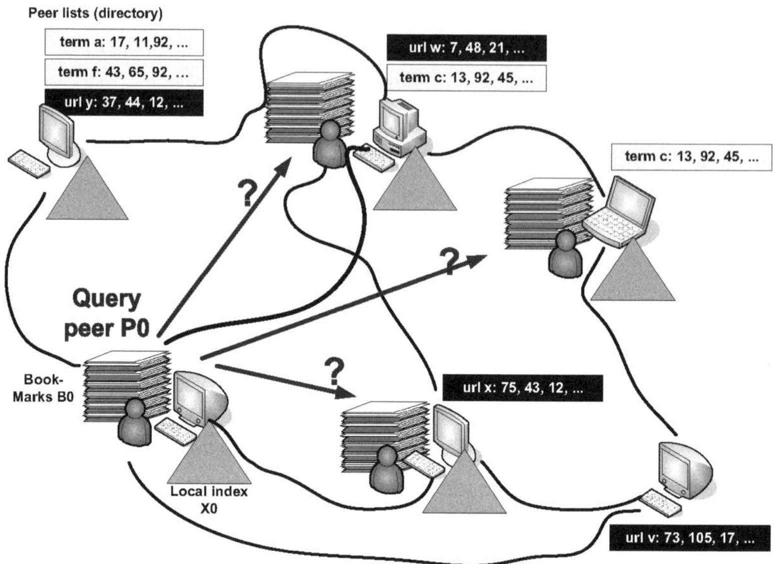

Figure 3. System Architecture for P2P Web Search

In Minerva, peers are connected by an overlay network based on a distributed hash table (DHT). Peers analyze their local information content and prepare compact statistical synopses that capture the relevance for specific query terms (i.e., keywords, stemmed words, or concepts onto which words are mapped), the richness, authority, and freshness of the content, the behavioral characteristics of the peer including the corresponding user's thematic interests, the peer's quality-of-service properties, etc. This metadata can also include the URLs of the locally bookmarked web pages as descriptors of the local profile. These synopses are posted into the overlay network: disseminated to specifically chosen (e.g., by the DHT hash function) peers, often in a redundant manner with judiciously chosen replicas on different peers, such that the overall network forms a conceptually integrated but physically massively distributed directory for metadata and statistical summaries.

To reduce the bandwidth consumption, each peer posts its metadata only for the terms that are statistically most characteristic for its local content and the URLs of its bookmarks that reflect the user's interests. The peer or the peers that are responsible for maintaining the directory entry for a given term or URL maintain ranked lists of peers that have good information about the term or have bookmarked the URL, respectively. The decentralized directory can efficiently be queried by all peers.

This overall system architecture is depicted in Figure 3. The prototype implementation, serving as an experimental platform has been coined *Minerva* [8,5,6,7].[4]

---

[4]Minerva is the Roman goddess of science, wisdom, and learning, and is also the icon of the Max Planck Society.

A user query is normally executed on the local index first, thus avoiding network costs unless involving other peers is justified by unsatisfactory local results. In the latter case, a query routing decision is made about which other peers should be contacted in order to evaluate the query. Clearly this is the technically interesting case, which would typically arise with advanced information demands of "power users" like scientists, students, or journalists. For dynamically selecting target peers, the originating peer can consult the directory and base its decision on the statistical summaries that have previously been posted. The originator may additionally use further information about the candidate peers' content, network bandwidth and latency, trustworthiness, and behavior that it has locally cached from previous interactions and observations. Once the target peers for executing the query are determined, the query is processed using a top-k algorithm, either by a) running the complete query on each selected peer and merging the search results, or by b) decomposing the query into individual subqueries, like one subquery per term, and using a network-conscious distributed top-k algorithm [37,38], where the extra difficulty is to reconcile the network costs (i.e., bandwidth consumption and latency) and the processing costs of the involved peers (i.e., CPU time, disk accesses, memory consumption). The respective local results are shipped to the query initiator, that merges the results into a single result list that is presented to the user. This step, commonly refered to as *result merging*, is another technical challenge, as the scores of documents returned from multiple autonomous sources are typically mutually incomparable.

The software architecture of the Minerva experimental platform is depicted in Figure 4. Note that all the major components shown in the figure can be replaced by alternative implementations, for experimenting with new models and algorithms.

The *local search engine* comprises:

- functions for *data import*, e.g., Web crawling, along with the necessary analysis of the data, e.g., parsing and extraction of terms,
- functions for managing *concept spaces* such as thesauri and ontologies or latent-concept spaces based on spectral analysis techniques, along with support for mapping words onto concepts with word sense disambiguation (WSD),
- the *index manager* that maintains inverted index lists for efficient lookups, including precomputed scores that capture the weight of individual terms in a document (based on probabilistic IR models such as Okapi BM25, advanced matrix decomposition techniques such as probabilistic LSI, or authority scores derived from analyzing the links in the Web graph),
- the local *query processor* that provides efficient top-k ranked retrieval, supports query expansion (based on thesauri, ontologies, and other concept spaces, possibly combined with relevance feedback and other means), and techniques for customizing the search engine to the interest profile and bias of the individual user.

The *collaborative search engine* communicates with other peers; it comprises:

- one or more *overlay networks*, which can be distributed hash tables, random graphs with particular properties (e.g., expander graphs with small diameter), or semantic overlay networks where the network topology reflects thematic similarities among peers,
- the *query router* that decides to which other peers a query by the local user should be forwarded for collaborative query processing, based on a variety of statistics-driven strategies, and

- the result merger that consolidates the query results obtained from different peers into a global ranking.

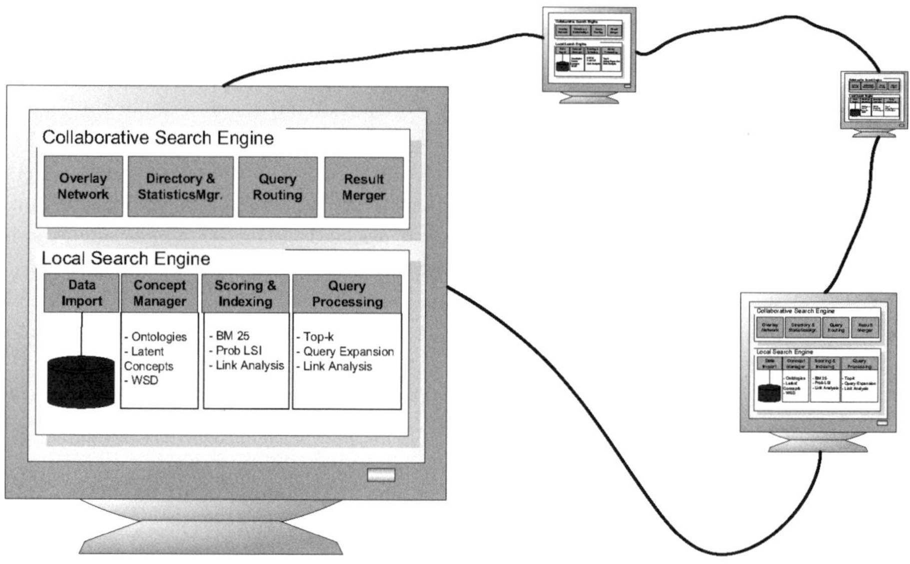

Figure 4. Architecture of the Minerva Experimental Platform

5. Query Routing and Processing in Minerva

Database selection has been a research topic for many years, e.g. in distributed IR and metasearch [15,35]. Typically, the expected result quality of a collection is estimated using precomputed statistics, and the collections are ranked accordingly. Most of these approaches, however, are not directly applicable in a true P2P environment, as

- the number of peers in the system is substantially higher (10^x peers as opposed to 10-20 databases)
- the system evolves dynamically, i.e. peers enter or leave the system autonomously at their own discretion at a potentially high rate
- the results from remote peers should not only be of high quality, but also complementary to the results previously obtained from one's local search engine or other remote peers

In [10,8], we have adopted a number of popular existing approaches to fit the requirements of such an environment and conducted extensive experiments in order to evaluate the performance of these naive approaches. As a second step, we have extended these strategies using estimators of mutual overlap among collections [5,36].

In Minerva, all queries are first processed by the query initiator itself on the locally available index. We expect that many queries will be answered this way without incurring any network costs. But when the user is not satisfied with the query result, the query will be forwarded to a small number of promising peers. In this situation selecting those peers merely on the basis of their data quality, like size of indexed data or freshness and authority of the data, and the "semantic" or statistics-based similarity to the thematic profile of the query initiator, does not work well. We may often end up choosing remote peers that, albeit having high-quality data, do not provide additional information, for their indexed data may overlap too much with the data that the query originator already searched in its own local index. Thus, overlap-awareness is crucial for cost-beneficial query routing. Experiments show that such a combination can outperform popular approaches based on quality estimation only, such as CORI [15].

We also want to incorporate the fact that every peer has its own local index, e.g., by using implicit-feedback techniques for automated query expansion (e.g., using the well-known IR technique of pseudo relevance feedback [14] or other techniques based on query logs [34] and click streams [50]). For this purpose, we can benefit from the fact that each peer executes the query locally first, and also the fact that each peer represents an actual user with personal preferences and interests. For example, we want to incorporate local user bookmarks into our query routing [8], as bookmarks represent strong recommendations for specific documents. Queries could be exclusively forwarded to thematically related peers with similarly interested users, to improve the chances of finding *subjectively* relevant pages.

5.1. Overlap-aware Query Routing

The rationale for the overlap-aware query routing strategies is based on the following three observations:

1. The query initiator should prefer peers that have *similar interest profiles* and are thus likely to hold thematically relevant information in their indexes.
2. On the other hand, the query should be forwarded to peers that offer *complementary results*. If the remote peer returns more or less the same high-quality results that the query initiator already obtained from its own local index, then the whole approach of collaborative P2P search would be pointless.
3. Finally, all parties have to be cautious that the *execution cost* of communicating with other peers and involving them in query processing is tightly controlled and incurs acceptable overhead.

We address the first two points by defining the *benefit* that a remote peer offers for the given query to be proportional to the thematic similarity of that peer and the query initiator and inversely proportional to the overlap between the two peers in terms of their local index contents. As for the third point, we aim to estimate the load and performance behavior of different peers, and then consider the *benefit/cost ratio* as the main criterion for making query routing decisions. For the benefit and cost estimation we utilize statistical summaries and metadata about peers. This information is maintained in a decentralized directory implemented as a distributed hash table (DHT).

More specifically, we assume that all peers have precomputed statistical summaries on their local data contents. These are organized on a per-term basis and would typically include measures such as the number of documents that the peer has for a given term, the average term frequency in these documents, and so on. Additionally, compact synopses about the identifiers (e.g., URLs), of the documents that each peer holds should be locally computed. These summaries are then posted to the distributed directory and conveniently accessible by every peer, with $O(\log N)$ communication costs per term where N is the network size.

An integrated, quality-overlap-aware query routing method can now estimate the content richness of candidate target peers, in terms of the similarity of the peers' contents to the given query (or the locally computed initial result), and the degree of novelty that a candidate peer would offer relative to the initial results that are already known to the query originator. We have developed an algorithm, coined *IQN routing* (for integrated quality and novelty) [36], that chooses target peers in an iterative manner, performing two steps in each iteration. First, the Select-Best-Peer step identifies the most promising peer regarding the product (or a weighted combination) of result quality and novelty. This step is driven by the statistical synopses that are obtained from the directory. Then, the Aggregate-Synopses step conceptually aggregates the selected peer's content with the previously selected peers' data collections (including the query originator's own local collection). This aggregation is actually carried out on the compact synopses, not on the full data. The two-step selection procedure is iterated until some performance and/or quality goals are satisfied (e.g., a predefined number of peers is reached, or a desired recall is estimated to be achieved).

The efficiency and effectiveness of the IQN routing method crucially depends on appropriately designed compact synopses for the peer-collection statistics. The synopses should be small to keep network bandwidth consumption and storage costs low, yet they must offer low-error estimations of quality and novelty (or overlap) measures. Furthermore, to support the Aggregate-Synopses step, it must be possible to combine multiple synopses published by different peers in order to derive a synopsis for the aggregated collection. We have developed detailed methods for using Bloom filters [11], hash sketches [22], and min-wise independent permutations [12] as the basis of our peer-summary synopses. Extensive experiments have shown that our methods do indeed combine very low overhead with high accuracy for quality-novelty estimation, and the IQN query routing strategy outperforms standard approaches such as CORI by a significant margin [5,36].

5.2. Query Processing Steps

This section describes the steps that are necessary for a peer to participate in the P2P network, submit queries, and benefit from the query routing and P2P query execution. These various steps are also reflected in the components of the Minerva GUI, as illustrated in Figure 5.

Peers Registering with Minerva

We present the process of peers registering with Minerva, i.e. joining the DHT-style directory and posting statistical information about local indexes to the network. Afterwards, users can instantly type arbitrary keyword queries into the GUI of any peer, just like in one of today's popular web search engines.

Query Routing

The system selects a tunable number of promising remote peers from the network by gathering the statistical information posted to the directory for each term and subse-

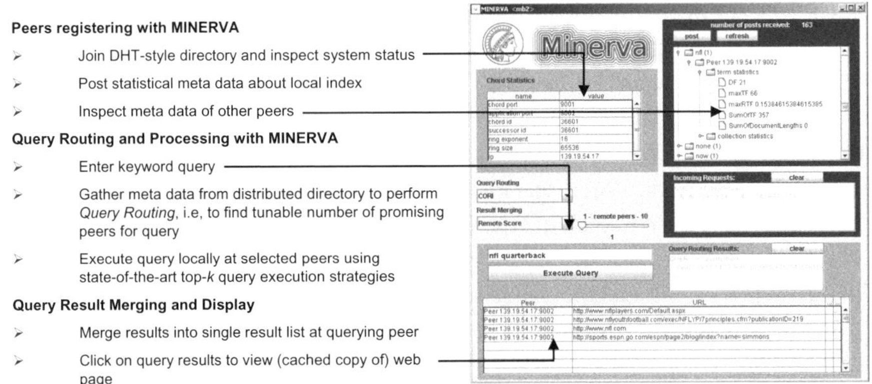

Figure 5. Minerva GUI

quently applying query routing strategies. The peers that have been selected indicate this fact in real-time in their graphical user interfaces, i.e. the user can interactively see which peers have been selected to answer the query.

Query Processing

The selected peers execute the query independently and in parallel, using state-of-the-art efficient top-k algorithms [21,37] for retrieving the k best results according to the local scoring model of each peer. In advanced settings, the query could decomposed into subqueries, for example, by partitioning the set of query keywords, such that each subquery is executed by a different set of most promising peers. In this case, distributed top-k algorithms are employed [17,37].

Query Result Merging and Display

At the peer initiating the query, the local results returned from each of these peers are merged into one global result list, which is displayed to the user. It indicates which remote peer has delivered the respective results. The user can easily click on the query results to open the original documents in order to verify their relevance to the query. The result merging either uses heuristics for re-scaling the - a priori incomparable - scores of the various peers. This can be done by using CORI-style peer scores for normalizing the document scores [15], or by estimating global document frequencies and computing globally valid scores for the final ranking.

5.3. Experiments

One pivotal issue when designing our experiments was the absence of a standard benchmark. While there are benchmark collections for centralized Web search, it is not clear how to distribute such data across peers of a P2P network. Some previous studies partitioned the data into many small and disjoint pieces; but we do not think this is an adequate approach for P2P search with no central coordination and highly autonomous peers. In contrast, we expect a certain degree of overlap, with popular documents being indexed by a substantial fraction of all peers, but, at the same time, with a large number of documents only indexed by a tiny fraction of all peers.

For our experiments we have taken the complete GOV document collection, a crawl of the .gov Internet domain used in the TREC 2003 Web Track benchmark (http://trec.nist.gov). This data comprises about 1.5 million documents (mostly HTML and PDF). All recall measurements that we report below are relative to this centralized reference collection. So a recall of x percent means that the P2P Web search system with IQN routing found in its result list x percent of the results that a centralized search engine with the same scoring/ranking scheme found in the entire reference collection.

For our P2P testbed, we partitioned the whole data into disjoint fragments, and then we form collections placed onto peers by using various strategies to combine fragments. In one strategy, we split the whole data into f fragments and created collections by choosing all subsets with s fragments, thus, ending up with $\binom{f}{s}$ collections each of which was assigned to one peer. In a second experiment, we have split the entire dataset into 100 fragments and used the following sliding-window technique to form collections assigned to peers: the first peer receives r (subsequent) fragments f_1 to f_r, the next peer receives the fragments f_{1+o} to f_{r+o}, where o is the offset, and so on. This way, we systematically control the overlap of peers.

For the query workload, we used the 50 queries from the TREC-12 Web Track benchmark. These are relatively short queries, with 2 to 4 keywords each; examples are "forest fire", "pest safety control", "marijuana legalization".

All experiments were conducted on the Minerva testbed described before, with peers running on a PC cluster. We compared query routing based on the CORI method which is merely quality-driven against the quality- and novelty-conscious IQN method. Recall that CORI is among the very best database selection methods for distributed IR. We measured the (relative) recall as defined above, for a specified number of peers to which the query was forwarded. In the experiments we varied this maximum number of peers per query. This notion of recall directly reflects the benefit/cost ratio of the different query routing methods and their underlying synopses.

Figure 6 shows the recall results (macro-averaged over all our benchmark queries), using the $\binom{f}{s}$ technique in the chart on the left side and the sliding-window technique on the right side. More specifically we chose $f = 6$ and $s = 3$ for the left chart, which gave us $\binom{6}{3} = 20$ collections for 20 peers, and we chose $r = 10$ and $o = 2$ for 50 collections on 50 peers in the sliding-window setup.

Our approach clearly outperforms CORI in terms of recall in this setting; in order to reach a recall of 80% in the sliding-window setup, for example, CORI on average needs to contact more than 20 peers, whereas our strategy achieves this goal by contacting only 7 peers. This clearly shows substantial improvements already and especially for a relatively small number of peers. This underlines the importance of a powerful collection selection strategy in a distributed search environment, where efficiency in terms of bandwidth consumption and latency mainly depends on the number of contacted peers.

More details on this experiment and additional, in-depth experimental studies can be found in [5,36].

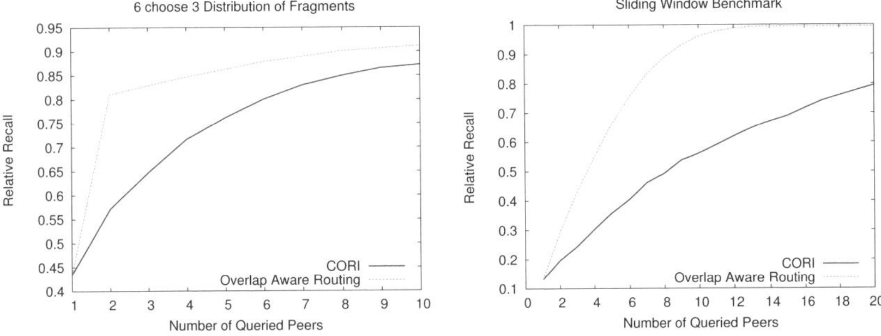

Figure 6. Performance of overlap-aware query routing

6. The Minerva∞ System

Minerva∞ peers are assumed to be members of G, a *global* DHT overlay network. Minerva∞ is designed with the goal of facilitating ultra scalability. For this reason, the fundamental distinguishing feature of Minerva∞ is its high distribution both in the data and computational dimensions. In this sense, it goes far beyond Minerva and the state-of-the-art in distributed top-k query processing algorithms, which are based on nodes storing complete index lists for terms and performing coordinator-based, top-k algorithms over these nodes accessing their local index lists. Minerva∞ involves sophisticated distributed query execution, engaging a large number of peers, which collectively store the accessed portions of a queried index list. To achieve ultra scalability, the key computations (such as the maintenance and retrieval of the data items) are engaging several different nodes, with each node having to perform small (sub)tasks.

6.1. Overlay Network

Our approach to materialize this design relies on the employment of the novel notion of *Term Index Networks* (TINs). A TIN can be conceptualized as a *virtual* node storing a *virtually global* index list for a term, which is constructed by the sorted merging of the separate complete index lists for the term computed at different nodes. TINs serve two roles: First, as an abstraction, encapsulating the information specific to a term of interest, and second, as a physical manifestation of a distributed repository of the term-specific data items, facilitating their efficient and scalable retrieval during top-k query processing. TINs are comprised of nodes which collectively store different horizontal partitions of this global index list. During the execution of a top-k query involving r terms, the query-initiator node (and any other node) never needs to simultaneously communicate with more than r other nodes. Furthermore, as the top-k algorithm is processing different data items for each query term, this involves gradually different nodes from each TIN, producing a highly distributed, scalable solution.

In general, TINs can form separate overlay networks, coexisting with the global overlay G. In practice, it may not always be necessary or advisable to form full-fledged separate overlays for TINs; instead, TINs may be formed as straightforward extensions of G: when a node n of G joins a TIN, only two additional links are added to the state of n linking it to its successor and predecessor nodes in the TIN. In this case, a TIN is simply a doubly-linked list of nodes.

6.2. Distributed Query Processing

The design of Minerva∞, and in particular the placement of data and nodes, is heavily influenced by the way the well-known, efficient top-k query processing algorithms (e.g., [21]) operate, looking for docIDs within certain ranges of score values. Thus, correspondingly the networks' $lookup(s)$ function, will be called using scores s as input, to locate the nodes storing docIDs associated with scores s.

For any highly distributed solution to be efficient, it is crucial to keep as low as possible the time and bandwidth overheads. To achieve this, Minerva∞ follows the principles put forward by top-performing, resource-efficient top-k query processing algorithms in traditional environments. Specifically, the principles behind favoring sequential index-list accesses to random accesses (in order to avoid random disk IOs) have been adapted in our distributed algorithms to ensure first that sequential accesses dominate, and second that they require at most a one-hop communication between nodes. In addition, random accesses require at most $O(logN)$ messages. To ensure the at-most-one-hop communication requirement for successive sequential accesses, Minerva∞ utilizes an *order preserving hash function*, $h_{op}()$. $h_{op}()$ has the property that for any two values v_1, v_2, if $v_1 > v_2$ then $h_{op}(v_1) > h_{op}(v_2)$. This guarantees that data items corresponding to successive score values of a term t are placed either at the same or at neighboring nodes of the TIN for $I(t)$. Similar functionality can be provided by employing for each $I(t)$ the SkipNets overlay.

Query Initiator

The query initiator calculates the set of *start nodes*, one for each term, where the query processing will start within each TIN. Also, it randomly selects one of the nodes (for one of the TINs) to be the initial coordinator. Finally, it passes on the query and the coordinator ID to each of the start nodes, to initiate the parallel vertical processing within TINs.

The following pseudocode details the behavior of the initiator.

Algorithm 1 Top-k QP: Query Initiation at node $G.n_{init}$

1: **input:** Given query $Q = \{t_1,..,t_r\}, k$:
2: **for** $i = 1$ to r **do**
3:      $startNode_i = I(t_i).n(s_{max}) = h_{op}(t_i, s_{max})$
4: **end for**
5: Randomly select c from $[1,...,r]$
6: $coordID = I(t_c).n(s_{max})$
7: **for** $i = 1$ to r **do**
8:      send to $startNode_i$ the data $(Q, coordID)$
9: **end for**

Query Processing Within Each TIN

Processing within a TIN is always initiated by the start node. There is one start node per communication phase of the query processing. In the first phase, the start node is the top node in the TIN which receives the query processing request from the initiator. The start node then starts the gathering of data items for the term by contacting enough nodes, following successor links, until a threshold number γ (that is, a batch size) of items has been accumulated and sent to the coordinator, along with an indication of the maximum score for this term which has not been collected yet, which is actually either a locally stored score or the maximum score of the next successor node. The latter information is critical for the coordinator in order to intelligently decide when the top-k result list has been computed and terminate the search. In addition, each start node sends to the coordinator the ID of the node of this TIN to be the next start node, which is simply the next successor node of the last accessed node of the TIN. Processing within this TIN will be continued at the new start node when it receives the next message from the coordinator starting the next data-gathering phase.

Algorithm 2 Top-k QP: Processing by a start node within a TIN

 1: **input:** A message either from the initiator or the coordinator
 2: $tCollection_i = \emptyset$
 3: $n = startNode_i$
 4: **while** $|tCollection_i| < \gamma$ **do**
 5:     **while** $|tCollection_i| < \gamma$ AND more items exist locally **do**
 6:         define the set of local items $L = \{(t_i, d, s)$ in $n\}$
 7:         send to $coordID : L$
 8:         $|tCollection_i| = |tCollection_i| + |L|$
 9:     **end while**
10:     n = succ(n)
11: **end while**
12: $bound_i = $ max score stored at node n
13: send to $coordID : n$ and $bound_i$

Algorithm 2 presents the pseudocode for TIN processing. Recall that because of the manner with which items and nodes have been placed in a TIN, following succ() links, items are collected starting from the item with the highest score posted for this term and proceeding in sorted descending order based on scores.

6.3. Putting Everything Together

In summary, the Minerva∞ design and processing are based on the following pillars.

1. Data items are (term, docID, score) triplets, posted to the underlying DHT network, using an order preserving hash function on the score value to identify the node which will store this item. This node then becomes a member of the TIN for the index list for the named term, using special gateway nodes (which are randomly selected for each TIN from the N nodes). This results in successive nodes of TIN storing items with successive scores.

2. The gateway nodes are easily identifiable since they are made to store dummy predefined score values. Hashing for one of these predefined score values yields the ID of a gateway node.

3. Once TINs are populated, queries are executed by having the query initiator node of G send, for each query term, a message to the node responsible for storing the highest score value (e.g., the value 1). This is achieved by hashing for the pair (term, 1) using the order-preserving hash function. In this way, the "top" nodes of each relevant TIN are identified and the query is sent to them.

4. Query processing is batched; it proceeds in communication phases, between the initiator and the TIN nodes, with each phase collecting a certain portion (batch size) of the index list stored in each TIN. This is essence creates a pipeline, defined by the TIN nodes that collaborate to collect the batch of index list entries for the current phase.

5. Communication between any two nodes in a TIN during this process requires one hop at a time; a consequence of order-preserving placement.

6. The initiator collects the batch size of index list entries from every TIN and then runs locally a top-k algorithm.

7. This process continues with the initiator collecting more batches of data from the TINs (accessing nodes further "down" in the TIN) until the top-k result can be computed.

The Minerva∞ design can leverage DHT technology to facilitate efficiency and scalability in key aspects of the system's operation. Specifically, posting (and deleting) data items for a term from any node can be done in $O(logN)$ time, in terms of the number of messages. Similarly, during top-k query processing, the TINs of the terms in the query can be also reached by the initiator in $O(logN)$ messages. Furthermore, no single node is over-burdened with tasks which can either require more resources than available, or exhaust its resources, or even stress its resources for longer periods of time. This follows since (i) no node is needed to communicate with more than r other nodes in a r-term query (regardless of the number of peers that crawled the web and constructed index lists for these terms) and (ii) the 'pipelined' processing within each TIN in essence facilitates the pulling together of nodes' resources to create 'virtual' nodes of a capacity close to the sum of the individual node capacities.

6.4. Experiments

Our implementation was implemented in Java. Experiments were performed on 3GHz Pentium PCs We simulated large network with 10,000 peers as separate processes on the same PC, executing the real Minerva∞ code. We used the GOV document collection from the TREC-12 Web Track, whose index lists were distributed across the peers by the DHT and TIN mechanisms.

For the workload we used the original 50 GOV queries from the Web Track's distillation task. As these are relatively short queries with up to 4 terms, we additionally constructed an extended setup, coined XGOV, with a larger number of query terms and associated index lists. The original 50 queries were expanded by adding new terms from synonyms and glosses taken from the WordNet thesaurus (http://www.cogsci.princeton.edu/~wn). The expansion increased the average query length by a factor of two; the largest expanded query had 18 keywords.

In the simulated wide-area network, we assumed a transfer bandwidth of 800 Kb/s. For network latency we used typical round trip times (RTTs) [48] set to 100 ms for large data transmissions and 30 ms for short messages such as query forwarding.

Figures 7 and 8 show the network bandwidth consumption, response times, and network hops (number of point-to-point messages) for the GOV and XGOV benchmarks, where all 50 queries for each of the two setups were sequentially submitted from a single peer. All performance figures refer to the entire batch of 50 queries. Note, that different query groups have in general mutually-incomparable results, since they involve different index lists with different characteristics (such as size, score distributions etc).

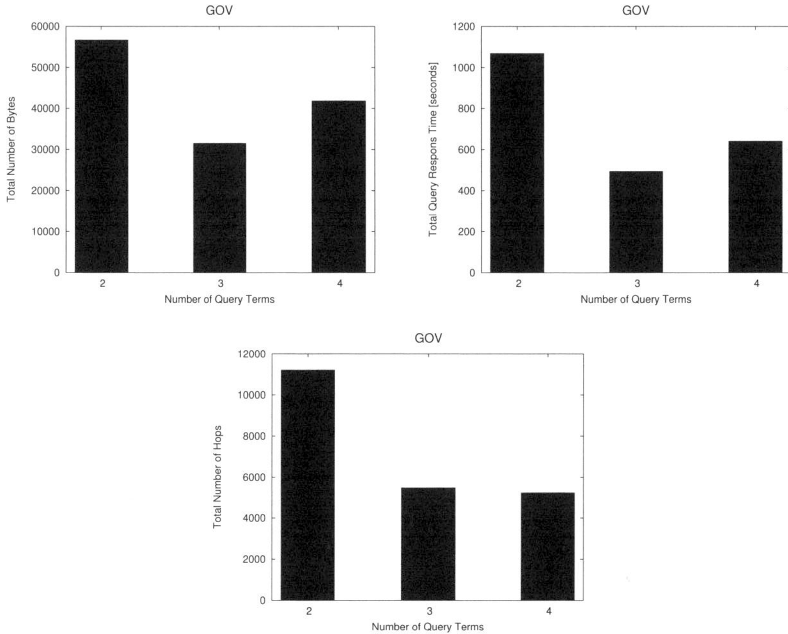

Figure 7. GOV Results: Bandwidth Consumption, Execution Time, and Number of Hops

The 2-term queries introduced the biggest overheads. There are 29 two-term, 7 three-term, and 4 four-term queries in GOV.

In XGOV the biggest overhead was introduced by the 8 seven-term and 6 eleven-term queries. Table 2 shows the total benchmark execution times, network bandwidth consumption, as well as the number of hops for the GOV and XGOV benchmarks.

Benchmark	Hops	Bandwidth(KB)	Time(s)
GOV	22050	130189	2212
XGOV	146168	744700	10372

Table 2. Total Benchmark GOV and XGOV Results

Generally, the performance of a query is determined by its number of terms and the size of the corresponding index lists. Additional experiments can be found in [38].

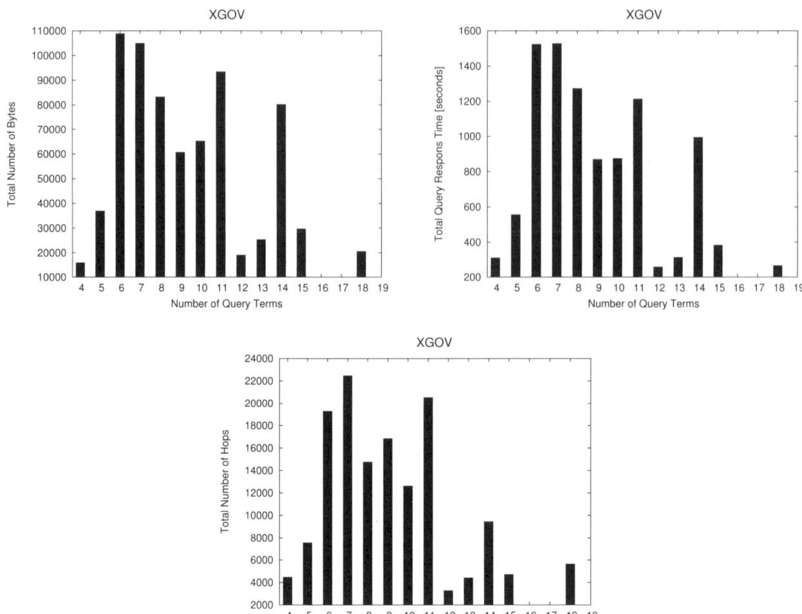

Figure 8. XGOV Results: Bandwidth Consumption, Execution Time, and Number of Hops

7. Conclusion

This paper has explored the design space for P2P Web search systems and has taken a closer look at two particular architectures, Minerva and Minerva∞. The two architectures emphasize different design criteria, most notably, peer autonomy in Minerva and "ultra-scalability" in Minerva∞. Hybrid architectures are conceivable, too, but would be subject of future research.

The Minerva prototype is a full-fledged system, and we plan to deploy it in a small-scale, real-life test environment. The goal is to gain more insights into user behavior in a P2P Web search setting. We plan to gather query logs and click streams, in order to develop more adaptive and personalized query routing strategies that leverage user-specific behavior and profile information.

References

[1] Karl Aberer, Philippe Cudre-Mauroux, Manfred Hauswirth, Tim Van Pelt: GridVine: Building Internet-Scale Semantic Overlay Network, International Semantic Web Conference (ISWC), Hiroshima, Japan, 2004.

[2] K. Aberer, F. Klemm, T. Luu, I. Podnar, M. Rajman: Building a peer-to-peer full-text Web search engine with highly discriminative keys, Technical Report, Ecole Polytechnique Federale de Lausanne, Lausanne, Switzerland, 2005.

[3] Karl Aberer, Magdalena Punceva, Manfred Hauswirth, Roman Schmidt: Improving Data Access in P2P Systems, IEEE Internet Computing, 6(1), 1089-7801, 2002.

[4] Karl Aberer, Jie Wu: Towards a Common Framework for Peer-to-Peer Web Retrieval, in: Matthias Hemmje, Claudia Niederée, Thomas Risse (Eds.): From Integrated Publication and Information Systems to Virtual Information and Knowledge Environments, Springer, 2005.

[5] Matthias Bender, Sebastian Michel, Peter Triantafillou, Gerhard Weikum, Christian Zimmer: Improving Collection Selection with Overlap Awareness in P2P Search Engines, ACM SIGIR Int. Conf. on R&D in Information Retrieval, Salvador, Brazil, 2005.

[6] Matthias Bender, Sebastian Michel, Peter Triantafillou, Gerhard Weikum, Christian Zimmer: Minerva: Collaborative P2P Search, Demo Paper, Int. Conf. on Very Large Data Bases (VLDB), Trondheim, Norway, 2005.

[7] Matthias Bender, Sebastian Michel, Peter Triantafillou, Gerhard Weikum, Christian Zimmer: P2P Content Search: Give the Web Back to the People, 5th International Workshop on Peer-to-Peer Systems (IPTPS), Santa Barbara, USA, 2006.

[8] Matthias Bender, Sebastian Michel, Gerhard Weikum, Christian Zimmer: Bookmark-driven Query Routing in Peer-to-Peer Web Search, ACM SIGIR Workshop on Peer-to-Peer Information Retrieval, Sheffield, UK, 2004.

[9] Matthias Bender, Sebastian Michel, Gerhard Weikum, Christian Zimmer: Das Minerva-Projekt: Datenbankselektion für Peer-to-Peer-Websuche,

[10] Matthias Bender, Sebastian Michel, Gerhard Weikum, Christian Zimmer: The Minerva Project: Database Selection in the Context of P2P Search, 11. GI-Fachtagung für Datenbanksysteme in Business, Technologie und Web (BTW), Karlsruhe, Germany, 2005.

[11] Burton H. Bloom: Space/time trade-offs in hash coding with allowable errors, Commun. ACM, 13(7), 0001-0782, 1970.

[12] Andrei Z. Broder, Moses Charikar, Alan M. Frieze, Michael Mitzenmacher: Min-Wise Independent Permutations, Journal of Computer and System Sciences, 60(3), 2000.

[13] Erik Buchmann, Klemens Böhm": How to Run Experiments with Large Peer-to-Peer Data Structures, 18th International Parallel and Distributed Processing Symposium, Santa Fe, USA, 2004.

[14] C. Buckley and G. Salton and J. Allan: The effect of adding relevance information in a relevance feedback environment, ACM conference on research and development in information retrieval (SIGIR), Dublin, Ireland, 1994.

[15] J. Callan: Distributed information retrieval, Advances in information retrieval, Kluwer Academic Publishers, 2000.

[16] James P. Callan, Zhihong Lu, W. Bruce Croft: Searching distributed collections with inference networks, ACM SIGIR Int. Conf. on R&D in Information Retrieval, Seattle, USA, 1995.

[17] Pei Cao, Zhe Wang: Efficient top-K query calculation in distributed networks, ACM Symposium on Principles of Distributed Computing (PODC), Newfoundland, Canada, 2004.

[18] Soumen Chakrabarti: Mining the Web: Discovering Knowledge from Hypertext Data, 1-55860-754-4, Morgan Kaufmann 2002.

[19] Francisco Matias Cuenca-Acuna, Christopher Peery, Richard P. Martin, Thu D. Nguyen: PlanetP: Using Gossiping to Build Content Addressable Peer-to-Peer Information Sharing Communities, 12th International Symposium on High-Performance Distributed Computing (HPDC), Seattle, USA, 2003.

[20] Ronald Fagin: Combining fuzzy information from multiple systems, J. Comput. Syst. Sci., 58(1), 0022-0000, Academic Press, Inc., 1999.

[21] Ronald Fagin, Amnon Lotem, Moni Naor: Optimal aggregation algorithms for middleware, J. Comput. Syst. Sci., 66(4), 0022-0000, 2003.

[22] Philippe Flajolet, G. Nigel Martin: Probabilistic Counting Algorithms for Data Base Applications, Journal of Computer and System Sciences, 31(2), 1985.

[23] Norbert Fuhr: A Decision-Theoretic Approach to Database Selection in Networked IR, ACM Transactions on Information Systems, 17(3), 1999.

[24] Prasanna Ganesan, Mayank Bawa, Hector Garcia-Molina: Online Balancing of Range-Partitioned Data with Applications to Peer-to-Peer Systems, Int. Conf. on Very Large Data

Bases (VLDB), Toronto, Canada, 2004.

[25] Luis Gravano, Hector Garcia-Molina, Anthony Tomasic: GlOSS: text-source discovery over the Internet, ACM Trans. Database Syst., 24(2), 0362-5915, 1999.

[26] Abhishek Gupta, Ozgur D. Sahin, Divyakant Agrawal, Amr El Abbadi: Meghdoot: content-based publish/subscribe over P2P networks, ACM/IFIP/USENIX international conference on Middleware, Toronto, Canada, 2004.

[27] David Hales: From Selfish Nodes to Cooperative Networks – Emergent Link-based Incentives in Peer-to-Peer Networks. IEEE Conf. on Peer-to-Peer Computing, Zurich, Switzerland, 2004.

[28] N. Harvey, M. Jones, S. Saroiu, M. Theimer, A. Wolman: Skipnet: A scalable overlay network with practical locality properties, USENIX Symposium on Internet Technologies and Systems (USITS), Seattle, USA, 2003.

[29] Ryan Huebsch, Joseph M. Hellerstein, Nick Lanham, Boon Thau Loo, Scott Shenker, Ion Stoica: Querying the Internet with PIER, Int. Conf. on Very Large Data Bases (VLDB), Berlin, Germany, 2003.

[30] Stratos Idreos, Manolis Koubarakis, Christos Tryfonopoulos: P2P-DIET: An Extensible P2P Service that Unifies Ad-hoc and Continuous Querying in Super-Peer Networks, ACM International Conference on Management of Data (SIGMOD), Paris, France, 2004.

[31] David Karger, Eric Lehman, Tom Leighton, Mathhew Levine, Daniel Lewin, Rina Panigrahy: Consistent Hashing and Random Trees: Distributed Caching Protocols for Relieving Hot Spots on the World Wide Web, ACM Symposium on Theory of Computing, El Paso, USA, 1997.

[32] John Kubiatowicz: Extracting Guarantees from Chaos. Communications of the ACM 46(2): 33-38, 2003.

[33] Jie Lu and, James P. Callan: Content-based retrieval in hybrid peer-to-peer networks, ACM International Conference on Information and Knowledge Management (CIKM), New Orleans, USA, 2003.

[34] Julia Luxenburger and Gerhard Weikum: Query-log based Authority Analysis for Web Information Search, 5th International Conference on Web Information Systems Engineering (WISE), Brisbane, Australia, 2004.

[35] Weiyi Meng, Clement Yu, King-Lup Liu: Building efficient and effective metasearch engines, ACM Comput. Surv., 34(1), 0360-0300, 2002.

[36] Sebastian Michel, Matthias Bender, Peter Triantafillou, Gerhard Weikum: IQN Routing: Integrating Quality and Novelty in P2P Querying and Ranking, 10th International Conference on Extending Database Technology (EDBT), Munich, Germany, 2006.

[37] Sebastian Michel, Peter Triantafillou, Gerhard Weikum: KLEE: Internet-scale Distributed Top-k Query Algorithms, Int. Conf. on Very Large Data Bases (VLDB), Trondheim, Norway, 2005.

[38] Sebastian Michel, Peter Triantafillou, Gerhard Weikum: Minerva Infinity: A Scalable Efficient Peer-to-Peer Search Engine, 6th ACM/IFIP/USENIX International Middleware Conference, Grenoble, France, 2005.

[39] Henrik Nottelmann, Gudrun Fischer, Alexej Titarenko, André Nurzenski: An integrated approach for searching and browsing in heterogeneous peer-to-peer networks, SIGIR workshop on Heterogeneous and Distributed Information Retrieval (HDIR), San Salvador, Brazil, 2005.

[40] Henrik Nottelmann, Norbert Fuhr: Evaluating Different Methods of Estimating Retrieval Quality for Resource Selection. ACM SIGIR Conf. on R&D in Information Retrieval, Toronto, Canada, 2003.

[41] Nikos Ntarmos, Peter Triantafillou: AESOP: Altruism-Endowed Self Organizing Peers, 3rd Int. Workshop on Databases, Information Systems and Peer-to-Peer Computing, Toronto, Canada, 2004.

[42] Nikos Ntarmos, Peter Triantafillou: SeAl: Managing Accesses and Data in Peer-to-Peer Data Sharing Networks, 4th IEEE Conf. in Peer-to-Peer Computing, Zurich, Switzerland, 2004.

[43] Nikos Ntarmos, Peter Triantafillou, Gerhard Weikum: Counting at Large: Efficient Cardinality Estimation in Internet-Scale Data Networks, IEEE International Conference on Data Engineering (ICDE), Atlanta, USA, 2006.

[44] Josiane Xavier Parreira, Gerhard Weikum: JXP: Global Authority Scores in a P2P Network, 8th Int. Workshop on Web and Databases (WebDB), Baltimore, USA, 2005.

[45] Sylvia Ratnasamy, Paul Francis, Mark Handley, Richard Karp, Scott Schenker: A scalable content-addressable network, ACM SIGCOMM Conference on Data Communication, San Diego, USA, 2001.

[46] Patrick Reynolds, Amin Vahdat: Efficient Peer-to-Peer Keyword Searching, ACM/IFIP/USENIX International Middleware Conference, Rio de Janeiro, Brazil, 2003.

[47] Antony Rowstron, Peter Druschel: Pastry: Scalable, Decentralized Object Location, and Routing for Large-Scale Peer-to-Peer Systems, IFIP/ACM International Conference on Distributed Systems Platforms (Middleware), Heidelberg, Germany, 2001.

[48] D. Salomoni, S. Luitz: High Performance Throughput Tuning/Measurement, http://www.slac.stanford.edu/grp/scs/net/talk/
High_Perf_PPDG_Jul2000.ppt, 2000.

[49] Luo Si, Rong Jin, Jamie Callan, Paul Ogilvie: A language modeling framework for resource selection and results merging, ACM International Conference on Information and Knowledge Management (CIKM), McLean, USA, 2002.

[50] Jaideep Srivastava, Robert Cooley, Mukund Deshpande, Pang-Ning Tan: Web Usage Mining: Discovery and Applications of Usage Patterns from Web Data, 6th ACM International Conference on Knowledge Discovery and Data Mining (SIGKDD), Boston, USA, 2000.

[51] Ion Stoica, Robert Morris, David Liben-Nowell, David R. Karger, M. Frans Kaashoek, Frank Dabek, Hari Balakrishnan: Chord: a scalable peer-to-peer lookup protocol for internet applications. IEEE/ACM Transactions on Networking 11(1): 17-32, 2003

[52] Torsten Suel, Chandan Mathur, Jo-wen Wu ,Jiangong Zhang Alex Delis, Mehdi Kharrazi, Xiaohui Long, Kulesh Shanmugasundaram: ODISSEA: A Peer-to-Peer Architecture for Scalable Web Search and Information Retrieval, 6th International Workshop on the Web an Databases (WebDB), San Diego, USA, 2003.

[53] Torsten Suel, Jiangong Zhang: Efficient Query Evaluation on Large Textual Collections in a Peer-to-Peer Environment, 5th IEEE International Conference on Peer-to-Peer Computing, Konstanz, Germany, 2005.

[54] Peter Triantafillou, Chryssani Xiruhaki, Manolis Koubarakis, Nikos Ntarmos: Towards High Performance Peer-to-Peer Content and Resource Sharing Systems, 1st Int. Conf. on Innovative Data Systems Research (CIDR), Asilomar, USA, 2003.

[55] Christos Tryfonopoulos, Stratos Idreos, Manolis Koubarakis: Publish/Subscribe Functionality in IR Environments using Structured Overlay Networks, ACM SIGIR Int. Conf. on R&D in Information Retrieval, Salvador, Brazil, 2005.

[56] Y. Wang, L. Galanis, and D. DeWitt: Galanx: An efficient peer-to-peer search engine system, Technical report, University of Wisconsin, Madison, USA, 2003.

[57] Zonghuan Wu, Weiyi Meng, Clement T. Yu and Zhuogang Li: Towards a highly-scalable and effective metasearch engine, International Word Wide Web Conference (WWW), Hong Kong, 2001.

[58] Hailing Yu, Hua-Gang Li, Ping Wu, Divyakant Agrawal, Amr El Abbadi: Efficient Processing of Distributed Top-k Queries, 16th International Conference on Database and Expert Systems Applications (DEXA), Copenhagen, Denmark, 2005.

Global Data Management
R. Baldoni et al. (Eds.)
IOS Press, 2006

From Web Servers to Ubiquitous Content Delivery

Guillaume Pierre [1], Maarten van Steen,
Michał Szymaniak, Swaminathan Sivasubramanian
Vrije Universiteit, Amsterdam, The Netherlands

Abstract. Hosting a Web site at a single server creates performance and reliability issues when request load increases, availability is at stake, and, in general, when quality-of-service demands rise. A common approach to these problems is making use of a content delivery network (CDN) that supports distribution and replication of (parts of) a Web site. The nodes of such networks are dispersed across the Internet, allowing clients to be redirected to a nearest copy of a requested document, or to balance access loads among several servers. Also, if documents are replicated, availability of a site increases. The design space for constructing a CDN is large and involves decisions concerning replica placement, client redirection policies, but also decentralization. We discuss the principles of various types of distributed Web hosting platforms and show where tradeoffs need to be made when it comes to supporting robustness, flexibility, and performance.

Keywords. Replication, Mirroring, Content delivery networks, Peer-to-peer

1. Introduction

Thanks to the expansion of the Internet, an ever-growing number of businesses and end users decide to publish information using the World-Wide Web. These documents can range from a set of simple HTML pages to multi-tiered Web-based applications, in which pages are generated dynamically at the time of a request.

The Web was initially designed with the idea that each page would be hosted by one server machine [9]. The resulting system model is extremely simple: to obtain a document, a browser is given a URL which contains the name of the server to contact, and the document path to request. The browser initiates a TCP connection with the requested server and specifies the required document path, after which the server returns the document and closes the connection.

Although this approach is extremely simple, taking a closer look at it also quickly reveals a number of shortcomings. The network connection between the client and the server can have arbitrarily poor performance, potentially leading to long connection setup and transfer delays. The server cannot control the rate of incoming requests, so it always runs the risk of overload when subject to high request rates. This issue can also lead to increased document retrieval delays, or even to servers refusing incoming connections.

---

[1]Correspondence to: Guillaume Pierre, Department of Computer Science, Vrije Universiteit, de Boelelaan 1081, 1081 HV Amsterdam, The Netherlands; E-mail: gpierre@cs.vu.nl.

Finally, a centralized Web server constitutes a single point of failure: it is sufficient that a server, or the network connection leading to it, fails for the documents it hosts to become unreachable. This situation is clearly unacceptable to most Internet-based businesses or even to demanding end users.

The solution to these issues is to decouple a Web *site* (i.e., a collection of documents related to each other) from the one or more *server machines* used to host it. For example, the Google Web site is believed to be hosted by over dozens of thousands of servers [7]. A large number of systems have been built to this aim, using different techniques ranging from caching or mirroring Web documents, to building high-performance server clusters, and building worldwide replicated hosting platforms known as content delivery networks. More recently, worldwide content delivery has witnessed additional development, with the advent of collaborative and peer-to-peer content delivery networks.

Although distributed Web hosting platforms are very different in their architecture, most of them follow a common goal, namely to share the burden of delivering the contents among multiple machines by way of replication. Replication involves creating copies of a site's Web documents, and placing these copies at well-chosen locations. In addition, various measures are taken to ensure consistency when a replicated document is updated. Finally, effort is put into redirecting a client to a server hosting a document copy such that the client is optimally served. Replication can lead to reduced client latency and network traffic by redirecting client requests to a replica closest to that client. It can also improve the availability of the system, as the failure of one server does not result in entire service outage.

The original nonreplicated system model of the World-Wide Web also imposes a transparency constraint to any Web hosting system. Since no specific support for replication is included in the Web protocols, it is a desired property that replication be transparent to the Web browsers. Otherwise, the complexity of the system must be revealed to the end users by asking them to select a server where requests should be sent to, or by requiring them to use nonstandard replication-aware browsers to access the information.

This chapter will detail the different types of Web hosting architectures, and discuss their relative merits and drawbacks. We will show that, although decentralization is a desirable property, it makes the implementation of advanced features such as latency-driven client redirection and dynamic Web application hosting more complex, or even impossible.

2. Content Delivery Networks

The shortcomings of centralized Web site hosting can be addressed by creating copies of (or *replicating*) a site's Web documents at well-chosen locations and redirecting client requests to a server hosting a document copy such that the client is optimally served. Replication can lead to reduced client latency and network traffic by redirecting client requests to a replica closest to that client. It can also improve the availability of the system, as the failure of one replica does not result in entire service outage.

The simplest form of Web-site replication is mirroring. As discussed in Section 2.1, mirroring requires very little technical sophistication but presents a number of issues due to the almost total lack of centralized control over the system.

A number of infrastructures known as content delivery networks have been developed to address the issues of mirroring by providing worldwide distributed resources that can be dynamically allocated to Web sites, and by advanced automation of system administration. Section 2.2 presents the general design of content delivery networks.

Many CDNs focus on replicating static Web pages only. However, an increasing fraction of Web contents are generated dynamically at the time of a request by applications that take, for example, individual user profile and request parameters into account when producing the content. Hosting such applications, and their associated databases, requires entirely different techniques than for hosting static contents. We present them in Section 2.3.

Finally, even though CDNs distribute Web contents at a worldwide scale, the management of these resources remains fundamentally centralized. Section 2.4 discusses the advantages and limitations of such an approach.

2.1. Mirroring vs. Content Delivery Networks

The simplest form of Web document replication is mirroring. Mirroring consists of creating copies of (a part of) a Web site at multiple servers. The servers hosting a mirror of a given site are chosen manually, usually by way of server administrators volunteering to mirror a popular Web site. Setting up replication is also done manually by periodically copying the files from the origin server to each of its mirrors. The origin server typically presents a list of mirror servers to its clients, who are expected to select "the best one" manually.

The popularity of mirroring techniques is certainly due to their extreme simplicity. However, this simplicity imposes many limitations in terms of server selection, consistency, availability guarantees, client redirection and administration.

The selection of servers hosting the content is constrained by the willingness of Web server administrators, rather than by the actual needs of the mirrored site. For example, a site may end up having many mirrors in an area where very few clients access the site, and on the other hand, lack mirrors in areas where it is most popular.

The consistency of document replicas is ensured by copying documents periodically, typically once every few hours or days. This limits the effectiveness of mirroring to sites with slow update rates, or which can tolerate the delivery of outdated content to its clients.

A mirrored site does very little to guarantee its availability in the presence of server or network failures. There is no automatic failover mechanism, so when a client notices the unavailability of one mirror, (s)he is expected to select another mirror manually. Furthermore, a failure of the origin server typically means that new clients cannot access the list of mirrors. The whole site then becomes unreachable, even though many mirrors may still work correctly.

Presenting a list of mirrors to a client requires the client to select "the best server" manually. Mirror lists are usually annotated with the geographical location, in the hope that a server geographically close to a client will deliver acceptable performance. However, it is notoriously difficult for a user to predict which server will deliver best performance, as geographical distance is a poor predictor of the performance of an Internet client-to-server network path [37]. In addition, geographical distance says nothing about the current load of the server. In some cases, it may be wise to (temporarily) switch to a farther, but better performing server.

Finally, the decentralization of control of a mirrored site can lead to a number of difficulties. Each mirror server is usually administrated by a different person, who needs to

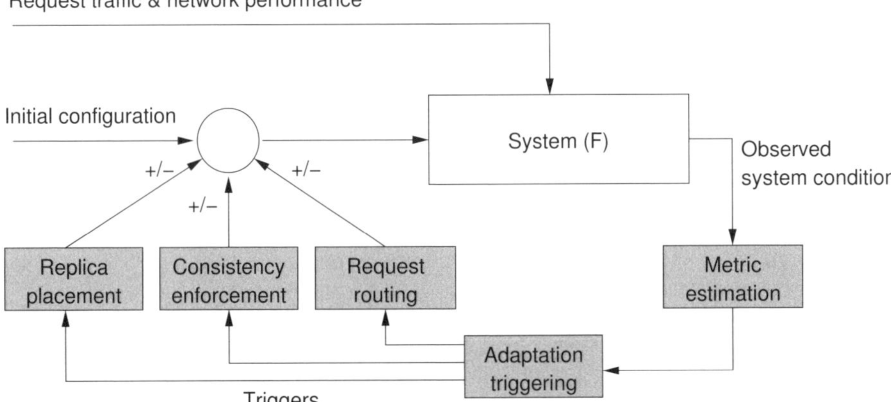

Figure 1. Abstract architecture of a content delivery network.

be contacted and convinced before any administrative task such as a change in configuration can take place. Similarly, each mirror maintains its own access log. Most mirrored sites do not require mirror servers to report their access logs to the origin server, which prevents the site owner from exploiting these logs for understanding the needs of clients or claiming revenue from advertisements embedded in the pages.

Most of the limitations of mirroring can be addressed by centralizing the control of replication, and automating a number of tasks. In particular, a popular Web site may buy servers, install them at well-chosen locations, and manage consistency maintenance itself across these servers. Additionally, a number of solutions can be implemented to automate the redirection of clients to one of the available servers. However, building such a worldwide system is very expensive, so from an economical point of view it often does not make sense to deploy a separate infrastructure for each Web site. This observation leads to the development of Content Delivery Networks (CDNs). A CDN provides many resources that can be dynamically allocated to the sites it is hosting, which allows to share the same infrastructure to host multiple unrelated sites. The next section describes the general design and architecture of most content delivery networks.

2.2. Content Delivery Networks Architecture

The best well-known commercial content delivery network is Akamai [4], but recent years have witnessed the development of many more [17]. Their detailed architecture is often considered a trade secret, but their general principles are known. Likewise, much academic research has been conducted in the domain [32,36].

The detailed architecture of content delivery networks is extremely diverse, but in essence every Web hosting system requires the same types of mechanisms. As illustrated in Figure 1, any content delivery network faces a continuously changing traffic of requests addressed by its clients and must deliver the requested documents via the Internet, whose performance also fluctuates. The goal of a CDN is to continuously adapt its configuration to provide a near-optimal quality of service at the lowest possible cost.

Such adaptation can affect the number and placement of replicas, the mechanisms used to maintain replicas consistent in the presence of updates, and the way client requests are directed to one of the replicas.

To take correct adaptation decisions, the system must monitor its own performance, such as the rate of requests addressed to each document and the location of clients. Although certain performance metrics are trivial to measure, others such as the inter-host network distance require specialized mechanisms [21,24,38].

Another issue is to decide when the system should adapt its configuration to maintain an acceptable level of performance. Adapting the configuration at regular time intervals allows the system to take into account long-term changes in the request traffic [30]. However, this technique does not allow a timely response to sudden changes in the request traffic. Large and abrupt changes in request rates do happen, and are known as flash crowds. To handle them, the system needs to quickly detect certain events which suggest that the situation is changing and that immediate adaptation is needed.

The actual system adaptation can take multiple forms, depending on the nature of the change in the request traffic and the network condition. The first possibility is to change the number or location of replicas. Multiple algorithms have been proposed to select replica placements that minimize the average client-to-replica distance, or to balance the load across replicas.

Another form of adaptation that a system can use is to change the way clients are redirected to replicas. Multiple mechanisms can be used to automatically redirect clients to a given replica, including DNS-based mechanisms [12,18], network-level packet redirection [33], and HTTP redirection. In addition, the system must define a policy to decide where each client should be redirected to. Many such policies have been defined [3,6,40].

Finally, the last type of adaptation is to change the way replicas are kept consistent in the presence of updates. We have shown that, for static Web documents, near-optimal performance can be attained by associating each document with the policy that suits it best [30]. Dynamic Web applications, which execute arbitrary code to generate documents upon each client request, clearly require different techniques, in particular when they access a backend database. Depending on the nature of an application and its client access pattern, different techniques such as fragment caching [13], database query result caching [11] and (partial) database replication [34] may be best employed.

Performance Evaluation Metrics

Evaluating the performance of a content delivery network is no easy task. In particular, there is no one metric that can capture the complexity of such a system. Instead, as shown in Table 1, there exists a wide range of metrics that can reflect the requirements of both the system's clients and the system's operator. For example, metrics related to latency, distance, and consistency can help evaluate the client-perceived performance. Similarly, metrics related to network usage and object hosting cost are required to control the overall system maintenance cost, which should remain within bounds defined by the system's operator.

Different metrics are by nature estimated in different manners. Certain metrics are trivial to measure in the CDN system itself, such as the amount of traffic generated over the network or the amount of storage resources currently in use. However, other relevant metrics such as the client-perceived download latency are much harder to evaluate from the point of view of the CDN and require dedicated measurement infrastructures. For

Table 1. Five different classes of metrics used to evaluate performance in content delivery networks.

Class	Description
Temporal	The metric reflects how long a certain action takes.
Spatial	The metric is expressed in terms of a distance that is related to the topology of the under-lying network, or region in which the network lies.
Usage	The metric is expressed in terms of usage of resources of the underlying network, notably consumed bandwidth.
Financial	Financial metrics are expressed in terms of a monetary unit, reflecting the monetary costs of deploying or using services of the replica hosting system.
Consistency	The metrics express to what extent a replica's value may differ from the master copy.

example, metric estimation services are commonly used to measure client latency or network distance. The consistency-related metrics are not measured by a separate metric estimation service, but are usually measured by instrumenting client applications.

Replica Placement

The performance of a CDN depends to a large extent on its ability to identify the location of its clients and to place replicas close to them. In conjunction with an appropriate request redirection mechanism, this allows to optimize the latency and/or bandwidth of the client-to-replica network path. For example, the delivery performance of typical small Web objects is mostly constrained by the network latency [44]. We have shown that a dozen of well-placed replicas can decrease the median client-to-replica latency by a ratio around 3 depending on the site's client population [39], which demonstrates the potential gain of well-placed replicas.

For a content delivery network, replica placement can be divided into two subproblems. The first one is *server placement*, which strives to select a number of locations where servers should be placed. Setting up a new server in a remote location takes time and clearly involves a significant financial cost. As a consequence, server placement typically tries to forecast interesting server locations regardless of the short-term needs of the currently hosted sites. Such algorithms base their decisions on the general topology of the Internet and try to optimize some cost metric without taking the location of actual clients into account.

The second subproblem is *replica placement*, which consists of deciding which of the existing servers should be used to host a particular piece of content [27]. Unlike server placement algorithms, content placement algorithms take as input fine-grain information about the localization of clients who access the particular piece of content to be placed. The cost involved by creating or deleting content replicas in existing servers is relatively low, so content placement algorithms can be executed often to follow the variations of request load as closely as possible.

Request Redirection

Placing replicas carefully can be useful only if clients actually access the replica closest to them. However, manual replica selection falls short of this requirement while it creates an unnecessary burden to the users. Instead, content delivery networks use a variety of mechanisms to automatically redirect clients to one of the replicas.

Request redirection first requires a redirection mechanism to instruct Web browsers of the server where they should issue their requests. Two mechanisms are commonly used. First, with HTTP redirection a redirector can decide on a per-page basis which replica server is to handle the request. To this end, the redirector returns the URL of the replicated page to the client. The drawback of HTTP redirection is the loss of transparency and control: as the client is effectively returned a modified URL, it can decide to cache that URL for future reference. As a consequence, removing or replacing a replica may render various cached URLs invalid. Alternatively, a second mechanism is DNS redirection. In this case, redirection is based entirely on a site's host name and the client's location. When the client resolves the site's host name, the redirector returns the IP address of the replica server closest to the client. In this case, redirection is done on a per-site basis as the DNS redirector has no means to differentiate between individual pages. On the other hand, DNS redirection is mostly transparent to the client, allowing for better control of replica placement. Most CDNs employ DNS redirection.

In addition to a redirection mechanism, one needs to define a redirection policy which decides where each client should be redirected to. Policies usually try to redirect clients to a replica server close to them. However, other criteria such as the respective load of replica servers may also be taken into account when taking this decision [19,26].

Consistency Maintenance

Creating copies of Web documents creates a new problem: when a document is updated, old copies need to be refreshed or destroyed so that no outdated information is delivered to the clients. A wealth of techniques have been developed to achieve this [42], but they can essentially be classified along three main dimensions.

The first dimension is the level of consistency that a specific consistency policy provides. Ideally, one would like no outdated document to be ever delivered to a client. Techniques to achieve this are however quite expensive in terms of necessary network traffic. To address this issue, many policies relax the consistency requirement by allowing some bounded level of inconsistency. Such inconsistency bounds are often expressed as a maximum time during which an outdated version is allowed to remain in the system, but they can also be expressed in terms of the number of outstanding updates or semantic distance between versions [43].

The second dimension is the nature of the update messages that are exchanged in the system. When a document is updated, the simplest form of update, called *state shipping*, consists of transferring the whole content of the new version. However, if only a few changes were applied to a long document, it might be more efficient to propagate those differences only, leading to *delta shipping*. Finally, *function shipping* carries the identity and parameters of an operation that must be applied to the outdated version to bring it up-to-date. Note that the latter two forms require that each replica server has a copy of the previous version available.

The third dimension is the direction in which updates are propagated. In some systems, the origin server *pushes* updates to its replicas. Other systems prefer replica servers to *pull* updates from their origin. Hybrid schemes also exist, and combine both approaches depending on the characteristics of the document [10].

An interesting form of document consistency was used in the Akamai CDN [28]. In this scheme, a hash of the content of a document is embedded in its URL. When a document is updated, the new version has a different hash value, so it is stored independently from the old version at a URL containing the new hash value. All other documents referring to it merely need to update their references to replace the old URL with the new one. The old document version can coexist with the new one, as these are in fact implemented as two different documents. The old one, which ceases to be requested, is rapidly evicted from the system. Although this mechanism is very elegant, it has one drawback: a document's URL changes at each update, which makes this technique applicable only to the replication of embedded contents (images, videos, etc.). HTML documents cannot be easily replicated using this technique, which perhaps explains why Akamai apparently does not use this consistency policy any more.

Adaptation Triggering

As mentioned previously, the goal of a CDN is to continuously monitor its own performance so that it can adapt its configuration to changes in the traffic of requests it handles, and maintain near-optimal performance over time. This raises the question: when should a CDN update its configuration? Adaptations usually involve a cost (e.g., in terms of performance during the transition or cost of increased network traffic) so an adaptation should take place only if its anticipated benefits exceed the involved costs.

The simplest adaptation triggering scheme consists of adapting the system on a periodic basis. We have shown that, provided that the access patterns do not change too quickly, periodically re-evaluating the configuration of a CDN allows one to maintain near-optimal performance over time [30]. In such a scheme, the system periodically collects information about its own recent behavior, and evaluates whether a different configuration would have offered a better performance. If so, it then updates its own configuration accordingly.

A major drawback of such an approach is that it relies on the assumption that recent past access patterns allow one to predict the near future with a reasonable accuracy. Should access patterns change dramatically between two periodic adaptations, such as upon the occurrence of a flash crowd, the system would be unable to react in a timely manner. Due to a variety of reasons, a server's request load can increase by several orders of magnitude within minutes, and decrease back to normal only after several hours [2].

Figure 2 shows the variation of load of four different Web sites. Figure 2(a) shows normal variations of load according to a day-and-night pattern. Even though the load does vary to a large extent, its variations are predictable enough to be efficiently handled by periodic adaptation. On the other hand, Figures 2(b), 2(c) and 2(d) show abnormal behavior with harder-to-predict huge load peaks. In such situations, a system cannot rely on periodic adaptation any more. What is needed is to detect the flash crowd at its earliest stage, *predict* its near-future characteristics, and proactively adapt the system accordingly [8]. Adaptation often consists of increasing the number of replicas of the concerned documents. However, adapting the consistency and redirection policies may also help to a certain extent, for example to switch from a proximity-based redirection policy to a load-balancing-based one.

2.3. Dynamic Document Hosting

With the development of Web forums, e-commerce sites, blogs and many others, an increasing fraction of Web content is not delivered from a static file but generated dynamically each time a request is received. Dynamically generating Web contents allows servers to deliver personalized contents to each user, and to take action when specific requests are issued, such as ordering an item from an e-commerce site.

     G. Pierre et al. / From Web Servers to Ubiquitous Content Delivery

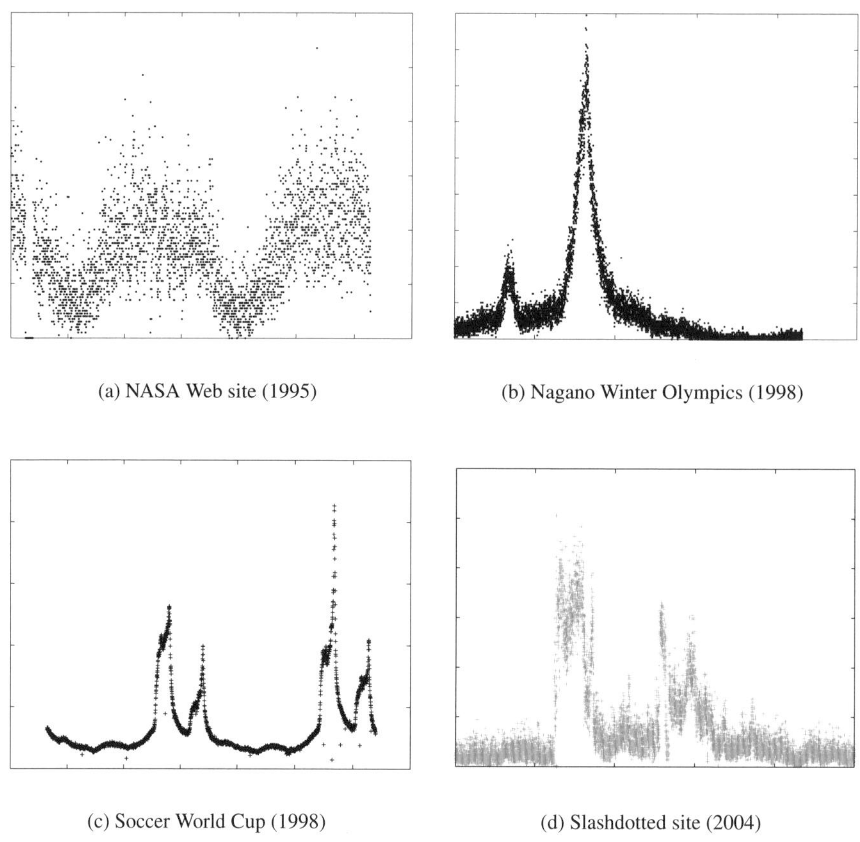

(a) NASA Web site (1995)   (b) Nagano Winter Olympics (1998)

(c) Soccer World Cup (1998)   (d) Slashdotted site (2004)

Figure 2. One normal server load, and three different flash crowds (adapted from [8]).

Dynamic Web applications are often organized along a three-tiered architecture, as depicted in Figure 3(a). When a request is issued, the Web server invokes application-specific code, which generates the content to be delivered to the client. This application code, in turn, issues queries to a database where the application state is preserved.

From the point of view of a content delivery network, it can be tempting to host such Web applications using similar techniques as for static content. One can indeed ignore the fact that documents are dynamically generated, and cache the content as it is generated by the application. However, this technique, called fragment caching, offers poor performance as it is often unlikely that the exact same request will be issued again at the same server. Moreover, maintaining the consistency of dynamic document copies is hard because any update in the underlying database can potentially invalidate a copy.

An improved solution consists of duplicating the application code at all replica servers while the database remains centralized. This allows each server to execute the application in reaction to client requests (see Figure 3(b)). Edge server computing, as it is called, allows servers to generate contents tailored to the specificities of each client request while distributing the computational load [16]. On the other hand, the central-

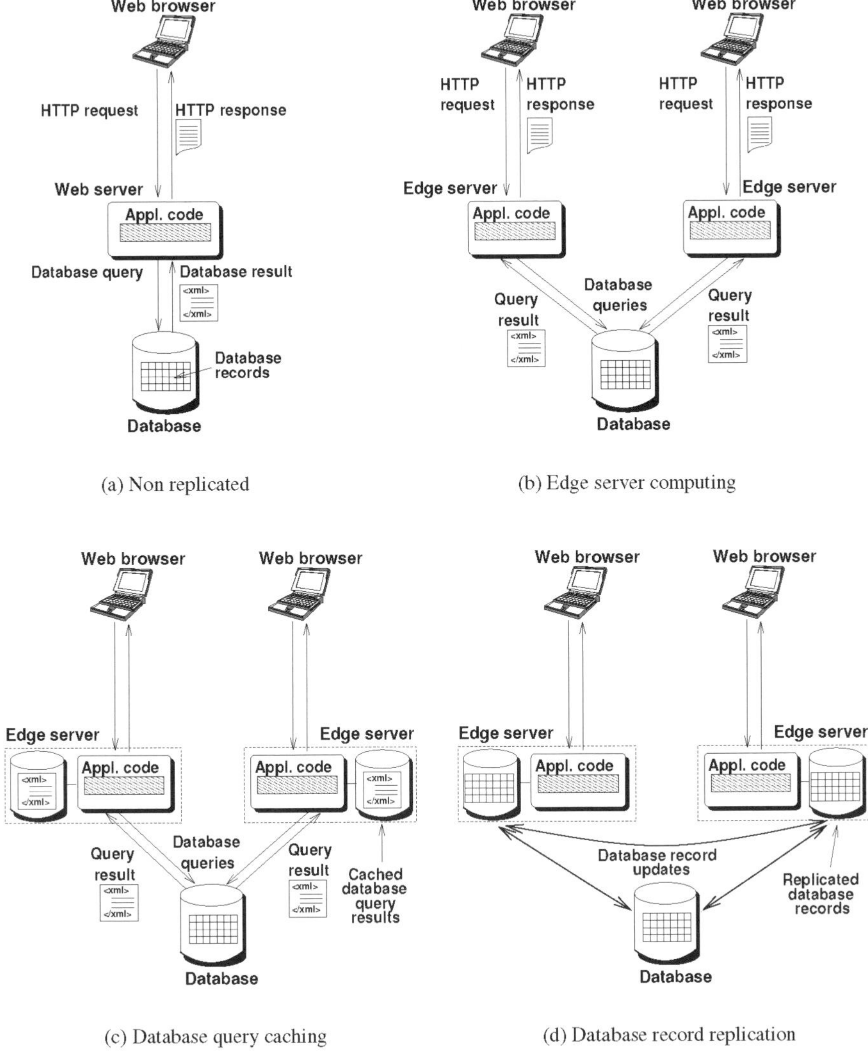

(a) Non replicated

(b) Edge server computing

(c) Database query caching

(d) Database record replication

Figure 3. Various Web application hosting techniques (adapted from [29]).

ized database often constitutes a performance bottleneck, which limits the scale that such systems can reach.

To overcome these limitations, it is necessary to move the data to the edge servers, thereby reducing the load of the database. To this end, two types of systems can be distinguished. First, it is possible to cache the results of database queries at the edge servers (Figure 3(c)). Content-aware caching requires each edge server to run its own database server which contains a partial view of the centralized database [5,11]. Each query is subject to a so-called 'query containment check' to determine if it can be answered from the locally-available data. When this is not the case, the query is issued to the central database. Results are subsequently inserted in the local database, before being returned to the application.

A second, simpler alternative to content-aware caching is content-blind caching, where the edge servers do not need to run a database server nor be aware of the database structure [35]. Instead, it stores query result structures independently from each other. This results in storing potentially redundant information at the edge servers. On the other hand, storing precomputed query results eliminates the database overhead of content-aware caching.

Finally, database caching techniques work well only for applications which repeatedly issue the same queries to their database. For applications which do not exhibit this behavior, it can be more efficient to replicate the whole database at the edge servers (Figure 3(d)). This guarantees that edge servers can always query their local database copy. On the other hand, database replication involves a lot of communication when the database is updated. One way to deal with this problem is to use partial database replication [34].

2.4. Discussion

As can be seen, content delivery networks are significantly more sophisticated than mirrored environments in terms of automation and control. Many issues that are typically handled manually in mirrored systems can in fact be best realized in a more automatic fashion, such as continuously evaluating the system's performance, selecting appropriate numbers and locations of replicas, redirecting requests and maintaining consistency. Also, only automatic systems are likely to deal with a flash crowd in a timely manner.

A different set of techniques must be used by CDNs to host dynamic Web applications. In comparison, mirroring techniques can only host very specific types of applications (such as an application containing only code, but no database).

CDNs also provide improved control over the system. While the administration of a mirrored system mostly relies on the good will of a multitude of administrators, CDNs offer more centralized control based on systematic performance evaluations and well-defined adaptation strategies. Such centralized control, however, is made possible mostly by the fact that a single entity (the CDN operator) owns and controls the whole server infrastructure, which may be dispersed across the Internet. Such an architecture restricts the operation of a CDN to large companies capable of investing the necessary funds, and which expect return on investments. In practice, this means that CDNs build commercial offers for the use of their infrastructure, which in turn limits the use of these technologies to a restricted class of Web site owners.

3. Collaborative Content Delivery Networks

Deploying CDN technology for only a single Web site is difficult as it requires that the owner has access to a large collection of machines placed at strategic locations in the Internet. Moreover, it is highly inefficient not to share this infrastructure as it effectively amounts to a gross overprovisioning of resources for just a single site.

On the other hand, it is not obvious why Web hosting for increased quality of service should be outsourced, as in many cases the necessary resources are already available elsewhere in the system. Certain users or organizations, such as a supermarket chain, may have multiple computers online, so the extra resources needed are generally already available in-house. Alternatively, several users can decide to build their own CDN and join their respective resources in order to average everyone's resource needs over all the provided servers. Consider, for example, a retail chain. Assuming that each shop will always have at least one computer online (most of the time), the extra resources needed are probably already available in-house. As another example, worldwide nongovernmental organizations may be able to connect the computers of their local branches and team up to jointly host a single fully distributed Web site, making effective use of their own resources. A similar argument holds for other groups of which the members may want to jointly host a Web site, such as many virtual online communities. We thus come up with a collaborative model where independent organizations team up their resources for each other's benefit.

Collaborative content distribution networks are similar in architecture to noncooperative CDNs as described in the previous section: they need to evaluate performance, handle replica placement, do request redirection, maintain consistency, and trigger adaptations in order to keep the system's performance as close as possible to the optimum. We shall not detail these issues here, as they are mostly identical to those discussed in Section 2. However, the fact that CCDNs are operated by a group of organizations rather than a single entity creates a number of issues. In a system such as Globule [29] and DotSlash [45], each Web site ends up being replicated at a collection of servers which belong to different organizations and may not have the same goals and policies regarding the system. This raises a number of new issues regarding system management and security.

3.1. Availability

In a CCDN, resources are typically contributed by many organizations independent from each other, with very few guarantees regarding their availability. Servers may become unreachable due to voluntary disconnection from their owner, or because of a hardware, software or network failure. For these reasons, CCDNs should expect any server to be unreachable a significant fraction of the time. Moreover, when the number of servers taking part in hosting a given site increases, the probability that at least one server is unreachable grows quickly. A CCDN therefore needs to make sure that a site will remain functional even when a fraction of its hosting servers fail.

The first problem to address is the availability of the redirector subsystem at the time of a client request. When using DNS redirection, this issue is easily solved. A DNS redirector is simply a DNS server responsible for the site's host name, and which returns responses customized to each client. The DNS protocol allows multiple redundant servers to be registered for the same name; if one server fails, then the other ones are automatically queried instead.

The second issue is to make sure that at least one server is available at any time, and has a copy of the contents to be delivered. This advocates some form of full replication, where a site's contents is fully replicated at a number of servers. The Web site as a whole cannot experience a failure as long as one of these servers remains available. Note that this does not rule out all forms of caching or partial replication. Globule, for example, supports two forms of replication simultaneously: full replication across a few 'backup servers' guarantees the site's availability, while partial replication across a potentially large number of 'replica servers' is in charge of optimizing the site's content delivery performance.

Finally, it is necessary that the redirector subsystem monitors the availability of the servers participating in hosting a given site. When one server fails, the redirector should redirect requests to a 'second best' server so that the failure is not perceived by the clients.

3.2. Brokerage

An important goal of a CCDN is to offer Web site owners suitable servers where to host their contents. However, in a CCDN servers may join or leave the system at any time. In such conditions, finding good servers where to host a site's content may prove difficult.

First, the definition of a 'good' server is more complex in a CCDN than in a commercial CDN. Clearly, criteria such as a server's location and network capacity are crucial. But other criteria such as the availability of specific dynamic document generation software, the identity of a server's owner and server-specific access right policies may also influence the choice. In particular, it is very important for server administrators to keep control over which site is hosted at their server.

One solution is to make administrators negotiate access rights manually, as done for example in DotSlash [45]. Such a choice is suitable for DotSlash, as this system is mostly concerned with handling flash crowds. In this system, peer servers are involved in delivering another site's content only upon a flash crowd. When this happens, the number and capacity of servers that take place in the 'flash-crowd rescue' are more important than their location.

However, when content replication is to be realized on a permanent basis and servers are expected to join and leave the system at will, such manual hosting negotiation is not practical any more. To address this issue, Globule proposes servers to register to a central repository so that queries can be issued to find suitable servers. Administrators can also specify policies to define who is authorized to host content at their server. Finally, they are proposed a number of servers with compatible access right policies to host replicas of their content.

3.3. Security

In a CCDN, a server will often host content that does not belong to its own administrator. In such situations, most administrators would demand guarantees that potentially malicious content cannot damage the server, by means of excessive resource usage, access to confidential information, or any other type of misbehavior. This threat is particularly present when hosting dynamic content, where arbitrary code can be executed to generate documents. This is a well-known problem, however, which is usually addressed by means of sandboxing techniques [1].

Another more difficult security issue is that a content owner expects guarantees that replica servers will actually perform their assigned task faithfully. A malicious replica server could, for example, reject incoming connections (creating a denial-of-service attack) or deliver modified versions of the original content. It is impossible for an origin server to check directly the content delivered by a replica server to a client without negating the benefits of replication. Instead, it is necessary to involve (some of) the clients in checking the contents and reporting misbehaviors to the origin server. When the site is made of static content, the origin server can sign documents and expect clients or client-side proxies to check signatures. When dynamically-generated content is involved, however, more sophisticated techniques become necessary [31].

3.4. Discussion

Collaborative CDNs allow individually contributed servers to team up resources in the form of storage capacity, bandwidth and processing power. In return, their Web content is transparently and automatically replicated according to quality-of-service demands regarding performance, availability, and reliability. In this way, a collaborative CDN offers the same service as a commercial CDN, but at virtually no extra costs beyond what a member is already paying for Internet connectivity.

Most implementation techniques used in CDNs can be used in CCDNs as well. However, CCDNs experience new issues due to distributed management and security concerns that do not appear in CDNs. Current solutions to these issues introduce some additional burden to the administrators, who are not necessarily professionals in the domain. These constraints drive the need for simpler content distribution technologies, even at the cost of very restricted functionality.

4. Peer-to-Peer Content Delivery Networks

A completely different approach to distributing Web content in a decentralized fashion is the use of peer-to-peer technologies. Unlike traditional CDNs, peer-to-peer systems spread the request load across all their members hosts, which makes them extremely resilient to node failures and load surges.

Although very similar in features to a content delivery network, traditional peer-to-peer systems such as Gnutella [23] and BitTorrent [14] have not been specifically designed to host Web content. They are only focused at large-scale delivery of large, static and immutable files such as music or video files. Web content, on the other hand, is much harder to deliver using this type of overlays because it is made of many small documents which are potentially updated frequently or even generated dynamically. Moreover, these systems are designed to be access using specific client applications rather than standard Web browsers, which breaks the transparency requirement discussed in the introduction. Finally, the way they route requests through the overlay is often not designed to optimize document access latency but to maximize the throughput and the scalability of the system.

A number of peer-to-peer-based systems have been built specifically to host Web content. Systems such as Coral [22] and CoDeeN [41] are in fact made of a (potentially large) number of Web caches that cooperate with each other by way of peer-to-peer technologies. This architecture allows to handle large amounts of traffic with significantly better performance than noncooperative caches. It also enables regular Web browsers to access them using the standard HTTP protocol.

It must be noted that Web-oriented peer-to-peer CDNs do not involve the browsing users into the content delivery itself. Instead, both systems mentioned above are actually operated over a relatively limited number of servers, all of which remain under the control of their respective programmers [15]. Although their architecture does not clearly impose such centralized control, peer-to-peer CDNs will need to solve the same issues as collaborative CDNs before they can really be deployed in a fully decentralized fashion.

The architectures of Coral and CoDeeN as Web caches have another important consequence: the origin server does not actively participate in these systems. Building a CDN independent from the origin servers allows the replication of any Web site with no intervention of the site owner. However, it also prevents the CDN from hosting dynamically generated content as all techniques described in Section 2.3 except fragment caching require specific support at the origin server. Dynamically-generated content is typically considered not cacheable, which is the reason why current peer-to-peer CDNs are effective at hosting static content only.

It must be noted that, although existing peer-to-peer CDNs cannot host dynamically generated content efficiently, there is no fundamental reason why this would be impossible. However, one would need to host both application code and data in a peer-to-peer network, and provide a rich interface to access and modify the data. A number of research efforts is being conducted in this direction [20,25] which might in the future allow peer-to-peer CDNs to efficiently host dynamic Web applications.

5. Conclusion

Replicating a Web site over a collection of servers can improve the site's access performance and availability. The simplest form of Web replication is mirroring in which all replication-related issues are handled manually. However, mirroring falls short in terms of systematic performance improvement, availability guarantees and ease of administration.

Content delivery networks provide Web sites with advanced replication techniques. Most aspects of replication are handled automatically, such as replica placement, consistency maintenance, request redirection, etc. CDNs also continuously evaluate their own performance to automatically adapt their configuration upon changes in the request traffic.

Collaborative content distribution networks allow independent people or organizations to cooperate in order to build their own content delivery network. If done right, such a system can provide the same features as a commercial CDN, but at virtually no extra cost beyond what each member is already paying for Internet connectivity. CCDNs use similar techniques to CDNs, but they also face additional specific issues regarding management and trust, which make them harder to operate.

Finally, a next step toward decentralization is represented by peer-to-peer content delivery systems. These systems have the advantage of spreading the request load across all their members hosts, which makes them extremely resilient to node failures and load surges. On the other hand, their architecture currently limits them to hosting static Web content. More complex data types such as dynamic Web applications are currently beyond the reach of these systems.

Decentralized Web site replication is very appealing for reasons of cost, robustness and reactiveness to flash crowds. However, the more decentralized the hosting platform, the more difficult it is to provide rich features such as dynamic document replication. Very active research is being conducted in this area, so we can expect future Web hosting systems to approach the goal of a true ubiquitous content delivery infrastructure.

References

[1] M. Achour, F. Betz, A. Dovgal, N. Lopes, P. Olson, G. Richter, D. Seguy, J. Vrana, and several others. *PHP Manual*, chapter 42: Safe Mode. PHP Documentation Group, 2005. http://www.php.net/features.safe-mode.

[2] S. Adler. The Slashdot effect: An analysis of three Internet publications. http://ssadler.phy. bnl.gov/adler/SDE/SlashDotEffect.html.

[3] A. Aggarwal and M. Rabinovich. Performance of replication schemes for an Internet hosting service. Technical Report HA6177000-981030-01-TM, AT&T Research Labs, Florham Park, NJ, October 1998.

[4] Akamai. http://www.akamai.com/.

[5] K. Amiri, S. Park, R. Tewari, and S. Padmanabhan. DBProxy: A dynamic data cache for Web applications. In *Proc. 19th Intl. Conf. on Data Engineering (ICDE)*, pages 821–831, Bangalore, India, March 2003.

[6] M. Andrews, B. Shepherd, A. Srinivasan, P. Winkler, and F. Zane. Clustering and server selection using passive monitoring. In *Proc. 21st INFOCOM Conference*, pages 1717–1725, New York, USA, June 2002.

[7] L.A. Barroso, J. Dean, and U. Hölzle. Web search for a planet: The Google cluster architecture. *IEEE Micro*, 23(2):22–28, March-April 2003.

[8] Y. Baryshnikov, E.G. Coffman, G. Pierre, D. Rubenstein, M. Squillante, and T. Yimwadsana. Predictability of web-server traffic congestion. In *Proc. 10th Intl. Workshop on Web Content Caching and Distribution*, pages 97–103, Sophia Antipolis, France, September 2005.

[9] T. Berners-Lee, R. Cailliau, A. Luotonen, H.F. Nielsen, and A. Secret. The World-Wide Web. *Communications of the ACM*, 37(8):76–82, August 1994.

[10] M. Bhide, P. Deolasee, A. Katkar, A. Panchbudhe, K. Ramamritham, and P. Shenoy. Adaptive push-pull: Disseminating dynamic Web data. *IEEE Transactions on Computers*, 51(6):652–668, June 2002.

[11] C. Bornhövd, M. Altinel, C. Mohan, H. Pirahesh, and B. Reinwald. Adaptive database caching with DBCache. *Data Engineering*, 27(2):11–18, June 2004.

[12] V. Cardellini, M. Colajanni, and P.S. Yu. Request redirection algorithms for distributed web systems. *IEEE Transactions on Parallel and Distributed Systems*, 14(4):355–368, April 2003.

[13] J. Challenger, P. Dantzig, A. Iyengar, and K. Witting. A fragment-based approach for efficiently creating dynamic Web content. *ACM Transactions on Internet Technologies*, 5(2):359–389, May 2005.

[14] B. Cohen. Incentives build robustness in BitTorrent. In *Proc. Workshop on Economics of Peer-to-Peer Systems*, Berkeley, CA, USA, June 2003.

[15] Coral frequently asked questions. Can I run a CoralCDN node? http://wiki.coralcdn.org/ wiki.php/Main/FAQ#runnode.

[16] A. Davis, J. Parikh, and W.E. Weihl. EdgeComputing: Extending enterprise applications to the edge of the Internet. In *Proc. Intl. World Wide Web Conference*, pages 180–187, New York, USA, May 2004.

[17] B.D. Davison. Web caching and content delivery resources. http://www.web-caching.com/.

[18] J. Dilley, B. Maggs, J. Parikh, H. Prokop, R. Sitaraman, and B. Weihl. Globally distributed content delivery. *IEEE Internet Computing*, 6(5):50–58, September 2002.

[19] C. Ferdean and M. Makpangou. A response time-driven replica server selection substrate for application replica hosting systems. In *Proc. Intl. Symposium on Applications and the Internet*, Phoenix, Arizona, USA, January 2006.

[20] W. Fontijn and P. A. Boncz. AmbientDB: P2P data management middleware for ambient intelligence. In *Proc. Workshop on Middleware Support for Pervasive Computing*, pages 203–208, Orlando, FL, USA, March 2004.

[21] P. Francis, S. Jamin, C. Jin, Y. Jin, D. Raz, Y. Shavitt, and L. Zhang. IDMaps: A global Internet host distance estimation service. *IEEE/ACM Transaction on Networking*, 9(5):525–

540, October 2001.

[22] M.J. Freedman, E. Freudenthal, and D. Mazières. Democratizing content publication with Coral. In *Proc. 1st Symposium on Networked Systems Design and Implementation*, pages 239–252, San Francisco, CA, March 2004.

[23] Gnutella. http://www.gnutella.com/.

[24] K.P. Gummadi, S. Saroiu, and S.D. Gribble. King: Estimating latency between arbitrary Internet end hosts. In *Proc. 2nd SIGCOMM Internet Measurement Workshop*, pages 5–18, Marseille, France, November 2002.

[25] R. Huebsch, B. Chun, J.M. Hellerstein, B.T. Loo, P. Maniatis, T. Roscoe, S. Shenker, I. Stoica, and A.R. Yumerefendi. The architecture of PIER: an Internet-scale query processor. In *Proc. Conference on Innovative Data Systems Research*, pages 28–43, Asilomar, CA, USA, January 2005.

[26] K.L. Johnson, J.F. Carr, M.S. Day, and M.F. Kaashoek. The measured performance of content distribution networks. *Computer Communications*, 24(2):202–206, February 2001.

[27] M. Karlsson and C. Karamanolis. Choosing replica placement heuristics for wide-area systems. In *Proc. Intl. Conference on Distributed Computing Systems*, pages 350–359, Tokyo, Japan, March 2004.

[28] F. Thomson Leighton and Daniel M. Lewis. Global hosting system. United States Patent, Number US6108703, August 2000.

[29] G. Pierre and M. van Steen. Globule: a collaborative content delivery network. Submitted for publication, November 2005.

[30] G. Pierre, M. van Steen, and A.S. Tanenbaum. Dynamically selecting optimal distribution strategies for Web documents. *IEEE Transactions on Computers*, 51(6):637–651, June 2002.

[31] B.C. Popescu, J. Sacha, M. van Steen, B. Crispo, A.S. Tanenbaum, and I. Kuz. Securely replicated web documents. In *Proc. 19th Intl. Parallel and Distributed Processing Symposium*, Denver, CO, USA, April 2005.

[32] M. Rabinovich and O. Spatscheck. *Web Caching and Replication*. Addison Wesley, Reading, MA, USA, 2002. ISBN: 0201615703.

[33] P. Rodriguez and S. Sibal. SPREAD: Scalable platform for reliable and efficient automated distribution. *Computer Network*, 33(1–6):33–46, 2000.

[34] S. Sivasubramanian, G. Alonso, G. Pierre, and M. van Steen. GlobeDB: Autonomic data replication for Web applications. In *Proc. 14th Intl. World-Wide Web Conference*, pages 33–42, Chiba, Japan, May 2005.

[35] S. Sivasubramanian, G. Pierre, M. van Steen, and G. Alonso. GlobeCBC: Content-blind result caching for dynamic Web applications. Submitted for publication, October 2005.

[36] S. Sivasubramanian, M. Szymaniak, G. Pierre, and M. van Steen. Replication for web hosting systems. *ACM Computing Surveys*, 36(3):291–334, 2004.

[37] L. Subramanian, V.N. Padmanabhan, and R.H. Katz. Geographic properties of Internet routing. In *Proc. Usenix Annual Technical Conference*, pages 243–259, Monterey, CA, USA, June 2002.

[38] M. Szymaniak, G. Pierre, and M. van Steen. Scalable cooperative latency estimation. In *Proc. 10th Intl. Conference on Parallel and Distributed Systems*, pages 367-376, Newport Beach, CA, USA, July 2004.

[39] M. Szymaniak, G. Pierre, and M. van Steen. Latency-driven replica placement. In *Proc. Intl. Symposium on Applications and the Internet*, pages 399-405, Trento, Italy, February 2005.

[40] L. Wang, V. Pai, and L. Peterson. The effectiveness of request redirection on CDN robustness. In *Proc. 5th Symposium on Operating System Design and Implementation*, pages 345–360, Boston, MA, December 2002.

[41] L. Wang, K. Park, R. Pang, V.S. Pai, and L. Peterson. Reliability and security in the CoDeeN content distribution network. In *Proc. Usenix Annual Technical Conference*, pages 171–184, Boston, MA, June 2004.

[42] J. Yin, L. Alvisi, M. Dahlin, and A. Iyengar. Engineering Web cache consistency. *ACM*

Transactions on Internet Technologies, 2(3):224–259, August 2002.

[43] H. Yu and A. Vahdat. Design and evaluation of a conit-based continuous consistency model for replicated services. *ACM Transactions on Computer Systems*, 20(3):239–282, August 2002.

[44] M. Zari, H. Saiedian, and M. Naeem. Understanding and reducing Web delays. *IEEE Computer*, 34(12):30–37, December 2001.

[45] W. Zhao and H. Schulzrinne. DotSlash: A self-configuring and scalable rescue system for handling web hotspots effectively. In *Proc. Intl. Workshop on Web Caching and Content Distribution*, pages 1–18, Beijing, China, October 2004.

Global Data Management
R. Baldoni et al. (Eds.)
IOS Press, 2006

CROSSFLUX: An Architecture for Peer-to-Peer Media Streaming

Marc Schiely and Pascal Felber

Computer Science Department, University of Neuchâtel
CH-2007, Neuchâtel, Switzerland
{marc.schiely, pascal.felber}@unine.ch

Abstract. The use of peer-to-peer (P2P) networks for distributing content has been widely discussed in the last few years and the most important properties have been identified: scalability, efficiency and reliability. With CROSSFLUX we propose a P2P system for media streaming which incorporates these properties starting from the design. In addition reliability is coupled with fairness by rewarding peers that contribute more with a higher number of backup links. This coupling can be achieved by using links (1) for content distribution in one direction and (2) as backup in the opposite direction. For maximizing the throughput and distributing the load among the participating nodes an adaptive join procedure and reorganization algorithms are being used. Our evaluation of CROSSFLUX shows that recovery of node failures is fast and efficiency is increased with the help of our techniques.

1. Introduction

With the increasing demand for media streaming over the Internet, there have been a number of academic and commercial initiatives for designing architectures to enhance the quality, improve the reliability, and decrease the cost of content distribution. One of the most promising approaches is based on peer-to-peer (P2P) networks, where the end systems participate actively in the dissemination of information, thus alleviating the need for costly server overlays (e.g., CDNs). File distribution systems like KaZaa, BitTorrent, or eMule have contributed to the popularity of the P2P technology. While a large number of P2P networks have been developed for sharing files, the distribution of time-sensitive streaming content has been mostly overlooked so far.

The major challenges of media streaming systems derive from their timing constraints. Although a media stream can be split into multiple chunks that are distributed independently among participating nodes, as in classical file distribution systems, each block must arrive before its scheduled playback time. This implies, for instance, that traditional mechanisms to deal with message loss (ack- or nack-based) are not readily applicable to media streaming. If the block arrives late, playback must be delayed or part of the stream must be discarded. This major difference has some important implications on the design of P2P media streaming architectures, as we shall discuss in this paper.

The scalability of a P2P media streaming architecture is directly related to its service capacity, i.e., the aggregate upstream bandwidth of participating peers, and the way this capacity is used and shared among the peers. Video content, for instance, needs sufficient bandwidth for being streamed in an acceptable quality. Here, the goal is to provide each peer with the same uniform bandwidth of highest capacity, unlike traditional file distribution systems that try to minimize individual download times. In a real environment, where nodes have heterogeneous and fluctuating bandwidth capacities, it is essential to develop adaptive mechanisms to dynamically update the network topology so as to maximize usage of the available bandwidth and minimize end-to-end latency. We shall discuss different approaches to reach that goal and present our solution based on the *HeapTop* [1] algorithm and uniform rate distribution strategies [2].

Another major problem that P2P systems have to deal with are node failures. As the different peers are under the control of randomly acting users and typically consist of low-end hardware, failures are expected to occur often. Therefore, the architecture must be able to withstand a significant number of ungraceful failures and recover with no interruption of the time-sensitive stream.

A number of approaches have been proposed to deal with the stringent requirements of media streaming. One of the most well-known system is SplitStream [3], which uses multiple description coding to split a stream into different stripes that can be distributed independently. A separate distribution tree is constructed on the same set of nodes for each of the stripes, in such a way that each peer is an inner node of at most one tree. This property guarantees that a single node failure affects only one tree. While SplitStream offers a promising approach, it suffers from a few drawbacks which we address in our system: (1) the SplitStream architecture is too rigid (it does not adapt well to the dynamics of the network), (2) the recovery of node failures may not be very fast and (3) the system is not well adapted to heterogeneity in node bandwidth.

With CROSSFLUX, we propose a scalable, efficient, and reliable architecture for P2P media streaming. As in SplitStream, the initial stream is split into multiple stripes. These stripes are distributed across a *mesh* interconnecting the peers. Under normal operation, a link between two peers p and q is used to transmit a single stripe s from p to q; in case of failure, it can also be used in the reverse direction to send other stripes (different from s) from q to p. This mechanism guarantees path redundancy between the source and any peer, and it rewards the peers with a high outdegree (big contributors) by providing them increased reliability.

During the construction process of the distribution topology, we try to place nodes in branches that are less loaded. We use adaptive algorithms to evenly distribute the load among the peers and to give sufficient bandwidth to each of them. These algorithms rely on passive measurements and information aggregation techniques. Dynamic reorganization is performed locally by the nodes in order to enhance the topology: nodes that have higher bandwidth capacities are moved closer to the source by pairwise exchanges with lower capacity nodes.

Evaluation of CROSSFLUX using the Modelnet [4] network simulator demonstrate its good scalability and performance even under high churn.

2. Challenges in P2P Media Streaming

While the use of P2P techniques for media streaming offers many benefits, it also comes with a number of challenges that have to be dealt with. In addition to the problems usually encountered in classical P2P systems, such as withstanding high churn, additional challenges are specific to media streaming. We take a closer look at these issues and discuss existing solutions.

2.1. Scalability

We usually distinguish between three types of P2P architectures: (1) systems that rely on a single central instance of a specific component, (2) fully decentralized architectures where each participating peer has the same role, and (3) hybrid or hierarchical models with some peers (usually called "superpeers") having a specific role. Obviously, the scalability of the first approach is limited by the capacity of the central instance, which also represents a single point of failure. The hybrid approach mitigates this problem by essentially replicating the service provided by the superpeers.

Fully decentralized architectures have the greatest potential for scalability and reliability, but they have to face additional complexity in their topology management protocols. As there is no global knowledge about the network, all operations have to be made locally. As we have seen for instance in [1], this may lead to slightly sub-optimal performance (when compared to centralized, omniscient algorithms) but this is a small price for having a scalable system. Further, as each peer has the same role, failures are not as critical as the failure of a centralized component or a super peer in a hybrid model. In environments with high churn, where many nodes join and leave the system, this property is essential.

2.2. Robustness

One of the major advantages of the P2P paradigm is also one of its biggest problem: the peers are acting in an unpredictable manner and independently of each others. The rate at which peers join and leave the system can be very high. Worse, departures may be ungraceful in the sense that peers fail or leave without prior notification. As a consequence, P2P system must incorporate some form of self-healing mechanisms and construct robust topologies (e.g., using redundant paths).

In general, the robustness of P2P networks can be increased by using either data redundancy or path redundancy. The most widely used techniques for data redundancy are *forward error correction* (FEC), *layered coding* and *multiple description coding* (MDC). FEC uses encoding techniques, such as Reed-Solomon codes, to encode a number of packets n into m packets where $m > n$. Any subset k $(k \geq n)$ of these m packets is enough to reconstruct the n original packets.

In layered coding, the original media stream is split into different layers with different importance. The base layer is the most important and must be received in any case. Each additional layer improves the quality of the stream but is not mandatory.

Finally, MDC is a combination of FEC and layered coding. First, layered coding is used to order groups of frames by their importance. Then, these groups are encoded with FEC where the redundancy factor is chosen according to the importance of the group of frames. With MDC, any subset of such encoded descriptions can be used to decode the original stream.

Redundancy in data alone does not help if a peer has only one neighbor serving the data. If this single data source fails then the peer does not get any data. A better strategy is to have multiple neighbors that serve different parts of the stream such that, if a subset of the neighbors fail, the remaining peers can still serve the data needed to play back the stream. Most existing P2P media streaming systems provide such support for path diversity, e.g., using redundant distribution trees or mesh-based topologies.

2.3. Latency

P2P media streaming architectures are based on application-level overlay networks. This means that messages from the source to a given peer typically follow a longer route than IP's shortest path. In order to minimize the network's stretch and the end-to-end latency, peers that are physically close should be neighbors in the logical overlay. Thus, the construction of the distribution architecture does not only need to take into account robustness, but also performance metrics. The neighbors of a node have to be selected in an intelligent way to optimize the chosen metrics.

2.4. Throughput Optimization

In traditional P2P file sharing systems, each peer tries to download content as fast as possible, i.e, maximize its effective bandwidth. In contrast, media streaming architectures must provide a constant download rate for a smooth play back of the stream. Multiple cooperating peers are needed to balance out bandwidth fluctuations, so that the loss or degradation of service from one peer can be compensated by the other peers.

The service capacity of the system consists of the aggregate upload bandwidth of all participating nodes. As this bandwidth is a scarce resource its usage must be optimized. In the optimal case, each peer can obtain a service capacity equal to the aggregate bandwidth divided by the number of nodes.

In [2] we analyzed different architectures that try to achieve optimal usage of the upload bandwidth. We make use of this knowledge in our implementation. Our topology is constructed in such a way that each peer has enough parents to receive the full stream and as many children as allowed by its upload bandwidth.

2.5. Timing Constraints

The second major difference between P2P file sharing and media streaming is the strict timing constraints of the latter. The chunks of the stream have to arrive before their play back time otherwise they are of no use. As we cannot rely on guarantees from the transport layer that a packet arrives on time, we need some over-provisioning of bandwidth to deal with small delays and limit the risk of missing some deadlines. This requirement is tightly coupled with the throughput optimization problem. The more download bandwidth each peer gets, the higher the probability that all blocks arrive on time.

In the construction process of the mesh, the peers try to get some spare parents to be used in the case the bandwidth drops under a certain threshold.

2.6. Fairness

An important observation made on current peer-to-peer file distribution systems is the existence of selfish peers, so-called freeriders [5]. These peers try to download from the system without serving other nodes. As peer-to-peer systems live from cooperation, this is an important problem that needs to be addressed.

Without any central instance that controls data flows in the system, the peers must have the ability to penalize peers that are unfair. Ideally, each peer should only get as much as it contributes, but this objective is not compatible with the uniform bandwidth requirement of media streaming. Yet, a peer that has high upload bandwidth shall get more advantages than a node that does not contribute at all.

In CROSSFLUX we try to establish some fairness in terms of reliability and latency. A node that provides much upload bandwidth to the system gets more backup links than a node that does not upload anything. Further, it is moved closer to the source.

3. Overview of Existing Systems

Although many proposals for P2P media streaming architectures exist, only few were implemented and are used in the real world. We can identify the following reasons for this slow growth:

1. A critical mass of users is needed for cooperation to be effective. If there are only few participants, then the media server can use traditional multicast communication. Given the almost synchronous property of content distribution, few media streams have the potential to attract enough users at the same time. The broadcast of live events can contribute to inverse this trend.
2. Most existing systems fail short of providing the properties users expect from media streaming architectures: (1) no interruptions and no jitter; (2) fast startup of the stream; and (3) quick recovery of failures such that the stream is played back continuously also under high churn.
3. P2P systems have to deal with legal and political issues. The owners of a stream lose the control of how the stream is being distributed. Further, any user with low-end equipment is able to serve streams, which opens the door to copyright infringement.

CoolStreaming: One of the most widely used systems is CoolStreaming [6], which has been deployed with up to 30,000 distinct users in 2004. Unlike many other systems, CoolStreaming is data-driven, considers bandwidth heterogeneity, and tries to reduce latency between pairs of peers. A set of backup nodes is maintained to deal with failures and adapt to changing network properties. Backup nodes are periodically contacted to see if they provide higher performance than some node currently serving the stream; in that case, both nodes may be exchanged. A limitation of this optimization strategy is that it is restricted to the nodes of the backup set. in contrast, the algorithms used in CROSSFLUX allow to perform "transitive" optimizations, i.e., not limited to the exchanges with direct neighbors.

End System Multicast: End System Multicast (ESM) [7] is a P2P media streaming solution that provides several desirable properties. An overlay mesh is initially constructed and multiple spanning trees, rooted at each possible source, are constructed on top of it. Narada then incrementally enhances the trees by adding or dropping additional links depending on a utility function.

In CROSSFLUX, we try to construct a good mesh from the beginning and incorporate performance metrics during the joining process of new nodes. In addition, CROSSFLUX introduces a notion of fairness by using links between nodes in one direction to serve streaming data and in the other direction as backup link.

PeerStreaming: PeerStreaming [8] differs from other systems in that it adapts the streaming bitrate dynamically to the available bandwidth, which directly depends on the number of serving peers. The clients reading the stream receive different parts from multiple altruistic serving peers. A new node joins the system by asking a list of serving peers and connects to a number of them. The main drawback is that there is no incentive for the serving peers to participate in the system and to help distributing the stream.

GnuStream: GnuStream [9] is built on top of the Gnutella P2P substrate. A peer in GnuStream queries the Gnutella network to locate multiple parents that have part of the stream. The stream is then requested from these parents and aggregated in the peer for playback. As GnuStream relies upon Gnutella, its implementation is very simple: joins and searches are mapped to the underlying protocols, while failure recovery is achieved by simply exchanging a failed source with another one. This simplicity comes at the price of some performance loss. Gnutella is not optimized for live media streaming and, therefore, may not perform as good as a system that has been designed specifically for that purpose.

SplitStream: SplitStream [3] is a P2P media streaming architecture that focuses on robustness. As in our model, the stream is split into multiple stripes that can be distributed independently. A distinct tree is constructed for each of these stripes on all the participating peers. The robustness in SplitStream comes from the fact that each node is inner node in at most one tree and leaf in all the other trees. Thus, if a peer fails, only one distribution tree is affected and has to be rebuilt. In CROSSFLUX, we can quickly recover from a failure on a tree by using the available backup links.

CollectCast: The CollectCast [10] architecture is built on top of a P2P DHT substrate, such as Chord, CAN, or Pastry. Failures or stream degradations are handled by exchanging active senders. Further, CollectCast tries to optimize the download rate at each peer by selecting the best performing peers out of a candidate set. In contrast, CROSSFLUX does not rely on fixed candidate sets but performs a more global optimization by moving peers across the trees.

CoopNet: CoopNet [11] combines a classical client-server model with a P2P architecture. The server is responsible for directing joining nodes to potential parents and for reconnecting peers upon failure of their parents. The central instance obviously limits scalability and represents a single point of failure.

NICE: NICE [12] also uses a hybrid architecture in which peers are clustered in a hierarchical layer structure. Each cluster has a leader, which also belongs to the next layer above. Latency can be optimized by selecting as leader a peer that is close to the center of the cluster. The system focuses on low-bandwidth streams distributed to a large receiver set. Thus, optimization of the available bandwidth is not a major objective of NICE and has not been explicitly addressed.

ZIGZAG: ZIGZAG [13] is another layer-based architecture. Like NICE, it constructs clusters that are grouped in a hierarchical structure. Unlike NICE, ZIGZAG dynamically adapts to the load of the cluster heads: if a node has too many children or no sufficient bandwidth capacity, it can distribute the load by reconfiguring the cluster. ZIGZAG does not use path redundancy and it is not clear how well it scales when distributing high-bandwidth streams.

4. The CROSSFLUX Architecture

We have designed and implemented a media streaming system, named CROSSFLUX, which tries to answer to the challenges identified in Section 2. To that end, we have incorporated properties of performance, robustness, scalability, self-adaptability, and extensibility from the ground up in the design of the architecture. These properties are not only considered during the construction phase of the overlay, but are also dynamically adjusted while content is being streamed.

4.1. Distribution Overlay

We initially consider the case where there is only one streaming source for a single stream. The architecture can be trivially extended to support multiple sources and streams (one distribution overlay is constructed per stream and per source).

In CROSSFLUX, we consider content as a sequence of chunks that are separated into m groups (stripes) and sent through m distinct spanning trees. The separation of the original file into stripes is performed by the source, which can optionally generate additional stripes for error correction. In its simplest form, the source can construct an "universal backup stripe" as an *xor* of all stripes. Subsequently, the loss of any stripe can be compensated by *xor*-ing all stripes but the missing one with this universal backup stripe. Of course, more sophisticated network coding techniques can be used. Error correction is orthogonal to the content distribution problem and the decision to encode redundant information in the stripes is left to the source: with that respect, the CROSSFLUX architecture is content agnostic. Obviously, source-driven data redundancy can be combined with CROSSFLUX' path redundancy to further increase end-to-end reliability.

To distribute the content from the source to the peers, we create distribution trees that act as long-lived virtual "circuits" along which all the chunks of a stripe are send. Distribution trees are dynamically updated upon failure or during optimization.

To cope with the inherent unreliability of the peers, we do not use single distribution trees but multiple trees (one per stripe) with additional backup links. We distinguish between two types of connections: (1) primary links used as active connections to send the content across the overlay; and (2) secondary, or backup links used to quickly route around the failure of a primary link. When a node fails, its neighbors only need to switch to a backup link that can provide the missing stripe while the primary links is being repaired. This strategy allows us to minimize the recovery time.

To ensure some fairness in the system, we use every link in both directions: a primary link responsible for serving a stripe s_i from peer p_i to peer p_j is used as a backup link (secondary link) for any other stripe $s_j \neq s_i$ in the opposite direction p_j to p_i. Constructing the mesh in this way provides incentives for contributing to content distribution, as peers get as many backup links as they are serving other peers. A selfish peer that does not serve any peers has no backup link and is more adversely affected by a failure. Peers that do not have sufficient bandwidth to obtain enough secondary connections and guarantee a certain level of robustness can create bi-directional backup links with each others (again, reciprocity is the incentive).

A backup link is *valid* for a given stripe s_i if it allows a peer p to tolerate the failure of its parent in the distribution tree of s_i, i.e., of the peer that serves s_i to p.

For being a valid backup, a link must satisfy the following *path diversity* property:

Property 1 (Path diversity) *A link from p to q for stripe s_i is a valid backup link from q to p for another stripe $s_j \neq s_i$ iff p's parent for s_j is not an ancestor of q in the distribution tree of s_j.*

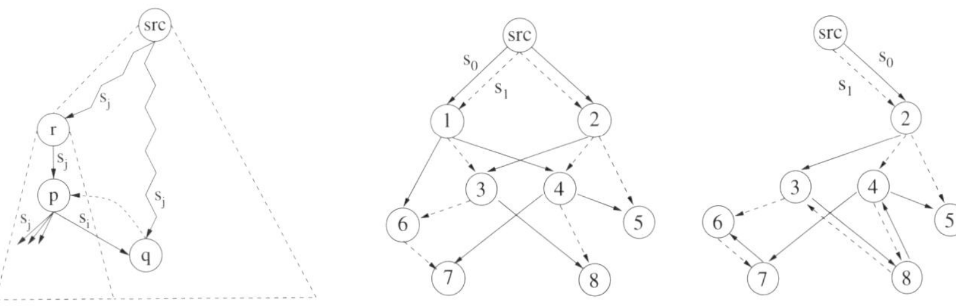

Figure 1. Illustration of the path diversity property.

Figure 2. Example of content distribution in normal mode (left) and backup mode after failure of node 1 (right).

Consider Figure 1. Peer p serves stripe s_i to q. In the reverse direction, the link from q to p is a valid backup for stripe s_j because the path from the source to q does not traverse p's parent for s_j (r). In other words, the failure of r will not prevent q from receiving s_j because q is not part of the distribution subtree for s_j rooted at r.

This property implies that the source needs to serve each stripe to at least two distinct peers, otherwise the grandchildren of the source would not have valid backup links. This requirement is not a major issue because a source typically has enough bandwidth to serve the whole streaming content multiple times in parallel.

Figure 2 shows an example of a forest constructed on 9 nodes and 2 stripes for both normal mode and backup mode after failure of node 1. The solid arrows show the distribution tree for stripe s_0, the dashed ones for s_1. In backup mode the affected nodes 3, 4 and 6 use one of their primary links for stripe s_i as backup for stripe $s_j \neq s_i$.

The algorithms for joining the system and optimizing the distribution trees guarantee that the path diversity property is always met on a link for at least some of the stripes.

A peer should actively transmit a small number of stripes on its outgoing primary connections, because sending the same stripe along multiple connections increases the degree of the distribution tree for that stripe and avoids it to degenerate into a linear chain (increased latency). On the other hand, transmitting only one stripe along all outgoing primary connections (as in SplitStream [3]) implies that no incoming secondary links can be used as a backup for that stripe (decreased reliability). Therefore, a good compromise is for a peer to forward two stripes to its direct neighbors (i.e., be inner node of the distribution trees for two stripes).

4.2. Joining the System

A peer that wants to participate in the system and receive the stream has to know the source of the system. This information can be obtained, for instance, from a Web page. The join procedure always starts at the source. We first outline its principle before describing it formally.

Upon arrival, a new peer p first contacts the source and asks for the number of stripes and stream rate. Then, it sends a join request message (JRQ) to the source for each stripe.

These messages traverse the associated distribution trees until "enough" potential parents for p are found. Finally, p connects to the "best" parent candidate for each stripe and starts receiving content.

A new peer connects to the distribution trees as a leaf. Therefore, it has no children and no backup link initially. This conscious design decision is motivated by the fact that, in typical P2P systems, many peers remain connected a very short amount of time: the longer a peer has been online, the higher the probability that it remains connected [14], [15]. Therefore, departures among the volatile population of newcomers will have limited impact. As peers remain in the system, they will accept children and consequently acquire backup links. This approach also acts as an incentive for peers to remain connected for long periods of time.

During the bootstrap phase, the source serves directly the first few peers in parallel. Thereafter, new peers connect deeper in the distribution trees. This seeming unfairness between early and late joiners is compensated over time by the *HeapTop* algorithm that continuously optimizes the distribution tree and changes the depth of the nodes.

Algorithm 1 Reception of $\mathrm{JRQ}(s_i, j)$ at peer p for stripe s_i and new peer j

---

if $f_p(s_i) \geq 1$ **and** $j \notin C_p$ **then**
    send $\mathrm{CAN}(p, h_p(s_i), source \rightarrow p)$ to j
end if
if $C_p \neq \emptyset$ **then**
    $c \leftarrow$ biased random node from C_p
    send $\mathrm{JRQ}(s_i, j)$ to c
end if

The join procedure is detailed in Algorithm 1. To join a distribution tree for stripe s_i, a peer p issues a join request JRQ to the stripe. We assume that each peer knows its upstream bandwidth. This value can be set by the user (e.g., by specifying a cap on the bandwidth that the application is allowed to use) or discovered at runtime by the application (e.g., by sending probe packets or using passive measurement techniques). Peers also keep track of the list of nodes on the path from the source. As the structure of the distribution trees may change due to failures or reorganizations, we embed in each message the sequence of traversed nodes so that these paths can be updated.

When a new peer joins the distribution tree for a stripe, we try to find a "good" location where to connect that peer to, according to the following criteria:

- Distribution trees should be balanced, i.e., all the leaves of the trees should have approximately the same depth.
- Peers should preferably join healthy branches with much spare capacity rather than branches with limited growth potential.
- A newcomer should try to connect to interior nodes first, if they have sufficient spare capacity, in order to maximize their utility and limit the depth of the trees.

The first criteria implies some fairness or randomness in the selection of the subtrees where to connect new nodes. The second criteria avoids directing newcomers toward branches that have limited service capacity, e.g., because they only contain peers with low bandwidth. The third criteria favors nodes high in the tree, given that they still have sufficient service capacity.

The join algorithm uses heuristics to meet these criteria. Each peer p maintains for each stripe s_i a "healthiness" value $h_p(s_i)$, which it periodically transmits to its parents in the distribution tree of s_i. healthiness is computed as the average of p's healthiness and the mean of its children's healthiness in the distribution tree of s_i. Formally:

$$h_p(s_i) = \begin{cases} \frac{1}{2}\left(f_p(s_i) + \frac{1}{|C_p(s_i)|}\sum_{c \in C_p(s_i)} h_c(s_i)\right) & : & |C_p(s_i)| > 0 \\ f_p(s_i) & : & |C_p(s_i)| = 0 \end{cases} \tag{1}$$

where $f_p(s_i)$ is the number of new children that p can accept for stripe s_i and $C_p(s_i)$ is the set of children of p for stripe s_i. One can note that the free capacity of p has more weight than that of its children. This allows us to favor new connections to nodes high in the trees. Note that a peer may return 0 for $f_p(s_i)$ if it still has enough upstream capacity but is already interior nodes of several distribution trees other than s_i. The healthiness of the nodes evolves over time as a result of peers joining and leaving, as well as reorganization of the distribution trees.

Join requests are sent to the source and traverse the distribution trees using biased random walks (which have only a fraction of the overhead of a broadcast). A join request JRQ for stripe s_i sent to the source by p is propagated along the distribution tree of s_i as follows. If the current node can accept p as a child for s_i, it sends a message CAN to p together with its healthiness h_p and the path from the root to p. Then, if it has children in s_i, it forwards the join request to a child chosen at random according to a biased distribution in which the probability of a child is proportional to its healthiness.

Joining node p typically receives several replies for a random walk. It then selects among the replies the node q closest to the root and, upon these, with the highest healthiness, under the condition that path diversity (Property 1) is satisfied for the connection from q to p. Note that the property can be verified using the path information embedded in the CAN message. The join procedure finishes when the new node starts receiving chunks from its parent.

If p receives no valid replies, it issues another join request that will likely follow a different path in the distribution tree. Although not shown in the algorithm, p can also request multiple random walks to be conducted in parallel to gather more candidates (parallel random walks fork as early as possible in the trees).

The behavior of the source differs from other peers in that it always tries to have the same number of children for each stripe. The source accepts a new child for stripe s_i if it has sufficient bandwidth *and* no other stripe has less children than are currently registered for s_i.

Note that the heuristics used to meet these criteria will *not* produce optimal distribution trees. The dynamic reorganization of the nodes in the trees (to be described shortly) has been precisely designed to improve the efficiency of the trees after their construction.

4.3. Content Distribution

The chunks of each stripe are forward along the associated distribution trees in a straightforward manner: each inner node of a distribution tree forwards incoming chunks to all of its children in that tree. We assume that the links between nodes are reliable (we use TCP in our implementation).

Peers buffer the chunks for some time, so that they can transmit them to their neighbors over secondary links in case of a failure. To dispose of buffered chunks, each peer regularly sends a notification to its backup neighbors indicating the last chunk it has received for each relevant stripe. This mechanism allows secondary sources to dispose of the chunks that they buffer for retransmission purposes. If the buffers of a peer are full, it may delete the chunks in its retransmission buffers even if the peers downstream secondary links have not yet acknowledged their reception.

4.4. Departures and Failures

When a node fails or leaves the systems, its children in each stripe have to find a new parent. This operation must be very fast to guarantee smooth playback of the media stream. CROSSFLUX relies on secondary links for quick failover: affected children ask their backup sources to send missing chunks.

By ensuring that each node has at least one valid secondary link for each stripe, we can quickly reconfigure the system after a failure while ensuring good load balancing: the children of a failed node will request the missing stripes from distinct peers with high probability. Obviously, backup sources must have spare bandwidth to send the missing stripes, even with degraded performance, until the primary link is restored. One should note, however, that the load of sending missing chunks can be shared among several backup nodes.

After promoting a secondary link to primary, the peers affected by the failure execute the join protocol to find a new parent and revert the status of the secondary link.

4.5. Overlay Optimization

A P2P network is a in constant evolution. Throughput optimization needs to take into account the dynamism of the underlying network and the heterogeneity in bandwidth. To that end, we use *HeapTop* [1] to dynamically move fast nodes up the trees toward the root. *HeapTop* is a fully decentralized algorithm that only performs local reorganizations based on local observations. When a peer has notably higher upload capacities than its parent, both peers exchange their position. Thus, the peers that can most help in content distribution are moved toward the root of the tree while the peers with low bandwidth capacities remain close to the leaves.

HeapTop is remotely inspired from the well-known HeapSort algorithm, where the nodes of a tree are reorganized by exchanging selected father-child pairs. The goal is to move the nodes with highest bandwidth closest to the root of the tree. The property maintained by our algorithm is that, for every node p other than the root and every child c of p, we have $u_p \geq u_c$ (with u_p and u_c being the effective upload bandwidth of p and c, respectively).

As we only want to perform local operations, the only way we can reorganize the tree is by exchanging the position of a node with its parent. This operation can be easily implemented because both nodes are directly connected with each other and they essentially have to exchange their respective neighbors.

The algorithm starts with a random initial tree. We assume that all nodes in the tree can estimate their bandwidth capacity and that of their parent, using a combination of active and passive measurements [1].

Algorithm 2 *HeapTop* algorithm at peer p

---

loop
  $q \leftarrow parent_p$
  if $q \neq root$ **and** $u_q < u_p$ **then**
    Exchange positions of p and q
  end if
end loop

Each node continuously executes the trivial operations shown in Algorithm 2. Peer p periodically compares its bandwidth capacity with that of its parent. If p's bandwidth is strictly bigger than its parent's bandwidth, then they switch positions, i.e., they exchange their neighbors. This operation can be performed efficiently as it is essentially local to p and its parent. The algorithm preserves the structure of the initial tree (even if it is not balanced), but the position of the nodes evolves over time.

For avoiding pairwise exchanges resulting from short bandwidth fluctuations, the estimations are based on a weighted moving average computed using the following formula:

$$u(t) = (1 - \alpha) \cdot u(t - 1) + \alpha \cdot u$$

The average bandwidth at time t is obtained by combining the latest sample u with the previous average value. The constant $\alpha \leq 1$ (typically $\frac{1}{8}$) is a smoothing factor that puts more weight on recent samples than on old samples and smooths out important variations.

In addition, in order to prevent unnecessary reorganizations of peers with similar bandwidth capacities, we shall only exchange the position of a peer p and its parent q if $u_q < \beta \cdot u_p$, with $\beta \leq 1$ (typically $\frac{9}{10}$).

Note that there is no synchronization between the peers (except between pairs of neighbors when positions need to be exchanged). This implies that nodes can move upward or downward the tree at different speeds, and distinct configurations can be obtained from the same initial tree. Figure 4 shows a possible configuration obtained from the execution of the algorithm on the tree in Figure 3 (the numbers indicate the bandwidth capacities of the peers: large numbers correspond to high bandwidth).

Given the special role of the root node, it appears clearly that the peers cannot move from one 1st-level subtree to another 1st-level subtree. Further, within any subtree, a node in one branch may be further from the root than some other node with less bandwidth in another branch (see nodes 9 and 10 in Figure 4). As such, the resulting distribution tree may be slightly sub-optimal but performing further optimizations would necessitate non-local operations and higher complexity.

If there is no bandwidth fluctuation, the tree will quickly reach a stable configuration. In the worst case, a node located at depth $d \geq 1$ (the root is at depth 0) can initiate $d - 1$ exchanges. The actual number of exchanges depends on both the initial configuration of the tree and the order in which exchanges are performed.

Several important considerations must be taken into account when using *HeapTop* to optimize the distribution trees in CROSSFLUX. First, the *HeapTop* algorithm is run independently in the distribution trees of each stripe. Second, we do not exchange a leaf

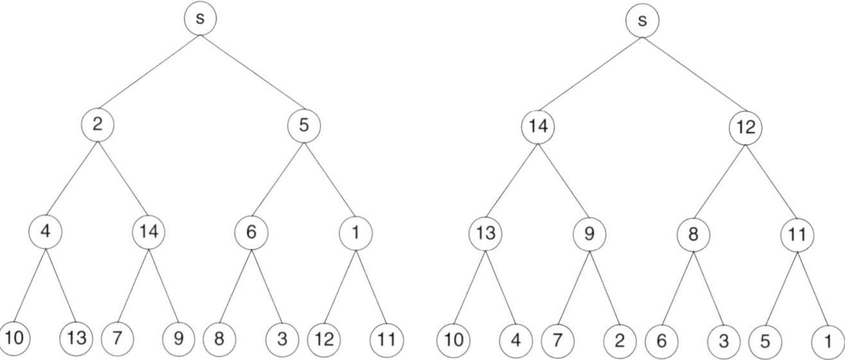

Figure 3. Original distribution tree (larger numbers mean more bandwidth).

Figure 4. One possible configuration obtained from executing the algorithm.

node with an inner node if the former is already inner node of several other trees. Finally, before performing any pairwise exchange, we verify that the path diversity (Property 1) will be preserved in the new configuration.

5. Evaluation

The CROSSFLUX architecture has been implemented in Java. We have evaluated its performance using the Modelnet [4] network simulator. We have also studied independently the effectiveness of *HeapTop*. Some of the results of our evaluation are discussed in this section.

5.1. Simulation Setup

Modelnet is a network simulator that emulates a virtual network on top of a set of machines (typically a cluster). The software to be evaluated is deployed on multiple virtual hosts residing on each machine. The traffic generated by these virtual hosts is routed through the simulator, which mimics the behavior of the modeled links (delay, throughput, loss) and forwards it to the destination.

In Modelnet, each end-to-end link in the topology can be assigned different values for bandwidth, latency, and loss rate. For our purpose, we used the Inet generator [16] to generate a random transit-stub topology of $4,000$ nodes with 50 CROSSFLUX clients spread across 19 stubs. The bandwidth of each link was chosen randomly in the range from 512 Kbit/s to 1024 Kbit/s. The number of stripes a node could serve was determined according to its connection speed.

A single streaming source has been used to serve an endless stream. This stream was split into chunks of 40 Kbit and distributed using 8 stripes. We fixed the streaming rate to 320 Kbit/s, thus each peer should receive at least 8 chunks per second.

5.2. Failure Recovery

A key requirement of P2P media streaming is fast recovery from failures. CROSSFLUX deals with that problem using backup links. In our first experiment, we compared the recovery time when switching over to backup links and when rejoining from the source. We terminated a node and observed the traffic at one of its children. The failure of the node was immediately discovered by the children upon socket disconnection, so that there is no noticeable delay in fault detection.

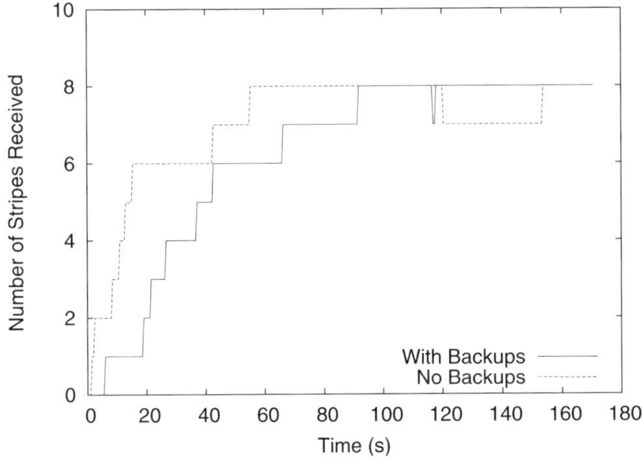

Figure 5. Comparison of Recovery Time with Backup Links and without.

Figure 5 shows the number of stripes received as a function of time for a node that must recover from its parent's failure. We observe that, when using backup links, the interruption is almost unnoticeable while it takes approximately 30 seconds to rejoin from the source. Note that, in both cases, the missing chunks were buffered and delivered after recovery.

5.3. Used Capacity

To evaluate the load balancing and fairness properties of the join procedure, we compared the number of stripes served by each node. To that end, we added all 50 nodes sequentially, with one new host joining every 5 seconds. Figure 6 shows the cumulative distribution function of the average used capacities after all nodes have joined. As one can see, the trees in CROSSFLUX are well balanced. About 50% of all nodes have no spare capacity and very few are almost idle, indicating that the capacity of the system is well used.

5.4. Dynamic Adaptation with HeapTop

As the structure of the distribution trees obtained with CROSSFLUX depends on many parameters than cannot be easily controlled (including random factors), we have studied the behavior of *HeapTop* using simulations that faithfully reproduce the operations of the algorithm and evaluate its efficiency. The main criterion considered is the average upload bandwidth capacity using the tree adapted by *HeapTop*, as compared with that of an initial randomly generated tree.

We have simulated three main classes of peers, chosen to match the observations we have made of real-world populations in an earlier study of the BitTorrent protocol [17]:

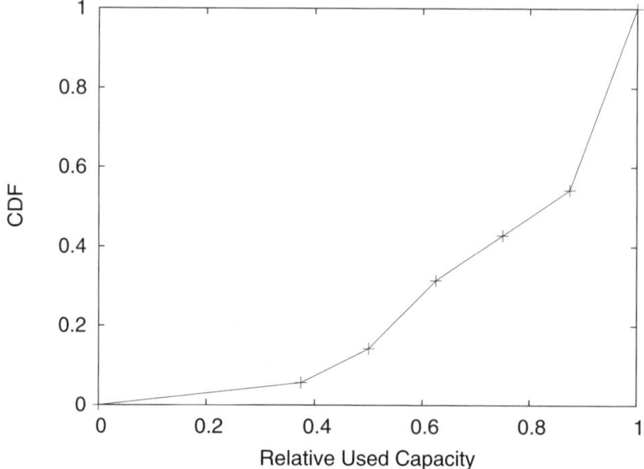

Figure 6. Cumulative Distribution Function of the Used Capacity.

- F: fast nodes with 1024 Kbit/s upload bandwidth.
- M: medium-speed nodes with 512 Kbit/s upload bandwidth.
- S: slow nodes with 128 Kbit/s upload bandwidth.

As the upload bandwidth is usually the limiting factor, we do not explicitly take into account download capacities (peers of classes M and S typically have asymmetric bandwidth).

Each peer has a given probability to fall in one of the considered classes. We constructed *binary* trees by iteratively adding each node at a valid position, chosen by traversing the tree from the root until a leaf or a node with a single child is encountered (a simpler join procedure than in CROSSFLUX). We experimented with both unbalanced and balanced trees. As the differences in the measurements were negligible, we only show results for balanced trees and note that they are also valid for unbalanced trees.

We have evaluated the improvement factor of *HeapTop* with different population sizes and various proportions of nodes in each class. To that end, we have used the class distributions shown in Table 1.

	Class F	Class M	Class S
$D1$	90%	5%	5%
$D2$	60%	30%	10%
$D3$	50%	25%	25%
$D4$	30%	60%	10%
$D5$	25%	25%	50%
$D6$	5%	90%	5%
$D7$	5%	5%	90%

Table 1. Distributions of peer classes for the simulations.

We simulated *HeapTop* by running it on the inner nodes of each stripe, as happens in CROSSFLUX. In other words, a leaf in the initial tree is never promoted to inner node.

Figure 7 shows the improvement factor for different population sizes and various class distributions. The improvement factor f is defined as the ratio of the average bandwidth $\overline{B}_{HT}$ of the tree generated by *HeapTop* to the average bandwidth $\overline{B}_R$ of the random initial tree: $f = \overline{B}_{HT}/\overline{B}_R$.

One can observe that the gain is significant (up to almost 400%). Figure 8 shows the best improvement factor observed during the simulations (up to 750%) and gives a measure of the potential benefits of *HeapTop* for CROSSFLUX.

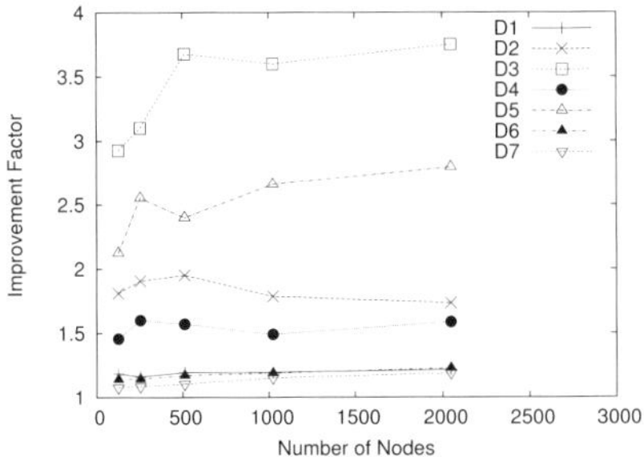

Figure 7. Average improvement factor with two parallel trees for different population sizes and various class distributions.

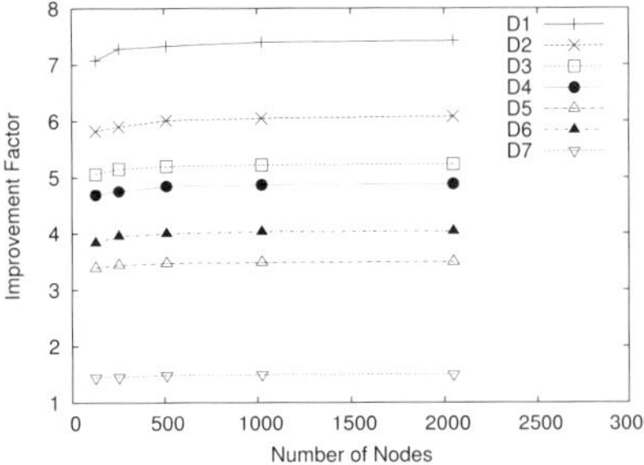

Figure 8. Best case improvement factor for two parallel trees for different population sizes and various class distributions.

6. Conclusion

We have presented CROSSFLUX, a peer-to-peer architecture specifically designed to satisfy the stringent requirements of media streaming. For distributing a stream from a single source to a large population of clients, the content is split into multiple stripes that are distributed over different trees. Altruistic peers that serve others are rewarded by additional robustness, as each connection can be used as a backup link in the reverse direction.

CROSSFLUX dynamically modifies the structure of the trees to adapt to bandwidth fluctuations and optimize the efficiency of the content distribution. Stable nodes with high bandwidth capacities are moved upwards the trees towards the root where they are most useful. Evaluation shows that CROSSFLUX can quickly deal with failures and produces balanced and efficient distribution trees.

Acknowledgements.   This work is supported in part by the Swiss National Foundation Grant 102819.

References

[1] M. Schiely, L. Renfer, and P. Felber, "Self-organization in cooperative content distribution networks," in *Proceedings of IEEE International Symposium on Network Computing and Applications (NCA)*, July 2005, pp. 109–116.

[2] M. Schiely and P. Felber, "Peer-to-peer distribution architectures providing uniform download rates," in *Proceedings of the International Symposium on Distributed Objects and Applications (DOA)*, Oct. 2005, pp. 1083–1096.

[3] M. Castro, P. Druschel, A.-M. Kermarrec, A. Nandi, A. Rowstron, and A. Singh, "SplitStream: High-bandwidth multicast in a cooperative environment," in *Proceedings of ACM Symposium on Operating Systems Principles (SOSP)*, Oct. 2003.

[4] A. Vahdat, K. Yocum, K. Walsh, P. Mahadevan, D. Kostic, J. Chase, and D. Becker, "Scalability and accuracy in a large-scale network emulator," in *Proceedings of 5th Symposium on Operating Systems Design and Implementation (OSDI)*, Dec. 2002, pp. 271–284.

[5] E. Adar and B. Huberman, "Free riding on gnutella," Oct. 2000. [Online]. Available: http://www.firstmonday.org/

[6] X. Zhang, J. Liu, B. Li, and T.-S. P. Yum, "Coolstreaming/DONet: A data-driven overlay network for peer-to-peer live media streaming," in *Proceedings of IEEE Infocom*, Mar. 2005.

[7] Y.-H. Chu, S. G. Rao, and H. Zhang, "A case for end system multicast," in *Proceedings of the 2000 ACM SIGMETRICS International Conference on Measurement and Modeling of Computer Systems*, 2000, pp. 1–12.

[8] J. Li, "Peerstreaming: A practical receiver-driven peer-to-peer media streaming system," Microsoft Research, Tech. Rep. MSR-TR-2004-101, Sept. 2004.

[9] X. Jiang, Y. Dong, D. Xu, and B. Bhargava, "Gnustream: A P2P media streaming system prototype," in *Proceedings of International Conference on Multimedia and Expo (ICME)*, vol. 2, July 2003, pp. 325–328.

[10] M. Hefeeda, A. Habib, B. Boyan, D. Xu, and B. Bhargava, "PROMISE: peer-to-peer media streaming using CollectCast," in *Proceedings of 11th ACM international conference on Multimedia*, Nov. 2003, pp. 45–54.

[11] V. N. Padmanabhan, H. J. Wang, and P. A. Chou, "Resilient peer-to-peer streaming," in *Proceedings of IEEE International Conference on Network Protocols (ICNP)*, Nov. 2003, p. 16.

[12] S. Banerjee, B. Bhattacharjee, and C. Kommareddy, "Scalable application layer multicast," in *Proceedings of ACM SIGCOMM*, Aug. 2002, pp. 205–220.

[13] D. Tran, K. Hua, and T. Do, "Zigzag: An efficient peer-to-peer scheme for media streaming," in *Proceedings of IEEE Infocom*, 2003.

[14] P. Gummadi, S. Saroiu, and S. Gribble, "A measurement study of napster and gnutella as examples of peer-to-peer file sharing systems," *Multimedia Systems Journal*, vol. 9, no. 2, pp. 170–184, 2003.

[15] S. Saroiu, P. Gummadi, and S. Gribble, "A measurement study of peer-to-peer file sharing systems," in *Proceedings of Multimedia Computing and Networking*, 2002, pp. 156–170.

[16] C. Jin, Q. Chen, and S. Jamin, "Inet: Internet topology generator," University of Michigan, Tech. Rep. CSE-TR443-00, 2000.

[17] M. Izal, E. Biersack, P. Felber, G. Urvoy-Keller, A. A. Hamra, and L. Garces-Erice, "Dissecting BitTorrent: Four months in a torrent's lifetime," in *Proceedings of 5th Passive and Active Measurement Workshop*, Apr. 2004.

Global Data Management
R. Baldoni et al. (Eds.)
IOS Press, 2006

Author Index